Historical Encyclopedia of U.S. Independent Counsel Investigations

Historical Encyclopedia of U.S. Independent Counsel Investigations

Edited by
Gerald S. Greenberg

Greenwood Press
Westport, Connecticut • London

Library of Congress Cataloging-in-Publication Data

Historical encyclopedia of U.S. Independent Counsel investigations / edited by Gerald S. Greenberg.
    p. cm.
    Includes bibliographical references and index.
    ISBN 0–313–30735–0 (alk. paper)
    1. Special prosecutors—United States. I. Title: Historical encyclopedia of US
Independent Counsel investigations. II. Greenberg, Gerald S.
    KF5107.5.H57 2000
    345.73'01—dc21   00–024522

British Library Cataloguing in Publication Data is available.

Library of Congress Catalog Card Number: 00–024522
ISBN: 0–313–30735–0

First published in 2000

Greenwood Press, 88 Post Road West, Westport, CT 06881
An imprint of Greenwood Publishing Group, Inc.
www.greenwood.com

Printed in the United States of America

The paper used in this book complies with the
Permanent Paper Standard issued by the National
Information Standards Organization (Z39.48–1984).

10 9 8 7 6 5 4 3 2 1

Contents

Preface and Acknowledgments

Whenever one identifies a subject of public interest for which there is little or no reference support, a volume is waiting to be written. Such was the case with the topic of U.S. independent counsel investigations. A constitutionally questionable legislative response to the Watergate scandal, the statute represented an attempt to restore public confidence in government. The office it created, however, was too frequently utilized as an effective political tool by both Democrats and Republicans. Investigations were often protracted, costly, and personally destructive. There seemed to be new inquiries called for on a daily basis. Political cartoonists depicted the independent counsel as a required accoutrement of residence in the nation's capital. Still, there was no place an interested researcher could go to examine the history and development of special prosecutors/independent counsels.

My education began with Philip A. Lacovara's article, "Independent Counsel," in the 1992 supplement to Macmillan's *Encyclopedia of the American Constitution*. There, the Teapot Dome affair and the tax scandals of the Truman administration were identified as historical precedents, and constitutional questions raised by the statute were discussed. The article's bibliography opened the door to further research. Examination of library catalogs revealed the existence of two monographs on the subject, Katy J. Harriger's *Independent Justice: The Federal Special Prosecutor in American Politics* (University Press of Kansas, 1992) and Terry Eastland's *Ethics, Politics and the Independent Counsel: Executive Power, Executive Vice 1789–1989* (National Legal Center for the Public Interest, 1989). These volumes proved to be invaluable sources of information and analysis.

Today's researchers are blessed with access to full-text, electronic databases that provide documentation on demand. Reed Elsevier's Lexis-Nexis served as an essential tool, providing the journalistic history of independent counsels and their probes. Although much maligned, our journalists continue to report the nation's history as it occurs. The best of them illuminate as they educate, and the story of the independent counsel statute's twenty-one-year lifespan has been explained most capably by our nation's finest news reporters.

Historians of presidents Ulysses S. Grant, Theodore Roosevelt, Warren G. Harding, Calvin Coolidge, and Harry S Truman provide us with instances in which federal special prosecutors were employed to investigate scandals in the pre-Watergate era. Such information helps us understand why the special prosecutor seemed a natural response to administrative corruption. The convenient solution, however, may not be a legal one. Care was taken in the crafting of the independent counsel statute to ensure that the unorthodox creation would still likely fit within our constitutional framework. A significant minority of legalists, however, continued to argue that the statute was impermissible. The debate surrounding this question was reflected in numerous law review articles that extended throughout the existence of the statute.

I thank the group of attorneys, historians, and political scientists whose contributions to this volume help illustrate the subject's interdisciplinary nature. All unsigned articles have been prepared by the editor.

The Ohio State University's institutional support for the research of its library faculty has been of significant assistance in the production of this work. Funding and time made available through the University Libraries' Advisory Committee on Research helped facilitate the timely completion of the project. Numerous individuals provided support and advice. In particular, I wish to acknowledge the research assistance of Ami Chitwood, the editorial expertise of Rachel Besen, and the problem-solving ability of my wife Melanie Pepper-Greenberg and daughter Meredith Greenberg.

Introduction

Whitewater independent counsel Kenneth Starr ends up investigating President Bill Clinton's sex life. Federal agents fan out across the country to question women who may have consorted with the president in the past. Venerable news analyst Daniel Schorr feels it necessary to express his regrets before offering commentary regarding the Monica Lewinsky affair. Veteran UPI White House Bureau Chief Helen Thomas seems somewhat uncomfortable appearing on a television news panel discussing the situation. How has a three-year-old investigation of a failed land development deal in Arkansas been transformed into this sordid scenario? Surely this is not what senators Sam Ervin and Abraham Ribicoff had in mind when, in the mid-1970s, they helped craft what they thought would be a statutory remedy to the conflict of interest that was apparent whenever the executive branch of government was called upon to investigate itself.

The independent counsel office was subjected to constant criticism: It was unaccountable; investigations consumed unconscionable amounts of time and funding; the independent counsel was too frequently partisan, turning investigations into vendettas; politics—not justice—drove the process; investigative power and authority were routinely abused. Many of these complaints were addressed when the Ethics in Government Act (1978), which established the Office of Special Prosecutor (later renamed Independent Counsel), was reformed during periodic reauthorizations. Yet, some maintain that the institution itself was fundamentally flawed and constitutionally unwarranted. Despite the cries of those who viewed the independent counsel as out of control, there remained those who insisted that the office was not independent enough. The attorney general still needed to trigger an investigation by choosing to conduct and validate a preliminary inquiry, thereby retaining significant control over the process. Indeed, it was this feature that many believed permitted the office to pass constitutional muster by maintaining an important element of executive oversight. More than one group of citizens initiated court action in attempting to force an attorney general to launch a preliminary investigation of a matter that the administration would have just as soon ignored. In addition, some critics wondered if it was reasonable to expect an attorney general to initiate potentially damaging inquiries aimed at the person who placed him/her in office.

Before the Ethics in Government Act, presidents were occasionally forced by circumstances to name a special investigator in order to examine, and possibly prosecute, executive branch misconduct. Calvin Coolidge named two special prosecutors to sort out the Teapot Dome scandal that occurred in Warren Harding's administration, and Harry Truman reacted similarly when scandal was uncovered among his tax collectors. Such *ad hoc* appointments, however, were exceptional responses to temporary public outrage. Those special prosecutors served at the president's pleasure and could be summarily dismissed (as Truman appointee Newbold Morris quickly discovered) if they incurred executive wrath. When Richard Nixon's firing of Watergate Special Prosecutor Archibald Cox appeared to be a transparent effort to mask presidential crimes, the public demanded an institutional answer to executive branch conflict of interest. After much debate concerning the nature of the prospective remedy, Congress created the independent Office of Special Prosecutor.

The first ten years of the Office's life were marked by continual challenges to the constitutionality of the new institution. Did the Office of Special Prosecutor/Independent Counsel, as crafted, violate the principal of separation of powers by vesting executive branch authority outside the direct control of the chief executive? Separation of powers case law and textual evidence offered no conclusive answer. Formalists and functionalists vigorously debated the issue, each armed with court decisions supporting their viewpoint. A string of cases in the 1970s and 1980s (*Buckley v. Valeo, Bowsher v. Synar*, and *INS v. Chadha*) predicted a short life for the independent counsel by demonstrating little tolerance for cross branch creations. The Supreme Court, however, abruptly reversed the trend, validating the office's existence in *Morrison v. Olson* (1988) and confirming their new direction in *Mistretta v. U.S.* the following year.

The lengthy, costly, and confounding investigation called Whitewater proved most unpopular, branching off on tawdry tangents, subjecting the process and the office to increasing criticism. Lawrence Walsh's Iran-Contra inquiry spanned six years and cost $40 million, but its ultimate futility might be attributed to congressional grants of immunity to principal targets and presidential pardons to those convicted. The excesses of Kenneth Starr's Whitewater/Travelgate/Filegate/Lewinsky investigation ultimately resulted in the demise of the Independent Counsel Office. By the spring of 1999, both political parties had been bludgeoned and bloodied by those who employed the independent counsel investigation as a political tool. The memory of Watergate could not support the concept indefinitely.

Largely forgotten is the fact that a fair number of independent counsel investigations either found no evidence of criminal wrongdoing or effectively prosecuted misconduct through a series of indictments and convictions that were clearly supported by evidence uncovered. The work of counsels Jacob Stein, Joseph DiGenova, and Robert Fiske was characterized by rather responsible restraint. Their probes stayed on track; they did not feel compelled to either indict or wander off on examinations that were only marginally related. Arlin Adams accumulated an impressive record of indictments and convictions while laboring in relative obscurity. When a mechanism functions as it should, it is frequently ignored. The complete picture should be examined before passing historical judgment on the independent counsel.

A

Abrams, Elliott (1948–) former Assistant Secretary of State, 1981–1989. Elliott Abrams was the first State Department official to face criminal charges in the Iran/Contra investigation. Shortly before the five-year statute of limitations would have expired, Independent Counsel LAWRENCE WALSH filed charges alleging that Abrams lied to Congress in testimony before the Senate Foreign Relations Committee and the House Intelligence Committee. In October 1986, Abrams testified that he knew nothing of OLIVER NORTH's activities to keep the Contras armed in Nicaragua in violation of a congressional ban. He also concealed the fact that he had secured a $10 million donation from the Sultan of Brunei to help fund the operation, depositing the money in a Swiss bank account managed by North. In October 1991, Abrams pleaded guilty to two misdemeanor counts. In doing so, Abrams avoided possible felony charges. He faced a maximum penalty of one year in prison and a $100,000 fine. On November 15, U.S. District Judge Aubrey Robinson, after hearing Associate Independent Counsel CRAIG GILLEN testify to Abrams's recent cooperation with the office, sentenced Abrams to two years probation, one hundred hours community service, and payment of a $50 fine.

Elliott Abrams became the youngest person in the twentieth century to serve as an Assistant Secretary of State when he came to Washington in 1981. He held three different Assistant Secretary posts, assuming responsibility for Central America in 1985. Abrams earned a reputation for aggressiveness by serving as an enthusiastic, and occasionally combative, spokesman for the new foreign policy agenda advanced by President RONALD REAGAN and Secretary of State GEORGE SHULTZ. He remained on the job after his conviction, winning the continual plaudits of Secretary Shultz. In his 1993 book, Abrams characterizes his congressional testimony as an appropriate method of protecting sensitive foreign policy matters. He also portrays many of the congressional members involved in the Iran/Contra hearings as unworthy of respect.

References:

Abrams, Elliott. *Undue Process: A Story of How Political Differences Are Turned into Crimes.* New York: Free Press, 1993.

Lardner, George, Jr. "Abrams Pleads Guilty in Iran-Contra Affair." *Washington Post,* 8 October 1991, p. A1.

————. "Abrams Sentenced to 2 Years' Probation." *Washington Post,* 16 November 1991, p. A20.

Adams, Arlin (1921–   ) Independent Counsel, HUD probe, 1990–1995. Arlin Adams was a 69-year-old retired federal appeals court judge when he was named independent counsel charged with investigating misappropriation of federal funds by the Department of Housing and Urban Development (HUD) during the Reagan administration. Adams conducted a deliberate, workmanlike, investigation that yielded sixteen convictions, and recovered $12 million ($6 million less than its cost) before resigning. Although Adams's principal target, former HUD Secretary Samuel Pierce, was not indicted, several of Pierce's staff members were implicated in influence peddling. In addition, a number of real estate developers were convicted of bribery.

Adams believed that HUD Secretary Pierce was derelict in his administration of his department, thereby fostering an atmosphere that invited misconduct. In the end, Pierce admitted as much, but Adams decided not to prosecute him citing lack of criminal intent as well as Pierce's age (72) and poor health. Instead, Adams won convictions against two of Pierce's top aides, Lance Wilson and Deborah Gore Dean. Real estate developers caught in Adams's net included: Benton Mortgage Company of Knoxville, Tennessee, which pleaded guilty to bribery of HUD officials in connection with low-income housing projects in Tulsa, Oklahoma, and Arlington, Texas; Philip Winn of Colorado (bribery), who agreed to pay a fine of $981,975; and Leonard Briscoe of Fort Worth who was sentenced to two years imprisonment and fined $50,000 for bribery. Adams also secured a conviction of Robert Olsen, a top staff member of the North Dakota Housing Finance Agency (bribery and conspiracy) for receiving over $50,000 from developers in return for directing federal funds to their projects.

Adams met with his share of defeats as well. Connecticut lawyer Victor Cruse was acquitted in 1993 of lying about his role in obtaining $1 million in HUD subsidies for a low-income housing project in Savannah, Georgia. Though Adams did obtain a 1993 plea bargain from Elaine Richardson, one-time aide to Edward Brooke, former senator from Massachusetts, his detailed investigation of Brooke himself was ultimately fruitless. Adams suspected Brooke of influence peddling on behalf of several Massachusetts companies that received large HUD housing subsidies in the 1980s. They included the Corcoran, Mullins, Jennison Co. of Quincy, Massachusetts, that developed the Harbor Point project in Dorchester (recipient of $20 million in HUD grants); Cobbet Hill Apartments that converted a former public school in Lynn (recipient of several million dollars in moderate rehabilitation funds); Summitt Hill Apartments in Springfield (recipient of $1.3 million in rent subsidies); and Royal Worcester Apartments in Worcester (recipient of HUD subsidies). Some believed the Cruse acquittal deterred Adams from prosecuting Brooke. In addition, it was considered that Adams's case against Brooke was not as strong as the one he had against Winn. Any prosecution of Brooke would also have had to contend with the former senator's considerable reputation.

Early in 1995, Adams brought an indictment against former Secretary of the Interior James Watt, charging him with perjury, obstruction of justice, and hiding subpoened documents relating to HUD misconduct in the Reagan administration. The indictment alleged that Watt lobbied HUD on behalf of developers after he left the cabinet in 1983 (receiving over $500,000 in return), lied about it, and initiated a cover-up of illegal activities. Adams's investigation of Watt enabled the government to recover $10 million targeted for a Virgin Island housing project, allegedly funded at Watt's request, but never expended as planned. Adams resigned his post in June, before resolution of the Watt case. His successor, Adams associate LARRY D. THOMPSON, accepted a plea bargain in January 1996. Watt pleaded guilty to misleading a grand jury, and was sentenced in March to five years probation, 500 hours of community service, and payment of a $5,000 fine.

Adams, never considered an activist judge during his service on the bench, had been mentioned as a possible Supreme Court appointee during the Nixon and Ford administrations. He believes that his decision to free an antiwar colleague, the radical priest Daniel Berrigan, may have caused him to be passed over in favor of Lewis Powell and William Rehnquist. He proved to be activist enough as independent counsel, leading a productive—if unsensational—investigation.

References:

Boot, Max. "Dakota Official Pleads Guilty in HUD Probe." *Christian Science Monitor*, 13 May 1993, p. 3.
———. "Uneven Results Mark HUD Corruption Cases." *Christian Science Monitor*, 17 February 1993, p. 3.
"Developer Gets 2 Years for Role in HUD Scandal." *Fort Worth Star-Telegram*, 30 April 1993, sec. C, p. 6.
"A Guilty Plea in HUD Case." *New York Times*, 9 June 1992, sec. D, p. 14.
Howlett, Debbie. "HUD Prober Not an 'Activist.' " *USA Today*, 11 April 1990, sec. A, p. 2.
"Independent Counsel in HUD Probe Quits." *Chicago Tribune*, 2 June 1995, p. 8.
"Judge Will Lead HUD Probe as Independent Counsel." *St. Petersburg Times*, 3 March 1990, sec. A, p. 8.
Kurkjian, Stephen, "Brooke Reportedly Is Focus of HUD Probe." *Boston Globe*, 22 August 1992, p. 1.
Wassenaar, Sheri L. "Watt Draws Probation in HUD Probe." *Los Angeles Times*, 13 March 1996, sec. A, p. 13.

Allen, Richard (1936–   ) former National Security Adviser 1981. In November 1981, it was reported that Reagan Administration National Security Adviser Richard Allen had received $1,000 from Japanese journalists and three watches from Japanese academic Tamotsu Takase in return for arranging an interview with Nancy Reagan. In addition, he had filed an inaccurate financial disclosure statement. These allegations resulted in a Justice Department investigation in order to determine whether a special prosecutor should be requested to look into the matter. At first, a White House spokesman had announced that the FBI found no wrongdoing. Within hours, however, it was realized that the ETHICS IN GOVERNMENT ACT (1978) required the attorney general to begin a preliminary investigation of such matters. This early test of the special prosecutor law was aborted, however, when Attorney General WILLIAM FRENCH SMITH's preliminary investigation judged the allegations to be unworthy of examination by a special prosecutor. Smith ruled that evidence of intent was lacking, therefore, 18 U.S.C. sections 201 (g) and (c), which bar public officials from accepting gifts for the performance of official acts, could not be said to have been violated. Elaborating upon his decision, Smith explained that the watches in question were presented to Allen in circumstances that would not lead a reasonable person to conclude that they represented payment in return for Allen discharging his duties. Regarding Allen's erroneous financial disclosure statement, Smith announced that an FBI investigation had determined that the mistakes were inadvertent. As a result, even a preliminary investigation was unnecessary. Smith believed that the relevant criminal statute, 18 U.S.C. section 1001, applied only to intentional falsification of reports. In addition, the attorney general stated that he did not feel the special prosecutor provision of the Ethics Act should be triggered when the violation of the criminal statute in question is merely technical. Nevertheless, in late November, Allen was placed on administrative leave, and six weeks later it was announced that Deputy Secretary of State William P. Clark would replace him.

Allen had briefly served in RICHARD NIXON's National Security Council during Henry Kissinger's tenure as Secretary of State. His work as an international business consultant in the 1970s gave rise to numerous allegations, including providing a Japanese businessman with inside information in order to develop lucrative personal contracts, receiving $60,000 from financier Robert Vesco for services as a "verbal consultant," introducing Vesco's attorney to then-Securities and Exchange Commission chairman WILLIAM CASEY at a time when Vesco was under investigation by that agency, and soliciting a $1 million contribution from Grumman Corporation to the Nixon campaign in return for a promise of the President's help in securing an airplane contract in Japan. Allen denied the last allegation when questioned by a Senate investigating committee, and RONALD REAGAN's advisers found no basis to deny Allen a place in the President's cabinet.

References:

Harriger, Katy J. *Independent Justice: The Federal Special Prosecutor in American Politics*. Lawrence: University Press of Kansas, 1992. Pages 128–129, "Richard Allen, Japanese Watches, and Financial Disclosure," explain the former NSC Adviser's brush with the special prosecutor law.

Kelly, James. "Allen Exit, Shake-Up at the White House." *Time*, 11 January 1982, p. 23.

"Picking and Choosing; Reagan Nearly Completes Cabinet and Selects Allen for NSC." *Time*, 5 January 1981, p. 56.

"The Right Response to $1,000." *New York Times*, 17 November 1981, sec. A, p. 30.

Altman, Roger C. (1946–   ) Deputy Treasury Secretary, 1993–1994. A friend of Bill CLINTON's from their days at Georgetown University, Roger Altman was one of the casualties of the WHITEWATER controversy. He resigned as Deputy Treasury Secretary on August 17, 1994, two weeks after his testimony before the Senate Banking Committee. While serving as acting chief of the Resolution Trust Corporation (RTC), Altman was in the awkward position of overseeing the investigation of JAMES McDOUGAL's failed Madison Guaranty and Loan, to which Clinton was connected, while simultaneously working in the administration's Treasury Department. Congressional hearings focused on the number and nature of contacts between Altman and the White House during the course of the RTC investigation. At an RTC hearing in February 1994, Altman admitted to contact with White House officials regarding RTC investigative procedures. Republican anger over this revelation of improper communication during an independent federal probe resulted in the issuance of subpoenas to White House and treasury officials on March 4. At the March 18 RTC hearing, Altman revealed that he had also met with White House officials to discuss recusing himself from RTC oversight of the Madison Guaranty investigation.

During the time when the independent statute had lapsed, ROBERT B. FISKE, JR. had been appointed independent counsel to investigate Whitewater on January 31, 1994, by Attorney General JANET RENO. Fiske conducted a four-month investigation, issuing his report on June 30. He found no evidence that any Treasury or White House official obstructed the RTC investigation of Madison Guaranty. Nevertheless, congressional hearings were scheduled in order to investigate matters in greater detail. Hearings before the House Banking Committee the week of July 25 operated under rules that strictly limited questioning. Former White House counsel BERNARD NUSSBAUM strongly defended the need for the White House to be briefed on RTC investigations in order to be able to respond to press inquiries regarding leaks. Nussbaum also admitted that he had helped convince Altman not to recuse himself from RTC's Madison investigation because it would set the undesirable precedent of recusal merely for the sake of appearances rather than when legally required. Senate hearings, which began on July 29, proved more contentious. Nussbaum faced harsh questioning over his interference with Altman's initial decision to recuse himself. Altman's nine hours of testimony on August 2 conflicted with the statements of both Treasury General Counsel JEAN HANSON and Treasury Chief of Staff Joshua Steiner regarding various Whitewater-related contacts with the White House. Whereas House Banking Committee Chairman Henry Gonzalez (D-Texas) effectively controlled proceedings, Senate Banking Committee Chairman Donald Riegle (D-Michigan), ranking Republican ALFONSE D'AMATO New York, and Paul Sarbanes (D-Maryland) were expansive in expressing their dissatisfaction with the explanations offered, Altman's testimony in particular was perceived as scripted and less than candid. In addition, his aggressive, unrepentant demeanor was offensive to many in Congress. (The fact that both Riegle and D'Amato had faced ethics charges in the past caused their rebuke of witnesses to appear ironic to some critics.)

At the conclusion of hearings, Riegle and Sarbanes told Secretary of Treasury Lloyd Bentsen that Altman's relationship with the Banking Committee had been irreparably damaged by his attempts to mislead Congress. Senate Republicans called for the resignation of Altman, Hanson, and Steiner. Altman and Hanson both stepped down. The House and Senate Banking Committee official reports, issued in January 1995, found no legal or ethical violations. The Republicans' accompanying report, however, flatly stated that Altman had intentionally lied to Congress.

Before joining the Clinton administration, Altman was an investment banker with Lehman Brothers, a firm with many Democratic contacts in Washington, where he was made a general partner within five years. As Assistant Treasury Secretary in the Carter administration, Altman was instrumental in securing federal bailouts for New York City and the Chrysler Corporation. In the late 1980s Altman was employed by the Blackstone Group, an investment firm headed by former NIXON Commerce Secretary Peter G. Peterson. Significant accomplishments during Altman's service in the Clinton administration included progress in federal deficit reduction and passage of the North American Free Trade Agreement (NAFTA). Some think that Altman's Treasury position could have been saved had Lloyd Bentsen rallied to his defense. Instead, the Treasury Secretary moved to separate himself from the problem.

References:

"Rough 'Whitewater' Ride for Clinton." *Congressional Quarterly Almanac* 1994: 104–115. Details Whitewater background, appointment of independent counsel Robert Fiske, his investigation and findings, Altman's role as RTC investigative overseer while serving in the Treasury Department, House and Senate hearings, and reports including Altman's testimony and resignation. Includes text of Robert Fiske's letter to congressional committees requesting postponement of their hearings in order to facilitate the independent counsel investigation, and descriptive chronology of contacts between Treasury officials and White House aides regarding RTC investigation of Madison Guaranty.

Ullmann, Owen. "Who Killed Roger Altman?" *Washingtonian* (October 1994): 71–75.

Discusses Altman's background. Suggests how his Treasury position might have been saved despite his congressional testimony.

American Bar Association (ABA). The ABA played a crucial role in the development of the independent special prosecutor office, actively offering proposals and testimony regarding constitutionally acceptable methods of investigating wrongdoing in the executive branch of government. In 1973, the ABA formed the Special Committee to Study Federal Law Enforcement Agencies aimed at effectively insulating law enforcement from partisan politics. William B. Spann, Jr. chaired the committee, which issued a preliminary report in 1975 calling for reform of the justice system. ABA testimony before Congress regarding Senator ABRAHAM RIBICOFF's Watergate Reorganization and Reform Act of 1975 (S. 495) is widely credited with crafting a mechanism for triggering the special prosecutor investigation that was able to withstand constitutional challenge. Rejecting the concept of a permanent special prosecutor/ public attorney favored by Ribicoff, Senate Watergate Committee chief counsel SAM DASH, and the administration of President GERALD FORD, the ABA recommended a procedure to be initiated by the attorney general whenever there was a perceived conflict of interest regarding investigation of executive branch misconduct. Although the ABA proposal left open the precise appointment details, allowing actual assignment of a special prosecutor to be made by either the attorney general or a special court panel, initiation of the procedure by the attorney general provided an element of executive control that would prove valuable.

The ABA has always considered legal and political reform to be integral to its organizational objectives. Self-regulation and self-governance are cornerstone principles in asserting the association's independence from governmental control. The ABA believes such independence necessary if the profession hopes to successfully challenge governmental abuse of legal authority whenever it appears. The WATERGATE scandal represented an outstanding example of such abuse, demonstrating the need for a solution to the political perversion of justice. The ABA expressed significant concern that so many lawyers were intimately involved in Watergate-related misconduct, and consequently was apprehensive about resulting public perception of the profession. Given the ABA's interest in independence and professional self-regulation, it was understandable that the mechanism recommended by the organization (and largely adopted by Congress) placed power in the hands of the attorney general and an independent lawyer/ prosecutor selected from the private sector. Along with COMMON CAUSE, the ABA exerted greater influence on the creation of the office of special prosecutor than any other organization external to government. After passage of the ETHICS IN GOVERNMENT ACT (1978), the ABA's role was reduced to passive monitoring of the statute's implementation. The organization did, however, play a more active role when the act was reauthorized in 1982 and 1987. Lobbying in favor of its continuance, the ABA opposed reforms that gave the attorney general greater authority at the first reauthorization, but generally approved of the work conducted by the independent counsel office, believing that public confidence in the nation's ability to investigate misconduct by the executive has been significantly restored since Watergate.

References:

Bertozzi, Mark. "Oversight of the Executive Branch: A Policy Analysis of the Federal Special Prosecutor Legislation." Ph.D. dissertation, State University of New York at Albany, 1980.

Harriger, Katy J. *Independent Justice: The Federal Special Prosecutor in American Politics*. Lawrence: University Press of Kansas, 1992. Chapter 3, "A Watergate Legacy," discusses the ABA's involvement in the crafting of legislation that created the special prosecutor office; Chapter 8, "Symbols and Politics," covers the organization's historical interest in self-government and regulation of the profession.

Arms Export Control Act (1968). Originally passed in 1968 (Pub. L. No. 90–629, 82 Stat. 1320), the Arms Export Control Act has been amended and codified in various sections of 22 U.S.C. Requiring congressional approval of large shipments of arms to foreign countries, this act is representative of a tendency in the past thirty years to codify large areas of foreign affairs law that, in the past, had traditionally been left to the discretion of the president. (Other examples would be the Hughes-Ryan Amendment of 1974, limiting covert operations by intelligence agencies; the Intelligence Oversight Act of 1980, mandating intelligence heads to inform congress of covert activities; and the War Powers Resolution Act of 1982, requiring congressional approval for sending troops to participate in hostilities.) The Arms Export Control Act played a crucial role in Independent Counsel LAWRENCE WALSH's IRAN-CONTRA investigation. Despite the fact that President Jimmy CARTER had banned all arms exports to Iran when American hostages were seized in 1979, the Reagan adminstration arranged for arms to be shipped to Iran with Israel serving as an intermediary. In return, Iran was to arrange for American hostages in Lebanon to be released. Two such shipments were made in 1985 with one hostage being freed. Walsh considered this arrangement to be a clear violation of the Arms Export Control Act. (The arrangement apparently fell apart when Israel mistakenly transported the wrong weapons, delivering arms with Israeli identification markings that were discovered by Iran.)

Like the BOLAND AMENDMENTS, the Arms Export Control Act presented obstacles to presidential administration efforts in aiding Contra overthrow of the Sandinista government in Nicaragua during the 1980s. After the collapse of the arms-for-hostages deal, American arms were sold to Iran. The profits were used to aid the Contras. When two American helicopter pilots were shot down and killed over Nicaragua attempting to supply the Contras in September 1984, Congressman JIM LEACH (R-Iowa), chairman of the Arms Control and Foreign Policy Caucus, explained that such activity violated section 38 of the Arms Export Control Act. That section required export licenses for the ammunition clips, camouflage uniforms, and even the military training provided by the Americans. The Americans, sponsored by an Alabama-based group, Civilian-Military Assistance, were apparently aided by the same U.S. government officials who should have been preventing them from proceeding because they weren't licensed. Defenders of the Contra supply operation interpreted the applicable law differently. They pointed out that the C123 helicopter that was shot down turned out to be carrying arms manufactured in eastern Europe; therefore it was not clear that they had been exported from the United States.

In February 1987, the TOWER COMMISSION REPORT generally supported the contention that the Reagan administration had violated the Arms Export Control Act in its support for the Nicaraguan Contras. Indicating that the NATIONAL SECURITY ACT, the Boland Amendment (to the Department of Defense Appropriations Act of 1985), and the Hughes-Ryan Amendment may also have been violated, the Arms Export Control Act represented the most serious transgression, because it was the only one that provided for criminal penalties—possible ten years of imprisonment and fines up to $1 million for each violation. The applicable provisions of the Arms Export Control Act specified that the President could not approve transfer of defense equipment valued at $14 million or more unless a report has been submitted to the Speaker of the House and the chairman of the Senate Foreign Relations Committee thirty days in advance. Fifteen days after the end of each calendar year, the President was also required to issue a report listing price and availability estimates made to each foreign country for possible future arms sales totalling $7 million or more. In addition, items on the United States Munitions List could not be exported to any country that the Secretary of State has determined to be providing support for acts of international terrorism. (Iran was such a country.)

At first Attorney General EDWIN MEESE indicated he did not think that dealings with Iran had violated any laws, because he was not sure that government funds were involved. The Tower Commission Report, however, appeared to influence his opinion otherwise. In a letter to Commission chair, former Senator John Tower (R-Texas), Meese stated that the CIA's delivery of arms to Iran in 1985 probably violated federal law. The question would be decided, Meese indicated, by Independent Counsel Lawrence Walsh.

During the summer of 1987, testimony before congressional Iran-Contra investigation committees addressed the question of Arms Export Control Act violations. Secretary of Defense CASPAR WEINBERGER indicated that he believed the arms-for-hostages arrangement to be in violation of the Arms Export Control Act. Weinberger's testimony supported that of Henry Gaffney, Jr., an official in the Defense Department's foreign arms sales unit, who had expressed similar sentiments a few weeks earlier. Weinberger's testimony also agreed with the Tower Commission's evaluation. Testimony by Weinberger, Meese, and former National Security Adviser JOHN POINDEXTER all indicated that concern over violating the Arms Export Control Act was responsible for a change in the method of arms transfer to Iran beginning in January 1986.

Meese testified that former Attorney General WILLIAM FRENCH SMITH had issued an opinion in 1981 indicating that covert arms sales through the CIA did not violate the Act. Further testimony raised additional questions regarding the letter and spirit of the Arms Export Control Act. Its provisions were the subject of creative interpretation. In the end, Independent Counsel Lawrence Walsh was left to evaluate testimony and apply the law as best he could. He would be significantly hampered, however, by grants of IMMUNITY that had been issued to key witnesses.

References:

"Aftermath of the Tower Report, Laws That May Have Been Violated." *Los Angeles Times*, 28 February 1987, p. 22.

Hayes, Andrew W. "The Boland Amendment and Foreign Affairs Deference." *Columbia Law Review* 88 (1988): 1534–1574. Argues that traditional deference to the President on matters of foreign affairs should not apply to statutory interpretation.

"How U.S. Law Limits Military Aid to Contras." *Washington Post*, 12 October 1986, sec. A, p. 25.

Leach, Jim. "Those International Vigilantes Were Wrong." *Washington Post*, 29 September 1984, sec. A, p. 17.

"Many Laws Bear on Deals." *New York Times*, 14 November 1986, sec. A, p. 8.

Ostrow, Ronald J. "Panel Suggests Four Possible Law Violations." *Los Angeles Times*, 28 February 1987, p. 1.

Picharallo, Joe. "Weinberger Highlights a Problem: Did '85 Sales to Iran Break Law?" *Washington Post*, 15 August 1987, sec. A, p. 10.

Walsh, Lawrence. "Political Oversight, the Rule of Law, and Iran-Contra." *Cleveland State Law Review* 42(1994): 587–597. The former independent counsel reviews the findings of his investigation and details its obstacles and frustrations in an address. He characterizes the experience as an exercise in balancing two protective systems: the rule of law as enforced by courts and lawyers and political oversight of the President as established by the Constitution and enforced by Congress.

B

Babbitt, Bruce (1938–) Secretary U.S. Department of the Interior, 1993– .
Former two-term Governor of Arizona (1979–1987), Bruce Babbitt was an unsuccessful candidate for the Democratic presidential nomination in 1988. An
attorney with a Harvard law degree, Babbitt served as a partner in the Phoenix
law firm of Steptoe and Johnson until being named Secretary of the Interior by
President Bill CLINTON. Babbitt brought with him a reputation as a popular,
effective administrator and a vocal conservationist. A decision made by Babbitt's department in July 1995 regarding a proposal for an Indian tribal casino
resulted in the initiation of an independent counsel investigation 31 months later.

Three groups of impoverished northern Chippewa Indians, the Red Cliff, Lac
Courte Oreilles, and Mole Lake, applied to the Department of the Interior for
the right to convert a failing dog racing track in Hudson, Wisconsin, into a tribal
gambling casino. An alliance of five wealthier tribes from Wisconsin and Minnesota opposed the proposal, because they believed the operation would harm
their own casinos. The department rejected the application, and the disappointed
Chippewas sued on the grounds that Babbitt's office was influenced by political
lobbyists and promise of large financial contributions to the Democratic Party.

The St. Croix Meadows Greyhound Racing Park had opened in Hudson in
June 1991. Built for $40 million, it had lost money from the beginning. In
October 1993, Fred Havenick, the track owner, joined with the three northern
Chippewa bands in a request for a permit to open a casino that was projected
to earn up to $80 million annually. The Minneapolis office of the Interior De-
partment's Bureau of Indian Affairs approved the application in November 1994,
despite the opposition of five bands of Indian tribes who already operated casinos in the area. In January 1995, the opposing tribes hired Patrick J. O'Connor
of O'Connor and Hannan, to lobby for them. O'Connor was a former Treasurer
of the Democratic National Committee and had been a successful fund-raiser
for them. He immediately began a lobbying campaign that effectively reversed

the decision of the Minneapolis office. O'Connor met with Babbitt's chief of staff Tom Collier in order to guarantee that a final decision would not be made until O'Connor had the opportunity to make his case. Next, the lobbyist approached President Clinton, who referred him to aide Bruce Lindsey. Lindsey brought the matter to another aide who dealt with Indian affairs. O'Connor went on to meet with Donald Fowler, Chairman of the Democratic National Committee. Fowler contacted associates in the White House and Interior Department as well.

When the Chippewa tribal officials met with Interior officials in Washington on May 17, 1995, there appeared to be no opposition to their proposal. They were joined at the meeting by Paul Eckstein, Babbitt's former law partner, now working for the Chippewas. The next day, Babbitt's assistant, Heather Sibbison, reported that the application was likely to be denied. Eckstein met with Babbitt on July 14, 1995, regarding the decision, and claimed he was told that there had been substantial lobbying against the application and that White House Deputy Chief of Staff Harold Ickes wanted a quick decision on the matter. The application was formally rejected later that day, citing community opposition. In September, O'Connor sent a fund-raising letter to the tribes for whom he had lobbied. They responded beginning in March 1995 with political donations to the Democratic Party totaling $230,000. In December 1995, the Chippewas filed suit, charging that improper political influence resulted in denial of their casino application. In July 1996, Senator John McCain (R-Arizona), Chairman of the Committee on Indian Affairs, questioned Babbitt about the nature of the comments made to Eckstein. After first denying Eckstein's version of the meeting, Babbitt admitted that he had mentioned Ickes's interest in resolution of the case, but had merely been trying to end the interview. Babbitt testified before Senator Fred Thompson's (R-Tennessee) committee investigating campaign contributions in October 1997. He stated that the application decision had been made by his associates, and that politics did not influence the outcome. Somewhat surprised by the aggressiveness of the questioning, Babbitt emerged from the encounter determined to defend himself in a more forceful manner. In February 1998, Attorney General JANET RENO requested appointment of an independent counsel to investigate whether Babbitt had lied to Congress regarding the manner in which the casino decision had been made. The court panel named CAROL ELDER BRUCE independent counsel in the Babbitt case on March 19, 1998. Her 19-month investigation ended on October 13, 1999 with a finding of insufficient evidence to warrant further action.

References:

Jackson, Robert L. "Special Counsel Named in Babbitt Probe." *Los Angeles Times*, 20 March 1998, sec. A, p. 18.
Lardner, George, Jr. "Crux of Babbitt Probe: Recollections in Conflict." *Washington Post*, 29 March 1998, sec. A, p. 8.

Van Natta, Don, Jr., and Jill Abramson. "Web of Influence." *New York Times*, 11 January
    1998, p. 1.

Baker, Howard H., Jr. (1925–   ) former senator (R-Tennessee), 1967–1985.
Having served as vice chairman of the Senate WATERGATE Committee, Howard Baker was expected, along with Committee Chairman SAM ERVIN (D-
North Carolina) to play an important role in the development of reform measures
that would help prevent future executive-branch misconduct. Accordingly, Baker
assumed a prominent role in addressing the issue. He opposed Senator ABRA-
HAM RIBICOFF's bill S. 495 (1975) on the grounds that judicial appointment
of a special investigator was unconstitutional. Instead, Baker, working with Senator CHARLES PERCY (R-Illinois), favored establishment of a new "Division
of Government Crimes" within the Justice Department. Introduced as an amendment to S. 495, the idea failed to be adopted when the bill died in the House.
Baker, however, remained an active participant in keeping alive the concept of
a legislative response to executive branch wrongdoing. He was among a group
of influential senators who demonstrated a willingness to compromise that was
necessary to the eventual adoption of the ETHICS IN GOVERNMENT ACT
in 1978.
    Baker and Percy had joined many other legislators in attempting to respond
to the Watergate crisis as it unfolded. Their bill S. 2734 (1973) was one of
thirty-five bills attempting to quickly address the issue and recapture public
confidence in government. During the televised Senate Watergate hearings,
Baker's leadership won him the respect of individuals on both sides of the
political aisle. After President RICHARD NIXON's resignation, Baker, influenced by former Solicitor General ERWIN GRISWOLD, argued unsuccessfully
that the Justice Department should be reformed in a manner that would facilitate
its handling of future executive-branch malfeasance. When President GERALD
FORD proposed establishment of a permanent office of special prosecutor within
the Justice Department in 1976, the Baker-Percy initiative was given new life.
The House of Representatives, however, was not receptive. There, Democrats
held out for the concept of a temporary special prosecutor. JIMMY CARTER's
election as president in November assured the success of this proposal. Although
the Ethics in Government Act created a court-appointed special prosecutor,
largely outside the control of the Justice Department, Baker went along in the
end.
    As Senate Minority Leader in 1979, Baker criticized Attorney General GRIF-
FIN BELL's decision to avoid naming an Ethics Act special prosecutor to investigate whether president Carter's peanut business had made illegal political
contributions to his presidential campaign. His comments helped prompt Bell to
arm special counsel PAUL CURRAN with powers at least equivalent to those
exercised by Watergate special prosecutors ARCHIBALD COX and LEON JA-
WORSKI.

After the election of President RONALD REAGAN in 1980, Baker served as Senate Majority Leader, leaving Congress in 1985. He returned as Reagan's Chief of Staff in 1987–1988. In September 1998, Baker joined with ROBERT DOLE in expressing the opinion that an extensive impeachment inquiry was called for in the CLINTON-LEWINSKY matter.

References:

Baker, Senator Howard H., Jr. "The Proposed Judicially Appointed Independent Office of Public Attorney: Some Constitutional Objections and an Alternative." *Southwestern Law Journal* 29 (1975): 671–683.
Bertozzi, Mark. "The Federal Special Prosecutor: Too Special?" *Federal Bar News & Journal* 29 (1982): 222–230.
Harriger, Katy J. *Independent Justice: The Federal Special Prosecutor in American Politics.* Lawrence: University Press of Kansas, 1992. Chapter 3, "A Watergate Legacy," discusses Baker's legislative initiatives in response to Watergate.
McGrory, Brian. "Dole, Baker Reject Talk of a Quick Deal on Clinton." *Boston Globe,* 28 September 1998, sec. A, p. 1.

Banzhaf v. Smith 737 F.2d 1167 (D.C. Cir 1984). On October 25, 1983, George Washington University law professor John F. Banzhaf III and public interest attorney Peter H. Meyers filed suit in U.S. District Court in an attempt to force Attorney General WILLIAM FRENCH SMITH to request appointment of an independent counsel. In a letter written on July 22, 1983, Banzhaf called Smith's attention to the fact that members of the Reagan campaign staff may have illegally obtained debate briefing papers from the Carter White House in 1980. Specific allegations involving possible theft of government property and interference with an election were made against officials covered by the ETHICS IN GOVERNMENT ACT (1978), including White House Chief of Staff James Baker and CIA Director WILLIAM CASEY. The Justice Department conducted an eight-month investigation before deciding that there was no evidence of criminal behavior by any of the officials named. Had the investigation been conducted under the provisions of the Ethics Act, a decision to appoint an independent counsel would have had to have been made after 90 days. The Justice Department, however, maintained that the allegations were not specific enough to trigger the Ethics Act provisions, because evidence was lacking.

On February 29, 1984, Federal District Court Judge Harold H. Greene ruled that the allegations involved were specific enough as evidenced by the Justice Department's own lengthy investigation. Greene further ruled that the attorney general was required to apply to the courts for an independent counsel in this case, as stipulated by the Ethics Act. Private citizen Banzhaf must have standing to sue, stated Greene, for if he did not, the Attorney General could not be held accountable for adhering to Ethics Act provisions.

On April 21, 1984, the Justice Department asked for dismissal of Banzhaf's suit by the District Court on the grounds that the Ethics Act did not allow the court to force action by the Attorney General. The Department also asked Judge

Greene to reconsider his decision permitting Banzhaf and Meyers to bring suit, because the Ethics Act does not provide for action by private citizens. Greene rebuffed the Justice Department's contentions, ruling instead that Smith must seek appointment of an independent counsel, because he had failed to act within the specified 90-day period allotted for the preliminary investigation.

On June 21, 1984, the Court of Appeals for the D.C. Circuit heard the case on an expedited basis with seven of the court's eleven justices in attendance. The fact that the case was not relegated the usual three-judge panel reflected the seriousness of the matter at hand. Among the justices were ROBERT BORK and RUTH BADER GINSBURG. ANTONIN SCALIA, not present, would participate in the court's decision. KENNETH STARR had disqualified himself, because he had been counsel to Attorney General Smith. Justice Department attorney John H. Cordes argued that judicial review of the Attorney General's decision was not permitted by the Ethics Act. Such review permitted charges to be publicized prematurely in the district court. Political pressure, not judicial, must provide the remedy for recalcitrant Attorneys General. In addition, Cordes maintained that Banzhaf and Meyers lacked standing to sue, because they had not suffered the type of injury required by law. Banzhaf countered that if the Attorney General could prevent appointment of an independent counsel in the current instance, there would be no mechanism for preventing another Watergate. Allowing the Attorney General such discretion was unwise given the fact that Watergate-era Attorneys General John Mitchell and Richard Kleindienst had committed federal crimes while in office. After deliberation, Chief Judge Spottswood W. Robinson III overturned Greene's decision, ruling that the district court lacked jurisdiction to hear the case. Congress did not intend to allow such judicial review initiated by a public request. In fact, early versions of the Ethics Act had contained clauses permitting private right of action, but they had been cut out of the final bill.

This decision by the Court of Appeals raised disturbing questions regarding the amount of discretion afforded the Attorney General, an aspect of the statute that was enhanced by amendments to the Ethics in Government Act approved in the reauthorization of 1982. How effective could the Ethics in Government Act be in eliminating conflict of interest if the executive branch continued to maintain such control over investigations of misconduct by officials in its own house? Discussions surrounding reauthorization of the Ethics Act in 1987 would have to address this issue.

References:

Brown, Jonathan P. "*Banzhaf v. Smith*: Judicial Review under the Independent Counsel Provisions of the Ethics in Government Act." *Iowa Law Review* 70 (1985): 1339–1352. Argues for judicial review of Attorney General's refusal to seek appointment of independent counsel in given cases.

Harriger, Katy J. *Independent Justice: The Federal Special Prosecutor in American Politics.* Lawrence: University Press of Kansas, 1992. Chapter 4, "Implementation and Oversight," discusses *Banzhaf* as it relates to specific provisions in the independent counsel law. Chapter 5, "Is the Special Prosecutor Constitutional?," points out that although the Court of Appeals never specifically addressed the question of constitutionality in *Banzhaf*, there were indications that at least some court members would have been sympathetic to the argument that the independent counsel law violated separation of powers doctrine.

"Inquiry on Carter Papers Sought." *New York Times*, 21 April 1984, p. 24.

"Lawsuit Seeks Prosecutor in Debate Case." *Washington Post*, 26 October 1983, sec. A., p. 3.

Mixter, Stephen Charles. "The Ethics in Government Act of 1978: Problems with the Attorney General's Discretion and Proposals for Reform." *Duke Law Journal* (1985): 497–522. Argues for limiting or removing Attorney General's power to short-circuit independent counsel mechanism by refusing to request appointment of investigator in certain cases. Also discusses *NATHAN V. ATTORNEY GENERAL* 557 F. Supp. 1186 (D.D.C. 1983) and *DELLUMS V. SMITH* 573 F. Supp. 1489 (N.D. Cal 1983).

Taylor, Stuart, Jr. "Judges Hear Case on 1980 Campaign Documents." *New York Times*, 21 June 1984, sec. B, p.9.

Barr, William P. (1950–   ) Attorney General 1991–1992. Nominated as a "caretaker" Attorney General on October 17, 1991, William Barr was considered a safe, sensible choice to succeed RICHARD THORNBURGH as head of the Justice Department. When Thornburgh decided to run for the Senate, President GEORGE BUSH looked for a noncontroversial successor. Clarence Thomas's emotionally exhausting confirmation hearings had ended just eighteen hours before Bush made his perfunctory announcement, naming Deputy Attorney General Barr as his choice. Barr was a career civil servant who had served as a lawyer in the Central Intelligence Agency in 1976–1977 when Bush was its director. Although associated with the policies of RONALD REAGAN, he had maintained a low profile and alienated few Democrats. His nomination received favorable reaction on both sides of the aisle. Bush believed that Barr concurred in the basic belief that Congress should not impinge upon executive privilege. Serving little more than one year as Attorney General, Barr would still be presented with several opportunities to initiate independent counsel investigations. In all but one case, he would decline.

When faced with calls for an independent counsel investigation of alleged abuses in the House of Representatives banking system, Barr opted for an internal examination instead. He named Malcolm Wilkey, a former appeals court judge in the D.C. circuit for whom Barr had clerked in the mid-1970s, as "special counsel" charged with investigating the situation. Wilkey's history as an active Republican drew criticism. He had been a delegate to the Republican convention in 1960, held a series of political posts, and was appointed to the bench by RICHARD NIXON. But, Wilkey was also in charge of federal forces that ensured the desegregation of the public schools in Little Rock, Arkansas, in 1958, and enjoyed a reputation for intelligence and integrity. His nine-month investigation of the House bank, beginning in March 1992, drew mixed reviews.

By issuing subpoenas for the banking records of over 500 current and past House members, Wilkey was accused of overzealousness and invasion of privacy. Some considered the act a violation of the House's constitutional status. Although enough questionable practices were uncovered to result in five indictments, some congressmen resented being classified as abusers for trivial overdrafts.

In July 1992, Democrats on the House Judiciary Committee called for the Attorney General to request an independent counsel to investigate possible administration involvement in $5 billion worth of illegal loans made by the Atlanta branch of Italy's Banca Nazionale del Lavoro (BNL) to Iraq before that nation's invasion of Kuwait. Some of those funds helped finance Iraq's arms buildup. U.S. District Court Judge Marvin H. Shoob concurred, expressing great doubt that Christopher Drogul, Atlanta branch bank manager, could have acted independently in such circumstances. The Bush administration acknowledged committing policy errors in attempting to convince Saddam Hussein to lead his nation in a manner more friendly to the west. Such errors, Bush claimed, do not constitute crimes. The Democrats, however, felt there was reason to believe that the administration actually approved of BNL's loans and Iraq's acquisition of sophisticated weapons technology. They also charged that after the Gulf War, a deliberate effort was made to cover up U.S. involvement in the arming of Iraq.

On August 11, 1992, the Attorney General formally announced that he would not request appointment of an independent cousel in order to investigate the BNL loans to Iraq. Barr ruled that the allegations of impropriety failed to provide sufficiently specific and credible information regarding the commission of any illegalities by high-ranking government officials. Predictably, Democrats accused Barr of stonewalling. Presidential candidate Bill CLINTON declared that Barr's action placed greater responsibility upon the Justice Department to fully investigate the situation. Judge Shoob believed that Barr's decision made it unlikely that the true BNL story would ever be uncovered. As questions continued to be raised, the CIA and the Justice Department issued statements accusing each other of having provided misleading information to Judge Shoob. In October, refusing to let matters rest, Senator Joseph Biden (D-Delaware) and Congressman Jack Brooks (D-Texas), chairmen of the Senate and House Judiciary Committees respectively, formally repeated the Democratic motion for request of an independent counsel. This new request posed a considerably narrower question, focusing on why relevant CIA documents weren't provided to Judge Shoob during the sentencing hearing for BNL Atlanta bank manager Christopher Drogul. In response to this request, Barr named retired U.S. District Judge Frederick B. Lacey to conduct a special Justice Department examination of the matter. Once again, Barr avoided initiating a full-scale Ethics Act investigation. Democratic leaders felt that Barr's appointment fell short of what was required. Barr indicated that should Lacey uncover serious wrongdoing, an independent counsel could then be requested. Lacey had been appointed to the bench by

Richard Nixon in 1971, but enjoyed a reputation for nonpartisan administration of justice. In December, Lacey reported that there was no need for an independent counsel. Mistakes had been made in the handling of classified messages between the CIA and Justice Department, but there was no evidence of criminal conduct. There matters rested as the independent counsel statute lapsed without renewal until 1994. Talk of resurrecting the BNL investigation preceded the statute's revival, but newer scandals took priority.

In November 1992, Senate Minority Leader ROBERT DOLE (R-Kansas) called upon Barr to request an independent counsel investigation of LAWRENCE WALSH. Dole claimed that Walsh's indictment of CASPAR WEINBERGER shortly before election day was timed to help defeat George Bush, who, according to Weinberger's notes, was involved in the IRAN-CONTRA scandal. Although Barr considered Walsh's investigation to be overly zealous, Barr rebuffed Dole. Barr was vocal in his dislike for the independent counsel office, believing that the Justice Department was capable of handling investigations of executive branch officials despite apparent conflict of interest. He particularly questioned the independent counsel selection process, which he believed failed to provide for appointment of individuals with adequate understanding of Justice Department standards. Barr also regarded the independent counsel as largely unaccountable, and the investigations, therefore, lacking in control and direction.

Shortly before leaving the Justice Department, Barr did request appointment of an independent counsel. One day before the governing statute expired on December 15, JOSEPH DiGENOVA was appointed by the Special Division panel of judges to investigate whether White House officials violated the law in their search of Bill Clinton's passport files. Republicans were attempting to uncover damaging information for use against Clinton during the presidential campaign. DiGenova's investigation, eventually concluded by MICHAEL ZELDIN in 1995, found no basis for indictments.

During the WHITEWATER investigation, William Barr joined with other former attorneys general in criticizing Democratic attacks upon independent counsel KENNETH STARR and his investigatorial methods. Vouching for Starr's integrity, Barr concurred in denunciation of efforts that served to interfere with the ongoing investigation.

References:

Atlas, Terry. "Barr Forced to Weigh Probe of Iraqi Loans." *Chicago Tribune*, 16 October 1992, sec. C, p. 3.
———. "Retired Judge Will Probe Iraq Loan Case." *Chicago Tribune*, 17 October 1992, sec. C, p. 1.
"Attorney General Barr Rejects Demands." *St. Louis Post-Dispatch*, 10 December 1992, sec. C, p. 5.
"Counsel Named to Probe Search of Clinton File Move Taken Day before Law Ends." *Atlanta Journal and Constitution*, 18 December 1992, p. 3.

Farrell, John Aloysius. "Special Prosecutor to Sift Iraq Aid Sought." *Boston Globe*, 10 July1992, p. 1.

Gurdon, Hugo. "Top Lawyers Denounce White House Starr 'War.' " *Daily Telegraph*, 7 March 1998, p. 15.

"Investigation of Walsh Sought." *Courier-Journal* (Louisville, KY), 12 November 1992, sec. A, p. 8.

"Judge Criticizes U.S. Attorney General." *Houston Chronicle*, 13 August 1992, sec. A, p. 5.

"No Special Counsel to Be Named in Iraq Probe." *Chicago Tribune*, 11 August 1992, sec. C, p. 3.

Ostrow, Ronald J. "William Barr." *Los Angeles Times*, 21 June 1992, sec. M, p. 3.

"Reopening Iraqgate." *Boston Globe*, 26 November 1993, p. 22.

Taylor, Stuart, Jr. "The Great House Bank Holdup Scandal Is Phony and the Inquiry Is Suspect." *San Diego Union-Tribune*, 31 May 1992, sec. C, p. 3.

"Wider Passport Scandal." *New York Times*, 26 December 1992, p. 20.

Barrett, David M. (1936–) Independent Counsel, Cisneros investigation, 1995– . David Barrett was an experienced federal prosecutor who had served as special counsel to the House Ethics Committee when he was named independent counsel in 1995. He was charged with investigating false statements made by Housing Secretary HENRY CISNEROS to the FBI regarding payments to his former mistress. Attorney General JANET RENO's preliminary investigation had determined that information provided by Cisneros during a background check in 1993 indicated that payments to Linda Medlar never exceeded $10,000 a year, when, in fact, they averaged between $42,000 and $60,000 annually. Reno requested appointment of an independent counsel in order to ascertain the materiality of Cisneros's false statements. She believed the key question to be whether or not the false statements would have had a substantial effect on Cisneros's ultimate confirmation. Reno also asked that the counsel investigate whether there was evidence of a cover-up.

Barrett was an active Republican who had headed Lawyers for Reagan in 1980. During the independent counsel investigation of the Department of Housing and Urban Development (HUD), Barrett had been identified as a major housing developer who had lobbied HUD officials in 1986–1987 for development contracts. An investigation by the House Government Operations Committee in 1990 determined that Barrett had continual contact with Assistant Secretary for Housing Thomas Demery between 1986 and 1988, and had received a $1.7 million contract for a Tulsa housing project in 1987. Congressman Tom Lantos (D-California) pointed out the irony in appointing someone who had likely benefited from HUD's influence peddling in the 1980s to investigate the current HUD secretary. Despite the fact that such information tended to cast doubt upon Barrett's actual independence, he had his supporters. Former U.S. attorney and independent counsel JOSEPH DiGENOVA and Congressman Bob Livingston (R-Louisiana) praised Barrett's selection. DiGenova felt that Barrett possessed the necessary judgment for the job. Livingston, who was cochair of the House Ethics Committee when Barrett helped prosecute Congressman Dan Flood (D-Pennsylvania) in 1980, stated that Barrett operated in a nonpartisan manner.

To his credit, Barrett conducted a low-profile investigation in which relatively little information was leaked to the public. Linda Medlar had secretly taped her conversations with Henry Cisneros during the winter of 1992–1993 in which there was discussion of the possible impact his payments to her might have on his confirmation as HUD Secretary. In 1994 she sold a transcript of tape excerpts to the tabloid television show *Inside Edition* for $15,000. Medlar also sued Cisneros for $250,000 claiming that he breached a verbal contract to support her and her daughter. Cisneros settled the suit in 1995 for $49,000. In May 1996, Barrett granted Medlar use IMMUNITY in return for her cooperation in his investigation. Cisneros resigned as HUD Secretary in November, but by that time Barrett was convinced that the information he sought from Medlar was not forthcoming. The FBI indicated to Barrett that the tapes Medlar had supplied were crude copies—not the originals. Barrett exercised a search warrant at Medlar's Texas home and subpoened her former attorneys. By the fall of 1997 the cost of Barrett's investigation had reached $4 million. Expanding his original probe, Barrett now secured a 28-count indictment against Medlar, her sister Patsy Wooten, and Wooten's husband, Allen. Medlar was charged with obsruction of justice, perjury, bank fraud, and money laundering (because the house was eventually sold for a profit of $8,462). The Wootens were accused of lying on a mortgage application. They had allegedly bought a house for Medlar's use, but stated that they had intended to occupy it.

In December, Barrett secured an indictment against Cisneros, Linda Medlar Jones, and two former Cisneros employees—Sylvia Arce-Garcia and John D. Rosales. Cisneros faced 18 counts of lying, obstruction of justice, and conspiracy for his testimony before the FBI. Cisneros's employees were charged with participation in the conspiracy. The indictment alleged that they cooperated with Cisneros in return for promised jobs. If convicted, Cisneros faced a five-year jail sentence on each count. Cisneros maintained that his erroneous testimony before the FBI was the result of faulty memory rather than a conspiracy, and his attorney predicted exoneration at trial. Some cited the serious charges contained in the indictment as vindication of Barrett's efforts. Others maintained that the whole affair was merely proof that Cisneros was an easy subject to blackmail. The Mexican American Legal Defense and Educational Fund, based in Los Angeles, decried the politicization of a personal indiscretion for which Cisneros had already paid a heavy price.

On the eve of her trial in January 1998, Linda Medlar Jones pleaded guilty to lying about the purchase of her house. She was sentenced to three and a half years in prison. A guilty verdict at trial might have resulted in a 25-year sentence. On September 7, 1999, over two months after the expiration of the independent counsel statute, Cisneros agreed to plead guilty to one misdemeanor count of lying to the FBI. He was fined $10,000.

References:

"Agents Reportedly Trying to Determine Whether Tapes of Cisneros Were Altered." *Dallas Morning News*, 15 December 1996, sec. A, p. 14.

Cannon, Carl M. "Probe of Cisneros Will Not Let Go." *Baltimore Sun*, 30 November 1997, sec. A, p. 1.

Jackson, Robert L., and Ronald J. Ostrow. "Ex-HUD Secretary Indicted, Accused of Lying to FBI." *Los Angeles Times*, 12 December 1997, sec. A, p. 1.

Johnston, David. "Lawyer Linked to 80's HUD Scandal Is Named to Investigate Housing Chief." *New York Times*, 25 May 1995, sec. B, p. 10.

Locy, Toni, and Guy Gugliotta. "Court Appoints D.C. Lawyer as Special Counsel in Cisneros Case." *Washington Post*, 25 May 1995, sec. A, p. 8.

————. "Independent Counsel, Witness in Cisneros Probe at Odds." *Washington Post*, 16 November 1996, sec. A, p. 4.

Ostrow, Ronald J, and Robert L. Jackson. "Investigator Grants Immunity to Cisneros Ex-Mistress." *Los Angeles Times*, 10 May 1996, sec. A, p. 11.

Savage, David G. "Cisneros Former Mistress Admits Lying to Buy Home." *Los Angeles Times*, 16 January 1998, sec. A, p. 13.

Shenon, Philip. "More Republican Lobbying of H.U.D. Is Disclosed." *New York Times*, 11 December 1989, sec. A, p. 21.

Bell, Griffin (1918–   ) lawyer, judge, Attorney General 1977–1979. A longtime friend of President Jimmy Carter, Griffin Bell assumed the post of Attorney General amid fears that he might not be able to run the Justice Department in an independent manner. The department, it was argued, would become politically influenced because its ties to the White House would be too close. Justice would suffer.

Some might have found evidence for this contention when, in November 1978, the FBI received reports indicating that Jimmy Carter and WALTER MONDALE had solicited funds to help repay campaign debts at a luncheon that the White House had hosted for prominent businessmen. Such behavior would violate 18 U.S.C section 603 prohibiting soliciting or receiving political contributions in a public area occupied by a public official conducting his/her duties. Pursuant to provisions of the ETHICS IN GOVERNMENT ACT (1978), Bell initiated a preliminary investigation that revealed the President had been present only for the first hour in order to thank those in attendance for past support. The Vice President was not present at all. Bell reported that the allegation was so unsubstantiated that it did not warrant further examination. He also stated that he believed the statute in question did not apply to the situation at hand, because section 603 was created to protect federal employees from being solicited for campaign funds. Apparently, Bell was disturbed that he had received news of this allegation rather belatedly, and as a result, had little time to conduct the preliminary investigation and decide if a special prosecutor should be requested. After the Carter-Mondale Luncheon Case, Bell required adoption of procedures that would result in earlier notification of misconduct allegations. To his credit, Bell requested that his report in this matter be made public in order to answer concerns that had been raised in news articles regarding the incident. Such openness was appreciated by Justice Department officials as well. It gave them reason to believe that difficult decisions would be supported and publicly defended.

Bell's association with the President was put to a sterner test when an ongoing investigation into Office of Management and Budget Director Bert Lance's alleged history of mishandling funds took an unexpected turn. Lance's activities at the National Bank of Georgia appeared to be connected to the Carter family peanut warehouse and Jimmy Carter's 1976 presidential campaign fund. The question arose whether money from the peanut warehouse business was illegally diverted into the Carter campaign.

Griffin Bell had never favored establishment of an independent special prosecutor. In fact, he had a distinct dislike for the term itself, preferring use of the title "counsel," which was later to be adopted. When Republicans received news that the White House was looking into a possible connection between Carter's business and campaign funds, they demanded appointment of a special prosecutor. COMMON CAUSE, influential in helping craft the special prosecutor statute, joined the call. Griffin Bell acceded to the demands on March 20, 1979, by naming PAUL CURRAN, a Republican lawyer from New York City, "special counsel" to investigate the issue. Bell argued that because the alleged misconduct being investigated occurred prior to passage of the Ethics in Government Act (1978), the provisions of that statute did not apply. Bell could appoint the investigator himself and decide precisely what powers would be vested in the investigator's office. Initially, Bell denied Curran the full authority enjoyed by WATERGATE special prosecutors. Curran, for example, would need approval of the Justice Department before seeking indictments. This arrangement immediately came under attack by a host of critics including *New York Times* columnist William Safire who dubbed Curran a "patsy prosecutor." Even Senate Majority Leader Robert Byrd (D-West Virginia) lamented that Curran was not protected from arbitrary dismissal. Republican leaders like Senate Minority Leader Howard Baker (R-Tennessee) called for a complete Watergate-style investigation. Bell was forced to backtrack, granting Curran the same authority that had been exercised by LEON JAWORSKI. In October 1979, Curran reported that there was no cause for criminal prosecution in this case.

After resigning as attorney general in 1979, Bell's path continued to cross those of various persons involved in independent counsel investigations. As the details of the IRAN-CONTRA affair were coming to light in 1986, Bell agreed to represent EUGENE HASENFUS, the American Contra supply courier who was shot down over Nicaragua. Bell, with little preparation and no knowledge of Nicaraguan legal procedures, made his case with the aid of a Nicaraguan attorney. Hasenfus was found guilty and sentenced to a lengthy prison term, but was released at Christmas after spending 73 days in maximum security.

In 1987, as the independent counsel statute was being considered for its second reauthorization, Griffin Bell joined two former Watergate assistant prosecutors in testifying against its renewal. Bell reiterated his initial dislike for the arrangement, but the life of the statute was extended nonetheless. This afforded Bell the opportunity to become further involved in the Iran-Contra investigation seven years later when President GEORGE BUSH called upon him. Bush was attempting to prevent independent counsel LAWRENCE WALSH from implicating him in the scandal. Bell's law firm, King & Spalding, prepared several reports in Bush's behalf. When Walsh issued his final report in 1994, no charges were brought against Bush.

In recent years Bell's name has surfaced in connection with the WHITE-WATER investigation as well. At first Bell was among those being proposed as an independent counsel, one who would be widely acceptable to Republicans as well as Democrats. Since KENNETH STARR has assumed responsibility for the investigation, Bell has been called upon to support both the independent counsel's conduct and charges of interference leveled against those who might not want to see the investigation pursued. In 1996, Bell supported Starr's claims that Arkansas state prosecutor Mark Stadola was under political pressure to bring charges against DAVID HALE, a key witness for Starr in his trial of former Arkansas Governor JIM GUY TUCKER and Whitewater officials JIM and SUSAN McDOUGAL. In March 1998, Bell joined other former attorneys general RICHARD THORNBURGH, EDWIN MEESE, and WILLIAM BARR in denouncing the CLINTON administration's attacks on Starr's investigation methods as improper.

Walter Mondale was among those who believed Griffin Bell would have been nominated to serve on the Supreme Court had President Carter served long enough to fill a vacancy. Although that opportunity never presented itself, Bell has remained an active presence in current affairs, continuing to address many of the compelling legal issues of the day.

References:

"Griffin Bell to Represent U.S. Captive in Nicaragua." *Chicago Tribune*, 18 October 1986, sec. C, p. 6.

Gurdon, Hugo. "Top Lawyers Denounce White House Starr 'War.'" *Daily Telegraph*, 7 March 1998, p.15.

Harriger, Katy J. *Independent Justice: The Federal Special Prosecutor in American Politics*. Lawrence: University Press of Kansas, 1992. Chapter 6, "The Attorney General and Conflict of Interest," describes Bell's handling of the Carter-Mondale Luncheon and CARTER PEANUT WAREHOUSE cases as well as their implications for the Justice Department's relationship with the Special Prosecutor's Office.

"It's No Longer Just Peanuts." *U.S. News & World Report*, 2 April 1979, p. 9.

"Let Law Naming Counsels Expire, Panel Is Urged." *Los Angeles Times*, 4 June 1987, p.16.

Lewis, Ephraim. "Tiptoeing Around Goobergate." *Businessweek*, 9 April 1979, Industrial ed., p. 129

Mantius, Peter. "Can 'Mr. Fixit' Solve Bush's Lingering Legal Woes? Griffin Bell Tackles Former President's Iran-Contra Problems." *Atlanta Journal and Constitution*, 24 January 1993, sec. A, p. 8.

Mathews, Tom, Elaine Shannon, and Susan Agrest. "A Peanut Prosecutor." *Newsweek*, 2 April 1979, p. 31.

Schmidt, Susan. "Interference Seen in Whitewater Case." *Washington Post*, 22 March 1996, sec. A, p. 19.

Totenberg, Nina. "For the U.S.: Griffin Bell, Esq.; A Closing Argument on the Departing Attorney General, Who Hopes to Leave a Legacy of Integrity, Patriotism and Nonpartisan Justice." *Washington Post*, 1 July 1979, magazine section, p. 10.

Weaver, Maurice. "Republican Clamour Grows for Whitewater Investigator." *Daily Telegraph*, 8 January 1994, p. 11.

Bennett, Robert S. (1939–   ) defense attorney Iran-Contra and Whitewater investigations. Frequently compared to legendary trial lawyer Edward Bennett Williams (dramatic defender of Jimmy Hoffa and John Connolly), Robert Bennett has built a reputation for success as a tough negotiator, skillful courtroom performer, and expert handler of the media. Along the way he has become involved in both the IRAN-CONTRA and WHITEWATER independent counsel investigations.

Robert and his brother William, former Secretary of Education and drug czar, were raised by their grandmother in the Flatbush section of Brooklyn where Robert won a reputation as an amateur boxer and occasional streetfighter. A debater in high school, Bennett went on to distinguish himself at Georgetown and Harvard Law Schools before assuming a judicial clerkship in Washington, D.C. He worked in the U.S. attorney's office in Washington, 1967–1970, where he met longtime partner and friend CARL RAUH. After working at Hogan & Hartson for five years, Bennett started his own firm—Dunnells, Duvall, Bennett & Porter, where he began to specialize in white-collar criminal work. Corporate clients included Boeing, BDM International, and Northrup Corporation. In 1990, Bennett and Rauh left Dunnells to join the D.C. office of the New York firm Skadden, Arps, Slate, Meagher & Flom. At Skadden, Bennett worked in many high-profile cases with political implications. He served as special counsel to the Senate Ethics Committee in its investigation of Senator David Durenberger (R-Minnesota) and banker Charles Keating; defended Clark Clifford and Robert Altman against charges related to their association with the Bank of Commerce and Credit International (BCCI); succeeded in obtaining leniency for Cincinnati Reds owner Marge Schott after her racial slurs ignited protests; and undertook the defense of Secretary of Defense CASPAR WEINBERGER when the cabinet member became a target of LAWRENCE WALSH's Iran-Contra investigation.

Bennett's defense of Weinberger demonstrated his ability to capitalize on opponents' questionable strategy. Walsh had waited until four days before the 1992 presidential election to announce an indictment of Weinberger on Iran-

Contra–related charges. Quotations from Weinberger's notes, obtained by Walsh, appeared to clearly implicate GEORGE BUSH in the scandal. Bennett characterized the maneuver as blatantly political, aimed at securing victory for BILL CLINTON. To bolster his argument, Bennett pointed to Walsh's recently appointed associate JAMES BROSNAHAN who had been hired to try the Weinberger case. Brosnahan, who had long been an active supporter of liberal causes, was dismissed by Bennett as a partisan Democrat, unfit for service in the office of an independent counsel. Having raised questions as to the true motivation behind the indictment, Bennett was able to successfully lobby the White House for a pardon, which arrived on Christmas Eve.

In May 1994, Bennett agreed to represent President Clinton in the sexual harassment lawsuit brought by former Arkansas state employee PAULA JONES. It appeared to some that Bennett may have exercized poor judgment in agreeing to make the President his client, because Bennett, at the time, was also representing congressman Dan Rostenkowski (D-Illinois) on federal charges. Negotiations with the Justice Department regarding the Rostenkowski case were ongoing, and Bennett's sudden representation of the president might well be seen as another lobbying opportunity for the opportunistic attorney. Despite such criticism, Bennett began his defense of the President with typical aggressiveness, portraying the charges as "tabloid trash." Five months later, when KENNETH STARR was appointed independent counsel for the Whitewater investigation, Bennett once again raised charges of partisanship—this time from the opposite end of the political spectrum. Starr had seriously contemplated filing a friend-of-the-court brief on behalf of the Paula Jones suit, and had been associated with many conservative causes. As Kenneth Starr's investigation concentrated increasingly on President Clinton's behavior in sex-related situations, Bennett's representation of the President in the Paula Jones suit brought him increasingly under the ever-widening probe that began as Whitewater.

Bennett's performance in the Jones case came under criticism in early 1998. Though he was successful in helping postpone the case until after the President's re-election and obtaining a gag order from Judge Susan Webber Wright limiting public statements about the case, critics wondered why a settlement was not engineered after victory was secured at the polls. Without such an agreement to end the matter, the President was forced to give a deposition that could be used as the basis for possible perjury charges. In addition, Bennett's motions for postponement of the case until after the end of Clinton's second term and dismissal of the case outright met with failure. Bennett was also unsuccessful in attempting to prevent Jones's attorneys from dropping defamation aspects of the suit. Without the defamation element, Bennett could not attack Jones's sexual history. Bennett's early aggressiveness was second-guessed. Some maintain that it was his acerbic criticism of LINDA TRIPP's credibility that led the White House informant to tape her conversations with MONICA LEWINSKY, thereby causing the President further difficulty. In defense of Bennett, others had pointed out that he was not working independently. It is possible that Clinton legal team members David Kendall and Lloyd Cutler, as well as HILLARY RODHAM CLINTON, all had significant input into the decisions that were frequently perceived as Bennett's alone.

In November 1998, Clinton settled with Jones for $850,000.

References:

Bendavid, Naftali, and Jan Crawford Greenburg. "Bennett's Legal Plan under Fire." *Chicago Tribune*, 27 January 1998, sec. N, p. 1.

Marcus, Ruth. "Dole and Mitchell Spar over Starr." *Washington Post*, 15 August 1994, sec. A, p. 9.

Taylor, Stuart, Jr., and Daniel Klaidman. "Bob Bennett Got to the Top by Doing a Great Job for His Clients. But He Failed Rostenkowski When He Said Yes to the President." *The American Lawyer* (July/August 1994): 65.

Taylor, Stuart, Jr., Daniel Klaidman, and William W. Horne. "What Kind of Lawyer Is Bob Bennett?" *The American Lawyer* (July/August 1994): 68.

Boland Amendments. The periodic efforts of Congressman Edward P. Boland (D-Massachusetts) to limit presidential prerogatives in the area of foreign affairs met with mixed success during the 34 years in which he represented Massachusetts's second district (1953–1988). A longtime colleague of Thomas P. "Tip" O'Neill, Boland exercised significant influence through his committee offices, but did not become a public figure the way O'Neill did. Boland's service on the House Iran-Contra Committee placed him in direct confrontation with the men who had worked to deliberately avoid the very limitations that Boland's amendment sought to impose.

Negative public reaction to the Vietnam War provided impetus to congressional efforts at restraining the president's ability to act independently in foreign affairs. In 1973, the War Powers Resolution Act mandated that the president notify Congress within 48 hours of his decision to send military forces into any situation likely to result in combat, and withdraw them within 60 days, unless Congress approved their stay; the Nelson-Bingham Amendments in 1974 permitted congressional veto of major arms sales; and the Clark Amendment of 1976 prohibited U.S. military aid to Angola. In recent decades, the executive branch of government has employed a variety of effective methods in order to avoid legislative attempts to limit the president's ability to wage war without congressional consultation. Sidestepping of legislative initiatives could be achieved by conducting covert actions and short-term military strikes. The National Security Council (NSC) and the Central Intelligence Agency (CIA) could be enlisted to run such operations. The Supreme Court's decision in *INS v. CHADHA* (1983) helped as well by ruling against the legislative veto. In fact, the president usually won such confrontations with Congress, because the executive branch was willing to seize the initiative in foreign affairs and Congress usually acquiesced. In addition, the courts traditionally tolerated such executive action. When legislative initiatives like the Boland Amendment succeeded in passing, they usually contained sunset provisions that limited their effectiveness.

They would have to be passed repeatedly in order to avoid providing the executive with windows of opportunity during which otherwise illegal activities could be carried out. Meanwhile, the ever-changing political alignment of Congress made such continual legislative renewals a difficult proposition.

The 1983 version of the Boland Amendment prohibited U.S. funding to aid in the overthrow of the Sandinista government in Nicaragua, including the use of neighboring Honduras as a conduit for military assistance. The provision expired in one year. The 1984 version banned aid to the Contra rebels whether or not it was specifically targeted for the overthrow of the government. This provision too would have a brief lifespan, expiring in October 1984. During the period of its effectiveness, however, it was discovered that the CIA had been circulating a manual that called for the Contras to overthrow the Sandinista government using kidnapping, blackmail, and assassination as recommended tactics. The House Intelligence Committee chaired by Boland conducted hearings in which the CIA was criticized. It was argued that the manual represented a clear violation of the Boland Amendment. Agency officials, including Head WILLIAM CASEY, repudiated the manual, but the CIA escaped without formal sanction or penalty. The Boland Amendment of 1985 extended the ban on Contra funding for another year.

As congressional hearings and the independent counsel investigation of LAWRENCE WALSH began to reveal the intricacies of the arms-for-hostages deal that succeeded in providing substantial assistance to the Contras, the Reagan administration's defenders began to argue that such activity did not in fact violate the Boland Amendment. It did not, they maintained, apply directly to the President or his National Security Council, but rather only to conventional intelligence agencies. President REAGAN expressed the opinion that there was nothing in the Boland Amendment that prohibited him from asking individuals to fund support for the Contras. The only restriction he observed applied to the use of budget funds for that purpose. These views, however, were at odds with the interpretation of many in Congress as well as that of former National Security Adviser ROBERT McFARLANE who testified before Congress that he believed the Boland Amendment applied to the NSC.

Subjected to extensive analysis by political commentators, journalists, and constitutional lawyers, the Boland Amendment's provisions were incapable of decisively answering the questions raised by the IRAN-CONTRA investigation. Instead, they represented one chapter in the long story of Congress's attempts to assert its influence in the conduct of foreign affairs. The Amendment's usefulness as a tool in the Iran-Contra crisis may have been somewhat hampered by the very personality of Edward Boland himself, who characteristically kept a low profile throughout situations that one would think called for a more confrontational response. Boland, a respected and honorable presence on Capitol Hill, always preferred to remain in the background. Even when confronting OLIVER NORTH face-to-face during congressional hearings, Boland barely mentioned the piece of legislation that bore his name. The fact that North's presence before him was a direct result of efforts to circumvent the Boland Amendment did not cause him to deviate from his traditional reserve. "It is the law," said Boland, and the most dramatic presentations and elaborate arguments could elicit no more vociferous discourse on his part.

In the end, the Boland Amendment did not provide Lawrence Walsh with the foundation he needed in order to win conspiracy convictions against those who had worked to circumvent it. Most of the independent counsel's successes would be related to the perjured testimony of the witnesses involved.

References:

Blumenthal, Sidney. "The Boland Achievement." *Washington Post*, 15 June 1987, sec. C, p. 1.

Brinkley, Joel. "House Panel Calls C.I.A. Manual Illegal." *New York Times*, 6 December 1984, sec. A, p. 3.

"Contra-Aid Opponent Calls It a Day." *Chicago Tribune*, 8 April 1988, sec. C, p. 24.

Hayes, Andrew. "The Boland Amendment and Foreign Affairs Deference." *Columbia Law Review* 88 (1988): 1534–1574. Maintains that the NSC violated Boland, because the executive should not be accorded free interpretation of statutes.

Koh, Harold Hongju. "Why the President (Almost) Always Wins in Foreign Affairs: Lessons of the Iran-Contra Affair." *Yale Law Journal* 97 (1988): 1255–1342. Argues that use of the legislative veto and power over appropriations represent the legislature's best chances for success in limiting executive action in foreign affairs.

Lee, Rex E. "Boland Does Not Apply to the President." *Los Angeles Times*, 22 June 1987, part 2, p. 5. Lee was Solicitor General of the U.S., 1981–1985.

McGrory, Mary. "SHHHH! Congress Doesn't Want to Wash Our Dirty Little War in Public." *Washington Post*, 16 December 1982, sec. A, p. 3.

Saikowski, Charlotte. "Iran-Contra Probe: Reagan's View of Law Called into Question." *Christian Science Monitor*, 21 May 1987, p. 1.

"A Sorry Record." *Time*, 18 April 1983, p. 31.

Taylor, Stuart, Jr. "Reagan's Defenders Arguing He Can Defy Congress's Ban." *New York Times*, 17 May 1987, p. 14.

Wallace, Don, Jr. and Allen Gerson. "The Dubious Boland Amendments." *Washington Post*, 5 June 1987, sec. A, p. 27.

Will, George. "The 'Spirit' of Boland, a Pseudo-Law." *Washington Post*, 24 May 1987, sec. D, p. 7.

Bonaparte, Charles J. (1851–1921) Special Prosecutor, Post Office investigation, 1903. The grandnephew of France's Emperor Napoleon, Charles Bonaparte was born in Baltimore, educated at Harvard, and made a career in the law. His work as a civil service reformer in the city of his birth brought him to the attention of THEODORE ROOSEVELT, who served on the Civil Service Commission under Presidents Benjamin Harrison and Grover Cleveland. After entering the White House upon the death of William McKinley, Roosevelt called upon Bonaparte for assistance in eliminating alleged corruption in the Post Office. During the summer of 1903, Bonaparte worked as special assistant in the

Justice Department. His recommendations in favor of personnel and procedural changes were largely adopted in the fall.

Bonaparte's appointment in 1903 followed the dismissal of Assistant Attorney General John N. Tyner who was suspected of destroying documents related to misconduct in the Postal Service. Bonaparte's presence served to support the internal investigation of Post Office corruption being conducted by Assistant Postmaster General Joseph L. Bristow. Roosevelt's head of the Post Office, Henry Clay Payne, was in ill health, and dealt feebly with the burgeoning scandal. The President, however, apparently found Payne useful as a political ally in his rivalry with Mark Hanna. Consequently, Payne remained Postmaster General until his death in 1904, while Bristow addressed the problems in the department. Bonaparte supported prosecution of Tyner, as well as Charles Emory Smith and Perry S. Heath, Postmaster General and first Assistant respectively in McKinley's administration. Tyner died in 1904, and the case against Heath was eventually dropped due to insufficient evidence. Nevertheless, the action that had been initiated appeared to serve effective notice that the Postal Service would conduct its internal affairs according to the merit system, and that politics would not drive the process. Numerous lower-level personnel changes occurred during the summer of 1903, adding to the general housecleaning of the department. While Roosevelt praised the manner in which Payne handled the affair, insiders understood that it was Bristow and Bonaparte who had effected the reform.

Bonaparte joined Roosevelt's cabinet as Secretary of the Navy in 1905. In December 1906, he was appointed attorney general. In this capacity, Bonaparte helped wage Roosevelt's war against the trusts. Twenty antitrust lawsuits were initiated by Bonaparte, eight of which were decided in the government's favor. The dissolution of the American Tobacco Company may have been Bonaparte's most notable accomplishment. Bonaparte returned to private law practice in Baltimore in 1909, but he remained active in reform politics as a Republican and a Roosevelt Progressive. He was one of the founders of the Municipal League and a frequent speaker for the cause of civic reform.

References:

Dictionary of National Biography, volume 1, p. 427–428. New York: Scribners, 1964.

Gould, Lewis L. *The Presidency of Theodore Roosevelt.* Lawrence: University Press of Kansas, 1991. Chapter 5, "The Square Deal," discusses the Post Office scandal and Bonaparte's role in its resolution.

National Cyclopedia of American Biography, volume 14, p. 22–23. Ann Arbor: University Microfilms, 1967.

Bork, Robert H. (1927–   ) lawyer, former Solicitor General, federal judge. When President RICHARD NIXON fired WATERGATE Special Prosecutor ARCHIBALD COX on October 20, 1973, it was the Justice Department's Solicitor General, Robert Bork, who accomplished what has since become known

as the "Saturday Night Massacre." Both Attorney General ELLIOT RICHARD-
SON and his deputy, WILLIAM RUCKLESHAUS, resigned rather than obey
the president's directive. Bork apparently gave serious consideration to following suit. He decided against such a course, because he believed that his own
resignation might fuel a flurry of such actions that would have brought down
the administration prematurely, perhaps sparking a constitutional crisis. In addition, Richardson had pointed out that if Bork resigned too, there would, in
effect, be no Justice Department. Of course, by staying, Bork allowed himself
to be associated with Nixon's attempt to cover up the WATERGATE scandal.

Bork's decision to remain in the Justice Department meant that he would play
an integral part in working with the Watergate Special Prosecuting Force
(WSPF) in its attempts to unravel the story of Watergate. Although Cox had
been dismissed, the public outcry that ensued required the appointment of a
successor who would carry on Cox's investigation. Although the Watergate Special Prosecutor enjoyed relatively independent status, he was technically a part
of the Justice Department. In actuality, both Cox and his successor, LEON
JAWORSKI, met with the attorney general on a regular basis in order to address
questions regarding investigative jurisdiction, cooperative efforts, and government policy. Jaworski negotiated the terms of his position with Bork, now Acting Attorney General, and on occasion conferred regarding clarification of his
position. Bork was in a considerably more difficult situation than Richardson
had been. Outrage over Cox's firing would make it difficult for the attorney
general (especially an acting one) to question the actions of the special prosecutor or seek to limit his investigation in any significant way. In addition, the
Senate Judiciary Committee exercised greater oversight of WSPF activity after
receiving reports that the White House had refused to provide Cox with evidence
he needed in order to conduct his investigation. This meant that Bork was called
upon by the Judiciary Committee to facilitate Jaworski's efforts at obtaining
such evidence. Bork duly instructed Jaworski to indicate to the committee all
requests for evidence that had not been honored. Bork's tenure as Acting Attorney General (1973–1974) was marked by general cooperation with the special
prosecutor. When William Saxbe was named attorney general, Bork reassumed
the duties of Solicitor General.

In 1982, Robert Bork was named judge of the U.S. Court of Appeals for the
District of Columbia Circuit. Two years later, he helped decide the case of
NATHAN V. ATTORNEY GENERAL in which private citizens sought appointment of an independent counsel to investigate an alleged cover-up of FBI involvement in the shooting of Communist Worker Party members during protests
in Greensboro, North Carolina. Attorney General WILLIAM FRENCH SMITH
contended that the citzens lacked standing to bring a suit in this matter, but the
district court disagreed. The court ruled that citizens had a procedural right to
bring charges against officials covered by the ETHICS IN GOVERNMENT
ACT (1978). If they did not, stated the court, the Act would be little more than
an empty political proclamation. The Court of Appeals, however, overturned the

decision. Judge Bork ruled that the Ethics in Government Act did not permit private citizens to compel action by the attorney general. In this case, the attorney general could not be forced to initiate a preliminary investigation that might result in requesting appointment of an independent counsel. Only the attorney general is permitted to trigger the process that may result in such an appointment. In addition, Bork established himself as a clear opponent of the concept of an independent counsel by declaring that all law enforcement power must reside in the executive branch of government. Therefore, the arrangement calling for court appointment of an independent counsel must be unconstitutional.

Judge Bork's unsuccessful candidacy for the Supreme Court in 1987 brought him great public attention. The Senate's refusal to confirm his nomination by President REAGAN could reasonably be interpreted as a rejection of the conservative theory of judicial restraint long advocated by Bork. The doctrine of judicial restraint, however, should not be interpreted to mean that Judge Bork was always content to permit Congress free reign. In 1988, Bork found himself in accord with the man he had dutifully dismissed fifteen years before. Both Bork and Cox appeared before a Senate committee to testify against a proposed bill that would have removed the issue of abortion from court jurisdiction.

References:

Bork, Robert H. "Against the Independent Counsel." *Commentary* (February 1993): 21. Bork argues against reauthorization of the independent counsel statute based on his evaluation of the office's record, which he characterizes as "abominable."

Carter, Betsy, Stephan Lesher, and Tony Fuller. "Saturday-Night Survivors." *Newsweek*, 20 October 1975, p. 14.

Harriger, Katy J. *Independent Justice: The Federal Special Prosecutor in American Politics*. Lawrence: University Press of Kansas, 1992. Chapter 3, "A Watergate Legacy: The Independent Counsel Provisions of the Ethics in Government Act," relates Bork's role in dismissal of Special Prosecutor Archibald Cox, and his relationship with Leon Jaworski. Chapter 5, "Is the Special Prosecutor Constitutional?," details his decision in the case *Nathan v. Attorney General* (1984).

"Next in Line for the Nine." *Nation*, 8 October 1984, p. 32.

Press, Aric, and Diane Camper. "A Justice-in-Waiting." *Newsweek*, 31 August 1981, p. 37.

Swire, Peter, and Simon Lazarus. "Reactionary Activism: Conservatives and the Constitution." *The New Republic*, 22 February 1988, p. 17.

***Bowsher v. Synar*, 478 U.S. 714 (1986).** This case held that Congress violated separation of powers principles in vesting certain functions in the Comptroller General of the United States under the Balanced Budget and Emergency Deficit Control Act of 1985 (better known as "Gramm-Rudman," after two of its primary senatorial sponsors). The functions at issue, according to the Court, were part and parcel of the execution of the laws, and could be delegated only to officers of the United States who were immune, except through impeachment, to any congressional role in their removal. By statute, however, the Comptroller

General is removable also by "joint resolution of Congress, after notice and an opportunity for a hearing, only for (i) permanent disability; (ii) inefficiency; (iii) neglect of duty; (iv) malfeasance; or (v) a felony or conduct involving moral turpitude" [See 31 U.S.C. § 703(e)(1)(B)]. Hence, the Court held, Congress overstepped separation of powers bounds by permitting the Comptroller General a role in executing the laws.

Gramm-Rudman embodied a complex congressional attempt to deal with the once-intractable problem of growing budget deficits. As part of the newly enacted process, both the Director of the Office of Management and Budget, a close presidential adviser, and the Director of the Congressional Budget Office, clearly a functionary of the legislative branch, were to develop projections of the likely budget deficit for each approaching fiscal year. They would report their projections to the Comptroller General of the United States, who would, in essence, perform two key functions. First, if the projections differed, the Comptroller General would have to reconcile them. Second, if the projected deficits exceeded a statutorily prescribed target, the Comptroller General would determine a figure by which the President would have to cut back on previously authorized spending through a process called "sequestration." Once the Comptroller General provided this information, the President was bound to issue the sequestration order. The Court determined that the Comptroller General's powers to determine a binding projection of the budget deficit and thus require the President to sequester funds in a particular matter amounted to participation in the execution of the laws.

In a highly formalistic opinion, the Court found it impermissible to vest such functions in any public official whom Congress could remove other than through impeachment—even though there was no practical showing that enacting a joint resolution of removal would have been a process less protective of the incumbent than impeachment. It was enough for the Court to observe:

> Congress cannot reserve for itself the power of removal of an officer charged with the execution of the laws except by impeachment. To permit the execution of the laws to be vested in an officer answerable only to Congress would, in practical terms, reserve in Congress control over the execution of the laws. [See 478 U.S. at 726.]

Pursuant to this reading of the Constitution, Congress, in providing for independent counsel, may protect such officers from the President's plenary powers of removal to the extent consistent with *HUMPHREY'S EXECUTOR v. UNITED STATES*, 295 U.S. 602 (1935), but may not reserve to itself any power other than impeachment with regard to the removal of the independent counsel. The same conclusion would follow from *MYERS v. UNITED STATES*, 272 U.S. 52 (1925), which held it impermissible to require Senate advice and consent to the removal of an official charged with helping to execute the laws.

References:

Cornell Law Review 72 no. 3 (1987). Entire issue is a symposium devoted to *Bowsher v. Synar.* Includes articles by Thomas O. Sargentich, Peter L. Strauss, L. Harold Levinson, Russell K. Osgood.

—PETER M. SHANE

Brosnahan, James J. (1934–   ) Associate Independent Counsel, Iran-Contra investigation. A controversial choice of LAWRENCE WALSH's to lead the prosecution of former Secretary of Defense CASPAR WEINBERGER, James Brosnahan was born in Boston but built his career in the San Francisco area. Recommended to Walsh by fellow San Francisco attorney JOHN KEKER, prosecutor of OLIVER NORTH, Brosnahan had long been associated with liberal/progressive causes. He had served in Robert Kennedy's Justice Department, defended sanctuary church workers who helped refugees escape right wing governments in Central America, and had been active in the anti-apartheid and abortion rights movements. A partner in the large San Francisco firm of Morrison & Foerster, Brosnahan's legal skills were well-established, but Walsh must have known that his new associate's political preferences would come under attack by the Republicans. Brosnahan's appointment might be interpreted as a sign of frustration by Walsh, himself a Republican, who found his investigation continually thwarted by the BUSH administration.

Brosnahan first appeared in the national news when he testified against the appointment of William Rehnquist to the Supreme Court in August 1986. He recalled an incident that occurred in Phoenix, Arizona, on election day in 1962. While investigating complaints of voter harassment, Brosnahan was informed that Rehnquist was aggressively and belligerently challenging the voting credentials of black and Hispanic voters in the South Phoenix election district. His testimony contradicted Rehnquist's denial of such activity, and precipitated an angry response from Senator Orrin Hatch (R-Utah) who accused Brosnahan of lying.

After the indictment of Weinberger in October 1992, Walsh associate CRAIG GILLEN was forced to recuse himself from the case. Weinberger's attorneys indicated that they intended to call Gillen as a witness in order to challenge prosecution assertions that Weinberger lied under oath. U.S. District Judge Thomas Hogan expressed concern about Gillen's continued participation on the prosecution team, prompting Gillen to retire. Walsh quickly replaced Gillen with Brosnahan who had just three months to prepare to face Weinberger defense attorney ROBERT BENNETT at trial.

In November, Senate Minority Leader ROBERT DOLE suggested that Walsh fire Brosnahan. Dole claimed that the credibility of the new prosecutor had been compromised when it was revealed that Brosnahan had contributed $500 to the CLINTON campaign. Walsh refused Dole's request in a written response, and expressed objections to such interference in a pending lawsuit. Brosnahan, it is clear, was entering a situation where tempers were already raised. Walsh's indictment of Weinberger had occurred a mere four days before the presidential election. Despite Walsh's claim that the filing deadline was known for over a month, the timing of the event seemed an act of political calculation to the Republicans. Dole called for an investigation into the timing of the Weinberger indictment. Attorney General WILLIAM BARR ordered such an investigation, but declined to name an independent counsel.

On Christmas Eve, Bush issued a pardon to Caspar Weinberger and five other IRAN-CONTRA defendants (ELLIOTT ABRAMS, DUANE CLARRIDGE, ROBERT McFARLANE, ALAN FIERS, and CLAIR GEORGE). Two days later, an angry James Brosnahan expressed his outrage. Claiming that history would ultimately condemn Bush's action, Brosnahan asserted that he had built a strong case against Weinberger that clearly implicated Bush as well. Brosnahan stated that Weinberger's own notes, which the former Secretary of Defense long insisted did not exist, placed both Bush and Weinberger at meetings of the National Security Council when the arms-for-hostages deal was discussed. Weinberger's notes, said Brosnahan, clearly demonstrated that he had lied to Congress when he claimed no knowledge of the Iran-Contra connection.

In January, Brosnahan spoke to the Santa Clara County Bar Association in his first public address since the pardon ended his Iran-Contra involvement. Brosnahan argued that Iran-Contra was a question of law, not politics. The prosecution sought to demonstrate that war cannot be waged in opposition to the wishes of Congress, and that "even the king is subject to the law." Brosnahan praised two Republicans he had interviewed as prosecutor, Senator WILLIAM COHEN (R-Maine) and former Senator Warren Rudman (R-New Hampshire), and defended Lawrence Walsh's efforts as independent counsel.

In January 1998, Brosnahan joined those who expressed concern over the direction in which Independent Counsel KENNETH STARR's WHITEWATER investigation was moving. Brosnahan claimed that Starr's efforts to uncover the truth of the MONICA LEWINSKY affair had taken him far afield from his original inquiry, and led one to ask if the investigation had turned into a personal vendetta against President Clinton. Brosnahan believed that the idea of an independent counsel still had merit, but further reform of the office was warranted in order to keep investigations on track.

References:

Brazil, Eric. "Ex-Special Prosecutor Doubts Starr's Goals." *San Francisco Examiner*, 27 January 1998, sec A, p. 7.

Halstuk, Martin. "Weinberger Prosecutor Lashes Out." *San Francisco Chronicle*, 26 December 1992, sec. A, p. 2.

Mintz, Howard. "Brosnahan to Prosecute Weinberger." *The Recorder*, 16 October 1992, p. 1.

Pincus, Walter. "Walsh Rejects Call to Fire New Prosecutor." *Washington Post*, 11 November 1992, sec. A, p. 18.

Taylor, Stuart, Jr. "4 Rebut Testimony of Rehnquist on Challenging of Voters in 60's."
    New York Times, 2 August 1986, p. 1.
Walsh, Mark. "Brosnahan Speech Tops Bar Installation Dinner." *The Recorder*, 25 January 1993, p. 3.

Brown, Ronald Harmon (1941–1996) Secretary of Commerce, 1993–1996. After serving as Democratic Party National Chairman (1989–1993)—the first African American to chair a major political party in the United States—Ron Brown was named to President CLINTON's cabinet as Commerce Secretary. In this capacity, he proved an energetic promoter of American business and industry. His success in this role made it difficult for Republicans, whose many supporters benefited from the international contracts Brown facilitated, to abolish the Commerce cabinet post as part of the cost-saving platform that gave them control of Congress in 1994.

Beginning in 1994, Brown's activities became the subject of federal investigation. In February of that year, the Justice Department briefly looked into allegations that Brown had accepted $700,000 in return for helping to lift the U.S. trade ban against Vietnam. They found nothing worthy of prosecution. More problematic allegations surfaced the following year when questions were raised about Brown's financial dealings with business partner Nolanda Hill. Brown held an interest in Hill's company, First International, Inc., until he divested himself in 1994, and admitted receiving over $400,000 in payments from her, including a $37,000 loan that she forgave and $190,000 that covered some of Brown's personal debts. It was alleged that Brown also filed inaccurate financial disclosure statements and a misleading mortgage application in connection with a town house that he wished to purchase. These charges were deemed substantial enough by Attorney General JANET RENO to request the appointment of an independent counsel. Accordingly, former federal prosecutor DANIEL PEARSON was named by the court panel to conduct the investigation.

Early in 1996, Pearson expanded his probe to include Ron Brown's son, Michael, who was paid $160,000 by Dynamic Energy Resources, an Oklahoma natural gas firm, to act as its lobbyist. Dynamic's former president was quoted as saying that the payments were made to curry favor with the Department of Commerce. In addition, it was reported that Brown had provided a job for the daughter of Dynamic's owners. By April 1996, the Internal Revenue Service was investigating whether First International had cheated on its tax returns, and reports were circulating that Brown had overspent his department travel budget.

As troublesome as this multitude of charges might appear, in truth Ron Brown's activities were little affected. Pearson had been appointed as independent counsel in July. It was September before his office was fully staffed, and the investigation proceeded in silence until the following March. Although Pearson had hired six attorneys, and was also employing experts from the FBI, IRS, and the Federal Deposit Insurance Corporation, he himself was not devoting all his time to the investigation, nor was any of this in the public eye. During this period, Brown continued to perform his duties as Commerce Secretary unhindered by the sort of harassing press inquiries that normally accompany investigation of federal officials. The Commerce Secretary functioned as the administration's spokesman on American trade and led a five-nation tour of Africa in February. This situation annoyed Republican critics such as Representative William Clinger (Pennsylvania), Chairman of the House Government Reform and Oversight Committee. Clinger had been raising ethical concerns regarding Brown's activities ever since the Commerce Secretary had taken office, and he had anticipated that his concerns would receive greater attention once the Republicans had won control of Congress in the 1994 elections. By pressing Janet Reno to request an independent counsel, however, rather than mount his own full-scale investigation, Clinger had inadvertently facilitated the silencing of the whole affair.

Despite the ongoing investigation, there was no anti-Brown sentiment visible when, on April 3, 1996, the airplane carrying Brown and his party crashed in Dubrovnik, Croatia, killing all 35 on board. Ron Brown was eulogized as a visionary who realized that the nation could never be truly great unless it rose to greatness in the arena of international trade. Reducing America's efforts to promote its exports was unconscionable, said Brown. His efforts in this area were praised by American labor, angry over jobs lost overseas, and by American business, eager to open up new markets for their goods. Ron Brown represented an African-American success story. He had grown up in Harlem, where his father was manager of the Theresa Hotel. He had distingushed himself at college in Vermont, breaking color barriers by becoming the first non-white member of his fraternity. His mentors included Mario Cuomo (his law professor at St. John's University), Vernon Jordan (who hired him as the Urban League's general counsel), Ted Kennedy (for whom he worked during the 1980 presidential campaign), and Jesse Jackson (for whom he was employed as a strategist in 1988). He became a partner in the influential Washington law firm of Patton, Boggs & Blow. As Democratic Party National Chair, he engineered a campaign that elected a rather obscure Arkansas governor president. He ascended to the cabinet, and aspired to the position of Secretary of State in a second Clinton term. Some say the "commercial diplomacy" he conducted as Commerce Secretary made him a logical choice. Whether his questionable financial dealings would have ultimately spelled disaster is unanswerable. The independent counsel investigation was terminated with Ron Brown's death.

References:

"Ex-Judge to Be Counsel in Ron Brown Inquiry." *Chicago Tribune*, 7 July 1995, p. 4.
Jones, Joyce. "The Best Commerce Secretary Ever." *Black Enterprise* (June 1996): 90.
Knight, Jerry. "Ronald Brown Probe Widens." *Washington Post*, 30 March 1996, sec. C, p. 1.
Rowan, Carl. "Lessons Americans Can Learn from the Life of Ron Brown." *Buffalo News*, 9 April 1996, sec. B, p. 3.

White, Jack E. "An Empty Seat at the Table: Ronald Harmon Brown, 1941–1996." *Time*, 15 April 1996, 72.

York, Byron. "Why Ron Brown Won't Go Down." *The American Spectator* (April 1996): 32–34.

Bruce, Carol Elder (1949–   ) Independent Counsel, Babbitt investigation. As a former Assistant U.S. Attorney in the District of Columbia (1975–1985), Carol Bruce brought over 100 felony investigations before grand juries and prosecuted a variety of other crimes. She specialized in white-collar crime and international terrorism cases. Bruce worked with President CLINTON's legal adviser and former WATERGATE Special Prosecutor CHARLES RUFF in helping successfully defend Senator John Glenn (D-Ohio) against charges that he had assisted savings-and-loan president Charles Keating in return for political contributions. She also helped prosecute former CIA agents Edwin Wilson and Frank Terpil who were accused of aiding Libyan terrorists. Wilson was later sentenced to 25 years in prison for attempting to murder Bruce and other law enforcement officials. Bruce also served as Deputy Independent Counsel during JAMES McKAY's investigation of possible misconduct by Attorney General EDWIN MEESE in 1987–1988. A Democrat, she was not active politically, and her appointment drew praise from former independent counsel JOSEPH DIGENOVA who testified to her skill as a litigator and vouched for her nonpartisan approach.

In March 1988, Bruce was charged with investigating whether Secretary of the Interior BRUCE BABBITT had lied to Congress regarding his department's denial of a gambling casino application presented by a group of Chippewa Indians in Wisconsin. Babbitt maintained that politics did not enter into the decision, but rival Indian tribes were substantial contributors to President CLINTON's re-election campaign. Bruce's charge allowed her to include in her probe examination of any other violations of federal criminal law that may have occurred, but did not accede to Republican requests that overall Democratic campaign contribution behavior be included.

Republicans were quick to condemn the appointment of Bruce. Jim Nicholson, Republican National Committee Chairman, expressed explicit objections to Bruce because of her association with Ruff as well as her participation in the Meese investigation. Meese was not indicted, but his behavior was criticized.

Babbitt pledged cooperation with Bruce, and expressed confidence in his vindication. It was suggested by some analysts, however, that Babbitt might eventually prove to be one of many possible targets for Bruce's investigation, and perhaps not the principal one. Congress delivered to Bruce a collection of messages, memoranda, and depositions that hinted at possible involvement of Babbitt's employees and White House officials in influencing the decision to deny the Chippewa casino application for political reasons. Specifically, Babbitt counsel John Duffy and former Chief of Staff Tom Collier appeared to be most closely involved as well as former White House official Harold Ickes. Both

Duffy and Collier took jobs with Babbitt's former law firm, Steptoe & Johnson, the year following the casino decision. In their new positions, they helped represent the Shakopee Sioux, one of the tribes that had opposed the casino. In addition, Duffy helped arrange a contribution of $50,000 from the Shakopees to the 1996 Clinton re-election campaign. Only the congressional testimony of Paul Eckstein, former associate and law school classmate of Babbitt's, appeared to implicate the Secretary of the Interior. Eckstein claimed that Babbitt alluded to an attempt by Ickes to influence the casino decision, and also acknowledged the sizable campaign contributions routinely donated by the tribes opposed to the casino during a meeting shortly before the decision was announced. Babbitt insisted that the Ickes remark was misinterpreted and denied discussing tribal campaign contributions at all.

Bruce's investigation, unresolved when the independent counsel statute expired on June 30, 1999, was concluded on October 13 when she dismissed all charges against Babbitt citing lack of evidence.

References:

Barker, Jeff. "Babbitt Case About More Than Just Interior Chief." *Arizona Republic*, 24 March 1998, sec. A, p. 2.

———. "Babbitt Investigator Draws GOP Fire." *Arizona Republic*, 20 March 1998, sec. A, p. 1.

"Independent Counsel Named to Investigate Babbitt's Casino Role." *Chicago Tribune*, 20 March 1998, sec. N, p. 3.

Jackson, Robert L, and Ronald J. Ostrow. "Special Counsel Named in Babbitt Probe." *Los Angeles Times*, 20 March 1998, sec. A, p. 18.

Salant, Jonathan D. "Ex-Associate of Clinton Aide to Probe Babbitt." *Buffalo News*, 20 March 1998, sec. A, p. 6.

Buckley v. Valeo, 424 U.S. 1 (1976). This case resolved a series of challenges to the constitutionality of the Federal Election Campaign Act of 1971 (FECA), a comprehensive effort to reform campaign finance practices associated with the election of federal officials. Part of that effort was Congress's creation of the Federal Election Commission, originally comprising eight members—the Secretary of the Senate and the Clerk of the House, both serving *ex officio*, plus two members each chosen by the President, the Speaker of the House, and the President *pro tempore* of the Senate, respectively. (All six voting members of the FEC were to be approved by majority votes of both Houses of Congress, and no appointing authority could choose both appointees from the same political party.) The plaintiffs successfully argued that the FEC's duties rendered its members "officers of the United States," who could be selected pursuant only to the four modes of appointment explicitly authorized in the Constitution, Art. II, § 2, par. 2. The Court's holding necessarily implies a similar limitation on Congress's capacity to provide for the appointment of independent counsel.

Article II of the Constitution provides that the President:

shall nominate, and by and with the Advice and Consent of the Senate, shall appoint Ambassadors, other public Ministers and Consuls, Judges of the Supreme Court, and all other Officers of the United States, whose Appointments are not herein otherwise provided for, and which shall be established by Law: but the Congress may by Law vest the Appointment of such inferior Officers, as they think proper, in the President alone, in the Courts of Law, or in the Heads of Departments.

These provisions thus contemplate four modes for appointing "Officers of the United States." The default position, compulsory for all officers who are not "inferior officers," is that the President shall nominate the officer and then, if the Senate consents, complete the appointment. With regard to "inferior officers," however, Congress may authorize their appointment by the President, by the courts, or by the "Heads of Departments," without requiring Senate consent to a prior act of nomination.

In enacting the FEC appointments scheme, Congress had implicitly taken the position that the specification of appointment methods in Article II should be read as illustrative, rather than as exhaustive, and that Congress should be permitted to improvise new methods of appointment should some such innovation be fitting for the particular officers and governmental functions involved. Congress defended the particular modes of FEC appointment that it enacted as appropriate to assure that no one party's point of view would predominate in policing campaign financing, and that allegiance to an appointing President would not unduly influence those charged with overseeing critical aspects of presidential elections.

The Supreme Court rejected Congress's position without according any weight to the rationality of Congress's point of view in this matter. The Court held that the Article II appointments methods had to be deemed exclusive in order to protect a larger principle—preventing the aggrandizement of Congress's role in administering the laws it enacted: "Not having the power of appointment, unless expressly granted or incidental to its powers, the legislature cannot ingraft executive duties upon a legislative office, since that would be to usurp the power of appointment by indirection" (424 U.S. at 139 [citation omitted]).

As a result, the Court held, should Congress provide for the appointment of a public functionary through some method other than those articulated in Article II, that functionary constitutionally cannot be deemed an "officer of the United States," and must be limited to "perform[ing] duties only in aid of those functions that Congress may carry out by itself, or in an area sufficiently removed from the administration and enforcement of the public law as to permit their being performed by persons not 'Officers of the United States' " (*Id.*). The Court stated: "Insofar as the powers confided in the Commission [were] essentially of an investigative and informative nature, falling in the same general category as those powers which Congress might delegate to one of its own committees," (*id.* at 137), Congress could innovate in designing the processes for the commissioners' appointments.

Congress was limited to the Article II methods of appointment, however, for any functionary authorized to perform "a significant governmental duty exercised pursuant to a public law" (*Id.* at 141). Among such powers vested in the FEC, the Court's primary example of a duty dischargeable only by an "officer of the United States" was "responsibility for conducting civil litigation in the courts of the United States for vindicating public rights" (*Id.* at 141). (The Court would plainly have reached the same conclusion if, like independent counsel, the FEC had power to conduct criminal litigation.) The Court reached the same conclusion with regard to the FEC's other significant administrative powers, "including rulemaking, advisory opinions, and determinations of eligibility for funds and even for federal elective office itself," even though "[t]hese functions, exercised free from day-to-day supervision of either Congress or the Executive Branch, are more legislative and judicial in nature than are the Commission's enforcement powers" (*Id.* at 140). So long as a public official is performing a significant public duty that Congress may not perform itself or through its committees, that official must be appointed pursuant to Article II, whether or not the official's duties are traditionally characterized as executive in nature.

Given the preeminent law enforcement functions vested in independent counsel, it must follow that such prosecutors may be appointed only by the President, with the advice and consent of the Senate, or, to the extent such a prosecutor is an "inferior officer," by the President, by the head of a department, or by a court of law. To remove the President from even an indirect role in selecting an independent counsel, Congress chose the last of these methods in enacting the ETHICS IN GOVERNMENT ACT.

References:

Simon, Donald J. "The Constitutionality of the Special Prosecutor Law." *University of Michigan Journal of Law Reform* 16 (1982): 45–74.
Tiefer, Charles. "The Constitutionality of Independent Officers as Checks on Abuses of Executive Power." *Boston University Law Review* 63 (1983): 59–103.

—PETER M. SHANE

Bush, George Herbert Walker (1924–   ) President of the United States, 1989–1993; Vice President, 1981–1989. George Bush quickly rose in the ranks of the Republican Party during the decade of the 1970s, assuming a variety of responsible posts of national importance: Congressman (R-Texas) 1971–1973; Ambassador to the United Nations 1973–1974; Chairman of the Republican National Committee 1974–1975; and Director of the Central Intelligence Agency 1976–1977. Serving as RONALD REAGAN's Vice President during the time in which efforts were being made to free American hostages in Lebanon and fund the Contras in Nicaragua, George Bush's knowledge of and involvement in these events were the subject of serious inquiry by LAWRENCE WALSH during the IRAN-CONTRA investigation. The extent to which Bush participated in the arms-for-hostages deal with Iran remained a question during his presidency, and may have contributed to his failure to win re-election in 1992.

By the end of President Reagan's second term, investigations into Iran-Contra had moved beyond lower-level government functionaries, and were beginning to evaluate roles played by National Security Council members. George Bush's presence at National Security Council (NSC) meetings called into question the extent of his participation in decisions made regarding Iran and Nicaragua. JOHN POINDEXTER and OLIVER NORTH, whose testimony before Congress was already being challenged as untrue, found themselves fighting prosecution and possible criminal penalties. George Bush, however, claiming ignorance of any wrongdoing, was seeking the presidency. There was speculation that Bush already felt tainted by independent counsel investigations of Attorney General EDWIN MEESE. Bush, it was said, desired Meese's resignation in order to avoid any further guilt-by-association.

Publication of the TOWER COMMISSION REPORT in 1987 led many to assume that Bush certainly had knowledge of the Iran-Contra affair, even if he was not an active participant. The report placed him at meetings where arrangements were discussed, but did not attribute to him any active role. Congressional hearings on Iran-Contra did not focus on the role of the Vice President. Rather, they aimed at uncovering whether President Reagan was involved. Still, key committee members were left with the assumption that Bush was a willing party to the affair. Early in President Bush's first term, Lawrence Walsh presented Oliver North's attorney, BRENDAN SULLIVAN, with a 42-page "admission of facts," stating that the Vice President had met with Honduran President Roberto Suazo Cordova in order to negotiate aid for the Nicaraguan Contras. The agreement that resulted called for Honduras to funnel military supplies to the Contras in return for America's promise to expedite economic and miltary aid for the nation. This information helped Sullivan portray North as a mere pawn in the Iran-Contra scheme, but clearly depicted Bush as disingenuous after having earlier stated that such arrangements would be in violation of the BOLAND AMENDMENT.

Lawrence Walsh's investigation, which continued throughout President Bush's presidential term, contended with unfavorable court decisions and problems occasioned by congressional grants of IMMUNITY to key witnesses. Four days before the presidential election of 1992, Walsh announced the indictment of former Secretary of Defense CASPAR WEINBERGER. Weinberger's handwritten notes of January 7, 1986, discovered the previous spring, implicated Bush along with former Secretary of State GEORGE SHULTZ in the arms-for-hostages planning. Announcement of the indictment was assailed by Republican leaders such as Bob DOLE who saw the timing as calculated to influence the election. Analysts generally believed that the news contributed to Bush's defeat, but was probably not decisive. The awkward timing of the indictment facilitated the Christmas Eve pardon of Weinberger and five other Iran-Contra defendants announced by Bush on December 24, 1992. Angered by the pardon, Walsh contemplated further action against Bush, but the outgoing president and his attorney, GRIFFIN BELL (former attorney general during the CARTER administration), were successful in fending off any further attacks. The independent counsel had to satisfy himself with reiterating the findings surrounding Bush's Iran-Contra role in his final report issued in 1994. Walsh regarded Bush's pardon as subverting the principal of equal treatment under the law by allowing superiors to avoid the penalties meted out to lower-level operatives. At least one legal analyst questioned whether Bush's Christmas Eve announcement amounted to self-pardon, and discussed whether such an action would be constitutionally permissible.

Two additional inquiries during the Bush presidency involved brushes with the independent counsel office. The Atlanta branch of Italy's government-owned Banca Nazionale del Lavaro, apparently with the knowledge and consent of its Rome headquarters, made over $5 billion in illegal loans to Saddam Hussein from 1985 to 1989. Significant portions of this money appeared to have funded Iraq's military arsenal, and there was circumstantial evidence that the White House was aware of the loans. Democratic calls for an independent counsel, however, were rebuffed by Attorney General WILLIAM BARR who preferred to order his own investigation into the matter. In 1992, Independent Counsel JOSEPH DiGENOVA was named to investigate the improper use of BILL CLINTON's State Department file by members of the Bush campaign. Clinton's trip to Prague as a student in 1969 was the subject of scrutiny by those who hoped to use any potentially embarrassing incidents for political ends. Bush campaign employees apparently received assistance from the Czech Federal Security and Information Service during their search. DiGenova's final report in 1995, however, found no evidence of criminal activity.

References:

"Awkward Timing." *Time*, 9 November 1992, p. 22.

Borger, Gloria, with Kenneth T. Walsh and Ted Gest. "White House Follies." *U.S. News & World Report*, 16 May 1988, p. 20.

Cohen, William S, and George J. Mitchell. *Men of Zeal.* New York: Viking, 1988. Concludes that Bush endorsed the arms-for-hostages sale as Vice President either out of loyalty to President Reagan or out of desire to obtain release of the hostages.

Corn, David. "Instant Karma—Eventually." *The Nation* 255 (1992): 532.

Friedman, Alan. "BNL Hell: An Iraqgate Primer." *New Republic*, 9 November 1992, p. 18.

Kalt, Brian C. "Pardon Me?: The Constitutional Case against Presidential Self-Pardons." *Yale Law Journal* 106 (1996): 779–809. Sees Bush's Christmas Eve pardon as dangerously close to self-pardon. Argues against such pardons as likely to undermine public confidence in the executive and the Constitution.

Madison, Christopher. "Old Scandal Rides Again." *National Journal* 14 (1992): 2620.

Magnuson, Ed. "Pawn among the Giants." *Time*, 17 April 1989, p. 22.

Shapiro, Walter. "Bush Bites Back." *Time*, 18 January 1988, p. 16.

Stein, Jonathan. "Czech It Out." *The Nation* 258 (1994): 149.

C

Carter, James Earl (1924–   ) President of the United States, 1977–1980. On October 26, 1978, President Jimmy Carter signed into law the ETHICS IN GOVERNMENT ACT, which included establishment of the Office of Special Prosecutor. The president's remarks upon signing made reference to the mechanism being set in place for appointment of a prosecutor, and stressed the protection being provided for the individual in the exercise of his/her duties. Well aware of the need to restore public confidence in the integrity of government following the WATERGATE scandal of recent memory, Carter declared his support for Senator ABRAHAM RIBICOFF's (D-Connecticut) Public Officials Integrity Act (S. 555) as the Senate Committee on Governmental Affairs opened hearings on May 3, 1977. Carter's support was a valuable asset to those who favored establishment of a statutory, independent prosecutor. President GERALD FORD had helped forestall such action by arguing against the proposed office's constitutionality. Once the executive dropped its objections, it became more difficult for the opposition to advance the constitutional argument.

The man who signed the Ethics Act was never himself the target of the type of investigation authorized by the statute. Allegations of possible impropriety did result in preliminary probes, but no evidence was ever found to warrant a full-scale inquiry. In fact, Jimmy Carter's career has been, and continues to be, one characterized by adherence to high standards of ethical conduct. His failure to win re-election as president in 1980 has been largely attributed to economic inflation at home and the Iran hostage crisis abroad. Ethical challenges played no role. Jimmy Carter had arrived on the national political scene as a representative of the "New South." A moderate Democrat with an enlightened outlook that made others believe the region's racial problems were a thing of the past, Carter had been a popular Georgia Governor (1971–1975) with national aspirations. After leaving the White House, Carter's reputation for fairness enabled him to lead international teams of observers that facilitated democratic elections in nations such as Panama, Nicaragua, the Dominican Republic, and Haiti. He also hosted peace negotiations in Ethiopia, and continues to devote much time to charitable and humanitarian causes.

During Jimmy Carter's presidency, special prosecutors were twice named to investigate possible misconduct by Carter appointees. Several other questionable incidents prompted calls for such investigations in vain. Special Prosecutors ARTHUR CHRISTY and GERALD GALLINGHOUSE were both named to investigate whether Carter associates HAMILTON JORDAN and TIMOTHY KRAFT were guilty of cocaine use. After separate grand jury investigations (Christy's, 1979–1980; Gallinghouse's, 1980–1981), it was determined that there was insufficient evidence to prosecute Chief of Staff Jordan and staff member Kraft.

On March 20, 1979, Attorney General GRIFFIN BELL appointed PAUL CURRAN as "special counsel" to investigate whether money from the CARTER PEANUT WAREHOUSE had been illegally diverted into the president's 1976 campaign fund. Not a formal Ethics Act investigation, the finding that there had been no wrongdoing seemed to satisfy the public. Similarly, 1978 allegations that President Carter and Vice President WALTER MONDALE had solicited funds at a White House businessmen's luncheon in order to help repay campaign debts resulted in an investigation that failed to produce evidence requiring the naming of a special prosecutor. The Department of Justice, however, did trigger Ethics Act provisions by authorizing a preliminary investigation that found insufficient evidence to pursue the matter further.

In July 1980, Billy Carter, Jimmy's younger brother, revealed that he had accepted $220,000 from the Libyan government, which he characterized as a loan. A subsequent Senate investigation revealed that ties between Billy and the government of Muammar Qaddafi had originated in 1978, Libya apparently believing they could influence U.S. policy by cultivating a relationship with the president's brother. Billy welcomed the attention and the money, even attempting to act as a middleman for the sale of Libyan crude oil. The Justice Department began an investigation of the situation, but Attorney General BENJAMIN CIVILETTI did not inform his own investigator all that he knew about the affair. Similarly, CIA Director Stansfield Turner concealed pertinent information from the FBI. Perhaps most curious was the fact that the administration attempted to use Billy's influence to gain release of the hostages in Iran. National Security Adviser Zbigniew Brzezinski, acting with the President's approval, had Billy arrange a meeting with Libyan diplomat Ali Houderi at the White House. As a result, Kaddafi issued an appeal for release of the hostages, to no avail. Billy Carter was persuaded to reveal all he knew about his Libyan arrangement and formally register as an agent of the Libyan government under the Foreign Agents Registration Act (1938). In return, the Justice Department investigation, headed by Michael Shaheen in the Office of Professional Responsibility, recommended against pressing either criminal or civil charges in the matter. A special prosecutor would not be requested. The Senate investigation criticized the administration's poor judgment, but found no illegalities or even serious improprieties. The incident, however, might have done further damage to Jimmy Carter's attempt to close the gap between himself and popular Republican presidential candidate RONALD REAGAN in the public opinion polls.

During the 1980 presidential campaign, Jimmy Carter's debate briefing papers disappeared. They eventually turned up in the hands of Reagan campaign officials. George Washington University professor John Banzhaf brought suit, attempting to force Attorney General WILLIAM FRENCH SMITH to name an independent counsel to investigate the matter. In *BANZHAF v. SMITH* (1984), the Court of Appeals reversed a district court decision that had ordered such an inquiry. A House subcommittee, headed by Donald Albosta (D-Michigan), appeared to implicate CIA Head WILLIAM CASEY, then Reagan campaign director, in the theft of the Carter papers.

The media directed increased attention to Jimmy Carter following the election of BILL CLINTON to the White House in 1992. Reporters wanted to record the thoughts of the last Democrat to occupy the executive office. Carter expressed disappointment that his old Attorney General, GRIFFIN BELL, had supported GEORGE BUSH in the presidential election. He went on to predict that Bush would be well-served by Bell, however, during LAWRENCE WALSH's IRAN-CONTRA investigation. Bush had hired Bell as his personal counsel in the matter. Carter also indicated that his wife, Rosalyn, was Bell's cousin, and that consequently she was more upset about the turn of events than he.

Because of his own experiences with special prosecutors, the former president was able to sympathize with Clinton's WHITEWATER troubles. Both Jimmy and Rosalyn contributed $1,000, the maximum allowed, to the legal defense fund established to help the Clintons pay their attorneys. In October 1997, Carter did join the call for an independent counsel to investigate campaign financing irregularities, but the former president made it clear that he believed Vice President Al Gore guilty of nothing more than participating in the type of regrettable behavior now practiced by politicians in both major political parties. Current rules must be changed, asserted Carter, and "soft money" contributions eliminated.

References:

"Debategate Rears Its Head Again." *U.S. News & World Report*, 4 June 1984, p. 14.

"Ethics in Government Act of 1978—Remarks on Signing S. 555 into Law. October 26, 1978." *Weekly Compilation of Presidential Documents* 14 (1978): 1854–1856.

Grove, Lloyd. "That Other Southern President." *Washington Post*, 14 January 1993, sec. C, p. 1.

Kurtz, Howard. "Evidence of Crime Distinguishes Watergate from Debate Case." *Washington Post*, 29 May 1984, sec. A, p. 4.

Kurylo, Elizabeth. "Carter Says Gore Deserves Support." *Atlanta Journal and Constitution*, 21 October 1997, sec. A, p. 11.

Mathews, Tom, with Holly Morris and Elaine Shannon. "Did Billy Cook His Books?"
    Newsweek, 26 March 1979, p. 50.
Mayer, Allan J., and Kim Willenson. "The Senators Scold Billy and Jimmy." *Newsweek*,
    13 October 1980, p. 47.
Mayer, Allan J., with Eleanor Clift, Elaine Shannon, Gloria Borger, Kim Willenson,
    Holly Morris, and Vern E. Smith. "A Storm over Billy Carter." *Newsweek*, 4
    August 1980, p. 14.
Nelson, Jack. "Clinton's Trust in Carter Rests on Long Relationship." *Los Angeles Times*,
    26 September 1994, sec. A, p. 1.
Pound, Edward T. "Carter Associates Still Under Inquiry." *New York Times*, 1 February
    1981, sec. A, p. 23.

Carter Peanut Warehouse Case. During a presidential administration remarkably devoid of scandal, one grand jury investigation in Atlanta threatened to
taint Jimmy Carter's fine record. In 1978–1979 PAUL CURRAN, special counsel to Attorney General GRIFFIN BELL, conducted an inquiry into whether
there had been improper ties between Carter peanut business funds and the
Carter presidential campaign. This investigation included examination of the
roles played by longtime Carter associate and Georgia banker Bert Lance (also
under investigation for questionable financial practices), Carter media adviser
Gerald Rafshoon, and Jimmy Carter's brother Billy, whose unpredictable activities were the source of embarrassing scrutiny throughout the Carter presidency.
In addition to Curran's inquiry, the Securities and Exchange Commission, the
Internal Revenue Service (IRS), and the National Bank of Georgia conducted
their own investigations.

The source of all these inquiries was a 1975 $1 million loan made by Bert
Lance's National Bank of Georgia (NBG) to the Carter family peanut business.
The funds were targeted for construction of a new warehouse and peanut sheller.
Carter claimed $1 million investment tax credit on his 1975 and 1976 income
tax returns. A contractor, however, later claimed that construction costs
amounted to no more than $700,000. That left $300,000 unaccounted for, funds
that critics theorized might have ended up in Carter campaign coffers, thereby
violating federal banking and campaign finance laws.

The series of investigations served to exonerate Carter. Attorney Charles
Kirbo, who administered the Carter peanut business as a blind trust during the
Carter presidency, explained that the NBG loan actually served to consolidate
two earlier loans totaling $900,000 with the extra money going to pay off an
earlier debt to the Citizens Bank in Americus, Georgia. Reports that the Carters
had received a "sweetheart loan" from NBG proved false upon examination. In
reality, the interest rate was 1.5% higher than the prime rate at the time. The
Carters' revolving credit line also came under attack. Increases in the line of
credit, however, appeared to be the result of corresponding growth in business
volume. In any case, the business only used a fraction of the credit that was
extended and paid it all back on time. An IRS audit added to Carter's good

news, upholding the legitimacy of his tax credit claim. The investigations did reveal, however, that NBG was quite lenient in its extension of credit to Carter, not requiring complete collateral to support all loans.

In April 1976, NBG granted Gerald Rafshoon a $155,000 line of credit. The Carter campaign owed Rafshoon $645,000 in unpaid bills at the time. Rafshoon's books were subpoenaed as part of the Bert Lance investigation. Examination discovered that the NBG loan had been used to pay off bills incurred by another Rafshoon client who had suffered bankruptcy. Carter's debt to Rafshoon was satisfied by August 1, 1976, in stark contrast to the usual scenario involving political candidates who typically carry forward large, unpaid campaign debts for many years.

Many questions were raised about the manner in which Billy Carter had run the family business. Before Charles Kirbo leased the business to Gold Kist, a southern agribusiness, Billy had entered into a curious string of financial arrangements involving poorly secured loans and questionable expenditures. These activities, however, appeared to be more closely connected to the Bert Lance investigation, having no discernible ties to the Carter campaign. In October 1979, Paul Curran announced that no improprieties had been uncovered in the investigation of the Carter peanut business. Curran's questioning of Carter during a four-hour deposition on September 5, 1979, was believed to be the first time a president had been examined under oath as part of a criminal investigation. Curran's appointment had not followed the procedures established by the ETHICS IN GOVERNMENT ACT. Attorney General Griffin Bell had reasoned that because the events in question had occurred before the Ethics Act had been passed in 1978, such a formal examination was unwarranted. Curran's report clearing Carter of any wrongdoing made any second-guessing of Bell's decision unnecessary. The two Ethics Act investigations that did occur during Carter's presidency, those of Carter associates HAMILTON JORDAN and TIMOTHY KRAFT by special prosecutors ARTHUR HILL CHRISTY and GERALD GALLINGHOUSE respectively, also concluded in exoneration. Only Bert Lance suffered the indignity of indictment.

Lance had served as Carter's Head of the Office of Management and Budget before resigning in 1977. By then, congressional hearings were being conducted regarding Lance's financial dealings as head of the First National bank of Calhoun, Georgia, and the NBG. It was charged that Lance's loan practices, which included unsecured funds extended to relatives and associates, had jeopardized the financial existence of the banks he administered. Lance's defenders maintained that his behavior was typical of small-town bankers across the nation. Ultimately, examination of nearly 400 bank loans resulted in Lance's indictment on conspiracy charges and 32 other counts. Charges were reduced to 12 felony counts by the judge during a 14-week trial. Lance was acquitted on 9 of the counts and the remaining 3 were dismissed when the jury could not reach a verdict. The Justice Department chose not to retry him. Lance demonstrated great resiliency. He regained control of the First National Bank in Calhoun in

1981, and was selected chair of Georgia's Democratic Party. In 1984, he headed
WALTER MONDALE's successful campaign for the Democratic Party presidential nomination.

References:

"Justice Clears Carter White House." *The National Journal*, 20 October 1979, p. 1783.
Mathews, Tom, with John Walcott, Elaine Shannon, Vern E. Smith, and Joseph B. Cum-
        ming, Jr. "Those Carter Loans." *Newsweek*, 12 February 1979, p. 33.
Thornton, Mary. "New Position Spotlights Lance's Past." *Washington Post*, 17 July 1984,
        sec. A, p. 7.

Casey, William J. (1913–1987) Director of the Central Intelligence Agency,
1981–1987. Trained as a lawyer, William Casey received his education in intelligence as a member of the Office of Strategic Services (OSS) during World
War II. Casey worked to plant spies in Nazi Europe under the tutelage of the
legendary General William "Wild Bill" Donovan. Forerunner of the Central
Intelligence Agency (CIA), the OSS produced a group of secretive intelligence
operatives whose dedication and sacrifice would influence the American intelligence community for decades.

Casey's name surfaced during the WATERGATE investigation when he was
suspected of providing perjured testimony. It was alleged that Casey, Head of
the Securities and Exchange Commission at the time, had provided NIXON's
Justice Department with 34 boxes of International Telephone and Telegraph
Company files and 13 boxes of potentially damaging office memos and letters
in order to keep them beyond the reach of congressional subpoenas. Casey was
never charged, apparently because the Watergate Special Prosecution Force
(WSPF) had larger targets in mind.

In 1980, Casey managed the presidential campaign of RONALD REAGAN.
In this capacity, he became a pivotal figure in the controversy surrounding the
manner in which President Jimmy CARTER's briefing book and other campaign
documents ended up in the possession of the Reagan campaign team. The incident was the subject of investigations by both the Justice Department and a
House subcommittee, and a lawsuit brought by professors John Banzhaf and
Peter Meyers (*BANZHAF v. SMITH*). Although the Justice Department concluded in February 1984 that there was no evidence of criminal activity, the
House subcommittee, headed by Donald Albosta (D-Michigan), disagreed. Its
report, issued in May, found Casey to be the likely culprit. The report based its
conclusion on the testimony of White House Chief of Staff James Baker who
had declared that he had received the Carter papers from Casey. The report also
charged that Casey had urged his staff to obtain and circulate material from the
Carter campaign, basing its conclusion on the minutes of a meeting Casey held
with his deputies in September 1980. Despite its findings, the question of how
the Carter papers were actually transferred was never answered. Casey testified
that he could not recall ever seeing the papers in question, and was never

charged in the matter. Banzhaf's effort to require the appointment of a special prosecutor to formally investigate the matter met with success at the district court level, but was overturned on appeal.

It was the IRAN-CONTRA investigation in which William Casey was identified by both investigators and witnesses as having played a crucial role in both the arms-for-hostages deal with Iran and the military supply of the Contras in Nicaragua. Assuming the leadersip of the CIA in 1981, Casey successfully increased the agency's budget and staffing, and was credited with improving the organization's analytical capabilities. In 1984, however, the agency suffered sharp criticism when it was revealed that it had mined Nicaraguan harbors and authored a handbook for the Contras that encouraged assassination and kidnaping of Sandinista leaders. By late 1986, the congressional investigation into the Iran-Contra affair had voiced its suspicions that Casey was behind many of OLIVER NORTH's activities. How else, it was reasoned, could a relatively low-level, inexperienced functionary like North succeed in managing such grandiose foreign policy initiatives in both the Middle East and Central America? In testimony before Congress, Casey acknowledged assisting North in the transfer of arms to Iran in hopes of obtaining release of American hostages, but denied knowledge of Contra supply. Casey stressed the importance of preventing Nicaraguan interference in El Salvador, a foreign policy goal with bipartisan support, but would not speak openly about the use of Honduras as a Contra staging ground for attacks on Nicaragua's Sandinista government.

Suspicions grew that Casey had engineered the covert operation that had circumvented congressional limitations on Contra aid, such as the BOLAND AMENDMENTS. One need only look at similar CIA operations in Afghanistan, Angola, and Cambodia. Perhaps he had also been behind the unprecedented delegation of authority to the National Security Council that enabled North and his cohorts to establish their financial/military network independent of normal governmental channels. Casey's appearances before congressional committees were punctuated by claims of memory lapse. He frequently mumbled, and left an impression of disorganization and carelessness. It has been suggested by critics and admirers alike that this persona served Casey's purposes well. Casey was preparing for further congressional testimony on December 16, 1986, when he was stricken with seizures that forced his hospitalization. Brain cancer was diagnosed, and surgery followed. Casey resigned as CIA Director on January 29, 1987. In and out of hospitals in the following weeks, he died on May 6, 1987. The family asked that those wishing to make contributions should direct them to Contra aid.

As the Iran-Contra story continued to unfold after Casey's death, witnesses came forward to address many of the charges involving the former CIA Director. Oliver North maintained that Casey knew all about the Iran-Contra connection, but EDWIN MEESE steadfastly supported Casey's claims of ignorance. In August 1987, Deputy CIA Director CLAIR GEORGE testified that Casey would bypass subordinates who complained about the use of Iranian middleman Manucher Ghorbanifar and retired Air Force Major General RICHARD SECORD in the arrangement of arms transfers to Iran. George viewed them as disreputable, but Casey was fixed on the plan as originally conceived. The testimony of ALAN FIERS, the CIA's Head of the Central American Task Force, attributed to Casey the idea to overcharge Iran for weapons and use the profit to support the Contras in Nicaragua. According to Fiers, Casey was well aware of North's projects. Independent Counsel LAWRENCE WALSH's findings place Casey at the organizational meetings that planned the Iran-Contra arrangement. The actual extent of Casey's knowledge and involvement may never be known, and it has been suggested that Casey would have wanted it just that way.

Casey's death did not lay to rest tales of his conspiratorial activities. It was alleged that he had played an important role in what has been termed the "October Surprise," a negotiated agreement with Iran to delay release of hostages until after the 1980 election. As Ronald Reagan's campaign manager, Casey was suspected of engineering such an arrangement. In 1993, a bipartisan House task force released a report clearing Casey of these charges. In what could be considered a tribute to William Casey's lasting reputation for masterminding covert operations, journalists and politicians continue to question the credibility of the report's findings.

References:

"Casey Ignored CIA Critics, Aide Testifies." *Chicago Tribune*, 27 August 1987, sec. C, p. 1.

"Casey Tied to Carter Papers." *San Diego Union-Tribune*, 23 May 1984, sec. A, p. 1.

"CIA's Casey Engineered Contra Aid, Report Says." *San Diego Union-Tribune*, 25 March 1987, sec. A, p. 1.

" 'Debategate' Rears Its Head Again." *U.S. News and World Report*, 4 June 1984, p. 14.

Elsasser, Glen. "Iran-Contra Figure Tells of Casey Ties." *Chicago Tribune*, 1 August 1992, sec. C, p. 10.

Jacoby, Tamar. "William Casey: Silent Witness." *Newsweek*, 18 May 1987, p. 46.

Magnuson, Ed. "Death of an Expert Witness." *Time*, 18 May 1987, p. 37.

Neikirk, William R., and Glen Elsasser. "Meese Disputes North on Casey's Role." *Chicago Tribune*, 30 July 1987, sec. C, p. 1.

Parry, Robert. "The Man Who Wasn't There." *The Nation* 256 (1993): 226. Questions the accuracy of the congressional report clearing Casey of involvement in the "October Surprise" by challenging alibis that place Casey at various locations when he could have been negotiating with Iranians for delay in release of the hostages.

"Won't Throw Casey, Regan 'To Wolves,' Reagan Says." *Los Angeles Times*, 7 December 1986, p.1.

Woodward, Bob. *Veil: The Secret Wars of the CIA 1981–1987*. New York: Simon and Schuster, 1987. The author claims he received a deathbed confession from Casey acknowledging, and providing concise justification for, his involvement in Iran-Contra.

Christy, Arthur Hill (1923–   ) Independent Counsel, Hamilton Jordan investigation, 1979–1980. New York attorney Arthur Christy became the first man to be named special prosecutor under the ETHICS IN GOVERNMENT ACT (1978) when he was selected by a panel of judges to investigate whether HAMILTON JORDAN, President Jimmy CARTER's Chief of Staff, had indulged in cocaine use on a visit to a New York discotheque. Attorney General BENJAMIN CIVILETTI did not place much credence in the allegations, but decided to request a special prosecutor nonetheless. Civiletti believed that the special prosecutor was better equipped to properly examine the situation, and such an investigation would allay any Republican concerns that executive misconduct was being disregarded or covered up.

Brooklyn-born Arthur Christy was an inactive Republican who had made his reputation during a brief tenure as U.S. Attorney for the Southern District of New York (1958–1959) during which he successfully prosecuted crime boss Vito Genovese. He had also assisted in the prosecution of organized crime member Frank Costello on income tax charges; directed the investigation of the assault on journalist Victor Riesel upon whom acid had been thrown; and helped in the prosecution of congressman Adam Clayton Powell (D-New York) on corruption charges. During the mid-1950s, Christy served as assistant U.S. Attorney to Edward Lumbard, one of the judges on the panel that would appoint him special prosecutor. Named to investigate the Jordan case on November 29, 1979, Christy was presented with a mandate somewhat broader in scope than the one originally defined by the attorney general. Christy was charged with determining whether Hamilton Jordan had used cocaine during a visit to the Studio 54 discotheque on June 27, 1978, and was given leave to examine "any other or related allegations." Christy made it clear upon his appointment that he would feel free to expand the investigation in any direction he saw fit. Listeners assumed that Christy was alluding to charges that had recently surfaced regarding Jordan's alleged cocaine use at a Beverly Hills party in October 1977. The original charge had been leveled by Studio 54 owner Steve Rubell, who was under indictment for income tax evasion at the time. Rubell said he saw Jordan use cocaine that was given to him by drug dealer John (Johnny C.) Conaghan. Conaghan admitted administering the drug to someone that night, but failed to identify the person as Jordan.

In March 1980, Christy convened a grand jury that met a total of 19 times and heard the testimony of 33 witnesses. The investigation concluded on May 21 when the grand jury concluded that there was insufficient evidence to warrant indictment. Christy's report characterized the testimony of both Rubell and Conaghan as unreliable. Their account of the New York incident was vague and subject to continual revision. Both witnesses admitted that they had themselves used drugs and/or alcohol on the night in question. In addition, Rubell's allegation appeared to be influenced by his desire to arrange a plea bargain for the tax charges he faced. Conaghan had appeared on the newsmagazine television show *20/20* the previous October, during which time he stated that he had administered cocaine to a man later identified to him as Jordan. Segments of the interview not televised, however, revealed Conaghan admitting that he had reasonable doubt that the man in question was really Jordan.

The Beverly Hills portion of Christy's investigation uncovered even less evidence of wrongdoing. Some witnesses claimed to have observed cocaine use, while others placed Jordan at the gatherings, but no one could positively identify Jordan as a user of the drug. Again, the veracity of witness testimony was subject to challenge, because of the likelihood that their powers of observation were compromised by drug indulgence. In the end, it was probably Jordan's lifestyle, one that had changed little from his pre–White House days, that had given rise to the charges of drug use.

Christy's handling of the investigation appeared entirely proper and responsible. It had not been colored by political partisanship. Christy felt that the manner in which he conducted the investigation would reflect the trust placed in him by the panel of judges, especially his mentor Judge Lumbard. The duration of the investigation was not unduly prolonged, and partly as a result, the cost ($182,000) was not exorbitant. The outcome was one that had been predicted by Attorney General Civiletti and many knowlegeable observers. The principal criticism raised was that the investigation was unnecessary. The crime being examined amounted to a misdemeanor, one that probably would not have precipitated any investigation had the subject not been a public and political figure.

References:

Lardner, George, Jr. "Grand Jury Clears Jordan." *Washington Post*, 29 May 1980, sec. A, p. 1.
———. "Prosecutor Appointed in Jordan Case." *Washington Post*, 30 November 1979, sec. A, p. 1.
Morganthau, Tom, and Elaine Shannon. "Ham Jordan's Prosecutor." *Newsweek*, 10 December 1979, p. 55.

Cisneros, Henry (1947–   ) Secretary, Department of Housing and Urban Development (HUD), 1993–1997. Former mayor of San Antonio, Henry Cisneros was serving as HUD Secretary in the cabinet of President Bill CLINTON when statements made regarding a past romantic affair led to the appointment of an independent counsel in 1995. DAVID BARRETT's investigation resulted in an 18-count indictment on charges of conspiracy, false statements, and obstruction of justice announced in December 1997.

Cisneros's troubles began in 1987, when he entered into an affair with Linda Medlar Jones from Lubbock, Texas, then a 38-year-old political fund-raiser and wife of a wealthy jeweler. Cisneros, the eldest of five children, rose from San Antonio's Mexican barrio to become the city's mayor in 1980, and was widely credited with revitalizing the community. He had married his high school sweetheart, Mary Alice Perez, and fathered three children, before earning a doctorate in public administration from George Washington University in 1975, and rising in the political ranks beginning with his election to San Antonio's city council that same year. WALTER MONDALE had seriously considered Cisneros as a possible running mate in 1984 when the young mayor's convention speech was enthusiastically received. His affair with Medlar was not a secret for long. San Antonio newspapers broke the story in October 1988. Cisneros suffered public humiliation and chose not to run for re-election as mayor. Mary Alice filed for divorce initially, then decided otherwise. Medlar attempted suicide and was hospitalized in a psychiatric ward.

Cisneros's affair with Medlar apparently continued until mid-1989. During this time, Medlar divorced her husband. Medlar maintained that she asked for no financial settlement in order to avoid a public dispute that would further harm Cisneros. Cisneros rented an apartment and lived part-time with Medlar. According to Medlar, they planned a future together, but Cisneros had a change of heart after seeking counseling and decided to return to his family. By the end of 1989, Cisneros and Medlar had negotiated a parting agreement. Two months later, Medlar began taping her conversations with Cisneros. Although Cisneros's affair with Medlar ended, he continued to support her financially. This connection would lead to Cisneros's greatest difficulties.

Afraid that fallout from his affair with Medlar would hinder his chances at winning elective office, Cisneros passed over opportunities to run for governor or senator. Instead, he accepted appointment to Clinton's cabinet as HUD Secretary. During an FBI background check, Cisneros acknowledged his continuing relationship with Medlar, but maintained his payments had been considerably less ($40,000) than they actually were ($200,000). Justice Department official WEBSTER HUBBELL found Cisneros to be frank about the Medlar affair. Medlar, however, felt betrayed by Cisneros's pending departure for Washington. Physical separation would probably be accompanied by decreased financial support, because Cisneros would be required to divest himself of lucrative investments and live largely on his government salary. Cisneros passed FBI muster, and confirmation hearings did not even touch on the Medlar matter. He was confirmed. Cisneros's payments to Medlar continued until October 1993, when they abruptly ceased.

Medlar, unable to afford to continue the lifestyle to which she had become accustomed, was forced to borrow from family members. When she was still unable to meet her mortgage payments, she decided to sue Cisneros for $250,000. Medlar claimed Cisneros had broken a promise to pay her $4,000 per month until her teenage daughter completed college. In December, Medlar sold her story to the tabloid television show *Inside Edition* for $15,000. Taped excerpts of Medlar's conversations with Cisneros, on which the two discussed plans to conceal the extent of the payments, were included. The lawsuit was settled out of court for $49,000, but the matter had now come to the attention of Attorney General JANET RENO, who decided to request appointment of an independent counsel. Republican lobbyist David Barrett was named in March 1995.

Although Medlar had quickly agreed to cooperate in the independent counsel's investigation of Cisneros in return for immunity, the independent counsel was ultimately dissatisfied with the extent of Medlar's cooperation. The taped conversations she turned over were found to be edited, and her testimony contained apparent lies. Her immunity was revoked, and when Barrett obtained his indictment against Cisneros, Medlar was charged on 28 counts involving bank fraud and money-laundering in connection with the transfer of her house to her sister and brother-in-law and its eventual sale.

The grand jury indictment of Cisneros included charges that he induced assistants Sylvia Arce-Garcia and John Rosales to lie about his connections to Medlar. Analysts believed that the independent counsel would need to prove that Cisneros was guilty of significant misstatements to the FBI; that had he told the truth, his confirmation as a cabinet member would not have been possible. Cisneros left the Cabinet early in 1997, assuming an executive position with the Spanish-language Univision Communications Corporation based in Los Angeles, where he now resides. One of his daughters has passed the bar exam and plans a career as a child services advocate. His other daughter teaches in the inner city. His son, troubled with a congenital heart defect, has undergone successful open-heart surgery. It is estimated that Cisneros's legal fees will eventually be counted in millions of dollars. Cisneros retained BRENDAN SULLIVAN, OLIVER NORTH's former counsel, to represent him. He also enjoys the active support of Los Angeles's Latino community in his legal struggles.

Cisneros's case was unresolved at the time of the independent counsel statute's expiration on June 30, 1999.

References:

Jones, Tamara. "Henry and Linda." *Washington Post*, 22 February 1998, magazine section, sec. W, p. 10.

Thomas, Evan, and Daniel Klaidman. "A Star's Fall from Grace." *Newsweek*, 22 December 1997, p. 70.

Civiletti, Benjamin (1935–   ) Attorney General, 1979–1981. Having served capably as Assistant Attorney General of the Criminal Division (1977–1978) and Deputy Attorney General (1978–1979), Benjamin Civiletti was President Jimmy CARTER's choice to succeed the departing GRIFFIN BELL as attorney general. This pleased Bell who had advocated for his assistant. Born in Peekskill, New York, Civiletti is most closely associated with the legal community in and around Baltimore. He completed his legal education at the University of Maryland, and had been associated with the large Baltimore firm of Venable, Baetjer & Howard for many years.

In the fall of 1979, Civiletti found himself faced with the task of deciding whether or not to invoke the ETHICS IN GOVERNMENT ACT's special prosecutor provisions in response to charges that President Carter's Chief of Staff, HAMILTON JORDAN, had used cocaine in a New York discotheque. The charge had been leveled by Studio 54 club owner Steve Rubell, who was being prosecuted for tax evasion. An investigation by the FBI did not support the charge. Although Civiletti considered the allegation of little consequence, he could not summarily dismiss it as frivolous because several witnesses refused to speak to him without a grant of immunity from prosecution. Civiletti could not make such a grant, but a special prosecutor could. Eager to avoid the appearance of political partisanship, Civiletti decided to request the appointment of a special prosecutor. He explained his reasons to President Carter who, although not pleased, was understanding.

Civiletti asked that the special prosecutor, ARTHUR CHRISTY, focus his investigation on the Studio 54 incident, but Christy elected to expand his original mandate by including a similar allegation concerning a party in Beverly Hills. Despite the broader inquiry, after seven months, a grand jury refused to indict Jordan, and the case was dropped. The problem, however, would not go away. Four months later, in September, TIMOTHY KRAFT, a former presidential aide, was under investigation for cocaine use. GERALD GALLINGHOUSE, a New Orleans Republican, was named special prosecutor. In November 1980, Kraft challenged the constitutionality of the special prosecutor's office in a lawsuit (*KRAFT v. GALLINGHOUSE*). The case was never decided, however, because Gallinghouse cleared Kraft of wrongdoing in March 1981 and legal proceedings ceased. To some it appeared that Civiletti's decision to invoke the Ethics Act in these cases had been vindicated. The process had been honored and justice served. Others felt that the Hamilton and Kraft cases were indicative of serious weaknesses in the special prosecutor mechanism. Civiletti would join those who called for reform of the process.

Before the Jordan case concluded, Civiletti was forced to confront congressional calls for an investigation of Treasury Secretary G. William Miller. In February 1980, Senators William Proxmire (D-Wisconsin) and Lowell Weicker (R-Connecticut) called for a special prosecutor to investigate whether Miller was aware of $5.4 million in payments made by Textron, Inc. to 11 different foreign countries in order to promote sales of its helicopters. Miller headed the firm between 1971 and 1978 when the questionable transactions occurred. Proxmire, Chairman of the Senate Banking Committee, maintained that Miller had committed perjury during confirmation hearings before the Senate. Miller disavowed knowledge of payments. Proxmire, however, cited a Securities and Exchange Commission (SEC) report that detailed payment of a $2.9 million bribe paid by Textron to Iranian Air Force General Mohammed Khatami and a similar transaction with officials in Ghana. He maintained that Textron officials who worked with Miller knew of the payments, and that documents related to the Ghanian transaction were destroyed as soon as the inquiry was announced. The SEC also reported the existence of a $600,000 slush fund at Textron for the purpose of entertaining Pentagon officials. In March, Civiletti responded to Proxmire by announcing that the Justice Department's investigation had found that Miller was unaware of any wrongdoing. Explaining that the department's inquiry had begun prior to passage of the Ethics Act, Civiletti stated that a special prosecutor could not be requested in this case under any circumstances. Senator ROBERT DOLE (R-Kansas), then a member of the Senate Judiciary Committee, characterized Civiletti's decision as politically motivated.

Billy Carter's relationship with Libya caused difficulties for Civiletti in the summer of 1980. The Justice Department began conducting an investigation into Billy Carter's activities on behalf of Libyan oil interests amid calls for a special prosecutor by Republicans in Congress. Because Billy Carter had failed to register as an agent of a foreign government, as required by the Foreign Agents Registration Act (1938), his activities were subject to criminal prosecution. At first, Civiletti made it clear that he was not communicating information regarding the Justice Department's investigation to the President. Later, however, the attorney general was forced to admit that he had a brief conversation with Jimmy Carter on June 17, 1980, during which time the President learned that his brother could probably avoid prosecution by belatedly registering as an agent of the Libyan government. Billy Carter did so and was never prosecuted. Civiletti's ethical lapse, and failure to admit it initially, was subject to widespread criticism. Rejecting the charge that his conduct was improper, Civiletti acknowleged that he was guilty of disservice to the President by initiating conversation regarding Billy's investigation.

After Jimmy Carter's failure to win re-election in November 1980, Civiletti returned to private practice. In 1994 he was mentioned as a principal candidate for independent counsel to investigate WHITEWATER. Attorney General JANET RENO would name the investigator herself, because the independent counsel statute had not been renewed after lapsing in 1992. It appears that one of the reasons Civiletti was passed over in favor of ROBERT FISKE concerns the relationship of his law firm (now Venable, Baetjer, Howard & Civiletti) to failed savings and loan institutions. The firm had been sued by the state of Maryland in the mid-1980s during the savings and loan scandals.

Civiletti's experience with the special prosecutor mechanism convinced him that reforms were necessary. He believed that the process was triggered too easily, and investigations launched over relatively minor incidents. We cannot rest, believing that WATERGATE reform legislation has solved all problems of government misconduct, warned Civiletti. Reformers must be pragmatists as well, examining what works in practice, and continually adjusting past solutions to fit current circumstances.

References:

Babcock, Charles R. "No Special Prosecutor Needed in Miller Case." *Washington Post*, 12 March 1980, sec. A, p. 2.

———. "Special Prosecutor Investigations Called 'Enormous Waste'." *Washington Post*, 21 May 1981, sec. A, p. 20.

Berry, John F. "Civiletti Affirms Miller Never Knew of Payments." *Washington Post*, 6 February 1980, sec. C, p. 1.

"Hamilton Jordan's Ordeal." *Washington Post*, 30 November 1979, sec. A, p. 14.

Isikoff, Michael. "N.Y. Lawyer Fiske Is in Line to Head Whitewater Inquiry." *Washington Post*, 20 January 1994, sec. A, p. 3.

Kiernan, Laura. "Jordan Cocaine Case Tests '78 Ethics Law." *Washington Post*, 3 September 1979, sec. B, p. 1.

Pear, Robert. "Civiletti Discloses He Spoke to Carter on Brother Case." *New York Times*, 26 July 1980, sec. A, p. 1.

Rich, Spencer. "Senator Is Insistent On Perjury Probe of Treasury Chief." *Washington Post*, 15 February 1980, sec. A, p. 16.

Clarridge, Duane R. (1932–) CIA Latin American division chief, 1981–1987. Duane "Dewey" Clarridge was an instrumental figure in the IRAN-CONTRA connection, having directed CIA efforts to supply the Nicaraguan rebels with arms both before and after the BOLAND AMENDMENTS attempted to limit such government aid. His testimony before the TOWER COMMISSION and congressional committees led to indictment by Iran-Contra Independent Counsel LAWRENCE WALSH on charges of perjury. Before his scheduled trial on March 15, 1993, outgoing President GEORGE BUSH included him in the Christmas Eve pardon of 1992.

In December 1981, WILLIAM CASEY transferred Clarridge from the CIA station in Rome in order to have him assume command of the Latin American division. President REAGAN had just authorized the CIA to direct a covert supply operation for the Contras, and Congress had agreed to fund it. Even though Clarridge's previous intelligence experience was limited to Europe and Asia, and he did not speak Spanish, his reputation for resourcefulness endeared him to the CIA chief. Under Clarridge's leadership, the Contras engaged in some of their most daring and controversial activities, including mining of Nicaraguan harbors at Sandino and Corinto and publication of the *Tacayan Manual*, which advocated assassination of Nicaraguan leaders. Mine damage to a neutral vessel resulted in an embarrassing World Court judgment against the United States. Revelations concerning the CIA's involvement in such activity prompted Congress in 1984 to pass the most restrictive version of the Boland Amendment to date. As a result, the CIA was forced to suspend its assistance to the Contras. Casey directed Clarridge to turn over command of Contra supply to OLIVER NORTH and the National Security Council.

When North began directing the arms-for-hostages arrangement with Iran, he called on Clarridge to help rescue a failed shipment of Hawk missiles by Israeli arms merchants who were acting as middlemen. Only 18 of the promised 80 missiles were delivered to Iran, and they were outdated and bore Israeli identification markings. Clarridge was unsuccessful in rectifying the situation, and his collaboration with North involved the CIA in activities forbidden by Congress. The agency attempted to correct the problem by having the president sign belated authorization for the operation that they characterized as assistance to "private parties" who were attempting to obtain freedom for the hostages.

In his testimony before investigating bodies, Clarridge maintained that he did not know missiles were being shipped. Instead, he stated, it was his belief that oil drilling equipment was involved. It was this denial that formed the basis of the case Independent Counsel LAWRENCE WALSH was building against Clarridge. Walsh had gathered evidence from CIA subordinates and documents refuting Clarridge's claims of ignorance. In addition, Walsh claimed to have proof of Clarridge's efforts to recruit the cooperation of another country in a weapons sale to benefit the Contras. With the death of Casey in May 1987, Clarridge, along with CLAIR GEORGE and ALAN FIERS, became the principal CIA targets in Walsh's investigation.

CIA Director William Webster dismissed Clarridge from his post as counterterrorism chief in December 1987 and encouraged him to retire because of his involvement in the Iran-Contra scandal. Clarridge left the CIA and was working as an executive with General Dynamics Corporation in San Diego on November 26, 1991, when the grand jury returned indictments on seven counts of perjury against him. Eleven months later, President George Bush included Clarridge in a pardon that effectively put a halt to what remained of Lawrence Walsh's investigation. His trial, scheduled for 1993, would never take place.

References:

"CIA Chief Reportedly Plans to Fire 2 Over Iran-Contra Scandal." *Chicago Tribune*, 19 July 1987, sec. C, p. 25.

Ostrow, Ronald J. "Ex-CIA Official Faces Iran-Contra Charges." *Los Angeles Times*, 27 November 1991, sec. A, p. 18.

"2 CIA Men Fired, 2 Officials Rebuked Over Iran Scandal." *Los Angeles Times*, 17 December 1987, sec. A, p. 1.

Walsh, Lawrence. *Firewall: The Iran-Contra Conspiracy and Cover-up*. New York: W. W. Norton, 1997.

Classified Information Procedures Act (1980). Created as a response to defendants who threatened to disclose government secrets if prosecuted (GRAYMAIL), the Classified Information Procedures Act (CIPA) proved incapable of solving the conflict of interest presented in the IRAN-CONTRA affair where the Justice Department and the intelligence agencies combined to thwart the independent counsel's prosecution. Ordinarily, invocation of CIPA facilitated compromise between the attorney general, who was attempting to prosecute a defendant, and intelligence agencies, which were trying to preserve national security. During Iran-Contra, the Justice Department's interest in preventing disclosure of covert operations frequently coincided with the CIA's.

CIPA required defendants to provide pretrial notification of intent to use classified information in the course of their defense. Such notification must be accompanied by a description of the type of information that was required and an explanation of its relevancy. CIPA specified that the court respond by conducting closed hearings to determine the relevance and admissibility of the information identified by the defendants, and the manner in which they intended to use it. Should the court rule that the classified information is necessary to the defense, the government may substitute summaries of the information in question, providing that the court does not believe such substitutions would violate the defendants' rights. If the government feels that disclosure of classified information would seriously damage national security, it can file an affidavit to that effect. At that point, the court must decide whether the case can continue without the information. If not, the court dismisses the indictment.

Although the independent counsel statute was crafted to exclude executive branch interference with the office's prosecution, CIPA provisions authorized such interference by empowering the Justice Department to deny to the independent counsel essential information. Consequently, Independent Counsel LAWRENCE WALSH was forced to abandon efforts to try Iran-Contra defendants such as OLIVER NORTH on conspiracy charges when Attorney General RICHARD THORNBURGH refused to permit disclosure of classified information that Judge GERHARD GESELL deemed essential to the defense. As a result, Walsh's remaining cases were built around isolated acts peripheral to the central offense in question. The subsequent proceedings lacked the unifying principal that a conspiracy count would have provided.

With the lapse of the independent counsel statute on June 30, 1999, it is possible that the unusual conflict of interest presented by the Iran-Contra prosecution may not reappear. Nevertheless, it would be useful to address CIPA's weaknesses in order to prevent conceivable problems in the future.

References:

Harriger, Katy J. *Independent Justice: The Federal Special Prosecutor in American Politics.* Lawrence: University Press of Kansas, 1992. Chapter 6, "Conflict of Interest," discusses CIPA and its effect on the Iran-Contra prosecutions.

Jordan, Sandra D. "Classified Information and Conflicts in Independent Counsel Prosecutions: Balancing the Scales of Justice after Iran-Contra." *Columbia Law Review* 91 (1991): 1651–1698. Argues that the government that classifies information is not in an objective position to determine whether disclosure of such information is in the public interest. Proposes that sensitive portions of trials be closed, the defendant being required to relinquish the right to a fully public trial in return for obtaining access to the classified information necessary for mounting an effective defense.

Salgado, Richard P. "Government Secrets, Fair Trials and the Classified Information Procedures Act." *Yale Law Journal* 98 (1988): 427–446.

Clines, Thomas (1930–   ) retired CIA agent; Contra supplier. The only Iran-Contra figure to serve a prison term, Clines was a principal participant in OLIVER NORTH's covert Contra supply network, using his European contacts to arrange for purchase and delivery of arms to the Nicaraguan rebels. Before retiring from the Central Intelligence Agency (CIA) in 1978, Clines was involved in a variety of controversial international intelligence operations, including "Operation Mongoose" in Miami that targeted Fidel Castro (1961–1965);

secret U.S. involvement in Laos, Thailand, and Vietnam (1965–1969); organized arms shipments to Egypt (1981); and collaboration with RICHARD SECORD and a Portuguese arms firm helping to supply the Contras (1982–1984).

Early in 1987, Independent Counsel LAWRENCE WALSH's investigation had identified Clines as a middleman in nine separate arms shipments to the Contras. Secord's purchases were shipped through Clines to Nicaragua at the request of North. Clines used the Portuguese arms supplier, Defex, Inc., and a former CIA-owned shipping company to deliver the weapons to the Contras. Secord found Clines's arrangement to be a distinct improvement over the Canadian supply organization he had been utilizing previously. As a result of his participation in the Contra arms purchases, Clines received 20 percent of the profits that were secreted in a Swiss bank account.

Walsh was successful in convincing the House committee investigating Iran-Contra to forgo any testimony by Clines, thereby avoiding granting him IMMUNITY. Walsh had discovered that retired CIA officer Felix Rodriguez (alias Max Gomez), hired by North to coordinate air attacks for the Contras, was accusing Secord and Clines of profiting from their arms sales. In actuality, Secord, Clines, and associate ALBERT HAKIM had received over $2.5 million in profits from the $10 million in arms deals they had engineered. Although the numbers raised serious questions, Secord, in his testimony before the House on May 5, 1987, characterized the markup as a routine commercial transaction in conformity with standard business practices.

Walsh decided to try Clines on the grounds that he had underreported his income and failed to pay taxes on his profits from the arms sales. During the summer of 1990, Walsh's associate counsel Stuart Abrams, Bill Treanor, and Geoff Berman represented the prosecution in Baltimore's U.S. District Court. On September 18, Clines was found guilty of four felonies: two counts of underreporting income to the Internal Revenue Service, and two counts of denying possession of foreign bank accounts. Judge Norman P. Ramsey sentenced Clines to 16 months in prison and ordered him to pay $400,000 in fines. A federal appeals court in Richmond, Virginia, upheld the conviction in February 1992, and Clines began serving his sentence at a minimum security facility in Schuylkill, Pennsylvania, in May. On June 22, the Supreme Court denied certiorari, allowing Clines's conviction to stand. At the time of his incarceration, Clines was an executive with Panex Corporation of McLean, Virginia, an international security consulting firm.

References:

"Ex-CIA Officer Clines First Iran-Contra Figure Going to Prison." *Los Angeles Times*, 25 May 1992, sec. A, p. 29.

"Family Ties: How the North Operatives Came to Know Each Other." *Newsweek*, 9 March 1987, p. 34.

Rosenbaum, David E. "Ex-CIA Aide Called a Principal in Iran Affair." *New York Times*, 23 April 1987, sec. A, p. 10.

Walsh, Lawrence. *Firewall: The Iran-Contra Conspiracy and Cover-up*. New York: W.W. Norton, 1997.

Clinton, Hillary Rodham (1947–   ) lawyer, First Lady of the United States, 1993–   . When Bill Clinton was elected president in 1992, accompanying him to the White House was a woman who was already an accomplished attorney and educator in her own right. She had served as an attorney with the Children's Defense Fund and the Carnegie Counsel on Children (1973–1974); worked as counsel on the impeachment inquiry staff of the House of Representatives Judiciary Committee (1974); and was Assistant Professor of Law and Director of Legal Aid at the University of Arkansas Law School in Little Rock (1974–1980) while functioning as a partner in the Rose Law Firm (1977–1992). Hillary Rodham Clinton promised to be a more active and involved First Lady than anyone since Eleanor Roosevelt. She appeared to play an influential role in the president's policy decisions on many issues, an opinion supported by the fact that she was formally charged with leading the Presidential Task Force on National Health Care Reform in 1993. After failure of that Clinton initiative, Hillary assumed a lower profile.

Hillary's professional association with her husband in Arkansas inevitably resulted in her being linked to the complex and convoluted scandalous morass that has come to be designated simply as WHITEWATER. As Rose Law Firm partner, Hillary did legal work for JAMES McDOUGAL's failed Madison Guaranty Savings and Loan. McDougal was also the Clintons' partner in the ill-fated Whitewater land development deal. Both ALFONSE D'AMATO's Senate Whitewater Committee and Independent Counsel Kenneth Starr have attempted to ascertain the exact extent of Hillary Clinton's involvement in McDougal's ventures. Hillary indicated that her work was minimal. Rose Law Firm billing records, discovered two years after the inquiries began, raised the possibility that her involvement was somewhat more significant. It has also been alleged that Hillary helped McDougal launder illegal cash payments to her husband by accepting money through the law firm for nonexistent legal services. Hillary was also questioned by the Resolution Trust Corporation (RTC) regarding the manner in which she helped structure a financial option for Madison Guaranty's Castle Grande real estate investment. This arrangement involved longtime Clinton associate WEBSTER HUBBELL's father-in-law, Seth Ward, and federal investigators had already implicated him in a series of fraudulent transactions with Madison Guaranty. Hubbell, thrice indicted by KENNETH STARR, has served a prison sentence for overbilling Rose Law Firm clients, and faces further charges. The intensity with which he has been prosecuted likely stems from the belief that Hubbell possesses knowledge implicating Hillary to a greater extent.

Continual attempts have also been made to implicate Hillary in the summary dismissal of White House Travel Office employees in May 1993 (TRAVELGATE), and the suicide of legal associate VINCENT FOSTER the following July. Foster cited concerns over the travel office issue in a note he left shortly before his death. Hillary denied knowledge of the reason for dismissal of the travel office employees, but some evidence indicated that she wanted to replace them with associates of her friend, producer Harry Thomason.

Hillary Clinton has long had to defend her husband against charges of marital infidelity. During the 1992 presidential campaign, Gennifer Flowers' allegations put the Clinton marriage in the spotlight. Hillary's steadfastness helped salvage Bill's candidacy. When the story of Bill's possible affair with former White House intern MONICA LEWINSKY surfaced in January 1998, while the president was still defending himself against PAULA JONES's sexual harrassment lawsuit, Hillary's reaction was less sanguine. Appearing on national television, she charged that a vast right-wing conspiracy was behind the continual personal attacks on her husband's presidency. While Hillary offered no evidence to support this contention, she indicated that future revelations would be forthcoming. Hillary's charge was granted surface credibility by those who pointed to Kenneth Starr's longtime connection to conservative causes and organizations such as the Federalist Society, as well as his offer of support to Paula Jones's attorneys. Paula Jones's allegations had also received heavy support from conservative publications and legal foundations such as the Rutherford Institute. Longtime Clinton strategists such as James Carville elaborated on this theme with regularity in media appearances. If Hillary's contention placed the prosecution on the defensive temporarily, it did not derail attempts to further document the president's philandering. Former White House staffperson Kathleen Willey appeared on television to relate in detail an alleged incident involving an unwanted sexual advance by the president. Again, official denials followed.

Hillary Clinton spent four hours testifying before a Washington, D.C., grand jury on January 26, 1996. She declared that there had been no attempt to obstruct justice during the independent counsel's Whitewater investigation. The billing records of the Rose Law Firm, she declared, had been misplaced. After they finally were discovered, no indictments were forthcoming. Whereas Webster Hubbell, the McDougals, and JIM GUY TUCKER have all paid a price for their involvement in Whitewater, evidence gathered did not make a case against the Clintons that satisfied Kenneth Starr. Starr abandoned further investigation into the Arkansas aspect of the investigation by permitting the Little Rock grand jury to disband. Some saw this as a vindication of Hillary Clinton. Whatever the nature of her activity as partner in the Rose Law Firm, she appears to be innocent of any crime. Had not Starr received permission, via depositions given in the Paula Jones lawsuit, to look into the Lewinsky affair, Whitewater might have been concluded. Instead, Hillary was forced to spend more of her time supporting her husband, and attempting to focus public attention on his presidency's policy achievements. Public opinion polls indicated that the majority of Americans were not greatly influenced by the embarrassing sexual revelations.

Because the president's claims to executive privilege concerning White House aides did not meet with success, the nature of Hillary Clinton's conversations with aide Sidney Blumenthal became the subject of prosecutors' examination. It is apparent that Hillary played a key role in White House efforts to limit political and legal damage caused by the Lewinsky matter. Starr's questioning of Blumenthal attempted to underscore this point. His case against the president, centering on perjury and obstruction of justice in his Paula Jones deposition, resulted in his impeachment in December 1998, but the Senate trial in February was brought to a quick conclusion when it became clear that the vote for removal would fall well short. Hillary's efforts to protect her husband, and his place in history, had a chance to succeed.

As Hillary Clinton's White House years neared their end, she began to explore the possibility of seeking elective office on her own. In the spring of 1999, she approved the formation of a committee to explore the possibility of running for the U.S. Senate seat being vacated by Daniel Moynahan (D-New York). Her candidacy was formally announced in early 2000.

References:

Barfield, Deborah. "Hillary Scorns Scandal." *Newsday*, 12 February 1998, sec. A, p. 7.

Borger, Gloria. "Scenes from a Marriage." *U.S. News & World Report*, 2 February 1998, p. 30.

Clines, Francis X. "Hillary Clinton Tells Grand Jury She Cannot Account for Records." *New York Times*, 27 January 1996, sec. A, p. 1.

"First Lady Blames Starr and Right-Wing Plot." *Minneapolis Star-Tribune*, 28 January 1998, sec. A, p. 1.

Germond, Jack, and Jules Whitcover. "Hillary Clinton's Chief Role May Be to Save Her Husband's Career." *Baltimore Sun*, 13 February 1998, sec. A, p. 17.

Lowther, William. "Standing By Her Man—Fiercely." *Macleans*, 9 February 1998, p. 28.

Rankin, Robert A. "The Case against Hillary." *Tampa Tribune*, 23 January 1996, p. 4.

Schmidt, Susan. "Executive Privilege Claim Covers First Lady's Talks with Blumenthal." *Washington Post*, 24 March 1998, sec. A, p. 6.

Stewart, James B. *Blood Sport: The President and His Adversaries*. New York: Simon & Schuster, 1996. Criticizes the Clintons, especially Hillary, for what the author perceives as a less-than-genuine attitude of innocence and persecution in the face of Whitewater-related allegations. Is not convinced that any actual crimes were committed, but is content to allow the independent counsel and grand jury to make that determination.

Zehren, Charles V. "Her Triple Threat." *Newsday*, 7 January 1996, p. A5. Concise explanation of Hillary Clinton's relationship to the intricate Whitewater issues and Travelgate.

Clinton, William Jefferson (1946–   ) U.S. President, 1993–   . Bill Clinton, former governor of Arkansas, was a leader of a movement that helped redefine the Democratic Party's position on the political landscape. Moving away from the liberal economic policies with which Democrats had traditionally been identified, Clinton successfully preached fiscal responsibilty, free trade, and deficit reduction as chair of the Democratic Leadership Council, 1990–1991. He combined such moderate/conservative economic initiatives with a more conventionally liberal social agenda to win the White House in the 1992 presidential election. Along the way, he was able to deflect charges of marital infidelity that caused some to question his ethical standards.

The independent counsel statute expired on December 15, 1992, shortly before Clinton took office. Reauthorization of the original 1978 ETHICS IN GOV-
ERNMENT ACT had taken place in 1983 and 1987 as Congress continued to
acknowledge the need for a mechanism to address executive branch misconduct
in a manner that would avoid apparent conflict of interest. By 1992, however,
WATERGATE was a less-vivid memory, and the seemingly interminable
IRAN-CONTRA investigation had yet to formally conclude after accumulating
over $30 million in expenses. Republicans, in particular, believed that the in-
dependent counsel had been used as a political weapon against the REAGAN
and BUSH administrations. Despite last minute revisions to both the House and
Senate reauthorization bills (H.R.5840 and S.3131, S.24), renewal efforts failed.
Senator WILLIAM COHEN (R-Maine) warned that his fellow Republicans
would regret their opposition to reauthorization should a Democrat be elected
president.

With the initiation of the WHITEWATER investigation in 1993, Republicans
began to rethink their opposition to the independent counsel mechanism. On
November 18, 1993, the Senate succeeded in passing the Independent Counsel
Reauthorization Bill (S.24), but it was the end of June before it was signed into
law. In the absence of an independent counsel statute, Attorney General JANET
RENO appointed Republican and former U.S. Attorney ROBERT B. FISKE,
Jr. as special counsel to begin the inquiry early in 1994. He would focus on the
nature of Bill and HILLARY RODHAM CLINTON's involvement in the failed
Whitewater Development Company's land venture in Arkansas during the
1980s. Fiske's initial report, issued on 30 June, found no wrongdoing by the
Clintons. Citing the fact that Fiske's appointment by Reno created the appear-
ance of a conflict of interest, congressional Republicans urged the court appointment of a different individual as independent counsel. Operating under the newly
reauthorized statute, the Court's Special Division named Republican and former
Appeals Court Judge KENNETH STARR in August. Starr's investigation resulted in the conviction of Clinton associates WEBSTER HUBBELL, JIM GUY
TUCKER, and JAMES and SUSAN McDOUGAL, but did not implicate the
Clintons. Collateral investigations by Starr delved into the 1993 suicide of Clinton associate VINCENT FOSTER and the dismissal of employees from the
White House Travel Office (TRAVELGATE). Neither inquiry revealed misconduct. A sexual harrassment lawsuit initiated by former Arkansas employee
PAULA CORBIN JONES, however, led to the expansion of the original investigation in early 1998. As a result, Starr became involved in trying to determine
whether Bill Clinton was guilty of obstruction of justice and/or subornation of
perjury for urging former White House intern MONICA LEWINSKY to lie
about a possible sexual relationship with the president in an affadavit provided
to Paula Jones's attorneys.

Clinton appealed to the courts numerous times in order to limit the scope of
Starr's investigation with mixed results. Although he was unsuccessful in having
the Paula Jones lawsuit postponed until after his presidency, Judge Susan Web-

ber Wright issued a summary judgment dismissing the case on 1 April 1998. Conjecture now centered around the issue of whether affidavits given in connection with a dismissed lawsuit could be the subject of a criminal investigation. Clinton's claims of executive privilege, reminiscent of RICHARD NIXON's attempts during the WATERGATE investigation, were denied. Consequently, presidential advisers such as Bruce Lindsey would be required to testify before a grand jury. Similarly, it was ruled that Secret Service agents who guard the president would be required to testify to anything they might have witnessed in the course of their duties that could contribute to the independent counsel's investigation. There was concern that such a ruling might encourage presidents to distance themselves from their assigned protectors, thereby placing themselves at risk. Some have suggested that the Secret Service issue would need to be addressed by Congress in the near future in order to resolve a dilemma that, to this point, had never presented itself. Without the capability of invoking executive privilege, would Clinton resort to the fifth amendment should he be called to testify before the grand jury? Would he move to quash any subpoena requiring his testimony? Kenneth Starr moved to expedite the normal appeals process by requesting that the Supreme Court quickly decide pressing legal issues related to his inquiry. Once again, Watergate provided precedent for such a move. The foray of the independent counsel into the sexual arena provoked much controversy. Though obstruction of justice and subornation of perjury are serious issues, the matter to which they may be connected—consensual sex— has hardly been a traditional subject of official concern. In addition, because ordinary citizens are rarely subject to criminal prosecution in such instances, some questioned the standard to which the president should be held.

Public opinion became an important factor in determining the ultimate disposition of the independent counsel's investigation. Whereas Kenneth Starr did not appear to allow Clinton's continuing popularity to influence the direction of his investigation, Congress, more cognizant of political realities, was reluctant to act in an aggressive manner when a public backlash was considered likely. Nevertheless, the House of Representatives succeeded in approving articles of impeachment against Clinton in December 1998. An abbreviated Senate trial in February 1999, however, failed to muster the votes necessary for his removal. On April 12, 1999, U.S. District Court Judge Susan Webber Wright found Clinton in civil contempt for his perjurious testimony in the Jones case. On July 28, Wright assessed a fine of $90,000, based upon legal fees incurred by Jones as a result of Clinton's false denial in the Lewinsky matter.

Kenneth Starr's prior ties to conservative Republican causes gave rise to more than the usual number of accusations of political partisanship. Indeed, shortly before being named independent counsel, Starr offered to file an *amicus* brief on behalf of Paula Jones's lawsuit. If nothing else, Starr's appointment focused attention on the political orientation of Special Division judges such as DAVID SENTELLE whose reputed advocacy on behalf of Starr has been attributed by some to his friendship with conservative North Carolina Senator Jesse Helms whose dissatisfaction with Fiske was a matter of public record. Clinton expressed his frustration with the manner in which Starr's investigation was unfolding by formally charging the independent counsel with responsibility for a steady series of leaks to the media that were proving to be a continual source of embarrassment for the president.

Many of Clinton's cabinet members have been targets of independent counsel investigations. These have included Secretary of Commerce RONALD BROWN, Secretary of Agriculture MIKE ESPY, Secretary of Housing and Urban Development HENRY CISNEROS, Secretary of the Interior BRUCE BABBITT, and Secretary of Labor ALEXIS HERMAN. The Brown inquiry was closed when the Secretary died in a plane crash on April 3, 1996; the other investigations were unresolved before expiration of the independent counsel statute on 30 June 1999.

Other difficulties periodically threatened the Clinton administration. Critics charged the president with solicitation of illegal campaign contributions and influence peddling during the 1996 campaign. In December 1997, however, Janet Reno rejected a call for an independent counsel to examine the issue. Congressional campaign finance reform, capable of addressing widespread abuses in a meaningful manner, was stalled due to political infighting by contentious Democrats and Republicans. In May 1998, charges were made that the Clinton administration pursued a trade policy favorable to China in return for political contributions from the Chinese. It was alleged that China obtained improved rocket technology in this manner. Attorney General Reno again decided against appointment of an independent counsel to handle this matter despite a Times-CNN survey that reported 58 percent of Americans sampled favored such a move.

References:

"Political Scandals." *CQ Researcher*, 27 May 1994, p. 459–479. Places Clinton's problems in historical context.

Pooley, Eric. "Red Face Over China." *Time*, 1 June 1998, p. 46.

Roberts, Robert N., and Marion T. Doss, Jr. *From Whitewater to Watergate: The Public Integrity War*. Westport, CT: Praeger, 1997. Chapter 12, "The Clinton Scandals," contends that Clinton failed to understand the nature of the present "public integrity war," and its political implications. The authors fault Clinton for expecting to enjoy any degree of privacy in the White House.

"Rough 'Whitewater Ride' for Clinton." *Congressional Quarterly Almanac* (1994): 108–115.

"U.S. President Clinton's Popularity Hits New High Despite Allegations of Affair and Coverup." *Facts on File*, 29 January 1998, p. 41–45.

"Whitewater Sparks New Hearings." *Congressional Quarterly Almanac* (1995): 1–57–1–60.

Cohen, William S. (1940–   ) U.S. Senator, 1979–1996; Secretary of Defense, 1996–   . A firm believer in the institutional value of the independent counsel office, William Cohen has argued for the continued existence of the mechanism by supporting three reauthorizations and defending controversial investigations.

Having served as mayor of Bangor, Cohen was elected senator from Maine one year after the ETHICS IN GOVERNMENT ACT created the Office of Special Prosecutor, and witnessed the early investigations of HAMILTON JORDAN and TIMOTHY KRAFT on questionable allegations of cocaine use. It was apparent to many that special counsel investigations were being triggered too quickly in response to relatively insignificant charges. Cohen became a leader of those who sought to rescue the statute through meaningful reform. In 1982, joined by Senator CARL LEVIN (D-Michigan) on the Subcommittee on Oversight of Governmental Management of the Committee on Governmental Affairs, Cohen proposed a series of amendments that promised to maintain the independence of the institution while assuring responsible operation of the statute's provisions. Cohen argued in favor of instituting an investigation only when the attorney general receives specific information, constituting sufficient grounds to investigate, that a person has committed a federal violation. The attorney general, said Cohen, should consider degree of specificity and credibility of the source of the allegations. In addition, Cohen proposed raising the standard for appointment of the special prosecutor. The attorney general should have reasonable grounds to believe that further investigation is warranted. Prosecution should not go forward if the attorney general can demonstrate that the U.S. Attorney in the district in which the alleged violation occurred would not prosecute such an offense. Cohen also proposed that the number of federal officials covered by the statute be limited to the president, vice president, cabinet members, CIA director and deputy, IRS commissioner, senior officials in the executive office and Department of Justice, and family members of the president. The period of coverage should be restricted to the president's incumbency plus one year. The attorney general should be able to remove the special prosecutor for good cause (subject to judicial review), if the decision is made public and reported to Congress. For those who suffer extraordinary financial hardship while defending themselves against investigation, Cohen suggested that the court award attorney's fees that would cover costs not likely to be incurred by private citizens. Finally, Cohen favored changing the title of "special prosecutor" (too closely associated with WATERGATE) to "independent counsel." These proposals formed the basis of the reauthorization amendments signed into law by President RONALD REAGAN on January 3, 1983.

In 1986, Republicans lost their majority in the Senate. Democratic Senator Levin took over leadership of the Subcommittee on Oversight of Government Management. His more confrontational style, combined with the presence of the controversial EDWIN MEESE in the Attorney General's office, served to fuel a series of reauthorization amendments that removed discretion from the Justice Department. Cohen remained an influential voice in the subcommittee's deliberations, but he may not have favored the extent to which the 1987 amendments weakened the hand of the executive branch in triggering independent counsel investigations.

During Independent Counsel LAWRENCE WALSH's IRAN-CONTRA investigation, most Republicans, led by ROBERT DOLE, attacked the legitimacy of the independent counsel office. Reagan administration officials of increasingly high rank appeared to be implicated in serious wrongdoing. Cohen did not join the critics. Instead, he joined fellow Maine Senator George Mitchell, a Democrat, in condemning congressional committee tactics that hindered Walsh's investigation. In particular, Cohen objected to an agreement between Republicans and Democrats that imposed a deadline on committee hearings so that the process would not spill over into the 1988 elections. This forced Walsh to gather evidence against Iran-Contra defendants OLIVER NORTH and JOHN POINDEXTER very quickly, before the congressional committee questioned them in public. Their public testimony would be immunized, and Walsh would be barred from using it in his investigation. Cohen and Mitchell also believed that agreeing to an arbitrary deadline encouraged those charged with offenses, and sympathetic administration officials, to delay. Refusal to cooperate became a strategy with a reasonable prospect of success, because the congressional phase of the investigation was guaranteed to end before the fall. When many Republicans held the BOLAND AMENDMENTS at least partly responsible for administration officials' misconduct by prohibiting legitimate aid to the Contras, Cohen refused to characterize the defendants' actions as either justified or necessary. When BRENDAN SULLIVAN, North's attorney, successfully negotiated favorable terms for his client's testimony before Congress, Cohen joined those who descibed the committee's capitulation as a "cave-in."

In 1992, Attorney General WILLIAM BARR was among the leaders who opposed reauthorization of the independent counsel statute. It was an insult to dedicated justice officials, Barr maintained, to claim that an impartial investigation of executive-branch misconduct could not be conducted by the Department. Cohen responded to this contention that there would always be an unacceptable appearance of a conflict of interest in any Justice Department investigation of an executive-branch official. To those who pointed to the mounting cost of independent counsel investigations, Cohen replied that the Justice Department had spent $19 million prosecuting Panamanian dictator Manuel Noriega in what appeared to be a case of much less complexity than Iran-Contra. A Republican-led filibuster ultimately prevented Cohen and Levin from bringing the reauthorization bill to a vote.

During the the early days of the WHITEWATER investigation, Cohen served as a voice of moderation. A supporter of the inquiry, he served to counterbalance the hyperbole of the volatile Senator ALFONSE D'AMATO (R-New York), who, it was believed by critics, might jeopardize congressional hearings into the matter because he lacked appropriate judicial temperament.

In 1996, Cohen joined the administration of President Bill CLINTON as Secretary of Defense. Cohen's moderate track record made him a likely choice for

Clinton who wanted to facilitate a working relationship with a Republican-led Congress. Certainly, Cohen's approach to the independent counsel issue has demonstrated his ability to work effectively in a bipartisan environment.

References:

Cohen, William S. "Reforming the Special Prosecutor Process." *American Bar Association Journal* 68 (1982): 278–281.

Cohen, William S., and George J. Mitchell. *Men of Zeal.* New York: Viking Press, 1988.

Harriger, Katy J. *Independent Justice: The Federal Special Prosecutor in American Politics.* Lawrence: University Press of Kansas, 1992.

McGrory, Mary. "What's It All About Alfonse?" *Washington Post,* 20 March 1994, sec. C, p. 1.

Walsh, Lawrence. *Firewall: The Iran-Contra Conspiracy and Cover-up.* New York: W. W. Norton, 1997.

Collins v. United States 14 Ct. Cl. 568 (1878). From 1855, when it was created by Congress, until 1982, when it was abolished by the Federal Courts Improvement Act, the Court of Claims served as a federal tribunal with original jurisdiction to decide actions brought against the national government. The judicial body heard cases disputing aspects of the Constitution, federal law, executive department regulations, and federal government contracts—either express or implied.

In 1878, the Court of Claims decided *Collins v. United States,* a separation of powers case that would have important implications for the eventual establishment of the independent counsel office. This case hinged on the court's interpretation of the appointments clause, found in Article II of the Constitution, which specifically permits Congress to vest the appointment of inferior officers with the President alone, the courts, or the heads of departments. In this instance, the President reinstated U.S. Army Major Joseph B. Collins to service eight years after he was forced to retire as part of an armed forces reduction act. The reappointment, pursuant to a special act of Congress, was designed to permit Collins to collect pay and benefits he would have received had he been allowed to serve out his time as he had planned. The government accounting office, however, refused to approve payment of past wages to Collins, because the President did not obtain the usual consent of the Senate before reappointing him to his office.

The Court of Claims held that the President need not seek the advice and consent of the Senate in this instance, because Article II permits inferior officers to be appointed by the President alone when Congress deems it fitting. The court defined "inferior officers" as those who are subordinate to the officers in whom appointment powers may be vested. The decision explicitly stated that the term "inferior officers" is not to be understood to mean unimportant or insignificant. In addition, according to the court, because an act of Congress authorized the President to act alone in reappointing Collins, the Senate already had the opportunity to participate in the decision. Now that the President has acted constitutionally, the executive offices involved must abide by his decision. Major Collins's pay should be issued.

The court cited *EX PARTE HENNEN* (1839) to support its opinion. Nearly a century later, the Supreme Court would see things differently in *BUCKLEY v. VALEO* (1976).

Reference:

Simon, Donald J. "The Constitutionality of the Special Prosecutor Law." *University of Michigan Journal of Law Reform* 16 (1982): 45–74. Names *COLLINS, UNITED STATES v. GERMAINE*, and *EX PARTE SIEBOLD* (1879) as all supportive of the special prosecutor/independent counsel concept, because they provide rationale for appointment of such an officer outside of normally prescribed constitutional patterns.

Commodity Futures Trading Commission v. Schor 478 U.S. 833 (1986). A case in which the Supreme Court anticipated *MORRISON v. OLSON* 487 U.S. 654 (1988) by adopting a functionalist approach to the issue of separation of powers, this more flexible stance to constitutional principle reversed a trend begun by the court with *BUCKLEY v. VALEO* 424 U.S. 1 (1976), and continued by *INS v. CHADHA* 462 U.S. (1983) and *BOWSHER v. SYNAR* 478 U.S. 714 (1986). *CFTC v. Schor* ruled that delegating judicial powers to a commission does not impermissibly violate the Constitution's vesting of judicial authority with the federal court system. In doing so, this case paved the way for *Morrison*, which legitimized the independent counsel statute two years later.

CFTC v. Schor addressed the question of whether it was proper for the CFTC to adjudicate state law counterclaims brought forward by petitioners. The Court of Appeals, while upholding most of the commission's judicial authority, ruled that the CFTC was authorized by the Commodity Exchange Act (CEA) to adjudicate claims arising out of CEA or CFTC rules violations only. Departing from these strict limits created serious Article III concerns. Writing for the Supreme Court, Justice Sandra Day O'Connor ruled that the CEA permits the CFTC to hear state law counterclaims in reparations proceedings. Neither the language of the statute in question nor legal history allows for distinguishing between common law counterclaims and counterclaims based on violations of statute. More importantly, O'Connor ruled that drawing such distinctions effectively defeats the Congress's purpose in creating the reparations proceedings mechanism in order to facilitate efficient resolution of disputes.

The integrity of the judiciary is not threatened, declared the Court, by allowing the CFTC jurisdiction over state claims that arise incidental to the federal cases it normally hears. Unlike *Bowsher*, this case does not present the Court with evidence of aggrandizement of one branch's power by another, according to O'Connor. In addition, parties involved in such cases effectively waive their right to trial in the federal court system by voluntarily electing to proceed under administrative law. Finally, the Court ruled that federalist principles were not violated, because federal courts may decide state claims under their ancillary jurisdiction.

Justices William Brennan and Thurgood Marshall dissented. Brennan, writing the dissent, stated that the Court recognizes three narrow exceptions only to the constitutional mandate vesting judicial powers in the federal court system: territorial courts, courts-martial, and courts that adjudicate certain public rights disputes. Because *CFTC* is not covered by any of those exceptions, its adjudication of state law counterclaims is impermissible. Citing the recent separation-of-powers decisions in *Buckley*, *INS*, and *Bowsher*, Brennan highlighted the apparent inconsistency in the Court's current ruling. Brennan also pointed to the Court's decision in *NORTHERN PIPELINE CONSTRUCTION COMPANY v. MARATHON PIPELINE COMPANY* 458 U.S. 50 (1982) for support. In that case the Court ruled that Congress had delegated overly broad judicial powers to bankruptcy courts in a 1978 statute. While Brennan agreed that the CFTC exercised significantly narrower authority, the principle involved was the same. Thus, the Court's decision should not vary. The Court majority, on the other hand, felt that the degree of authority granted by Congress to such quasi-judicial bodies was an important—even, perhaps, a determining factor—in their decision. Brennan defined the issue as one in which legislative convenience and efficiency, on the one hand, must be weighed against the principle of judicial independence on the other. For Brennan and Marshall, the principle must prevail.

The formalist dissent of Brennan and Marshall in this case would be seized upon and expanded by ANTONIN SCALIA two years later in *Morrison*. The decision to favor expediency in this case is characterized as turning away from one's judicial obligation by Brennan. The majority's willingness to entertain practical legislative solutions to pressing problems, however, would serve to make constitutional room for the office of the independent counsel.

References:

Brown, George D. "When Federalism and Separation of Powers Collide—Rethinking *Younger* Abstention." *George Washington Law Review* 59 (1990): 114–156.

Dudley, Earl C. *"Morrison v. Olson*: A Modest Assessment." *American University Law Review* 38 (1989): 255–274. Discusses *CFTC v. Schor* in terms of two crucial questions: Does statute prevent one branch of government from carrying out constitutionally assigned functions? If so, is this justified by an overriding need to promote constitutional objectives?

Verkeuil, Paul R. "Separation of Powers, The Rule of Law and the Idea of Independence." *William and Mary Law Review* 30 (1989): 300–341.

Common Cause. Founded in 1970 by psychologist and education reformer John W. Gardner, Common Cause was formed to respond to a perceived decline of public support for government. John Gardner, as Secretary of Housing, Education and Welfare (1965–1968), had seen the Vietnam War policy of Lyndon Johnson destroy a presidency. Many progressive social programs died with it.

As a result, Gardner's new organization devoted its early years to opposing the Vietnam War and the social cost such hostilities entailed.

Common Cause was only two years old when the WATERGATE break-in occurred. The genesis of this scandal coincided with Common Cause's shift in focus to reform of political processes and structure, rather than concentration on specific issues. As public anger mounted in response to new Watergate-related revelations, Common Cause realized several early successes: a lawsuit that forced the Committee to Re-elect the President to reveal the contibutors to its campaign (1973); passage of the Federal Election Campaign Amendments (1974); and approval of the sunshine law (1975). Perhaps its greatest success, however, was passage of the ETHICS IN GOVERNMENT ACT in 1978. Common Cause and the AMERICAN BAR ASSOCIATION (ABA) were instrumental in helping craft and support the legislation that included the office of special prosecutor.

Common Cause was an influential player in post-Watergate reforms, because during its relatively brief existence, it had succeeded in building a reputation for accurately reflecting public concern for honest government. Testifying before Congress in December 1975, Common Cause president David Cohen voiced support for the ABA's proposal calling for the institution of a temporary special prosecutor to investigate executive branch misconduct on a case-by-case basis. Cohen urged quick action on the measure in order to restore confidence in the government.

Shortly after passage of the Ethics Act, President CARTER became the subject of an investigation into a possible connection between his family's peanut business and his campaign funding. Common Cause joined those who called for Attorney General GRIFFIN BELL to name a special prosecutor to conduct an investigation. Avoiding early implementation of Ethics Act provisions, Bell instead appointed his own special counsel, PAUL CURRAN, who cleared the president of any wrongdoing. In 1980, Carter associate TIMOTHY KRAFT became the subject of a special prosecutor investigation when it was alleged that he had indulged in cocaine use. In defending himself against the charge, Kraft challenged the constitutionality of the special prosecutor mechanism (*KRAFT v. GALLINGHOUSE*). Because the Justice Department chose not to formally support the legitimacy of the special prosecutor, Common Cause filed an *amicus* brief on behalf of Special Prosecutor GERALD GALLINGHOUSE. Gallinghouse's investigation cleared Kraft before the case could be heard; eight years would pass before the matter would be adjudicated again in *MORRISON v. OLSON*.

In 1980, former Watergate special prosecutor ARCHIBALD COX was named chairman of Common Cause. For the next 12 years, he would epitomize an image of rectitude and principle valued by the organization. Sometimes this image would find few followers on Capitol Hill, as when Cox lectured the Senate on the inadvisability of consenting to the appointment of EDWIN MEESE as attorney general in 1984. Although Independent Counsel JACOB

STEIN's report contained no evidence of criminal misconduct, Cox believed the ethical lapses that were detailed made Meese a poor choice to head the Justice Department. At the very least, Meese's apparent indifference to the appearance of conflict of interest should raise questions concerning his suitability for the office. Unfortunately for Cox and Common Cause, few senators bothered to read Stein's actual findings, and only Howard Metzenbaum (D-Ohio) chose to join Cox in vociferous opposition to popular President RONALD REAGAN's selection. Meese was confirmed. Cox continued to advise and speak for Common Cause after stepping down as chairman in 1992. He was succeded by Ned Cabot, president of Housing All Americans, a New York based organization that advocates for affordable housing.

Throughout the years, Common Cause's committment to the concept of an independent counsel has remained firm. Amendments to the statute that were adopted in reauthorization of the law in 1982 and 1987 were not of great concern to the organization. Common Cause regarded such reform as tinkering. The central concept was the important matter, and it was this idea that consistently summoned the organization's support. When the next constitutional challenge to the independent counsel office surfaced, Common Cause was ready. The D.C. District Court ruled the office constitutional in 1987 (*IN RE SEALED CASE*), Judge Aubrey E. Robinson finding that the independent counsel represented an appropriate response to concerns regarding the executive branch investigating its own misconduct. Common Cause joined the ABA and Public Citizen in filing an *amicus* brief in support of the district court decision when it was appealed. Judge SILBERMAN's reversal in the Court of Appeals would be overturned by the Supreme Court.

In June 1992, Common Cause revisited an issue that has, through the years, been a focal point for the organization—campaign finance reform. The issue was the centerpiece of a broad anti-corruption campaign launched by the organization. President Fred Wertheimer formally asked Attorney General WILLIAM BARR to request an independent counsel in order to investigate possible violations of federal campaign finance laws by Republican Party contributors at a fund-raising event in April. In announcing his request, Wertheimer alluded to reports of donations coerced from employees and heavily indebted contributors whose contributions were of questionable origin. Common Cause was quick to attack the proliferation of "soft money" contributions that were supposedly barred from use in federal campaigns. Similarly, six months later, Wertheimer asked House Ethics Committee chairman Louis Stokes (D-Ohio) to investigate whether House Ways and Means Committee chairman Dan Rostenkowski (D-Illinois) used campaign funds for his personal use. Common Cause was reacting to a report in the *Chicago Sun-Times* that Rostenkowski and his sisters collected $73,000 in payments from his campaign committee over the past six years for rental of an office. Common Cause urged Stokes to retain outside counsel to review the facts. The organization was not successful in convincing the attorney general to name an independent counsel to investigate GOP campaign funding, but did help contribute to congressman Rostenkowski's exit from office as it did in the case of Senator Bob Packwood (R-Oregon). Common Cause's 1992 call for an independent counsel investigation of allegations that Packwood sexually harassed many of his female aides helped focus attention on the issue and facilitate Packwood's departure.

Common Cause supported permanent reauthorization of the independent counsel statute in 1992, but found itself in the distinct minority. Congress let the law lapse until 1994 when Democratic President Bill CLINTON found himself the subject of the WHITEWATER investigation. Responding to widespread reports of campaign funding violations by both major political parties in 1996, Common Cause urged appointment of an independent counsel, only to be disappointed when Attorney General JANET RENO decided against such a move. Common Cause president Ann McBride argued that political advertisements aired by both the Democratic and Republican National Committees were in fact presidential campaign ads for Clinton and DOLE. Such ads were financed by "soft money" that is legally barred from use in candidates' campaigns. McBride's request for an independent counsel was criticized by those who, while acknowledging the problem to be addressed, questioned the suggested remedy. They did not believe that campaign financing violations amounted to crimes or that the independent counsel should be used to remedy such offenses. Reno's denial of the organization's request was accompanied by news that the Justice Department had created a new campaign finance unit to examine the issues Common Cause had raised.

Recently, critics have questioned Common Cause's effectiveness, even its continued existence. Membership, at 250,000, has dropped. Its dues and donations income ($10.5 million) is down. Some question what the organization has really accomplished in 25 years. Campaign finance reform, Common Cause's signature issue, is a hot topic, but its popularity has not resulted in concrete reform. Perhaps, as some suggest, Common Cause enjoys greater popularity when faced with the intransigence of a conservative presidential administration. Maybe the organization needs to return to its grass-roots origin. Some say it has become too much of a Beltway institution. Rejecting such criticism, Ann McBride maintains that Common Cause continues to be what it always has been, a force for "good government."

References:

"Challenging the Big Wink." *New York Times*, 11 October 1996, sec. A, p. 38.

"Fat-cat Watch." *The National Journal*, 13 June 1992, p. 1423.

Harriger, Katy J. *Independent Justice: The Federal Special Prosecutor in American Politics*. Lawrence: University Press of Kansas, 1992. Chapter 8, "Symbols and Politics," discusses Common Cause's constructive role in the development of the independent counsel office.

"Inquiry Is Rejected on Campaign Funds." *New York Times*, 10 November 1996, sec. A, p. 24.

Lewis, Ephraim. "Tiptoeing Around Goobergate." *Business Week*, 9 April 1979, p. 129.

Marcus, Ruth. "Common Cause Seeks Independent Counsel Probe of Parties' Spending." *Washington Post*, 10 October 1996, sec. A, p. 23.

McGrory, Mary. "One More Battle of Principle." *Washington Post*, 20 December 1984, sec. A, p. 2.

Pianin, Eric. "Common Cause Calls for Probe of Rostenkowski." *Washington Post*, 22 December 1992, sec. A, p. 19.

Victor, Kirk. "Lost Cause?" *National Journal*, 1 March 1997, p. 410.

Zaradich, Linda. "Outside Counsel Urged in Ethics Case." *The Courier-Journal*, 4 May 1989, sec. A, p. 6.

Coolidge, Calvin (1872–1933) U.S. President 1923–1928. Calvin Coolidge built a national reputation by standing strongly against a 1919 strike by Boston policemen who sought to unionize. Governor of Massachusetts at the time, Coolidge was acclaimed as the man who repudiated those who would jeopardize public safety for private interest. Nominated for president at the Republican convention of 1920, Coolidge settled for second place on the ticket, and became vice president when WARREN G. HARDING of Ohio won the election. With Harding's death in office on August 2, 1923, Coolidge ascended to the presidency.

At the time of Harding's death, it had become public knowledge that corruption pervaded the administration. Perhaps the most outstanding example of such malfeasance was the TEAPOT DOME SCANDAL. In May 1921, President Harding had signed an executive order that unconstitutionally transferred naval oil reserves form the Department of the Navy to the Department of the Interior. Secretary of the Interior ALBERT FALL subsequently leased the oil reserves to oil company presidents EDWARD L. DOHENY and HARRY F. SINCLAIR in return for substantial bribes. It was left to Coolidge to dispose of this debacle.

Congressional investigations in the fall of 1923 uncovered the details of Teapot Dome. On February 2, 1924, the Senate passed a resolution calling for cancellation of the oil leases and appointment of a special counsel, independent of the Justice Department, to investigate the situation. The House of Representatives expressed concurrence the next day. Coolidge concluded that action of some sort was necessary. If for no other reason, action of some sort was necessary to create an atmosphere favorable to re-election in 1924. Initially, he considered appointing two of Attorney General HARRY DAUGHERTY's associates to investigate the scandal. The Justice Department, however, had already been tainted. Next, Coolidge decided to name Republican SILAS H. STRAWN and Democrat THOMAS W. GREGORY as special prosecutors. Unfortunately, both men had ties to oil companies. Gregory had been an attorney for an oil company, and had even once received payment from Doheny in return for services related to Mexican oil properties. Strawn was rumored to be connected to a bank that had helped to float Sinclair's oil stock and had ties to Standard Oil. Understandably, the Senate balked at confirmation. Finally, Coolidge settled on appointment of two distinguished lawyers, former Senator ATLEE POMERENE (D-Ohio) and Philadelphia Republican OWEN J. ROB-

ERTS, a future Associate Justice of the Supreme Court. The appointment of Pomerene and Roberts was approved after some debate, and as special prosecutors, the two men conducted a successful investigation resulting in the convictions of Fall and Sinclair.

Coolidge's appointment of special prosecutors is widely regarded, along with President HARRY S TRUMAN's use of a similar appointment in the TAX SCANDAL of the 1950s, as the principal, historical precedent for eventual establishment of the statutory independent counsel office.

References:

Busch, Francis X. *Enemies of the State*. Indianapolis: Bobbs-Merrill, 1954. A compilation of notable American trials. Chapter 2 discusses the Teapot Dome Case and describes how Doheny's admission of $100,000 payment to Fall prompted the Senate to call for a special investigation.

Ise, John. *The United States Oil Policy*. New Haven: Yale University Press, 1926. Chapter 25 covers the oil leasing scandal and discusses the irony of Strawn and Gregory's oil connections, which made them unsuitable as special prosecutors in this instance. This chapter also covers the congressional criticism of successful appointees Pomerene and Roberts.

Noggle, Burl. *Teapot Dome: Oil and Politics in the 1920's*. Baton Rouge: Louisiana State University Press, 1962. Chapters 5 and 6 discuss Coolidge's gradual decision to take action and his difficulty in obtaining Senate approval for his appointees. Chapters 7 and 9 describe the suits filed by Pomerene and Roberts in response to malfeasance uncovered.

Stratton, David Hughes. "Albert B. Fall and the Teapot Dome Affair." Ph.D. dissertation, University of Colorado, 1955. Chapter 10 discusses the political implications of Coolidge's prosecutor appointments. The investigation of Pomerene and Roberts is detailed in Chapter 11.

Cox, Archibald (1912–   ) Watergate Special Prosecutor, 1973. Among the best known of all the federal independent counsels, Archibald Cox was the first counsel to be appointed since the Teapot Dome scandal in the 1920s. Cox was appointed to investigate numerous allegations stemming from events surrounding the break-in at the Democratic National Committee headquarters on June 17, 1972, at the WATERGATE office and apartment complex in Washington, D.C. After serving more than six months, Cox became the principal target in the infamous "Saturday Night Massacre," wherein President RICHARD NIXON accepted the resignations of the top two persons in his Justice Department after they declined to fire Cox, who was in turn fired by the department's third ranking member. Immediate public outcry—featuring three million protest messages being sent to Congress—in response to the "massacre" accelerated the process leading to President Nixon's resignation in disgrace a year later.

A native of Massachusetts, Cox already had a distinguished public service and legal career before becoming Special Prosecutor. After studying American history and economics at Harvard, Cox entered the university's law school, and graduated with highest honors in 1937. He subsequently served as clerk for a prominent federal appellate judge, Learned Hand. Next he entered private practice before joining the Harvard Law faculty, where he became full professor in 1946. Cox served as head of the Wage Stabilization Board in the TRUMAN administration. Later, he was Solicitor General for President John Kennedy. An expert on both labor and constitutional law, Cox frequently was called upon to deliver lectures and arbitrate labor disputes around the nation. He also was published extensively in academic journals and public periodicals. His well-received books include: *Cases on Labor Law* (1948, through eight subsequent editions), *Civil Rights, the Constitution, and the Courts* (1967), *The Warren Court: Constitutional Decision As an Instrument of Reform* (1968), *The Role of the Supreme Court in American Government* (1976), and *The Court and the Constitution* (1987).

After announcing the resignation of two top aides, H.R. Haldeman and John Erlichman, and his attorney general, Richard Kleindienst, and the firing of another aide, John Dean, Richard Nixon was under growing pressure to "do something" about the Watergate scandal. He selected ELLIOT RICHARDSON to become attorney general with jurisdiction over the Watergate investigation and authorized him, if he thought necessary, to name a special prosecutor for the scandal. Then, during his confirmation hearings Richardson promised the Senate Judiciary Committee that he would name a Special Prosecutor and give him maximum independence. Richardson, after being turned down by four others, selected Cox, one of his Harvard law professors.

Cox moved quickly to hire a staff of attorneys (collectively known as the Watergate Special Prosecution Force), set up an office in a private building not far from the White House itself, and begin the investigation. He divided his attorneys into four teams, each of which focused on an aspect of the Watergate allegations: the Watergate break-in and cover-up, the "Plumbers" break-in cases, campaign "dirty tricks" allegations, and the collection and distribution of campaign funds. All teams spent most of their time scrambling to uncover and win release of documents, particularly from the White House itself. Cox and his teams would have the added weapon of a federal grand jury.

Meanwhile, Senator SAM ERVIN (D-North Carolina) and his congressional committee investigating the scandal tended to dominate the public's attention with their televised hearings. Although unsuccessful in his efforts to prevent the hearings from having further live television coverage, Cox immediately subpoenaed the President to win custody of selected audiotape recordings of White House conversations, once their existence was made public during an Ervin Committee hearing. Cox's subsequent successful legal effort in Federal District Court to win release of selected audiotapes ultimately led to his being fired as Special Prosecutor. President Nixon clearly did not want to relinquish the tapes and fired Cox as a last, desperate measure.

Throughout its existence, the Watergate Special Prosecution Force remained technically part of the Department of Justice. Yet when Richardson offered the top position to Cox, both men agreed that it would be an essentially independent legal force. The men continued to struggle defining the nature of this independence throughout their remaining time in office. From the beginning, Cox won two noteworthy concessions: first, that he would be free to make any public explanation or defense of his investigation; and second, that he would not be obligated to submit reports to Richardson.

Later, during negotiations over whether Cox could investigate allegations concerning money spent on President Nixon's home in San Clemente, California, each man argued that it was within his power to screen allegations and determine if they fell within the jurisdiction of the Watergate Special Prosecution Force. The two men reached an agreement that Cox would examine allegations of activities occurring between January 1971 and the time of his appointment in May 1973, unless the allegation involved a possible tampering with the Special Prosecutor's investigation.

Cox also had some limited struggles with Ervin's Senate committee investigating Watergate. The Special Prosecutor failed not only in attempts to end live television coverage of the committee hearings but even in his attempts to have the committee postpone its investigation until after Cox and his group had finished theirs. Despite these differences, the Special Prosecutor's office and the Senate committee and their staff continued to share valuable information throughout the time of the scandal.

Yet the greatest challenge Cox would confront to the powers and jurisdiction of his office involved the issue of executive privilege.

In essence, Cox argued that the importance of learning the contents of some of the White House audiotapes, in order to determine the roles played by President Nixon and those in his administration in the scandal, outweighed traditional claims of executive privilege made by presidents through the years. The president's attorney, Charles Alan Wright, countered by arguing that no president in history had ever been obligated to relinquish such sensitive material. Cox won the initial case, argued before Federal District Court Judge JOHN SIRICA, who ruled that he would first listen to each tape in question and screen out any information he thought protected by executive privilege. President Nixon protested the ruling and appealed to the United States Appeals Court where he again lost.

President Nixon, possibly frustrated by his court defeats and fearful of another setback upon appeal to the Supreme Court, sought to fire Cox. Richardson, Cox's immediate superior in the Department of Justice, said he felt obligated to his agreement with the Senate Judiciary committee upon his appointment and declined to fire the Special Prosecutor. Instead, he resigned. Moreover, Richardson's second in command, WILLIAM RUCKLESHAUS, also resigned rather than fire Cox. Finally, the third in the department's chain of command, Solicitor General Robert Bork, was summoned. He subsequently fired Cox.

President Nixon and his cohorts clearly failed to anticipate the breadth and depth of outrage in the public response to this action. The subsequent outcry stemming from the public, news media, and members of Congress (including those from the President's own party) enormously eroded whatever support the President previously had enjoyed. The President was suffering major setbacks in the political as well as the legal arena. In sum, Cox lost his job and Nixon lost his presidency.

Not long after taking the job, Cox was asked what he thought of his new position. He quickly responded that he thought it "a bit awesome" and that "in a way, I'm being asked to play God" (Doyle, 49). Of particular concern to Cox was the possibility of negotiating a settlement with the President over release of the White House tapes. Cox feared making an error in going to either of two extremes: excessively compromising and letting the President edit the released tapes to his satisfaction, or being excessively confrontational by stubbornly rejecting a legitimate compromise from the President.

Some outsiders occasionally had an entirely different perspective. Undergoing continuous critical assessment throughout his time in office, Cox was accused both of being too easy and of being excessively partisan on behalf of his fellow Democrats. Of particular concern for President Nixon was Cox's close association with the Kennedy family. Some liberal Democrats saw Cox as being aloof and arrogant; they were uncomfortable with his establishment Boston Brahman background. Yet, on the whole, most observers gave Cox high marks for both his independence from all outside pressure and for being aggressive to an appropriate degree.

References:

Ben-Veniste, Richard, and George Frampton, Jr. *Stonewall: The Real Story of the Watergate Prosecution*. New York: Simon and Schuster, 1977. This is an account written by a pair of attorneys on the Watergate Special Prosecution Force.
Cox, Archibald. *Papers*. His public papers are housed in the Special Collections section of the Harvard University Law School Library, Cambridge, Massachusetts.
———. "Reflections on a Firestorm," *Saturday Review*, 9 March 1974, pp.12–14, 56. Here Cox presents his views on how the Watergate scandal affected the nation and makes a recommendation about what best can be done to prevent such tragedies in the future.
Doyle, James. *Not above the Law: The Battles of Watergate Prosecutors Cox and Jaworski*. New York: William Morrow, 1977. This is a narrative account of the Special Prosecutor's Task Force written by the group's press officer.
Gormley, Ken. *Archibald Cox: Conscience of a Nation*. Reading, MA: Addison-Wesley, 1997. Eight of 22 chapters in this biography are devoted to Cox's time as Watergate Special Prosecutor. The book's foreword is written by Elliot Richardson.
Harriger, Katy J. *Independent Justice: The Federal Special Prosecutor in American Politics*. Lawrence: University Press of Kansas, 1992. An analytic study of the Federal Special Prosecutor's Office throughout the twentieth century.

—*ROBERT E. DEWHIRST*

Curran, Paul Jerome (1933–   ) Special Counsel, Carter Peanut Warehouse Investigation, 1979. Paul Curran was a Manhattan attorney with the Park Avenue law firm of Kaye, Scholer, Fierman, Hays & Handler when he was selected by Attorney General GRIFFIN BELL as special counsel. He was charged with determining whether loans from Bert Lance's National Bank of Georgia to the Carter family peanut business were illegally diverted to Jimmy CARTER's presidential campaign fund. Bell, reasoning that the alleged improprieties occurred before enactment of the ETHICS IN GOVERNMENT ACT (1978), did not choose to request a court-appointed special prosecutor. Instead, he named Curran "special counsel" on March 10, 1979, and vested him with limited powers for investigation. Curran would be unable to seek indictments without Justice Department approval. When public reaction to such limitations proved negative, Bell reconsidered. On March 23, Curran was granted all the powers that had been enjoyed by WATERGATE prosecutor LEON JAWORSKI.

A New York Republican, Curran was raised in Manhattan. His father, also an attorney, was an associate of New York Governor Thomas Dewey. Following his father into politics, Curran served three terms as state assemblyman in Albany during the 1960s. It was as U.S. Attorney for the Southern District of New York, however, that Curran's activities attracted the attention of state and national leaders. His 1974 prosecution of organized crime figure Carmine "Mr. Gibbs" Tramunti on narcotics charges won plaudits from New York Governor Nelson Rockefeller and President GERALD FORD. Curran was known for winning his cases through meticulous preparation. Not a dramatic courtroom performer, he relied on a logical and thorough presentation of the facts to convince judge and jury.

Upon being named special counsel, Curran announced that he intended to complete his investigation within a year, but was prepared to stay on the job longer if necessary. The statute of limitations on campaign finance violations was three years, noted Curran, and the alleged misconduct had occurred during the 1976 campaign. These facts appeared to present the special counsel with a mandate. He would run the investigation out of a government office building in New York with the assistance of three attorneys and an accountant. He had received applications from lawyers nationwide to serve on his staff.

Six prior federal investigations of a limited nature had not revealed any connection between the $680,000 in loans from the National Bank of Georgia and the Carter campaign. It appeared that the $1,013,422 construction loan was spent as intended on the peanut warehouse. Similarly, two commodity loans totaling $5,850,000 appeared legitimate, and were repaid on schedule. There were also questions being raised concerning a National Bank of Georgia loan to Carter media adviser Gerald Rafshoon in 1975. Curran's investigation would be the first thorough examination of the entire situation.

When Carter associate and banker Bert Lance was indicted in May 1979, there was no accompanying allegation linking the Carter campaign to any violations. Billy Carter, Jimmy's brother and peanut business manager, was alleged to have mishandled company funds, but it was not believed that any business funds had found their way into the campaign. Curran's focus was likely to be bank records that were vague concerning the extent of the Carter family debt early in 1976, which is when the Jimmy Carter was forced to float over $1 million in personal loans in order to keep the campaign alive. There also appeared to be a curious delay between the time the peanut business repaid its commodity loans and when the bank used the money to fund loans to three smaller state institutions. Might some of the loan money have found its way into the cash-strapped Carter campaign during the interim? Curran would have to decide. There was some indication that Lance's bank had been involved in covering a few minor Carter campign debts, but the bank denied it, explaining away the apparent evidence as clerical errors. In any case, by granting the Carter peanut business $9 million in credit, Lance's bank had certainly increased the potential borrowing power of Jimmy Carter. All of this had to be considered by Curran.

After a relatively brief six-month investigation, Curran released a 239-page report in October exonerating the President. Curran claimed to have traced all monies in and out of the Carter peanut warehouse, and found no connection to the Carter campaign. Testimony elicited by the Curran investigation had included a four-hour session with Jimmy Carter. Curran found a pattern of sloppy business practices by peanut business manager Billy Carter, and favorable treatment by the National Bank of Georgia, but no violation of campaign funding regulations. It appeared that the bank permitted Billy Carter to repay debts with checks drawn on insufficient funds. The bank would merely hold them until they could be covered. The bank also allowed the Carter business to violate loan agreements by releasing peanuts that had been pledged as collateral. Finally, Curran reported that the Carter business had understated its income for the years 1975–1977. As a result, there had probably been income tax matters to settle. Nevertheless, there were no campaign law transgressions.

Curran's investigation, although not an Ethics-Act-driven examination, led the public to believe that the special prosecutor statute might very well work to restore confidence in the government. Here was a Watergate-type investigation that had, by all accounts, thoroughly examined the facts surrounding an allegation of executive branch misconduct, efficiently allocated its resources ($360,000 spent), concluded its work in a reasonable time, and released a relatively concise report explaining its findings. The HAMILTON JORDAN and TIMOTHY KRAFT investigations would prove discouraging to some in the near future, because they dealt with what many would characterize as trivialities. Curran, however, had demonstrated that a serious allegation could be handled in a professional manner.

References:

Hendrickson, Paul. "Counsel at the Warehouse Door." *Washington Post*, 9 April 1979, sec. C, p. 1.

Mayer, Allan J., and Elaine Shannon. "The Peanut Probe: Case Closed." *Newsweek*, 19 October 1979, p. 35.

Morganthau, Tom, John Walcott, and Elaine Shannon. "The Carter Warehouse Probe." *Newsweek*, 4 June 1979, p. 23.

D

D'Amato, Alfonse (1937–   ) Senator (R-New York), 1981–1998. As leading Republican, and later Chairman, of the Senate Committee on Banking, Housing and Urban Affairs, Alfonse D'Amato played a prominent role in the congressional hearings on WHITEWATER held in 1994 and 1995. Working alongside Committee Chairman Donald W. Riegle, Jr. (D-Michigan) in 1994, D'Amato aggressively challenged the Clinton administration version of the manner in which Treasury officials interacted with the Resolution Trust Corporation's (RTC) investigation of Jim McDOUGAL's failed Madison Guaranty Savings & Loan. D'Amato's attack upon the veracity of Deputy Treasury Secretary ROGER C. ALTMAN's testimony helped lead to that official's resignation shortly after the hearings. The following year, as Chairman, D'Amato led hearings that focused on the death of White House attorney VINCENT FOSTER and the fate of documents contained in Foster's office. D'Amato used the proceedings to successfully press for release of more government records that might shed additional light on Whitewater-related transactions. Democrats claimed that many of the documents sought were protected by attorney-client privilege.

Born in Brooklyn, New York, D'Amato was educated at Syracuse University, receiving his law degree in 1961. He occupied a number of increasingly responsible positions in Long Island, New York, while rising in the Republican ranks (Administrator of Nassau County, 1965–1968; Tax Collector, Town of Hempstead, 1971–1977; Presiding Supervisor and Vice Chairman of County Board of Supervisors, Town of Hempstead, 1977–1980). As Senator, D'Amato earned a reputation as pugnacious and combative, characteristics that caused many of the targets of his verbal assaults to rejoice when he was condemned by an ethics panel in 1991 for allowing his brother, a lobbyist, use of his Senate office.

The Senate Whitewater hearings of August 1994, featured testimony by former White House Counsel BERNARD NUSSBAUM, Treasury General Counsel

JEAN HANSON, Treasury Chief of Staff Joshua Steiner and Altman. D'Amato accused Altman of lying about his role in leaking information to the Clinton administration regarding RTC's probe of Madison Guaranty. He also charged that Altman, by contradicting the testimony of Hanson and Steiner, was attempting to attribute responsibility to them for his own misdeeds. A scathing Republican report of the committee's findings led directly to the resignations of both Altman and Hanson. Upon ascending to the Chairmanship of the Senate Banking Committee following the elections of November 1994, D'Amato sent Independent Counsel KENNETH STARR a letter requesting further investigation into testimony given by White House aides Harold Ickes and George Stephanopoulos, as well as Treasury Department officials Altman, Hanson, and Steiner.

As Chairman of the Senate Banking Committtee in 1995, D'Amato led four weeks of Whitewater-related hearings that began on July 18. Concentrating on the events surrounding the suicide of White House attorney Vince Foster in 1993, D'Amato called high-profile witnesses, such as former Associate Attorney General WEBSTER HUBBELL, White House adviser Susan Thomases, and Nussbaum. Although inconclusive in its findings, the Senate's proceedings effectively upstaged Representative JIM LEACH's better-documented House probe into the documentary history of the Whitewater affair, which took place at the same time. It was generally agreed that D'Amato successfully tempered his approach in conducting the 1995 hearings, adopting a more judicial demeanor than he had the previous year. D'Amato's investigative efforts were successful in eventually forcing the administration to turn over notes taken by Associate White House Attorney William Kennedy III during a Whitewater-related meeting on November 5, 1993. D'Amato believed the information contained in those missives might help in determining whether administration officials had illegally used information obtained from other government agencies to defend themselves against Whitewater-related charges.

D'Amato's tenure in Congress did not outlive the Whitewater investigation. Seeking a fourth term, he was defeated in the 1998 elections by Democrat Charles Shumer.

References:

"Rough Whitewater Ride for Clinton." *Congressional Quarterly Almanac* (1994): 108–115.
"Whitewater Sparks New Hearings." *Congressional Quarterly Almanac* (1995): 1–57–1–61.
Zehren, Charles V. "Fonz in with a Splash." *Newsday*, 30 November 1994, p. A24.

Dash, Samuel (1925–   ) lawyer; Chief Counsel, Senate Watergate Committee 1973–1974. Sam Dash had established a reputation as a distinguished lawyer in Philadelphia, both in the district attorney's office (1952–1956) and private practice (Dash & Levy, 1958–1963), and as a professor at the Georgetown University Law School in Washington (1965–   ) when he was called upon to serve as Chief Counsel to the U.S. Senate Select Committee on Presidential Campaign Activities (Senate Watergate Committee). His active participation during the WATERGATE investigation enabled him to play a crucial role in the crafting of legislation that resulted in the establishment of the special prosecutor. A staunch defender of the institution, Dash would regularly speak in favor of the mechanism's reauthorization. Recently he has served as ethical adviser to Independent Counsel KENNETH STARR, whose WHITEWATER inquiry was subject to intense criticism due to aggressive prosecutorial tactics.

Dash's work with the Senate Watergate Committee during its public hearings in the spring and summer of 1973 included functioning as liaison with the Watergate Special Prosecuting Force (WSPF) and its head, ARCHIBALD COX. Dash and the Senate Watergate Committee performed the important function of capturing public attention and mobilizing it in favor of the Watergate Investigation. Cox and his team acknowledged as much in their report. Tension existed, however, between the Senate and WSPF investigations, because testimony before the Senate Committee was obtained in return for grants of IMMUNITY to witnesses. These grants significantly hindered Cox's investigation and prosecution of Watergate. This would pose a serious problem for future independent counsels as well, especially LAWRENCE WALSH and his IRAN-CONTRA INVESTIGATION. At first, Cox attempted to halt the Senate hearings without success. Next, he tried to limit congressional grants of immunity only to those witnesses who testified in executive session. Judge JOHN SIRICA refused to allow such limitation. Dash objected to Cox's approach, which he perceived as arrogant. Dash's meetings with Cox, who had been his labor law professor at Harvard, left him with the distinct impression Cox wanted the Senate Committee to step aside and allow him to conduct the investigation alone. Dash felt that Cox looked upon the Senate's inquiry as hopelessly tainted by the political atmosphere in which it operated. Cox's pursuit of justice would end in October 1973 when he was fired by President RICHARD NIXON who objected to the Special Prosecutor's demands for release of taped White House telephone conversations. Dash's work continued.

The Senate Watergate Committee concluded its hearings, and was ready to release its report in February 1974. LEON JAWORSKI, Cox's successor, prevailed upon Dash to delay the Senate's report until March, when the WPSF would issue its indictments. Dash complied with the request, and went on to develop a close working relationship and friendship with Jaworski. The Senate Committee's files, turned over to the Senate Rules Committee, served as a valuable source of documents for the WSPF's continuing activities. Perhaps Dash's most important contribution to the evolution of the special prosecutor/independent counsel mechanism was his efforts to ensure that the special prosecutor be truly independent. Senator ABRAHAM RIBICOFF introduced the Watergate Reorganization and Reform Act of 1975 (S.495) at the start of the 94th Congress. It called for establishment of a permanent office of public attorney appointed by a panel of judges with the advice and consent of the Senate. It would be charged with investigating allegations of executive branch misconduct, cases referred by the Justice Department due to conflict of interest, criminal cases referred by the Federal Election Commission, and allegations of federal election and campaign law violations. Senators CHARLES PERCY (R-Illinois) and Howard Baker (R-Tennessee) introduced an amendment that called for the public attorney to be placed within the Department of Justice. Dash agreed with the establishment of a permanent office. It should receive and investigate complaints from individuals who believe that they have been victims of executive branch misconduct. The public attorney would function essentially as an ombudsman, referring legitimate cases to the attorney general for action. Should the attorney general fail to act, the public attorney could take the matter to a federal district court in order to obtain an order requesting the attorney general to show cause why the public attorney should not become special prosecutor for the case in question. Dash believed, however, that S.495 described a public attorney with too much discretion operating in too broad a jurisdiction.

When general sentiment grew for a temporary public attorney, Dash accurately predicted the course that events would follow. He stated that the Senate would support a temporary public attorney appointed by a court panel if the House passed it. President GERALD FORD would be forced to accept such a plan for political reasons, declared Dash, and if Jimmy CARTER won the election, he was certain to support it. Senator Ribicoff's Public Officials Integrity Act (S.555), introduced in February 1977, created the Office of Special Prosecutor largely in the manner Dash had forecast.

Dash remained a firm supporter of the independent counsel office for the next two decades. Testifying before the Senate Governmental Affairs Committee in May 1993 with JANET RENO and Arthur Liman, then counsel to the Senate/House Iran-Contra Committee, Dash asserted that the independent counsel office carried out its responsibilities in an objective, impartial manner. Its costs, though high, did not compare unfavorably with Justice Department expenditures in the prosecution of high-profile figures such as Panamanian dictator Manuel Noriega.

Unlike many in the political arena, Dash's support of the office did not change whenever the party affiliation of the target did. As a result, in October 1994, Dash readily accepted an offer from Whitewater independent counsel Kenneth Starr to add ethical credibility to an unpopular investigation. Starr's association with persons and organizations openly hostile to President Bill CLINTON caused many to question his impartiality as independent counsel. Dash's presence on Starr's team was calculated to ease such concerns. By 1996, Dash's association with Starr was becoming difficult. Some saw Starr as using Dash's reputation as cover for his politically influenced investigation of Clinton. When Dash's unusually high consulting fee of $3,200 a week was leaked to the press, it appeared to support critics' contentions. In interviews, Dash tried at times to objectively criticize aspects of Starr's investigations while remaining loyal to the man who was retaining his services—an impossible balancing act to maintain. Yes, mused Dash, it might have been better to keep Fiske as independent counsel for the Whitewater investigation, but that was not Starr's fault. Yes, it would be wiser if Starr was a full-time independent counsel, but maintaining a private practice was not improper. Dash, perhaps tiring of the pressures involved, took a two-month leave from his position in May 1996 to teach at Heidelberg University Law School in Germany.

References:

Grove, Lloyd. "Say It Again Sam." *Washington Post*, 23 April 1996, sec. D, p.1.
Harriger, Katy J. *Independent Justice: The Federal Special Prosecutor in American Politics.* Lawrence: University Press of Kansas, 1992. Chapters 3 ("A Watergate Legacy") and 4 ("Implementation and Congressional Oversight") discuss Dash's contributions to crafting of the statute that created the special prosecutor office.
Schorr, Daniel. "Even an Ethicist Can Get Splashed by Whitewater." *Christian Science Monitor*, 3 May 1996, p. 19.
Tackett, Michael. "Reno Asks to Renew Special Prosecutors but Dole Says Law Wastes Money." *Chicago Tribune*, 15 May 1993, sec. N, p. 3.

Daugherty, Harry M. (1860–1941) Attorney General, 1921–1924. One of the first U.S. officeholders to be targeted by a special prosecutor's investigation, Harry Daugherty was forced out of President CALVIN COOLIDGE's Cabinet in 1924 because of his association with the TEAPOT DOME SCANDAL. Although never convicted of any scandal-related crimes, his failure to act while those around him were accepting bribes and leasing public land to large oil companies was sufficient to end his political career.

A native of Washington Court House, Ohio, Harry Daugherty earned his law degree at the University of Michigan in 1881, then returned to practice in his small hometown. He won election to the state legislature as a Republican in 1890, serving two terms as representative of Fayette County. In 1893, Daugherty moved his law practice to Columbus, establishing the firm of Daugherty, Todd & Rarey in 1902. Although his practice would continue until 1921, increasingly, Republican politics occupied his time and energy. Daugherty's association with the popular educator and journalist WARREN G. HARDING began in the century's first decade. He engineered the personable Ohioan's successful candidacy for lieutenant governor, but failed to secure his election as governor in 1910. Harding's election as senator in 1914, however, boosted Daugherty's fortunes as well as his own. By 1919, Daugherty was widely considered to be in charge of Republican machine politics in the state. At the Republican convention of 1920, Daugherty, acting as campaign manager for WARREN G. HARDING, successfully positioned the senator from Ohio as a compromise candidate. He was selected on the party's tenth ballot, and his victory in the fall secured a Cabinet post for Daugherty.

When lawyer and conservationist Harry A. Slattery and progressive Wisconsin Senator Robert M. La Follette began raising public consciousness regarding Secretary of the Interior ALBERT B. FALL's leasing of the nation's oil reserves in 1922, Daugherty saw no cause for alarm. When Fall resigned in March 1923, Daugherty stated that the Senate's pending investigation of oil policy played no part. Early in 1924, after the Senate's hearings had continued for several months, President Coolidge directed Daugherty's Department of Justice to monitor the proceedings. The Attorney General was instructed to examine evidence produced by the hearings in order to determine if any further action was indicated. Daugherty, having served under Harding when Fall's oil leases were negotiated and approved, was in an awkward position. Surely he had been aware of the situation. His failure to oppose the arrangement appeared to suggest concurrence. This was also a presidential election year. Coolidge could not afford to appear soft on corruption. On January 26, 1924, Coolidge announced his intention to appoint a special counsel to investigate the Teapot Dome Scandal. Jurisdiction over the alleged wrongdoing would be removed from Daugherty's department. Daugherty stated that he understood his presence along with Fall in Harding's cabinet created a perceived conflict of interest, and, consequently, he approved of Coolidge's action.

Although the Democrats aggressively accused Daugherty of complicity in disposing of the nation's oil reserves, the Attorney General proclaimed his innocence and resolved to stay on. Fall was called before the Senate in February and invoked his Fifth Amendment privileges. As the public clamored for action, ATLEE POMERENE and OWEN J. ROBERTS began their investigation as special prosecutors. Daugherty offered them all the assistance of the Justice Department. On February 18, Secretary of the Navy EDWIN DENBY resigned. He had acquiesced in transfer of the naval oil reserves to the Department of the Interior. Daugherty now remained as the last prominent target of investigators and critics.

Coolidge refused to comply with the mounting chorus calling for Daugherty's dismissal, but he let it be known that he would not reject his resignation. When prominent Republican Senators William Borah (Idaho) and Joseph T. Robinson (Arkansas) joined the call, the pressure on Coolidge increased. Daugherty, having demanded a hearing, was vigorously attacked by Senate Democrats during testimony on February 28. Most Republicans refused to come to his defense. On March 12, Roxie Stinson, ex-wife of Daugherty's deceased friend Jesse Smith, testified before the special counsel that the Attorney General had hosted meetings where corrupt deals were arranged. On March 28, after several meetings with Coolidge, Daugherty resigned. Coolidge, apparently annoyed by Daugherty's long delay, issued a taciturn acceptance statement. Daugherty continued to explain and defend his record verbally and in writing. He viewed Coolidge's insistence on his departure as driven by expediency and lacking in principle.

References:

Daugherty, Harry M., and Thomas Dixon. *The Inside Story of the Harding Tragedy*. New York: Churchill, 1932. Appendix contains correspondence between Coolidge and

Daugherty regarding his resignation and Special Counsel Atlee Pomerene's letter of July 22, 1931, indicating that Daugherty was not involved in the leases and contracts transferring naval oil reserves to private control.

Noggle, Burl. *Teapot Dome: Oil and Politics in the 1920's*. Baton Rouge: Louisiana State University Press, 1962.

Deaver, Michael K. (1938–   ) Deputy Chief of Staff to the President, 1981–1985. The subject of an investigation by Independent Counsel WHITNEY NORTH SEYMOUR, Michael Deaver was convicted of perjury for lying about his contacts with government officials on behalf of business clients. Former government employees like Deaver are specifically forbidden from such association by the ETHICS IN GOVERNMENT ACT (1978). Deaver became the first former government official convicted as a result of an independent counsel investigation.

Michael Deaver was born in Bakersfield, California, and received a B.A. in Public Administration from San Jose State University in 1960. He successfully combined a career in public relations with service to Republican administrations both in the state of California and in Washington, D.C. White House service enabled him to acquire an intimate knowledge of the way in which government works. His contacts with influential government figures during his tenure in Washington placed him among the most well-positioned individuals in public relations to lobby on behalf of persons seeking favors. When Deaver used government influence as a public relations lobbyist, he was following in the footsteps of many other former administration employees, including Democratic insiders like Clark Clifford and Robert Strauss. It was the aggressiveness, pervasiveness, and unparalleled lucrativeness of the practice that was new. Some believed as well, that Deaver practiced his craft in an ostentatious, brazen manner, flaunting his influence and advertising his success. Others see Deaver as a product of the 1980s when the entrepreneurial spirit, in all its manifestations, appeared more virtuous.

In early March 1986, the news media began reporting that Michael Deaver had become a millionaire within nine months of leaving a $72,000 a year government position by representing the interests of wealthy corporate clients. Deaver & Associates counted among their clients CBS, TWA, and Philip Morris. The firm also successfully negotiated $1.7 million in contracts with the government of South Korea and connected businesses. Deaver's longtime association with President RONALD REAGAN was undoubtedly attractive to many clients. Deaver also was permitted to maintain his White House pass after leaving his government position. Clearly, he would continue to be a welcome visitor. In April, on a complaint from congressman John Dingell (D-Michigan), the General Accounting Office began an inquiry into whether Deaver's consulting agreement with the government of Canada influenced the U.S. settlement on the issue of acid rain. Deaver's firm also signed a $1.5 million contract with Saudi Arabia, reportedly aimed at facilitating acquisition of military equipment. Having quickly succeeded in building a profitable firm, Deaver was now reported to be negotiating its sale to the British company of Saatchi & Saatchi, close advisers of Margaret Thatcher, for $18 million. In May, Congress began hearings on a proposed Integrity in Post Employment Act aimed at curbing the perceived excesses of former employees like Deaver. Senator Robert Byrd (D-West Virginia) called on Attorney General EDWIN MEESE to request an independent counsel to examine Deaver's dealings. He was joined by David Martin, head of the Government Ethics Office, who asked the Justice Department to probe Deaver's relationship with the government of Canada. It was reported that the sale of Deaver's firm was now on hold. The negative publicity, however, did not seem to have a deleterious effect on his relationship with the White House. It was reported that he continued to receive a copy of the president's daily schedule. Some concern appeared to be developing among White House insiders that Deaver's growing problems might reflect negatively on the President.

On May 29, 1986, Whitney North Seymour was named independent counsel to investigate alleged misconduct by Deaver. Seymour's investigation was not, however, limited to the two incidents cited by the Justice Department: the acid rain issue involving Deaver's lobbying for Canada, and Deaver's reported approach to Security Adviser ROBERT McFARLANE in order to facilitate a tax break for Puerto Rico. Deaver's business suffered during Seymour's ten-month investigation as his legal costs mounted. On February 25, 1987, Deaver secured a temporary restraining order forestalling his indictment. He contended that the Ethics in Government Act was unconstitutional, violating the priciple of separation of powers. On March 11, the U.S. District Court in *DEAVER v. SEYMOUR*, decided not to intervene in the case. There would be no injunction preventing indictment. Constitutional questions would be resolved on appeal of any conviction. In late March 1987, Seymour announced an indictment. Deaver was charged with five counts of perjury involving his testimony before a federal grand jury and Congress. The indictment charged that Deaver lied about his representation of the Canadian government during acid rain discussions; his arrangement of a meeting between the President and Kim Kihwan, a representative of the South Korean government; and his lobbying efforts for the Smith Barney company and Trans World Airlines (TWA). Deaver denied all charges. The indictment meant that Deaver would not be eligible for reimbursement of legal expenses.

Although there was speculation that evidence of Deaver's reputed problems with alcohol might be presented during trial, Deaver's attorneys, led by Herbert J. Miller, Jr. elected to present no defense during the seven weeks of proceedings. The tactic backfired when Deaver was convicted on three counts of perjury. The jury deliberated for 27 hours before returning their verdict on December 17, 1987. The decision found Deaver guilty of lying about arranging the visit of South Korean emissary Kim Kihwan to the White House, efforts to influence administration officials on behalf of TWA, and attempts to secure a tax break for Puerto Rico. Deaver faced a possible sentence of 15 years in prison. In late September 1988, Deaver was given a three-year suspended sentence and fined $100,000.

Although his book *Behind the Scenes* (Morrow, 1987) apparently caused some temporary ill-feeling because of its controversial portrait of the Reagans, Deaver has been able to maintain his ties with prominent Republicans. In August 1991, Deaver helped open the Reagan Library, and he was involved in planning the Republican convention in 1996. He has frequently been called upon to comment on political affairs and public image.

References:

"Access, My Foot." *New Republic*, 28 April 1986, p. 6.

Alterman, Eric. "Scandal Sheet." *New Republic*, 20 April 1987, p. 17. Contains details of Deaver indictment.

Beckwith, David. "The High Price of Friendship." *Time*, 28 December 1987, p. 23.

"Cashing In on Top Connections." *Time*, 3 March 1986, p. 28.

Church, George J. "Acid Raining on Deaver's Parade." *Time*, 5 May 1986, p. 20.

"Delving into Deaver's Details." *Time*, 9 June 1986, p. 33.

DeMott, John S. "The Bill Comes Due for Deaver." *Time*, 30 March 1987, p. 23.

Doan, Michael, and Patricia A. Avery. "Michael Deaver." *U.S. News & World Report*, 14 April 1986, p. 8.

McAllister, Bill. "Deaver Is Found Guilty of Lying about Lobbying." *Washington Post*, 17 December 1987, sec. A, p.1.

Shapiro, Walter, Thomas M. DeFrank, Gloria Borger, and Howard Fineman. "Has Mike Deaver Gone Too Far?" *Newsweek*, 14 April 1986, p. 23.

Shapiro, Walter, Margaret Garrard Walker, and Howard Fineman. "Cashing In on Reagan." *Newsweek*, 3 March 1986, p. 21.

"United States of America v. Michael K. Deaver." *Washington Post*, 26 September 1988, sec. A, p. 13. Contains excerpts of Independent Counsel Whitney North Seymour's presentencing memo that, among other things, criticizes the *Washington Post*'s editorial acceptance, and implicit approval of, the type of activities that brought Deaver to trial. Also contains excerpts of U.S. District Court Judge Thomas Penfield Jackson's sentencing statement that expresses the opinion that Deaver knew he was lying, but acted not entirely out of mercenary considerations.

Deaver v. Seymour 656 F. Supp. 900 (1987). Former Deputy Chief of Staff during the administration of President RONALD REAGAN, MICHAEL K. DEAVER sought to prevent an investigation of his lobbying activities by Independent Counsel WHITNEY NORTH SEYMOUR. After learning that Seymour was about to indict him for perjury, based on testimony before a federal grand jury and congressional subcommittee, Deaver applied to the U.S. District Court for an injunction based on the contention that the independent counsel statute is unconstitutional. Deaver claimed that the arrangement was in violation of the constitutional principle of separation of powers. As a result, Seymour's inquiry should be ended and evidence collected to date impounded. Judge Thomas Penfield Jackson issued a temporary restraining order on February 25, 1987, in order to consider Deaver's petition for injunction.

On March 11, 1987, Jackson denied Deaver's request. Before addressing the argument presented by Deaver, Jackson noted that the plaintiff had created a confusing procedural situation by filing a motion for summary judgment and requesting consolidation of that motion with his petition for injunction. The judge did not wish to delay Seymour's investigation any further than was absolutely necessary, believing that it was in the public interest to dispose of Deaver's challenge quickly. Consequently, Jackson elected to dismiss Deaver's motion to consolidate, allowing the court to rule promptly on the injunction request.

The court decided that an injunction was unnecessary for several reasons. First, another remedy was readily available to Deaver; he could move for dismissal of charges prior to trial based on defects in the prosecution. This was the argument advanced by Seymour. Secondly, and most important, Jackson declared that it appeared unlikely Deaver would succeed on the merits of the case. True, the judge acknowledged, the independent counsel was an unusual institution that combined aspects of more than one branch of government in a curious manner, but available legal authority seemed to suggest to Jackson that the mechanism was likely to withstand constitutional scrutiny. The court indicated that *EX PARTE SIEBOLD, BANZHAF v. SMITH, WIENER v. UNITED STATES*, and *HUMPHREY'S EXECUTOR v. UNITED STATES* all served to argue in favor of the independent counsel's legality. Because it was incumbent upon Deaver, in bringing the motion, to demonstrate a likelihood of success in this regard, the court could not grant the injunction.

Jackson considered that the issue of the independent counsel statute's constitutionality would ultimately be decided on appeal. Meanwhile, counsel should be permitted to speedily prosecute any apparent violations of the the criminal code committed by the plaintiff.

OLIVER NORTH would bring a similar challenge to the institution of the independent counsel before *MORRISON v. OLSON* would settle the matter in 1988.

References:

Harriger, Katy J. *Independent Justice: The Federal Special Prosecutor in American Politics*. Lawrence: University Press of Kansas, 1992. Chapter 5, "Is the Prosecutor Constitutional?," discusses the case.

Dellums, Ronald V. (1935–   ) Congressman (D-California), 1971–1998 Oakland, California, Congressman Ron Dellums joined other left/liberal activists in the 1980s seeking to test the usefulness of the independent counsel statute by attempting to force the attorney general to employ the mechanism in specific instances.

After early investigations under the statute, such as the HAMILTON JOR-

DAN and TIMOTHY KRAFT cases, proved trivial in nature, reauthorization of the statute in 1982 raised the standard by which such investigations could be triggered. Revision stipulated that the attorney general was to consider the credibility of evidence presented as well as the specificity of the information received. The attorney general could also refuse to request appointment of an independent counsel if he/she found no reasonable grounds to believe that further investigation was warranted. Previously, guidelines instructed the attorney general to appoint a special prosecutor unless the incident in question was so unsubstantiated that it did not warrant further examination.

Under the new guidelines, Democrats found the REAGAN administration unresponsive when presented with allegations that might well call for investigation by an independent counsel. Those pressing for action resorted to the courts. Ron Dellums initiated such a suit in response to the Reagan administration's support of the Contras in Nicaragua. Contending that the government's military operations in support of the Contra rebels violated the Neutrality Act of 1982, Dellums was joined in his action by Eleanor Ginsberg, a resident of Dade County, Florida, where paramilitary training centers were located, and Myrna Cunningham, a physician residing in Nicaragua who allegedly was kidnapped and raped by Contra members. *DELLUMS v. SMITH* (1983) met with success in the district courts, as did two companion cases, *BANZHAF v. SMITH* (1984) and *NATHAN v. ATTORNEY GENERAL* (1983). The district court found that Dellums and his fellow plaintiffs had standing to sue, and that the attorney general should have initiated a preliminary investigation into the charges presented to him. The ETHICS IN GOVERNMENT ACT (1978) did not permit him the prosecutorial discretion that would justify dismissing the allegations without further inquiry. On appeal, however, Judge Thomas E. Fairchild of the Seventh Circuit Court ruled that the plaintiffs lacked standing to sue, because the Ethics in Government Act did not intend private citizens to monitor the investigative and prosecutorial decisions rendered by the Justice Department. Citizen participation in the process was limited to reporting of alleged offenses. Both the *Banzhaf* and *Nathan* cases met with a similar fate.

On February 5, 1987, Dellums announced that he was formally dropping his suit. The appointment of Independent Counsel LAWRENCE WALSH to investigate the IRAN-CONTRA scandal was seen by Dellums as at least partial vindication of his allegations. Although Walsh was empowered to examine only activities occurring after 1984, Dellums hoped that the scope of the investigation might be expanded to include incidents before that date, and he asked Walsh to seek such authority. Although Walsh was not named independent counsel in direct response to Dellums's suit, it was believed by some that the suit served to help persuade Attorney General EDWIN MEESE to request appointment of such counsel.

Trained as a psychiatric social worker, Dellums also served in the Marines before entering politics. When Ron Dellums joined Congress in 1971, he appeared to personify the angry, black radical of the 1960s era. Veteran members of Congress were unsure whether they would be able to work constructively with him. Similarly, Dellums was not confident of finding a place for himself in Washington. Gradually, Dellums won the respect of his colleagues by wisely choosing when and where to fight for his causes, and by demonstrating appreciation for opposing viewpoints. When Dellums announced his retirement from Congress in February 1998, he found himself the subject of laudatory testimonials from members on both sides of the aisle. Much of Dellums's congressional achievements were facilitated by his long tenure on the House Armed Services (now the National Security) Committee, and his 17-year stint on the Appropriations Subcommittee. As chairman of the Armed Services Committee, 1993–1995, Dellums worked with conservative colleagues like John Kasich (R-Ohio) to limit the number of expensive B-2 bombers that were produced. Such action was hoped for by the congressional Black Caucus when it convinced Dellums to seek appointment to the Armed Services Committee instead of one that dealt with the social issues that initially brought him to Congress. Other projects that occupied Dellums during his congressional service included initiation of sanctions against South Africa during its long apartheid era.

Dellums himself came under investigation for alleged drug use in 1982, and as a principal offender in the House Banking scandal, which identified over 300 members as having written checks against insufficient funds. No criminal action was taken in either case. Dellums plans a book on his congressional career with longtime aide Lee Halterman.

References:

"Dellums Drops Suit Seeking Prosecutor on Neutrality." *San Diego Union-Tribune*, 5 February 1987, sec. A, p. 5.

Rosenfeld, Megan. "A 21-Gun Send-off, California's Ron Dellums Departs House with Bittersweet Memories and Fond Farewells." *Washington Post*, 7 February 1998, sec. B, p. 1.

Dellums v. Smith 797 F.2d 817 (1986). One of three court challenges posed by plaintiffs attempting to force REAGAN administration Attorney General WILLIAM FRENCH SMITH to initiate independent counsel investigations in response to citizen-reported allegations of executive-branch misconduct, this case was brought by Rep. RON DELLUMS (D-California). He was joined by Eleanor Ginsberg, a resident of Dade County in Florida, and Myrna Cunningham, a physician residing in Nicaragua. The plaintiffs' suit demanded that the U.S. Justice Department trigger the independent counsel mechanism in order to determine if the United States had violated the Neutrality Act of 1982 during its activities in Nicaragua on behalf of the Contras.

In January 1983, the plaintiffs reported to the attorney general that they had information indicating that the Reagan administration policy in Nicaragua was in violation of several federal, criminal statutes. Specifically, it was alleged that President Reagan, former Secretary of State Alexander Haig, Assistant Secretary of State GEORGE SHULTZ, Assistant Secretary of State Thomas Enders, Secretary of Defense CASPAR WEINBERGER, Assistant Secretary of Defense Nestor Sanchez, and Central Intelligence Agency Director WILLIAM CASEY were guilty of misconduct. The plaintiffs alleged that they had violated the Neutrality Act of 1982 by conducting military operations against a nation with whom the United States was at peace, a related statute prohibiting conspiracies aimed at the destruction of foreign government property, and a statute prohibiting unlicensed arms shipments. Congressman Dellums's coplaintiffs had both been in position to observe U.S. misconduct. Ginsberg lived nearby five U.S. military training facilities where Contras were prepared for battle, and Cunningham was a physician who was allegedly kidnapped and raped in Nicaragua by Contra members.

In March 1983, Attorney General Smith responded to the plaintiffs by formally denying their request. He had decided not to conduct a preliminary investigation into the allegations. In response, the plaintiffs filed suit. Along with the companion lawsuits, *BANZHAF v. SMITH* (1984) and *NATHAN v. ATTORNEY GENERAL* (1983), *Dellums v. Smith* met with success at the district level. The district court ruled that the Administrative Procedure Act (APA) of 1982 provided the plaintiffs with standing to request judicial review. Having reviewed the Attorney General's decision, the court found that the ETHICS IN GOVERNMENT ACT (1978) required a preliminary investigation in this instance, because the plaintiffs had provided the Justice Department with specific information of wrongdoing from a credible source. The Attorney General did not have discretion to ignore such a complaint. The attorney general proceeded to file a post-judgment motion arguing that a preliminary investigation was not warranted, because the Justice Department had established a non-prosecution policy for Neutrality Act violations. In addition, the argument continued, the Neutrality Act was not applicable to paramilitary actions authorized by the President. The district court denied the motion. Non-prosecution policies are only permissible, stated the court, when government officials would be in danger of being prosecuted for offenses that would not place a private person at risk. The district court's interpretation of Ethics Act language also did not allow presidential paramiltary expeditions against nations with whom the United States was at peace. Granting the attorney general authority to act as final interpreter of statute language, ruled the court, would defeat the purpose of the Ethics Act. Apparently, Judge Stanley A. Weigel believed that the 1982 reauthorization reforms that had called for the attorney general to more carefully monitor the investigations that were initiated, had resulted in Justice Department excesses.

The attorney general appealed the district court's decision. As in *Banzhaf* and *Nathan*, the appeals court reversed the district court's decision. The appeals court ruled that the plaintiffs lacked standing to bring the case. In order to satisfy the requirements of the APA, stated the court, plaintiffs must demonstrate injury-in-fact. Because the plaintiffs could not show such injury, their interest in the matter amounted to mere abstract concern. This, stated the court, was insufficient to confer standing. In addition, the court ruled that private citizens did not possess the procedural right to monitor the actions of the attorney general. The public may report alleged violations to the Justice Department. The Department is obligated to investigate such charges when specific information is provided by credible sources. It is the duty of congressional judiciary committees, however—not the general public—to ensure that the Justice Department carries through the investigation in accordance with Ethics Act provisions. The public has a right to report alleged executive-branch misconduct, but does not possess the correlative right of having its allegations investigated. Accordingly, the appeals court dismissed the case.

In 1987, Dellums formally withdrew his suit. The appointment of independent counsel LAWRENCE WALSH to investgate IRAN-CONTRA enabled the plaintiffs to declare partial victory. Walsh was charged with investigating all allegations of executive wrongdoing after 1984.

References:

Brown, Jonathan P. "*Banzhaf v. Smith*: Judicial Review under the Independent Counsel Provisions of the Ethics in Government Act." *Iowa Law Review* 70 (1985): 1339–1352. Calls for amendment of Ethics in Government Act to specifically allow judicial review of attorney general's rulings.

Mixter, Stephen Charles. "The Ethics in Government Act of 1978: Problems with the Attorney General's Discretion and Proposals for Reform." *Duke Law Journal* (1985): 497–522. Discusses *Banzhaf*, *Dellums*, and *Nathan* cases. Argues for judicial review of attorney general's discretion with regard to independent counsel decisions. Considers the possibility of removing independent counsel matters from attorney general control entirely.

Denby, Edwin (1870–1929) Secretary of the Navy, 1921–1924. Implicated in the TEAPOT DOME SCANDAL, although never formally charged with improprieties, Edwin Denby resigned from President CALVIN COOLIDGE's Cabinet because he believed his continued presence in the administration was a cause of embarrassment. In doing so, Denby became the second casualty (after Interior Secretary ALBERT FALL) of an executive-branch scandal to be investigated by special prosecutors.

Born in Evansville, Indiana, Denby spent most of his adolescence in China, where his father served as U.S. minister. Denby spent seven years working in the Chinese imperial maritime customs service under Sir Robert Hart before returning to the United States to study law. He received his degree from the University of Michigan in 1896. Physically powerful, Denby was a standout football player at Michigan, and served in both the Spanish-American War and World War I. In the latter conflict, he entered the Marine Corps as a 47-year-old private and rose to the rank of major. Representing Michigan as a Republican congressman (1905–1911), Denby was an advocate of military preparedness, and he worked to create a strong sea force by upgrading the naval militia. He also defended Theodore Roosevelt's acquisition of the Panama Canal zone, but favored payment of compensation to Colombia. Upon demobilization, Denby was named chief probation officer of the recorder's court in Detroit and the circuit court in Wayne County before entering President WARREN HARDING's cabinet in 1921.

Conservationists opposed Denby's appointment as Secretary of the Navy from the start. Forestry expert, and later Pennsylvania governor Gifford Pinchot, and his associate, Washington, D.C. lawyer Harry Slattery, viewed Denby as an enemy of the conservation movement. As a congressman, Denby had supported Secretary of the Interior Richard Ballinger during his controversial conflict with Pinchot over conservation policy in 1909. Soon after entering the Cabinet, Denby took action that in the eyes of conservationists justified their early concerns. Convinced that private oil companies on land adjacent to naval oil reserves were draining government oil, he decided to permit the private development of such reserves by large oil companies with whom the government would negotiate leasing contracts. To facilitate this arrangement, Denby recommended transfer of the oil reserves to the Department of the Interior, because that agency already was leasing millions of acres of public land to private companies. This meant that the oil reserves would come under the control of Interior Secretary Albert Fall, a man whose previous record indicated a tendency to favor transfer of public land to private interests. Denby apparently considered his actions legally sound and prudent. Congress had passed legislation in 1920 permitting such transfers of naval oil. Denby stated that the transfer would solve a pressing drainage problem and benefit the nation. He didn't foresee that the contracts negotiated by Fall would be found to involve large-scale exploitation and bribery.

Before Congress, following the lead of Progressive Wisconsin Senator Robert LaFollette, began to fully investigate leasing of the naval oil reserves, Fall resigned as Secretary of the Interior early in 1923. He did not mention the oil issue as reason for his exit. Investigation revealed that Fall had secretly leased the large Teapot Dome oil reserve to HARRY SINCLAIR of the Mammoth Oil Company. Congressional hearings in late 1923 and early 1924 elicited testimony describing a well-concealed $100,000 loan from EDWARD DOHENY of the Pan American Petroleum and Transport Company to Fall. Denby's innocent transfer took on the appearance of a conspiracy to defraud the American public, and Democrats called for his resignation.

On January 28, 1924, Senator THOMAS J. WALSH (D-Montana) called upon Denby to resign for surrendering the oil reserves to Fall. Senator Joseph T. Robinson (D-Arkansas) introduced a resolution to that effect. The next day, President Coolidge named SILAS STRAWN and THOMAS GREGORY as special counsel, subject to Senate approval, to investigate the burgeoning scandal. Denby stated that he would not step aside, and asked that all senators express their opinion on the issue of his resignation in a public vote. In the Senate, Walsh continued to demand Denby's resignation. He did not agree with some who called for the impeachment of Denby, however, because he characterized the offense as stupidity rather than criminality. On February 11, the Senate passed the Robinson Resolution 47 to 34 calling for Denby's resignation. Later that day, Coolidge stated that he would wait for special counsel's findings on the matter before asking for anyone to leave office. The special counsel investigation would be delayed as both Strawn and Gregory would eventually step aside for ATLEE POMERENE and OWEN J. ROBERTS. Denby, however, did not choose to wait. On February 18, he offered his resignation for the good of the administration. He defended his record and accused the Senate of practicing slander while shielded by congressional immunity. Coolidge accepted Denby's resignation with a statement expressing appreciation and friendship. Denby's record, asserted the President, had not been besmirched. Reaction to Denby's exit was mixed. Herbert Hoover proclaimed him a victim of political persecution. Democrats felt that Denby had been negligent and lacking in the vigilance necessary to the protection of the nation's resources. No one believed he was a criminal. Subsequent findings of the Senate and the Supreme Court cleared Denby of any wrongdoing.

After leaving the Cabinet, Denby formed the law firm of Denby, Kennedy & O'Brien in Detroit.

References:

National Cyclopedia of American Biography, volume 21, under "Denby, Edwin," pp. 486–487.

Noggle, Burl. *Teapot Dome: Oil and Politics in the 1920's*. Baton Rouge: Louisiana State University Press, 1962.

DiGenova, Joseph E. (1945–   ) Independent Counsel, Clinton passport file search, 1992–1995. A former U.S. Attorney for the District of Columbia (1983–1988), Joseph DiGenova conducted a three-year independent counsel investigation of the manner in which Bill CLINTON's passport files were used by President GEORGE BUSH's campaign officials in 1992. Though concluding that Bush administration personnel acted foolishly and inappropriately, DiGenova found no basis for criminal prosecution. DiGenova himself argued that his own investigation, which cost over $2.5 million, helped demonstrate that the independent counsel mechanism was overused.

As U.S. Attorney, DiGenova, a Republican, fell into disfavor with Washington, D.C., mayor Marion Barry. Barry held DiGenova and former Attorney General EDWIN MEESE responsible for information leaks that embarrassed the mayor. Barry went so far as to urge city employees to boycott public appearances by DiGenova. Earning Barry's enmity did not hinder DiGenova's career. After leaving government service, he became a partner in the law firm of Bishop, Cook, Purcell & Reynolds (1988–1990), then switched to Manatt, Phelps & Phillips (1991–1995) before starting his own firm (DiGenova & Toensing) with wife Victoria Toensing in 1996.

DiGenova was named independent counsel at the request of Attorney General

WILLIAM BARR, shortly before expiration of the statute in December 1992. In their zeal to uncover information embarrassing to Bill Clinton during the 1992 presidential election, officials in the Bush campaign made unauthorized use of Clinton's State Department passport file. They were examining Clinton's 1969 trip to Eastern Europe when he was a student involved in antiwar activities. Their findings helped fuel accusations by extremists on the Republican right like Robert Dornan, who cast aspersions on Clinton's patriotism.

DiGenova's investigation, dubbed "Filegate" (not to be confused with the CLINTON administration's own FILEGATE controversy), encountered an early obstacle in January 1993 when the Justice Department ruled that the State Department Operations Center practice of routinely monitoring phone calls was illegal. The State Department's own investigation into the matter had relied partly on such phone calls when it concluded that former Secretary of State James Baker and aide Janet Mullins were aware of the passport search. DiGenova was able to build his own investigation by relying on interviews with 147 witnesses, and examination of computer records at the White House and on Air Force One. Those interviewed included Bush, Baker, former National Security Adviser Brent Snowcroft, former Vice President Dan Quayle, and former Assistant Secretary of State Elizabeth Tamposi. DiGenova also dispatched investigators to ascertain the nature of reported collaboration between the Bush campaign, working through the State Department, and Czech intelligence personnel. Jaroslav Basta, former Deputy Director of the Czech Federal Security and Information Service (FBIS), had stated that the Bush campaign requested an investigation of Clinton's contacts during his 1970 trip to Prague. Reportedly, the inquiry was carried out, and results were provided to Bush officials. Basta's account was confirmed by Miroslav Polreich, former Czech ambassador to the Conference for Security and Cooperation in Europe. DiGenova's examination of the incident could conceivably have uncovered violations of the Federal Election Campaign Act.

On November 30, 1995, DiGenova issued a report of his findings. Though criticizing Bush administration officials for lack of judgment, the investigation uncovered no basis for criminal indictment. The incident had proved an embarrassment. Apparently, James Baker had offered to resign as Chief of Staff after the election. Though never clearly identifying the person who leaked information about Clinton's passport applications, DiGenova concluded that Baker became aware of the affair but did not engineer it. The investigation was concluded by Independent Counsel MICHAEL ZELDIN.

DiGenova and his law partner/wife, Victoria Toensing, have been frequent guests on television news programs that monitored independent counsel investigations such as WHITEWATER. Although never advocating frequent use of the statute, DiGenova was critical of JANET RENO's decision not to request an independent counsel to investigate Democratic campaign finance practices. He has also charged that he and his wife have been targeted by private investigators working for Bill Clinton, presumably because of his public criticism of the president's behavior in the PAULA JONES and MONICA LEWINSKY affairs. In the most high-profile case involving their professional collaboration, DiGenova and Toensing were hired to investigate the legitimacy of the Teamsters Union election in 1996.

References:

Cerio, Gregory. "Tainted Evidence." *Newsweek*, 4 January 1993, p. 7.

Fenyvesi, Charles. "Washington Whispers." *U.S. News & World Report*, 26 September 1994, p. 40.

Hickey, Jennifer G. "The Last Refuge of a President." *Washington Times*, 23 March 1998, p.14. Reports DiGenova's charge that Clinton hired private investigators to uncover a scandal involving the private lives of him and his wife. Article alleges a pattern of such behavior by Clinton.

Stein, Jonathan. "Czech It Out." *Nation* 258 (1994): 149.

"Three Years, $2.3 Million—No Crime." *Newsweek*, 4 December 1995, p. 6.

Victor, Kirk. "On the Firing Line." *National Journal* 29 (1997): 828. Mentions DiGenova's criticism of Reno's decision to eschew an independent counsel in campaign finance matter. DiGenova characterizes the Attorney General as "an independent, stubborn cuss."

Doheny, Edward L. (1856–1935) petroleum producer. A pivotal figure in the TEAPOT DOME SCANDAL, Edward Doheny's testimony before Congress on January 24, 1924, served to implicate Interior Secretary ALBERT FALL in apparent bribery while transferring U.S. naval oil reserves to private control. Doheny himself was never convicted of misconduct.

The son of an Irish immigrant father and Canadian mother, Doheny was born in Fond du Lac, Wisconsin. He worked briefly as a surveyor in Indian country, but left to prospect for gold. From 1872 to 1892, Doheny worked in Arizona, New Mexico, and California, with occasional success. His interest switched to oil in 1892 after noticing large amounts of petroleum mixed with soil being used as factory fuel ouside of Los Angeles. The well he constructed with partner Charles Canfield marked the beginning of the Los Angeles oil industry. Doheny proceeded to strike oil in Fullerton and the Kern river valley before moving on to Mexico where he established wells west of Tampico and along the Tamesi River. The Mexican Petroleum Company was established, and the country's first commercial oil was produced. After incorporating as the Pan-American Petroleum & Transport Company, Doheny went on to rival John D. Rockefeller as an oil magnate.

The activities of Secretary of the Interior Albert Fall were closely scrutinized by conservationists from the time he assumed office on 1921. Fall's past association with developers alarmed conservation activists like Gifford Pinchot and Harry Slattery. When Fall obtained control of the naval oil reserves through the cooperation of Naval Secretary EDWIN DENBY, and promptly leased drilling rights for one section to Doheny on July 12, it was feared that large-scale exploitation was to follow. On April 25, 1922, Fall's deputy Edward C. Finney announced the lease of the Teapot Dome oil rights to HARRY SINCLAIR's Mammoth Oil Company and further California reserve oil to Doheny. In return for receiving the navy's royalty oil, Doheny agreed to construct oil storage tanks at Pearl Harbor. Docks and wharves would also be established in order to fuel the nation's fleet. The contract that specified these terms also stipulated that Doheny would receive preferential treatment regarding any future leases of naval oil in California. When Doheny was issued a further contract for all of the huge Elk Hills, California, oil reserve, it was not announced.

Wisconsin's progressive Senator Robert La Follette carried Harry Slattery's suspicions of malfeasance to the congressional floor in the spring of 1922, and an investigation by the Senate's Public Lands Committee ensued. Fall resigned from the cabinet in early 1923, but Senator THOMAS J. WALSH (D-Montana) kept the issue alive. By closely examining Fall's finances, Walsh forced him into embarrassing attempts to explain or cover-up property acquisitions that coincided with oil lease grants. Fall was eventually caught trying to explain receipt of a $100,000 loan that he attributed to the generosity of *Washington Post* publisher Edward McLean. At first, Walsh suspected that it was a bribe paid by Harry Sinclair in return for the Teapot Dome oil lease. On January 24, 1924, Doheny testified that he had loaned the money to Fall. His son, Edward, Jr., had carried the cash to him "in a little black bag." Fall's lie was exposed, and the transaction appeared as a bribe. Doheny stated that he hadn't previously concealed the loan because no one had asked him a pertinent question regarding it. In addition, he did not believe that the loan was relevant to any of the lease agreements that had been signed. The money used for the loan belonged to Doheny, not his oil company. Doheny and Fall had been friends for years, and Doheny was pleased to make the loan in order to enable Fall to purchase a ranch in New Mexico. Doheny invited the government to examine the oil contracts. If they found them to be less than correct, he offered to repay all interest and profits that had accrued, asking only to be compensated for expenses incurred. Doheny maintained that the agreements were wise and advantageous to all parties concerned. He had received the contracts because he had submitted the best bid. Doheny offered to locate all documentation in support of his testimony and place it before the committee for inspection.

On February 1, Doheny was recalled for further testimony. Committee members wanted to know if Doheny's wealth had been used to influence present or past government officials. Under questioning, Doheny acknowledged that he had hired several former cabinet members as employees. Among those was former attorney general THOMAS GREGORY, who had been recently nominated special counsel to investigate Teapot Dome by President CALVIN COOLIDGE. Within days Gregory withdrew as nominee. During this testimony, Doheny produced part of a note that he claimed represented Fall's obligation to repay the $100,000 loan. Fall's signature was missing. Doheny said his wife held the lower half of the note. This unusual precaution, testified Doheny, ensured that Fall would not be pressed for repayment at an inconvenient time should Doheny die before the obligation had been discharged. Doheny's son was familiar with the arrangement, and should both Doheny and his wife die before repayment, Fall was trusted to supply a new note to Edward, Jr. The peculiarities of this procedure only served to further test the committee's credulity.

The investigation of special counsels ATLEE POMERENE and OWEN J. ROBERTS resulted in civil and criminal trials. On May 25, 1925, the U.S. District Court in Los Angeles held that Doheny's loan to Fall constituted a bribe. Doheny and Fall were found guilty of fraud and conspiracy. The Appeals Court in San Francisco affirmed the decision, and on February 28, 1927, the Supreme Court ordered Doheny to return the oil reserves to the government. Doheny, said the court, was not entitled to repayment for any expenditures. In the criminal trial, Doheny and Fall were acquitted of conspiracy on December 16, 1926. Although Fall was convicted for receiving a bribe in 1929, Doheny was acquitted of paying one the following year. Perhaps Doheny's willingness to testify helped him. Fall would not do so. Others suggest that Doheny's wealth and businessman/hero image saved him. It has also been pointed out that offering a bribe and accepting one are separate offenses under the U.S. criminal code. In Doheny's mind, payment of the loan may not have been intended as a bribe.

Doheny sold all his oil interests outside California and, in retirement, engaged in many philanthropic enterprises, including the establishment of the Memorial Library on the campus of UCLA and of St. Vincent's Church in Los Angeles, and the financing of numerous archaeological expeditions in New Mexico and Arizona.

References:

Busch, Francis X. *Enemies of the State.* Indianapolis: Bobbs-Merrill, 1954.
National Cyclopedia of American Biography, edition volume 29, under "Doheny, Edward L." pp. 238–239.
Noggle, Burl. *Teapot Dome: Oil and Politics in the 1920's.* Baton Rouge: Louisiana State University Press, 1962.

Dole, Robert (1923–) Republican Senator from Kansas, 1969–1996. Although never directly involved in an independent counsel investigation, Robert Dole played an instrumental role in helping to determine the manner in which individual inquiries and the office itself were publicly perceived. As the leader of his party in the Senate during the years 1987–1996, Dole gave voice to Republican concern over the direction of LAWRENCE WALSH's IRAN-CONTRA investigation. He was also a leading figure in helping to defeat renewal of the independent counsel statute in 1992, but reversed himself two years later when Democratic President Bill CLINTON found himself the target of the WHITEWATER investigation.

Born in Russell, Kansas, Bob Dole overcame serious injuries suffered in World War II to build a successful career in law and politics. A recipient of the Bronze Star and Purple Heart for his wartime service, Dole served as Russell

County Attorney (1953–1961) before winning election to Congress representing Kansas's 6th District in 1961. He was returned to office three more times as representative of the 1st District before winning his Senate seat in 1969.

Dole played no role in the crafting of the ETHICS IN GOVERNMENT ACT (1978). He seems to have been more interested in the political ramifications of the special prosecutor issue. During the 1976 presidential campaign, CHARLES RUFF, the last of four WATERGATE Special Prosecutors, was presented with allegations that Republican candidate GERALD FORD was tainted by the Watergate Scandal. Dole apparently believed that Ruff used the situation to benefit the Democrats by not immediately clearing Ford of wrongdoing. As a result, when Ruff was nominated for the post of Deputy Inspector General in the Department of Health, Education, and Welfare by President Jimmy CARTER, Dole took the opportunity to retaliate. As a member of the Senate Finance Committee, Dole held up action on the appointment during the months of September and October 1977 before allowing confirmation to proceed.

When the Iran-Contra affair surfaced late in 1986, Dole urged President RONALD REAGAN to quickly call for a special session of Congress in order to form a select committee to investigate the matter. Democratic Senate leader Robert Byrd (D-West Virginia) favored appointment of an independent counsel. Though he agreed with Dole that Congress needed to take effective, cooperative action on the matter, he preferred to wait until the special session of Congress convened in January 1987. Politics again was a major factor in this debate, because Democrats would control the Senate with Byrd assuming Dole's position as majority leader.

Lawrence Walsh's six-year, $40 million Iran-Contra Investigation infuriated Dole. Walsh's investigation became increasingly damaging politically as it targeted officials of greater responsibility each year. Ironically, Walsh was a Dole Republican who supported his 1988 presidential candidacy. By 1991, however, Dole's open criticism of Walsh had angered the independent counsel, and during the last three years of the investigation, the two confronted each other frequently in bitter exchanges. In May 1991, Walsh decided to continue his prosecution of OLIVER NORTH even though the Supreme Court had refused to review the Appeals Court decision setting aside North's conviction. Dole responded to Walsh's persistence by formally calling upon Attorney General RICHARD THORNBURGH to fire him. Thornburgh took no such action, presumably because Walsh had committed no violations that would have allowed dismissal under the terms of the statute. Walsh's investigation threatened to derail the appointment of Robert Gates as the new director of the Central Intelligence Agency in the summer of 1991, when witness ALAN FIERS indicated that Gates was aware of the arms-for-hostages deals. The Senate Intelligence Committee postponed hearings, angering Dole. (The hearings convened in September, and Gates was confirmed the following month.) When Walsh's conviction of JOHN POINDEXTER was overturned by the Court of Appeals in November, Dole asked the Department of Justice once again to dismiss Walsh.

When Walsh's investigation began concentrating on former Secretary of Defense CASPAR WEINBERGER in 1992, Dole envisaged further political repercussions. Weinberger's notes had been recently discovered by Walsh investigators. At a meeting in mid-November 1986, Weinberger quoted Dole as asking Reagan if contacts with Iran didn't amount to trading arms for hostages. The President responded that the contacts would have taken place even had there been no hostages. During the time in which Walsh's investigation was moving toward an indictment of Weinberger, Congress prepared to debate the renewal of the independent counsel statute. Dole, characterizing many investigations as little more than exercises in partisanship, cited Walsh's inquiry as the worst manifestation of the problem. In the end, Dole organized a credible filibuster threat that defeated efforts by Senators WILLIAM COHEN (R-Maine) and CARL LEVIN (D-Michigan) to maintain the independent counsel office. Walsh's first indictment of Weinberger in June 1992 was dismissed. His persistence, however, resulted in a second indictment, announced a mere four days before the 1992 presidential election. The indictment clearly implicated President GEORGE BUSH in the Iran-Contra scandal. Dole's fears were realized with the Republicans' defeat at the polls. He charged that the timing of the Weinberger indictment was politically motivated. To support his contention, Dole pointed to Walsh's recently hired assistant, JAMES BROSNAHAN, who had contributed to Bill Clinton's presidential campaign. Dole also called for a formal investigation of Walsh and his actions, and urged President Bush to pardon Weinberger as well as all those convicted in the investigation. Bush granted Dole's request on Christmas Eve. Walsh responded by comparing Dole unfavorably with 1950s Communist witch-hunter Senator Joseph McCarthy (R-Wisconsin). McCarthy, stated Walsh, at least had the support of a congressional committee, and never spoke as his party's Senate leader. Walsh found Dole's attacks during the Weinberger case especially despicable, because they continued even after the jury had been instructed to report for trial.

By 1993, Dole's view of the independent counsel office underwent a profound change. As President Clinton was faced with allegations of misconduct regarding his dismissal of White House Travel Office employees, and possible involvement in the failed Whitewater land deal while he was governor of Arkansas, Dole called for the appointment of an independent counsel. Without statutory provision for the office, Attorney General JANET RENO named ROBERT FISKE on her own initiative. Dole helped pass a new independent counsel statute in 1994. He has continued to support the mechanism after leaving the Senate and losing in his bid for the presidency in 1996. In 1997, Dole joined fellow Republicans in calling upon Janet Reno to request an independent counsel to examine Democratic campaign financing tactics, a call she did not heed.

References:

Devroy, Ann, and Helen Dewar. "Republicans Seek Travel Office Probe." *Washington Post*, 12 June 1993, sec. A, p. 5.

"Dole Relents; Ruff to Get HEW Post." *Washington Post*, 20 October 1977, sec. A, p. 3.

"Dole Requests Broader Probe." *San Diego Union-Tribune*, 1 December 1986, sec. A, p. 1.

"Dole Says Reno 'Dragging Feet' on Inquiry." *Los Angeles Times*, 3 January 1994, sec. A, p. 10.

Hayward, Ed. "Dole Favors Independent Probe into Dem Funds." *Boston Herald*, 16 April 1997, p. 15.

Jackson, Robert L. "Dole Calls for Investigation of Iran-Contra Counsel." *Los Angeles Times*, 9 November 1992, sec. A, p. 23.

Walsh, Lawrence. *Firewall: The Iran-Contra Conspiracy and Cover-up*. New York: W. W. Norton, 1997. Chapter 25, "Bob Dole, Pardon Advocate," addresses Dole's role in facilitating what Walsh considers the Iran-Contra defendants' escape from justice.

Donovan, Raymond J. (1930–   ) Secretary of Labor, 1981–1985. Raymond Donovan's four-year term in the Cabinet of President RONALD REAGAN was a difficult one. He was continually the subject of allegations regarding his past contacts with organized crime. As Executive Vice President of the Schiavone Construction Company in Secaucus, New Jersey, it was alleged that Donovan maintained regular financial and organizational ties with organized crime figures and their companies, but an eight-month investigation by Special Prosecutor LEON SILVERMAN in 1982 did not uncover evidence of sufficient credibility to warrant criminal prosecution. When New York State brought charges against Donovan in 1985, he resigned from the Cabinet.

Born and raised in a Catholic, working-class family in Bayonne, New Jersey, Donovan grew up in a home that revered Franklin Roosevelt. He studied for the priesthood, but following the death of both his parents, Donovan entered the business world to help raise his younger siblings. There, he switched allegiances to the Republican Party. He became active politically in 1976, raising funds for the state Republican gubernatorial campaign. Donovan's efforts for Reagan in 1980 were instrumental in capturing nearly all the state's delegates for the candidate. After Reagan's election, Donovan was named Secretary of Labor.

Donovan's confirmation was delayed while the Senate Labor and Human Resources Committee investigated reports that the FBI had turned up evidence indicating that the Schiavone Construction Company had bribed union officials to guarantee peace with labor. Testifying on January 12, 1981, Donovan denied allegations that Schiavone Construction Company hired a "ghost" foreman whose pay was collected by the Teamsters union, or accepted false invoices in return for payment to the union. When an FBI report, dated January 23, 1981, largely exonerated Donovan, he was appointed to the Cabinet. Although the FBI report did not specifically implicate Donovan in any improper activity, it did contain information on a disturbingly large number of allegations involving the Schiavone Construction Company. This would pose a problem for the special prosecutor as well. Months after Donovan's confirmation, new information would surface from FBI field reports serving to support charges that Schiavone Construction did business with organized crime. These new disclosures proved embarrassing to FBI Director William Webster and frustrating to Orrin Hatch (R-Utah), Chairman of the Senate Labor and Human Resources Committee.

With new information available, the Justice Department began a preliminary investigation. Attention was focused on an alleged $2,000 payment that was made to union official Louis Sanzo at a Long Island City restaurant in June 1977. Donovan reportedly was present. This specific charge, and many others that would surface, were made by an informant with a criminal record. In this instance, former union official Mario Montuoro testified that the money represented a bribe paid by the company to prevent a competing union with a higher wage scale from gaining jurisdiction over a Schiavone construction project. Attorney General WILLIAM FRENCH SMITH, at the invitation of Donovan, requested appointment of a special prosecutor to investigate this charge. On December 29, 1981, the New York Court of Appeals named New York attorney Leon Silverman. He was charged with investigating the alleged payoff and any other possible violations of federal criminal law that presented themselves during the course of the inquiry.

On June 11, 1982, the body of former union official Fred Furino was found in the trunk of a car. Furino had been interviewed by Silverman as a potential witness in the Donovan case. Salvatore Briguglio, a crime figure with whom the Schiavone Construction Company allegedly did business, had been murdered in 1978. Briguglio had been a suspect in the disappearance of Teamster leader Jimmy Hoffa. Clearly, this ETHICS IN GOVERNMENT ACT investigation was unlike any of those that had preceded it. In one respect, the Donovan probe resembled the HAMILTON JORDAN and TIMOTHY KRAFT investigations; it did not involve alleged misconduct related to performance of government duties. Because it involved possible ties to organized crime, there are those who believed that the Justice Department, experienced in such matters, was better equipped to examine the case. Prior to reauthorization reforms enacted in 1982, however, the attorney general was not allowed the discretion to reserve such cases for departmental handling.

On the same day that Furino's body was found, Senate Labor and Human Resources Committee members Hatch and Edward Kennedy (D-Massachusetts) received an FBI report, dated January 12, 1981, stating that the FBI had information, independently corroborated, that Donovan maintained close personal and business ties with organized crime figures. Charges were made by Democrats that the information had been intentionally suppressed in order to secure Donovan's appointment to the Cabinet. On June 16, Chairman Hatch called for Donovan to resign. Although there was no evidence of Donovan's criminal involvement, the prevailing sentiment held that those doing business with criminals should not occupy Cabinet posts. Donovan refused to step down. Instead, he chastized those in elective office who insisted on judging him in advance of any legal proceedings.

On June 29, 1982, Leon Silverman reported that there was "insufficient credible evidence" to charge Donovan with any crimes. A federal grand jury in Brooklyn had declined to indict him on June 8. Silverman appeared to be concerned about the number of allegations that had been made, but none had proved worthy of prosecution. Silverman's findings were contained in a 1,025-page report, edited to 709 pages for public consumption. Donovan declared that he had been exonerated. Reagan announced that Donovan would continue as Secretary of Labor. On August 2, however, it was announced that the FBI was looking into a new series of allegations involving Donovan. The next day, Silverman reopened his investigation. Donovan had no comment on this new turn of events. The second phase of his probe would concentrate on reports that Donovan had met with two known criminals, William Maselli and Albert Facchiano, near Miami in January 1979 for the purpose of setting up fictional jobs at Schiavone Construction sites. Facchiano, who was serving a prison term in Alabama for loan sharking, was overlooked by Silverman in the first phase of his investigation.

On August 24, Nat Maselli, William's son, was murdered in his car. Donovan was questioned by Silverman early in September and emerged confident that he would be exonerated of any wrongdoing. On September 13, Silverman declared his investigation at an end. He had investigated a total of fourteen new allegations and found no credible evidence of misconduct by Donovan. One informant who had made seventeen separate charges against Donovan had recanted. With the investigation over, Donovan expressed anger at the treatment he had received by his accusers and the press. Among the charges Silverman had investigated were allegations that Donovan maintained false companies in order to launder money; that Donovan helped arrange sewer contracts for a corrupt longshoreman's union; and that Donovan helped distribute $20 million contributed by the Teamsters to the Reagan campaign in return for pardons promised for crime figures Anthony Provenzano and Russell Bufalino.

In October 1984, Donovan was indicted in New York along with nine co-defendants. They were charged with 137 violations of state law involving transfer of state money to an allegedly crime-controlled construction company. Donovan was placed on unpaid leave, and he resigned in March when ordered to stand trial. Eight months later, Donovan was cleared.

As Secretary of Labor, Donovan worked to implement the conservative agenda championed by Reagan. He cut the department budget and staff; and he sought to remove government regulation of labor, health, and safety standards. He incurred the wrath of organized labor and usually declined invitations to explain government labor policy to congressional committees. Among his most important achievements Donovan counted: settlement of the 1981 baseball strike, return of $6.5 million spent improperly by trustees of the Teamsters Central States Pension Fund, and removal of a 40-year ban on home employment of workers.

After leaving government, Donovan rebuilt Schiavone as its president. Current independent counsel investigations have prompted him to reflect on how cruel life in the nation's capital can be. In particular, the suicide of CLINTON associate Vince FOSTER prompted many of Donovan's friends to ask if it brought back unpleasant memories. Apparently many of those memories linger, because Donovan has stated that he would not have entered politcs had he known the toll it would take on his family. Perhaps Donovan is best known for having asked where he could go to get his reputation back after having been cleared of wrongdoing. A number of independent counsel investigation targets have expressed similar sentiments in recent years.

References:

Blumenthal, Ralph. "Inquiry on Donovan Again Yields 'Insufficient Evidence' to Prosecute." *New York Times*, 14 September 1982, sec. A, p. 1.

"Darkening Cloud over Donovan." *Time*, 28 June 1982, p. 44.

Horning, Jay. "Donovan's Government Experiences Haven't Soured His Labors." *St. Petersburg Times*, 10 October 1993, sec. A, p. 7.

Kelly, James. "Donovan Probe." *Time*, 11 January 1982, p. 23.

Lardner, George, Jr. "FBI Told Reagan Staff Donovan Had Mob Ties." *Washington Post*, 15 June 1982, sec. A, p. 1.

———. "Insufficient Credible Evidence." *Washington Post*, 14 September 1982, sec. A, p. 1.

———. "No Basis Found for Prosecution of Donovan." *Washington Post*, 29 June 1982, sec. A, p. 1.

———. "Silverman Confirms New Donovan Probe." *Washington Post*, 3 August 1982, sec. A, p. 7.

Pear, Robert. "F.B.I. Is Said to Be Checking New Allegations on Donovan." *New York Times*, 2 August 1982, sec. A, p. 8.

"Ray Donovan." *Economist*, 23 March 1985, p. 41.

Rowan, Roy. "The Payoff Charges against Reagan's Labor Secretary." *Fortune*, 31 May 1982, p. 80. Contains detailed account of allegations leveled by paid informants including William Maselli and Mario Montuoro. Responding to critics who disparaged the character of those providing information, Senator Thomas Eagleton (D-Missouri) stated, "You do not usually get Pope John Paul II as an informant."

Thornton, Mary, and George Lardner, Jr. "Court Names Prosecutor in Donovan Case." *Washington Post*, 30 December 1981, sec. A, p. 1.

E

Ervin, Sam J., Jr. (1896–1985) Chairman Senate Select Committee on Watergate, 1973–1974. Sam Ervin represented the state of North Carolina as its senator for twenty years (1954–1974). During that time, as a conservative Southern Democrat, he built a reputation for integrity and adherence to principle, although his political philosophy did not always provide the answers he sought on particular issues. Ervin was a fiscal conservative, but he led the fight against President RICHARD NIXON's effort to curb spending by impounding money appropriated by Congress. Similarly, he was a fervent civil libertarian who opposed federal civil rights legislation in the South, and he departed from his anticommunist stance long enough to help achieve the Senate's censure of Senator Joseph McCarthy (R-Wisconsin).

Ervin's lawyer father instilled in him a love and respect for the law. Sam junior graduated from the University of North Carolina in 1917, and entered the Army. He served 18 months in France during World War I, where he was twice wounded and awarded the Silver Star and Distinguished Service Cross. He was admitted to the North Carolina bar after "reading law" in an attorney's office, but went on to Harvard Law School in order to receive more formal training. Ervin effectively combined a folksy manner and penchant for storytelling with an impressive command of the classics when he did battle in the political arena. He did not receive national attention, however, until he was chosen by Senator Mike Mansfield (D-Montana) to chair the Senate's special committee investigating the WATERGATE scandal.

Mansfield wanted someone who did not aspire to higher political office, enjoyed the respect of both Democrats and Republicans, and had substantial judicial experience. Ervin, a former state supreme court justice, qualified on all counts. At a time when public distrust of political figures was reaching new heights, Ervin's search for the truth about Watergate, captured on television, raised him to the level of folk hero in the eyes of many. In addition, his committee's cooperation with the Watergate Special Prosecution Force (WSPF) helped establish the credibility of an independent prosecutorial body in dealing with executive branch misconduct. Ervin was generous in his praise of AR-CHIBALD COX, LEON JAWORSKI, HENRY RUTH, and CHARLES RUFF, the four special prosecutors who, in turn, led the WSPF. During his last year in the Senate, 1974, he also made significant contributions to the crafting of a statutory remedy aimed at preventing future Watergates.

Ervin did not favor removing future special prosecutors entirely from the executive branch. He agreed with those who saw Watergate as a threat that had been successfully met, to a great extent, by existing governmental remedies. Yes, the WPSF had been created to help deal with the problem, but there was nothing unusual about that. Past crises such as TEAPOT DOME and the TRU-MAN TAX SCANDAL had resorted to similar mechanisms. There was no need for a statutory creation that would confuse the existing constitutional separation of powers. What was needed, Ervin believed, was a special prosecutor appointed by the President with the consent of the Senate. Ervin suggested a six-year term in his bill, S.3652 (1974). His proposal represented an attempt to balance the special prosecutor's office with the authority of existing institutions. In this effort, Ervin was joined by Charles Ruff, whose ideas on the subject were similar. Characteristically, Ervin occupied a moderate position in the debate. Senators ABRAHAM RIBICOFF (D-Connecticut) and CHARLES PERCY (R-Illinois) were among those who sought to remove the special prosecutor completely from control of the executive, and the memory of Watergate was fresh enough to lend their ideas great influence. There were still those, like Senator Edward Gurney (R-Florida), who insisted that the special prosecutor would be an abusive persecutor. Ervin's proposal, although not adopted, made a useful contribution to the debate by demonstrating that creative compromise was an option.

Ervin retired in 1974 at the age of 77, four years before the ETHICS IN GOVERNMENT ACT created an independent office of special prosecutor.

References:

Bertozzi, Mark. "Oversight of the Executive Branch: A Policy Analysis of Federal Special Prosecutor Legislation." Ph.D. dissertation, State University of New York at Albany, 1980. Discusses Ervin's special prosecutor proposal and compares it to other bills addressing the issue.

Ervin, Sam, Jr. *Preserving the Constitution: The Autobiography of Senator Sam Ervin.* Charlottesville: Michie, 1984. Chapter 23, "Watergate," discusses Ervin's work on the Senate Select Committee. Significant material is excerpted from his book *The Whole Truth.*

―――. *The Whole Truth: The Watergate Conspiracy.* New York: Random House, 1980.

"Former Sen. Sam Ervin, 88, Watergate Folk Hero, Dies." *Los Angeles Times,* 24 April 1985, p. 1.

Espy, Mike (1953–   ) Secretary of Agriculture, 1993–1994. The subject of an investigation by Independent Counsel DONALD SMALTZ, Mike Espy became the first CLINTON administration official to be indicted when he was charged with soliciting gratuities, fraud, and making false statements on August 27, 1997.

Mike Espy grew up in Yazoo City, Mississippi, where his family ran a funeral home business. After graduating from Howard University (B.A., Political Science, 1975) and earning a law degree at the University of Santa Clara (1978), he returned to serve in Mississippi state government in Jackson as Assistant Secretary of State (1980–1984) and Assistant Attorney General (1984–1985). He was elected to Congress in 1986 as a Democrat, representing Mississippi's Second District and twice won re-election. As a member of the House Agriculture Committee, Espy worked to effectively serve many of his district's poor farmers while maintaining good relations with large growers. He boosted consumption of Mississippi's pond-raised catfish by persuading the military to add the product to its weekly menu and increased appropriations for small farmers through his work as chairman of the Lower Mississippi Delta Congressional Caucus. Some were predicting that Espy would become the state's first African American governor when he was named Secretary of Agriculture by President Bill CLINTON, the youngest person ever to hold that post and the first of his race.

Espy assumed administration of the fourth largest federal bureaucracy with wide-ranging responsibilities, including the nation's food-stamp program. Upon taking office, he quickly suspended Republican plans to close 1,200 Agriculture Department field offices. Instead, he announced plans to cut staff at the Washington, D.C., headquarters. This move was welcomed by farm-state legislators. After further examining the situation, however, Espy became convinced of the necessity to consolidate operations. In November 1993, he reduced department agencies from 43 to 30 and announced the closing or consolidation of 1,215 county offices. Other initiatives instituted by Espy included a plan to require use of ethanol in gasolene as a means of improving farm income, upgrading inspection of the nation's meat, and updating nutritional standards in school lunches. He also succeeded in obtaining $23.5 billion in flood relief funding targeted for farmers who suffered crop losses in Mississippi during the summer of 1993. Espy would have few additional opportunities to build on his record. In March, reports had surfaced indicating that Tyson Foods, a large contributor to the Clinton campaign, had favored Espy with numerous gifts, receiving favorable treatment by the government in return. By July, the Justice Department and Congress had begun investigating the matter.

On September 9, 1994, former Assistant U.S. Attorney in Los Angeles and Republican Donald Smaltz was named Independent Counsel for the Espy investigation. Attorney General JANET RENO had requested and received a mandate that would allow the independent counsel to broaden the inquiry beyond the immediate allegations relating to specific gratuities. At first, it appeared that the subject under consideration concerned tickets to sporting events, rides on corporate airplanes, and lodging at resorts. The largest gift involved appeared to be a $1,200 scholarship arranged for Espy's girlfriend. It soon became apparent, however, that these immediate favors might be indicative of a larger pattern of corporate bribery. Accordingly, Smaltz, after initially predicting a six-month inquiry, expanded his probe to include the relationship that has long existed between Tyson Foods and Bill Clinton in Arkansas. Espy, attempting to make restitution, began to reimburse Tyson and other corporations from whom he had accepted gifts. This was perceived, however, as an attempt to cover his tracks. In December, Espy's resignation was requested and received.

After a three-year investigation, Smaltz began to bring indictments. Crop Growers Corporation, an insurance company, was charged with making illegal campaign contributions to Henry Espy, Mike's brother. Henry was an unsuccessful candidate for Congress. Smaltz charged that the donation was aimed at currying favor with the Department of Agriculture. John J. Hemmingson and Gary A. Black, Crop Grower executives, were acquitted in a trial held in February 1997. The August indictment of Mike Espy specified 39 counts that included sporting event tickets, lodging, and meals; violations of the Meat Inspection Act (1907) that forbids accepting gratuities from any business subject to governmental regulation; mail and wire fraud committed in the course of covering up the arrangements; lying to investigators; and witness tampering (by ordering an employee to alter a travel itinerary sought by an investigator). Businesses charged with particpating, other than Tyson Foods, included Sun-Diamond Growers of California, Oglethorpe Power Corporation of Georgia, Smith-Barney Investment of New York, EOP Group of consultants in Washington, D.C., and Quaker Oats of Chicago. The grand jury found that Espy arranged unnecessary trips and lied about the true nature of his travels in order to conceal the gifts he accepted. The indictment, however, did not charge that Espy had returned favors for the gifts received. Unless Smaltz could ultimately demonstrate that this was the case, Espy's conviction at a scheduled Washington, D.C., trial was in doubt. Washington juries have demonstrated skepticism toward government prosecutors in the past.

On September 10, 1997, Mike Espy pleaded not guilty to the charges and vowed to clear his name. While Mike Espy returned to the practice of law in Mississippi, Smaltz successfully negotiated plea agreements with corporations charged in the indictment. Tyson Foods pleaded guilty and agreed to pay $6 million in fines, acknowledging payment of $12,000 in gifts to Espy. On December 16, Federal District Court Judge Ricardo M. Urbina dismissed charges that Espy violated the Meat Inspection Act, ruling that the law applied only to rank-and-file inspectors, not the Secretary of Agriculture. On March 3, 1998, District Court Judge Thelton E. Henderson dismissed charges against a Sun-Diamond Corporation lobbyist, because the case should have never been brought in California. Espy attorneys charged that Smaltz sought to avoid a Washington jury, because the lobbyist, Richard Douglas, is African American. Smaltz denied that race was a factor and stated that California was the only common ground for the counts in the indictment. On March 18, Espy aide Ronald H. Blackley was sentenced to two years and three months in prison for lying under oath about gifts he received while in office. District Court Judge Royce C. Lamberth departed from sentencing guidelines that suggested probation in such cases.

On December 2, 1998, Espy was acquitted on all counts when it could not be conclusively demonstrated that received gratuities were repaid with official acts.

References:

Babcock, Charles R. "Lobbyist's Conviction Thrown Out in Espy Case." *Washington Post*, 4 March 1998, sec. A, p. 7.

Behar, Richard. "On Fresh Ground." *Time*, 26 December 1994, p. 111.

Locy, Toni. "Ex-Agriculture Secretary Indicted." *Washington Post*, 28 August 1997, sec. A, p. 1.

Miller, Bill. "Espy Pleads Not Guilty." *Washington Post*, 11 September 1997, sec. A, p. 10.

————. "Espy's Former Chief of Staff Sentenced to 27 Months." *Washington Post*, 19 March 1998, sec. A, p. 5.

Novak, Viveca. "Chasing Good-Time Charlie." *Time*, 8 September 1997, 58.

"Tyson Foods to Pay Fine in Gifts Case." *New York Times*, 30 December 1997, sec. A, p. 14.

The Ethics in Government Act (1978). This act was passed in 1978 in the wake of the WATERGATE scandal. It was the product of five years of congressional hearings and debate about how to solve the problems of official misconduct that were brought to light during the scandal. The most famous part of the statute is the provision for a judicially appointed special prosecutor to investigate allegations of misconduct against executive branch officials, but the legislation also established broad new ethics rules for the executive branch.

Almost immediately upon the firing of Watergate Special Prosecutor ARCHIBALD COX, Congress began to consider statutory mechanisms for insulating the prosecutor from control by the executive. NIXON's dismissal of Cox in the infamous "Saturday Night Massacre" provoked a public outcry that shifted public opinion against Nixon and convinced Congress that some kind of legislative response was necessary. Eventually Congress decided that the new prosecutor appointed to replace Cox, LEON JAWORSKI, was sufficiently independent to complete the Watergate investigation. Nonetheless, efforts continued to find a long-term solution to the perceived problem.

In its final report, the Senate Select Committee on Presidential Campaign Activities (also known as the Senate Watergate Committee) recommended that a permanent office of public attorney be established. This new investigator would be appointed by a panel of federal judges with the advice and consent of the Senate. After extensive hearings and debate, the weight of opinion seemed to be against a permanent office. There was fear that this would create an office looking for work and might have the potential of becoming too powerful and dangerous in its own right. In addition, there were constitutional concerns raised about whether an officer wielding permanent law enforcement powers could be appointed by judges when law enforcement power was generally seen as resting with the executive branch. Also, the Department of Justice under President GERALD FORD was opposed to the office for constitutional reasons. It wanted any new public prosecutor to be appointed by the president. Though there was sympathy for this position in the Senate, there was little in the House, which supported a temporary, judicially-appointed office. These competing forces kept any Watergate reform legislation from being passed in 1975 or 1976.

In November of 1976, the Democrats recaptured the White House with the election of Jimmy CARTER, who had campaigned on a platform of ethics reform. In addition, they expanded their majority in Congress. In February 1977 the Public Officials Integrity Act was introduced in the Senate, and hearings were held that spring. It included a temporary special prosecutor mechanism, an Office of Government Crimes, and provided for legal counsel for Congress. When the hearings began in May, President Carter announced his support for the legislation and sent a message to Congress requesting ethics legislation requiring financial disclosure by executive branch officials. Most of these hearings addressed the financial disclosure issue as it seemed that by this time, and with the president's support, a consensus had emerged on the temporary special prosecutor mechanism. After some delay in the House caused by a controversy over whether Congress should be covered by the statute, the legislation was finally passed in the fall of 1978.

The Ethics in Government Act of 1978 established new financial disclosure rules for executive branch officers. It also created the Office of Government Ethics, an executive agency charged with overseeing the enforcement of the new rules. Its most visible and controversial provision was the establishment of a temporary special prosecutor arrangement. When the attorney general received allegations of criminal misconduct by covered executive branch colleagues, the statute required a preliminary investigation by the Department. If after 90 days the Department concluded that further investigation or prosecution was necessary, the attorney general was to request the appointment of a special prosecutor by a panel of three federal judges from the U.S. Court of Appeals. The panel of judges was charged with making the appointment and defining the jurisdiction of the prosecutor. At the conclusion of the investigation, the special prosecutor was required to file a report with the panel. The panel would decide whether or not to make that report public. The special prosecutor was removable by the attorney general but only for "extraordinary impropriety." Finally, the statute contained a "sunset provision," requiring Congress to reauthorize the provisions every five years.

In 1982 and 1987 Congress reauthorized the provisions, amending the statute in a number of ways. For example, in 1982, the name was changed from special prosecutor to independent counsel in order to remove the Watergate stigma and acknowledge that not all investigations led to prosecutions. In addition, the 1982 amendments gave the attorney general more discretion in triggering the Act and allowed for the reimbursement of attorneys' fees for targets of investigation who were not indicted. In 1987, as an expression of its dissatisfaction with Attorney General EDWIN MEESE's interpretation of the Act, Congress imposed new restrictions on the attorney general's discretion. In 1992, the provisions were allowed to lapse amid controversy about the length and expense of Independent Counsel LAWRENCE WALSH's investigation of the Iran-Contra scandal. The provisions were reauthorized in 1994 after allegations of President Bill CLINTON's dealings in the WHITEWATER scandal created new interest among congressional Republicans in an independent mechanism. The provisions were due for reauthorization in 1999 but the controversy surrounding KENNETH STARR's investigation of Clinton raised new doubts about whether the statute could survive. These concerns proved justified when the statute was allowed to expire on June 30, 1999.

References:

Eastland, Terry. *Ethics, Politics, and the Independent Counsel.* Washington, D.C.: National Legal Center for the Public Interest, 1989.
Harriger, Katy J. *Independent Justice: The Federal Special Prosecutor in American Politics.* Lawrence: University Press of Kansas, 1992.

—KATY J. HARRIGER

Ex Parte Hennen 38 U.S. 230 (1839). A Supreme Court case that addressed the issue of appointment and removal of inferior officers, the *Ex Parte Hennen* decision argued against the the type of interbranch arrangement constructed by the framers of the independent counsel statute. Justice Smith Thompson's opinion hinges on the contention that the Appointments Clause of the Constitution calls for inferior officers of the government to be appointed by that department of government to which the officer being appointed most appropriately belongs. By such reasoning, it is unlikely that an independent counsel, performing functions normally reserved for the executive branch's Department of Justice, could be appointed by a judicial panel.

Ex Parte Hennen concerned the arbitrary removal of Duncan N. Hennen as clerk of the Circuit Court for Eastern Louisiana by Judge Philip K. Lawrence who replaced him with John Winthrop, a personal friend. There was no indication that Hennen's job performance was in any way unsatisfactory. On the contrary, it appeared that Hennen had performed his duties in an excellent manner. Refusing to vacate his office, Hennen presented himself for duty the next time court was in session. Because Hennen's appointed successor, Winthrop, also reported for duty, the Circuit Court found it could not conduct its business. Circuit Court judges differed as to who was the actual clerk. Contending that his removal was unconstitutional and antirepublican, Hennen petitioned the Court for a writ of mandamus restoring him to his position.

Justice Thompson held that Hennen held his position at the pleasure of the appointing judge. Such is the case when the Constitution is silent on the issue of removal, as it is in this instance, when the tenure of office is not specified or limited by law. The power of removal accompanies the power of appointment, stated Thompson, unless otherwise indicated by the Constitution or specified by statute. Again, such is the case in this instance. The Supreme Court cannot take issue with Hennen's removal when the power to appoint and remove has been properly vested in the lower courts, and the office was held at their discretion. Thompson refused to address the question of whether Judge Lawrence had abused his power by dismissing Hennen without good cause, because the Supreme Court was not the proper forum for such an inquiry and could not provide redress for such a grievance even should the complaint prove meritorious. The application for writ of mandamus was denied.

Subsequent decisions such as *U.S. v. GERMAINE* (1878) and *EX PARTE SIEBOLD* (1879) would provide a more liberal interpretation of interbranch appointments, one more welcoming to the mechanism devised by the ETHICS IN GOVERNMENT ACT (1978) for the establishment of the Office of Special Prosecutor/Independent Counsel.

References:

O'Keefe, Constance, and Peter Safirstein. "Fallen Angels, Separation of Powers, and the Saturday Night Massacre: An Examination of the Practical, Constitutional, and Political Tensions in the Special Prosecutor Provisions of the Ethics in Government Act." *Brooklyn Law Review* 49 (1982): 113–147. Discusses Appointments Clause cases including *Ex Parte Hennen* in arguing for renewal of a revised independent counsel statute.

Ex Parte Siebold 100 U.S. 371 (1879). A case used to justify the constitutionality of the independent counsel statute, *Ex Parte Siebold* established that court appointment of election supervisors in order to guarantee free and fair congressional elections was legitimate. The Supreme Court held that judicial appointment of executive officers can occur when the official being appointed exercises functions that may not be entirely executive in nature, and when no incongruity is evident in such an arrangement.

The petitioners in *Ex Parte Siebold* were Baltimore election judges who had been imprisoned for violations committed during the congressional elections of 1878. Several of them participated in stuffing ballot boxes with invalid ballots. All of them obstructed federal election supervisors who were attempting to prevent the type of activities in which the petitioners were engaged. After ruling the Supreme Court competent to exercise appellant jurisdiction in this matter, Justice Joseph P. Bradley proceeded to declare constitutional the Enforcement Act of May 31, 1870. This act contained several sections referred to as "The Elective Franchise," which provided for judicial appointment of federal election supervisors authorized to ensure the integrity of elections.

Bradley devoted much of his decision to discussion of whether federal and state regulations can coexist. He ruled that such cooperation was proper, principally because Congress maintained the power to enforce its legislative decisions. State and federal authority are not mutually exclusive. One does not exclude the other except in such cases where they cannot be executed at the same time. The petitioners, in this instance, declared Bradley, were called upon to obey regulations of the United States as well as those of the state of Maryland. Surely, the federal government possessed authority to compel such obedience.

The final point addressed by Bradley was the one later seized upon by advocates of the independent counsel statute. The petitioners claimed that the courts cannot be charged with appointment of federal election supervisors because such function is not judicial in character. Furthermore, election supervisors charged with performing purely executive duties must be appointed by the executive branch. Bradley rejected both arguments. He considered election supervisors to be inferior officers whose appointment may logically be vested in the judiciary. In fact, stated Bradley, the court was the most competent authority to make such appointments in this instance. The Court found nothing incongruous in judicial appointment of election supervisors, thereby rejecting *EX PARTE HENNEN* as precedent. Justices Nathan Clifford and Stephen J. Field dissented.

Following WATERGATE, congressmen who sought to create a truly independent prosecutor to investigate future cases of alleged executive-branch misconduct, relied on the *Ex Parte Siebold* decision. On the one hand, they found nothing incongruous in vesting the judiciary with the power to appoint a special prosecutor. On the other hand, the notion that the executive branch should be charged with appointing a special prosecutor to investigate its own possible misconduct appeared replete with incongruity.

References:

Eastland, Terry. *Ethics, Politics and the Independent Counsel: Executive Power, Executive Vice 1789–1989*. Washington, D.C.: National Legal Center for the Public Interest, 1989. Chapter 4, "The Search for Law: 1973–1976," discusses *Ex Parte Siebold* as precedent for the independent counsel statute. Mentions FORD administration Deputy Attorney General Harold Tyler's characterization of the Watergate Reorganization and Reform Act of 1975 (S.495) as about as clear an example of incongruity as one could imagine. The idea that a court should appoint a special prosecutor who was independent of presidential control appeared ludicrous to Tyler. In Chapter 8, "Is the Law Constitutional?," Eastland finds *Siebold* a questionable precedent for the ruling in *MORRISON v. OLSON*. However one might care to characterize the nature of election supervisors' duties, declares Eastland, the function of the independent counsel is clearly executive.

O'Keefe, Constance, and Peter Safirstein. "Fallen Angels, Separation of Powers, and the Saturday Night Massacre: An Examination of the Practical, Constitutional, and Political Tensions in the Special Prosecutor Provisions of the Ethics in Government Act." *Brooklyn Law Review* 49 (1982): 113–147. Describes standard established by *Siebold*: would appointment power exercised by a court be "incongruous, improper or inconvenient?"

Tachmes, Alexander I. "Independent Counsels under the Ethics in Government Act of 1978: A Violation of the Separation of Powers Doctrine or an Essential Check on Executive Power?" *University of Miami Law Review* 42 (1988): 735–765. Argues that judicial appointment of the independent counsel is justified by the *Siebold* precedent, because such appointment does not adversely affect successful performance of the prosecutor's duties, and may even be essential to it.

F

Fall, Albert B. (1861–1944) Secretary of Interior, 1921–1923. An instrumental figure in the TEAPOT DOME SCANDAL during President WARREN G. HARDING's administration, Albert Fall was tried and sentenced to prison following investigation of the matter by special prosecutors ATLEE POMERENE and OWEN J. ROBERTS.

Born in Frankfort, Kentucky, Fall was educated in country schools and worked as a school teacher from 1879 to 1881. He moved to the New Mexico Territory in 1886, where he prospected for gold and silver. His activity took him into northern Mexico. He gradually built significant holdings in mines, railroads, and timber throughout the southwest. Although he had little formal education, he read law and practiced as an attorney from 1889–1904, serving as general counsel to William C. Greene, who owned large investments in northern Mexico. Fall's contacts with Greene enabled him to enrich his own portfolio. He relocated to Three Rivers, a large ranch near Tularosa, in 1904. Entering New Mexico politics as a Democrat in 1904, he switched parties two years later, perhaps seeing greater opportunity for advancement in the largely Republican region. When New Mexico became a state in 1912, Fall was elected to the U.S. Senate and re-elected in 1918. Fall presented himself as a courageous, combative frontiersman: a self-made ambitious man who brooked no opposition.

In the Senate, Fall befriended Ohio's Warren Harding and was rewarded with a cabinet post when Harding was elected president in 1921. Conservationists like Gifford Pinchot and Harry Slattery were stunned that Fall was named Secretary of Interior. Fall had built his wealth and reputation through private development of the nation's resources. He had sided with the exploiters, and had actively opposed the conservation movement. In June 1921, Fall secured control of the Navy's oil reserves when their administration was transferred to the Department of the Interior. Pinchot was not immediately concerned, because he was occupied in monitoring Fall's control of the nation's forests, which he was convinced were at risk. Slattery, however, anticipated trouble. In a visit to Theodore Roosevelt, Jr., Assistant Secretary of the Navy, he warned that Fall might well be poised to turn the naval oil reserves over to private exploitation. Roosevelt, however, considered Fall a family friend. Fall had been a member of his father's Rough Riders, and Roosevelt expressed anger at Slattery's derogatory insinuations.

On April 14, 1922, it became public knowledge that Fall had leased the Teapot Dome naval oil reserves to HARRY SINCLAIR's Mammoth Oil Company. Fall would maintain that this was part of a policy to prevent loss of government oil through leaks and neglect. Offset wells needed to be drilled to prevent additional loss. Although Wisconsin's Progressive Senator Robert LaFollette began raising questions regarding mishandling of the oil reserves, and the Senate's Committee on Public Lands and Surveys scheduled hearings, Teapot Dome had not captured widespread public attention when Fall announced his resignation in March of 1923. It was reported that Fall was disappointed at his inability to either maintain leadership of New Mexico politics while in Washington, or assume leadership of Harding's Cabinet where CHARLES EVANS HUGHES proved most influential.

Senate hearings, led by THOMAS WALSH (D-Montana), uncovered a $100,000 loan to Fall that the Interior Secretary used to increase his livestock holdings. Fall at first attributed the loan to *Washington Post* publisher Edward McLean. This statement proved false when, on January 24, 1924, EDWARD DOHENY of Pan American Petroleum and Transport, testified that he had loaned the money to Fall. This revelation raised the specter of bribery and resulted in President CALVIN COOLIDGE's appointment of a special prosecution team to investigate the scandal. Secretary of the Navy EDWIN DENBY and Attorney General HARRY DAUGHERTY would be forced to resign from the cabinet as a result of Teapot Dome.

After a series of civil and criminal trials prosecuted by special appointees Pomerene and Roberts, Fall was convicted of conspiracy on October 25, 1929, and sentenced to prison and ordered to pay a $100,000 fine. Due to extensive litigation of the matter, Fall exhausted his wealth, and he eventually lost his ranch. Suffering from tuberculosis, Fall was permitted to serve his sentence in New Mexico. He entered prison on July 20, 1931, and was released on May 9, 1932. The fine was never paid. In his last years, Fall lived modestly, supported by his wife Emma, who continued to insist that her husband had been wrongly convicted.

Fall's conviction was viewed by many as evidence that appointment of special prosecutors was a viable option, especially when the attorney general may be implicated in the matter under investigation. HARRY TRUMAN would follow a similar course when faced with scandal in his administration. President NIXON's involvement in WATERGATE would eventually result in an attempt at a statutory solution to questions calling for special prosecution.

References:

Busch, Francis X. *Enemies of the State*. Indianapolis: Bobbs-Merrill, 1954.
Noggle, Burl. *Teapot Dome: Oil and Politics in the 1920's*. Baton Rouge: Louisiana State University Press, 1962.
Stratton, David Hodges. "Albert B. Fall and the Teapot Dome Affair." Ph.D. dissertation, University of Colorado, 1955. Chapter 11, "Oil Scandal in Court," concentrates on the investigation of special prosecutors POMERENE and ROBERTS. Chapter 3, "The Ambitions of Secretary Fall," deals with conservationists' view of Fall and his motives.

Fernandez, Joseph F. (1937–   ) CIA Station Chief in Costa Rica, 1984–1986. The highest ranking CIA officer ever to be charged with criminal wrongdoing, Joseph Fernandez was accused of conspiracy and obstruction of justice for his role in the IRAN-CONTRA affair. Independent Counsel LAWRENCE WALSH maintained that Fernandez played an instrumental role in a covert operation aimed at supplying arms to the Nicaraguan Contras during a period of time when such activity was prohibited by Congress. Prosecution of Fernandez ultimately failed, however, when the CLASSIFIED INFORMATION PROCEDURES ACT (CIPA) of 1980 was unable to satisfactorily resolve questions involving use of classified documents considered necessary to the Fernandez defense.

On June 20, 1988, a federal grand jury indicted Fernandez for conspiring to defraud the U.S government by deceitfully and illegally assisting in the Contra resupply effort. The indictment also alleged that Fernandez made false statements to CIA officials during an internal investigation of his activities and lied to the TOWER COMMISSION regarding the true nature of his involvement in Contra supply. Fernandez was a 20-year veteran of the CIA who firmly believed that his actions on behalf of the Contras were sanctioned by the White House. He maintained faith in the principle of "loyalty up, loyalty down," and did not anticipate facing a situation where he would be left alone to answer for actions taken in violation of the law.

Fernandez became a principal subject early in the Iran-Contra investigation when his telephone number was found on the person of EUGENE HASENFUS, a passenger on a Contra supply aircraft, after it was shot down by the Nicaraguan Army in October 1986. Walsh's investigation succeeded in translating a series of encrypted messages that passed between Fernandez and OLIVER NORTH in which Fernandez indicated that the CIA intended to establish a 2,500-man armed force in southern Nicaragua. In the course of his activities, Fernandez assisted RICHARD SECORD's Contra supply operation by arranging for construction of an airstrip. Much of Fernandez's efforts were aimed at opening a southern front in the Contra uprising against the Nicaraguan Sandinista government. To this end, he worked closely with Contra leader Alfonso Rubello, and had some success in persuading Contra soldiers to leave established Contra commander Eden Pastora in favor of Pedro "Blackie" Chamorro, who was more compliant to CIA directives. Fernandez, who employed the pseudonym Tomas Castillo during this time, answered directly to ALAN FIERS, who also became a target of Walsh's investigation.

Trial Judge Claude M. Hilton, after conferring with counsel regarding CIPA specifications for dealing with classified information, decided to allow Fernandez to specifically name and locate CIA stations during his trial testimony. Walsh had hoped that Hilton would have ruled that a more general reference to such facilities, agreeable to the CIA, would have sufficed. Now Walsh realized that his case against Fernandez might well be dismissed, if Attorney General RICHARD THORNBURGH determined that the names and locations of CIA facilities could not be publicly revealed. Still, he hoped that some provision less severe than dismissal could be arranged. After extended negotiations, no mutually agreeable substitutions were agreed upon for the specific information Fernandez planned to reveal in his testimony. As a result, on November 22, 1989, Attorney General Thornburgh and the CIA filed a CIPA affidavit refusing to produce the classified information requested by Judge Hilton. The case against Fernandez was dismissed by Hilton on the grounds that the defendant was unable to defend himself. A prosecution appeal was unsuccessful. Walsh contended that the classified information was in actuality already public knowledge. He also had offered, without success, to drop charges related most closely to the classified information in question.

CIPA was designed to deal with the threat of GRAYMAIL by criminal defendants who claimed that classified information was necessary to their defense. Its crafters did not envision its use by the Justice Department and agencies such as the CIA in cases brought by an independent counsel. CIPA's failure to effectively handle such situations can be measured by the dismissal of the case against Fernandez and the severe limitations placed on the prosecution's cases against Oliver North and JOHN POINDEXTER. The prospect of the attorney general and the CIA working together to thwart the case of the independent counsel appeared, at times, as an absurdity.

Walsh did secure Fernandez's testimony after the Court of Appeals affirmed the case's dismissal. In November 1990, testifying under IMMUNITY, Fernandez admitted that he had lied to the Tower Commission.

Fernandez repeatedly maintained that his activities were legal. He insisted that he had obeyed the BOLAND AMENDMENTS limiting aid to the Contras, and had reported all his activities (which he characterized principally as information gathering) to his superiors. Thomas E. Wilson, Fernandez's attorney, expressed the opinion that all CIA operatives involved in Contra aid were presented with the difficult choice of either remaining loyal to the President or being truthful with Congress. After it was over, Fernandez continued to express great affection for the CIA, but admitted that his feelings were tempered somewhat by bitterness over the manner in which he was treated by his superiors.

References:

Drew, Christopher. "Iran-Contra Charge for CIA Aide." *Chicago Tribune*, 21 June 1988,
    sec. C, p. 3.
Harriger, Katy J. *Independent Justice: The Federal Special Prosecutor in American Pol-
    itics*. Lawrence: University Press of Kansas, 1992. Pages 134–137 discuss CIPA
    problems such as those faced in the Fernandez case.
"Iran-Contra; Case Dismissed." *Economist*, 2 December 1989, 28.
"Iran-Contra Case against Key Official Dismissed." *Los Angeles Times*, 24 November
    1989, sec. P, p. 2.
Johnston, David. "Ex-Agent Is Bitter over Iran Affair." *New York Times*, 26 November
    1989, sec. A, p. 31.
Jordan, Sandra D. "Classified Information and Conflicts in Independent Counsel Prose-
    cutions: Balancing the Scales of Justice after Iran-Contra." *Columbia Law Review*
    91(1991): 1651–1698. Argues that the government, which classifies information,
    is not in an objective position to determine whether disclosure of such information
    is in the public interest.
Walsh, Lawrence. *Firewall: The Iran-Contra Conspiracy and Cover-up*. New York: W.
    W. Norton, 1997. Chapter 12, "Deniability Triumphant," discusses the Fernandez
    case.

Fiers, Alan D., Jr. (1939–   ) CIA Chief of Central American Task Force,
1984–1988. As successor to DUANE CLARRIDGE, Alan Fiers assumed major
responsibility for support of the Nicaraguan Contras' armed opposition to the
Sandinista government. In this capacity, Fiers became aware of, and involved
in, OLIVER NORTH's efforts to circumvent congressional limitations on aid to
the rebel forces. Due to his participation in this arrangement, Fiers became a
target of Independent Counsel LAWRENCE WALSH's IRAN-CONTRA investigation. The Walsh investigation determined that Fiers had knowledge of
North's activities, and participated in concealing it from congressional investigators. On July 9, 1991, Fiers pleaded guilty to two misdemeanor counts of
withholding information from Congress in return for IMMUNITY from further
prosecution. His admission temporarily placed in jeopardy confirmation of President BUSH's Deputy National Security Adviser Robert Gates's appointment as
Head of the CIA, because Gates's tenure and position at the CIA raised serious
questions about his knowledge of Iran-Contra. Fiers's testimony at the trial of
his CIA supervisor CLAIR GEORGE in July 1992 proved dramatic and damaging. Five months later, Fiers was included in President Bush's Christmas Eve
pardon of those implicated in Iran-Contra misdeeds.

Alan Fiers was raised in Indiana, the son of an evangelical minister. He played
football for Coach Woody Hayes at the Ohio State University and joined the
Marine Corps after college. As a Marine lieutenant, he was sent to the Domin-
ican Republic in 1965 to curb civil unrest. There he earned a Bronze Star and
Purple Heart for his part in an heroic rescue of a wounded civilian. By 1969,
Fiers was working for the CIA. His service took him to Istanbul, Ankara, and
Karachi before being appointed station chief in Riyadh, Saudi Arabia.

When Fiers assumed command of the CIA's Central American Task Force, Oliver North was already deeply involved in arming the Contras. Although similar in many respects, Fiers and North found themselves at odds over Contra policy. North's activities included sidestepping the limitations mandated by the BOLAND AMENDMENTS. Fiers was not cognizant of any agency mandate requiring support for such illegal activity. Rather, his instinct was to protect the CIA from questionable wildcat operations. Fiers soon discovered, however, that North's operation was supported by those in authority, and he made the decision to participate in concealing the facts from investigators.

North advised Fiers that he would be better off not knowing about Contra resupply activities. According to the Walsh investigation, however, by 1986 Fiers was part of a "restricted interagency group" consisting of Assistant Secretary of State ELLIOTT ABRAMS, Assistant Secretary of Defense Richard Armitage, and North that helped direct Contra supply operations. Under Fiers's direction, CIA Costa Rican Station Chief JOSEPH FERNANDEZ arranged for construction of an airstrip to facilitate RICHARD SECORD's air supply operation. As Fiers's involvement in these activities was revealed, both he and Duane Clarridge received negative internal CIA reviews and left the agency in 1988.

Following the downing of a Contra supply plane manned by EUGENE HASENFUS, Fiers was called to testify before the House Intelligence Committee. His denials regarding the Contra supply operation were subsequently demonstrated to be false by the Walsh investigation. Faced with the Independent Counsel's evidence, Fiers agreed to plead guilty to two false statements in return for immunity. Walsh would use Fiers as a witness in his trial of Clair George. On July 28 and 29, 1992, Fiers testified that George had advised him to lie before the Senate Foreign Relations Committee when asked the identity of "Max Gomez" (actually CIA employee Felix Rodriguez), identified by Hasenfus as his superior. Fiers also stated that George had ordered him to fabricate testimony that would conceal North's Contra supply operation. When asked to testify about his personal relationship with George, Fiers wept openly in court, and was unable to fully recover his composure for the next twenty minutes, during which time he recalled the citations and awards he had received from his supervisor as compensation for his distinguished agency service.

Fiers's testimony, damaging though it was, could not convict George. A mistrial was declared when the jury was unable to reach a verdict. Walsh retried George, but Bush's blanket pardon on December 24, 1992, ended the matter. After leaving the CIA, Fiers joined W.R. Grace & Company, a multinational corporation with headquarters in Washington, D.C.

References:

Lewis, Neil A. "Ex-CIA Official Testifies Boss Knew About Iran-Contra Affair." *New York Times*, 29 July 1992, sec. A, p. 1.
———. "Former Spy Weeps at Iran-Contra Trial." *New York Times*, 30 July 1992, sec. A, p. 10.

McDonald, Marci. "A Superspy Comes Clean." *Macleans*, 22 July 1991, p. 28.
Walsh, Lawrence. *Firewall: The Iran-Contra Conspiracy and Cover-up.* New York:
   W.W. Norton, 1997.
Wines, Michael. "Washington at Work: Quintessential Spy Undone by His Own Loy-
   alty." *New York Times*, 30 July 1991, sec. A, p. 12.

Filegate. While investigating the manner in which the CLINTON administration had dismissed members of the White House Travel Office (resulting in a controversy dubbed TRAVELGATE), Congress discovered that the FBI file of former Travel Office head Billy Dale had been requested by the White House. The fact that Dale had already left his position raised curiosity. Further investigation discovered that 481 files in all had been requested, most of them belonging to former Republican administration employees.

In June 1996, Congress began hearings on the matter. It was established that Craig Livingstone, a Clinton appointee, had been asked to create a list of employees from previous administrations who still needed access to the White House. Livingstone hired Anthony Marceca, a civilian Army investigator, to work on the project. Working from a list of names apparently obtained from a retiring government employee, Marceca requested the FBI files of the individuals named. During testimony, he admitted to requesting 300 more files than were originally anticipated. The FBI granted his request. They began producing the requested material between December 1993 and February 1994. Included on the list were fomer Secretary of State James Baker III and White House spokesperson Marlin Fitzwater.

On June 18, 1996, Attorney General JANET RENO asked the FBI to look into the matter. Republicans claimed that the file transfer represented a sinister attempt to slander Billy Dale and the other Travel Office employees, thereby justifying their dismissal after the fact. On June 20, Reno requested an independent counsel, and the matter was turned over to KENNETH STARR, Independent Counsel for WHITEWATER. Starr, it was reasoned, already had an investigatorial organization established. On June 26, 1996, Livingstone resigned. Whereas FBI Director Louis Freeh characterized the file transfers as "egregious violations of privacy," past and present Clinton administration officials described it as a "bureaucratic snafu." Former White House Counsel BERNARD NUSSBAUM, former Associate Counsel William Kennedy, and Livingstone all offered apologies to the persons whose files had been obtained. The FBI acknowledged lapses in their security that facilitated the file transfers and promised to institute new procedures aimed at preventing future mishaps.

In March 1997, FBI General Counsel Howard Shapiro acknowledged erroneously passing along background information on Craig Livingstone to the White House, rather than to the independent counsel. A Justice Department report censored Shapiro for his actions. The information in question indicated that HILLARY CLINTON had been influential in the hiring of Livingstone.

The independent counsel's office has been silent on the filegate matter. Questions remaining unanswered include: How was the list of names compiled? Did the information in the files consist of summaries, or were actual documents included? Was the information obtained entered into White House databases before being returned to the FBI?

References:

Feldmann, Linda. "What's Behind the Latest White House Scandal?" *Christian Science Monitor*, 21 June 1996, p. 4.
Fletcher, Martin. "Clinton Aide Quits as Inquiry Begins into Files Scandal." *The Times*, 27 June 1996.
Safire, William. "Unclosed Filegate." *New York Times*, 23 July 1998, sec. A, p. 25.
Zehren, Charles V. "FBI Counsel Rapped." *Newsday*, 29 March 1997, sec. A, p. 13.

Fiske, Robert B., Jr. (1930–   ) Independent Counsel, Whitewater Investigation, 1994. Named as independent counsel to investigate allegations surrounding the CLINTONs' involvement in the Arkansas land development deal known as WHITEWATER, Robert Fiske assumed his duties during a period when the independent counsel statute had lapsed. Republican opposition to the mechanism following Independent Counsel LAWRENCE WALSH's lengthy and expensive IRAN-CONTRA investigation had defeated efforts to renew the law at the end of 1992. When newly elected Democratic President Bill Clinton became the target of charges alleging his involvement in a questionable Arkansas investment arrangement during the time he was the state's governor, Attorney General JANET RENO was called upon to appoint a special prosecutor to examine the matter. On January 20, 1994, Reno selected Fiske. After five months, he released a preliminary report indicating that there was no evidence of wrongdoing by any Clinton administration officials. Conservative Republicans, convinced that Fiske's investigation was lacking in vigor, urged his replacement under the terms of the newly reauthorized independent counsel statute. The federal appeals court's Special Division agreed, naming KENNETH STARR the new independent counsel on August 5, 1994.

A widely respected attorney who specialized in civil litigation and criminal law, Robert Bishop Fiske, Jr. is the son of a lawyer who was named Assistant Secretary General of NATO by President Dwight D. Eisenhower in 1959. Shortly after receiving his law degree from the University of Michigan in 1955, Robert Fiske, Jr. began a long associaton with the Wall Street law firm of Davis, Polk & Wardell. Appointed U.S. Attorney for the Southern District of New York in 1976 by President GERALD FORD, Fiske stayed on to serve in the same capacity under President Jimmy CARTER. Fiske's record as U.S. Attorney was most praiseworthy. He successfully prosecuted labor racketeers Anthony Scotto and Anthony Anastasio, as well as Harlem heroin dealer Leroy (Nicky) Barnes.

Stepping down in 1980, he returned to private practice. In 1984, Fiske became chairman of the AMERICAN BAR ASSOCIATION's Committee on the Federal

Judiciary. During this period, the committee demonstrated occasional displeasure with President RONALD REAGAN's judicial selections. This criticism was perceived as obstructionist by a number of Conservatives who believed that Fiske's leadership was at least in part responsible for interfering in Reagan's attempt to establish a less-activist federal judiciary. Fiske was no longer chair of the ABA committee when it issued a somewhat critical report on Supreme Court nominee ROBERT BORK in 1987. Still, the failure of Bork's candidacy was part of a pattern that some conservatives traced to Fiske's leadership of the committee.

When Lawrence Walsh became independent counsel for the Iran-Contra investigation in 1986, he conferred with Fiske, his former law partner, before naming associate counsels. At the time, such an innocent association would not have raised concern among conservatives, but six years later, Walsh was regarded as a renegade Republican who had wreaked havoc during the Reagan and Bush administrations. In retrospect, the Fiske-Walsh connection appeared somewhat sinister to some. Conservatives had the opportunity to register their opposition to Fiske in April 1989 when Attorney General RICHARD THORN-BURGH nominated him as one of his deputies. In addition to objections already raised, conservatives now also echoed a complaint voiced by the National Right to Life Committee that Fiske had submitted the names of potential Reagan judicial nominees to the liberal Alliance for Justice's Judicial Selection Project for their perusal. Fiske said he wanted to determine if any of those named had histories of bias toward women or minorities. Conservatives claimed that such notification permitted liberals to mount negative campaigns against the nominees even before their selections were announced. By early July, Thornburgh bowed to critics' pressure and abandoned plans to name Fiske to the Justice Department. Opposition to Fiske had been led by Senator Strom Thurmond, White House Chief of Staff John Sununu, and Paul M. Kamenar of the Washington Legal Foundation. A total of 14 Republican senators had spoken publicly against the nomination. Although the numbers were not overwhelming, many of those who had voiced their opposition were needed by the Reagan administration to support future nominees such as Clarence Thomas.

Many Republicans still held Fiske in high regard. Senator John Danforth (R-Montana) stated that Fiske had been victimized by those who had little understanding of his actions. In fact, Danforth asserted, Fiske should have passed the Conservatives' "acid test," because he had actually supported Bork's nomination. Fiske's appointment as Whitewater investigator received general support from the majority of Republicans. Senator ALFONSE D'AMATO (R-New York), personally acquainted with Fiske, characterized him as an honorable and skilled attorney, while Senate Majority Leader ROBERT DOLE (R-Kansas) described the prosecutor as well-qualified, but noted that there was some opposition to his appointment.

Fiske was presented with a broad mandate that included any possible wrongdoing associated with the Whitewater Development Corporation and Madison

Guaranty Savings & Loan. The 1993 suicide of Clinton associate VINCENT FOSTER would be included in the probe. Reno pledged that he need not answer to the Justice Department, but rather to the American people. Fiske anticipated questioning both the President and First Lady. Clinton stated that he welcomed the inquiry. Indeed, he had responded to critics by asking Reno to appoint an investigator.

Hoping to avoid one of the serious problems encountered by Walsh, Fiske formally requested the Senate and House Banking Committees to delay their hearings in order that overlapping investigations did not compromise his efforts. He was particularly concerned that congressional witnesses were likely to be granted immunity in return for congressional testimony, thereby making prosecution by the independent counsel difficult, if not impossible. Congressional leaders acceded to Fiske's request.

Fiske's preliminary report was issued on July 30, 1994. He announced that there was no evidence to warrant charging administration officials with interference with the federal probe, via the Resolution Trust Corporation (RTC), of Madison Guaranty. This finding no doubt surprised some who witnessed the contentious RTC hearings that resulted in the resignation of White House counsel BERNARD NUSSBAUM in February. In addition, Fiske did not find any indication that Vince Foster had been the victim of foul play. His investigation supported the report of U.S. Park Police who had ruled the death a suicide. Fiske found no indication that Foster's death was related to Whitewater. Not yet completed was Fiske's examination of the manner in which Foster's Whitewater-related papers were removed by White House officials shortly after his death. Fiske's report cleared the way for congressional hearings to begin. These hearings would be more far-ranging, allowing examiners to address issues of propriety separate from criminal considerations. Before they were completed, Deputy Treasury Secretary ROGER ALTMAN and Treasury General Counsel JEAN HANSON would be forced to resign.

In June, the independent counsel statute had been reauthorized. Days after Fiske released his preliminary report, Reno asked the federal appeals court to officially appoint him as independent counsel for the Whitewater investigation. Conservatives asked the court to choose someone else, arguing that Fiske's appointment by Reno left him appearing less than independent. Letters to the court also complained of Fiske's past friendliness with departed Clinton counsel Nussbaum. Spurning Reno's request, the court's Special Division replaced Fiske with Kenneth Starr, a jurist more closely identified with partisan conservative causes. The manner in whch Starr's appointment was arranged became the subject of controversy when it was learned that Special Division Judge DAVID SENTELLE had met with Starr advocates Senators Lauch Faircloth (R-North Carolina) and Jesse Helms (R-North Carolina) shortly before the appointment was made. Those displeased by Fiske's replacement asserted that entrusting the independent counsel's appointment to the courts did not guarantee that politics was removed from the process.

References:

Brill, Steven. "Anonymity and Dignity." *American Lawyer* (September 1994): 5. Portrays Fiske as a model of integrity unlikely to be matched by Starr in that regard.
"Declarations of Independence." *Economist*, 13 August 1994, p. 25. Discusses the difficulty in removing politics from the process of independent counsel selection.
Jackson, Robert L. "GOP Lawyer Picked to Probe Whitewater." *Los Angeles Times*, 21 January 1994, sec. A, p. 30.
Labaton, Stephen. "Reno Is Said to Choose New Yorker as Counsel." *New York Times*, 20 January 1994, sec. A, p. 12.
Malone, Julia. "Whitewater: Good News So Far." *Atlanta Journal and Constitution*, 1 July 1994, sec. A, p. 10.
"Reno Asks Court to Appoint Fiske as Independent Counsel." *Los Angeles Times*, 2 July 1994, sec. A, p. 27.
"Whitewater Round Goes to Whitehouse." *Chicago Tribune*, 30 June 1994, sec. N, p. 8.
Wines, Michael. "Thornburgh Abandons Choice for Top Justice Post." *New York Times*, 7 July 1989, sec. A, p. 1.
———. "Thornburgh Choice for Deputy Is Under Fire." *New York Times*, 30 April 1989, sec. A, p. 25.

Ford, Gerald R. (1913–) U.S. President, 1974–1976. Gerald R. Ford, the only President of the United States never elected president or vice president, was very much a part of the history of the development of the Office of Special Prosecutor (later known as the independent counsel), both during the WATERGATE investigation and in his own unelected Presidency, during which he eventually sought election to a term in his own right. Indeed, it could be argued that the then-newly-formed Office of the Special Prosecutor played an important role both in his ascension to the Presidency and his departure from it.

The future President Ford was born Leslie Lynch King, Jr. on July 14, 1913, in Omaha, Nebraska. Less than a year later, his parents, Dorothy Gardner King and Leslie Lyncy King, Sr., divorced, and his mother took him to live with her parents in Grand Rapids, Michigan. In 1916, Dorothy King remarried to Gerald R. Ford, Sr., whose name Ford legally took on at the age of twenty-one. During his youth, Gerald Ford, Jr. attended Grand Rapids' South High School, where he excelled in football. Ford continued his stellar football career in college, and was recruited by two professional teams. He turned both offers down, and instead graduated in 1935, with a B.A. in liberal arts, before paying his way through Yale law school by working as both an assistant football coach and head boxing coach. Shortly after his 1941 graduation, he returned to Grand Rapids to open a law firm, but before he could really develop a law practice, World War II broke out. In 1942, Gerald Ford enlisted in the Navy, with a commission of ensign. After spending his first year in the service training recruits at the Navy's V-5 flight school in North Carolina, Ensign Ford was eventually reassigned to serve on the U.S.S. Monterey In 1946, Ford was discharged from the Navy with the rank of Lieutenant.

Two years into his return to civilian life, Ford made his first run for Congress.

In the 1948 Republican primary he defeated the Michigan Fifth District's four-term incumbent, Bartel Jonkman, an old-style isolationist, by 9,300 votes, and went on to defeat his Democratic opponent in the general election. Ford's career in the U.S. House of Representatives was long and productive. He established his reputation as an internationalist in foreign policy, an economic conservative, and a social moderate. Although Ford never achieved his goal of becoming Speaker of the House during his years in Congress, he served on the Public Works and Appropriations Committees, became House Minority Leader in 1965, and actively supported other Republican candidates for office (including lobbying to keep RICHARD NIXON on the 1952 Presidential ticket in the wake of the "Fund Crisis"), among other accomplishments. In 1963, President Lyndon B. Johnson selected Ford to serve on the President's Commission to investigate the Assassination of President Kennedy (a.k.a. the "Warren Commission"). In the resulting published report, *Portrait of an Assassin*, which he coauthored, he concluded that Oswald had acted alone. In 1968, Ford served as the Permanent Chairman of the Republican National Convention and was offered the vice-presidential slot on the 1968 Republican ticket, which he declined. The following year, he led an investigation into the conduct of Supreme Court Justice William O. Douglas that lasted nearly a year. No charges were finally filed against Douglas, and Ford called the investigation a "whitewash." The very politicized nature of the investigation, followed on the heels of the Senate rejection of Nixon's Supreme Court nominees, both Southern conservatives. Though Ford was seen as merely acting on the orders of others, he did not escape the resulting political fallout.

It was not long afterwards, however, that Ford would begin his long, and sometimes reluctant role in bringing a resolution to Watergate, a scandal which not only shook American faith in the political system, but first launched the Office of Special Prosecutor to public prominence. Ford's first official act in the whole affair, though, was to intervene in order to slow down the financial investigation of the House Banking and Currency Committee (a.k.a. the "Patman Committee") into Watergate, not long after the initial report of the break-in. Throughout the early investigation, Ford continued to defend Nixon, proclaiming his unshaken belief in Nixon's innocence, although he also publicly supported the resignation and firings of others as a "necessary first step . . . in clearing the air." Ford also urged Nixon to release his tapes of phone conversations in order to clear his name.

The turning point in the Watergate scandal came with the Presidential order to fire Special Prosecutor ARCHIBALD COX, and the resulting resignations over the order, popularly known as the "Saturday Night Massacre." The firing was precipitated by the discovery of the tapes of Oval Office conversations, and Cox's subsequent attempt to obtain eight of the tapes deemed important to the Watergate investigation. When Nixon refused to voluntarily surrender the tapes, Cox requested a judicial subpoena, which Nixon's lawyers attempted to block, pleading national security and executive privilege. District Court Judge JOHN

SIRICA then ordered Nixon to surrender the eight tapes to him to determine whether or not they fell under the protection of executive privilege. Rather than complying, Nixon attempted to cut a deal by providing the Special Prosecutor with written summaries of the contents of the tapes, rather than the tapes themselves (with Senator John Stennis, a conservative Democrat from Mississippi, checking the accuracy of the summaries against the actual tapes), provided that Cox agreed to no more subpoenas of presidential papers or tapes. When Cox rejected this "compromise," Nixon ordered Attorney General ELLIOT RICHARDSON to fire Cox. Richardson resigned rather than do so, Assistant Attorney General WILLIAM RUCKELSHAUS was fired for his refusal to do the same, before he could submit a resignation. Finally Solicitor General and Acting Attorney General ROBERT BORK carried out Nixon's order. During this time, Nixon also tried to abolish the Office of Special Prosecutor.

These actions precipitated calls for impeachment, causing Nixon to temporarily reverse his stance, surrendering the tapes and announcing Bork's forthcoming appointment of a new special prosecutor. Yet the Watergate scandal continued to grow and to increasingly take up national attention. After the resignation of Vice President Spiro Agnew, following a plea of *nolo contendere* to income tax evasion charges, Nixon asked Ford to poll House Republicans concerning their preference for Agnew's replacement. That same night, Nixon advisor Melvin Laird called Ford to ask if he would accept the nomination for Vice President, which he did.

Immediately following the nomination, Ford was thoroughly investigated by the House Rules and Senate Judiciary Committees. Ford cooperated fully, providing every available record or witness to his personal, financial, and political conduct, and the result was an investigation that turned up no genuine "skeletons." During the course of the preconfirmation investigation, the Senate Rules Committee members questioned him repeatedly about his views on issues that included official separation of powers, executive privilege, and the independence of the next Special Prosecutor. He was also asked whether he believed that a sitting president had the right to withhold potential evidence in the event of a criminal investigation of the executive branch, to which Ford answered that he did not believe that the president should have "unlimited authority" through executive privilege, and that evidence concerning "serious allegation" of criminal activity should be made available to the investigator. Most crucially, Ford was asked whether, if Nixon did resign, he would do anything to stop further investigation into the President's conduct in office, to which Ford responded: "I don't think the public would stand for it."

On December 6, 1973, Ford was sworn in as the first unelected vice president in a brief ceremony televised from the House chamber. Although Ford had made it clear at the time that he had no intention of running for president, he was clearly selected with the full consideration of the possibility that he might eventually take on the presidency in the event of Nixon's resignation, causing public speculation as to the likelihood of his running in 1976, as well as the more immediate possibility of a presidential resignation. In any case, even Ford's ascension to vice president failed to halt the growing scandal as the Watergate investigation continued.

As Nixon continued to find ways to forestall the release of the tapes that provided the hard evidence of his wrongdoing, Vice President Ford lived with the increasingly difficult dilemma of supporting and remaining loyal to Nixon versus distancing himself from the increasing political quagmire. Even as Ford's actions moved from supporting to distancing, he scrupulously avoided any calls for Nixon's resignation or similar statements that would have made it look as though he were angling for the Presidency. Nonetheless, a group of Ford's closest political associates formed a "Secret Transition Team" well in advance of the announced resignation, without his knowledge or consent. Ford did his utmost to avoid any discussion of a pardon for Nixon, although Nixon's aides had drafted one a couple of months before the resignation.

On August 9, 1974, Ford was sworn in as President in the East Room of the White House. Ford's inauguration was a quiet, low-key event, with efforts made to leave no impression of celebrating on Nixon's political grave. It was most memorable for Ford's inaugural speech, in which he proclaimed that "our long national nightmare is over," and assured the nation that "our Constitution works; our great Republic is a government of laws and not of men." Ford's inauguration indeed seemed to signal a return to open, honest government, and initially his presidency was welcomed by Americans of all political stripes.

The drama of Watergate hardly ended with Ford's inauguration, however. As Special Prosecutor LEON JAWORSKI (Cox's successor) was deciding whether or not to pursue Nixon's prosecution for obstruction of justice, Ford decided to issue Nixon a pardon before even an indictment took place, while (as he saw it) the nation was still in the mood for reconciliation and moving beyond Watergate. When Ford made his decision to issue a pardon before the formal investigation could begin, he saw it as a compassionate move, to spare both the ailing and already disgraced ex-president and the politically fractured nation the long drawn-out process of a trial, as well as to speed the nation toward healing. In no sense did Ford anticipate the firestorm of criticism that resulted from his pardon, or the accompanying insinuations that he and Nixon had "cut a deal" in advance of Nixon's resignation. Although Ford tried to "balance" the pardon with a conditional pardon for Vietnam War draft evaders and deserters, his program of partial clemency failed to mollify any of his critics. Ford's press secretary, Jerald terHorst, resigned in protest after only a month in office. Notably, terHorst submitted his resignation as soon as he found out about the Nixon pardon, before it was formally announced. Jaworski, however, affirmed Ford's constitutional right to grant the pardon (although he had not been consulted on the matter), and shared Ford's view that given the vast publicity, there was no way that Nixon could have received a fair trial.

And though Ford did a thorough job of explaining his reasons for the pardon to both Congress and the general American public (taking the unprecedented step of testifying before a Congressional committee), it unquestionably ended whatever Presidential "honeymoon" he had, and may have contributed to his defeat at the polls, when he decided to run for a regular term as president. Ford's brief presidency was, in any case, not an easy one, beset by both domestic problems, most notably inflation, and by foreign crises, including the Cambodian invasion in the dying stages of the Vietnam War. Also, aside from the controversy surrounding the pardon, Ford's presidency was further dogged by the shadow of Watergate due to his initial decision to keep most of Nixon's surviving Cabinet (even those whom he later replaced).

Although Ford had initially taken on the vice presidency, and then the presidency with the intention to retire when his term was over, he soon changed his plans and declared his candidacy for the 1976 election. Far from being a case of newfound ambition, Ford's decision to run in 1976 was motivated in large part by the realization that it would be necessary for him to be seen as something more than a "caretaker" President. As a result, he ran on the campaign theme of allowing the Ford administration to complete its work. The 1976 campaign, however, was a very tough one for Gerald Ford, still in the shadow of the Nixon pardon and facing a serious challenge from within his own party by then California Governor RONALD REAGAN.

During July 1976, Congress debated the merits of establishing a statutory special prosecutor, independent of the executive. The Ford administration argued in favor of a permanent special prosecutor appointed by the president to a three-year term. Although the Ford proposal found support temporarily, it was rejected in favor of the more independent model two years later with the adoption of the ETHICS IN GOVERNMENT ACT.

In the end, Ford narrowly lost the election to his Democratic opponent, former Georgia Governor Jimmy CARTER, who effectively stole Ford's thunder concerning honest and open government. This loss signaled the end of Ford's political career.

References:

Cannon, James. *Time and Chance: Gerald Ford's Appointment with History.* New York: HarperCollins, 1994.

Ford, Gerald R. *A Time to Heal: The Autobiography of Gerald R. Ford.* New York: Harper and Row, 1979.

Greene, John Robert. *The Presidency of Gerald R. Ford.* Lawrence: University Press of Kansas, 1995.

Kutler, Stanley I. *The Wars of Watergate: The Last Crisis of Richard Nixon.* New York: Alfred A. Knopf, 1990.

Mollenhoff, Clark R. *Game Plan for Disaster: An Ombudsman's Report on the Nixon Years.* New York: Norton, 1976.

———. *The Man Who Pardoned Nixon.* New York: St. Martin's Press, 1976.

Reeves, Richard. *A Ford, Not a Lincoln.* New York: Harcourt Brace Jovanovich, 1975.

Schapsmeier, Edward L., and Frederick H. Schapsmeier. *Gerald R. Ford's Date with Destiny.* New York: Peter Lang Publishing, 1989.

Schoenbaum, Eleanora W., ed. *Political Profiles: The Nixon/Ford Years*. New York: Facts on File, Inc., 1979.

terHorst, Jerald. *Gerald Ford and the Future of the Presidency*. New York: The Third Press, 1974.

—SUSAN ROTH BREITZER

Foster, Vincent W., Jr. (1945–1993) Deputy White House Counsel, 1992–1993. Born in Hope, Arkansas, Vince Foster was a childhood friend of Bill CLINTON. He entered the law and became a partner at the Rose Law Firm in Little Rock before coming to Washington with the Clintons. As Deputy Counsel to BERNARD NUSSBAUM, Foster dealt extensively with Hillary Clinton's legal records, including those relating to WHITEWATER. He was also involved in clearing Clinton Cabinet nominees before the confirmation process. The failed nominations of Zoe Baird, Kimba Wood, and Lani Guinier reflected badly on Foster's work. In addition, Foster was implicated in the firing of White House Travel Office employees, a burgeoning scandal that was dubbed TRAVEL-GATE. The fervor with which each embarrassment was seized upon, examined, and publicized by the media was disturbing to Foster, a man who had exhibited symptoms of emotional distress and depression in the past. On July 20, 1993, Foster was found dead in Fort Marcy Park overlooking the Potomac River, the victim of an apparent suicide. Analysts immediately began theorizing that Foster's death was in some way related to Clinton misconduct in the WHITE-WATER affair. Some claimed that Foster had been murdered. These charges were further fueled by the fact that White House aides apparently removed papers from Foster's office shortly after his death.

Five separate investigations into Foster's death between 1993 and 1997—one by U.S. Park Police, one each by Independent Counsels ROBERT FISKE and KENNETH STARR, and two by the Congress—all concluded that it was a suicide. The investigation by Park Police was significantly hampered by Clinton aides who interfered with attempts to interview Foster family members and prevented entry to Foster's office while sensitive papers were gathered and removed. Because police did not have immediate access to Foster's office and its papers, skepticism greeted police findings that Foster had committed suicide.

In July 1994, Robert Fiske issued a 58-page report on Foster's death. Fiske's report documented Foster's bouts with depression while still in Arkansas. The pressure of his job in Washington had caused physical and psychological ailments, according to Fiske. White House Counsel Bernard Nussbaum stated that Foster had virtually ceased to function at work by the summer of 1993. Foster attempted to reach a psychiatrist shortly before his death. The Fiske report identifies Travelgate as Foster's most troublesome concern. He had been pressured by Hillary Clinton to replace the Travel Office staff with Clinton loyalists. Foster apparently dreaded being called by Congress to testify, in part because he had served as Hillary Clinton's personal attorney in Arkansas and was upset about a conflict of interest. Shortly before his death, Foster had tried to secure the services of Denver attorney James Lyons, a lawyer who had helped the Clintons deflect questions about Whitewater during the 1992 campaign. Fiske's investigation included interviews with the Clintons. His verdict concurred with the findings of the Park Police.

On October 10, 1997, Kenneth Starr's report on Foster's death was unsealed by the courts. In addition to confirming Foster's emotional fragility and documenting his contacts with physicians, Starr's report refutes the contentions of conspiracy theorists on several points: the gun found in Foster's hand, a .38-caliber revolver, was the murder weapon, and it belonged to Foster; carpet fibers found on Foster's body were consistent with samples taken from the carpet in Foster's home (arguing against those who believed his body had been wrapped and moved); there was a large amount of blood in and around the body, and there was soil on Foster's shoes (contrary to earlier rumors), indicating that death occurred in the park; and the absence of a suicide note was not significant, because most suicide victims do not leave one. Foster had committed suicide, according to Starr.

A few Foster conspiracy theorists remain unconvinced. Led by Reed Irvine of Accuracy in Media and journalist Christopher Ruddy, author of *The Strange Death of Vincent Foster* (Free Press, 1997), they found the Starr report a worse blow than Fiske's. Though the manner of Vince Foster's death appears certain, the contents of the papers removed from his office still hold interest for Whitewater investigators. Travelgate appears to have played the greater role in pushing Foster toward self-destruction, but it is conceivable that documents in his possession might have implicated the Clintons in Whitewater-related misconduct.

References:

Isikoff, Michael. "The Night Foster Died." *Newsweek*, 17 July 1995, p. 20.
Isikoff, Michael, and Mark Hosenball. "Why Vince Foster Died." *Newsweek*, 11 July 1994, p. 17.
Labaton, Stephen. "A Report on His Suicide Portrays a Deeply Troubled Vince Foster." *New York Times*, 11 October 1997, sec. A, p. 1.
Sidey, Hugh. "Did Washington Kill Vincent Foster?" *Time*, 23 August 1993, p. 76.
York, Byron. "Vince Foster, in the Park, with the Gun." *Weekly Standard*, 27 October 1997, p. 25.

G

Gallinghouse, Gerald J. (1920–   ) Independent Counsel, Timothy Kraft investigation, 1980–1981. In an investigation that mirrored that of White House Chief of Staff HAMILTON JORDAN, Gerald Gallinghouse was named special prosecutor to examine whether President Jimmy CARTER's campaign manager, TIMOTHY KRAFT, had used cocaine during visits to New Orleans and San Francisco in 1978. Following a six-month inquiry, during which his constitutional authority was challenged in legal proceedings, Gallinghouse concluded that there was insufficient evidence to warrant further action.

Gallinghouse was appointed to investigate the allegations involving Kraft on September 9, 1980, pursuant to the request of Attorney General BENJAMIN CIVILETTI. A former U.S. Attorney in New Orleans during the period 1970–1978, he had coordinated an investigation of corruption in the grain export trade that resulted in convictions of many companies and individuals in the mid-1970s. Gallinghouse, a Republican, had also been involved in a successful prosecution of the Louisiana attorney general for perjury, and a failed attempt to convict Orleans Parish District Attorney Jim Garrison of accepting bribes to protect illegal gambling. Although cleared of the charges, voters rejected Garrison at the next election.

Tim Kraft had rallied to the defense of Hamilton Jordan in August 1979 when Jordan came under investigation for alleged cocaine use. Independent Counsel ARTHUR H. CHRISTY found insufficient evidence for an indictment. The following year, Kraft found himself facing similar charges. Testimony alleging his drug use had surfaced during the investigation of Jordan. Reportedly, the source of the allegations was Evan S. Dobelle, Deputy Chairman of the Democratic National Committee. Dobelle had been relieved of most of his campaign duties when Kraft was appointed. Unlike Jordan, Kraft resigned his post while Gallinghouse conducted his investigation. Stepping down on September 14, 1980, Kraft hired Washington attorney Thomas C. Green to defend him. Kraft did not want his situation to reflect badly on President Carter's upcoming re-election bid. Gallinghouse, also mindful of the possible political repercussions of his inquiry, delayed further action on his probe until after the elections.

Gallinghouse's appointment had charged him with investigating specific allegations of cocaine use occurring on or about August 10, 1978, in New Orleans and on or about November 18, 1978, in San Francisco, as well as any other related allegations. His inquiry was two months old when Kraft's attorneys filed a lawsuit in U.S. District Court challenging his authority. *KRAFT v. GALLINGHOUSE* contended that the ETHICS IN GOVERNMENT ACT (1978) unconstitutionally deprived the President and Justice Department of their prosecutorial responsibilities. Kraft's attorneys, Green and A. Raymond Randolph, Jr., characterized Gallinghouse as a *de facto* attorney general with one target—Kraft. The lawsuit also charged that Gallinghouse's recent service as U.S. Attorney made him ineligible for appointment as special prosecutor.

Before the case could be heard, Gallinghouse announced on March 25, 1981, that the evidence against Kraft was insufficient to establish probable cause of criminal wrongdoing. The investigation was ended. Also ended was Kraft's legal action against Gallinghouse's authority. Kraft's exoneration removed any cause for action. Although Kraft subsequently complained about the expense and trauma associated with the investigation, and Civiletti argued that the Jordan and Kraft investigations were proof that the special prosecutor statute was ill-advised, history would prove Gallinghouse's investigation to be comparatively quick and relatively painless. Its course also remained remarkably private with few leaks to embarrass the parties involved. The relative frivolousness of the charge helped fuel calls for revision of the special prosecutor statute in order to allow the attorney general greater discretion in deciding whether an allegation merits further action.

References:

Babcock, Charles R. "Special Prosecutor Investigations Called 'Enormous Waste.' " *Washington Post*, 21 May 1981, sec. A, p. 20.

Brown, Warren. "Carter Aide Steps Down Amid Probe." *Washington Post*, 15 September 1980, sec. A, p. 1.

Kiernan, Laura A. "Former Carter Aide Challenges Constitutionality of Ethics Law." *Washington Post*, 20 November 1980, sec. A, p. 4.

Pound, Edward T. "Inquiry Set on Alleged Drug Use by Kraft, Carter Campaign Aide." *New York Times*, 14 September 1980, sec. A, p. 1.

———. "Kraft Charge Laid to an Aide of Party's." *New York Times*, 17 September 1980, sec. A, p. 1.

Rich, Spencer. "Kraft Is Cleared of Allegations He Used Cocaine." *Washington Post*, 25 March 1981, sec. A, p. 1.

"2nd Charge Studied in Inquiry on Kraft." *New York Times*, 14 October 1980, sec. A, p. 16.

George, Clair E. (1930–   ) CIA Chief of Operations Directorate, 1984–1987. A 33-year veteran of the Central Intelligence Agency, Clair George advanced to the third ranking position in the organization before his involvement in the IRAN-CONTRA affair resulted in his 1992 conviction for lying to Congress during its investigation of the matter. Independent Counsel LAWRENCE WALSH obtained the testimony of George's subordinate ALAN FIERS to help convict George in the second of two trials, the first having ended in a hung jury. Weeks later, President GEORGE BUSH included George in his Christmas Eve pardon shortly before leaving office.

Raised in the steel town of Beaver Falls, Pennsylvania, George worked nights at the steel mill to help support his family after the death of his father, a dairy chemist, in 1947. His mother worked as an administrative aide to the mayor. George majored in Political Science at Pennsylvania State University, where he was a champion debater, earning his degree in 1952. He was accepted to Columbia University's Law School but decided to enlist in the Army instead. After studying Chinese at the Army's language school in Monterey, California, George served in the Counterintelligence Corps in Asia. In 1955 he joined the CIA.

Although the agency, just eight years old at that time, consisted mostly of Ivy League recruits and veterans of the World War II Office of Strategic Services (OSS), George managed to fit in by demonstrating great energy and commitment. George served in Hong Kong and Paris before gaining his first station chief post in Mali in 1964. He began to build a record of Cold War accomplishment while serving in the less-glamorous outposts. After a stint in India, George was promoted to Chief of Operations-External in the Soviet Division at CIA headquarters, where he supervised the recruitment and training of all Soviet agents outside the Eastern Bloc. In 1975, George was appointed station chief in Beirut, a nation in the process of deconstruction that dissolved into civil war the following year. George managed to keep the agency functioning in a period of civil war and terrorism. In 1976, he moved on to Athens after the assassination of station chief Richard Welch. There he helped lower the agency's profile and facilitate dialogue with opposing factions. Three years later, he returned to Washington as Division Chief for Africa. When WILLIAM CASEY was named CIA Director by President RONALD REAGAN in 1981, George became deputy to Casey's Chief of Covert Operations, Max Hugel.

George's involvement in Iran-Contra can be traced to his efforts as William Casey's adviser during the CIA chief's testimony before the Senate Intelligence Committee in 1984. It had been revealed that the CIA had been involved in the mining of Nicaraguan harbors as part of its support for the Contra war against the Sandinistas. Opinions differed as to George's influence. Some, like Intelligence Committee Chief Counsel Victoria Toensing and House Intelligence Committee Chairman Representative Edward BOLAND (D-Massachusetts) considered George to be a truthful source of information, someone who was trying to repair the damage Casey had done by embarking on illegal activities in Central America. Others, like Rob Simmons, Senator Barry Goldwater's Chief of Staff and a former CIA officer, felt that George participated in deliberately misinforming Congress. Casey, obviously pleased with George's assistance, whatever its true nature, promoted him to Chief of the Operations Directorate in July 1984. In this new capacity, George oversaw covert operations in Afghanistan, Angola, Ethiopia, and Cambodia, as well as Central America. His budget exceeded $1 billion, and he directed the activities of 2,500 employees. (Indeed, in defending himself against Iran-Contra charges, George's attorney would later claim that his client was too busy to be personally aware of possible transgressions in Nicaragua.)

On October 5, 1986, a cargo plane carrying supplies to the Contras was shot down over Nicaragua. Surviving crew member EUGENE HASENFUS claimed to be working for a CIA officer named Max Gomez. Because such aid to the Contras had been forbidden under the Boland Amendments, Congress began hearings into the incident. In appearances before congressional hearings on October 10 and 14, George denied knowledge of the Contra supply operation and disavowed any involvement by the CIA. He also professed no knowledge of the identity of Max Gomez. One year later, with the Iran-Contra scandal raging, George modified his testimony by explaining that he had answered questions narrowly to protect the agency. His responses had been intended to convey the fact that the CIA was not institutionally involved in the illegal Contra supply effort. Yes, he had been less than truthful when he had professed ignorance of the entire operation. George proceeded to apologize to Congress for misleading them. Although an internal CIA probe cleared George of any wrongdoing, Director William Webster, who assumed his duties following the death of Casey in May 1987, relieved him of his position. George was offered another job with the agency, but elected to retire.

The investigation of Iran-Contra Independent Counsel Lawrence Walsh led to the indictment of George on September 6, 1991, on charges of lying to Congress and obstructing justice. Walsh's investigation had revealed that George knew "Max Gomez" was, in fact, former CIA officer Felix Rodriguez; that OLIVER NORTH was running the supply operation; and that retired Air Force General RICHARD SECORD was involved. George, faced with the choice of cooperating with Walsh or facing legal proceedings himself, chose to fight the charges. Alan Fiers elected to cooperate, and became Walsh's chief witness against George. George's first trial ended with the announcement on August 26, 1992, that the jury had deadlocked on all nine charges. A poll of jurors indicated that most had favored acquittal. In interviews, jurors appeared to hold Fiers and Casey more responsible than George for Iran-Contra misdeeds.

In George's second trial, he was convicted on two counts of lying to Congress after eleven days of jury deliberation. The verdict, announced on December 9, 1992, found George guilty of false testimony to the House Permanent Committee on Intelligence on October 14, 1986, when denying knowledge of Felix Rodriguez's role in the supply operation, and to the Senate Intelligence Committee on December 3, 1986, when claiming ignorance of the roles played by North and Secord. George faced five years imprisonment and fines of $250,000 on each count. Judge Royce C. Lamberth scheduled sentencing for February 18.

Prosecuting attorney CRAIG E. GILLEN pointed out that this marked the first time that a senior CIA official had been convicted for crimes committed while functioning as an agency official. George's lawyer, Richard A. Hibey, announced that he would appeal.

President George Bush's pardon of December 24, 1992, brought an abrupt halt to the proceedings against George.

References:

Lewis, Neil A. "Ex-Spy Chief Is Convicted of Lying to Congress on Iran-Contra Affair." *New York Times*, 10 December 1992, sec. A, p. 1.
———. "Iran-Contra Trial of Ex-CIA Man Ends in a Deadlock." *New York Times*, 27 August 1992, sec. A, p. 1.
Walsh, Lawrence. *Firewall: The Iran-Contra Conspiracy and Cover-up*. New York: W. W. Norton, 1997.
Weiser, Benjamin. "Company Man." *Washington Post*, 17 May 1992, sec. W, p. 10. Comprehensive, 11,000-word account of George's career.
———. "Ex-CIA Operative Chooses to Stand and Fight Charges." *Washington Post*, 8 September 1991, sec. A, p. 27.

Gesell, Gerhard A. (1910–1993) U.S. District Court Judge, D.C., 1968–1993. Judge Gerhard Gesell's tenure as D.C. District Court Judge spanned both the WATERGATE and IRAN-CONTRA eras. Though he did participate in some decisions related to the former affair, his impact was greatest on the latter, especially in the 1989 trial of OLIVER NORTH. Judge Gesell's decisions facilitated dismissal of the conspiracy charges brought against North by allowing the defendant to claim that large amounts of classified information were necessary to his defense. Even though Gesell refused to dismiss the case against North, the subsequent CLASSIFIED INFORMATION PROCEDURES ACT (CIPA) affidavits filed by Attorney General RICHARD THORNBURGH ultimately resulted in dismissal of the most important charges.

Born in Los Angeles, Gerhard Gesell built his legal reputation in Washington, D.C., as Dean Acheson's law partner in the firm of Covington & Burling between the years 1941 and 1967. As a litigator, he specialized in complex cases. He was a hardworking, demanding judge, respected by the attorneys who argued cases in his court. Gesell was nearing his 78th birthday when the Iran-Contra cases were presented to him. He initially did his best to expedite matters. After North and codefendants JOHN POINDEXTER, RICHARD SECORD, and AL- BERT HAKIM pleaded not guilty on March 24, 1988, Gesell announced that a preliminary hearing would occur on April 12 in order to determine whether evidence collected by Independent Counsel LAWRENCE WALSH during his investigation would be admissible. He was determined to quickly rule on the question of whether Walsh had succeeded in making his case without recourse to the immunized testimony of the defendants during their appearances before congressional investigative committees. Gesell stated that he hoped to try the defendants before the November elections.

Complicating matters was a January ruling by a panel of the U.S. Court of Appeals to the effect that the ETHICS IN GOVERNMENT ACT (1978) was unconstitutional. Independent Counsel Lawrence Walsh appeared to be protected from this decision by a backup appointment awarded to him by the Justice Department after he had begun his work in December 1986. (*MORRISON v. OLSON* would reverse the appeals court decision later in 1988.)

Gesell had difficulty determining how a successful conspiracy trial could be held given the nature of the immunized testimony involved. Testimony at trial by any of the defendants entitled the others to use their immunized testimony during cross-examination, stated Gesell. On the other hand, trying the defendants separately was unacceptable, according to Gesell, because none of the defendants would receive the benefit of the others' testimony.

By June, Gesell had determined that the classified information issue posed an issue that was more serious than the question of immunized testimony. Unless the defendants were allowed to reveal that the conduct for which they were being tried represented usual procedures that had been employed in other covert operations, then their defense would be seriously hampered. Walsh maintained that the defense was exaggerating the problem. A simple code, utilizing numbers and letters to represent countries or individuals, could be used as it had been during congressional testimony. Rejecting a defense challenge to the constitutionality of CIPA, Gesell gave North until July 11 to specify precisely which classified information he intended to use in court. An interagency task force would have until August 1 to review North's list and determine if disclosure of the information would endanger national security.

Gesell complained of delays caused by both the REAGAN administration and the independent counsel's office. The administration was taking too much time declassifying government information for use during trial, and the independent counsel was requesting an additional month in order to get an additional 150,000 pages of classified documents cleared for release. As the November election deadline passed, Gesell tried in vain to arrive at a compromise that would protect national security while allowing the conspiracy charge to be tried. Along the way, he contemptuously dismissed a defense contention that the BOLAND AMENDMENT, barring aid to the Contras, did not apply to the National Security Council. During pretrial hearings on December 2, Gesell ruled that certain National Security Agency reports were vital to North's defense. Because the reports in question were received by North's superiors, they would be useful in arguing that North's actions were sanctioned by the administration. Walsh's appeal to Thornburgh proved fruitless. The attorney general would not allow disclosure of the information in question. By the end of December, the prosecution agreed to drop the conspiracy count.

Oliver North's trial on the peripheral charges of lying to Congress, destroying documents, and accepting an illegal gratuity began on January 30, 1989. On May 4 the jury found the defendant guilty on three of the nine counts. Although Gesell instructed the jury that North failed to demonstrate that he had acted with the authorization of his superiors, the jury had apparently found persuasive the defense argument that he had. On July 5, Gesell sentenced North to pay a fine of $150,000 and perform 1,200 hours of community service. Concurrent jail sentences of one, two, and three years were suspended. In explanation of his sentence, Gesell made it clear that he believed that North, although not explicitly authorized, was in fact carrying out the wishes of his superiors.

Gesell's decisions in the Iran-Contra cases served to weaken the hand of the independent counsel by permitting the attorney general to prevent prosecution based on CIPA considerations. As a result, it was clear that the Office of Independent Counsel did not solve all possible conflict of interest questions in the prosecution of executive branch misconduct.

References:

"Confidence in Judge Gesell." *Washington Post*, 11 February 1989, sec. A, p. 24.
Elsasser, Glen. "North Judge Reluctant to Call Bush, Reagan." *Chicago Tribune*, 28 January 1989, sec. C, p. 4.
Harriger, Katy J. *Independent Justice: The Federal Special Prosecutor in American Politics*. Lawrence: University Press of Kansas, 1992.
"Judge Blasts North, Rejects Dismissal Plea." *Chicago Tribune*, 11 November 1988, sec. C, p. 4.
"Judge Gives North Trial a Push." *Chicago Tribune*, 23 June 1988, sec. C, p. 5.
"Judge: Immunity Clouding Iran-Contra Trial." *Chicago Tribune*, 27 May 1988, sec. C, p. 9.
"Judge Scolds Iran-Contra Prosecutors." *Los Angeles Times*, 12 April 1988, sec. A, p. 2.
"Judge Sees Barrier in Iran-Contra Case." *Chicago Tribune*, 7 June 1988, sec. C, p. 4.
"Judge Wants Iran Arms Figures Tried before November Voting." *San Diego Union-Tribune*, 25 March 1988, sec. A, p. 3.
"Judge Warns of Risks of North Trial." *Chicago Tribune*, 22 November 1988, sec. C, p. 4.
Walsh, Lawrence. *Firewall: The Iran-Contra Conspiracy and Cover-up*. New York: W.W. Norton, 1997.

Gillen, Craig (1952–) Deputy Independent Counsel, Iran-Contra investigation. Hired by IRAN-CONTRA Independent Counsel LAWRENCE WALSH in December 1989, Craig Gillen was initially added to the independent counsel's team in order to take charge of the investigation's conclusion. Walsh had already secured convictions against OLIVER NORTH and JOHN POINDEXTER. The investigation appeared to be approaching its end. During the following two years, however, Gillen's prosecutorial zeal helped reinvigorate the inquiry. He was rewarded with increasing responsibility, spearheading the prosecution of CIA officials ALAN FIERS, DUANE CLARRIDGE, and CLAIR GEORGE. In December 1991, Walsh, having received official permission from the D.C. Circuit judges who had appointed him, formally named Gillen Deputy Independent Counsel. By the start of 1992 Gillen was looking forward to prosecuting the highest-ranking official yet targeted by the inquiry, former Secretary of Defense CASPAR WEINBERGER.

Educated at the University of North Carolina and Emory University Law School, Gillen joined the U.S. Attorney's Office in 1978. As Assistant U.S. Attorney for the Northern District of Georgia, he had his greatest impact as lead attorney for the office's Organized Crime Drug Enforcement Task Force. Gillen's successes included helping convict cocaine smuggler Harold Rosenthal, racketeer Michael J. Thevis, and Henry County Sheriff Jimmy Glass (on public corruption charges). In 1989, Gillen's work drew national attention when he successfully prosecuted Representative Patrick Swindall (R-Georgia) for lying to a federal grand jury regarding his connections to money launderers involved in drug trade. Gillen's aggressiveness and tenacity, coupled with his experience in politically related cases impressed U.S. Attorney LARRY D. THOMPSON, later an independent counsel himself. Thompson recommended Gillen to Walsh.

Charged with reviewing documentation assembled earlier in the Independent Counsel's investigation, Gillen uncovered numerous inconsistencies and gaps in the record. Gillen convinced Walsh that the testimony of former Assistant Secretary of State ELLIOTT ABRAMS warranted closer scrutiny. Gillen's suggested avenue of investigation proved instrumental in uncovering the extent to which the CIA was implicated in concealing the Iran-Contra connection. Walsh was pleased enough to grant Gillen lead prosecutor status in cases involving former CIA officials Fiers, Clarridge, and George. Gillen's review of the inquiry's existing record also pointed investigators in the direction of former Secretary of State GEORGE SHULTZ and Vice President GEORGE BUSH. Subsequent examination of both brought the investigation very close to the President. Weinberger was indicted, and Bush appeared to be implicated. Walsh indicated that Gillen would take charge of the case against Weinberger.

Gillen was pitted against Weinberger's attorney ROBERT BENNETT. The experienced criminal defense attorney quickly moved to have Gillen disqualified from the case, because one of the counts in the indictment concerned a conversation between Gillen and Weinberger in which it was alleged that Bennett's client had lied. How could Gillen prosecute a case in which he was likely to be called as a witness? Walsh argued against Gillen's disqualification on the grounds that the apparent conflict did not reach the required standard of compelling necessity. Nevertheless, indications were that Gillen might very well be forced to step aside. With this in mind, Walsh replaced him with San Francisco trial attorney JAMES BROSNAHAN.

Gillen's political instincts told him that indicting Weinberger in the fall of 1992 would appear to be a calculated effort to hurt Bush's chances of being elected president. Gillen disagreed with Brosnahan's decision to ignore the political ramifications of his conduct in the matter, but did not want to intrude. As a result, in advancing the case against Weinberger, the office released evidence implicating Bush. This was seized upon by the CLINTON campaign for whatever political advantage it afforded them. The inevitable charges of political partisanship ensued.

The Weinberger trial never occurred because the Iran-Contra investigation was effectively terminated with Bush's Christmas Eve pardon of the inquiry's principal targets at the end of 1992. Gillen returned to practice law in Georgia.

References:

Klaidman, Daniel, and Ann Woolner. "Craig Gillen Takes the Stage in Iran-Contra." *Legal Times*, 22 June 1992, p. 1.

Walsh, Lawrence. *Firewall: The Iran-Contra Conspiracy and Cover-up*. New York: W. W. Norton, 1997.

Ginsburg, Ruth Bader (1933–) Associate Justice, U.S. Supreme Court, 1993– . While serving as U.S. Court of Appeals Judge for the D.C. Circuit (1972–1993), Ruth Bader Ginsburg participated in a 1988 decision that temporarily invalidated the ETHICS IN GOVERNMENT ACT (1978) that created the Office of Independent Counsel. In dissenting from her colleagues Judge LAURENCE H. SILBERMAN, author of the majority opinion, and Judge Stephen F. Williams, Judge Ginsburg upheld the constitutionality of the independent counsel mechanism. She characterized it as a reasonable attempt to deal with possible abuse by the executive branch of government. Ginsburg believed that the attorney general continued to maintain enough authority over the process to honor the constitutional principle of separation of powers.

Originally considered an unlikely case to test the constitutionality of the independent counsel law, ALEXIA MORRISON's investigation of former Assistant Attorney General THEODORE OLSON provided the opportunity, when Olson, joined by former Justice Department officials Edward Schmults and Carol Dinkins, challenged the legality of the statute. Morrison's investigation centered around whether Olson had misled Congress during that body's probe of the Environmental Protection Agency's Superfund scandal. After U.S. District Court Judge Aubrey E. Robinson upheld its constitutionality, Ginsburg was named to the three-judge panel that would hear the appeal.

On January 22, 1988, Judge Silberman, joined by Judge Williams, issued the majority ruling in *IN RE SEALED CASE* that held the independent counsel statute to be unconstitutional. Because the independent counsel is not required to operate under Justice Department guidelines, argued Silberman, the statute represents an unacceptable incursion into the executive's prerogatives and an unconscionable invasion of the individual's liberty. Judge Ginsburg, however, in her dissent, highlighted the significant authority that remained with the attorney general under the independent counsel statute: the power to initiate a preliminary investigation, and the power to decide if further investigation by an independent counsel is warranted. In addition, Ginsburg argued, the attorney general is not required to explain a decision against seeking appointment of an independent counsel in any detail. Nor are the attorney general's initial decisions regarding the independent counsel subject to judicial review. Furthermore, Ginsburg noted, the attorney general was vested with the authority to remove an independent counsel for cause. Finally, the attorney general's application for appointment of an independent counsel allows boundaries to be set for the investigation. In her analysis, Ginsburg clearly rejected the formalistic approach to separation of powers questions represented by *BOWSHER v. SYNAR* (1986), and allied herself with the more functional interpretation of *COMMODITY FUTURES TRADING COMMISSION v. SCHOR* (1986). Ginsburg's arguments, though not decisive at the appeals court level, would be validated by the Supreme Court later that year in MORRISON v. OLSON.

When Ginsburg was nominated for a seat on the Supreme Court by President Bill CLINTON in 1993, she was hailed as a likely consensus builder, a healing influence promising to bring together an ideologically fractured Court. The first nominee by a Democratic president since Thurgood Marshall in 1967, and the first Jewish justice since Abe Fortas (1969), Ginsburg's record was still moderate enough to win the support of mainstream Republicans like ROBERT DOLE. A graduate of Cornell University and Harvard and Columbia Law schools, Ginsburg taught law at Rutgers and Columbia Universities. While heading the American Civil Liberties Union's Women's Rights Project, Ginsburg argued six landmark sex discrimination cases before the Supreme Court, winning five of them. She was successful in influencing the judges to employ equal protection principles to strike down laws that discriminated against women. Ginsburg was named to the D.C. Circuit Court of Appeals by President Jimmy CARTER in 1980. Her service on the Court of Appeals, however, identified her as a moderate who frequently joined conservative judges such as Laurence Silberman and KENNETH STARR in divided decisions. Ginsburg's mixed record helped identify her as a new Democrat, representative of a new more moderate liberalism favored by the President.

References:

Biskupic, Joseph. "Looking at Human Problems with Judicial Restraint." *Washington Post*, 20 July 1993, sec. A, p. 1.

Marcus, Ruth. "Judge Ruth Ginsburg Named to High Court." *Washington Post*, 15 June 1993, sec. A, p. 1.

———. "Judges Weigh Independent Counsel Law." *Washington Post*, 17 September 1987, sec. A, p. 19.

Rosen, Jeffrey. "The New Look of Liberalism on the Court." *New York Times*, 5 October 1997, sec. F, p. 60.

"Ruth Bader Ginsburg in Her Own Words." *Legal Times*, 21 June 1993, p. 12.

Salans, Marc R. "Independent Counsel: The First Ten Years." *George Washington Law Review* 56 (1988): 900–936. A significant portion of the article is devoted to the Olson decisions including Ginsburg's dissent.

Giuliani, Rudolph W. (1944–   ) Mayor, New York City, 1994–   ; U.S. Attorney, U.S. District Court, Southern District, New York, 1983–1989; Associate

Attorney General, 1981–1983. During his service with the Justice Department and the U.S. District Court, Rudolph Giuliani participated in the investigations of two individuals who were targeted for possible examination by special prosecutors/independent counsels—RICHARD ALLEN and LYN NOFZIGER. He also worked for an attorney general who himself became the subject of investigations by Independent Counsel—EDWIN MEESE. Giuliani's experiences enabled him to view the special prosecutor/independent counsel mechanism from various perspectives, and develop informed opinions regarding its effectiveness. He freely communicated his thoughts in public forums when called upon to do so.

Giuliani's first experience with an investigation that had special prosecutor potential was the probe of President RONALD REAGAN's National Security Adviser Richard Allen in November 1981. Allen had accepted a gift in return for arranging an interview between a Japanese journalist and Nancy Reagan. He was quickly cleared of wrongdoing by a cursory FBI investigation. Soon after, it was realized that the ETHICS IN GOVERNMENT ACT (1978) required a more careful preliminary investigation by the Justice Department. Giuliani, then associate attorney general, joined other Justice Department officials in requesting the FBI to conduct a more thorough investigation of the Allen matter. The Justice Department could not complete its inquiry until the Bureau's field work was in order. The Department wanted to produce a report that would not be subject to question. After completion of the preliminary investigation, Attorney General WILLIAM FRENCH SMITH deemed the matter unworthy of further investigation, because Allen's error was inadvertent. No special prosecutor was requested.

In April 1982, Giuliani appeared before a Senate subcommittee considering REAUTHORIZATION of the Ethics in Government Act. Though acknowledging that the proposed amendments to the act, which would make it more difficult to trigger the process, were an improvement, he voiced the opinion that there was no need for the law. Giuliani contended that the statute represented a lack of faith in the ability of the Justice Department to do its job. The attorney general alone, stated Giuliani, should determine the appropriate course of action in sensitive cases. In rare cases where an independent investigation was warranted, the attorney general should be allowed to appoint one. Under the current system, Giuliani maintained, the entire Justice Department was being asked to recuse itself in certain cases. Giuliani considered it an absurdity that no one in the department was considered capable of handling cases of executive-branch misconduct. He hoped in vain that the House would hold its own hearings on the issue, and conceivably build momentum for the law's repeal. Despite support from former WATERGATE-era Attorney General ELLIOT RICHARDSON, Giuliani's views were rejected. The majority echoed the sentiments of Senator Thomas Eagleton (D-Missouri) that the appearance of impropriety needed to be avoided. Consequently, the statute was renewed, with amendments, for another five years.

In 1986, Giuliani conducted the Justice Department's preliminary investigation of former Reagan aide Lyn Nofziger. Nofziger was suspected of lobbying his former government colleagues on behalf of the Washington, D.C., public relations firm for whom he worked, securing a $31 million Army contract for Wedtech Corporation as a result. If true, such behavior stood in violation of the Ethics in Government Act, which mandated a one-year waiting period before initiating such contact. Nofziger's case closely resembled that of former Reagan aide MICHAEL DEAVER. Giuliani's investigation demonstrated that the allegations against Nofziger were substantial enough to warrant the request of an independent counsel. JAMES McKAY was assigned to the case.

Giuliani's investigation of Nofziger introduced him to the many attempts by Wedtech to lobby government officials for contracts. When Attorney General Edwin Meese came under investigation, Giuliani was placed in an awkward position. Although Independent Counsel James McKay eventually determined that the evidence of wrongdoing was insufficient to justify indictment of Meese, Giuliani joined others in criticizing Meese's behavior. He felt that Meese's disregard for ethical proprieties made him ill-suited to head the Justice Department. During the Wedtech-related trial of Rep. Mario Biaggi (D-New York) in July 1988, Giuliani apparently authorized the prosecutor's characterization of Meese as "a sleaze" for unethical dealings with the corporation. Meese resigned as attorney general in August.

After leaving federal government service in 1989, Giuliani practiced private law until his election as New York's mayor in 1994. Two of Giuliani's top assistants while U.S. Attorney, David Zornow and Michael Bromwich, served on the staff of IRAN-CONTRA Independent Counsel LAWRENCE WALSH.

References:

Jackson, Robert L. "Nofziger Faces Inquiry on Lobbying." *Los Angeles Times*, 5 November 1986, sec. A, p. 16.

Jackson, Robert L., and Ronald J. Ostrow. "Allegations Covered by Ethics Act, Justice Dept. Rules." *Los Angeles Times*, 25 November 1986, sec. A, p. 17.

Lardner, George, Jr. "Administration, Senators Air Ethics Law Changes." *Washington Post*, 29 April 1982, sec. A, p. 5.

———. "Prosecutor Labels Meese 'a Sleaze.' " *Washington Post*, 23 July 1988, sec. A, p. 3.

Maitland, Leslie. "Revision of Law on Special Prosecutors Is Backed." *New York Times*, 9 September 1982, sec. B, p. 14.

Pound, Edward T. "Agents of F.B.I. Told to Resume Inquiry on Allen." *New York Times*, 21 November 1981, sec. A, p. 1.

Smith, Jeffrey R., and Howard Kurtz. "Meese Was in Wrong Job." *Washington Post*, 17 February 1989, sec. A, p. 25.

Grant, Ulysses S. (1822–1885) U.S. President, 1868–1877. The veneration of (Hiram) Ulysses Simpson Grant following the victory of the Union Army in the Civil War resulted in his unanimous nomination for the presidency at the Republican convention and easy election over his Democratic opponent in 1868.

Unfortunately, his administration, especially during his second term, would be continually subject to scandal. Historians generally consider Grant to have been nearly as unfit for the presidency as WARREN HARDING, although at least one recent biographer takes a kinder view (Frank Scaturro, *President Grant Reconsidered*, University Press of America, 1998). In 1875, the Whiskey Scandal erupted in St. Louis where federal agents were implicated in fraudulent practices concerning collection of the federal liquor tax. Grant's personal secretary and close friend, Orville Babcock was said to be involved. In May, Grant appointed former senator JOHN BROOKS HENDERSON (R-Missouri) special counsel to help prosecute violators. This represented the first instance in which a special federal prosecutor was named to investigate executive branch misconduct. Henderson's tenure lasted only until December when he was dismissed by Grant, who believed the inquiry was becoming too critical of his administration. Treasury Secretary Benjamin Bristow concluded the investigation, bringing many of the offenders to trial in 1876.

Serving purely at the pleasure of the president, Henderson was easily disposed of when his remarks made the White House uncomfortable. Bristow, however, successfully prosecuted and won convictions against Revenue Supervisor John McDonald, his assistant John Joyce, Chief Clerk of Internal Revenue in Washington William Avery, and St. Louis political boss William McKee. Babcock was tried and found not guilty. A congressional probe in 1876 concluded that Grant had heard of the Whiskey Ring's existence, and Babcock's likely involvement in it, but chose not to believe such reports. While many of the scandals that erupted in Grant's administration, including the Credit Mobilier railroad scandal and the Whiskey Ring, originated before Grant's presidency, they were uncovered during Grant's tenure in the White House, and greatly damaged his reputation and that of the Republican Party.

The appointment/dismissal scenario originating with Grant's selection of Henderson in 1875 would be re-enacted when HARRY TRUMAN charged NEWBOLD MORRIS with addressing the TAX SCANDAL in 1952 and RICHARD NIXON delegated investigation of WATERGATE to ARCHIBALD COX in 1973. The obvious inability of a non-independent prosecutor to conduct an unfettered investigation of the executive eventually helped give rise to the independent counsel statute in 1978.

References:

Eastland, Terry. *Ethics, Politics, and the Independent Counsel Executive Power, Executive Vice 1789–1989*. Washington, D.C.: National Legal Center for the Public Interest, 1989. Chapter 2, "The History Before the Law," mentions Grant's appointment of Henderson in listing five pre-Watergate appointments of special prosecutors. Eastland refers to David A. Logan's 35-page study, *Historical Uses of a Special Prosecutor: The Administrations of Presidents Grant, Coolidge and Truman* (Congressional Research Service, 1973). This volume is held only at the U.S. Senate Library.

McFeeley, William S. *Grant: A Biography*. New York: W. W. Norton, 1981. Chapter 24, "Wedding and Whiskey," addresses the Whiskey Ring scandal.
Seematter, Mary E. "The St. Louis Whiskey Ring." *Gateway Heritage* (Spring 1988): 32–42.

Graymail. A legal strategy, successfully employed during the IRAN-CONTRA trials of OLIVER NORTH and JOHN POINDEXTER, "graymail" forces the prosecution to abandon part or all of its case against defendants who threaten to reveal government secrets during court proceedings. While the Iran-Contra trials brought the tactic to the attention of the public, it had been employed by espionage defendants frequently in years past with considerable success. Because such cases invariably involved classified information, it appeared to many prosecutors that they were effectively prevented from acting precisely against those whose crimes were of greatest import. Offenders whose acts subverted the democratic process (but were occasionally committed in the name of national interest), could not be charged because their defense required the use of sensitive documents.

In 1980, a legislative solution to this quandary was adopted in the form of the CLASSIFIED INFORMATION PROCEDURES ACT (CIPA). It attempted to place limits on the amount of documentation that defendants could reasonably claim was vital to their defense. It also specified procedures to be employed for the use of classified information during trial. Trial judges were encouraged to employ creative substitutions for sensitive material that would allow defendants to claim documentary support for actions being challenged without divulging specific details. Problems posed by CIPA include significant increase in the time needed to prepare for trial, as well as constitutional concerns raised by defendants who claim that their Fifth and Sixth Amendment rights are being infringed.

CIPA, successfully utilized in the early 1980s, was an insufficient answer to the challenges posed in the prosecution of the Iran-Contra defendants. Approximately 30,000 pages of classified information was deemed relevant to the case, but none of it could be publicly revealed in its original form. Judge GERHARD GESELL worked with Independent Counsel LAWRENCE WALSH and North defense attorney BRENDAN SULLIVAN in an effort to accommodate reasonable use of classified information, or acceptable substitutions thereof at trial. In December 1988, Gesell contended that much of the voluminous material demanded by the defense was irrelevant. The judge found defense tactics obstructive. He accused them of employing "graymail." Walsh, however, appeared to be compliant with all court orders. Gesell characterized the independent counsel's actions as generous toward the defense. In crucial rulings, however, Gesell ruled that sensitive material used by the defense would have to be presented in its entirety at trial. Only the source of the material and the method by which it had been obtained could be excised. Under these terms, the government refused to release the documents in question, and Walsh was forced to drop the most serious charges—conspiracy and theft—in January 1989.

Graymail proved an effective tactic during the Iran-Contra affair, because it highlights a problem yet to be satisfactorily addressed in certain instances. How can a defendant's constitutional guarantees be protected in proceedings that call for full and fair disclosure of large amounts of classified information? CIPA represents a partial solution. It remains for creative scholars and jurists to build upon this foundation.

References:

Holmes, Steven. "Giving in to 'Graymail.' " *Time*, January 16, 1989, p. 24.
Lacovara, Philip A. " Graymail, Secrets and the North Trial." *Los Angeles Times*, 5 January 1989, sec. B, p. 7.
Strasser, Fred. "North Case Appears On Course for Trial." *National Law Journal* (26 December 1988): 3.

Gregory, Thomas Watt (1861–1933) Nominated Special Prosecutor Teapot Dome Affair, 1924. Having served as President Woodrow Wilson's attorney general (1914–1919), Thomas Gregory was selected by President CALVIN COOLIDGE, along with SILAS STRAWN, to conduct an investigation of the TEAPOT DOME Affair. Coolidge, reacting to congressional pressure, felt the necessity of initiating an inquiry into the questionable sale of Naval oil reserves to private companies. Before Gregory's appointment could be confirmed by the Senate, it was revealed that he had previously been retained by EDWARD L. DOHENY, oil magnate implicated in the Teapot Dome Affair.

The son of a Virginia physician who died of pneumonia while serving in the Confederate Army, Gregory was raised by his maternal grandparents in Mississippi. After receiving his law degree from the University of Texas in 1885, he practiced in Austin, entering into partnership with Lynn Batts in 1900. Gregory & Batts successfully represented the state of Texas in its suit against the Waters-Pierce Oil Company, winning a settlement of $1,800,000. As attorney general during World War I, Gregory led enforcement of the nation's emergency alien, sedition, and sabotage acts, while assisting in administration of the military draft. He defeated efforts to substitute military tribunals for normal court proceedings when hearing violations of the emergency acts, because he believed that the war did not mandate suspension of citizenship rights. After resigning from the Cabinet on March 4, 1919, Gregory served on Wilson's second industrial conference during the following year.

Gregory had returned to Texas to practice law in Houston when he was chosen by President Coolidge on January 29, 1924, as a special prosecutor to examine the Teapot Dome Affair. Coolidge decided to appoint a pair of counsels, one Democrat and one Republican. Gregory's Republican partner would be Chicago attorney Silas Strawn. Gregory's candidacy would be short-lived, however, expiring along with the presidential aspirations of California Democrat William Gibbs McAdoo during Senate hearings held on January 31.

Senator James A. Reed (D-Missouri) had Edwin Doheny recalled for questioning, apparently for the purpose of implicating McAdoo in the Teapot Dome scandal. Reed, with presidential designs of his own, needed to eclipse front-runner McAdoo. Accordingly, he requested that Senate Public Lands Committee Chairman Irvine Lenroot ask Doheny whether he had ever employed any cabinet officers subsequent to their government service. Doheny revealed that he had hired both McAdoo and Gregory on separate occasions. Gregory had performed services related to Doheny's Mexican oil properties. Reed's design succeeded in sinking not only McAdoo's presidential campaign but also Gregory's pending appointment. Now tied by testimony to Doheny's oil interests, Gregory's appointment as Teapot Dome investigator appeared as a clear conflict of interest. As a result, Gregory withdrew his candidacy on February 4.

Reed's machinations did not secure the nomination for himself. Instead, he incurred the wrath of party leader and early Teapot Dome congressional investigator Senator THOMAS J. WALSH (D-Montana). The nomination went to John W. Davis. Strawn, indirectly linked to oil interests, stepped aside not long after Gregory. Coolidge replaced them both with OWEN J. ROBERTS and ATLEE POMERENE, who conducted a successful investigation and prosecution of government officials implicated in the scandal. Gregory was eminently qualified to do the same. It is unlikely that his ties to Doheny would have influenced his prospective prosecutorial service, but his investigation's findings might well have been received with skepticism.

References:

National Cyclopaedia of American Biography, volume 27, under "Gregory, Thomas Watt."
Ise, John. *The United States Oil Policy*. New Haven: Yale University Press, 1926. Chapter 25, "The Naval Reserves and the Teapot Dome Investigation," covers Gregory's appointment and discovery of his ties to Doheny.
Noggle, Burl. *Teapot Dome: Oil and Politics in the 1920's*. Baton Rouge: Louisiana State University Press, 1962.

Griswold, Erwin N. (1904–1994) Solicitor General of the United States, 1967–1973. As solicitor general during the administration of President RICHARD NIXON, Erwin Griswold argued unsuccessfully that the federal government had a right to halt publication of the Pentagon Papers in order to protect national security interests during the Vietnam War. In 1975, his broad judicial and political experience was called upon by the crafters of the ETHICS IN GOVERNMENT ACT (1978) who sought advice on creation of a statutory remedy to executive-branch misconduct. In his last years, Griswold continued to offer commentary on the direction of the nation's judiciary while practicing law with the Washington, D.C., firm of Jones, Day, Reavis & Pogue.

A self-described liberal Republican, Griswold was a Harvard law professor and dean for 33 years (1934–1967). During that time, he spoke out against Senator Joseph McCarthy's (R-Wisconsin) attacks on suspected Communists, and helped plan the 1954 desegregation of the nation's public schools. Lyndon

Johnson selected him as solicitor general, and he stayed on under President Nixon who called upon him to convince the Supreme Court that publication of the Pentagon Papers, which called into question the official version of America's entry into the Vietnam War, should cease. Griswold's national security argument was rejected in a 6–3 vote. In later years, Griswold came to realize that the actual documents published did not pose a threat. Those that might have were never released to the media.

Griswold's tenure in the Justice Department extended into the WATERGATE era. Leaving the administration not long before President Nixon ordered the firing of Special Prosecutor ARCHIBALD COX, Griswold nearly had to face the decision left to his replacement, ROBERT BORK, in October 1973 after Attorney General ELLIOT RICHARDSON and Deputy WILLIAM RUCKLE-SHAUS resigned rather than comply. Griswold's legal experience and proximity to the Watergate saga convinced the Senate Committee on Government Operations to seek his advice on a possible legislative remedy to future executive-branch wrongdoing. The committee was about to consider ABRAHAM RIBICOFF's Watergate Reorganization and Reform Act of 1975 (S. 495). Griswold argued against removing responsibility for maintaining executive-branch integrity from the Justice Department. Instead, maintained Griswold, the executive must be held more strictly accountable for carrying out such duties. Griswold's sentiments were echoed by Clark Clifford, Philip Lacovara, Elliot Richardson, and Harold Seidman, all of whom also responded to the committee's request. Griswold favored creation of a new "Division of Government Crimes" within the Justice Department to be supervised by an assistant attorney general. The division would oversee the conduct of all three branches of government. Congress would be notified if investigations were hampered. This idea was given legislative identity by Senators HOWARD BAKER (R-Tennessee) and CHARLES PERCY (R-Illinois) as S. 2734. Unfortunately for Griswold, prevailing opinion in the wake of Watergate mandated defeat of this initiative. Concepts that could allow for conflict of interest generally met with failure.

During his long career, Griswold argued over 125 cases before the Supreme Court, his first in 1934 before Chief Justice CHARLES EVANS HUGHES (whom he regarded as the best he ever faced). Justice Felix Frankfurter had been one of his law school professors. Although a supporter of current Chief Justice William Rehnquist's original candidacy for the Court in 1986, Griswold came to regard his tenure as overly conservative. Griswold testified against the candidacy of Clarence Thomas for the Court, and during his last years, Griswold expressed concern that *Roe v. Wade* (1973) and federal civil rights legislation might be struck down.

References:

Baker, Howard H. "The Proposed Judicially Appointed Independent Counsel Office of Public Attorney." *Southwestern Law Journal* 29 (1975): 671–683. Credits Griswold with providing Senators Baker and Percy with the ideological basis for their legislation.

Harriger, Katy J. *Independent Justice: The Federal Special Prosecutor in American Politics*. Lawrence: University Press of Kansas, 1992. Chapter 3, "A Watergate Legacy," includes discussion of Griswold's advice to those seeking to craft a legislative preventative to future Watergates.

"A Lawyer Who Spoke Up." *New York Times*, 23 November 1994, sec. A, p. 22.

Torry, Saundra. "At 87, Erwin N. Griswold Is the Dean of Supreme Court Observers." *Washington Post*, 15 July 1991, sec. F, p. 5.

H

Hakim, Albert A. (1936–   ) Iranian-American businessman and arms supplier to the Contras. Partner of retired Air Force General RICHARD SECORD, Albert Hakim participated in the effort headed by White House aide Colonel OLIVER NORTH to supply the Nicaraguan Contras with weapons. During 1985 and 1986, Hakim assisted in arranging a series of six weapons purchases through the use of false foreign corporations. The money involved was secured through private contributions, enabling those involved to claim that they did not violate the BOLAND AMENDMENTS barring government aid to the Nicaraguan rebels.

During the 1970s, Albert Hakim was a supplier of electronic equipment to the Shah of Iran. Hakim's company in California's "silicon valley" produced the products employed by the Iranian secret police and air force. Hakim traveled regularly to Teheran in arranging the commercial transactions. In his travels, Hakim became acquainted with former CIA operative Edwin P. Wilson, a competitor for Iranian contracts, and Richard Secord, a military adviser to the Shah's air force. Wilson would later be convicted of illegally supplying arms to Libya's Muammar Qaddafi. Secord resigned from government service in 1982, after it was suspected that he was involved in a plan to overbill the pentagon for arms sales to Egypt. This EATSCO (Egyptian American Transport and Services Corporation) scandal involved the same sort of Swiss bank accounts and layers of dummy corporations utilized by arms suppliers during the IRAN-CONTRA affair. After his resignation, Secord went to work for Hakim's company, Stanford Technology Trading International. Hakim became a naturalized American citizen after the fall of the Shah. Accustomed to operating in an environment where monetary rewards were expected in return for government services, Hakim agreed to assist Secord in establishing a financial system for supplying the Contras.

Independent Counsel LAWRENCE WALSH encountered significant obstacles in attempting to prosecute Hakim for his role in the Iran-Contra affair. Hakim, like many other Iran-Contra defendants, was offered IMMUNITY in return for his testimony before Congress. Walsh could not use such testimony, or even leads obtained from such testimony, against the defendant. Hakim's use of Swiss bank accounts posed further problems. Even if Walsh were able to obtain release of such records (after an anticipated lengthy delay, during which Hakim could employ a number of techniques aimed at blocking such release), it would be questionable whether he could transmit the records to Congress without special permission of the Swiss authorities.

Initially, Walsh was hopeful that testimony secured from Swiss banker Willard I. Zucker in return for immunity might be useful. Hakim had recruited Zucker of the Compagnie de Services Fiduciairies (CSF) to construct a hidden financial network for financing the Contras and to handle the profits that accrued. Zucker also testified that Hakim authorized him to open a $200,000 investment account for Oliver North's wife after she had complained that her husband's work was insufficiently compensated to provide for the educational needs of the couple's four children. Had Hakim lost North as his White House connection, many of the arms deals may have been terminated.

Hakim fled to Europe in early 1987, while his lawyers attempted to negotiate immunity deals from both Congress and the Independent Counsel Office. Immunity was arranged from Congress in return for Hakim's testimony in June. Walsh could not view Hakim's appearance before the Iran-Contra committee. Hakim confirmed Zucker's description of the account established for North's wife, denying that it represented a kickback. He also testified that after EUGENE HASENFUS's plane had been shot down on October 5, 1986, North had departed a negotiation session with the Iranians, authorizing Hakim to conclude arrangements. Hakim, in opposition to the administration's stated policy of not dealing with terrorists, settled for the Iranian pledge to release a sole hostage before election day in the United States. He also promised to arrange a method for releasing seventeen Iranian-backed prisoners being held in Kuwaiti prisons, all members of Islamic Call, a terrorist group based in Lebanon. Critics commented on Hakim's lack of sensitivity. During testimony, when asked if he felt like Secretary of State for the day while negotiating with the Iranians, Hakim responded that his position was much better, because his achievements could include millions of dollars in profits. Some committee members questioned North's judgment in recruiting someone like Hakim.

Hakim was included in an indictment secured by Walsh on March 16, 1988, charging involvement in a scheme to defraud the government while supplying the Contras with funds secured by sale of arms to Iran. Unable to secure confirmation testimony to support Zucker's, however, Walsh ultimately decided to broker a deal with Hakim. Following Secord's plea bargain on November 8, 1989, Hakim agreed to plead guilty to a misdemeanor charge of aiding and abetting the corruption of Oliver North; and one of his corporations, the Panamanian-based Lake Resources, pleaded guilty to a felony charge of converting $16.2 million in U.S. property to the benefit of the Contras. Lake Resources was dissolved, and Hakim dropped claims to most of his Swiss funds. Judge GERHARD GESELL, noting Hakim's pledge to cooperate in future investigations, sentenced him to two years of probation and payment of a $5,000 fine. In a civil agreement accompanying his plea bargain, Hakim also agreed to pay the United States $7.8 million remaining in Lake Resources accounts. This agreement was never honored.

References:

Maas, Peter. "Oliver North's Strange Recruits." *New York Times*, 18 January 1987, sec. F, p. 20. Discusses RICHARD SECORD, THOMAS CLINES, and Theodore Shackley, as well as Hakim. Maas's findings are based on research conducted for his book, *Manhunt* (Random House, 1986), about Edwin P. Wilson.

Walsh, Lawrence. *Firewall: The Iran-Contra Conspiracy and Cover-up.* New York: W. W. Norton, 1997.

Hale, David (1941–   ) municipal judge, investment company head, Whitewater witness. As head of Capital Management Services Corporation, David Hale was licensed to provide loans, backed by the Small Business Administration (SBA), to the economically disadvantaged in Arkansas. Instead, he extended hundreds of thousands of dollars to the state's power brokers, who used the funds to finance their own investments. Hale contends that he was pressured to make these fraudulent loans by the state's Democratic political leaders, banker JAMES McDOUGAL, future governor JIM GUY TUCKER, and then-Governor Bill CLINTON. Convicted of fraud, Hale served 20 months in prison. Intimately acquainted with the financial dealings of his associates, he helped convict McDougal and Tucker of misconduct related to WHITEWATER investments, and poses a threat to implicate Clinton in the matter.

Hale was a respected member of the Little Rock community when he began Capital Management in 1979. A former prosecutor and national head of the Jaycees, he was named judge of a new municipal court that same year. Hale's company was licensed by the SBA as a Minority Enterprise Small Business Investment Company, charged with providing capital to people who otherwise would not have access to it. Hale's company was the only one licensed by the SBA in the state, and Governor Bill Clinton viewed it as a valuable asset to his economic program. It could help bring more SBA money to Arkansas, creating jobs and easing rural poverty.

Because the written guidelines were vague and individual loans unmonitored, Hale was not prevented from acceding to the requests of associates like James McDougal who, in 1985 and 1986, asked him for assistance. Hale maintains that he did not ask for specifics before loaning McDougal the money with which he hoped to extricate his bank, Madison Guaranty Savings & Loan, from economic disaster. McDougal presented the matter as an urgent need by the "political family." Next, Tucker obtained two loans, one of which he used to invest in a doomed real estate venture of McDougal's. One final loan of $300,000 to Jim McDougal's wife Susan was requested, Hale claims, by Clinton.

As Madison Guaranty began to fail, Hale saw his borrowers default on their loans. McDougal helped Hale extort additional funding from the SBA by temporarily depositing cash in Capital Management, and encouraging Hale to represent the money as new investment capital. The SBA matched those funds, enabling Hale's company to stay afloat. Hale estimates that he extended $765,000 in loans that were lost in Madison's collapse. The SBA provided Hale with $900,000 under false pretenses, and this resulted in Hale's indictment in September 1993.

After the independent counsel statute had lapsed in 1992, ROBERT FISKE was appointed by Attorney General JANET RENO to investigate allegations of President Clinton's involvement in the Madsion-backed Whitewater land deal. Hale's loans came under scrutiny once again. His claim of Clinton's involvement apparently did not convince Fiske, whose preliminary report in the summer of 1994 failed to implicate the president. KENNETH STARR took over when the independent counsel statute was reauthorized in 1994. He successfully used Hale's testimony to help convict Jim McDougal and Jim Guy Tucker of Whitewater-related misconduct. Starr's report to Congress in September 1998, however, did not include Hale's allegations against Clinton. Instead, it concentrated almost exclusively on the MONICA LEWINSKY affair.

Explanation for the reluctance of independent counsel investigations to use Hale's testimony against Clinton point to Hale's fraud conviction, his reduction in sentence in return for cooperation with the Starr investigation, and to allegations that he has received financial payments from persons associated with Clinton opponent Richard Mellon Scaife and the conservative publication *American Spectator*. Perhaps Fiske and Starr have been reluctant to rely on Hale's charges without independent confirmation. With the death of Jim McDougal (whose previous testimony was subject to frequent revision) and the determined silence of his ex-wife Susan, such confirmation proved difficult to obtain.

References:

Bowermaster, David J., and Greg Ferguson. "The Clinton-Fiske Face-Off." *U.S. News & World Report*, 4 April 1994, p. 20.
Lacayo, Richard. "Hale Storm Rising." *Time*, 13 April 1998, p. 54.
Schneider, Howard. "Ex-Judge: SBA Loans Mocked Law." *Washington Post*, 15 February 1994, sec. A, p. 1.

Hanson, Jean E. (1949–   ) General Counsel, U.S. Treasury, 1993–1994. When the Resolution Trust Corporation (RTC) began to investigate what remained of JAMES McDOUGAL's failed Madison Guaranty Savings & Loan in 1993, Treasury Department General Counsel Jean Hanson found herself at the center of the developing WHITEWATER controversy. On several occasions in September and October of 1993, Hanson communicated with White House officials regarding the RTC probe of Madison Guaranty. It was alleged that Madison deposits were invested in the failed Whitewater land venture, which was undertaken by McDougal and then-Arkansas Governor Bill CLINTON. As a result, Hanson's contacts could be seen as an attempt to assist the President in evading or halting the inquiry. After her testimony before the Senate Banking Committee on August 1, 1994, contradicted statements by top departmental officials Lloyd Bentsen and ROGER ALTMAN, she was forced to resign.

Hanson graduated from the University of Minnesota Law School with honors in 1976, joining Fried, Frank, Harris, Shriver & Jacobsen in New York, where she became a partner seven years later. Earning a reputation as a specialist in corporate finance, her legal work helped facilitate Proctor & Gamble's $1.25 billion acquisition of Richardson-Vicks, Inc. in 1985; Tri-Star Picture's takeover of Coca Cola's entertainment sector in 1987; and Campeau's acquisition of Federated Department Stores the following year. Hanson was one of only ten women included in the *National Law Journal*'s list of the nation's 50 most influential attorneys released in 1989. Unfortunately, Hanson was not active politically and had no government experience when she applied for the position with the Treasury at the urging of former Fried, Frank cochair Robert Mundheim, who had held the post during the CARTER administration.

Three months after assuming her duties at the Treasury Department, Hanson learned that the RTC was planning on naming Bill and HILLARY CLINTON as possible witnesses in its investigation of Madison Guaranty when RTC senior vice president William Roelle contacted her on September 27, 1993. Two days later, Hanson notified White House Counsel BERNARD NUSSBAUM. Nussbaum designated staff attorney Clifford Sloan as Hanson's White House liaison, and the two conversed several times in the following days regarding the RTC probe. On October 7, Hanson was told by Roelle that the *Washington Post* was planning a story on Whitewater. She reported this information to Sloan. On October 14, Hanson attended a meeting between Treasury officials and White House representatives to discuss the growing press interest in Whitewater. She was also present on February 2, 1994, when Altman, functioning as acting RTC head, briefed White House aides on the investigation's procedural policies.

Once news of the Treasury-White House contacts became public, Republicans, led by Senator ALFONSE D'AMATO (R-New York) began calling for Hanson's dismissal. Independent Counsel ROBERT FISKE, who had assumed his post in January, subpoenaed testimony related to the matter. Lloyd Bentsen formally asked the Office of Government Ethics to review the situation. Clearly, Washington viewed Hanson's behavior as a serious development in the Whitewater saga. Fiske's preliminary report issued on June 30 was good news for Hanson. The independent counsel found no basis for criminal action against anyone whose actions impacted on the RTC inquiry. The respite was temporary, however. Although the Office of Government Ethics report released on July 31 found that no government ethics laws had been violated, it characterized as "troubling" the conduct of Treasury Department officials. Such criticism reflected badly on Hanson. As the department's chief lawyer, she was expected to lead the department clear of ethical quandaries.

On August 1, Hanson attempted to defend her behavior before the Senate Banking Committee. She testified that her conduct was appropriate, because White House aides needed to defend the president against the inevitable press leaks regarding Whitewater. When confronted with discrepancies between her testimony and that of Altman and Bentsen concerning when and to whom information was communicated, Hanson presented written documentation that supported her version of events and contradicted Altman's. At the same time, she maintained that such contradictions were not important because the fact remained, said Hanson, that no one attempted to interfere with the RTC investigation. Hanson's testimony did not please Democrats on the committee any more than it did Republicans. Barbara Boxer (D-California) and Donald Riegle (D-Michigan) were openly critical. Of special concern was the fact that Hanson had not attempted to correct Altman's earlier testimony before Congress. The previous February, Altman had given the impression that contact between the Treasury Department and the White House had been limited to one meeting. In her defense, Hanson responded that she intended to supplement Altman's testimony after reading the official transcript, but before she could do that, Fiske issued his subpoenas, and she was advised by her counsel to remain quiet.

The White House expressed continued confidence in the ability of the Treasury Department employees to do their job following the Senate hearings, but made it clear that Bentsen would take appropriate action in the matter. Her lack of experience in politics an obvious handicap, Hanson had managed to alienate Altman, Bentsen, and congressional Democrats, the very people who might have shielded her against partisan Republican attacks. Her resignation was submitted on August 18, one day after Altman's.

References:

Chandler, Clay. "For Treasury's Top Lawyer, Cross-Examination Awaits." *Washington Post*, 1 August 1994, sec. A, p. 19.

Gordon, Greg. "Minnesotan Is Cleared in Telling White House about Probe." *Minneapolis Star Tribune*, 1 July 1994, sec. A, p. 7.

———. "Whitewater Briefing Defended by Lawyer." *Minneapolis Star Tribune*, 2 August 1994, sec. A, p. 1.

"Rough 'Whitewater' Ride for Clinton." *Congressional Quarterly Almanac* (1994): 108–115.

Schmickle, Sharon. "Minnesota Native at Storm's Center Built Reputation as Brilliant Lawyer." *Minneapolis Star Tribune*, 9 March 1994, sec. A, p. 1.

Harding, Warren G. (1865–1923) President of the United States, 1921–1923. A weak president, repeatedly manipulated by Republican Party leaders, Warren Harding's careless stewardship of the nation and its resources set the stage for the TEAPOT DOME scandal. In May 1921, Secretary of the Interior ALBERT FALL succeeded in persuading Harding to approve the transfer of massive naval oil reserves at Teapot Dome and Elk Hills to his department's control. Fall proceeded to lease the reserves to private oil companies owned by EDWARD L. DOHENY and HARRY F. SINCLAIR. Congressional investigation of the oil transfer began within weeks but did not capture the public's attention until after Harding's death on August 2, 1923. CALVIN COOLIDGE, Harding's successor, appointed special prosecutors ATLEE POMERENE and OWEN J. ROBERTS to investigate the transaction. Their inquiry, and the legal proceedings that ensued, set an early precedent for the eventual establishment of the Office of Independent Counsel.

Albert Fall and Warren Harding were colleagues in the U.S. Senate before Harding's election as president. Harding supported Fall's attacks upon President Woodrow Wilson's Mexican policy. Fall had substantial economic interests in Mexico, and therefore opposed any initiatives that would serve to limit American economic prerogatives there. Fall paid Harding several visits during the fall of 1920 when the president-elect was considering his Cabinet selections. Harding labored over the process, and did not announce Fall as Secretary of the Interior until March 1, 1921. His choice immediately alarmed conservationist leaders Gifford Pinchot and Harry Slattery, who identified Fall as an exploiter, opposed to all conservation measures that had come before him in the Senate.

Led by Progressive Wisconsin Senator Robert LaFollette, Congress slowly became aware of the nature of Fall's tenure as Interior Secretary and its consequences. Pressed by the Senate to release documents detailing his handling of the oil reserves in June 1922, Fall delivered a truckload containing thousands of pages explaining the matter. Accompanying the delivery was a letter from Harding attesting to his approval of the arrangement. Fall and Secretary of the Navy EDWIN DENBY had secured the President's agreement prior to the transfer of the reserves from the Department of the Navy, stated Harding. There remains some question as to whether Harding ever paid much attention to Fall's extensive explanation of his oil policy, but he did officially endorse it, and having done so, shared responsibility for the scandal that followed.

The special prosecutors' investigation ended with Fall's conspiracy conviction in 1929. Harding's death six years earlier came at a time when Teapot Dome as well as other scandals were closing in on the administration. These involved the Justice Department (rumored extortion of money from Prohibition law violators), the Alien Property Custodian, and the Director of the Veteran's Bureau (both involving reported looting). He was also said to be greatly troubled by publicity surrounding a daughter born to his mistress Nan Britton. There has always been conjecture that had Harding lived, he might have faced impeachment. Historians have generally characterized Harding as a man of limited abilities who, due to his social skills and convivial manner, rose to an office for which he was ill-equipped.

Born in Morrow County, Ohio, Harding was a capable journalist with some oratorical ability who built a political career by attracting the friendship of Republican machine politicians like George B. Cox of Cincinnati. He was viewed as a safe, conservative choice by party leaders who supported his successful Senate and presidential campaigns in 1915 and 1920 respectively. Harding may well have been ignorant of the corruption surrounding him, but as president, he assumes a good share of the historical responsibility for it. The rest must be shouldered by those who helped place him in office.

References:

Dictionary of American Biography, volume 4, under "Harding, Warren G."
Noggle, Burl. *Teapot Dome: Oil and Politics in the 1920's*. Baton Rouge: Louisiana
    State University Press, 1962.

Harper, James (1918–   ) Independent Counsel, W. Lawrence Wallace investigation, 1987. Atlanta tax attorney James Harper was named independent counsel to investigate possible violation of tax regulations by former Assistant Attorney General W. LAWRENCE WALLACE on August 17, 1987. The inquiry had been sealed by the Special Division, the panel of judges responsible for appointing the independent counsel. The investigation was suspended on March 30 when original Independent Counsel CARL RAUH resigned due to problems with conflict-of-interest regulations instituted by the Justice Department. Harper completed the investigation, issuing a report on December 17 that exonerated Wallace.

Little information on the Wallace investigation was available during the course of the inquiry. Because of the sealed nature of the case, the Justice Department refused to even acknowledge the existence of the investigation. When the Justice Department made it clear that it would prevent independent counsels from representing other clients with cases pending before the Department for one year after their special appointment, it became most difficult to locate a qualified attorney to serve as independent counsel. Most veteran tax attorneys had clients with cases pending before the Department of Justice. After five months of searching, the court settled on James Harper.

Harper, who received his law degree from Northwestern University in 1951, had served as Senior Appellate Attorney and Supervising Attorney at the Atlanta regional office of the Internal Revenue Service between 1957 and 1960. He was associated with the Atlanta office of the Houston-based law firm Chamberlain, Hrdlicka, White, Johnson & Williams. Perhaps most important, he did not have a client with matters pending before the Justice Department.

After a four-month investigation, Harper determined that Wallace had committed a "technical" violation of the tax laws by failing to file a tax return for two years. When notified of his obligation, however, Wallace filed returns indicating that he was due a refund. Harper reasoned that because the government had incurred no harm, there was no basis for prosecution. If anyone had been harmed, it was Wallace, whose refund had been delayed.

Harper's investigation, clothed in anonymity, was completely overshadowed by Independent Counsel LAWRENCE WALSH's IRAN-CONTRA investigation, which was gathering momentum in 1987. Independent Counsel ALEXIA MORRISON's investigation of former Assistant Attorney General THEODORE OLSON, begun the previous year, would also command great attention, as it resulted in a legal challenge to the existence of the independent counsel office.

References:

Freiwald, Aaron. "New Prosecutor Takes Over Wallace Probe." *Legal Times*, 7 December 1987, p. 4.

Marcus, Ruth. "Justice Official Won't Be Charged in Tax Case." *Washington Post*, 19 December 1987, sec. A, p. 3.

Hasenfus, Eugene (1941–   ) Contra supply courier, 1986. Lone survivor of a C-123 aircraft shot down over Nicaragua on October 5, 1986, Eugene Hasenfus's capture by the Nicaraguan Sandinista government brought to public attention the effort, led by National Security Council staff member OLIVER NORTH, to secretly fund the Contra rebellion in that country. The congressional hearings and LAWRENCE WALSH's independent counsel investigation proceeded to uncover many of the details concerning the manner in which profits from the sale of weapons to Iran were used to fund covert operations in Nicaragua.

Hasenfus, a former Marine, and William Cooper, the Contra supply plane's pilot, had flown missions for Civil Air Transport, also called "Air America," during the Vietnam War. Unlike Hasenfus, pilot Cooper and copilot Wallace Sawyer were not wearing parachutes when a SAM-7 missile hit their plane. Only Hasenfus was able to escape with his life. After capturing Hasenfus, Sandinistas searching the plane's wreckage discovered ammunition, uniforms, and medicine intended for the Contra rebels. They also found an identification card connecting Cooper with Southern Air Transport, a company owned by the CIA. Other documents identified the airplane's owner as Corporate Air Services based in Pennsylvania. Its crew was identified as American employees. Upon questioning, however, Hasenfus claimed to be working for a "Max Gomez" of the CIA. In truth, Corporate Air Services was owned by RICHARD SECORD, who was helping Oliver North avoid the restrictive BOLAND AMENDMENTS that forbade government assistance to the Contras. "Max Gomez" was actually Felix Rodriguez, a former CIA employee and associate of Donald Gregg, Vice President GEORGE BUSH's National Security Adviser. The capture of Hasenfus undercut the statements Oliver North had made during the summer, denying the existence of such Contra supply operations.

Former Attorney General GRIFFIN BELL was retained as Hasenfus's legal representative, but his efforts were unsuccessful in preventing a guilty verdict and lengthy prison sentence. Hasenfus served 73 days in maximum security before being released on December 17. One week earlier, Walsh had been selected as independent counsel to investigate the Iran-Contra connection. Walsh's investigation made clear that flights such as the one manned by Hasenfus originated at the military air base in Ilopango, El Salvador. Pilots such as Cooper were provided with information that facilitated their avoidance of Sandinista positions, but flights were not canceled due to threat of antiaircraft fire. Typically, the arms being distributed by crews like Hasenfus's had been flown in from Portugal. The distribution flights were organized by Secord and North employees Richard Gadd and his successor Robert Dutton. North's efforts were supported by National Security Adviser JOHN POINDEXTER and other REAGAN administration officials.

Hasenfus, joined by the family of flight copilot Wallace Sawyer, filed suit against Richard Secord and Southern Air Transport for damages suffered as a result of their ill-fated flight. Money sought would have covered legal fees incurred by Hasenfus, and provided death benefits to the Sawyer family. In August 1990, a jury decided that although there did exist a joint venture relationship between the plaintiffs and defendants, there was no entitlement to further money. The decision was based on the absence of any contract governing the activities of Hasenfus and Sawyer.

In 1996, Congress refused to act on a bill first filed by Representative Toby Roth (R-Wisconsin) asking compensation of $805,209 for injuries and legal fees incurred by Hasenfus. President CLINTON indicated his opposition to the bill on the basis that Hasenfus was not an employee of the federal government and the United States bore no responsibility for the plane crash.

Hasenfus, living in Marinette, Wisconsin, did not believe that he would pursue his claim further. Hasenfus's fate contrasts sharply with that of Oliver North who is well-paid for his public appearances and may yet have a political future. Hasenfus is an occasional construction worker. His legal representatives point out the contradiction inherent in the government's continuing attempts to obtain $8 million found in Swiss bank accounts belonging to Richard Secord and ALBERT HAKIM. If they were government employees, how could Hasenfus not be?

References:
Gugliotta, Guy. "Iran-Contra Figure Shot Down Again." *Washington Post*, 18 June 1996, sec. A, p. 11.
"Jury Rejects Contra Operative's Suit for Damages." *Chicago Tribune*, 28 August 1990, sec. C, p. 6.
Morgan, Peter W. "The Undefined Crime of Lying to Congress: Ethics Reform and the Rule of Law." *Northwestern University Law Review* 86 (1992): 177–258. Author's introduction discusses Hasenfus's ill-fated flight and administration officials' reaction that included President Reagan's comparison of "private" efforts in support of the Contras to American volunteers' participation in the Abraham Lincoln Brigade that fought to preserve the Spanish Republic against Francisco Franco's fascist-backed rebellion in the late 1930s.
Walsh, Lawrence. *Firewall: The Iran-Contra Conspiracy and Cover-up*. New York: Norton, 1997.

Henderson, John Brooks (1826–1913) Special Prosecutor of Whiskey Ring, 1875. Appointed as special counsel to facilitate investigation and prosecution of persons involved in violating whiskey revenue laws in St. Louis, John Brooks Henderson was dismissed within seven months for criticizing President GRANT's associates.

In May 1875, Henderson was named to assist the U.S. district attorney in acting against participants in the St. Louis Whiskey Ring that had just been broken by agents working for Secretary of the Treasury Benjamin Bristow. Representing the latest in a shameful series of scandals that had occurred during the Grant administration, this matter appeared to immediately implicate Revenue Supervisor John McDonald and his assistant John Joyce. Grant's friend and personal secretary, Orville Babcock, also came under suspicion. Criticism of Babcock, however, was difficult for Grant to countenance.

Henderson did not feel obligated to respect such sensitivities in the conduct of his investigation. His political independence had been well-established prior to his appointment as special prosecutor. Henderson had frequently dissented from the majority in the Democratic Party when serving in the Missouri state legislature (1848–1849; 1856–1857) and as a presidential elector (1856; 1860). Appointed senator as a Republican in 1862 and elected to a full term the following year, he angered former states-rights allies by supporting Lincoln's emancipation of the slaves and proposed plan of reconstruction. A strong critic of President Andrew Johnson, Henderson nevertheless voted against his removal from office during the president's impeachment trial in 1868. This act of conscience ended his senatorial career. Henderson's reputation for independence certainly helped lend integrity to Grant's Whiskey Ring investigation but should also have alerted the president that the inquiry would be uninfluenced by personal considerations.

On September 26, 1875, Bristow's associate, Treasury Solicitor Bluford Wilson, sent Henderson a letter stressing the importance of revealing the true extent of the revenue scandal, regardless of who might be implicated. Although this was probably an unnecessary piece of advice, it may have encouraged Henderson to believe that the administration was giving him free rein to conduct his probe as he saw fit. Candid in his comments regarding the case's progress, Henderson made it clear that he judged the evidence to likely implicate Babcock in misconduct. As far as Grant was concerned, criticism of Babcock's conduct was an unwarranted personal attack of suspicious origin. Grant believed that political enemies were using criticism of Babcock to further discredit the Grant administration. Consequently, Henderson was dismissed in December.

Bristow continued the investigation that culminated in a series of trials in 1875 and 1876. Several convictions resulted, including those of McDonald and Joyce. Babcock, however, was acquitted. He resigned from the Cabinet at the insistence of Secretary of State Hamilton Fish. Shortly after his resignation, new reports appeared to link Babcock to illegal gold speculation. He drowned in 1884, at age 48, while working as a lighthouse inspector.

Henderson had only reluctantly supported Grant's candidacy for a second term in 1872. He had attempted during 1867 and 1868 to steer the president clear of individuals likely to involve him in political corruption. Grant appeared unable or unwilling to clean his political house. At the time of Henderson's appointment in 1875, too much damage had already been done. Following his dismissal, Henderson remained politically active by serving as president of the Republican National Convention in 1884, where he championed the candidacy of General William T. Sherman. In 1889, he moved to Washington, D.C. There, he was a delegate to the Pan-American Congress (1889) and served as regent for the Smithsonian Institution (1892–1911).

References:

Dictionary of American Biography, volume 4. under. "Henderson, John Brooks."
Hyde, William. *Encyclopedia of the History of St. Louis*, volume 2, pp. 1016–1017. New York: Southern History Company, 1899.
McFeely, William S. *Grant: A Biography*. New York: W. W. Norton, 1981. Chapter 24, "Wedding and Whiskey," mentions Henderson's role in the Whiskey Ring investigation and discusses Babcock.

Heney, Francis J. (1859–1937) Special Prosecutor, Oregon land fraud cases, 1903–1910. Selected by President THEODORE ROOSEVELT's Attorney General Philander Knox to investigate and prosecute persons involved in land grant fraud in Oregon, Francis Heney obtained indictment and conviction of some of the region's most powerful figures. These included Oregon Senator John H. Mitchell and U.S. Attorney John H. Hall. Although Heney's aggressiveness angered the state's Republican Party, Roosevelt's support of the investigation remained steadfast. Without Heney's determination to target those individuals in positions of greatest authority, the land fraud prosecutions might well have been limited to only those officials directly involved in the fraudulent transactions. Those who willfully subverted justice by permitting and encouraging such corruption would likely have avoided responsibility.

In November 1903, Heney was appointed to assist U.S. Attorney Hall in prosecution of the Oregon land fraud cases. Knox refused to honor Hall's recommendation of prominent Oregon Republican D. J. Malarkey. Knox's appointment of Heney, a San Francisco Democrat, was unpopular locally. This dissatisfaction was exacerbated when Knox named C. A. S. Frost as Heney's assistant. In 1901, Frost had been convicted of involvement in a conspiracy in Nome, Alaska, although he was subsequently pardoned.

Heney was raised in the "South of the Slot" section of San Francisco, populated by poor immigrants. Although associated with street gangs as a youth, he completed his education and worked as a school teacher. Traveling across the Pacific Northwest, he tried mining and mill work before landing a job as a law clerk in Idaho. There, without the benefit of legal training, he secured the dismissal of charges against a man accused of murdering a gambler. Convinced that law was his calling, he returned to San Francisco and enrolled in the Hastings School of Law in 1883. He graduated in 1884 and was admitted to the California bar. Heney opened a law office in Tucson in 1889, participating in litigation of Mexican land grant disputes. He argued three such cases before the Supreme Court. Heney also acted as attorney for the wife of John C. Handy, a prominent physician working for the Southern Pacific Railroad Company. Handy had threatened to kill the lawyer who undertook his wife's defense. He subsequently made an unsuccessful attempt on Heney's life and was shot and killed in the process. Heney was exonerated, and an attempt to indict him failed. After serving as attorney general of the Arizona Territory (1893–1894), Heney returned to private practice in San Francisco.

When Heney assumed his duties in Oregon, U.S. Attorney Hall had begun prosecution of fraud cases originating in the Eugene Land Office. Marie Ware, U.S. Commissioner for that office, had been indicted along with timber speculator Horace G. McKinley, lumber assessor Steven A. Puter, and local attorney Dan Tarpley. Senator Mitchell and Land Office Commissioner Binger Hermann had both expedited the fraudulent claims. When Hall proved uncooperative, Knox named Heney special assistant attorney general in charge of the prosecutions. Heney enlisted the assistance of Secret Service agent William J. Burns who had worked on land fraud cases in California. (Burns would later found the Burns Detective Agency and serve as predecessor to J. Edgar Hoover at the FBI.) Further investigation convinced Heney and Burns that the Oregon congressional delegation as well as U.S. Attorney Hall were implicated in the frauds.

On December 6, 1907, a jury convicted the principals involved in the first of two cases originating in the Eugene Land Office. During a postponement of the second trial, Heney received support for a plan to act against Senator Mitchell and Binger Hermann for their acquiescence in the land frauds. From December 1904 until April 1905, a single grand jury returned indictments that resulted in four major cases. In addition to Mitchell and Hermann, these cases involved Congressman John Williamson and state Senators George Sorenson, Willard Jones, H. A. Smith, and F. P. Mays.

On July 3, 1905, Mitchell was convicted, but the jury recommended leniency. On July 25, he was sentenced to six months in jail, fined $1,000, and disbarred. On December 8, before his appeal could be heard, Mitchell died of complications from a tooth extraction. On September 28, 1905, Williamson and two associates were convicted. On September 13, 1906, convictions were secured against Mays, Jones, and Sorenson. The jury was unable to reach a verdict in the fourth principal case.

Heney returned to San Francisco in 1907. He did not return to Oregon until after meeting with Attorney General CHARLES J. BONAPARTE in December. Heney requested to be relieved of any further land fraud prosecutions. Bonaparte agreed if Heney would promise to handle the government's case against Hall. Hall had been removed by Roosevelt on January 1, 1905, for his involvement in the land frauds. In court, Heney succeeded in demonstrating that Hall had intentionally failed to prosecute land companies that were involved in fraudulent practices. In addition, Heney proved that Hall used evidence of others' involvements in land fraud to his own political advantage, in one case forcing an opponent out of a political contest by threatening disclosure of such facts. On February 8, 1908, Hall was found guilty by the jury.

Heney's involvement with the land fraud cases, however, did not end with the Hall conviction. In January 1910, he returned to Oregon to prosecute Binger Hermann. Heney argued that Hermann approved fraudulent land deals in order to win favor with Oregon state politicians who could elect him to Congress. Heney recognized that his case against Hermann was less than conclusive. The principal witness for the prosecution had been convicted in an earlier trial, and Heney relied heavily on his cross-examination of Hermann to prove his case. On February 11, 1910, the jury reported that it could not reach a verdict. Eleven members had voted for conviction, one for acquittal.

Heney's prosecution of the land fraud cases resulted in substantial reform of the Forest Reservation Act of 1905. Provisions that invited fraudulent land transfers by speculators were repealed on March 3, 1905. Heney's prosecutions also helped reinforce President Roosevelt's commitment to national conservation. Heney's personal experience with widespread fraud involving public officials informed his own development as a progressive who advocated public ownership of railroads, telegraph and telephone, and insurance companies.

Heney's effectiveness as a special prosecutor was in part attributable to President Roosevelt's support. Roosevelt granted him the independence to act against even the most influential individuals in the Republican party. Heney enjoyed much the same investigative freedom extended to statutory independent counsels after 1978. In addition, Roosevelt's own independence from political influence meant that Heney did not need to fear the political consequences of his investigation.

References:

Messing, John. "Public Lands, Politics, and Progressives: The Oregon Land Fraud Trials, 1903–1910." *Pacific Historical Review* 35 (1966): 35–66.
National Cyclopedia of American Biography. Ann Arbor: University Microfilms, 1967, volume 33, pp. 391–392.

Herman, Alexis M. (1947–) Secretary of Labor, 1997– . Alexis Herman became the fifth CLINTON Cabinet member to be the subject of an independent counsel investigation, in May 1998. After a Justice Department inquiry, Attorney General JANET RENO was satisfied that there was sufficient evidence to warrant further investigation into charges that between 1994 and 1996, Herman, then White House public liaison officer, had accepted payments in return for use of her influence to further business ventures. On May 26, 1998, the Special Division of the D.C. Court of Appeals named RALPH LANCASTER independent counsel charged with investigating whether Herman was guilty of influence peddling that raised $250,000 that may have been deposited in Democratic campaign coffers.

Born in Mobile, Alabama, Herman received a bachelor's degree from Xavier University in 1969. She embarked on a career in social service, helping to direct a variety of programs aimed at training and employing minorities and women. These included the Black Women's Employment Program (1972–1974), the Department of Labor Recruitment Training Program (1973–1974), and the Women's Program for Minority Employment in Atlanta (1974–1977). Herman also served as Director of the Department of Labor's Women's Bureau (1977–1981) and in 1981 founded her own consulting business, A. M. Herman & Associates. The election of Bill Clinton in 1992 provided Herman with a series of political opportunities. She was awarded posts on the Democratic National Convention Committee and the Presidential Transition Team, and served as White House aide before being nominated secretary of labor in 1997.

In January 1998 it was announced that the Justice Department's Public Integrity Section was conducting a preliminary investigation into allegations that Herman had been guilty of influence peddling. These charges had first surfaced the previous year during Herman's confirmation hearings. They were brought by Cameroon businessman Laurent Yene, a former friend of Herman's business partner, Vanessa Weaver. Republicans at first threatened to block Herman's nomination because of the allegations but dropped their opposition after President Clinton agreed to withdraw an executive order expressing preference for contracting with unionized companies. This political arrangement cleared the way for Herman's appointment but did not silence her accuser.

Yene's new charges provided additional details and some documentary support. He now claimed to have delivered an envelope of cash to Herman, and he was willing to supply federal investigators with bank documents that supported his assertions. In particular, Yene charged that he and Weaver had introduced Herman to Singapore businessman Abdul Rahman in May 1996. Yene maintained that Herman accepted a kickback in return for intervening with the Federal Communications Commission (FCC) in support of Rahman's application for a communications satellite license. Investigators determined that someone in Herman's office did contact the FCC about the application, which was eventually denied.

In response to Yene's charges, Vanessa Weaver's attorneys characterized the matter as a vindictive effort to obtain vengeance for the collapse of a personal and professional relationship. Weaver's representatives portrayed Yene as an embezzler who fabricated his story in order to extort money in return for his silence. Herman emphatically denied Yene's charges, and the President expressed confidence in her innocence.

Nevertheless, on May 11, 1998, Attorney General Reno announced that her department's investigation had gathered enough information to indicate the need for an independent counsel. Testimony of witnesses, said Reno, was conflicting and subject to change. Other information appeared to provide some support for the charges. She could not say with certainty that the allegations were unsubstantiated. Two weeks later, Lancaster was named independent counsel for the Herman investigation.

Initiation of the independent counsel investigation came nine months after Herman's most significant accomplishment. She had been widely credited with using her skill and influence to help arrange a settlement in the 1997 Teamsters strike against United Parcel Service.

References:

Bendavid, Naftali. "Reno OK's Counsel to Probe Labor Secretary." *Chicago Tribune*, 12 May 1998, sec. N, p. 3.

Jackson, Robert L. "Prosecutors Urge Special Counsel for Alexis Herman." *Los Angeles Times*, 9 May 1998, sec. A, p. 10.

Labaton, Stephen. "Labor Secretary's Nemesis Now Finds Himself Impugned." *New York Times*, 16 January 1998, sec. A, p. 18.

Ostrow, Ronald J. "Labor Secretary Comes Under Scrutiny." *Los Angeles Times*, 15 January 1998, sec. A, p. 4.

Hubbell, Webster L. (1948–   ) Associate Attorney General, 1993–1994. A longtime friend and associate of Bill CLINTON, Webster Hubbell was a prime target of WHITEWATER Independent Counsel KENNETH STARR. As head of the litigation section at the Rose Law Firm, Hubbell was present when the questionable financial and real estate transactions surrounding Whitewater were concluded. In addition, Hubbell's father-in-law, businessman Seth Ward, played an integral part in securing financing for the project. In 1993, Hubbell was appointed associate attorney general. His past association with fellow Rose Law partners HILLARY CLINTON and VINCENT FOSTER quickly made him a subject of interest to Whitewater investigators. Unable to secure information that would directly connect Hubbell or the Clintons to illegal Whitewater activities, Starr successfully prosecuted Hubbell for fraudulent billing practices while at the Rose Law Firm. Hubbell served 17 months in prison. After his release, Starr indicted him for income tax evasion, a charge later dismissed by a federal judge who believed that the indictment violated a previous immunity agreement.

Six years after receiving his law degree from the University of Arkansas in 1973, Hubbell was elected mayor of Little Rock at the age of 31. He was already serving on the city's Board of Directors. By 1984, he was Chief Justice of Arkansas's Supreme Court. It was Hubbell's activities at the Rose Law Firm, however, that would become the center of attention once the Whitewater affair became the subject of scrutiny. Hubbell's father-in-law, Seth Ward, was instrumental in assisting JAMES McDOUGAL and his Savings and Loan in financing the acquisition of land that formed the basis of the Whitewater Development Corporation—the Castle Grande land deal. In an intentionally confusing series of loans involving local judge and banker DAVID HALE, McDougal and Ward succeeded, at least temporarily, in skirting federal banking regulations, while raising the necessary funding for their real estate schemes. Wasn't it reasonable to assume that Hubbell knew the details of these arrangements?

After assuming his duties at the Justice Department, Hubbell's contacts extended to include Clinton friends and advisers Vernon Jordan and Mickey Kantor. Starr's investigation viewed Hubbell's association with these individuals as protective of the Clintons. Starr hoped to use his investigation of Hubbell and McDougal in a manner similar to the way in which LAWRENCE WALSH utilized the testimony of CIA and National Security Council officials during the IRAN-CONTRA investigation. Eventually, the prosecutorial trail might lead to the White House. Unfortunately for Starr, Hubbell remained silent concerning anything damaging he might know regarding the Clintons. As a result, Starr resorted to prosecuting Hubbell for fraudulent billing practices uncovered during investigation of the Rose Law Firm records.

Hubbell resigned his position in the Justice Department in March 1994. Following negotiations with the Independent Counsel Office, he pleaded guilty to two felony counts related to his billing activities, and in June 1995 was sentenced to 21 months in prison. After serving 17 months of that sentence, Hubbell was reindicted by Starr in April 1998 for income tax evasion. Starr's office viewed payments made to Hubbell by Vernon Jordan and Mickey Kantor as incentive to remain silent concerning Whitewater-related matters. It was this money upon which Starr based his new charges. In July 1998, however, U.S. District Court Judge James Robertson ruled that the independent counsel had wandered too far from his authorized mandate. Hubbell had turned over the records upon which Starr had based his latest charge with the understanding that they would not be used against him. Judge Robertson viewed the new indictment against Hubbell as a violation of an IMMUNITY agreement. This ruling negated, at least temporarily, Starr's further attempts to coerce Hubbell's cooperation in the Whitewater investigation.

Conversations taped while Hubbell was in prison were released by Congressman Dan Burton (R-Indiana) as part of his committee's investigation of Democratic Party campaign financing practices. Burton, chair of the House's Government Reform and Oversight Committee, was attempting to prove that the Democrats had received large sums of campaign money from foreign sources, in particular the Riady family of Indonesia. Transcripts of Hubbell's conversations seemed to indicate the presence of a cover-up. Subsequent examination revealed that the conversations had been edited in a manner that encouraged that interpretation. Congressman Burton publicly apologized for release of the incomplete transcript but maintained that conclusions originally drawn from the conversations were still valid.

Hubbell may yet prove a source of further Whitewater revelations. Starr's report to Congress, however, delivered in September 1998, included no such information.

References:

Cohen, Richard. "What's His Secret?" *Washington Post*, 28 March 1997, sec. A, p. 29.
Henry, John C. "Judge Dismisses Hubbell Charges, Rebukes Starr." *Houston Chronicle*, 2 July 1998. sec. A, p. 1.
Sherman, Mark, and Rebecca Carr. "Whitewater Investigation Prison Tapes Controversy." *Atlanta Constitution*, 6 May 1998, sec. A, p. 10.
Simon, Roger. "Counsel Indicts Clinton Friend a 2nd Time." *Chicago Tribune*, 1 May 1998, sec. A, p. 1.
Von Drehle, David. "Key Clinton Player Finally on the Program." *Washington Post*, 3 April 1993, sec. A, p. 1.

Hughes, Charles Evans (1862–1948) Republican Governor of New York, 1906–1910; Associate Justice of the Supreme Court, 1910–1916; Secretary of State, 1921–1925; Chief Justice of the Supreme Court, 1930–1941. Although defeated for the presidency by Woodrow Wilson, who was reelected to a second term in 1916, Charles Evans Hughes came within 23 electoral votes of upsetting the Democratic incumbent. Having established a record of achievement as a popular and efficient governor as well as a respected jurist, President Wilson called upon Hughes to assume a position as special assistant to the attorney general, charged with investigation of delays in aircraft production during World War I. Predating President CALVIN COOLIDGE's selection of special prosecutors to examine the TEAPOT DOME scandal, this appointment represents an even earlier precedent for the establishment of an independent counsel office.

After resigning from New York State's Draft Appeals Board in May 1918 to assume his duties as special assistant to Attorney General THOMAS W. GREGORY, later himself a candidate as special prosecutor of the Teapot Dome affair, Hughes was provided with offices and hearing rooms within the Department of Justice in order to conduct his investigation. With the assistance of Meier Steinbrink, later New York State Supreme Court judge, Hughes examined over 200 witnesses and visited many aircraft plants. Attorney General Gregory and Solicitor General William L. Frierson did not interfere with Hughes's inquiry, but they were present throughout the proceedings. Witnesses were examined in private in order to avoid any public disclosures that might harm the war effort.

Hughes released a report of his findings at the end of October. It cited specific causes of delays, all of which might reasonably be addressed and corrected. Because the war ended on November 11, earlier than anticipated at the time, the corrective measures suggested by Hughes's report were never instituted. Aircraft production, however, had increased during the time the investigation was taking place.

Because Hughes's inquiry was conducted within the Justice Department, it can be argued that it should not be characterized as "independent" or even "special" in the WATERGATE prosecutors' sense of the word. Hughes was not armed with all the authority later extended to LEON JAWORSKI. His appointment, however, certainly was unusual and irregular. It was special in the sense that it vested investigatorial authority in an adjunct body created to operate outside the normal Justice Department framework. Its creation can be seen as a small step in the direction of establishing an independent mechanism for such investigations. Its appearance was in response to a complaint of minor magnitude. It would take a Watergate to prompt reform of major proportions.

Reference:

Danelski, David J., and Joseph S. Tulchin, eds. *The Autobiographical Notes of Charles Evans Hughes.* Cambridge: Harvard University Press, 1973. Chapter 13, "1917–1921," discusses Hughes's experience as special assistant to the attorney general.

Humphrey's Executor v. United States, 295 U.S. 602 (1935). This case was a successful suit for back pay brought by the estate of William E. Humphrey, a Herbert Hoover-appointed member of the Federal Trade Commission. President Franklin Roosevelt had purported to remove Humphrey from the FTC because of their differing economic philosophies. The Federal Trade Commission Act, however, had authorized the President to remove FTC commissioners only on grounds of "inefficiency, neglect of duty, or malfeasance in office." Because Roosevelt's dismissal order was based on none of these things, his dispute with Humphrey presented the question whether Congress could limit what presumably would otherwise have been the President's plenary authority to remove a principal administrative official from his or her office. The resolution of this question is key to the permissibility of creating a statutorily authorized independent counsel who could likewise be shielded from discharge "at will" by the President.

In understanding the contemporary meaning of *Humphrey's Executor*, it is important to distinguish the Supreme Court's precise constitutional holding—namely, that Congress could limit the president to the removal of FTC commissioners only for cause—from the rationale offered by the Court in 1935 to explain its holding. The Court's holding that permits Congress to limit the removability of FTC members necessarily supports the general proposition that it is permissible under the Constitution to immunize some significant federal administrators from complete presidential policy control. In enacting the ETHICS IN GOVERNMENT ACT, Congress implicitly relied on that proposition in authorizing the appointment of independent criminal prosecutors who would be subject to no more than limited presidential removability. (To be precise, the Ethics in Government Act does not directly authorize the president's removal of independent counsel at all. Instead, the attorney general—an official whom the President may remove at will—has exclusive authority to remove independent counsel "only for good cause, physical or mental disability . . . or any other condition that substantially impairs the performance of the independent counsel's duties" [28 U.S.C. § 596(a)(1)]).

The Court's 1935 rationale, however, might have been thought to raise significant doubt about whether *Humphrey's Executor* would pertain to independent criminal prosecutors. The Court stated: "Whether the power of the President to remove an officer shall prevail over the authority of Congress to condition the power by fixing a definite term and precluding a removal except for cause will depend upon the character of the office" (295 U.S. at 631). Only nine years earlier, in *MYERS v. UNITED STATES*, 272 U.S. 52 (1926), the Court had held that Congress could not require the President to secure the Senate's consent in order to discharge a postmaster. The 1935 Court distinguished *Myers* on the ground that the president's plenary powers to discharge administrative officers at will was limited to what the Court in *Humphrey's Executor* called "purely executive officers." Thus, the Court stated, the reason why the president did not have sole and plenary authority to remove FTC members was that FTC members (unlike postmasters, the Court implied) were not "purely executive" but were more accurately characterized as "quasi-judicial" or "quasi-legislative" in their functions. In a famous passage, the Court wrote:

The Federal Trade Commission is an administrative body created by Congress to carry into effect legislative policies embodied in the statute in accordance with the legislative standard therein prescribed, and to perform other specified duties as a legislative or as a judicial aid. *Such a body cannot in any proper sense be characterized as an arm or an eye of the executive.* Its duties are performed without executive leave and, in the contemplation of the statute, must be free from executive control. In administering the provisions of the statute in respect of "unfair methods of competition," that is to say, in filling in and administering the details embodied by that general standard, the commission acts in part quasi-legislatively and in part quasi-judicially. . . . To the extent that it exercises any executive function, as distinguished from executive power in the constitutional sense, it does so in the discharge and effectuation of its quasi-legislative or quasi-judicial powers, or as an agency of the legislative or judicial departments of the government. [295 U.S. at 627–628 (emphasis added)]

This passage poses a puzzle for any Congress intent on creating an office of independent counsel that would be immune from plenary presidential removal power. The puzzle arises because it would hardly be plausible, within the American governmental tradition, to characterize a criminal prosecutor as quasi-legislative or quasi-judicial. By tradition, federal criminal prosecutors have virtually always functioned "as an arm of the executive." The question thus is posed: Isn't a criminal prosecutor precisely the kind of "purely executive officer" to whom the holding of *Humphrey's Executor* does not apply?

In *MORRISON v. OLSON*, 487 U.S. 654 (1988), which upheld the special prosecutor provisions of the Ethics in Government Act, the Supreme Court resolved this conundrum. The Court held that "the determination of whether the Constitution allows Congress to impose a 'good cause'-type restriction on the President's power to remove an official cannot be made to turn on whether or not that official is classified as 'purely executive' " (487 U.S. at 689). Instead, the Court said: "[T]he real question is whether the removal restrictions [enacted by Congress] are of such a nature that they impede the President's ability to perform his constitutional duty . . ." (*Id.* at 691). Rejecting its earlier form of analysis, which rested the Court's conclusions regarding removability on the categorization of an office as "purely executive" or as quasi-legislative or quasi-judicial, the *Morrison Court* concluded:

Although the counsel exercises no small amount of discretion and judgment in deciding how to carry out his or her duties . . . we simply do not see how the President's need to control the exercise of that discretion is so central to the functioning of the Executive Branch as to require as a matter of constitutional law that the counsel be terminable at will by the President. . . . We do not think that [the limitation on removal] as it presently stands sufficiently deprives the President of control over the independent counsel to interfere impermissibly with his constitutional obligation to ensure the faithful execution of the laws. (*Id.* at 692–693)

The Court's analysis in *Morrison* thus resulted in a new and different rationale for its holdings in *Myers* and in *Humphrey's Executor*. What was wrong with Congress's attempt, rejected in *Myers*, to require Senate consent for removing a postmaster was not its interference with some categorical, plenary removal power of the president over executive officers. The problem was that Congress was trying to augment its own institutional role in the removal process. The Court has since held that the only roles Congress may constitutionally play in removing officers of the United States are the roles of impeachment and removal after trial, which are explicitly authorized in Article I. Congress could, however, limit the president's capacity to discharge FTC members at will for two reasons. First, the statutory limit on the president's removal power did not aggrandize Congress's own role in the removal process. Second, the removal restrictions for Federal Trade Commissioners do not "impede the president's ability to perform" any constitutionally imposed executive duty.

References:

Cromer, Brian A. "Prosecutorial Indiscretion and the United States Congress: Expanding the Jurisdiction of the Independent Counsel." *Kentucky Law Review Journal* 77 (1989): 923–950. Cites *Humphrey* in justifying creation of the independent counsel by restricting the president's control over quasi-legislative/quasi-judicial agencies.

O'Keefe, Constance, and Peter Safirstein. "Fallen Angels, Separation of Powers, and the Saturday Night Massacre: An Examination of the Practical, Constitutional, and Political Tensions in the Special Prosecutor Provisions of the Ethics in Government Act." *Brooklyn Law Review* 49 (1982): 113–147.

Sherry, Suzanna. "Separation of Powers: Asking a Different Question." *William and Mary Law Review* 30 (1989): 287–300.

—PETER M. SHANE

Hungate, William L. (1922–   ) former congressman (D-Missouri), 1963–1977. After serving on the House Judiciary Committee and supporting some of the articles of impeachment with which President RICHARD NIXON was presented during the WATERGATE crisis, Congressman William Hungate participated in

the crafting of a proposed statutory remedy to future executive-branch misconduct. His 1976 bill, H.R. 14476, was an attempt to revive the concept of a
temporary special prosecutor at a time when the notion of a permanent one
seemed to be winning favor.

Senator ABRAHAM RIBICOFF's (D-Connecticut) Watergate Reorganization
and Reform Act, S. 495 (1975) called for establishment of a permanent office
of public attorney that would function as a special prosecutor of executive-
branch malfeasance. During hearings in March 1976, most witnesses argued
against the idea of a permanent special prosecutor. As a result, the bill was
amended to call for a temporary office of the type proposed by the AMERICAN
BAR ASSOCIATION. Before the House received the legislation, President
GERALD FORD revived the permanent prosecutor concept. FORD's plan, however, called for the office to be contained within the Department of Justice.
Nevertheless, when the House received the bill as amended, the special prosecutor, as described, was a permanent institution. Hungate's response was to
attempt to resurrect the temporary prosecutor concept.

On July 23, 1976, hearings began on Hungate's H.R. 14476. The bill called
for the attorney general to appoint the temporary special prosecutor subject to
the approval of a judicial panel. During hearings, Attorney General EDWARD
LEVI argued against Hungate's bill, expressing doubts as to the constitutionality
of the temporary prosecutor. He also disliked the possibility of multiple special
prosecutors operating simultaneously, each with a single case and all of them
independent of the Department of Justice. Levi urged adoption of the president's
plan. The House itself was divided over the issue. President Ford's amendment
of S. 495 had surprised the legislators. In addition, the November election was
nearing. No action was taken on the special prosecutor legislation.

With the election of Jimmy CARTER, the special prosecutor concept was
revived. New legislation was offered favoring the temporary concept that had
been suggested by Hungate. Although appointment of the special prosecutor
would be assigned to the judiciary, not the attorney general, Hungate's efforts
the previous year had helped preserve a fundamental feature of the new mechanism, one now guaranteed to become part of the new office.

After leaving Congress, Hungate served as U.S. District Court judge for Eastern Missouri, 1979–1992. He captured his life as a legislator in *It Wasn't Funny
at the Time* (1994), which he published himself.

References:

Bertozzi, Mark. "The Federal Special Prosecutor: Too Special?" *Federal Bar News and
Journal* 29 (1982): 222–230.
Harriger, Katy J. *Independent Justice: The Federal Special Prosecutor in American Politics.* Lawrence: University Press of Kansas, 1992. Chapter 3, "A Watergate Legacy," discusses the context within which Hungate's bill was developed and the
reception it received.

I

Immunity. An independent counsel typically will use a grand jury to collect evidence during the investigation. A grand jury can issue a subpoena to a witness, demanding that the person appear before the grand jury to testify. This is a powerful tool, and it is often the centerpiece of an independent counsel's investigation.

However, there is a major constitutional limit on the use of grand jury subpoenas. The Fifth Amendment to the U.S. Constitution provides that no person "shall be compelled in any criminal case to be a witness against himself." A witness asked to testify before the grand jury (or even in a noncriminal proceeding such as a civil trial or testimony before Congress) cannot be forced to provide evidence that would tend to expose the witness to later criminal charges.

The privilege against self-incrimination could amount to an enormous barrier to the work of the grand jury and the independent counsel. Given the breadth of federal and state criminal codes, testimony on many subjects could potentially help the government prove a criminal charge against the witness. Over the years, however, the legal system in the United States has developed a technique to make the self-incrimination privilege less costly. That technique is known as a "grant of immunity." If the independent counsel wants to obtain incriminating grand jury testimony from a witness, it must promise that no government agent will use that congressional testimony to further a later criminal prosecution against the witness. Once the government makes this promise, a judge will order the witness to testify, despite any self-incrimination claim. If the witness refuses, the judge can declare the witness to be in "contempt of court" and can order the witness to be held in prison until he or she does testify.

There are three basic types of immunity. The earliest federal immunity statute, passed in 1857, conferred "transactional" immunity on the witness. When a prosecutor granted transactional immunity to a witness, the government could not prosecute the witness for any "transaction" described during the compelled testimony. Even after a grant of transactional immunity, the government could still prosecute—for perjury or false statements—any witness who deliberately lied during the immunized testimony or during later testimony. Nevertheless, many viewed transactional immunity as overly generous to witnesses, because it allowed them to take an "immunity bath" by testifying to as many criminal transactions as possible. Arguably, transactional immunity made compelled witnesses better off than they would have been if they had remained silent.

An 1862 amendment to the immunity statute provided more limited protection to witnesses, called "simple use" immunity. Simple use immunity prevents the use of the compelled testimony itself as evidence, but the government reserves the right to prosecute the witness based on evidence other than the witness's testimony. The government could even develop investigative leads based on the compelled testimony, and use any evidence that derives from those leads in the later criminal case.

In 1892, the Supreme Court struck down the "simple use immunity" statute and declared that transactional immunity was necessary to protect the constitutional privilege against self-incrimination. See *Counselman v. Hitchcock*, 142 U.S. 547 (1892). As a result, for most of this century, the federal immunity statutes conferred transactional immunity on witnesses.

The federal immunity laws changed again in 1970. Congress, as part of the Crime Control Act of 1970, rewrote the immunity statutes to provide a narrower form of immunity for witnesses, known as "use-derivative use immunity." This form of immunity also goes under the shortened label of "use immunity." Unlike transactional immunity, a grant of use immunity still allows the government to prosecute the witness for a crime described in the compelled testimony. However, unlike "simple use" immunity, "use-derivative use" immunity prevents the government from using either the compelled testimony itself (a "direct" use) or any evidence derived from that testimony (an "indirect" or "derivative" use) as part of the later criminal case against the witness. It is still possible under this statute for the government to prosecute an immunized witness for the crime he testifies about, so long as the prosecution can prove that it built its case exclusively on evidence from independent sources.

Although the federal system now employs use immunity, several state systems grant the more generous transactional immunity to witnesses who are compelled to testify. Furthermore, federal and state investigators do not rely solely on use immunity statutes to force witnesses to waive their privilege against self-incrimination. The investigators will sometimes offer the equivalent of transactional immunity simply by promising the witness—in the form of a letter— that the government will not prosecute the witness if he/she testifies truthfully. This practice is known as "informal" or "letter" immunity. An informal immunity agreement might also grant the same protections as use immunity, while saving the government the logistical problems of obtaining a court order to compel the testimony. Lawyers for the government and the witness might also negotiate some customized form of protection that falls in between transactional and use immunity.

The Supreme Court heard a challenge to the 1970 federal immunity statutes in *Kastigar v. United States*, 406 U.S. 441 (1972). The Court decided that the use immunity offered under that statute is "coextensive" with the Fifth Amendment privilege against self-incrimination, because use immunity leaves the witness in substantially the same position as if she had claimed the privilege and remained silent. Transactional immunity, the Court said, offered broader protection than was necessary under the Fifth Amendment. According to *Kastigar*, the government can prosecute an immunized witness if prosecutors can convince the trial court, during a pretrial hearing, that all of the evidence they propose to use came from legitimate independent sources.

It is very difficult for prosecutors to show that a criminal case against an immunized witness was based on independent evidence rather than on the compelled testimony. Prosecutors who attempt to file charges against formerly-immunized witnesses keep careful records of the independent sources leading to each witness or other piece of evidence. Ideally, they prefer to "can" the testimony: that is, record all the available testimony against an individual before the targeted individual is granted immunity to testify. Prosecutors also usually try to prove that none of the attorneys, investigators, or others on the prosecutorial team was ever exposed to tainted testimony. The office will assign separate attorneys to handle the compelled testimony of the witness (usually in a grand jury proceeding) and the later criminal trial of the witness.

Because of the high hurdles to bringing a criminal case after an immunity grant, prosecutors rarely try to charge an immunized witness with a crime, so long as the witness testifies truthfully. Although there is a legal distinction between transactional immunity and use immunity, the difference is more apparent than real. For all practical purposes, an immunized witness who testifies truthfully is beyond the reach of a criminal prosecution for the crimes described in the testimony.

Because a grant of immunity normally bars a later criminal prosecution against the witness, independent counsels (like other federal prosecutors) have been very reluctant to use this tool. They typically extend grants of immunity to low-level wrongdoers who have unique knowledge about the wrongdoing of more-important targets. These immunity grants therefore tend to appear late in the investigation, after the investigators have explored all the other alternative sources of evidence.

Despite this reluctance, most independent counsels do ultimately immunize at least a few witnesses. Immunity grants are important enough to warrant discussion in the final reports of most independent counsels. For instance, the final report of LAWRENCE WALSH (the independent counsel for the IRAN-CONTRA affair) discussed grants of immunity to 12 witnesses, out of the hundreds of witnesses questioned both inside and outside the grand jury.

These immunity grants have cost independent counsels some potential criminal convictions. It is rare for individuals to face criminal charges about matters discussed during their testimony after they have received immunity from the independent counsel. There are, however, a few exceptions. For instance, prosecutions after immunity have occurred when the Department of Justice brings a criminal prosecution separate from the independent counsel investigation. In such a case, the ordinary prosecutors can show more easily than attorneys within the Independent Counsel's Office that they did not benefit at all from the immunized grand jury testimony that the independent counsel obtained. John Huang, for instance, received immunity from Independent Counsel KENNETH STARR and nevertheless faced criminal charges for illegal campaign contributions, charges filed by election law prosecutors in the Department of Justice.

Some independent counsels are willing to give immunity on terms more generous than those set out under the federal immunity statute. An independent counsel might grant such a "letter" or "informal" immunity to obtain fuller cooperation from a witness who might otherwise be reluctant and evasive during testimony. MONICA LEWINSKY, one of the most infamous witnesses in Kenneth Starr's WHITEWATER investigation, negotiated an informal grant of immunity which offered her greater protection than statutory use immunity.

Independent counsels are not alone in holding the power to immunize witnesses. Other criminal prosecutors could obtain a court order to compel testimony, and, thereby, make it difficult for the independent counsel to prosecute that witness later. Federal prosecutors obtain a few thousand compulsion orders for witnesses every year (for instance, 2,775 witnesses in 1995). State prosecutors have the same power under state law, and the testimony compelled through the state process could taint a federal prosecution. Administrative agencies can also grant immunity in exchange for testimony. Similarly, Congress can obtain a court order that compels a witness to testify in a congressional hearing despite the existence of the self-incrimination privilege. Congress immunizes far fewer witnesses than criminal prosecutors do: Congress has immunized just over 300 witnesses since the federal "use immunity" statute began operation in 1970.

However difficult it is to prosecute a witness after compelling his/her testimony before the grand jury, it is even more difficult to prosecute a witness after Congress compels her testimony during a public hearing. Grand jury testimony—the most common form of compelled testimony—remains secret except for the government attorneys immediately involved in the proceedings. As long as the attorneys from the independent counsel's staff who will ultimately prosecute the criminal case are not formally involved in the grand jury investigation, they will not be exposed to the immunized testimony. Testimony before Congress, however, is likely to be very widely reported and available. Indeed, when the hearings receive the press coverage we have come to expect on matters such as Iran-Contra or Whitewater, it is difficult for any interested person to avoid exposure.

These special difficulties in prosecuting witnesses who have received immunity from Congress played a major role in the prosecutions of OLIVER NORTH and JOHN POINDEXTER, two of the leading figures in the Iran-Contra affair. In *United States v. North*, 920 F.2d 940 (D.C. Cir. 1990), and *United States v. Poindexter*, 951 F.2d 369 (D.C. Cir. 1991), the appeals court overturned the convictions of Oliver North and John Poindexter because the prosecutor, Independent Counsel Lawrence Walsh, made improper use of the immunized congressional testimony of North and Poindexter.

Walsh took extensive precautions to prevent any prosecutorial exposure to the immunized testimony. The lawyers assigned to the cases canceled newspaper subscriptions and stopped watching broadcast news. They also filed with the court "canned" versions of those witness interviews completed before the congressional testimony.

The difficulty in the case came not in the exposure of prosecutors to immunized testimony, but in the exposure of grand jury and trial witnesses for the prosecution. Many of the witnesses closely followed the testimony of Oliver North and John Poindexter during televised congressional hearings.

North and Poindexter claimed that this witness exposure to the immunized testimony influenced the witnesses's testimony at trial and in the grand jury. The appeals court agreed. (Every judge who voted to overturn the convictions was an appointee of a Republican president, while every judge voting to sustain the convictions was an appointee of a Democratic president.) The appeals court held that the trial judge had not taken adequate steps to determine whether the content of witness testimony was tainted. The trial court in such a setting must review the testimony of each witness, line-by-line, to make this determination.

Prosecutors will have an extremely difficult time going forward with criminal cases under this standard. The independent counsel in the North and Poindexter cases did not even try to make the required showing when the cases returned to the trial court after the appeal. Very often, prosecutors will be unable to "can" the testimony of key witnesses, because they either will not agree to interviews or will invoke their own Fifth Amendment privileges. Prosecutors may also have difficulty predicting, early in an investigation, the identity of witnesses they will need later in the investigation or at trial. After the Iran-Contra investigation, it became clear that an immunity grant compelling a person to testify before a congressional hearing will block any later criminal prosecution of that witness for crimes described in the testimony.

Grants of immunity will always play a role in the investigations of independent counsels. Without them, the self-incrimination privilege of the Fifth Amendment would block much of the grand jury testimony that the independent counsel needs to hear. But, immunity is costly. Once a witness receives immunity, it is extremely unlikely that he/she will face criminal charges for the matters he/she describes in his/her testimony. As a result, independent counsels take special care in deciding which witnesses should receive immunity. They also urge other bodies with the power to grant immunity to make the decision cautiously.

References:

Barth, Alan. *Government by Investigation.* New York: Viking Press, 1955.
Beale, Sara Sun, William C. Bryson, James E. Felman, and Michael J. Elston. *Grand Jury Law and Practice.* 2nd ed., §§ 7:1 to 7:12. St. Paul: West Group, 1997.
Walsh, Lawrence E. "Final Report of the Independent Counsel for Iran/Contra Matters." Washington, D.C.: GPO, 1993.
Wright, Ronald F. "Congressional Use of Immunity Grants after Iran-Contra." *Minnesota Law Review* 80 (1995): 407–468.

—*RONALD F. WRIGHT*

In re Sealed Case 838 F. 2d 476 (1988). Although it was not initially anticipated that ALEXIA MORRISON's investigation of Assistant Attorney General THEODORE OLSON would result in the court decision that would decide the constitutionality of the Office of Independent Counsel, none of the earlier challenges to the ETHICS IN GOVERNMENT ACT provisions succeeded in reaching the Supreme Court. Before *MORRISON v. OLSON* settled the matter, the Court of Appeals for the D.C. Circuit ruled that the independent counsel mechanism was an unconstitutional encroachment upon the authority of the executive. Judge LAURENCE H. SILBERMAN delivered the opinion for the majority. Judge RUTH BADER GINSBURG dissented.

On August 19, 1987, District Court Judge Aubrey E. Robinson, Jr. upheld the constitutionality of the independent counsel statute. Article II permitted the courts to appoint inferior officers such as the independent counsel. Robinson found no violation of the separation of powers principle, because precedent demanded a flexible reading of the doctrine. Robinson cited *HUMPHREY'S EXECUTOR v. U.S.* (1935), *WEINER v. U.S.* (1958), and *U.S. v. Nixon* (1974) in support of his ruling.

On January 22, 1988, the Court of Appeals saw things differently. In a 2–1 ruling, Judge Silberman did not see the independent counsel as an inferior officer, because the office was independent of, rather than subservient to the attorney general. Furthermore, the independent counsel provision violates the separation of powers doctrine, ruled Silberman, because it authorizes an officer who is unaccountable to any elected official with the power to prosecute lawbreakers. In addition, because the independent counsel could be removed only for "good cause," Silberman considered that the mechanism improperly intruded upon the president's authority to remove purely executive officers at will. Nor did Silberman find the role played by the special court panel to his liking. Appointment and supervision of the independent counsel should not be governed by a judicial body, stated Silberman, because it violated the concept of a neutral judiciary charged with resolving disputes in a nonpartisan manner.

Silberman also found fault with the manner in which the office had operated to that point. The independent counsel appeared to be under intense pressure to obtain indictment and conviction. The target of the investigation was alone in facing all the resources at the disposal of the independent counsel, who had no other cases. Lack of an indictment was equated with failure. In addition, because the independent counsel was not required to operate under Department of Justice guidelines, prosecution was much more likely in the course of such an inquiry than it would be if the attorney general was in charge of the investigation. Probable cause that a crime had been committed governed the independent counsel's decisions, while the Department of Justice paused to consider whether an unbiased jury would be likely to convict before beginning prosecution. Silberman considered that the independent counsel posed a serious threat to the concept of individual liberty. Judge Stephen F. Williams concurred with Silberman.

Judge Ginsburg in her dissent found that the attorney general continued to retain significant control over the independent counsel office by virtue of the authority to conduct a preliminary investigation and request appointment of an independent counsel. These powers served to substantially limit the extent to which the independent counsel intruded upon traditional executive prerogatives. Some intrusion is warranted, stated Ginsburg, in order to prevent the likelihood of abuse inherent in situations where the executive branch is called upon to investigate itself.

The Court of Appeals's decision in *In re Sealed Case* might have threatened the continuation of Independent Counsel LAWRENCE WALSH's IRAN-CONTRA investigation but for the fact that Walsh had secured a backup appointment from the attorney general in March 1987. This appointment had been affirmed by the District Court on July 10 and the Court of Appeals on August 10. Still, Walsh feared problems arising from matters that had occurred prior to his Justice Department appointment. He also did not enjoy operating his inquiry solely at the pleasure of the attorney general. In June 1988, *Morrison v. Olson* established the constitutionality of the independent counsel, permitting investigations to continue.

References:

"Excerpts from Court Opinion Invalidating Law on Independent Counsel." *New York Times*, 23 January 1988, sec. A, p. 8.

Glitzenstein, Eric R., and Alan B. Morrison. "The Supreme Court's Decision in *Morrison v. Olson*: A Common Sense Application of the Constitution to a Practical Problem." *American University Law Review* 38 (1989): 359–382. Argues that the *In re Sealed Case* decision erred when discussing separation of powers, because *NIXON v. ADMINISTRATOR OF GENERAL SERVICES* (1977) established the principle that a statute that regulates, but does not disrupt or usurp executive power is permissible. Cites *YOUNG v. U.S.* (1987) ruling that there is no usurpation of executive power when court appoints officers as prosecutors.

Gressman, Eugene. "Introduction." *Hofstra Law Review* 16 (Fall 1987): 1–10. Discusses

Silberman's literal reading of the appointment clause and theorizes that the judge would have the President appoint all principal officers of the United States—not just ambassadors and Supreme Court justices.

Harriger, Katy J. *Independent Justice: The Federal Special Prosecutor in American Politics*. Lawrence: University Press of Kansas, 1992. Chapter 5, "Is the Special Prosecutor Constitutional?," discusses *In re Sealed Case* and its implications for the independent counsel office.

INS v. Chadha 462 U.S. 919 (1983). Following the Supreme Court decision in *BUCKLEY v. VALEO* (1976) and preceding the one in *BOWSHER v. SYNAR* (1986), *INS v. Chadha* helped to advance a formalist approach to separation of powers questions. Opponents of the independent counsel statute found support in these cases for the view that the Constitution does not permit legislative-initiated investigation of the executive branch.

The court's ruling in *INS v. Chadha* declared unconstitutional Section 244 c (2) of the Immigration and Nationality Act. This provision authorized resolutions by either house of Congress that served to invalidate decisions of the executive branch relating to deportation of aliens. In this instance, the attorney general sought to allow a deportable alien to remain in the United States in violation of the Act. The court ruled that it is the prerogative of the executive branch to make such decisions. The legislature is not permitted to take action that alters the legal rights and duties of executive branch officials. In this case, the attorney general would have been forced to deport a resident alien even though it was the considered judgment of the Department of Justice that the person in question should be allowed to remain in the country. The court held that the constitutional principle of separation of powers precluded such convenient congressional vetoes of executive decisions.

INS v. Chadha's formalist approach to the separation of powers issue was at odds with past decisions such as *HUMPHREY'S EXECUTOR v. U.S.* (1935), *WEINER v. U.S.* (1958), and *U.S. v. NIXON* (1974). *Buckley*, *Chadha*, and *Bowsher* seemed to usher in a new, more rigid interpretation of the separation of powers doctrine—one that would disallow cross-branch creations such as the independent counsel statute. *MORRISON v. OLSON* (1988), however, reversed the trend, and returned the court to a more traditional, functional reading of the issue. It was clear, though, that the separation of powers issue would likely remain contentious in years to come. Appeals Court Judge LAURENCE H. SILBERMAN supported *Chadha*'s reasoning in *IN RE SEALED CASE* before being overturned in *MORRISON*.

References:

Elliott, E. Donald. "Why Our Separation of Powers Jurisprudence Is So Abysmal." *George Washington Law Review* 57 (1989): 506–532. Criticizes *Chadha* decision because it does not address purposes of procedures in question.

Gerwitz, Paul. "Realism in Separation of Powers Thinking." *William and Mary Law*

Review 30 (1989): 343–354. Believes that *Chadha* decision describes a rigid legalistic world that experience teaches us to be false.

Gressman, Eugene. "Introduction." *Hofstra Law Review* 16 (Fall 1987): 1–10. The attorney who argued *Chadha* before the Supreme Court places the case in perspective before the *Morrison* decision.

Gwyn, William B. "The Indeterminacy of the Separation of Powers and the Federal Courts." *George Washington Law Review* 57 (1989): 474–505. Suggests that courts are working in a vacuum while trying to determine the permissible level of intrusion among branches of government, because there is no historical agreement on the definition of terms such as "executive," "legislative," and "judicial."

Schoenbrod, David. "How the Reagan Administration Trivialized Separation of Powers (and Shot Itself in the Foot)." *George Washington Law Review* 57 (1989): 459–473. Asserts that the Reagan administration challenged power grab attempts by Congress, but condoned those by the executive.

Sherry, Suzanna. "Separation of Powers: Asking a Different Question." *William and Mary Law Review* 30 (1989): 287–300. Argues for practical, flexible approach to separation of powers questions.

Strauss, Peter L. "Was There a Baby in the Bathwater? A Comment on the Supreme Court's Legislative Veto Decision." *Duke Law Journal* (1983): 789–819.

Verkuil, Paul R. "Separation of Powers, the Rule of Law and the Idea of Independence." *William and Mary Law Review* 30 (1989): 300–341. States that interbranch separation of powers crisis created by functionalists may be a more pressing problem than the type of intrabranch conflict of interest they are attempting to remedy.

Iran-Contra. The Iran-Contra scandal originated from two secret foreign policy initiatives developed and implemented by high-ranking officials in the administration of RONALD REAGAN. When the Iran-Contra operations became public in November 1986, many Americans expressed serious concerns about the conduct of foreign policy in the Reagan White House. The ensuing independent counsel investigation, which lasted nearly seven years and cost over $40 million, resulted in few indictments and even fewer convictions. Although some observers hailed Independent Counsel LAWRENCE E. WALSH as an "American hero" for his determination to discover the truth in the face of significant obstacles, critics pointed to Walsh's investigation as proof that the independent counsel provisions of the ETHICS IN GOVERNMENT ACT should be allowed to expire.

The first foreign policy initiative provided assistance to the Contras, an insurgent group dedicated to toppling the Sandinista government in Nicaragua. Fearful that the leftist Sandinistas would promote communist influence in Central America, President Reagan took a personal interest in assisting the Contras, and his administration enthusiastically supported covert operations to aid them. Although Congress initially appropriated funds for these operations, some legislators became skeptical about Contra activities and moved to limit aid, a process that culminated in 1984 with the passage of an amendment to the 1985 Defense Appropriations bill. Known as BOLAND II because it was the second amendment limiting aid to the Contras that Representative Edward P. Boland (D-Massachusetts) had sponsored, the amendment prohibited the Central Intelligence Agency (CIA), the Department of Defense, or "any other agency or entity of the United States involved in intelligence activities" from using funds to support "directly or indirectly, military or paramilitary operations in Nicaragua by any nation, group, organization, movement, or individual."

Despite the congressional ban, members of the executive branch decided to continue funding Contra activities. Lieutenant Colonel OLIVER NORTH, a Marine assigned to the staff of the National Security Council, coordinated this effort. ROBERT C. McFARLANE, national security adviser until December 1985, and his successor, Admiral JOHN M. POINDEXTER, were familiar with all the operations that North conducted. He raised funds from private sources, supplied intelligence information that the CIA had gathered to the Contra leaders, and employed RICHARD SECORD, a retired Air Force major general, to purchase arms and ship them to Nicaragua. Other administration officials solicited funds from third countries such as Saudi Arabia.

North also directed a second secret foreign policy initiative, that of trading arms for hostages with Iran. In 1984, the United States had designated Iran as a sponsor of terrorists and had promoted an international embargo on arms sales to Iran, which was embroiled in brutal war with neighboring Iraq. In addition, President Reagan had publicly declared that the United States would not bargain with terrorists. Nonetheless, his concern for American hostages held in Lebanon led Reagan to seek some accommodation with Iranian moderates who might be able to affect the release of the hostages. When Robert McFarlane suggested arms sales as one means of promoting goodwill with these moderates, both Secretary of State GEORGE P. SHULTZ and Secretary of Defense CASPAR W. WEINBERGER protested. Despite their objections, Reagan sanctioned a plan whereby Israel would sell American missiles to Iran.

Following the president's approval, Israel made two weapons shipments to Iran in late summer of 1985. When problems arose regarding a shipment of Hawk antiaircraft missiles in November 1985, Oliver North and Richard Secord obtained logistical support and the use of an aircraft from the CIA to make the delivery. Because CIA involvement required presidential authorization, President Reagan signed a presidential finding on December 5, 1985, that retroactively approved the CIA's role in the November arms shipment. This finding also explicitly stated that the arms sales were intended to bring about hostage releases. On January 17, 1986, Reagan signed a finding that allowed for direct transactions between the United States and Iran. North controlled these operations, which continued well into 1986. Although the ARMS EXPORT CONTROL ACT of 1976 required the president to inform Congress about such activities in a "timely fashion," Congress remained unaware of the arms sales.

The American people began to learn about their government's clandestine activities on October 5, 1986, when Sandinista forces shot down a cargo plane carrying arms for the Contras. They took EUGENE HASENFUS, an American who was the only survivor among the plane's crew, as a prisoner. Hasenfus incorrectly stated that he worked for the CIA. Administration officials immediately denied Hasenfus's claim, but also declared falsely that they had no knowledge of the arms sales. In fact, the plane was part of Secord's arms delivery operation. However, the administration's denial satisfied Congress, which passed a bill authorizing $100 million in Contra aid less than two weeks after the incident. However, the covert operations in Nicaragua would not remain secret much longer, ironically because news of the arms sales to Iran soon became public. On November 3, the Lebanese weekly *Al-Shiraa* published an account of the U.S. arms sales to Iran, creating a furor in the American press and a crisis within the Reagan White House.

While the White House struggled to define its public position regarding the Iran operation, Justice Department officials discovered a memorandum in which North discussed diverting funds from the Iranian arms sales to purchase weapons for the Contras, thus linking the two covert operations together. Attorney General EDWIN MEESE III realized that keeping this information might have disastrous consequences for the president, including the possibility of impeachment. Thus, after informing congressional leaders on November 25, Reagan and Meese held a press conference in which they revealed the diversion to the American people.

Their announcement set in motion a number of investigations into the Iran-Contra affairs. On November 26, Reagan appointed a special review board to examine the workings of the National Security Council, while Meese authorized the Federal Bureau of Investigation to begin a criminal investigation of the funds diversion. Both houses of Congress announced the establishment of committees to hold hearings on the matter. On December 2, Reagan called for the appointment of an independent counsel; two days later Meese filed a petition requesting such an appointment. The Special Division of Appeals of the United States Court of Appeals for the District of Columbia appointed Lawrence Walsh, a former deputy attorney general and a Republican, as independent counsel on December 19. The court directed Walsh and the Office of the Independent Counsel to investigate the funding and shipment of arms to Iran, the diversion of funds from the Iran sales to the Contras, and, against the wishes of the the attorney general, the Contra operation itself.

In February 1987, Oliver North attempted to block the Office of Independent Counsel investigation with a lawsuit challenging the constitutionality of the independent counsel provisions (a matter not resolved until the 1988 Supreme Court decision in *MORRISON v. OLSON*). Walsh requested an appointment from the attorney general paralleling that of the court. Recognizing that failure to do so would raise allegations that the administration was not supporting the Office of Independent Counsel, Meese announced the parallel appointment on March 5, thus allowing Walsh to proceed with his investigation without fear of an adverse decision from the courts.

The Office of Independent Counsel had few conflicts with the president's

special review board, called the TOWER COMMISSION after its chairman,
former Texas senator John Tower. Designed to protect the president, the commission concluded in its final report of February 26, 1987, that the covert operations were essentially an aberration, the result of inappropriate actions by
specific personnel rather than a flaw in the policy process. President Reagan
was responsible only in so far as his lax management style permitted subordinates to operate beyond the bounds of their responsibilities. Walsh later maintained that the Tower Report made his task more difficult because it fixed in
the public mind the notion of a "rogue operation" within the administration,
thus relieving many high officials of responsibility for policy decisions.

The Office of Independent Counsel's dealings with Congress were problem-
atic. Because Congress wanted to offer legislative remedies to prevent future
scandals, it had little interest in prosecuting individuals for crimes related to the
Iran-Contra operations. As such, Congress's goals conflicted with those of the
Office of Independent Counsel, which was charged with pursuing a criminal
investigation. Moreover, the joint congressional committee had given itself a
ten-month deadline to ensure that the investigation did not extend into 1988, an
election year. Thus, Congress wished to move quickly to resolve legislative
issues, whereas Walsh wanted to proceed deliberately in order to build criminal
cases against specific individuals.

The conflict between Office of Independent Counsel and the congressional
committees became apparent in the debate over granting immunity to Oliver
North and John Poindexter. Although Walsh was willing to offer immunity from
prosecution to people who had played apparently minor roles in the scandal, he
hoped to prosecute key players, especially North and Poindexter. Congress perceived securing the testimony of these two men as essential to completing its
mission in a timely manner. Both men had thus far refused to testify, exercising
their Fifth Amendment right against self-incrimination. When Congress expressed a willingness to grant them use IMMUNITY, which would preclude
prosecution based upon testimony given to the committee, Walsh protested. In
March 1988, Congress and the Office of Independent Counsel reached a compromise. Congress agreed to delay its grant of use immunity until the Office of
Independent Counsel had the opportunity to build a case against the two men.
Attorneys in the Office of Independent Counsel had to rush in order to acquire
evidence against North and Poindexter before Congress heard their testimony.
Walsh later complained that "no adverse factor shaped or constricted Independent Counsel's criminal investigation more than congressional immunity grants
made to North, Poindexter and [Albert] HAKIM" (who was a business partner
of Richard Secord).

The Office of Independent Counsel also met with opposition from executive
branch officials and agencies. Several administration officials withheld personal
notes taken during meetings about the Iran operations, and some agencies were
slow to deliver documents relevant to the investigation. Walsh preferred to make

document requests rather than to rely upon subpoenas because he feared that subpoenas would lead to litigation, which would slow his investigation at a time when he was racing to compile information prior to the pending congressional grants of immunity. Nonetheless, he threatened to subpoena CIA officials when that agency proved reluctant to comply with the document requests.

The Office of Independent Counsel and other executive branch agencies battled over the use of classified documents in criminal trials. The CLASSIFIED INFORMATION PROCEDURES ACT of 1980 (CIPA) was intended to prevent defendants from "GRAYMAILing" the government by threatening to use classified information as part of the defense. The law granted the attorney general the unrestricted authority to determine if classified documents can be used in a trial. Thus, the attorney general had the power to thwart any criminal proceeding that relied upon classified documents, a possibility that Walsh later claimed occurred in regard to the conspiracy charges against Oliver North, which were dropped, and in the charges against JOSEPH FERNANDEZ, a CIA official in Costa Rica, which were dismissed. Many observers concluded that the CIPA procedure limited the powers of the independent counsel in cases involving national security to an overwhelming and unfortunate degree.

Completed in August 1993, the Office of Independent Counsel's final report was made public on January 18, 1994. Walsh concluded that the 1985 arms sales to Iran may have violated the Arms Export Control Act, and were carried out with the knowledge of administration officials, including President Reagan. The Contra operations, which violated Boland II, were conducted with the knowledge of high-level officials. Walsh also concluded that the administration had deceived the American people in its explanations of the Iran-Contra affairs after the operations became public in 1986.

Public reaction to the final report was minimal, in part because the investigation had lasted so long, in part because the major figures in the scandal had already left office. Despite his weighty conclusions, Walsh had little to show for his efforts. As he had feared, the convictions of North and Poindexter were reversed on appeal because of the use immunity grants. Efforts to try Defense Secretary Weinberger for perjury and false statements came to a halt when President GEORGE BUSH pardoned him and five other officials, including Robert McFarlane, in December 1992. The few convictions that Walsh obtained regarded money transactions or "cover-up" efforts involving perjury.

Walsh left behind a mixed legacy. Some observers argued that the investigation had greatly contributed to the historical understanding of the Iran-Contra scandals and had illuminated the workings of the federal government. However, detractors accused Walsh of conducting a witch hunt in order to ruin the Republican party, especially after he indicted Weinberger on a charge of withholding evidence from Congress just days before the 1992 presidential election. Their negative perceptions of Walsh prompted Republicans in Congress to block reauthorization of the independent counsel provisions of the Ethics in Government Act in December 1992. They were reenacted in June 1994, when President William CLINTON faced allegations regarding his conduct in the Whitewater affair.

References:

Cohen, William S., and George J. Mitchell. *Men of Zeal: A Candid Inside Story of the Iran-Contra Hearings*. New York: Viking, 1988. In addition, several individuals including Oliver North and Richard Secord have published their accounts of the Iran-Contra affair.

Draper, Theodore. *A Very Thin Line; The Iran-Contra Affairs*. New York: Hill and Wang, 1991. Offers a detailed examination of the scandal.

Koh, Harold Hongju. *The National Security Constitution: Sharing Power after the Iran-Contra Affair*. New Haven: Yale University Press, 1990. Includes a brief but insightful discussion of the failures of the various investigations of Iran-Contra.

Kornbluh, Peter, and Malcolm Byrne, eds. *The Iran-Contra Scandal: The Declassified History*. New York: The New Press, 1993. Includes incisive essays and copies of pertinent documents.

Walsh, Lawrence. "Final Report of the Independent Counsel for Iran/Contra Matters." Washington, D.C: Government Printing Office, 1993. Includes Walsh's summary and responses from several individuals involved in Iran-Contra.

———. *Firewall: The Iran-Contra Conspiracy and Cover-up*. New York: W. W. Norton, 1997.

—THOMAS CLARKIN

J

Jaworski, Leon (1905–1982) Watergate Special Prosecutor, 1973–1974. Leon Jaworski reluctantly agreed to become chief special prosecutor investigating Watergate scandal allegations 12 days after the nationwide political firestorm ignited by President RICHARD NIXON's infamous "Saturday Night Massacre" firing of ARCHIBALD COX in October 1973. Jaworski subsequently gained fame as the federal special prosecutor who won the Supreme Court ruling forcing release of President Nixon's audiotapes. Jaworski directed the investigation that ultimately led to the prosecution and conviction of many of the White House defendants uncovered in the WATERGATE scandal. The scandal stemmed from investigation of events ignited by the capture of burglars breaking into the Democratic National Committee headquarters on June 17, 1972, at the Watergate office and apartment complex in Washington, D.C.

At the time of his nomination to become special prosecutor, Jaworski was a well-known attorney with extensive trial experience who was at the peak of his career. A native of Texas, he became a lawyer after graduating at the top of his law class at Baylor University in Waco at age 18 and then earning a Master of Laws from George Washington University. Later serving as an Army officer, he had been an early member of the prosecution team during the Nuremberg war crimes trials following World War II, subsequently earning the nickname "colonel" from family and friends. By the 1970s, Jaworski was widely regarded as a leading member of the nation's political and legal "establishment." Jaworski had served a term as president of the AMERICAN BAR ASSOCIATION and became a senior partner in one of the four largest law firms in the nation. As a generally conservative Democrat who reported twice voting for Nixon for president, Jaworski had extensive connections within both major political parties. A resident of Houston, Jaworski was a confidant of President Lyndon Johnson, who appointed him to the Warren Commission investigating the murder of President John Kennedy. He also was an acquaintance of John Connolly, a former governor of Texas and President Nixon's Secretary of the Treasury.

With Washington ablaze following the Saturday Night Massacre, Jaworski was, not surprisingly, extremely reluctant to replace Cox. Suggested by the White House's Al Haig and quickly endorsed by ROBERT BORK, the acting attorney general, Jaworski became the nominee. He agreed to take the position only after receiving assurance that President Nixon would not fire him without the consent of a majority of the Senate Judiciary Committee. Moreover, he would be free to pursue the case wherever it led, including taking the president himself to court.

Once in office, Jaworski continued the organizational arrangement of the Special Prosecutor's Task Force of attorneys created by his predecessor. The group of lawyers had been divided into five task forces in accordance with the subjects of their investigations: Watergate, "plumbers," campaign contributions, political espionage, and ITT (International Telephone and Telegraph). However, the group of lawyers had been assembled by Cox, to whom their primary allegiance ran, rather than Jaworski. Hence, both Jaworski and the lawyers themselves were initially, and justifiably, concerned about how well they would be able to work together. Moreover, many of the lawyers were concerned about the possibility of conflicts of interest involving Jaworski. First, he was a friend of some defendants in the Task Force's investigation of allegations of campaign contributions to the president made by the Associated Milk Producers. In addition, the new special prosecutor was an acquaintance of Connolly, in private life a member of a law firm neighboring Jaworski's in Houston.

Jaworski immediately set out to establish a good working relationship with the attorneys. He retained everyone on staff, declined to add any of "his" people to the task force, and promised to disqualify himself on any cases involving possible conflicts of interest. In addition, he gave task forces (and especially their leaders) much more independence than had Cox. And, although his subsequent relationship with Task Force attorneys was at times strained, Jaworski generally retained their professional respect. A continuing major point of contention between Jaworski and the attorneys was the issue of who should be indicted on criminal charges in connection with the Watergate cover-up. Although Jaworski prevailed, several of his decisions were tempered by arguments made by dissenting attorneys. In a few cases, dissenting attorneys resigned after Jaworski declined to accept their recommendations.

Each of the teams directed its efforts toward gathering evidence and then determining if there was sufficient cause to indict offenders. Their chief weapon was a federal grand jury. Jaworski continued the practice begun by Cox of assembling a parade of administration, and particularly White House officials, to testify before the grand jury. In addition, Jaworski and his team cooperated with the Senate committee, chaired by SAM ERVIN (D-North Carolina), investigating allegations in the Watergate scandal. Finally, after declining to indict President Nixon, Jaworski shared valuable information with the House Judiciary

Committee, chaired by Representative Peter Rodino (D-New Jersey), which ultimately reported out three articles of impeachment on the president.

Moreover, Jaworski was immediately confronted with an even more serious obstacle. President Nixon, delivering the annual State of the Union address to Congress and the nation, announced that "one year of Watergate is enough." The president said he would stop cooperating with both congressional and special prosecutor investigations of Watergate. Undaunted, Jaworski pressed ahead with his investigation. He continued subpoenaing White House operatives to testify before the federal grand jury. He also continued seeking release of the White House audiotapes and, in July 1974, won a unanimous Supreme Court verdict ordering the president to release them. The subsequently released tapes revealed that President Nixon was an early and active participant in the cover-up conspiracy. Moreover, key parts of the tapes of important White House meetings were missing. With this and other evidence in hand, the House Judiciary Committee, less than a week later, voted out three articles of impeachment. On August 8, 1974, President Nixon resigned rather than face the continued pressure of the investigation and a likely Senate impeachment trial. Exactly one month later President GERALD FORD pardoned Nixon. Jaworski resigned not long after that, having served as special prosecutor for about 11 months.

One of Jaworski's most serious obstacles was that many observers feared that he was "the president's man." They quietly questioned the depths of his independence and dedication. With this in mind, Jaworski immediately renewed Cox's quest for the White House tapes and continued to press the issue as hard as he could, all the way to the Supreme Court.

One issue that haunted Jaworski and his staff of lawyers was whether they could legally indict the President of the United States. Moreover, if they could do so legally, should they, considering the political and social turmoil such an act might precipitate in the nation as a whole. Jaworski remained skeptical that a president could be indicted while in office and was unwilling to risk losing a challenge by Nixon before the Supreme Court. Instead, Jaworski preferred to list President Nixon as an unindicted co-conspirator in the list of indictments in connection with the Watergate scandal and let the president confront a likely impeachment trial in the Senate.

The struggle between the special prosecutor and President Nixon over the release of the White House tapes clearly was the focal point, both legally and politically, of the Watergate scandal. The stakes—the future and legacy of the Nixon presidency—were high, and the confrontation had all the drama of a fictional best-seller. President Nixon, when initially successfully challenged by the special prosecutor in federal court, promptly responded by trying to throw the issue into the political arena. He fired the special prosecutor, Archibald Cox, and promised to end cooperation with both the prosecutor task force and the Senate committee investigating Watergate allegations. Undaunted, the new special prosecutor, Leon Jaworski, quickly resumed the quest for the tapes. Once again, President Nixon presented a political response; he proposed to release selected (by him) printed versions of the taped conversations. Jaworski eschewed entering the political arena in favor of pressing his case through the federal court system. The special prosecutor's unanimous victory before the Supreme Court forced President Nixon to release the tapes. Although some of the tapes were found to be missing—such as a mysterious 18-minute gap in one—evidence gathered from them revealed that President Nixon had been actively involved in the cover-up from the start. Such documentation made virtually untenable the president's defense in a likely impeachment hearing before the Senate. President Nixon's subsequent resignation led to Jaworski's stepping down as special prosecutor not long afterward and immediately returning to Houston.

Much like his immediate predecessor, Jaworski was simultaneously criticized by the president's supporters as being too aggressive and by White House critics as being an "establishment" figure himself and, hence, inherently sympathetic to the troubles of those in power. He carefully reveals his views of the position, and why he accepted the task to begin with, in his special prosecutor memoirs, *The Right and the Power*. In sum, Jaworski took the thankless job because of a sense of duty and patriotism rather than to advance his career. He did not need the position as a stepping-stone toward something else; he had already completed a distinguished career and was at an age when most men were retired.

References:

Ben-Veniste, Richard, and George Frampton, Jr. *Stonewall: The Real Story of the Watergate Prosecution*. New York: Simon and Schuster, 1977. An account written by a pair of attorneys on the Watergate Special Prosecution Force.

Doyle, James. *Not above the Law: The Battles of Watergate Prosecutors Cox and Jaworski*. New York: William Morrow, 1977. A narrative account of the Special Prosecutor's Task Force written by the group's press officer.

Harriger, Katy J. *Independent Justice: The Federal Special Prosecutor in American Politics*. Lawrence: University Press of Kansas, 1992. An analytic study of the Federal Special Prosecutor's Office throughout the twentieth century.

Jaworski, Leon. *Papers*. Texas Collection at Baylor University, Waco, Texas. Jaworski's public papers written in connection during his term as chief federal special prosecutor.

———. *The Right and The Power: The Prosecution of Watergate*. New York: Reader's Digest Press, 1976. Jaworski's memoirs wherein he provides his account of the Watergate investigation and prosecution.

—ROBERT E. DEWHIRST

Jones, Paula Corbin (1966–   ) Arkansas state government employee, 1991–1993. A small-town girl from rural Arkansas, Paula Corbin Jones brought sexual harassment charges against President Bill CLINTON in 1994. The matter remaining unresolved four years later, Independent Counsel KENNETH STARR was able to expand his WHITEWATER inquiry to include investigation of possible perjurious testimony offered by former White House intern MONICA LEWINSKY in her deposition related to Jones's lawsuit. Subsequent examination of Clinton's relationship with Lewinsky resulted in the president's impeachment.

In January 1994, the *American Spectator* magazine ran a story by David Brock detailing former Arkansas Governor Bill Clinton's alleged habit of employing state troopers to procure female companionship for him. In the story, Paula Corbin Jones was identified by her first name. Fearing that she would be easily identified in this manner, and angry that her apparently sordid encounter with Clinton was being resurrected and publicized, she decided to file formal charges against the president. Jones, supported in this endeavor by many of Clinton's political enemies, announced her allegations at a meeting sponsored by the Conservative Political Action Conference. Clinton supporters retaliated by portraying Jones as "trailer trash" whose lies were being used for political reasons.

The incident that sparked Jones's charges occurred on May 8, 1991. Jones, a clerk at the Arkansas Industrial Development Commission, stated that she was brought to Clinton's room at Little Rock's Excelsior Hotel by a state trooper. Clinton proceeded to make sexual advances, exposing himself in the process. Jones filed a $700,000 lawsuit against Clinton and state trooper Danny Ferguson in May 1994. She charged sexual discrimination under 42 U.S.C. Sections 1983 and 1985, defamation of character and intentional infliction of emotional distress. From the outset, analysts questioned whether Jones was likely to succeed on these bases. The fact that the alleged conduct occurred briefly, did not recur, and did not result in any apparent job penalty would prove difficult obstacles to overcome. Success under Section 1983 would require Jones to demonstrate the presence of a conspiracy to deprive her as a woman of equal protection, another formidable hurdle. Legal analysis aside, Jones's lawsuit certainly provided political problems for Clinton, and many viewed the matter strictly in this light.

After hiring ROBERT BENNETT to handle the Jones action, Clinton attempted to obtain immunity from prosecution while he was a sitting president. The district court granted Clinton temporary immunity, *Jones v. Clinton* 869 F. Supp 690 (E.D. Ark 1994), but the Eighth Circuit Court of Appeals reversed this decision in January 1996 by a 2–1 vote, ruling that defense against Jones's lawsuit would not distract him from his official duties. The rebuff did not prove a factor in Clinton's 1996 re-election, as had been feared by some. On May 27, 1997, the Supreme Court unanimously concurred with the appeals court decision to permit continuation of the Jones lawsuit. Subsequent events, however, proved that the Jones matter would indeed occupy a great amount of the president's time, especially after the Lewinsky deposition.

Jones's original team of lawyers withdrew from the case in the fall of 1997 after their client rejected a proposed settlement offer. In their place, Jones retained attorneys recommended and partially financed by the Rutherford Institute, a legal advocacy group with religious fundamentalist leanings. In April 1998, it appeared that Jone's decision to reject the settlement offer was a poor one when

Arkansas District Court Judge Susan Webber Wright dismissed the Jones suit for lack of merit. Even if Jones's allegations were admitted as true, ruled Wright, she would not have an actionable case. Revelations surrounding the Lewinsky deposition and her apparent sexual relationship with the president, however, encouraged Jones and her attorneys to seek reinstatement of her case. Meanwhile, Starr's use of the information formed the basis of his report to the House of Representatives in September.

In October 1998, Jones's lawyers argued their case before district court. Negotiations over a possible settlement continued behind the scenes. When Jones failed to respond to another settlement offer in early November, her attorneys indicated their intention to also withdraw from the case. Shortly afterward, however, on November 13, an out-of-court settlement was arranged. Clinton agreed to settle with Jones for $850,000. The arrangement did not require an admission of guilt by Clinton, nor did it require an apology. On January 13, 1999, having been impeached and facing trial in the Senate, Clinton's check arrived ending the Jones matter.

On April 12, 1999, Judge Wright held the president in civil contempt for having offered false testimony in the Paula Jones case. Clinton's characterization of his relationship with Lewinsky was ruled to have been intentionally false. This ruling, and the financial sanctions imposed, marked an end to both the Jones and Lewinsky affairs. Many regarded it as an appropriate response to the misconduct involved. Unlike the attempt to characterize Clinton's behavior as justifying his removal, the penalty appeared in proper proportion to the nature of the misdeed. The fact remained, however, that the Jones affair had set in motion a series of events that posed a grave threat to the Clinton presidency.

References:

Amar, Akhil Reed, and Neal Kumar Katyal. "Executive Privileges and Immunities: The Nixon and Clinton Cases." *Harvard Law Review* 108 (1995): 701–726. Argues that Clinton should be immune from prosecution while president.

"Excerpts from Wright's Order." *Washington Post*, 13 April 1999, sec. A, p. 6.

Isikoff, Michael. "The Paula Problem." *Newsweek*, 26 January 1998, p. 24.

Kilberg, William J. "Jones v. Clinton." *Employee Relations Law Journal*, 22 September 1994, p. 173.

Lacayo, Richard. "Jones v. The President." *Time*, 16 May 1994, p. 44.

Matraia, Michael T. "Running for Cover behind Presidential Immunity: The Oval Office as Safe Haven from Civil Suits." *Suffolk University Law Journal* 29 (1995): 195–231. Argues that immunity should not protect president from consequences of pre-presidential conduct.

Taylor, Stuart, Jr. "Her Case against Clinton." *American Lawyer*, November 1996, p. 57. This 15,000 word essay recants the author's original disbelief of Jones's charges and provides a penetrating comparison between Anita Hill's allegations against Clarence Thomas and Jones's contentions against Clinton. Maintains that Jones's charges are both more serious and plausible.

Thomas, Evan, and Michael Isikoff. "Clinton v. Paula Jones." *Newsweek*, 13 January 1997, p. 26.

Jordan, Hamilton (1944–   ) White House Chief of Staff, 1979–1980. Appointed President Jimmy CARTER's chief of staff on July 17, 1979, Hamilton Jordan quickly found himself facing charges that he had indulged in cocaine use at New York's Studio 54 discotheque in June 1978. Although skeptical, Attorney General BENJAMIN CIVILETTI reluctantly initiated the first ETHICS IN GOVERNMENT ACT investigation of an executive branch official when he requested that an appeals court panel name a special prosecutor to investigate the matter. On November 30, 1979, New York Republican ARTHUR CHRISTY was appointed to lead the inquiry. Seven months later, a grand jury cleared Jordan of wrongdoing. This first test of the Ethics Act special prosecutor provisions left many with the impression that the investigation had been initiated too quickly by allegations that lacked proper credibility. A similar probe of presidential aide TIMOTHY KRAFT would shortly serve to support this belief.

Jordan was a student at the University of Georgia when he first met Jimmy Carter. He served as manager of Carter's gubernatorial campaign in 1970, and remained as adviser and executive secretary to the Governor. After managing Carter's successful presidential campaign in 1976, Jordan was named Chief Political Adviser to the President. He was just 32 years old when he came to Washington as a presidential aide. No stranger to big city night life, Jordan had been accused of various breaches of etiquette at Washington social affairs in 1977 and 1978 before being named in 1979 as the person to whom drug dealer John Conaghan had administered cocaine. Jordan denied all accusations. The cocaine charges were brought by Studio 54 owners Steve Rubell and Ian Schrager, both of whom were tying to extricate themselves from federal charges of tax evasion, obstruction of justice, and conspiracy.

The FBI began an investigation of the cocaine charge, expanding it in September to include new charges that Jordan had been observed using the drug at a Beverly Hills party in October 1977. White House Press Secretary Jody Powell asserted that the charges against Jordan, which had been circulating for the past year, were unsubstantiated and generally ignored by the press, because they could not be corroborated. Rubell and Schrager resurrected the matter, and the FBI initiated an investigation that the press now found obligated to cover. Powell believed Jordan to be the victim of a smear campaign. The Beverly Hills aspect of the inquiry was based on the rather vague recollections of Leo Wyler, a California aerospace executive who was heading a dump-Carter movement called Democrats for Change. Though not specifically implicating Jordan, Wyler testified that the group that included Jordan was using cocaine at a party Wyler was hosting.

President Carter and presidential adviser Robert Strauss urged Jordan to remain as chief of staff in the face of these charges. Jordan agreed to do so although he worried that his continued presence was damaging to the Carter presidency. The FBI probe found the charges against Jordan to be without foundation, but Attorney General Civiletti did not believe that he could dismiss the affair without subjecting the Carter administration to charges of political favoritism. In addition, Civiletti's own inquiry could not be completed, because several witnesses refused to speak without grants of immunity—something only a special prosecutor could provide. As a result, New York attorney Arthur Christy was appointed to investigate the affair in November 1979. By May 1980, he was able to report that a grand jury had dismissed the charges against Jordan.

Although exonerated, Jordan suffered personal damage to his reputation and incurred sizable legal fees. Both consequences were addressed when the Ethics Act provisions were reauthorized in 1982. Investigations became more difficult to trigger, because the specificity of charge and credibility of source would have to be considered before launching an inquiry. As a result, the sort of charges brought against Jordan would be unlikely to result in a damaging inquiry. In addition, legal fees would be reimbursable if an investigation did not result in an indictment. These reforms came too late to help Jordan who remained in debt for years afterward.

Perhaps disillusioned with conventional politics, Jordan assisted Ross Perot during the 1992 presidential campaign. He has also worked as an official with the ATP professional tennis organization and with Whittle book publishers.

References:

Babcock, Charles R., and Tom Sherwood. "New Cocaine Allegation Cited in Jordan Inquiry." *Washington Post*, 14 September 1979, sec. A, p. 3.

"Justice for Mr. Jordan." *Washington Post*, 2 September 1983, sec. A, p. 20.

Schram, Martin. "Jordan Affair: A Dilemma for Carter, Media, Justice Dept." *Washington Post*, 25 September 1979, sec. A, p. 7.

Williams, Robert H. "FBI Investigating Alleged Cocaine Use by Jordan." *Washington Post*, 25 August 1979, sec. A, p. 1.

K

Keker, John W. (1944–   ) Associate Independent Counsel, Iran-Contra Investigation. Recommended to IRAN-CONTRA Independent Counsel LAWRENCE WALSH as the best criminal trial lawyer in San Francisco, John Keker joined the investigation in 1987, when plans were being formulated for its conduct. Although considerably more liberal than Walsh, a Republican, and most of his legal team, Keker impressed the independent counsel with his aggressive analysis of the case during strategy sessions. In addition, Keker's status as an ex-Marine who had been wounded in Vietnam would neutralize OLIVER NORTH's military credentials in any courtroom confrontation. Accordingly, Walsh assigned the prosecution of North to Keker. After a four-month trial that began in January 1989, the jury found North guilty of 3 of the 12 counts with which he was charged.

A graduate of Princeton University with a law degree from Yale (1970), Keker clerked for Supreme Court Chief Justice Earl Warren after graduation. Relocating to California in 1971, he worked in the Public Defender's office (1971–1973) before entering private practice (Kipperman, Shawn & Keker, 1973–1978; Keker & Brockett, 1978–   ). In partnership with William Brockett, a law-school classmate and Vietnam veteran, Keker specialized in defense of white-collar criminals and business litigation. Keker sought a spot on Walsh's team, because he was offended by North's actions. He called upon Chevron Corporation executive Charles Renfrew for a recommendation. Renfrew, who, like Walsh, was a former federal judge and deputy U.S. attorney general, touted Keker's courtroom skills and suggested that the team be assembled around him. Keker was one of Walsh's first selections.

North's defense team would benefit from IMMUNITY that had been granted to him in return for his congressional testimony. They would also successfully employ the tactic of GRAYMAIL, threatening release of sensitive government documents unless the prosecution agreed to drop specific charges. Faced with these formidable obstacles, Walsh's team needed to agree on a strategy that still promised a reasonable degree of success. Keker argued that North's fund-raising for the Contras amounted to a concerted effort aimed at undermining the BO-LAND AMENDMENTS. Prosecutorial efforts should focus on this conspiracy, even though Boland specified no penalties for violation. Keker insisted that North's actions had frustrated the will of the American people as represented in Congress.

During the trial of Oliver North, Keker characterized the defendant as a man who lied repeatedly in order to cover up crimes he had committed. Patriotism should not entail subversion of our democracy, and keeping secrets should not require telling lies, Keker maintained. Although evidence was introduced indicating that funds raised by North's organization were misappropriated, Keker stressed the dishonest nature of North's conduct and its detrimental effect upon a free society. North was more concerned, asserted Keker, with establishing democracy in Nicaragua than in abiding by the democratic procedures established in his own country. The verdict of the jury was a disappointment to Keker. The jury's findings indicated that it had probably found the arguments of North's attorney BRENDAN SULLIVAN persuasive. Sullivan maintained that the White House had authorized North's activities. President RONALD REAGAN had referred to North as a hero before dismissing him. This appeared to lend credence to Sullivan's contention that the White House supported North's activities but was now using him as a scapegoat.

North's conviction on 3 counts (aiding in preparation of false testimony; destruction of National Security Council documents; and acceptance of an illegal gratuity) was important to Walsh's investigation. Had North been acquitted on all 12 counts, the Iran-Contra inquiry would probably have been ended. In addition, evidence and leads that had surfaced during the trial helped provide the prosecution with new areas for investigation. Taking solace in the fact that North was not completely vindicated, Keker told reporters that the verdict demonstrated no man was above the law. Many said that the case could never be tried, Keker reminded the press. That, at least, had been accomplished.

Keker did not play a major role in the remainder of the Iran-Contra investigation. It was upon his recommendation, however, that Walsh hired San Francisco attorney JAMES BROSNAHAN to conduct the prosecution of former Secretary of Defense CASPAR WEINBERGER. In recent years, Keker has returned to his San Francisco law practice. He served as President of the civilian-run San Francisco Police Commission in 1997.

References:

Morain, Dan. "Ready for Combat." *Los Angeles Times*, 12 January 1989, sec. A, p. 1.
        Profiles Keker's career and his preparation for the North trial.
"Prosecutor Opens Attack on North." *San Diego Union-Tribune*, 21 February 1989, sec.
        A, p. 1.

Walsh, Lawrence. *Firewall: The Iran-Contra Conspiracy and Cover-up.* New York: W. W. Norton, 1997.

Kendall v. United States 37 U.S. 524 (1838). An early separation of powers case involving payment due to contract mail carriers, the Supreme Court's decision in this matter is considered part of the historical foundation supporting the independent counsel statute. Justice Smith Thompson's ruling served to allow Congress to impose executive duties upon officers without presidential interference.

When Amos Kendall became postmaster general of the United States in 1835, he refused to fully honor contracts that had been negotiated by his predecessor William T. Barry. Contract mail carriers William B. Stokes, Richard C. Stockton, Lucius W. Stockton, and Daniel Moore, dissatisfied with Kendall's refusal to fully reimburse them for services rendered, petitioned Congress. Congress passed an act, approved by the president on July 2, 1836, authorizing solicitor of the Treasury Virgil Maxcy to consider claims for additional payment due to the petitioners. Although Maxcy certified that additional funds were due to the mail carriers, Kendall disagreed and refused to act. The petitioners appealed to the President who, in December 1836, referred the dispute back to Congress. The mail carriers presented Congress with a memorial requesting resolution of their claim. The Senate referred the memorial to the Judiciary Committee. On January 20, 1837, the Committee issued its report supporting the award recommended by Maxcy.

On June 7, 1837, the District Court of the County of Washington issued a writ of mandamus ordering Kendall to comply with Congress's decision. Kendall's appeal was filed on June 24. It stated that the Constitution does not confer upon the Judiciary authority to interfere with executive branch functions; the circuit court does not have authority to issue a writ of mandamus in this case; and the court's order to the postmaster general cannot be legally carried out. On July 13, 1837, the Circuit Court for the District of Columbia directed that a writ of mandamus be issued to the postmaster general. Kendall appealed to the Supreme Court.

Kendall pressed the argument that the Judiciary was assuming power reserved exclusively for the executive branch of government. The court may not interfere with the president's Constitutional prerogatives. If the president is dissatisfied with the postmaster's decisions in matters such as the one in question, he may ask for his resignation or remove him from office.

The Supreme Court's reply highlighted the fact that the validity of the contracts held by the mail carriers is unchallenged. Kendall's defiance of Congress, the Judiciary, and the solicitor of the treasury has no legal basis because a writ of mandamus is an appropriate remedy in this case. It is the only available option that will satisfy the parties who have been damaged. Furthermore, the Constitution allows the courts to be vested by Congress with authority to issue writs directing an officer to do his duty. Article I directs Congress to oversee delivery of the mail, and Article III assigns to the Judiciary the comprehensive task of adjudicating all disputes arising from constitutional questions. When Congress creates an office like the postmaster general, may it not decide who shall enforce the responsibilities of that office?

Justice Thompson, speaking for the majority, ruled that the court's writ did not interfere with executive authority in any manner, because it did not attempt to direct or control the postmaster. It merely sought to enforce performance of a ministerial act. In this case, the postmaster attributes too much power to the president. The chief executive's authority to faithfully see the law executed does not include the power to refuse execution of the law. In any case, the president in this instance referred the matter to Congress, and that body issued directives that the postmaster now refuses to obey. Thompson ruled that Kendall must honor the contracts.

Dissenters led by Justice Roger B. Taney, concurred in most respects with the majority decision, but did not agree that the Circuit Court had the authority to issue a writ of mandamus to an officer of the federal government. There was no disagreement regarding Congress's constitutional power to call upon the proper court when attempting to coerce an executive officer into doing his duty. This view would later serve to support the creation of an independent counsel mechanism that relied on cross-branch cooperation.

References:

Dudley, Earl C. "*Morrison v. Olson*: A Modest Assessment." *American University Law Review* 38 (1989): 255–274. Cites *Kendall* as building on Madison's (*Federalist Paper* no. 47) explanation of a less-than-rigid separation of powers principle by which our government should be guided. Sees *YOUNGSTOWN SHEET & TUBE v. SAWYER* (1952) and *COMMODITY FUTURES TRADING COMMISSION v. SCHOR* (1986) as continuing the flexible approach to the issue.

Kraft, Timothy (1941–   ) White House Aide and Campaign Manager, 1976–1980. In a scenario resembling the allegations brought against President Jimmy CARTER's White House chief of staff HAMILTON JORDAN in 1979, one year later Campaign Manager Timothy Kraft was charged with cocaine use on a visit to New Orleans in 1978. As in the Jordan case, which had been dismissed in May 1980, the nature of the allegation hardly seemed worth the effort involved in mounting a costly, time-consuming investigation led by a special prosecutor operating under the provisions of the new ETHICS IN GOVERNMENT ACT. In this instance, however, the target of the inquiry filed a lawsuit in U.S. District Court (*KRAFT v. GALLINGHOUSE*) challenging the constitutionality of the special prosecutor's office.

A native of Indiana, Kraft graduated Dartmouth and served in the Peace Corps before turning to politics. During Independent Counsel ARTHUR CHRISTY's investigation, Kraft supported Hamilton Jordan's claim of innocence. Kraft had accompanied Jordan to the Studio 54 discotheque on June 27, 1978, and vouched for the fact that Jordan had not indulged in cocaine usage. Three months after Jordan was cleared of the charges, Kraft found himself under investigation by the FBI. The allegations against Kraft grew out of the Jordan investigation and were apparently supported by the testimony of Evan Dobelle, deputy chairman of the Democratic National Committee. Dobelle had been replaced as Carter Campaign Manager by Kraft. Unlike Jordan, Kraft resigned from the Carter campaign when his case was referred to a special prosecutor by Attorney General BENJAMIN CIVILETTI. GERALD GALLINGHOUSE was named to investigate the matter on September 14, 1980. A second charge of cocaine use was added to the inquiry in October when it was alleged that Kraft had indulged at a party in San Francisco on November 18, 1978.

On November 20, 1980, Kraft filed suit challenging the constitutionality of the special prosecutor mechanism. Kraft's attorneys, Thomas C. Green and A. Raymond Randolph characterized Special Prosecutor Gallinghouse a *de facto* attorney general with Kraft as his only target. They also asserted that Gallinghouse was ineligible for appointment as special prosecutor under the terms of the Ethics in Government Act, because he had served as a U.S. Attorney for Louisiana until February 1978. (The independent counsel may not hold "any office of profit or trust under the United States." 28 U.S.C. Sec. 593 b2.)

On March 25, 1981, Gallinghouse announced that there was insufficient evidence to support any criminal charges against Kraft. Because Kraft's case was now settled, his legal challenge to the constitutionality of the special prosecutor's office was dismissed as moot. Lessons of the Hamilton Jordan matter, however, were reinforced by the Kraft experience. It was apparent to many observers that special prosecutor investigations were being triggered too quickly. Sentiment also favored allowing the attorney general greater discretion in handling the process. Critics felt that too many relatively minor governmental officials were covered by the provisions. These concerns were to be addressed in reauthorization of the special prosecutor statute the following year.

Kraft, who moved to Albuquerque in 1981, worked in Ross Perot's 1992 presidential campaign along with Hamilton Jordan.

References:

Babcock, Charles R. "Special Prosecutor Investigations Called 'Enormous Waste.' " *Washington Post*, 21 May 1981, sec. A, p. 20. The Kraft case is cited as justification for radically altering or abolishing the Office of Special Prosecutor.

Brown, Warren. "Carter Aide Steps Down Amid Probe." *Washington Post*, 15 September 1980, sec. A, p. 1.

Harriger, Katy J. *Independent Justice: The Federal Special Prosecutor in American Politics.* Lawrence: University Press of Kansas, 1992. Chapter 4, "Implementation and Oversight," discusses the Kraft case and its implications.

Pound, Edward T. "Inquiry Set on Alleged Drug Use by Kraft, Carter Campaign Aide." *New York Times*, 14 September 1980, sec. A, p. 1.

————. "Kraft Charge Laid to an Aide of Party." *New York Times*, 17 September 1980, sec. A, p. 1.

Rich, Spencer. "Kraft Is Cleared of Allegations He Used Cocaine." *Washington Post*, 25 March 1981, sec. A, p. 1.

"2nd Charge Studied in Inquiry on Kraft." *New York Times*, 14 October 1980, sec. A, p. 16.

L

Lancaster, Ralph I. (1930–) Independent Counsel, Alexis Herman investigation, 1998–1999 and present. On May 27, 1998, Ralph Lancaster was named independent counsel to investigate whether Labor Secretary ALEXIS HERMAN had used her influence to benefit a friend's consulting business and/or raise illegal campaign contributions.

An attorney from Maine, Lancaster is a Republican who, on occasion, has supported Democratic candidates. Educated at Holy Cross (A.B., 1952) and Harvard University (LL.B., 1955), Lancaster has long been a partner in the Portland, Maine, law firm of Pierce Atwood. He has also lectured at the University of Maine and its law school, and served as legal adviser to Martindale Hubbell publishers. Lancaster was chair of the AMERICAN BAR ASSOCIATION (ABA) committee that evaluated and made recommendations regarding the competency of Supreme Court candidates David Souter and Clarence Thomas. This role subjected him to considerable political pressure from groups whose agendas included ensuring that Supreme Court vacancies were filled by individuals whose views coincided with theirs. During this period, Lancaster frequently resorted to taping conversations with reporters in an effort to guarantee an accurate record of the proceedings. In 1996, Lancaster hosted a tribute in honor of WILLIAM COHEN, then Republican senator from Maine, who had just been named President Bill CLINTON's Secretary of Defense.

References:

Leavitt, Paul, Tom Squiteri, and Bill Nichols. "Maine Lawyer Appointed to Investigate Herman." *USA Today*, 27 May 1998, sec. A, p. 6.
Mauro, Tony. "ABA Begins Study of Court Nominee." *USA Today*, 15 July 1991, sec. A, p. 3.

Leach, Jim (1942–) Congressman (R-Iowa), 1977- present. As ranking Republican and Chairman of the House Banking and Financial Services Committee, Jim Leach was among those leading the call for appointment of an independent counsel to investigate the WHITEWATER affair. Attorney General JANET RENO's appointment of ROBERT FISKE in January 1994 (during the period when the independent counsel statute had lapsed) satisfied this demand. Considered a moderate, Leach at first favored limited congressional hearings on Whitewater that acknowledged the primacy of Fiske's investigation. After presiding over a 21-month investigation, however, Leach was convinced that the CLINTONs had committed serious offenses that needed to be communicated to the public. During the course of his committee's investigation, Leach became its chairman, and KENNETH STARR replaced the more moderate Fiske as independent counsel for Whitewater.

Educated at Princeton University (B.A., 1964), Johns Hopkins (M.A., 1966) and the London School of Economics (1966–1968), Leach served as chairman of the board of Abdel Wholesalers in Bettendorf, and Director of the Federal Home Loan Bank in Des Moines before being elected representative from Iowa's first congressional district in 1977. He worked on the Arms Control and Foreign Policy Caucus, the Congressional Arts Caucus, and the Foreign Affairs and Urban Affairs Committees before rising to prominence as a result of Whitewater.

In January 1994, Leach was convinced that the burgeoning Whitewater affair warranted investigation by an independent counsel. It did not appear to Leach, however, that a major scandal was about to erupt. Rather, he saw the matter as a relatively minor indiscretion that was unworthy of a dramatic confrontation. The House Banking Committee's developing investigation as well as increasing politicization of Whitewater gradually served to alter Leach's outlook. Republicans planned to use a Banking Committee hearing scheduled for March 24 to publicly examine whether the Clinton administration was interfering with the Resolution Trust Corporation's (RTC) disposal of JAMES McDOUGAL's bankrupt Madison Guaranty Savings & Loan. Sensing that the scheduled meeting might be used to the Republicans' political advantage, then-Chairman Henry B.Gonzalez (D-Texas) postponed it. Lacking the forum that a committee meeting would have provided, Leach took to the floor of the House in order to charge that money from Madison Guaranty had been illegally funneled into the Whitewater Development Corporation; the Clintons had profited from their Whitewater investments, contrary to their claims of losses; and that federal officials were acting to protect Clinton by interfering with banking regulators' investigation into Madison Guaranty and Whitewater.

During the week of August 1, congressional hearings probed more deeply into Whitewater. Leach charged that Treasury General Counsel JEAN HANSON had acted to delay RTC criminal referrals in order to provide pro-administration attorneys with time to argue against the action. Questioning of the roles played by both Hanson and Deputy Treasury Secretary ROGER C. ALTMAN in the RTC investigation led directly to their resignations.

In August 1995, Leach anticipated that his committee's hearings would clearly define the nature of the Whitewater affair for the American public. The task of interpreting the 330,000 pages of documents in a manner that made the matter both comprehensible and compelling would be a daunting one. The attempt was rendered more difficult by the fact that Senate hearings had been underway for four weeks before the House proceedings convened. In addition, the Senate concentrated on the sensational death of White House attorney VINCENT FOSTER, challenging the official finding that it was a suicide. In contrast, Leach was attempting to tell the story of an obscure Arkansas land deal and its connection to a failed savings and loan several years ago. Witnesses called were relatively obscure bank officials and examiners.

In his opening statement, Leach characterized Whitewater as an unconscionable fraud perpetrated against poor, rural Americans by cynical Arkansas businessmen who intentionally misappropriated tax money for their own purposes. Responding to administration protestations of innocence, Leach claimed that his committee's findings demonstrated that at least $88,000 was transferred from Madison Guaranty into the Whitewater land deal; the Clintons were active participants in the fraud and benefited from it; Bill Clinton actively aided Jim McDougal in his illegal schemes; and Clinton's actions in Whitewater undercut his professed regard for both affirmative action policies and environmental protection law. Attempting to overcome public cynicism and apathy with regard to politics-as-usual in America, Leach pointed out that Whitewaters do not occur regularly in most states. This is not the way business is done, asserted Leach, in Nebraska or Iowa, and the American public should be outraged, because it is their tax money that was misappropriated by Clinton and his cronies.

Unfortunately, the promise that was implicit in Leach's opening statement was not realized in the week of hearings. Public attention remained focused on the Senate proceedings presided over by the more flamboyant ALFONSE D'AMATO (R-New York). Testimony did not register as clearly as Leach's opening remarks indicated it might. The Clintons' investment in the Whitewater Development Corporation was detailed through the use of 158 documents (primarily letters, calendars, and phone messages). The failure of McDougal's Madison Guaranty Savings & Loan was described, as well as its cost to taxpayers. In addition, Hillary Clinton was depicted as more closely involved in the bank's affairs than was previously believed. Still, it was possible for Democrats to make the argument that the hearings demonstrated nothing more than the fact that the Clintons had behaved carelessly, not criminally, with regard to their personal finances. Certainly, the hearings did not capture the public's imagination in a manner that would defeat the prevailing apathy. While Leach had moved beyond his initial impression that Whitewater was a less than dramatic affair, the public had not.

References:

"Leach: Whitewater Is 'Case Model in How Not to Handle Scandal.' " *Washington Post*, 8 August 1995, sec. A, p. 10.

Merida, Kevin. "Explaining Whitewater; Leach Vows 'Straightforward House Hear-
   ings.' " *Washington Post*, 7 August 1995, sec. A, p. 1.
————. "Republicans' Dive into Whitewater Scores Some Points." *Washington Post*, 14
   August 1995, sec. A, p. 1.
"Rough 'Whitewater' Ride for Clinton." *Congressional Quarterly Almanac* (1994): 109–
   115.

Levi, Edward H. (1911–   ) Attorney General, 1975–1977. As President GER-
ALD FORD's attorney general, Edward Levi represented the administration's
thoughts concerning Congress's proposed establishment of a Special Prosecutor's Office during the summer of 1976. Some believe that Levi's arguments in
opposition to the concept of a temporary special prosecutor effectively postponed its inception for two years. The constitutional objections and practical
considerations raised by Levi proved influential in the Senate where ABRA-
HAM RIBICOFF's S. 495 initiative was amended to reflect administrative criticism. The House of Representatives, however, balked at the changes, and,
consequently, no special prosecutor bill was passed in 1976.

A native of Chicago, Levi received his law degree (1935) and joined on the
faculty at the University of Chicago (1936–1940; 1945–1975), serving as the
Law School's Dean from 1950 until 1962. He was named university president
in 1968, a position he held until his appointment as attorney general in 1975.

In the summer of 1976, Levi maintained that the Senate's proposal for establishment of a special prosecutor was unconstitutional, because of the appointment authority it vested in the judiciary. The fact that S. 495 had been crafted
in consultation with the AMERICAN BAR ASSOCIATION did not convince
Levi of its legality. Successfully championing the Ford administration's plan for
a permanent special prosecutor within the Department of Justice, Levi prompted
the Senate to revise its bill. The new version called for the president to appoint
a special prosecutor, who was clearly not independent, to a three-year term. This
revised Watergate Reorganization and Reform Act was passed by the Senate on
July 21, 1976, 91–5.

The concept of a permanent special prosecutor, however, met with considerable opposition in the House of Representatives, which was considering its
own temporary special prosecutor bill, H.R. 14476. There, Elizabeth Holtzman
(D-New York) voiced concern that the jurisdiction of the proposed permanent
special prosecutor was too narrow; Henry Hyde (R-Illinois) suggested that a
permanent investigator might be more likely to behave like a demagogue. In his
appearance before the House, Levi, in addition to repeating his concerns regarding the constitutionality of a court-appointed temporary special prosecutor,
expressed reservations that might later be considered prescient. He feared that
reputations might be seriously damaged due to the fact that considerations regarding confidentiality did not appear to be satisfactorily addressed in the House
bill. In addition, the specter of multiple investigators operating independent of
the Justice Department, argued Levi, would likely result in unequal justice. With

an eye on the upcoming presidential election, the House, badly spilt on the special prosecutor issue, did not come to agreement on the matter.

When the ETHICS IN GOVERNMENT ACT was passed in 1978, the special prosecutor provisions resembled the temporary model that Levi worked so diligently to defeat. The unpopular investigations that ensued, however, caused critics to echo the very same concerns to which Levi gave voice in 1976.

After leaving Washington, Levi served as visiting professor at the University of Colorado and Stanford Law School. He was named Glen A. Lloyd Distinguished Service Professor at the University of Chicago in 1985. In 1986, Levi was elected president of the American Academy of Arts and Sciences. Founded in 1780 by John Adams, the Academy had never before selected a president from outside the Boston area.

Reference:

Harriger, Katy J. *Independent Justice: The Federal Special Prosecutor in American Politics.* Lawrence: University Press of Kansas, 1992. Chapter 3, "A Watergate Legacy," discusses Levi's role in influencing Congress to temporarily reject the concept of an independent, court-appointed special prosecutor.

Levin, Carl M. (1934–   ) U.S. Senator, 1978–   . A four-term Democratic senator from Michigan, Carl Levin is widely regarded as his party's authority on the independent counsel statute, due largely to his long service on the Oversight of Government Management Subcommittee (Committee on Government Affairs). Assuming the chairmanship of that body following the elections of 1986, Levin helped craft the 1987 revisions to the statute that weakened control exercised by the attorney general over the process. Despite the perceived excesses of many inquiries, he remained an advocate of an independent counsel mechanism capable of investigating and prosecuting misconduct in office by the president, vice president, or attorney general.

Born in Detroit, Levin was educated at Swarthmore (B.A., 1956) and earned a law degree from Harvard (1959). After working as an attorney in Detroit (1959–1964), he served as assistant state attorney general and general counsel for the Michigan Civil Rights Commission (1964–1967). Levin was elected to Detroit City Council in 1970, where he served for seven years, the last three as its president. He has also taught at Wayne State University and the University of Detroit.

At the time of the independent counsel statute's first reauthorization in 1983, Levin was the ranking minority member on the Government Oversight Subcommittee. Working cooperatively with the subcommittee's chairman, Senator WILLIAM COHEN (R-Maine), he helped secure continuation of the office by assisting in the institution of reforms. Chief among these was granting the attorney general greater discretion in triggering independent counsel investigations. The probes of HAMILTON JORDAN and TIMOTHY KRAFT, instigated by allegations of illegal drug use, were considered by most to be ill-advised.

They prompted critics to call for provisions that would allow the Justice Department to dismiss charges considered unworthy of such intensive inquiry. President RONALD REAGAN signed the reauthorized statute into law on January 3, 1983.

The tenure of Attorney General EDWIN MEESE (1985–1988) caused Levin to regret the 1983 reforms. The Democrats having recaptured control of the senate after the 1986 elections, Levin assumed the chairmanship of the Government Oversight Subcommittee. Despite Independent Counsel JAMES McKAY's decision not to indict Meese for his actions on behalf of Wedtech, a government contractor, it was clear to Levin that the independent counsel statute permitted an attorney general like Meese too much room within which to operate. Unless specifically mandated to do otherwise, an attorney general of questionable ethics might choose to ignore, or even venture to participate in, executive branch misconduct. During 1987, an investigation by Levin's subcommittee was uncovering numerous ethical transgressions by Meese: violations of White House policy by assisting Wedtech to procure a contract with the Army; formation of a lucrative financial partnership with Wedtech consultant W. Franklynn Chinn; failure to disclose this relationship as required by federal law; failure to disclose this partnership in his list of personal holdings; failure to disqualify himself from the Justice Department's investigation of Wedtech; failure to disqualify himself from the Justice Department's investigation of former coworker and Deputy Attorney General Edward Schmults; and failure to disqualify himself from Justice Department decisions involving regional Bell Telephone operating companies despite continuing to own stock in the firm. Throughout his department's handling of potential independent counsel cases, Levin's subcommittee found that Meese frequently misinterpreted statute provisions and failed to apply others in order to avoid launching investigations. For all these reasons, Levin called for Meese's resignation. He also was determined to reimpose limits on the attorney general's discretion at the 1987 reauthorization of the independent counsel statute.

The statute's reauthorization revisions in 1987 were aimed at eliminating the attorney general's practice of freely interpreting its provisions. The attorney general would be required to initiate a preliminary inquiry whenever there was credible evidence that a law may have been violated. Indication that a crime had been committed was no longer necessary. Limits were placed on threshold inquiries conducted to screen potential cases before initiating a preliminary investigation. This would result in funneling more cases directly into the triggering process. Critics of the 1987 reauthorization revisions maintained that the attorney general was now being required to assume criminal intent on the part of accused individuals. Such an assumption violated established Justice Department guidelines.

Levin, joined by Cohen, attempted to prevent the independent counsel statute's demise in 1992. Recalling the specter of WATERGATE, he argued that the statute had restored public confidence in the government. Citing Meese's request for an independent counsel investigation in order to clear him of wrongdoing at the time of his confirmation hearing, Levin demonstrated that even the statute's opponents had called upon its provisions when needed. Yes, the IRAN-CONTRA investigation was lengthy and costly, but given the serious nature of the charges involved it was understandable. The government's prosecution of Manuel Noriega had been as expensive. Levin also accurately predicted that even Republicans opposed to reauthorization might find the statute valuable should a Democrat be elected president in 1992. Although the statute was not reauthorized before its expiration that December, it was quickly resurrected after Clinton's ties to WHITEWATER were revealed.

In 1994, Levin called for a court review of KENNETH STARR's appointment as independent counsel for the Whitewater investigation, replacing ROBERT FISKE. Levin contended that Starr's past affiliation with Republicans strongly opposed to President CLINTON caused one to seriously question his impartiality. In addition, Levin asserted, Starr was involved in providing assistance to PAULA JONES's legal team regarding her sexual harassment lawsuit against Clinton.

As the independent counsel statute prepared to lapse once again in 1999, Levin called for substantial revisions that would permit its continuation in some form. The need for a mechanism to independently investigate and prosecute wrongdoing by the president, vice-president, or attorney general was essential, Levin maintained. Offenses those three persons might commit in office cannot be satisfactorily addressed in any other fashion. A scaled-down version of the statute must be retained for this reason, argued Levin.

References:

Eastland, Terry. *Ethics, Politics, and the Independent Counsel: Executive Power, Executive Vice, 1789–1989*. Washington, D.C.: National Legal Center for the Public Interest. Chapter 7, "The Second Amendments to the Law: 1987," discusses the reforms Levin helped craft.

Harriger, Katy J. *Independent Justice: The Special Federal Prosecutor in American Politics*. Lawrence: University Press of Kansas, 1992. Chapter 4, "Implementation and Oversight," discusses Levin's role in the 1987 revisions to the independent counsel statute.

Lardner, George, Jr. "Senate Chairman Favors End to Independent Counsel Law." *Washington Post*, 11 December 1998, sec. A, p. 29. Includes Levin's arguments that the statute must not expire.

Levin, Carl. "A Record of Shame: Why Meese Must Resign." *Washington Post*, 22 May 1988, sec. C, p. 1.

Levin, Carl, and Bill Cohen. "Save the Special Prosecutor Law." *Washington Post*, 27 September 1992, sec. C, p. 7.

Lewis, Neil A. "The Nation: How to Build a Better Independent Counsel." *New York Times*, 17 May 1998, sec. D, p. 1.

"Senator Wants Court Review of New Counsel." *St. Louis Post-Dispatch*, 13 August
    1994, sec. B, p. 4.

Lewinsky, Monica (1974–   ) White House Intern, 1995–1996. Participant in
an extramarital affair with President Bill CLINTON, Monica Lewinsky quickly
became the focus of Independent Counsel KENNETH STARR's expanded
WHITEWATER investigation. Her denials of both the affair and any attempts
by the president to influence her testimony in PAULA JONES's sexual harassment lawsuit against Clinton contradicted taped telephone conversations obtained by the Independent Counsel Office. This led Starr to believe that he could
build a case for perjury and obstruction of justice against the president. This
case formed the basis of the report Starr delivered to the House of Representatives in September 1998.

Raised in Beverly Hills, Lewinsky attended Lewis & Clark College in Portland, Oregon, before obtaining a White House internship in June 1995, thanks
to the efforts of family friend and Democratic Party contributor Walter Kaye.
In April 1996, she was transferred to a job in the Pentagon after Deputy Chief
of Staff Evelyn Lieberman became convinced that Lewinsky was spending too
much time arranging to be present at presidential functions. At the Pentagon,
Lewinsky became friendly with LINDA TRIPP, a career civil servant in whom
the younger woman confided.

On May 27, 1997, the Supreme Court ruled that the Paula Jones case could
proceed to trial. Because she had reportedly witnessed a sexual encounter between the President and White House aide Kathleen Willey, Linda Tripp began
to worry that she might be subpoenaed to testify in the matter. Jones's attorneys
were attempting to establish a pattern of sexual misconduct by the President. If
she denied knowledge of Lewinsky's affair, she could be charged with perjury.
If she related Lewinsky's story, she feared losing her job. As a result, she began
taping her telephone conversations with Lewinsky. In December, both Lewinsky
and Tripp were subpoenaed by the Jones attorneys. On January 7, 1998, Lewinsky testified that she did not have a sexual relationship with the president, and
was not promised a job in return for any such relationship. On January 12, Tripp
contacted the Independent Counsel Office. She claimed that her tapes demonstrated both Clinton and his friend, attorney Vernon Jordan, had advised Lewinsky to lie about the affair. Starr quickly received permission from the Special
Division of the Appeals Court to expand his probe once again. Starr's office
obtained further taped information on January 13 by having the FBI wire Tripp
and record her lunch conversation with Lewinsky. On January 14, Lewinsky
presented Tripp with printed "talking points," suggesting testimony to be given
to the Jones attorneys. Starr's office viewed this effort as evidence of subornation of perjury, and suspected that Jordan and the White House were behind it.

On January 16, Lewinsky was taken into custody by the FBI and Starr's
deputies. She was presented with the contradictions existing between her Jones
deposition and Tripp's telephone tapes. The Independent Counsel Office indi-

cated that Lewinsky would be charged with perjury unless she agreed to co-operate with their investigation. Her cooperation would likely involve secretly taping White House personnel such as presidential secretary Betty Currie. Lewinsky was detained for approximately 12 hours, at which point she was joined by her mother, Marcia Lewis. Lewis called family attorney William Ginsburg who assumed responsibility as Lewinsky's legal representative for the next five months.

Ginsburg, with little experience as a criminal attorney, failed in his efforts to arrange a satisfactory deal with Starr. At first apparently courting such an arrangement, Ginsburg angrily broke off negotiations once it became clear that Starr would not offer his client IMMUNITY from prosecution, unless she testified to more than a mere sexual liaison with the president. The Independent Counsel Office wanted evidence supporting their belief that the White House had engaged in subornation of perjury and obstruction of justice, possibly impeachable offenses. Ginsburg, frequently appearing on television talk shows that were now devoted to the burgeoning scandal, took an increasingly hostile stance toward the Independent Counsel Office. Critics maintained that Ginsburg's behavior would prove harmful to his client who, unlike SUSAN McDOUGAL and WEBSTER HUBBELL, was unwilling to defy legal authority in order to protect her privacy.

In June, Lewinsky obtained new legal counsel. Plato Cacheris and former Independent Counsel JACOB STEIN, both experienced criminal attorneys, replaced Ginsburg. Operating largely out of the public eye, an agreement was negotiated with Starr's office. Lewinsky was offered transactional immunity in return for her testimony before a grand jury. Her testimony in August offered graphic description of oral sexual encounters with the President, but was not as explicit regarding alleged White House efforts to suborn perjury. Nevertheless, Lewinsky's testimony formed the basis of Starr's report to the House of Representatives on September 9, and proved central to the movement aimed at Clinton's removal from office.

References:

Isikoff, Michael, and Evan Thomas. "Clinton and the Intern." *Newsweek*, 2 February 1998, p. 30–34.

"Scandal Chronology." *Congressional Quarterly Weekly Report*, 24 October 1998, p. 2890.

Starr, Kenneth. "Starr Report to the House of Representatives." 9 September 1998.

M

Mann, James R. (1920–   ) former congressman (D-South Carolina), 1969–1978. Author of what was termed the "House version" of the special prosecutor statute, James Mann's 1977 legislative initiative was joined with the Senate's Public Officials Integrity Act, as amended by President Jimmy CARTER, to create the 1978 ETHICS IN GOVERNMENT ACT containing provision for an independent special prosecutor.

The election of President Carter in 1976 ensured that the post-WATERGATE push to create a statutory remedy to executive-branch misconduct would find a receptive audience in the White House. Carter supported Senator ABRAHAM RIBICOFF's (D-Connecticut) S.555 introduced in 1977. It called for a temporary special prosecutor. President Carter called for the addition of stronger financial disclosure provisions. On June 27, S.1446, incorporating the president's request, passed in the Senate by a vote of 74–5. While the Senate was preparing its bill, Mann was introducing H.R.9705 in the House of Representatives. Also providing for a temporary special prosecutor, it met with opposition from House members, led by Elizabeth Holtzman (D-New York), who wished to include Congress under the special prosecutor's jurisdiction. Holtzman's initiative was given impetus by the revelation that a number of congressmen were implicated in a bribery scheme involving South Korean businessmen. For obvious reasons, few congressmen were anxious to vote against Holtzman's proposal, although it did not have wide support.

Mann's bill was further delayed by other versions of the special prosecutor bill still being debated in various House committees. Finally, on June 19, 1978, H.R.9705 was approved by the House Judiciary Committee. Significant opposition, however, was still evident. Holtzman continued to argue that Congress's behavior should be monitored by the special prosecutor, and five members of the committee remained entirely opposed to the concept of a special prosecutor. They maintained Watergate demonstrated that executive branch malfeasance could be successfully addressed without one. When the House passed Mann's bill on September 27, the special prosecutor provision had been removed. Members of the Senate and House met to reconcile their two bills on October 6. The resulting compromise, containing the special prosecutor, passed the Senate on October 7 and the House five days later. Mann did not stand for re-election in 1978.

Educated at the Citadel, Mann served in World War II and received his law degree from the University of South Carolina Law School in 1947. He worked as solicitor for the Thirteenth Circuit of South Carolina (1954–1962), and in the Greenville County Planning Commission (1963–1967) before entering Congress. Interviewed in December 1998, Mann characterized RICHARD NIXON's offenses as of much greater import than those of Bill CLINTON. Mann's stand against Nixon was so unpopular in Greenville that his home required full-time protection by deputies. Mann cites the bipartisan support that existed for action against Nixon in arguing that Clinton's offenses, stemming from a relatively insignificant Arkansas civil matter, are not comparable.

References:

Bertozzi, Mark. "The Federal Special Prosecutor: Too Special?" *Federal Bar News & Journal* 29 (1982)—222–230.

Harriger, Katy J. *Independent Justice: The Federal Special Prosecutor in American Politics.* Lawrence: University Press of Kansas, 1992. Chapter 3, "A Watergate Legacy," discusses Mann's H.R.9705 and its path through the House.

"Watergate Congressman Says Clinton's Problems Don't Match Up to Nixon's." Associated Press, 20 December 1998.

McDougal, James (1941–1998) Arkansas banker and real estate developer. A friend and supporter of Bill CLINTON in Arkansas, Jim McDougal embarked on a series of questionable real estate ventures during the 1970s and 1980s. These operations and the dubious methods he created for their financing attracted the attention of federal bank examiners. Their investigation resulted in the closing of McDougal's Madison Guaranty Savings & Loan in 1989. Because Bill and HILLARY CLINTON were investors in McDougal's WHITEWATER land development scheme, this particular venture attracted the attention of congressional investigators as well as Independent Counsels ROBERT FISKE and his successor KENNETH STARR.

McDougal became acquainted with Bill Clinton during the late 1960s when they both worked for Democratic Senator J. William Fulbright. McDougal, a political veteran who had worked with Governor Orval Faubus, served as mentor to the 21-year-old novice. When Fulbright lost a re-election bid in 1974, McDougal turned his attention to real estate while Clinton became more deeply involved in politics. While teaching a political science class at Ouachita Baptist College in 1974, McDougal met his future wife Susan, who was one of his students. They were married in 1976 and formed a real estate business partnership in which Jim located the deals and Susan promoted them. In 1978, the McDougals purchased 230 acres along the White River in northern Arkansas, christening it "Whitewater." The Clintons were invited to become investors. McDougal viewed the offer as a gift to his friends. The money could be borrowed and the land, turned into vacation homes, would be sold at great profit. In actuality, few lots were sold and the project became an embarrassing failure.

Clinton became governor of Arkansas in 1980. In 1982, McDougal acquired Woodruff Savings & Loan in Augusta, renamed it Madison Savings & Loan, and moved it to Little Rock. The Clintons remained close to the McDougals who now, as prominent financiers and land developers, belonged to the Arkansas elite. Madison Guaranty became the vehicle for McDougal's increasingly grandiose development schemes. Government banking regulations did not appear to be an inhibiting factor. In 1984, the Federal Home Loan Bank Board issued a report that was most critical of Madison Guaranty's banking practices. The bank was required to enter a supervisory agreement that would monitor the institution's lending practices. This did not prevent McDougal from engineering the Castle Grande deal one year later, a scheme emblematic of the sort of financial obfuscation that defies complete comprehension.

Conceived as yet another opportunity for turning rural land into affordable housing units, Castle Grande consisted of 1,000 acres purchased for $1.75 million. McDougal planned to divide the land into half-acre lots containing double-wide trailers. Working-class families could secure a home for a small investment and a 5 percent down payment. McDougal would borrow the money he needed for the venture from his own bank. Because state regulations prohibited investing more than 6 percent of the institution's assets, McDougal involved Seth Ward, a friend and WEBSTER HUBBELL's father-in-law, in the plan. Ward would supply the remaining $1.15 million by obtaining a nonrecourse loan from Madison Guaranty. This arrangement clearly violated the supervisory agreement under which the bank had been operating for the previous year. In order to conceal the true nature of Castle Grande's financing, McDougal and municipal court judge DAVID HALE engineered a series of complicated loans involving future Arkansas Governor JIM GUY TUCKER, his partner R. D. Randolph, and former Senator Fulbright. The effect of these transactions was to conceal Seth Ward's involvement in Castle Grande's financing by buying out his holdings. The scheme involved use of Hale's Capital Management Services, a Small Business Investment Corporation (SBIC) which received matching federal funds from the Small Business Administration (SBA). As a result, Madison Guaranty profited from the devious arrangement that effectively funneled tax dollars, intended for use by needy small businesses, into the hands of McDougal's speculative associates. This arrangement was called the "Dean Paul loan." It is named for a friend of Hale's who formally applied to Madison Guaranty for a loan of $825,000 that set in motion the transactions just summarized here. The involved procedure was not successful in deceiving federal regulators who arrived early in March 1986. After an examination lasting several months, the McDougals were forced to sever their association with Madison Guaranty in July.

Under investigation by Independent Counsel Kenneth Starr, Hale would later testify that Governor Clinton had lobbied for SUSAN McDOUGAL to receive a $300,000 loan from the proceeds of the Dean Paul arrangement. Clinton denied any such role. McDougal at first denied that Clinton was involved, but later confirmed Hale's account as part of a plea bargain arranged with Starr's office. It was also revealed by investigators that Hillary Clinton, working for the Rose Law Firm, had drafted the legal papers for the Seth Ward loan. Subsequent examination has attempted, largely without success, to determine the extent of her involvement in McDougal's many similar schemes.

Jim McDougal's health failed badly along with his financial and real estate investments. In the late 1980s, he suffered a stroke and underwent open heart surgery. He was also diagnosed as manic depressive. Susan's final attempts to avoid bankruptcy proved unsuccessful. In 1989 McDougal was charged with bank fraud related to aspects of the Castle Grande deal. Unlike most Savings & Loan defendants, he was acquitted following a trial in 1990. By this time, Bill Clinton had severed his connections with McDougal, although it wasn't until 1992 that he divested himself of all of his worthless Whitewater holdings. Susan separated from Jim, moving to California to become personal assistant to the wife of symphony conductor Zubin Mehta.

In 1996, Independent Counsel Kenneth Starr's Whitewater investigation led to new charges against McDougal. Seeking information related to the Clintons' involvement, Starr was successful in winning indictment and conviction of both McDougal and Governor Jim Guy Tucker on fraud and conspiracy charges. McDougal agreed to cooperate with Starr in return for a reduced, three-year sentence, which he began serving in June 1997. In contrast, Susan was sentenced to prison for refusing to testify before a grand jury.

McDougal died of a heart attack in prison on March 8, 1998. Whatever information McDougal provided to Starr has not apparently been regarded as particularly valuable. None of it was included in his report to the House of Representatives in September 1998.

References:

Schneider, Howard. "Down the Whitewater Rapids." *Washington Post*, 13 January 1994, sec. C, p. 1.

Stewart, James B. *Blood Sport: The President and His Adversaries*. New York: Simon & Schuster, 1996.

Wilkie, Curtis. "Remembering a Southern Rogue." *Newsweek*, 23 March 1998, p. 35.

Young, Rick. "The Castle Grande Deal." From the PBS television program *Frontline*, episode "Once Upon a Time in Arkansas." www.pbs.org/wgbh/pages/ frontline. Segment of series episode that investigates McDougal's behavior in the Castle Grande deal in explaining the dynamics of public life in Arkansas. Related segments identify key players in McDougal's real estate and banking schemes as

well as their relationship to the Castle Grande and Whitewater stories. A chronology and key documents (Rose Law firm billing records) are included.
Zehren, Charlie. "McDougal Lived Life Large." *Newsday*, 11 March 1998, sec. A, p. 33.

McDougal, Susan Henley (1955–) Arkansas banking and real estate partner of husband James. As business promoter and helpmate, Susan McDougal assisted her husband James in developing and selling the WHITEWATER real estate project in which Bill and HILLARY CLINTON were coinvestors. The failure of that venture, combined with violations of banking regulations committed by the McDougals' Madison Guaranty Savings & Loan, spelled economic disaster for the couple. Unlike her husband, however, Susan refused to cooperate with Independent Counsel KENNETH STARR's WHITEWATER investigation. As a result, she served an 18-month jail sentence for civil contempt and faced additional criminal charges related to her continued intransigence.

The daughter of a career military officer, Susan Henley was born in Germany but raised in rural Camden, Arkansas. She married her husband, fourteen years her senior, after a courtship that began at Ouachita Baptist College, where James was her political science instructor. At first, Susan's relationship to James continued as student to teacher. Susan was educated in James's extravagant approach to real estate and banking ventures. Initial success, or at least the appearance of the same, encouraged the pair frequently to ignore or sidestep legal details like record keeping. The Whitewater land development scheme originated in 1978. The bonanza that the McDougals, and their partners the Clintons, hoped to realize in the sale of Ozark vacation homes, never materialized. Instead, delays in surveying and needed improvements coupled with poor sales led to failure.

Increasingly throughout the 1980s, James's grandiose land ventures, imaginatively financed by Madison Guaranty, began to founder. Bank regulators sanctioned Madison for irregular loan practices in 1984. In addition, James's health began to fail. He suffered a stroke and was diagnosed with manic depression. Susan accepted greater responsibility for salvaging the McDougals' enterprises. She fraudulently obtained a Small Business Association (SBA) loan for $300,000 from DAVID HALE's bank. Hale, a municipal judge and friend of the McDougals and Clintons, later told the Independent Counsel Office that Bill Clinton had lobbied in favor of the loan. The money itself had been obtained by Hale's institution illegally. In one of Jim McDougal's last schemes, he had enlisted the assistance of Hale and his associate Paul Dean, to obtain a loan of $825,000, which qualified for matching federal funds through the SBA. Part of this money was funneled back to McDougal in order to finance a last real estate venture called Castle Grande.

Susan maintained ignorance of the fact that SBA loans were intended only for small business persons ordinarily prevented from obtaining any other financing. She thought that, as a woman, she might reasonably qualify for such assistance. The loan was used for yet another real estate project that might conceivably extricate the McDougals from the morass of debt accumulating around them. Susan purchased a large tract of land south of Little Rock from the International Paper Company. The Flowerwood Farms development succeeded, but profits could not cover losses elsewhere. The McDougals' marriage failed along with their economic enterprises, and they lost control of their bank in the fall of 1986.

In 1996, Susan and James McDougal were convicted of fraud and conspiracy related to the SBA loan Susan obtained in 1986. While James agreed to cooperate with the Starr investigation, Susan remained silent. She insisted that the independent counsel was pressuring her to falsely implicate the Clintons in return for her freedom. As a result, Susan was sentenced to prison for civil contempt. At any time during her incarceration she could have been released in return for her agreement to testify. Continuing to spurn such an arrangement, she served 18 months before being released in June 1998 for medical reasons. One month before her release, Susan was indicted on criminal contempt charges for her continuing refusal to testify. While Mark Geragos, Susan's attorney, claimed such legal action amounted to violation of the constitutional prohibition against double jeopardy, the Independent Counsel Office explained that the most recent charge was a clearly separate event resulting from the defendant's insistence on ignoring her civic duty to testify before the grand jury. Legal analysts described the situation as unusual, and perhaps unprecedented. Observers also suggested that Starr's treatment of Susan McDougal and WEBSTER HUBBELL was an indication of the frustration his investigation had encountered in its effort to connect the Clintons to any of the violations committed by their business partners in Arkansas.

On November 23, 1998, Susan McDougal was acquitted in California on charges that she had embezzled $50,000 while working as bookkeeper and personal assistant to Nancy Mehta, wife of symphony conductor Zubin Mehta. Susan maintained that the charges were encouraged by Kenneth Starr in his continuing attempt to force her testimony on Whitewater. Susan McDougal's acquittal along with MIKE ESPY on December 2 appeared to represent a public repudiation of the protracted nature of independent counsel investigations, some of which range far from the initial event they were called to examine.

In April 1999, Susan McDougal's criminal contempt trial ended when the jury acquitted her of obstruction of justice and deadlocked 7–5 in favor of acquittal when unable to agree on two contempt charges.

References:

Frieden, Terry. "McDougal Criminal Contempt Trial Rescheduled for February." *CNN Interactive.* cnn.com/ALL POLITICS/stories/1998/11/16/mcdougal/

Kranish, Michael. "Still-Silent Susan Is Indicted." *Boston Globe*, 5 May 1998, sec. A, p. 1.

Schneider, Howard. "Down the Whitewater Rapids." *Washington Post*, 13 January 1994, sec. C, p. 1.

Stewart, James B. *Blood Sport*. New York: Simon and Schuster, 1996.

Van Natta, Don. "Testing of a President: The Prosecutor; Hardball Tactics Appear to
    Fall Short against a Defiant McDougal." *New York Times*, 6 May 1998, sec. A,
    p. 20.

McFarlane, Robert C. (1937–), National Security Adviser 1983–1985. A
graduate of the United States Naval Academy, "Bud" McFarlane commanded
the first U.S. Marine battery landing in Vietnam. He completed two tours of
duty in Vietnam and received the Bronze Star before resigning from the Marines
as a Lieutenant Colonel. During the NIXON years, he served as a military aide
to National Security Adviser, Henry Kissinger.

In the REAGAN administration he was counselor to Secretary of State Alexander M. Haig, Jr., and then deputy to his predecessor as national security
adviser, William Clark. As national security adviser, McFarlane headed the National Security Council, the top advisory body for the coordination of U.S.
national security policy. The NSC was not an operational body, though under
McFarlane's supervision it took on an operational role (with covert actions) in
the IRAN-CONTRA affair.

In the early 1980s, Congress exercised its right to check presidential policy.
Using the power of the purse, members of the House and Senate passed a series
of amendments (BOLAND AMENDMENTS) that prohibited U.S. assistance
(including money, intelligence, and military aid) to the anti-Sandinista Contras
in Nicaragua. Frustrated by congressional restraint on his foreign policy, Reagan
directed McFarlane to keep the Contras alive "body and soul" until appropriations could be restored. McFarlane charged Marine Lieutenant Colonel OLIVER
NORTH, his deputy director of political-military affairs on the NSC staff, to
find ways of doing so. North's subsequent actions violated the Boland Amendments and raised the specter of a direct subversion of the Constitution by the
executive branch, though Reagan later insisted that he had meant McFarlane to
do whatever was possible within the bounds of the law to keep the Contras
alive.

To make up for the lost appropriations, North sought outside sources of funding for the Contras. He began soliciting funds from third countries, including
Israel, Saudi Arabia, and Taiwan. Solicitations of wealthy Americans who supported the policies of President Reagan were expanded. The money was deposited into Swiss bank accounts set up by North and controlled by RICHARD
SECORD, who then directed the funds and supplies purchased for the Contras
through his Enterprise Corporation. In high-level administration meetings, the
question arose as to whether these solicitations, especially from third-party countries, could be considered an impeachable offense for the President. It was decided that they were not, as long as it was made clear that these countries would
not receive repayment or special favors from the United States. However, the
question still remained whether the third-party countries might expect some sort
of special treatment.

Though North directed the Contra operation on a day-to-day basis, he kept

McFarlane generally informed of its progress. However, McFarlane later claimed that he knew little about the actual efforts of North. At Congressional inquiries into the matter in 1985, McFarlane denied any knowledge of North's activities and told Senate and House members that no NSC staff member had aided or solicited funds for the Contras.

McFarlane was also involved in the arms-for-hostages sales to Iran. After the fall of the Shah of Iran and the taking of American hostages in 1979, the United States barred the sale of weapons to Iran. In 1984, the United States placed Iran on the list of countries considered sponsors of international terrorism, and therefore it was illegal to sell arms to Iran under the ARMS EXPORT CONTROL ACT. President Reagan also strongly discouraged other countries from selling arms to Iran. However, in 1985 some in the administration, including McFarlane, favored a revision of policy and argued that arms sales to Iran could be used to affect relations with a post-Ayatollah Khomeini regime. To aid Iran in its war with Iraq, the United States would use the sale of arms to strengthen the hand of moderate factions in Iran. The hope, then, was that American-Iranian relations would improve following Khomeini's death. In the meantime, the sale of arms could assist in the release of hostages (an issue of much concern to the president). However, some questioned if the sale of arms was really an attempt to influence future relations with Iran or if they simply constituted a straightforward arms for hostages deal.

In the spring of 1985, McFarlane dispatched Michael Ledeen, an NSC consultant, to sound out Israeli officials about making contact with moderate factions in Iran. In July 1985, McFarlane informed Reagan that a transfer of arms to Iran could help bring the release of U.S. hostages being held in the Middle East. McFarlane claimed, though others denied it, that out of his concern for the U.S. hostages, Reagan gave his oral approval to the plan. McFarlane again turned to North for help in arranging the transfer of funds, setting up bank accounts, and making contacts. In August of 1985, Israel transferred 96 TOW missiles from its own stocks to Iran. The United States planned to replenish the Israeli stocks, allowing the United States not to be directly involved in the sale of arms to Iran. The next month, Israel transferred 408 TOW missiles to Iran, and the first hostage, Benjamin Weir, was released. In November, the wrong missiles (Hawks) were shipped to Iran, and no hostages were released. The mishap upset the Iranians, but also created new problems, as this sale involved the use of a CIA proprietary plane and, therefore, required a presidential finding approving the use of CIA property. The finding was issued retroactively but later raised the question of when Reagan first knew of the arms sale. This finding, along with two others that followed, raised additional questions regarding the purpose of the arms sales. The first finding indicated an arms-for-hostages deal, whereas the subsequent findings portrayed the sales as an attempt to improve relations with Iran.

In December 1985, McFarlane resigned as NSC Adviser. However, a week later he met with Manucher Ghorbanifar, the Iranian middleman with connections to moderate factions in Iran, regarding future arm sales. McFarlane did not trust Ghorbanifar, and did not believe he had contacts with moderate factions in Iran. Upon his return from the London meeting, McFarlane advised the president against using Ghorbanifar as the middleman and suggested cutting off the operation completely. Despite McFarlane's opposition, the United States then decided to go it alone and deal directly with Iran rather than go through Israel.

Despite his resignation, McFarlane continued to consult with North regarding the Contra operation and remained involved in the development of the arms sales to Iran. In May 1986, he went on a secret mission to Tehran to try and open up direct negotiations with moderate factions in Iran. He brought Hawk missile spare parts with him, though the remainder of the shipment stayed in Israel until hostages were released. He spent three days in fruitless talks with the Iranians. No hostages were released. On his return as he passed through Tel Aviv, North told McFarlane that he and Secord had overcharged the Iranians for the missiles. Furthermore, he informed his former superior that the profits had been diverted to support the Contras (North's Contra operation had been shut-down after the downing of a supply plane carrying an American had drawn the attention and inquiry of Congress and the public). After this trip, McFarlane once again advised Reagan to abandon the operation. The president remained unconvinced, and more missile sales were carried out through 1986.

Once the Iran-Contra scandal broke in late 1986, a major question that emerged was whether or not the President knew of the diversion of funds to the Contras. In November 1986, Attorney General EDWIN MEESE disclosed knowledge about the diversion, but said that only McFarlane, JOHN POINDEXTER (then National Security Adviser) and North knew about it. Later Reagan claimed that he "just didn't know." The TOWER COMMISSION's 1987 investigation into the Iran-Contra affair blamed Reagan's management style and concluded that North had been running a rogue operation within the government. However, Independent Counsel LAWRENCE WALSH surmised just the opposite. By the conclusion of his investigation, he speculated that Reagan was aware of everything and that his administration had simply tried to cover up the president's knowledge in order to protect him and avoid the possibility of an impeachment.

In March of 1988, McFarlane pleaded guilty to four misdemeanor counts of withholding information from Congress during its initial inquiries into the Iran-Contra affair. McFarlane was fined $20,000 and given 200 hours of community service and two years probation in 1989. The charges stemmed from his denial that North had given funding and military assistance to the Contras. He was not charged with any crimes relating to the Iranian affair. As part of the plea bargain, McFarlane agreed to cooperate with the Independent Counsel's Office, and he gave valuable evidence regarding the arms sales. In return, Walsh's office gave up the chance to prosecute McFarlane as a member of a conspiracy to defraud the United States with an unauthorized covert activity (though he was an unindicted coconspirator in the March 1988 conspiracy indictment against North,

Poindexter, Secord and ALBERT HAKIM), making false statements to Congress, and obstructing a congressional investigation (all felonies). Though McFarlane was considered an imperfect witness, he was crucial in linking people with events during an investigation made difficult because of classified information, matters of national security, and grants of immunity to those involved. The fact that McFarlane had attempted suicide in February 1987 and seemed remorseful also affected Walsh's decision in this regard. President Bush pardoned McFarlane in 1992.

McFarlane sued *Esquire* magazine for libel after the magazine printed an article about his possible involvement in a shady deal with Israel to delay releasing American hostages from Iran until after the 1980 presidential election. McFarlane lost on appeal in January 1996 when he could not prove malice.

References:

Draper, Theodore. *A Very Thin Line: The Iran-Contra Affairs*. New York: Hill & Wang, 1991.
Final Report of the Independent Counsel for Iran/Contra Matters. GPO: Washington, D.C., 1993.
"Former National Security Adviser Loses Appeal in Libel Suit." www.gannet1.com/go/newswatch/96/nw0218–6.htm.
McFarlane, Robert C., and Zofia Smardz. *Special Trust*. New York: Cadell & Davies, 1994.
Walsh, Lawrence E. *Firewall: The Iran-Contra Conspiracy and Cover-up*. New York: W. W. Norton & Company, 1997.

—*JACLYN STANKE*

McGrath, James Howard (1903–1966) Attorney General, 1949–1952. A political ally of President HARRY S TRUMAN, J. Howard McGrath was named attorney general following Truman's upset victory over Thomas E. Dewey in the 1948 presidential election. In 1951 and 1952, however, McGrath's department was compromised when charges of tax-fixing were leveled at the Tax Division of the Department of Justice as well as the Bureau of Internal Revenue (BIR). The president hired New York reformer NEWBOLD MORRIS as special assistant to McGrath, charged with investigating the tax scandals. When Morris adopted an approach that was regarded as overly aggressive, McGrath dismissed him. In response, Truman immediately obtained McGrath's resignation. McGrath had exercised the prerogative of the executive branch against a special prosecutor who did not enjoy the privileges of independence. He himself became a casualty, because Morris's dismissal was viewed as too abrupt.

Born in Woonsocket, Rhode Island, McGrath was raised in Providence. After graduating with a bachelor's degree from that city's college (1926), he earned a law degree at Boston University (1929). He served as U.S. district attorney for six years (1934–1940), then entered politics where he succeeded in building a liberal Democratic machine that took him to the statehouse as governor (1940–1945). McGrath returned to the law as U.S. solicitor general (1945–1946) before capturing a Senate seat in 1946. In 1948, he was called upon to succeed the ailing Democratic party national chairman Robert H. Hannegan. In that capacity, McGrath helped engineer Truman's surprising electoral victory.

When allegations of misconduct by officials in the BIR surfaced in 1951, congressional investigations ensued. Hearings uncovered widespread tax collection irregularities that led to dismissal of 66 BIR officers. In 1952, the former BIR commissioner and his assistant were implicated as well. Because investigations revealed complicity by the Justice Department's Tax Division, McGrath was instructed to dismiss the assistant attorney general in charge, T. Lamar Caudle. McGrath was somewhat compromised by the misdeeds of his department. It surprised some when Truman decided to have him assume responsibility for mounting a special investigation of the matter. After Truman failed in his attempt to have Alger Hiss prosecutor Judge THOMAS F. MURPHY and Philadelphia clergyman Reverand DANIEL POLING accept responsibilty as special prosecutors, McGrath named former New York City Council President Newbold Morris as his special assistant, charged with getting to the bottom of the tax scandal. Some observers felt that that job had already been accomplished after the recent rash of firings and prosecutions, but Congress clamored for stronger action.

Morris began his work at the end of January 1952. With the assistance of the New York City Department of Investigation, Morris composed a questionnaire that required detailed financial disclosure by respondents. While the administration anticipated that all attorneys would be surveyed, Morris made it clear that he expected everyone, including the president and attorney general, to respond. McGrath concluded that Morris had exceeded his mandate and dismissed him on April 3. That same day Truman, judging the matter had been poorly handled, asked for, and received McGrath's resignation. The president, although displeased with Morris's aggressiveness, apparently did not intend that McGrath dispose of him in such a precipitous manner. The firing of Morris and McGrath helped the Republicans make corruption a key issue in the 1952 presidential election.

After leaving office, McGrath advised his successor, Federal District Court Judge James P. McGranery to pack a pair of asbestos trousers for use in Washington. In 1956, McGrath served as campaign manager for Senator Estes Kefauver (D-Tennessee) who made an unsuccessful bid for the party's presidential nomination. Four years later, McGrath released the contents of a note Truman had sent him in 1955, regretting (if not apologizing for) the politically motivated dismissal of the attorney general.

References:

Dunar, Andrew J. "All Honorable Men: The Truman Scandals and the Politics of Morality." Ph.D. dissertation, University of Southern California, 1981.

Harriger, Katy J. *Independent Justice: The Federal Special Prosecutor in American Politics*. Lawrence: University Press of Kansas, 1992. Chapter 1, "The Special Prosecutor and the Separation of Powers," discusses McGrath's role in investigation of the Truman tax scandal.

Obituary, *New York Times*, 3 September 1966, p. 23.

McKay, James C. (1917–   ) Independent Counsel, investigations of Theodore Olson (1986); Lyn Nofziger and Edwin Meese (1987–1988). James McKay was appointed independent counsel on two different occasions. Named to examine former Justice Department official THEODORE OLSON's testimony before the House Judiciary Committee in 1983, McKay resigned after one month due to conflict of interest. That probe, continued by McKay's associate, ALEXIA MORRISON, ultimately proved to be the test case that determined the constitutionality of the independent counsel statute. In 1987, McKay was named independent counsel to investigate possible lobbying violations by former White House official LYN NOFZIGER. This examination was expanded to include Attorney General EDWIN MEESE. McKay's investigation resulted in Nofziger's indictment and conviction (later overturned on appeal). Although he recommended no indictment against Meese, McKay's report was highly critical of the attorney general's behavior in office. Its condemnation of Meese led to the attorney general's resignation, and prompted many to suggest that the prosecutor acted irresponsibly in charging Meese with illegalities when indictments were not forthcoming.

After receiving his law degree from Georgetown Law School, McKay served as an assistant U.S. attorney in the 1940s. He built a reputation as a skillful trial lawyer with the law firm Covington & Burling in Washington, D.C. He has been politically affiliated with the Democrats.

Conflict of interest problems plagued both of McKay's investigations. Appointed independent counsel for the Olson investigation in April 1986, McKay resigned in May because a member of his law firm had given advice that could have conceivably been interpreted to cause a conflict of interest. Similar allegations would resurface during McKay's investigation of Nofziger, but would not result in his departure.

On February 2, 1987, McKay was named independent counsel to investigate former White House aide Lyn Nofziger at the request of Deputy Attorney General Arnold Burns. (Attorney General Meese was recused.) McKay also accepted a parallel appointment from the Justice Department, an offer that was extended following OLIVER NORTH's legal challenge to the independent counsel statute's constitutionality. This improved the chances that McKay's investigation would proceed even if the independent counsel mechanism was found to be unconstitutional.

It was alleged that Nofziger had violated Ethics Act provisions barring officials from lobbying the first year after leaving office. Nofziger was charged with seeking White House support for the Welbuilt Electronic Die Corporation (WedTech) in their effort to win government contracts. McKay's investigation implicated Meese in the affair. It was alleged that the attorney general had

benefited materially from use of his influence on behalf of WedTech. Consequently, three months later, McKay's charge was formally expanded to include
the attorney general. McKay's investigation encountered some difficulty in coordinating its efforts with the U.S. attorney for the Southern District of New
York, who was simultaneously proceeding with a larger probe of the Bronx-
based WedTech organization. On most occasions, however, McKay's efforts
were granted priority. McKay's investigation of Nofziger resulted in indictment
and conviction for violation of Ethics Act lobbying restrictions. In April 1988,
Nofziger was sentenced to a 90-day prison term and fined $30,000. In August,
1989, however, the conviction was overturned on appeal. The appeals court cited
lack of clarity in the Ethics Act language that applied to lobbying activities as
reason for reversal of the lower court's decision.

McKay's investigation of Meese concluded in July 1988. Although no indictment was sought, McKay's report cited numerous instances of questionable,
and probably illegal, activities on the part of the attorney general. McKay asserted that Meese would likely have been found guilty of violating federal tax
law related to sale of securities in 1985, had the case been pursued. In addition,
McKay believed that Meese had violated federal conflict of interest law by
failing to sell stock he held in Bell Telephone regional companies while the
Justice Department ruled on cases affecting those businesses. Other allegations
that had been publicized during McKay's investigation included the charge that
Meese might well have violated the Foreign Corrupt Practices Act of 1977 by
continuing to support an oil pipeline project in the Middle East after it apparently
included the payment of a bribe to the Israeli government. Meese's ability to
continue in office was severely compromised by the publicity surrounding these
charges. The explicit statements included in McKay's report came under attack
by many who believed that when the circumstances surrounding a probe do not
justify seeking an indictment, a prosecutor should remain silent regarding possible guilt on matters no longer being pursued. Because McKay speculated that
Meese might well have been engaged in criminal activity, much of the public
perceived him to be an unindicted criminal. Meese resigned his office in July
1988, shortly before McKay's report was released.

After concluding his investigation, McKay returned to private practice.

References:

Eastland, Terry. *Ethics, Politics, and the Independent Counsel: Executive Power, Executive Vice: 1789–1989*. Washington, D.C.: National Legal Center for the Public
Interest, 1989. Chapter 9, "Amending the Law," discusses anger over McKay's
criticism of Meese in the absence of an indictment.
Harriger, Katy J. *Independent Justice: The Federal Special Prosecutor in American Pol-
itics*. Lawrence: University Press of Kansas, 1992. Chapter 7, "Accountability,"
discusses problems encountered by McKay during his investigations.
Shenon, Philip. "Independent Counsel Is Named in Inquiry over E.P.A. Documents."
New York Times, 25 April 1986, sec. A, p. 13.
Thornton, Mary. "Independent Counsel Quits to Avoid Conflict." *Washington Post*, 30
May 1986, sec. A, p. 17.

Meese, Edwin, III (1931–   ) Attorney General, 1985–1988. The subject of two separate independent counsel investigations, Edwin Meese, while attorney general, also twice requested the appointment of independent counsels and was forced to recuse himself as two others were appointed at the request of his Justice Department. A vocal opponent of the mechanism, Meese was, nonetheless, obligated to operate under its provisions. Not surprisingly, he was reluctant to trigger its mechanism and quick to limit its scope whenever possible. It is likely that Meese would have been the target of a third probe had Independent Counsel LAWRENCE WALSH succeeded in obtaining specific documents earlier in his IRAN-CONTRA investigation. Before leaving office in 1988, Meese issued a short-lived order subjecting Congress to the independent counsel system.

A native of Oakland, California, Meese graduated from Yale University (1953). After serving in the Army during the Korean War, he received his law degree from the University of California (1958). Meese served for eight years as deputy district attorney in Alameda County. He became involved politically while working in RONALD REAGAN's successful gubernatorial campaigns. During Reagan's tenure as governor of California, Meese served in the positions of secretary of clemency and extradition, executive assistant, and chief of staff. After Reagan's election as President in 1980, Meese was named the president's counselor with responsibility for overseeing policy matters. In 1984, Reagan named Meese Attorney General, replacing the departing WILLIAM FRENCH SMITH.

During the Senate confirmation hearings, investigation by Senator Howard Metzenbaum (D-Ohio) and his assistant Roy Meyers uncovered several instances in which persons who performed services for Meese were rewarded with government appointments. These included persons who had helped Meese sell his home and loaned him money. Allegations also touched upon Meese's Army Reserve promotion, which had been found improper by the Inspector General's Office. Questions were also raised concerning whether Meese had knowledge of how the Reagan campaign obtained possession of President Jimmy CARTER's notes in advance of their debate. In response, Meese requested appointment of an independent counsel to clear his name.

In April 1984, the Special Division of the D.C. Court of Appeals named JACOB STEIN independent counsel for the Meese investigation. Stein had built his reputation as a criminal defense attorney and was widely considered to be apolitical. In addition to the allegations already raised, Stein would be asked to investigate whether Meese failed to declare many trips he had taken at the expense of nongovernmental groups, as well as the nominee's role in a tax-exempt 1980–1981 Reagan transition fund that failed to reveal the source of its funding and the manner in which the money was spent.

After a five-month investigation, Stein issued a report on September 20 concluding that there was no basis for prosecution of Meese. Although critical of Meese's sensitivity to ethical concerns and lack of attention to detail, the report found no evidence of bribery. Meese's associates who had received federal appointments might well have obtained them by legal means. In addition, there was no indication that Meese had played a role in illegally obtaining Carter campaign documents prior to the presidential debates in 1980. Following Reagan's re-election, and in the face of continued Democratic criticism, Meese was appointed attorney general.

Given Meese's own encounter with the independent counsel, and the adversarial relationship that developed as a result of his testimony before his Senate critics, it was to be expected that the new attorney general's approach to independent counsel investigations would be under close scrutiny.

On December 12, 1985, the House Judiciary Committee requested that Meese seek appointment of an independent counsel to investigate whether three Justice Department officials—Assistant Attorney General Carol Dinkins, Assistant Attorney General THEODORE OLSON, and Deputy Attorney General Edward Schmults—had either lied or obstructed justice during a House investigation. The House's probe related to possible political manipulation of the Environmental Protection Agency's (EPA) Superfund Program charged with cleanup of toxic waste. A House report charged the Justice Department with complicity in refusal to turn over documents necessary to the investigation. After a preliminary investigation, the Public Integrity Section of the Justice Department recommended that an independent counsel be named to investigate Dinkins, Olson, and Schmults. Assistant Attorney General for the Criminal Division John C. Keeney disagreed, recommending that only Olson be the target of such a probe. Because there had been a large number of recusals in this matter due to personal interests, Meese appointed U.S. Attorney for Massachusetts William Weld to offer advice. Weld recommended proceeding against Olson and Schmults, but not Dinkins. In the end, Meese asked that only Olson be investigated.

On April 23, 1986, JAMES McKAY was named independent counsel to investigate Olson. One month later, he resigned because it appeared that he had a conflict of interest. ALEXIA MORRISON replaced him. Meese refused Morrison's request of November 14 that information regarding the Dinkins and Schmults allegations be forwarded to her. Although Morrison did not appear to believe that Olson's testimony before Congress by itself constituted a violation that could be prosecuted, she continued her investigation long enough for Olson to formally challenge the constitutionality of her authority. As a result, in *MORRISON v. OLSON*, the Supreme Court ultimately validated the independent counsel statute in 1988.

During 1986, several allegations of misconduct by U.S. ambassador to Switzerland FAITH WHITTLESEY reached Meese. Whittlesey, a personal friend of the attorney general, was charged with misusing funds, bribery, and obstruction of justice. After an investigation by the Justice Department, Meese ruled that there was no need for an independent counsel probe. It appeared that Meese violated provisions of the Ethics Act in terminating the Whittlesey matter so abruptly. Despite the fact that there appeared to be "specific and credible" evidence of wrongdoing, a preliminary investigation was never initiated, and, therefore, a report was never made to the Special Division.

In May 1986, MICHAEL DEAVER, a former White House colleague of Meese, became the subject of an independent counsel investigation. Meese recused himself while Deputy Attorney General D. Lowell Jensen brought the request for appointment before the Special Division. Deaver, who was investigated on charges of violating lobbying restrictions after leaving the White House, was eventually indicted for perjury. This represented the first indictment to result from an independent counsel investigation.

In December 1986, Meese requested appointment of an independent counsel to examine OLIVER NORTH's role in the Iran-Contra affair. On December 19, LAWRENCE WALSH was named to investigate the matter. Walsh believed that Meese had approved the sale of arms to Iran knowing that the transaction violated the ARMS EXPORT CONTROL ACT. In addition, because of the attorney general's long association with President Reagan, Walsh viewed Meese as personally involved in shielding the chief executive from harm. Walsh cited numerous reasons that he believed facilitated Meese's ability to evade implication in Iran-Contra: reliance on document requests rather than subpoenas, delay in obtaining cabinet members' meeting notes, and IMMUNITY grants made by Congress to witnesses that necessitated a narrowing of the investigation. In retrospect, Walsh considered Meese to be the architect of a successful Iran-Contra cover-up that permitted him to escape the fate of RICHARD NIXON's attorney general, John Mitchell.

North, in response to Walsh's investigation, challenged the constitutionality of the independent counsel's authority. Before *NORTH v. WALSH* was heard in court, Meese offered all independent counsels parallel appointments from the Justice Department. This would ensure that existing investigations could continue, even if the court ruled the Ethics Act provisions unconstitutional. These probes, however, would proceed under the control of the attorney general who had made clear his opposition to independently conducted investigations. Lawrence Walsh accepted Meese's offer.

In January 1987, Meese again was recused as Deputy Attorney General Arnold Burns asked the court to appoint an independent counsel to investigate White House aide LYN NOFZIGER for violating lobbying restrictions. Nofziger was charged with soliciting White House aid for the Welbuilt Electronic Die Corporation (Wedtech) within one year after leaving office. James McKay was named independent counsel. (McKay would also accept a parallel appointment from the Justice Department in response, as Walsh had done.) In May, Meese was implicated in McKay's investigation and formally became a target. It was alleged that Meese associate E. Robert Wallace received substantial payments from Wedtech, possibly for access to the attorney general. McKay concluded both investigations within the year. Nofziger was indicted, but Meese was not. Nevertheless, McKay's report alluded to several instances of unethical, and perhaps illegal, behavior by the attorney general. Early in July 1988, before the report became public, Meese resigned from the Cabinet.

Meese's continual encounters with the independent counsel—both as target, and as close associate of those being targeted—helped craft revisions to the statute in 1987. Critics were convinced that the 1982 reauthorization granted the attorney general too much discretion in deciding which cases merited referral to an independent counsel. Meese's antagonistic attitude toward Congress (originating in his confrontational confirmation hearing), as well as his demonstrated ability to circumvent Ethics Act restrictions, further convinced legislators of the need to facilitate independent counsel appointments. Once appointed, the counsels needed to operate in an effective manner. Meese attempted to require all employees of the independent counsel office to operate under the same conflict of interest regulations that governed Justice Department personnel. Had this requirement been enforced, it would have effectively stripped the office of many of its investigators, because they were simultaneously employed by law firms that handled cases in which the U.S. government was a party. The 1987 revisions to the independent counsel statute defeated Meese's attempt to enforce these stringent conflict of interest regulations on independent counsel employees. They also succeeded in requiring the attorney general to refer more cases to the Special Division for independent counsel appointment, although some supporters of this amendment would later regret it.

References:

Eastland, Terry. *Ethics, Politics, and the Independent Counsel: Executive Power, Executive Vice: 1789–1989.* Washington, D.C.: National Legal Center for the Public Interest, 1989. Chapter 7, "The Second Amendments to the Law: 1987," discusses Meese's encounters with the independent counsel and discusses his influence on revisions to the statute.

Harriger, Katy J. *Independent Justice: The Federal Special Prosecutor in American Politics.* Lawrence: University Press of Kansas, 1992.

Kmiec, Douglas W. *The Attorney General's Lawyer: Inside the Meese Justice Department.* New York: Praeger, 1992. The author, who served in the Office of Legal Counsel during Meese's tenure as attorney general, characterizes the independent counsel statute as "a malevolent political weapon." Chapter 1, "Surmounting the Independent Counsel," and Chapter 9, "Ethics, Give Us More Ethics," address the Stein and McKay investigations. Meese's record is strongly defended throughout.

Walsh, Lawrence. *Firewall: The Iran-Contra Conspiracy and Cover-up.* New York: W. W. Norton, 1997. Chapter 20, "The President's Protector," discusses Meese's involvement in Iran-Contra.

Mistretta v. United States 488 U.S. 361 (1989). In this case, the Supreme Court upheld the constitutionality of permitting the Judiciary to set mandatory criminal sentencing guidelines, a function usually performed by the legislative branch. The *Mistretta* decision served to reinforce the flexible approach to separation of powers questions articulated in *MORRISON v. OLSON* three years earlier, thereby adding to the body of case law supporting the concept of a judicially appointed independent counsel mechanism.

The United States Sentencing Commission, created as part of the Sentencing

Reform Act of 1984, was established in response to concerns that federal judges were not acting in an equitable manner when sentencing offenders who had committed similar violations. In addition, there were serious disparities regarding release dates set by federal parole officials. The Act revised the existing sentencing process by consolidating the power of the sentencing judge and the Parole Commission regarding the punishment prescribed for offenders; specifying that prisoners are to serve their complete sentences less time deducted for good behavior only; making the Commission guidelines binding on the courts (departure permissible only when the judge finds aggravating circumstances not considered by the Commission); and authorizing limited appeal of sentences (those that are either outside specified guidelines or reflective of incorrect guideline application).

The petitioner Mistretta had been sentenced to a guideline-mandated sentence of 18 months in prison for conspiracy to distribute cocaine. His conviction was appealed to the District Court on the grounds that establishment of the Commission violated the constitutional separation of powers doctrine, and that Congress had delegated too much authority to the Commission in formulating sentencing guidelines. The District Court ruled against the petitioner on both counts. The Supreme Court granted petitioner certiorari before the Court of Appeals could hear the case in order to settle the question of the Commission's constitutionality.

Justice Harry Blackmun delivered the majority opinion. Expressing great faith in the Judiciary to resolve the considerable problem of sentence disparity, Blackmun declared that there was nothing in the Constitution prohibiting the legislature from delegating to the Judiciary the authority necessary to address this situation. Rather, the Judiciary is the appropriate branch to which such problems should be referred, because they possess the expertise required to properly consider such questions. Blackmun distingushed between the creation of "unusual hybrid" structures by the legislature and blatantly unconstitutional ones. The Sentencing Commission, declared Blackmun, belonged to the former category. In order for the Commission to be unconstitutional, it would have to perform functions that more properly belong to nonjudicial branches of government or those that serve to undermine the judiciary's integrity. Neither was the case in this instance. Cases cited in support of the majority opinion included *Morrison v. Olson* 487 U.S. 654 (1988), *COMMODITY FUTURES TRADING COMMISSION v. SCHOR* 478 U.S. 833 (1986), and Justice Brandeis's dissent in *MYERS v. UNITED STATES* 272 U.S. 52 (1926).

As in *Morrison*, Justice ANTONIN SCALIA provided the lone dissent. The perception that a new structure would prove currently useful does not justify its creation if the Constitution does not permit it, reasoned Scalia. In this case, the Commission does not represent a permissible degree of interbranch cooperation. Instead, Scalia stated, it amounts to "a sort of junior varsity Congress," exercising powers that do not belong to the courts. Scalia viewed the majority decision as the *HUMPHREY'S EXECUTOR* of the judicial branch.

The *Mistretta* decision served to affirm the Supreme Court's return to a functional approach regarding separation of powers questions. As such, it served to lend additional legitimacy to the independent counsel statute.

References:

Harriger, Katy J. *Independent Justice: The Federal Special Prosecutor in American Politics*. Lawrence: University of Kansas Press, 1992. Chapter 5, "Is the Prosecutor Constitutional?," discusses *Mistretta*'s buttressing of the *Morrison* decision.

Schoenbrod, David. "How the Reagan Administration Trivialized Separation of Powers (and Shot Itself in the Foot)." *George Washington Law Review* 57 (1989): 459–473. Criticizes Reagan Administration for invoking separation of powers doctrine selectively—whenever Congress sought to appropriate more power (*CHADHA, BOWSHER, MORRISON* decisions), but never when Congress delegated power elsewhere (*Mistretta*).

Sherry, Suzanna. "Separation of Powers: Asking a Different Question." *William and Mary Law Review* 30 (1989): 287–300. Opines that *Mistretta*, following on the heels of *Morrison*, likely signals that the formalist approach to separation of powers questions has fallen into disfavor.

Susolik, Edward. "Separation of Powers and Liberty: The Appointments Clause, *Morrison v. Olson*, and the Rule of Law." *Southern California Law Review* 63 (1990): 1515–1567. Argues against functional approach to separation of powers question implicit in *Mistretta* decision. Maintains that strict separation of powers is the highest manifestation of the Rule of Law, and therefore, necessary to political liberty.

Mondale, Walter F. (1928–   ) Vice President, 1977–1981. As a member of the U.S. Senate (1964–1977), Walter Mondale (D-Minnesota) was a supporter of ABRAHAM RIBICOFF's 1975 bill calling for establishment of a permanent office of public attorney to handle cases of alleged misconduct in the executive branch of government. After three years of debate and revision, the independent counsel statute was born. As President Jimmy CARTER's vice president, Mondale was the subject of an ETHICS IN GOVERNMENT ACT–mandated preliminary investigation into alleged illegal fund-raising. What could have become the first test of the special prosecutor mechanism was dismissed when Attorney General GRIFFIN BELL judged the charges to be unfounded. Recently, Mondale has joined those who favor a ban on "soft money" donations to political campaigns.

Senator Ribicoff (D-Connecticut) introduced the Watergate Reorganization and Reform Act of 1975 (S.495) at the start of the 94th Congress. Mondale joined Senator Lowell Weicker (R-Connecticut) in testifying in favor of the permanent prosecutor concept. Although the legislation eventually adopted rejected the idea of a permanent mechanism, Mondale's support of S.495 helped sustain the idea championed by Weicker that concrete action was necessary to prevent future WATERGATE scandals. By 1975, there was a genuine fear that no real reform would occur, because public attention was no longer focused on the crisis. Mondale's testimony helped ensure that this fear would not become reality.

Mondale was educated at the University of Minnesota, receiving his law degree in 1956. He served as Minnesota's attorney general (1960–1964) before election to the U.S. Senate. After election to the vice presidency, Mondale also served on the National Security Council.

In November 1978, the FBI was informed that President CARTER and Vice President Mondale had hosted a White House luncheon for friends of the Democratic Party at which funds had been solicited to help the party retire its 1976 campaign debt. If true, this could have represented a violation of 18 U.S.C., section 603, which forbids solicitation of political contributions in public officials' offices. The Justice Department determined that the allegations were sufficient to trigger the Ethics Act provisions, and a preliminary investigation ensued. The investigation determined that the gathering in question was called in order to thank contributors for donations already made. In addition, President Carter was present only during the first hour, and Mondale was not in attendance at all. In his report, the attorney general noted that section 603 was intended to prevent solicitation of political donations from federal employees, a substantially different scenario than the one with which the department was being presented in this instance. For these reasons, Attorney General Bell decided that the charges did not merit appointment of a special prosecutor.

The unsuccessful Democratic candidate for president in 1984, Mondale returned to private law practice in Minneapolis (Winston & Strawn, 1981–1987; Dorsey & Whitney, 1987–1993) before being named U.S. ambassador to Japan (1993–1996).

In 1997, Mondale and former Senator Nancy Kassebaum Baker were asked by President Bill CLINTON to study and report on the problems posed by current campaign finance practices. Mondale and Kassebaum Baker both recommended banning "soft money" contributions, because such huge donations undermine public trust in the system. The question of public confidence was crucial to establishment of the Ethics in Government Act, the concept of which Mondale helped support in 1975. Twenty-two years later, he was seeking a legislative remedy to another problem that threatened to undermine trust in a similar manner.

References:

Harriger, Katy J. *Independent Justice: The Federal Special Prosecutor in American Politics.* Lawrence: University Press of Kansas, 1992. Chapter 3, "A Watergate Legacy," notes Mondale's contribution to Ribicoff's 1975 bill, S.495. Chapter 6, "Conflict of Interest," discusses the Carter-Mondale Luncheon case.

Rowley, James. "Mondale, Kassebaum Baker Urge Ban on 'Soft Money' Gifts." *Buffalo News*, 30 September 1997, sec. D, p. 12.

Morris, Newbold (1902–1966) Special Assistant to the Attorney General, tax scandal, 1952. Appointed as special assistant to Attorney General J. HOWARD

MCGRATH on February 1, 1952, Newbold Morris was charged with investigating corruption within the Bureau of Internal Revenue (BIR). His lack of
independence was plainly evident when he was dismissed two months later. His
aggressive approach to the problem, which included distribution of a questionnaire demanding disclosure of detailed financial information, had alarmed government officials. McGrath's dismissal of Morris quickly resulted in his own
departure when President HARRY TRUMAN asked for his resignation.

Newbold Morris was a direct descendant of Richard Morris, a loyal follower
of Oliver Cromwell who, in the seventeenth century, purchased the section of
the Bronx known as "Morrisania." Morris was educated at Yale, receiving his
law degree in 1928. Introduced to former Congressman Fiorello La Guardia in
1933 by City Chamberlain Adolf A. Berle, Morris helped forge the Fusion Party
organization that succeeded in electing La Guardia mayor of New York in November of that year. Morris was rewarded with an administrative appointment
that involved him in the drafting of a new city charter, one that granted the city
a degree of autonomy from the state. In 1938, Morris was elected president of
City Council. Working with LaGuardia, he proceeded to assert his independence
from traditional machine politics by refusing to take direction from political
leaders or appoint political regulars to government jobs. He also cut his own
budget from $70,000 to $40,000. Re-elected City Council president in 1941,
Morris helped unify the city's subway system and establish the New York City
Center of Music and Drama before the end of LaGuardia's administration in
1945. Morris was an unsuccessful mayoral candidate that year and in 1949,
losing to Democrat William O'Dwyer on both occasions.

During 1951 and 1952, tax scandals in the Truman administration led to the
dismissal of 66 BIR employees and Assistant Attorney General of the Tax Division T. Lamar Caudle. A former commissioner of the BIR and his assistant
were convicted in a tax-fixing conspiracy. Congressional investigators pressed
for additional measures. Responding to Congress, Truman at first determined to
name a three-man investigative panel headed by Alger Hiss prosecutor Judge
THOMAS F. MURPHY, and Philadelphia clergyman DANIEL POLING. Dis-
agreements over the organization of the panel, followed by Murphy's resignation, spelled the end of that concept. Truman delegated recruitment of the next
investigator(s) to McGrath, who named Morris.

Morris's appointment was well-received at first. New Yorkers hailed him as
an honest reformer capable of cleaning house in a forthright, independent manner. Unfortunately, independence was not a distinguishing feature of his appointment. On March 18, 1952, Congress refused to grant Morris the subpoena
powers that Truman recommended. Lacking such authority, Morris began his
inquiry by formulating a questionnaire intended to ascertain detailed information
regarding government employees' incomes and expenditures. Developed with
the assistance of former La Guardia associates Harold Seidman and Willard
Carmel, the survey was 16 pages long. According to critics, its intrusive nature

constituted invasion of privacy. Apparently, the questionnaire was originally conceived as an instrument with which to survey government attorneys only. Morris, however, intended it for wide distribution, suggesting that the president and attorney general set the example. He hoped to survey the top 10,000 federal employees before concluding his investigation.

Morris presented McGrath with 596 copies of the questionnaire for distribution to Department of Justice employees. Objecting to Morris's aggressive approach, McGrath dismissed him on April 3. Truman, apparently not anticipating McGrath's precipitous decision, or at least the political fallout that occasioned it, fired McGrath. Some attribute this unusual series of events to the fact that Morris's appointment created a confusing chain of command, an understandable by-product of special investigative appointments. Morris apparently believed that he was working for Truman. McGrath, however, understood that he was in charge. Before departing Washington, Morris indicated that he would make recommendations aimed at preventing future corruption in government, but his experience led him to believe that they would not be followed.

Morris must be ranked alongside JOHN BROOKS HENDERSON, appointed by President ULYSSES S. GRANT to investigate the St. Louis Whiskey Ring in 1875, as the least two successful special federal prosecutors. Their ineffectiveness, however, cannot be attributed to a lack of investigative skill. Rather, they both managed to quickly offend the presidents who had appointed them, a scenario to be avoided when one's position is dependent on the pleasure of the chief executive or his attorney general. Morris, in particular, attacked his mission with an unusual degree of zeal that was bound to offend. He seemed oblivious to the consequences of his actions, and displayed no interest in culitivating a political sensibility. Perhaps such precautions were unnecessary when working for LaGuardia, because the New York mayor was an enthusiastic reformer. Truman was more of a political realist, the product of Tom Pendergast's political machine in Kansas City. Morris was apparently unaware of the consequences of such distinctions.

After leaving Washington, Morris returned to the private practice of law with the Wall Street firm of Lovejoy, Morris, Wasson & Huppuch.

References:

Abels, Jules. *The Truman Scandals*. Chicago: Henry Regnery, 1956. Chapter 1, "President Truman and Corruption—I," discusses Morris's role in the tax scandals. *Current Biography*, 1952, p. 441–443.

Dunar, Andrew. "All Honorable Men: The Truman Scandals and the Politics of Morality." Ph.D. dissertation, University of Southern California, 1981.

Harriger, Katy J. *Independent Justice: The Special Federal Prosecutor in American Politics*. Lawrence: University Press of Kansas, 1992. Chapter 2, "Ad Hoc Appointment," covers the Truman tax scandals and Morris's role.

Morris, Newbold. *Let the Chips Fall: My Battles against Corruption*. New York: Appleton-Century-Crofts, 1955. Chapter 1, "How to Lose Friends in Washing-

ton," details Morris's activities as special assistant to the attorney general.
Appendix includes Morris's letter of appointment, press release describing Morris's charge, and his notice of dismissal.

Morrison, Alexia (1948–) Independent Counsel, investigation of Assistant
Attorney General Theodore Olson, 1986–1989. Hired initially as assistant to
Independent Counsel JAMES McKAY, Alexia Morrison was appointed primary
counsel in the investigation of former Justice Department official Theodore Olson on May 29, 1986, after McKay stepped aside, citing conflict of interest. The
issue before Morrison involved the truthfulness of Olson's testimony before
Congress three years earlier during the House Judiciary Committee's examination of the Environmental Protection Agency (EPA). After Olson's lawsuit challenging the authority of the independent counsel was upheld by the Court of
Appeals for the D.C. Circuit, it became clear that Morrison's investigation of
Olson would likely settle the question of the independent counsel statute's constitutionality.

Born in Los Angeles, Morrison received her law degree from George Wash-
ington University in 1972. She worked as a legal assistant at the Department of
Justice (1972–1973) before becoming an assistant U.S. attorney (1973–1981).
During 1981–1985, Morrison worked as chief litigation counsel at the Securities
and Exchange Commission, then joined the Washington law firm of Swidler &
Berlin as a partner in 1985.

In 1986, Morrison inherited a case in which the REAGAN Justice Department
was suspected of using the EPA to politically manipulate the Superfund program
that was intended to clean up toxic waste. Assistant Attorneys General Olson
and Carol Dinkins as well as Deputy Attorney General Edward Schmults, it was
believed, obstructed Congress's investigation by either lying or refusing to produce relevant documents. Despite calls for a far-ranging probe, Attorney General
EDWIN MEESE requested an independent counsel to examine the actions of
Olson only. Because it was believed by many that Olson was part of a wider
conspiracy, Morrison formally requested an expansion of her original jurisdiction in a letter to the attorney general on November 14, 1986. After being
rebuffed by Meese, she appealed to the Special Division of the Court of Appeals.
The court panel ruled that it lacked jurisdiction to overrule the attorney general
on this matter. It did, however, grant permission for Morrison to examine
whether Olson had been part of a wider conspiracy.

In June 1986, Morrison convened a grand jury and issued subpoenas to Olson,
Dinkins, and Schmults. The recipients moved to quash the subpoenas by challenging Morrison's constitutional authority as independent counsel. On August
19, 1987, the U.S. District Court upheld Morrison's authority in *IN RE SEALED
CASE*. The Court of Appeals for the D.C. Circuit reversed the District Court's
decision on January 22, 1988, jeopardizing all independent counsel investigations. On June 29, 1988, the Supreme Court voted 7–1 to reverse the Court of

Appeals, establishing the constitutionality of the independent counsel mechanism.

Free to continue her investigation, Morrison concluded her work in March 1989. Her report found no basis for prosecution of Olson. His testimony before Congress in 1983 was described as less than forthcoming, but not untruthful. Nor did Morrison find evidence that Olson had participated in a conspiracy to obstruct justice. Morrison's investigation, however, was subject to criticism for both its length, three years, and its cost, $2.1 million. Morrison responded to critics in her report, citing the fact that she did not receive the case until Olson's testimony was already 38 months old. In addition, 14 months were consumed while the federal courts decided on her office's constitutionality. Add five months during which Morrison sought unsuccessfully to expand her jurisdiction to include the activities of Dinkins and Schmults, and the period of her active investigation of Olson is reduced to little more than nine months.

JACOB STEIN, former independent counsel during the 1984 investigation of Meese, was counsel for Carol Dinkins. He was among those who believed that the length and expense of Morrison's investigation were excessive. Olson incurred over $1 million in defense expenses, but was entitled to reimbursement in the absence of an indictment. Stein expressed the viewpoint that investigations of the type conducted by Morrison would have a chilling effect on those persons considering public service careers. Though Morrison's investigation might have seemed excessive to some in 1989, its length and expense pale before the subsequent inquiries of LAWRENCE WALSH and KENNETH STARR.

Following the Olson investigation, Morrison returned to private practice with Swidler & Berlin.

References:

Harriger, Katy J. *Independent Justice: The Federal Special Prosecutor in American Politics.* Lawrence: University Press of Kansas, 1992. Chapter 5, "Is the Prosecutor Constitutional," discusses Morrison and the importance of her case.

Ostrow, Ronald J. "Independent Counsel Explains Why She Didn't Prosecute Figure in '83 EPA Probe." *Los Angeles Times,* 21 March 1989, sec. A, p. 17.

Morrison v. Olson, 487 U.S. 654 (1988). This case arose as a result of a Congressional investigation into the Reagan administration's alleged political manipulation and nonenforcement of the Superfund program. Congress had subpoenaed enforcement documents from the Environmental Protection Agency, to be produced during hearings before the House. The EPA refused to produce the documents, and the Reagan administration asserted executive privilege.

The controversy over the documents was resolved, but the House conducted an investigation into the Justice Department's role in the refusal. As part of that investigation, THEODORE OLSON, assistant attorney general for the Office of Legal Counsel, testified. Congress issued a 3,000-page report that accused a number of Department of Justice officials, including Theodore Olson, of lying to the Congressional subcommittee during the investigative hearings (Harriger, 95–96).

Pursuant to the Act, the House Judicial Committee chair, Peter Rodino, requested that an independent counsel investigation be undertaken of Olson and two other officials. Attorney General EDWIN MEESE referred only the allegations against Olson to the Special Division, which appointed JAMES C. McKAY as independent counsel. Due to a conflict of interest, he resigned; his deputy, ALEXIA MORRISON, was appointed in his stead (Harriger, 96). Morrison requested a referral to include two other justice department officials. Meese declined to refer these matters to the Special Division. Morrison took her case directly to that court. The Special Division ruled that they had no power to increase the independent counsel's jurisdiction, but that her mandate included the ability to investigate whether Olson had conspired to obstruct Congress with the other individuals. The court also ruled that the statute was constitutional.

Morrison opened a grand jury investigation and subpoenaed Olson. Olson refused to appear and moved to quash the subpoena, alleging that the statute that created the independent counsel was unconstitutional. The ETHICS IN GOVERNMENT ACT, 28 U.S.C. Sections 591–599, was upheld by the district court. On appeal, it was found to be unconstitutional by the Circuit Court of Appeals, in an opinion authored by LAURENCE SILBERMAN, with Judge RUTH BADER GINSBURG dissenting. The United States Supreme Court granted certiorari (Harriger, 97).

Olson challenged the independent counsel legislation on three fronts: (1) The act violated Article II of the Constitution relating to appointments by virtue of the fact that Article II vested appointment power of "principal" government officers in the president and "inferior" government officers in Congress. Olson argued that the independent counsel was not an "inferior" officer; (2) the activities of the special appointing panel violated Article III of the Constitution requiring that the judiciary remain independent from the other branches of government; inasmuch as the act imposed administrative duties of a nonjudicial nature on the Special Division; and (3) the act was an unconstitutional violation of the Separation of Powers Clause because the constitutional authority for conducting law enforcement is housed in the executive by that clause in the Constitution vesting in the president the duty to "take care" that the laws are faithfully executed. The Act's limitation on the attorney general's power to remove the independent counsel only for good cause was an intrusion on the executive branch's power over an executive branch official.

The High Court had decided a similar issue in *BUCKLEY v. VALEO*, 424 U.S. 1 (1976), holding only principal officers of the United States, appointed by the president with the advice and consent of the Senate, could sue to enforce the laws of the United States. The court ruled that the Federal Election Commission, as it was originally constituted, violated the separations of power, because its members, who were inferior officers, appointed only by Congress, would be permitted to sue (Clayton, 97).

Olson saw no significant conflict between *Buckley* and the Ethics in Government Act, which authorized the independent counsel. Morrison was an inferior officer, appointed by the courts, who could not conduct criminal prosecutions, an exclusively executive function. If an inferior officer, a member of the FEC, could not sue in civil court, as in *Buckley*, an inferior officer, the independent counsel, should not be permitted to pursue criminal actions.

Other participants in the case raised more-practical concerns. In their amicus brief, three former attorneys general—WILLIAM FRENCH SMITH, GRIFFIN BELL, and EDWARD LEVI—warned that the independent counsel "is designed to heighten . . . all of the occupational hazards of the dedicated prosecutor, the danger of too narrow a focus; of loss of perspective, of preoccupation with the pursuit of one suspect to the exclusion of other interests" (Martin and Zerhasen, 537). The attorneys general were concerned about the lack of accountability of the independent counsel, and the lack of collegial tempering from which other prosecutors benefit.

In an opinion authored by Chief Justice Rehnquist, and joined by six other justices, the statute was upheld. The court, focusing on the legal ramifications of the statute, found that the Appointments Clause of Article II permitted Congress to vest the appointment of "inferior" officers in the "President, the Courts of Law or in the Heads of Departments." Rehnquist, C.J. found the independent counsel was "inferior" a) because he or she was subject to removal by the attorney general, b) as he or she had limited jurisdiction, and c) because he or she had nonpolicymaking duties.

Similarly, the court rejected the Article III argument. The opinion narrowly construed the scope of the Special Division's ability to define the independent counsel's jurisdiction. In order to remain constitutional, the "jurisdiction that the court decides upon must be demonstrably related to the factual circumstances that gave rise to the attorney general's investigation and request for appointment of the independent counsel in the particular case" (*Morrison*, at 679).

The other duties of the Special Division, including their right to receive reports, were also narrowly construed, suggesting that those duties are ministerial in nature and do not impair the independence of the judiciary. Rehnquist was apparently troubled by the language in the statute that permitted the Special Division to "terminate" the independent counsel. However, he interpreted this section in such a manner that the court had little discretion, concluding that the Special Division would only "close the books" at the end of the investigation. He suggested that the Special Division would "terminate" the investigation only if there was virtually nothing left for the independent counsel to investigate, or if the counsel, having finished, refused to relinquish his or her post.

The majority, in addressing Olson's third argument, decided that the trespassing of one branch of government onto the territory of another does not violate the Separation Clause, as long as the function of the branch suffering the intrusion is not impaired. They found that the intrusion of the independent counsel was minor, it alleviated the potential problem of the administration investigating itself, and it would not affect the functioning of the executive branch.

The majority, according to Peter Shane, would fall into a category of individuals who view encroachment of one branch of government into the Constitutional realm of another as acceptable as long as the function of the imposed upon branch continues to be able to function. He refers to this group as "checks and balances separationist" (Shane, 37). This group is distinguished from what Shane would call "categorical separationists" such as the lone dissenter, ANTONIN SCALIA, who believe that there should be a wall separating the various branches of government.

The majority opinion sidestepped or ignored *Buckley*. They found the independent counsel to be an "inferior officer" despite his/her obvious involvement in prosecution of a lawsuit and the limited control anyone exercised over him/her. The Court suggested that the executive branch retained sufficient "control" by virtue of the part of the statute that permitted the attorney general to terminate the independent counsel but gave the Judiciary the right to review the action at the request of the terminated prosecutor.

Dissenting, Justice Scalia argued that every function of the government should be held by one of the three branches of government and that the paths of these offices should be kept separate and distinct (Fried and Bator, 1671). Scalia suggested that law enforcement is an executive function and that Congress and the courts cannot impinge on that process by naming an officer that is unaccountable to the executive branch.

Focusing on the practical implications of the statute, Justice Scalia, issuing dire warnings about the involvement of the courts in the process, suggested that the independent counsel could damage the office of the president "by substantially reducing the President's ability to protect himself and his staff" (*Morrison*, at 713).

He saw the potential for use of the independent counsel as a political tool, as one that would erode the public's support for the president, "Nothing is so politically effective as the ability to charge that one's opponents and his associates are not merely wrong-headed, naïve, ineffective but in all probability are 'crooks' " (Wolfe, 20). The heart of his dissent is his view that the courts should not become embroiled in what is essentially a political process.

The Justice suggested that the potential for abuse would be great, including a politically motivated court appointing a politically motivated independent prosecutor.

What if they are politically partisan, as judges have been known to be, and select a prosecutor antagonistic to the administration, or even to the particular individual who has been selected for this special treatment? There is no remedy for that, not even a political one. Judges, after all have life tenure, and appointing a surefire enthusiastic prosecutor could hardly be considered an impeachable offense. So if there is anything wrong with the selection, there is effectively no one to blame. (*Morrison*, at 730)

The Justice also took up the concerns of the former Attorneys General:

What would normally be regarded as an investigation that has reached the level of pursuing such picayune matters that it should be concluded, may be to him or her an investigation that ought to go on for another year. How frightening it must be to have your own independent counsel and staff appointed, with nothing else to do but to investigate you until investigation is no longer worthwhile. . . . And to have that counsel and staff decide, with no basis for comparison, whether what you have done is bad enough, willful enough, and provable enough, to warrant indictment. (*Morrison*, at 732)

Justice Scalia criticized the majority for their narrow focus on the language of the statute and their abandonment of the political ramifications of the statute.

Morrison's investigation continued for a number of years after the Supreme Court's decision. Olson was not indicted for the alleged offenses after a three-year, multimillion dollar investigation, and he went on to become part of another independent counsel case, representing former judge DAVID HALE in WHITE-WATER.

References:

Clayton, Cornell W. *The Politics of Justice: The Attorney General and the Making of Legal Policy*. Armonk, N.Y.: M. E. Sharpe, Inc., 1992.

Epstein, Lee, and Thomas G. Walker. *Constitutional Law for a Changing America: Institutional Powers and Constraints*. Washington, D.C.: CQ Press, 1995.

Fried, Charles, and Paul M. Bator. "Debate: After the Independent Counsel Decision: Is Separation of Powers Dead?" *American Criminal Law Journal* 26 (1989): 1667–1681.

Harriger, Katy J. *Independent Justice: The Federal Special Prosecutor in American Politics*. University Press of Kansas, 1992.

Martin, Thomas S., and David E. Zerhusen. "Independent Counsel—Checks and Balances." *George Washington Law Review* 58 (1990): 536–548.

Shane, Peter M. "Presidents, Pardons and Prosecutors: Legal Accountability and the Separation of Powers." *Yale Law and Policy Review* 11 (1993): 361–406.

Wolf, Stephen A. "In Pursuit of Power without Accountability: How the Independent Counsel Statute Is Designed and Used to Undermine the Energy and Independence of the Presidency." *South Dakota Law Review* 35 (1990): 1–39.

—CYNTHIA CLINE

Murphy, Thomas F. (1905–1995) Provisional Special Prosecutor, tax scandal, 1951. In response to congressional pressure following revelation that the Bureau of Internal Revenue (BIR) was implicated in tax-fixing schemes, President HARRY TRUMAN decided to name a special panel to investigate the matter. Truman's first selections were U.S. District Court Judge Thomas F. Murphy and Philadelphia clergyman DANIEL POLING. Murphy, nationally renowned as the prosecutor of former State Department official Alger Hiss, initially accepted the appointment. Following a disagreement over the organization of the panel and the opposition of his fellow judges, Murphy withdrew. Truman then delegated selection of a special prosecutor to Attorney General J. HOWARD McGRATH, who named NEWBOLD MORRIS.

A native of New York City, Murphy was educated in Manhattan's parochial schools, attended Georgetown University (B.A., 1927), and received his law degree from Fordham University Law School in 1930. He practiced law with the New York firm of Alcott, Holmes, Glass & Paul for 12 years (1930–1942), handling tax and business cases. In 1942 he was named assistant U.S. attorney for the Southern District of New York, being promoted to head of the criminal division in 1944. Successfully convicting 99.1 percent of his cases over the next five years, Murphy earned a reputation as one of the nation's top government lawyers. This led to his selection as chief prosecutor of Alger Hiss, former official in President Franklin D. Roosevelt's administration, accused of falsely denying transmission of documents to Communist courier Whittaker Chambers. The atmosphere surrounding the start of the Cold War meant that great attention would be focused on Hiss's two trials in 1949–1950. Murphy secured a conviction in the second trial and seemed destined for a political career. Support from the Democratic Party, however, never materialized, and he accepted appointment as New York City Police Commissioner in September 1950. After nine months, during which time he worked to end police collusion in the city's gambling activities, Truman named Murphy U.S. District Court judge for Southern New York.

In December 1951, the president appointed Murphy to a special three-man commission charged with investigating corruption in the BIR. Although 66 agents had already been dismissed, Congress pressed for further action. Murphy's reputation transcended partisan politics. He seemed to be an excellent choice for the job. He would be joined on the panel by Reverend Daniel Poling and an unnamed "prominent Chicago attorney." Murphy accepted the appointment, but his decision met with opposition from his associate judges on the bench. In addition, there appeared to be confusion regarding who would chair the panel. These factors led Murphy to reconsider, and he declined the appointment. After Murphy's withdrawal, it was revealed that the Tax Division of the Justice Department was also involved in the tax scandal. Further resignations and indictments were secured before Newbold Morris was named to assume responsibility for the tax scandal investigation in February 1952.

Perhaps the problems that had led to the tax scandal had been successfully addressed before Newbold Morris began his ill-fated attempt at investigation. Certainly, Truman's Justice Department had acted decisively to eliminate many of the implicated BIR agents in addition to reforming their own Tax Division. If further action was warranted, Murphy appeared to be an excellent choice to lead the investigation. It is likely that his approach to the inquiry would have been less sensational than Morris's. His history was one of dogged, low-profile, thorough investigative work, even when the case involved high-profile figures. An inquiry run by Murphy probably would not have met with the sort of opposition Morris encountered. The likelihood of corrective reorganization and reform within the BIR, and perhaps the Justice Department would have been greater. Murphy's nine months as New York's Police Commissioner saw a massive reallocation of personnel, as officers tainted by allegations of gambling collusion were replaced or reassigned. BIR officials might well have experienced the same fate, whether or not their performance merited indictment. In any case, it appears that Murphy's impact on the situation would have to have been greater than Morris's, whose overaggressiveness resulted in dismissal after two months. If Murphy was forced to work with the crusading Poling, however, their investigation might also have exceeded what Truman had in mind.

References:

Abels, Jules. *The Truman Scandals*. Chicago: Henry Regnery, 1956.
Dunar, Andrew J. "All Honorable Men: The Truman Scandals and the Politics of Morality." Ph.D. dissertation, University of Southern California, 1981.
Current Biography, 1951, p. 447–449.
Van Gelder, Lawrence. "Thomas Murphy, Police Head and Prosecutor of Hiss, 89." New York *Times*, 31 October 1995, obituary. Obituary and biographical overview.

Murray's Lessee v. Hoboken Land Improvement Company 59 U.S. (18 How.) 272 (1856). In deciding whether a distress warrant issued by the solicitor of the treasury was constitutional, the Supreme Court considered the argument that the executive branch had illegally constituted itself as a judicial body in attempting to press its warrant. The Court acknowledged that if the plaintiff was correct in characterizing the processing of a distress warrant as a judicial act, then the procedure would be unconstitutional, because the officers executing this duty could not properly perform judicial functions. The distress warrant in question was authorized by an act of Congress passed on May 15, 1820 (3 Stats. at Large 592). In this respect, one can recognize that the reasoning in *Murray's Lessee* could argue against the constitutionality of the independent counsel statute, where the executive power of appointment is delegated to the courts.

Justice Benjamin R. Curtis's decision in *Murray's Lessee* rejected the formalist argument presented by the plaintiff. Reasoning that not all acts that involve "the exercise of judgment upon law and fact" fall under the judicial power, Curtis ruled that the defendant had not been denied due process by the warrant in question, even though the judiciary was not involved in the procedure. Nevertheless, it can be argued that the Court's reasoning in this case might well have supported rejection of expressly stated executive powers to the judiciary. What one cannot estimate is the effect a political scandal with constitutional implications, such as WATERGATE, might have had upon the Court's decision.

Murray's Lessee was a combination of three New Jersey cases involving a mortgaged estate sold under a distress warrant. The Court, in ruling that the warrant was constitutional, rendered other aspects of the case moot. Justice Curtis relied upon an expansive discussion of English common law in deciding that due process had not been denied by the distress warrant or the statute that authorized it.

Justice Curtis was best known for his strong dissent in the Dred Scott case, and his participation as counsel in the defense of President Andrew Johnson during his 1868 impeachment trial.

Reference:

Liberman, Lee S. "*Morrison v. Olson*: A Formalistic Perspective on Why the Court Was Wrong." *American University Law Review* 38 (1989): 313–358. Discusses *MYERS v. U.S.* and *NIXON v. ADMINISTRATOR OF GENERAL SERVICES* as well as *Murray's Lessee* in arguing against the constitutionality of the independent counsel statute.

Myers v. United States 272 U.S. 52 (1926). A Supreme Court decision that has helped support the arguments of independent counsel opponents, *Myers v. U.S.* held that it was necessary for the president to be able to remove at will persons performing purely executive functions in order to guarantee faithful execution of the laws. Appeals Court Judge LAURENCE SILBERMAN relied on the *Myers* decision in ruling the independent counsel statute unconstitutional in *IN RE SEALED CASE* (1988). The *Myers* decision was significantly modified by Supreme Court rulings in *HUMPHREY'S EXECUTOR v. UNITED STATES* (1935) and *WIENER v. UNITED STATES* (1958), cases that took a closer look at the nature of the duties performed by the officer in question before determining whether the president might dismiss the individual at will.

Because section 6 of the Act of July 12, 1876, 19 Stat. 80, provided that postmasters could only be dismissed by the president with the approval of the Senate, Frank S. Myers sued when he was terminated without senatorial consent. The Supreme Court heard the case on appeal from a Court of Claims decision that denied Myers satisfaction because it was maintained that he had delayed in filing his lawsuit. Although the Supreme Court did not agree with the Court of Claims on this point, Chief Justice William Howard Taft ruled against Myers nonetheless. He held that the Act of 1876 was unconstitutional for placing restrictions on the president's ability to remove executive officers. The president's power to execute the laws, as stated in Article II, includes authority to remove executive employees from office, states Taft. However, Taft added, the Senate's advise and consent function cannot reasonably be extended to include performance of such a role in removal situations. Justices Willis Van Devanter, George Sutherland, Harlan Stone, and Edward Sanford concurred; Louis Brandeis, James McReynolds, and Oliver Wendell Holmes dissented.

When the Congress was considering establishment of an Office of Special Prosecutor in 1977, Assistant Attorney General for the Office of Legal Counsel John Harmon, testifying before the Senate Committee on Governmental Affairs, stated that the new proposed mechanism was constitutionally permissible because *Humphrey* and *Wiener* had modified *Myers*'s prohibition against such an arrangement. Although the precise nature of a special prosecutor's function was not entirely clear, Harmon believed that the government should be willing to experiment with limiting the president's removal power in this instance.

In 1986, the Supreme Court ruled in *BOWSHER v. SYNAR* that although *Myers* might be modified to permit limitations on the president's removal power, officials exercising executive authority cannot be removable only by Congress. Some felt that this decision heralded a return to Taft's reasoning in *Myers*. Silberman's decision reinforced this view. Only months later, however, *MORRISON v. OLSON* made it clear that limitations on the president's removal power would not invalidate the independent counsel statute in the eyes of the Supreme Court.

References:

Eastland, Terry. *Ethics, Politics, and the Independent Counsel Statute: Executive Power, Executive Vice 1789–1989*. Washington, D.C.: National Legal Center for the Public Interest, 1989. Chapters 4 ("The Search for Law") and 5 ("The Law of Title VI: 1977–1978") discuss *Myers*'s place in the formation of the independent counsel statute.

Harriger, Katy J. *Independent Justice: The Federal Special Prosecutor in American Politics*. Lawrence: University Press of Kansas, 1992. Chapter 5, "Is the Prosecutor Constitutional?," discusses *Myers*.

Liberman, Lee S. *"Morrison v. Olson*: A Formalistic Perspective on Why the Court Was Wrong." *American University Law Review* 38 (1989): 313–358. Discusses *Myers* in arguing against constitutionality of independent counsel statute.

O'Keefe, Constance, and Peter Safirstein. "Fallen Angels, Separation of Powers, and the Saturday Night Massacre: An Examination of the Practical, Constitutional, and Political Tensions in the Special Prosecutor Provisions of the Ethics in Government Act." *Brooklyn Law Review* 49 (1982): 113–147. Stresses the *Humphrey/Wiener* revisions to *Myers* in arguing in favor of the independent counsel statute.

Tiefer, Charles. "The Constitutionality of Independent Officers as Checks on Abuses of Executive Power." *Boston University Law Review* 63 (1983): 59–103. Doesn't believe *Myers* prevents necessary "oversight framework laws" such as the independent counsel statute.

N

Nader, Ralph (1934–) consumer advocate, attorney. Through his organization, Public Citizen, Inc., Ralph Nader has for almost three decades championed the causes of consumers and consistently advocated measures that would subject the political process to greater public scrutiny. In 1973, Nader joined with Representatives Bella Abzug (D-New York), Frank Moss (D-Utah), and Jerome Waldie (D-California) in challenging Acting Attorney General ROBERT BORK's dismissal of WATERGATE Special Prosecutor ARCHIBALD COX. Although Nader was later dropped from the suit because it was ruled that he lacked standing, U.S. District Court Judge GERHARD GESELL found that Cox's dismissal was illegal. Through the years, Nader continued to spearhead efforts at forcing release of documents related to scandals such as WATERGATE and IRAN-CONTRA.

After Attorney General ELLIOTT RICHARDSON and his assistant WILLIAM RUCKLESHAUS both resigned rather than comply with President RICHARD NIXON's order to dismiss Cox, Solicitor General Bork agreed to perform the task. On October 29, 1973, Nader filed suit in Washington's District Court. On November 9, Gesell agreed to hear the case, ruling on November 14 that Cox had been illegally discharged, because Justice Department regulations prohibited such action "except for extraordinary improprieties." The decision did not require Cox's reinstatement, but served to strengthen the hand of new Watergate Special Prosecutor LEON JAWORSKI.

Born in Winsted, Connecticut, Nader graduated from Princeton in 1955, and received his law degree from Harvard in 1958. He practiced law in Hartford and lectured in History and Government at the University of Hartford from 1961 to 1963. Nader's book *Unsafe at Any Speed* (Grossman, 1965) exposed the automobile industry's disregard for public safety and launched his campaign for consumer rights upon a national stage. In addition to Public Citizen, other activist organizations founded by Nader include Center for Responsive Law, Public Interest Research Group, Center for Auto Safety, Clean Water Action Project, Disability Rights Center, Pension Rights Center, and Project for Corporate Responsibility.

Nader has been particularly vocal concerning the manner in which regulatory agencies have frequently become de facto advocates for the corporations they are charged with regulating. He attributed this "theory of regulatory capture" to the fact that regulators are commonly recruited from the ranks of corporate America. In addition, Nader contended, influence peddling and lack of integrity pervade the process.

In 1999, Nader's Public Citizen lobbied for reform of the independent counsel statute. Displeased with the manner in which Independent Counsel KENNETH STARR proceeded in the WHITEWATER and MONICA LEWINSKY investigations, Nader's organization called for appointment of truly nonpartisan judges to oversee the independent counsel, and for requiring the independent counsel to meet higher standards of ethical conduct and accountability.

References:

Lardner, George, Jr., and Walter Pincus. "Notebook Reveals North-Bush Meeting." *Washington Post*, 9 May 1990, sec. A, p. 1. Discusses Public Citizen's role in securing the release of 1,400 pages of Oliver North's notes.

Nader v. Bork, Civil Action No. 1954–73, U.S. District Court for the District of Columbia.

Roberts, Robert N., and Marion T. Doss. *From Watergate to Whitewater: The Public Integrity War*. Westport, CT: Praeger, 1997. Chapter 6, "Regulatory Rebels," discusses Nader's contribution to the "theory of regulatory capture."

"Suit Seeks Nixon Tapes from Archives." *Chicago Tribune*, 20 March 1992, sec. C, p. 20.

Nathan v. Attorney General 557 F. Supp. 1186 (D.D.C. 1983). In 1982, the legal representatives of persons killed and injured during a protest demonstration in Greensboro, North Carolina, brought to Attorney General WILLIAM FRENCH SMITH evidence they believed demonstrated that federal officials had facilitated efforts to deprive the protestors of their civil rights. The Justice Department refused to conduct a preliminary investigation, ruling that the information provided was not specific enough to support the allegation that anyone covered by ETHICS IN GOVERNMENT ACT (1978) provisions had been guilty of any violations.

Along with the cases *BANZHAF v. SMITH* 588 F. Supp. 1498 (D.C. Cir. 1984) and *DELLUMS v. SMITH* 573 F. Supp. 1489 (N.D. Cal 1983), *Nathan* challenged the attorney general's discretion to dispose of potential independent counsel inquiries. Revision of the independent counsel statute at the time of its first reauthorization in 1983 had provided the attorney general with expanded authority to decide such matters. This reform was in response to the first independent counsel cases involving relatively frivolous accusations against CARTER administration officials HAMILTON JORDAN and TIMOTHY KRAFT.

It was believed that the attorney general should not be required to trigger an independent counsel investigation involving alleged offenses that would probably be ignored by the Justice Department.

Plaintiffs in the *Nathan* case claimed that Justice Department officials had participated in an effort to conceal the fact that the FBI was involved in the shooting of the demonstrators in Greensboro. Those demonstrating were members of the Communist Workers Party. Their attackers were white supremacists who objected to the protestors' support of a group of African-American workers during a labor dispute. Plaintiffs filed suit after the attorney general failed to initiate a preliminary investigation into the incident. They sought a writ of mandamus ordering the attorney general to carry out his obligations under the Ethics Act. Attorney General Smith claimed that the private citizens bringing the case lacked standing to sue.

Federal District Court ruled that the independent counsel statute provided the private citizen with a procedural right to initiate legal action in such instances. If such were not the case, the court held, the statute would amount to little more than a cynical political initiative aimed at providing false comfort to a public anxious over WATERGATE abuses. Smith was ordered by the court to begin a preliminary investigation into the incident.

In 1984, the Court of Appeals reversed the lower court's decision. Judge ROBERT BORK agreed with Attorney General Smith's assertion that the plaintiffs lacked standing to sue. In addition, Bork contended that Congress lacked authority to place prosecutorial power in the hands of an independent counsel, because the executive branch is vested by the Constitution with all law enforcement power. This separation of power argument would be rejected by the Supreme Court in *MORRISON v. OLSON* four years later.

Nathan helped fuel the argument that the authority retained by the attorney general in the independent counsel process represented an unacceptable conflict of interest. To remove the attorney general from the process completely, however, would have likely resulted in failure of the mechanism to pass constitutional muster. Further tinkering with the statute in an effort to fine-tune the procedure appeared probable before the next reauthorization in 1987.

References:

Harriger, Katy J. *Independent Justice: The Federal Special Prosecutor in American Politics.* Lawrence: University Press of Kansas, 1992. Chapter 5, "Is the Special Prosecutor Constitutional?," discusses the *Nathan* case and its relevance to the independent counsel mechanism.

Mixter, Stephen Charles. "The Ethics in Government Act of 1978: Problems with the Attorney General's Discretion and Proposals for Reform." *Duke Law Journal* (1985): 497–522. Argues that *Nathan* helped demonstrate that the attorney general's role in the independent counsel process served to subvert the administration of independent justice.

National Security Act. (1947) Independent Counsel LAWRENCE WALSH's IRAN-CONTRA investigation determined that the arms-for-hostages plan initiated by REAGAN administration officials was in violation of the BOLAND AMENDMENTS, the ARMS EXPORT CONTROL ACT, and the National Security Act (NSA). The latter, codified in sections 401–432 of 50 U.S.C., specified that Congress be notified regarding arms sales to foreign nations. Attorney General EDWIN MEESE argued that the arms sale was permissible, because notification could be made following the anticipated release of hostages. In addition, Meese contended, the NSA allowed arms sales when authorized as covert actions by a presidential finding.

In 1985, Israel acted as intermediary for U.S. arms sales to Iran. After Israel erroneously shipped arms with Israeli markings, the Reagan administration decided upon a new strategy: The CIA was authorized to obtain arms from the Defense Department and sell them directly to Iran. Because the Arms Export Control Act prohibited shipment of arms from one recipient country to another, the arrangement with Israel had been illegal. This new arrangement, however, did not meet notification requirements of the NSA. The Arms Export Control Act also required notification of Congress if sales exceeded specified limits.

The administration's creative interpretation of the arms-for-hostages arrangement helped rationalize the manner in which congressional restrictions had been avoided. Walsh's efforts at prosecuting such transgressions, however, were thwarted in part by Congress itself when the body offered testimonial IMMUNITY to principal participants like OLIVER NORTH and JOHN POINDEXTER.

References:

Koh, Harold Hongju. "Why the President (Almost) Always Wins in Foreign Affairs: Lessons of the Iran-Contra Affair." *Yale Law Journal* 97 (1988): 1255–1342.

Walsh, Lawrence. *Firewall: The Iran-Contra Conspiracy and Cover-up.* New York: W.W. Norton, 1997.

———. "Political Oversight, the Rule of Law, and Iran-Contra." *Cleveland State Law Review* 42 (1994): 587–597.

Nixon, Richard M. (1913–1994) U.S. President, 1969–1974. President Richard Nixon's involvement in the WATERGATE break-in of June 17, 1972, and its subsequent cover-up served as the impetus for establishment of an office of special prosecutor independent of the executive branch. Nixon's dismissal of Watergate Special Prosecutor ARCHIBALD COX on October 20, 1973, and his refusal to turn over tapes of his telephone conversations until forced to do so by court order, convinced many that executive-branch misconduct could not be investigated internally.

Nixon was implicated in the Watergate break-in by the testimony of White House attorney John Dean, when he appeared before Congress in March 1973. About the same time, an aide to White House Chief of Staff H. R. Haldemann revealed that Nixon maintained a complete set of audiotapes containing all his telephone conversations. These tapes became the focal point of the Watergate investigation. ARCHIBALD COX, the first Watergate special prosecutor, was dismissed on Nixon's order after refusing to accept a summary of the tapes for investigative purposes in place of the tapes themselves. This "Saturday Night Massacre" of October 20 convinced a large majority of Americans that the president could not be trusted to supervise an investigation of executive-branch misconduct.

The second Watergate special prosecutor, LEON JAWORSKI, was appointed on November 5, 1973, to continue the investigation. He experienced no interference from the Nixon White House as he pressed the case for release of the tapes. On July 24, 1974, in *United States v. Nixon* 418 U.S. 683 (1974), the Supreme Court ruled against Nixon's attempt to avoid subpoena of the tapes. Chief Justice Warren Burger ruled that Nixon could not claim absolute privilege in this matter. The requirements of our criminal justice system, stated Burger, outweigh the president's need for privacy of communication if we are to ensure its integrity. Nixon's claim under separation of powers doctrine was similarly rejected by the Court. Citing Justice Robert Jackson's opinion in *YOUNGS-TOWN SHEET & TUBE COMPANY v. SAWYER* (1952), Burger declared that such separation required accommodation for interdependence and reciprocity between branches of government in order that the government may function correctly. The Court unanimously concluded that any claim to presidential privilege in this matter must yield to "the legitimate needs of the judicial process." Justice William Rehnquist was absent.

On July 27, 1974, the House Judiciary Committee voted for impeachment of Nixon on grounds of abuse of power, obstruction of justice, and refusal to comply with subpoenas. On August 5, Nixon turned over transcripts of conversations taped on June 23, 1972 that demonstrated his involvement in the Watergate coverup. Three days later he resigned his office. Although it may be argued that the system worked in the end, public outrage over Nixon's perceived attempt to employ his personal political power to defeat justice, coupled with the two-year national agony caused by the president's desperate effort to save himself, convinced many that existing mechanisms were ill-equipped to deal with such eventualities. Consequently, Congress began its search for legislation that would create a special, independent office to investigate and prosecute future misconduct by the executive.

On September 8, 1974, President GERALD FORD pardoned Nixon in advance of his possible indictment for any Watergate-related crimes. For many, this gesture validated their belief that justice was not possible under the existing system. It was widely thought that Nixon either should have been made to answer for his actions, or at least required to acknowledge wrongdoing and ask for forgiveness. In 1977, Nixon was forced to permit government archivists access to his papers when the Supreme Court ruled, in *NIXON v. ADMINIS-TRATOR OF GENERAL SERVICES*, that such incursion was constitutionally permissible. This decision helped the independent counsel statute pass constitutional scrutiny.

Nixon attempted to play the role of elder statesman during the last twenty years of his life, with mixed success. Though he received credit primarily for foreign policy achievements such as establishment of relations with China, Watergate continued to cast a long shadow over his career. He died of a stroke on April 23, 1994.

References:

Doyle, James. *Not above the Law: The Battles of Watergate Prosecutors Cox and Jaworski*. New York: Morrow, 1977.

Eastland, Terry. *Ethics, Politics and the Independent Counsel: Executive Power, Executive Vice 1789–1989*. Washington, D.C.: National Legal Center for the Public Interest, 1989. Chapter 3, "Watergate: The Origins of the Law," discusses the effect of Nixon's actions on creation of the independent counsel statute.

Harriger, Katy J. *Independent Justice: The Federal Special Prosecutor in American Politics*. Lawrence: University Press of Kansas, 1992. Chapter 2, "Ad Hoc Appointment," covers Watergate, emphasizing the effect Nixon's behavior had on public opinion.

McNeely-Johnson, K. A. "*United States v. Nixon*, Twenty Years After: The Good, the Bad and the Ugly—an Exploration of Executive Privilege." *Northern Illinois University Law Review* 14 (1993): 251–301. Argues that the judiciary needs to check overuse of executive privilege by use of *in camera* inspection of material in question. Maintains that only national security concerns should exempt material from *in camera* examination. Discusses *NORTH v. WALSH* 656 F.Supp. 414 (D.D.C. 1987) and JOHN POINDEXTER'S case as well as *Nixon*.

Nixon v. Administrator of General Services 433 U.S. 425 (1977). One year before passage of the ETHICS IN GOVERNMENT (1978), which established the independent counsel, the Supreme Court ruled in *Nixon v. Administrator of General Services*, that a statute regulating—but not disrupting or usurping—executive power is constitutionally permissible. This decision helped pave the way for establishment of the independent counsel statute by sanctioning moderate incursion upon executive authority.

After RICHARD NIXON resigned as president in 1974, he negotiated a depository agreement with the Administrator of General Services providing for the storage of an estimated 42 million pages of documents and 880 tape recordings accumulated during his tenure in the White House. These materials would be located near his home in California, and neither Nixon nor the General Services Administration (GSA) could gain access to them without the other's permission. The agreement stipulated conditions governing accessibility of the documents and eventual disposal of the tapes. Three months later, Congress passed the Presidential Recordings and Materials Preservation Act (Pub.L. 93–526) that effectively abrogated Nixon's agreement with the GSA. Signed into law by President GERALD FORD on December 19, 1974, it provided for government archivists to screen Nixon's materials. Those deemed of historical value would be retained, made available for use in judicial proceedings, and rendered accessible to the public, subject to specified regulations. On December 20, Nixon filed suit in U.S. district court challenging its constitutionality. The suit claimed that the law violated separation of powers, presidential privilege, privacy interests, First Amendment rights of association, and amounted to a bill of attainder.

The District Court ruled that the constitutional challenges to the Act were without merit and dismissed the complaint. The court held that separation of powers was not violated because Presidents FORD and CARTER both approved of the arrangement; control over the materials in question continued to be exercised by the executive branch as represented by GSA and the government archivists; and the Act did not prevent the executive branch from performing its constitutional functions. In addition, the court found that the Act protected the ex-president's confidentiality, did not invade his privacy or limit his right of association, and did not represent a bill of attainder.

On June 28, 1977, Justice William Brennan delivered the opinion of the Supreme Court. In upholding the district court's decision, Brennan referred to Justice Robert Jackson's definition of separation of powers enunciated in *YOUNGSTOWN SHEET & TUBE CO. v. SAWYER* 343 U.S. 579 (1952). Separation of powers, stated Jackson, was not intended to be absolute. Brennan reminded Nixon that the Court had rejected his attempt to define separation of powers strictly just three years previously in *U.S. v. Nixon* 418 U.S. 683 when considering the president's duty to obey subpoena by the WATERGATE special prosecutor. Brennan also found most relevant the fact that the presidential documents remained in the hands of the executive branch. Confidentiality provisions are protected by the Act, stated Brennan, and the decision permitting regulated public access to such documents is founded on strong precedent (Freedom of Information Act, 1970; Sunshine Act, 1976). Justices Byron White, John Paul Stevens, Harry Blackmun, and Lewis Powell concurred.

Dissents were filed by Chief Justice Warren Burger and Justice William Rehnquist. They asked how the majority's current decision can be reconciled with the Court's ruling in *BUCKLEY v. VALEO* 424 U.S. 1 (1976) where a more formal approach to separation of powers was approved. The dissenters also contended that it mattered little whether Congress allowed the executive branch, as represented by GSA, to maintain control of the president's documents. They had still violated the constitutional prerogatives of the president by impermissibly disposing of his papers.

Nixon v. Administrator of General Services demonstrated that the Watergate crisis would serve to justify a pragmatic approach in dealing with the potential of executive-branch misconduct. This proved an accurate predictor of success for the independent counsel statute the following year.

References:

Glitzenstein, Eric R., and Allan B. Morrison. "The Supreme Court's Decision in *Morrison v. Olson*: A Common Sense Application of the Constitution to a Practical Problem." *American University Law Review* 38 (1989): 359–382. Refers to *Nixon v. Administration of General Services* as a pivotal case in establishing the constitutionality of a statute that regulates, but does not disrupt, executive power.

Goodpaster, Gary. "Rules of the Game: Comments on Three Views of the Independent Prosecutor Case." *American University Law Review* 38 (1989): 383–393. Rejects idea of *Nixon v. Administrator of General Services* as a balancing test in cases where a statute regulates the executive. Finds such balancing tests subject to unprincipled manipulation. Predicts independent counsel will be unaccountable.

Tiefer, Charles. "The Constitutionality of Independent Officers as Checks on Abuses of Executive Power." *Boston University Law Review* 63 (1983): 59–103. Counts *Nixon v. Administrator of General Services* among the historical cases that support the existence of "oversight framework laws" such as the independent counsel statute.

Nofziger, Franklyn C. (1924–   ) White House Communications Director, 1981–1982. The subject of an investigation by Independent Counsel JAMES McKAY, Franklyn (Lyn) Nofziger was convicted of violating lobbying provisions contained in the ETHICS IN GOVERNMENT ACT. His conviction in 1987 was overturned in 1989 when the Court of Appeals ruled that Nofziger did not knowingly violate the law.

A longtime associate of RONALD REAGAN, Nofziger was trained as a journalist. Educated at San Jose State University, he served at the statehouse in Sacramento during Reagan's tenure as governor. In 1972, Nofziger ran RICHARD NIXON's presidential campaign, and stayed on to serve in the White House. After Reagan's election as president in 1980, Nofziger came to Washington with him as an aide and adviser. In January 1982, Nofziger resigned his position. Four months later, acting as lobbyist for the Welbuilt Electronic Die Corporation (Wedtech), he enlisted the assistance of administration official James E. Jenkins in helping to win a $32 million Army contract for the firm. Nofziger's action was in apparent violation of the Ethics in Government Act provision that bars former administration officials from lobbying the government for one year after leaving office. For this reason, an independent counsel appointment was requested. The request was made by Deputy Attorney General Arnold I. Burns, because Attorney General EDWIN MEESE was recused.

The Nofziger investigation was similar to Independent Counsel WHITNEY NORTH SEYMOUR's 1986 probe of former White House official MICHAEL DEAVER. In both cases the subjects were accused of using their government contacts for personal economic gain. Independent Counsel James McKay, named to investigate Nofziger on February 2, 1987, had briefly served as investigator of former Assistant Attorney General THEODORE OLSON before stepping aside due to conflict of interest. ALEXIA MORRISON replaced McKay as independent counsel, and Olson's challenge to her authority eventually resulted in the Supreme Court case that affirmed the constitutionality of the independent counsel statute.

When McKay's investigation of Nofziger was three months old, Attorney General Meese was implicated. McKay's investigation was formally expanded to include any possible violations by Meese. The Nofziger investigation resulted in his indictment in July 1987 and conviction on February 11, 1988. On April 18, he was sentenced to 90 days in prison and fined $30,000. In August 1989, however, the conviction was overturned on appeal. The court cited language of the Ethics in Government Act that stipulated that the violator must "knowingly" commit the specified transgression. It had not been demonstrated to the court's satisfaction that Nofziger had known that he was in violation while he was lobbying on behalf of Wedtech. Nofziger was unsuccessful in an attempt to obtain government reimbursement for his legal fees. Nofziger's investigation had been conducted in a timely manner at a relatively reasonable cost ($2,796,000). His successful appeal demonstrated the danger in employing vague language when crafting legislation.

Nofziger has continued to remain active in Republican politics. In 1994, he worked in Michael Huffington's unsuccessful effort to unseat California's Democratic Senator Dianne Feinstein. In 1992, Nofziger published his autobiography, *Nofziger* (Regency Gateway).

References:

Beinstein, Debra. "Making the Case against Nofziger." *The American Lawyer* (September 1987): 117. Highlights the role of McKay's assistant, Lovida Coleman, in building the case against Nofziger.

Eastland, Terry. *Ethics, Politics, and the Independent Counsel: Executive Power, Executive Vice, 1798–1989*. Washington, D.C.: National Legal Center for the Public Interest, 1989. Chapter 7, "The Second Amendments to the Law: 1987," discusses the course of the Nofziger case.

"Ethics and Virtue; Lyn Nofziger Conviction Overturned." *National Review*, 4 August 1989, p. 14.

Radcliffe, Donnie. "The Notable Nofziger." *Washington Post*, 12 April 1981, sec. L, p. 1. Traces Nofziger's personal and political history.

Raines, Howard. "Nofziger Leaves Reagan: Take Three." *New York Times*, 23 January 1992, sec. A, p. 9.

North, Oliver L. (1943–   ) National Security staff member during Iran-Contra. Oliver North was a career military officer who emerged as one of the central figures in Independent Counsel LAWRENCE WALSH's investigation of the IRAN-CONTRA scandal. North would ultimately be indicted on 16 different counts relating to the scandal. North was born in 1943, in Texas, but his family moved to Philmot, New York. In 1961, after graduation from high school, North was accepted at both Holy Cross and Notre Dame. Financial constraints, however, prevented him from attending either university, and North instead went to Brockport State University. In 1963, he entered the Naval Academy. After graduation in 1968, he was commissioned a lieutenant in the Marine Corps. That same year he married Betsy Stuart, and the couple later had four children. North went on to serve in Vietnam and was decorated several times. He rose through the ranks and was promoted to lieutenant-colonel. In 1981, he was assigned to the National Security Council (NSC) staff.

North was appointed deputy director for politico-military affairs on the NSC staff. This position was a mid-level appointment, but from his post, North would become a central figure in overseeing both the arms-for-hostages deals with the Iranians and the covert operation to supply the Nicaraguan Contras. As a marine officer, North technically did not have the authority to command or control activities within the NSC or to direct the operations of other government agencies such as the CIA or the Defense Department. Nonetheless, North was able to assume a degree of authority that exceeded what would normally be associated with his office because of a number of factors. President RONALD REAGAN assigned his National Security Adviser ROBERT McFARLANE the task of keeping the Contras operational during the period when U.S. aid was cut off to the rebel group because of the BOLAND AMENDMENT (1984–1986). McFarlane then allowed the NSC staff to undertake operational duties that were clearly beyond the scope of the organization's mandate. In doing so, North and those involved on the NSC staff shielded the rest of the administration, including the president, the CIA, and the State Department, from many of their activities. Nonetheless, North kept both McFarlane and his successor, Admiral JOHN POINDEXTER, informed of his actions and claimed to have worked closely with CIA director WILLIAM CASEY. North also created the impression among others that he acted with the full knowledge and approval of the president.

During the course of his investigation, the independent counsel found that North had been involved in three broad categories of activities relating to scandal. North helped manage the arms-for-hostages deal with Iran and the resultant cover-up of the operation. North also took over the U.S. effort to supply the Contras after the CIA was forced to end its endeavors because of the Boland Amendment. Finally, North engaged in attempts to gain third-party support for the Contras, both from domestic figures and from foreign entities.

In the summer of 1985, North became involved with the ongoing operation to sell weapons to Iran in exchange for the release of U.S. hostages held by Iranian-backed Islamic extremist groups in Lebanon. U.S. weapons, including sophisticated Hawk and TOW missiles, were sold to Israel and then secretly transferred to Iran. After three shipments to Iran in 1985, one U.S. hostage was released. The delivery of five more shipments of missiles and missile parts in 1986, led to the release of two more hostages. During these operations, North coordinated the weapons transfers and even gained the unknowing cooperation of the State Department in pursuing clearances for the shipments through European nations.

North's participation in the weapons-for-hostages deals led to his development of the diversion scheme to transfer the profits of the sales to the Contras. In November of 1985, North found that there remained some $800,000 from the initial arms transfers to Iran. North authorized the use of these funds by the Contras. This marked the beginning of the diversion efforts. North subsequently found that the Iranians were willing to pay as much as $10,000 for TOW missiles, while he negotiated a selling price of $3,700 from the Department of

Defense. As more shipments were made to the Iranians, the profits from the sales were transferred to operations that North was overseeing to supply and equip the Contras.

With the Congressional cutoff of aid, North began to look for outside sources to fund the Contras. In May of 1984, McFarlane had convinced the Saudis to aid the Contras, and North arranged a covert bank account to transfer funds from the Middle East to the Contras. North turned to retired Air Force general RICHARD SECORD to aid him in his efforts. Secord was appointed to oversee the resupply operation (which was given the codename "Enterprise") and began buying weapons and supplies, as well as hiring aircrew and planes to drop supplies to the Contras and renting warehouse space for the equipment. North entered into negotiations with friendly governments in the region to aid the Contras by providing staging bases and other assistance in exchange for U.S. aid. North also coordinated aid from nations such as Brunei and Panama, in addition to directing a significant amount of funds from individuals and groups to the Contras.

In November of 1986, when revelations about the Iran-Contra operations surfaced, the decision was made to relieve North of his duties. On November 25, Reagan and Attorney General EDWIN MEESE announced in a press conference the details of the unfolding scandal and disclosed that North had been fired. During the congressional investigations that followed, North was offered limited IMMUNITY guaranteeing that anything he told Congress could not be used against him in criminal proceedings. The colonel's subsequent testimony on national television had the unexpected result of making him a hero to a number of conservative groups and factions within the United States as he portrayed himself as a simple soldier following orders and doing what he perceived to be correct under the contemporary circumstances.

Walsh quickly realized that the case against Oliver North was central to the success of the entire investigation. When North refused to enter into plea bargain negotiations with the Office of the Independent Counsel, Walsh decided to proceed with the prosecution of the former NSC staffer. North's immunity complicated the effort to prosecute and raised serious legal questions as to whether he could even be brought to trial. In addition, Walsh and his staff realized that North's defense might depend upon certain classified information that could not be disclosed for national security reasons.

Nonetheless, the prosecution's effort proceeded, and on March 16, 1988, the grand jury returned a 23-count indictment against North, Poindexter, Secord, and ALBERT HAKIM who worked with Secord on the Enterprise operation. All were charged with conspiracy to defraud the government, theft, and wire fraud. In addition, North was charged with obstruction of justice relating to his misstatements to Congress and efforts to destroy or alter official documents. North was also charged with acceptance of an illegal gratuity for a home security system that Secord gave him and with tax-fraud conspiracy.

The independent counsel wanted to try all four cases together, but the defense teams were able to gain a severance of the cases. For Walsh, this represented a major setback in his prosecution since he correctly presumed that the defendants would endeavor to shift the responsibility for their actions to each other. Furthermore, the separation of the cases created a delay of a year before Walsh and his team could finish their questioning of all of the accused. He decided to try North first as he was the most important of the four defendants. Walsh agreed to dismiss one count against North, and the court ordered the dismissal of another, so when the ex-marine went to trial, he faced 12 individual charges.

As jury selection began in the North trial, the issue of classified information became a key to the course of the case. Judge GERHARD GESELL attempted to deviate from the CLASSIFIED INFORMATION PROCEDURES ACT (CIPA) in order to allow testimony deemed essential by North's defense team. However, the administration was able to block the publication of certain information relating to national security. This led to the withdrawal of 100 prosecution team exhibits and approximately 10,000 pages of documents that were to be used in North's defense. After Judge Gesell ruled that the independent counsel had protected its case from undue influence by immunized testimony and that it shielded the members of the grand jury from immunized materials, North's lawyers immediately appealed. Although the independent counsel effectively opposed the appeals, they would form the basis for the appellate court's later actions.

In addition to these factors, the independent counsel team faced a range of other problems in prosecuting North. Most of its witnesses were hostile and opposed North's prosecution. During his testimony, North was able to effectively cast himself as a victim of circumstances who endeavored to carry out what he perceived to be the policies of the administration. He claimed that all of his actions were the result of higher authorization. His defense team was able to establish that many of his activities were conducted with the knowledge and approval of his superiors. However, the judge rejected North's effort to subpoena former President Reagan. Furthermore, North was unable to explain why he destroyed certain documents and why he removed others from his office after his dismissal. He was also unable to explain certain funds that were given to him or the gift of the home security system. One of the most important details to emerge from the trial was North's account of personally witnessing Poindexter's destruction of the sole copy of the presidential directive that authorized the 1985 transfer of missiles to Iran.

The jury began its deliberations on April 22, 1989. They found North innocent on nine counts but convicted him of obstructing a congressional inquiry, destroying and altering official documents, and receiving an illegal gift. Although the independent counsel recommended jail time for North on these three convictions, Judge Gesell instead sentenced him to two years probation, 1,200 hours of community service, and a $150,000 fine. North appealed his convictions, and on July 20, 1990, the Court of Appeals set aside the convictions on a 2–1 vote. The Court disagreed with Judge Gesell and the independent counsel over the use of immunized testimony and held that North's immunity prevented him from being tried. The independent counsel appealed the ruling, but on May 28, 1991, the Supreme Court denied Walsh's petition.

After his convictions were overturned, North ran unsuccessfully for a U.S. Senate seat from Virginia. He then went on to be a political commentator, first with his own radio show and then on national television.

References:

Bradlee, Ben. *"Guts and Glory": The Oliver North Story.* New York: D. I. Fine, 1988.
Draper, Theodore. *A Very Thin Line: The Iran-Contra Affairs.* New York: Hill and Wang, 1991.
Fagen, Richard R. *Forging Peace: The Challenge of Central America.* New York: Basil, 1987.
North, Oliver. *Under Fire: An American Story.* New York: HarperCollins Publishers, 1991.
Reagan, Ronald W. *An American Life: The Autobiography.* New York: Simon & Schuster, 1990.
Walsh, Lawrence E. *Firewall: The Iran-Contra Conspiracy and Cover-up.* New York: Norton, 1997.
————. *Iran-Contra: The Final Report.* New York: Times Books, 1994.
Weinberger, Caspar W. *Fighting for Peace: Seven Critical Years in the Pentagon.* New York: Warner, 1990.

—TOM LANSFORD

North v. Walsh 656 F.Supp. 414 (D.D.C. 1987). On February 24, 1987, OLIVER NORTH formally challenged the legitimacy of Independent Counsel LAWRENCE WALSH's IRAN-CONTRA investigation, claiming that separation of powers doctrine had been violated. Judge Barrington D. Parker proceeded to dismiss the suit, because it had been filed prematurely—North had not yet been indicted. In additional comments, Parker indicated that he believed that the independent counsel statute would withstand constitutional scrutiny.

North's attorney, BRENDAN SULLIVAN, argued that judicial appointment of a prosecutor was unconstitutional; that the executive must maintain prosecutorial authority; and that the judiciary's power was restricted to deciding cases—not determining who should bring them to court. Because Walsh had not yet brought charges against North, he did not feel immediately threatened by this action. He was more concerned about former Deputy Chief of Staff MICHAEL DEAVER's challenge to Independent Counsel WHITNEY NORTH SEYMOUR's investigation, which closely followed North's. After Deaver's suit resulted in a temporary suspension of Seymour's investigation, Walsh obtained a backup appointment from the Department of Justice that would enable him to proceed regardless of court action on the North and Deaver suits. North responded to Walsh's strategy by arguing, in a second challenge, that the attorney general did not possess the authority to make such an appointment. In addition, North maintained, officers wielding executive power such as Walsh must be removable at will by the president. In this instance, Walsh could only be dismissed for "good cause."

After ruling that North had failed to demonstrate that he had suffered hardship justifying the court's examination of the independent counsel statute's constitutionality at this point, Judge Parker proceeded to dismiss North's suit. In his ruling, he proceeded to offer ample evidence that he considered similar challenges of the independent counsel's constitutionality likely to fail. Parker indicated that North's formalistic arguments were also at odds with the long-standing practice of vesting executive power in independent agencies. In addition, Parker considered it ill-advised to intervene early during a criminal investigation. If he did elect to intervene, however, it was made clear that Parker considered existing case law at odds with North's separation of powers arguments. The judge's discussion also mentioned the role played by the attorney general in the process, preserving an important element of executive control, and pointed out the statutory limitations already constraining independent counsel investigations.

North v. Walsh provided an early and accurate indication that the independent counsel statute would survive constitutional scrutiny. The decision in *DEAVER v. SEYMOUR* would echo this prediction. The North defense team would have greater success manipulating the CLASSIFIED INFORMATION PROCEDURES ACT (CIPA) to their advantage in avoiding the most serious charges facing their client.

References:

Harriger, Katy J. *Independent Justice: The Federal Special Prosecutor in American Politics.* Lawrence: University Press of Kansas, 1992. Chapter 5, "Is the Prosecutor Constitutional?," discusses *North v. Walsh* and its implications for the independent counsel statute.

Walsh, Lawrence. *Firewall: The Iran-Contra Conspiracy and Cover-up.* New York: W. W. Norton, 1997. Chapter 5, "The Bramble Bush," describes North's constitutional challenge to Walsh's investigation.

Northern Pipeline Construction Company v. Marathon Pipeline Company 458 U.S. 50 (1982). An important case in establishing a trend toward formalist interpretation of the separation of powers principle from the mid-1970s until mid-1980s, *Northern Pipeline* ruled on the constitutionality of congressionally created bankruptcy courts. The Supreme Court, in declaring such creations unconstitutional, encouraged those who predicted a short life for the independent counsel statute.

The Bankruptcy Act of 1978 established a bankruptcy court in each judicial district of the United States. Judges were to serve 14-year terms, their salaries set by statute and subject to adjustment. When Northern Pipeline Construction Co. filed suit against Marathon Pipeline Co. in 1980, charging breach of contract, misrepresentation, coercion, and duress, Marathon responded by claiming that the Bankruptcy Act was unconstitutional because it transferred judicial power to judges who did not enjoy life tenure and protection against reduction in salary. The Bankruptcy Court denied Marathon's motion to dismiss, but the U.S. District Court granted it on appeal.

Justice William Brennan's decision upheld the District Court's. He ruled that Congress's bankruptcy courts clearly violated Article III's provision that judicial power must be placed in the hands of judges who have tenure for life and are protected against diminution of salary. Arguments in favor of the bankruptcy court's legitimacy, stated Brennan, err by failing to acknowledge any limiting principle that would prevent Congress from replacing an independent judiciary with a series of specialized legislative courts. Expediency should not be the governing principle in this instance. The powers granted to bankruptcy court judges greatly exceeded those extended to administrative agencies that decide cases of more limited scope. This represented an unacceptable encroachment upon judicial authority. Joining Brennan in this ruling were Justices Harry Blackmun, Thurgood Marshall, and John Paul Stevens. Justices Sandra Day O'Connor and William Rehnquist concurred in a separate decision, more limited in scope.

Justice Byron White, joined by Chief Justice Warren Burger and Justice Lewis Powell, dissented. Powell saw no reason why bankruptcy proceedings should not be included with all the other issues arising from federal law that are routinely decided by congressionally created tribunals. Bankruptcy proceedings, White maintained, cannot be separated into those claims based on state law and those based on federal, in order to determine the proper forum for adjudication. The great majority of creditor claims in such cases originate at the state level. Citing *MURRAY'S LESSEE v. HOBOKEN LAND AND IMPROVEMENT COMPANY* 59 U.S. (18 How.) 272 (1856), White stated that whether or not an issue may be decided by a non-Article III court is dependent upon the will of Congress and the validity of Congress's reasons for departing from standard practice. The Bankruptcy Act will not upset the separation of powers, because the issues decided there are of little political interest. Given the fluctuating nature of bankruptcy proceedings, there is practical value in allowing Congress the flexibility to deal with adjudication of such questions. There is also adequate provision, White declared, for appellate review of any questionable rulings made by the bankruptcy courts.

The formalist approach to separation of powers questions enunciated in *Northern Pipeline* began with the ruling in *BUCKLEY v. VALEO* (1976). It would continue with the Court's decisions in *INS v. CHADHA* (1983) and *BOWSHER v. SYNAR* (1986) before *MORRISON v. OLSON* (1988) abruptly reversed the trend while legitimizing the independent counsel statute.

References:

Gerwitz, Paul. "Realism in Separation of Powers Thinking." *William and Mary Law Review* 30 (1989): 343–354. Includes *Northern* among decisions that describe rigid, false universe that bears little resemblance to the world in which we operate. Calls for more realistic approach.

Sherry, Suzanna. "Separation of Powers: Asking a Different Question." *William and Mary Law Review* 30 (1989): 287–300. Argues against formalist approach to separation of powers questions. Sees *Northern* as having begun modern trend in this erroneous direction.

Nussbaum, Bernard W. (1937–   ) former Counsel to the President, 1993–1994. Attorney Bernard Nussbaum played an important role in two aspects of the WHITEWATER investigation of Independent Counsels ROBERT FISKE and KENNETH STARR. At the inception of the Whitewater inquiry in the spring of 1993, Nussbaum began receiving reports from Deputy Treasury Secretary ROGER ALTMAN regarding the Resolution Trust Corporation's (RTC) probe of JAMES McDOUGAL's Madison Guaranty Savings & Loan. President CLINTON's financial ties to McDougal had been well-established. In addition, following the apparent suicide of Deputy White House Counsel VINCENT FOSTER on July 20, 1993, Nussbaum prevented federal agents from examining document files in Foster's office. His behavior helped fuel critics' charges that the administration was participating in an effort to conceal the President's participation in Whitewater-related misconduct.

Nussbaum was born and raised in New York City's lower east side, the son of Polish immigrants. Educated at Columbia University and Harvard Law School, he worked as a federal prosecutor for U.S. Attorney Robert Morgenthau and as a partner with the law firm of Wachtell, Lipton, Rosen & Katz. During WATERGATE, Nussbaum served as Associate Counsel to the House Judiciary Committee, where he met HILLARY CLINTON. In 1992, he helped raise funds for Clinton's presidential campaign and was offered the position of White House Counsel after the election.

In March 1993, an RTC senior vice president notified Altman that the RTC had made criminal referrals to the FBI and U.S. Attorney's Office the previous September. The referrals called for additional investigations of the Madison Guaranty Savings & Loan and named Bill Clinton as a possible beneficiary of Madison's misconduct. Altman alerted Nussbaum to the situation. On September 29 and October 14, Nussbaum participated in meetings organized by Treasury General Counsel JEAN HANSON during which additional RTC referrals were discussed. On February 2, 1994, Altman decided to recuse himself from involvement in any further RTC cases involving Madison, because of his close personal relationship with the President. Nussbaum, however, convinced Altman to reconsider his decision. Nussbaum believed that such recusal, when not mandated, would set an undesirable precedent.

Robert Fiske was appointed Whitewater independent counsel in January 1994 by Attorney General JANET RENO, during the period in which the governing statute had lapsed. Congressional investigators, unhappy with Altman's explanations of Treasury Department contacts with the White House regarding

RTC's referrals, also served to focus attention on Nussbaum's role. When Fiske issued subpoenas to everyone involved in the RTC investigation, it became apparent that the White House–Treasury Department meetings might have criminal implications. On March 5, with the approval of the president, Nussbaum resigned. The resignations of Altman and Hanson would follow after congressional hearings during the summer. At the same hearings, Nussbaum staunchly defended his actions, claiming nothing improper had transpired during any of the meetings between the Treasury Department and White House officials. He also continued to maintain that Altman's recusal was unnecessary.

Following the apparent suicide of Vince Foster in a Washington, D.C. park on July 20, 1993, Nussbaum decided to prevent the police from immediately examining Foster's office. Nussbaum attempted to balance concerns for the privacy of Foster and the Clintons with the desire to avoid the appearance of a cover-up. Eventually, he decided to permit law enforcement officials to observe as Nussbaum himself sifted through Foster's papers. Nussbaum sorted them into three categories: material to be examined by police; Foster's personal materials to be turned over to Foster's lawyer, James Hamilton; and materials relating to Foster's clients, the Clintons, which were to be turned over to their lawyers at the firm of Williams & Connolly. Nussbaum's control of the situation was criticized by Associate Attorney General WEBSTER HUBBELL, who questioned the counsel's authority in this situation. As Nussbaum had feared, his delay in permitting access to Foster's office was perceived as a transparent effort to hide evidence that might have implicated the Clintons in Whitewater-related misconduct and/or Foster's death. After several investigations, including one by KENNETH STARR's office, Foster's death was confirmed a suicide.

Although there has been no demonstrated misconduct resulting from any of Nussbaum's actions or as a result of his advice while serving in the White House, it appears that he may have been insufficiently sensitive to the appearance of impropriety in permitting contact with Treasury officials during the RTC's probe of Madison Guaranty. The mere appearance of possible misconduct has served as just cause for initiating more than one independent counsel investigation in our post-Watergate world.

References:

"Rough Whitewater Ride for Clinton." *Congressional Quarterly Almanac* (1994): 108–115.

Schmidt, Susan, and Serge F. Kovaleski. "Hubbell Says Nussbaum Kept Probers From Files." *Washington Post*, 20 July 1995, sec. A, p. 1.

Stewart, James B. *Blood Sport*. New York: Simon & Schuster, 1996. Parts 2 and 3, "The Road to Scandal" and "A Death in the White House" discuss Nussbaum's background and influence as White House counsel during the Whitewater investigation.

Zehren, Charles V. " 'I Was Right': Senators Hear Nussbaum's Side." *Newsday*, 10 August 1995, sec. A, p. 3.

O

Olson, Theodore B. (1940–) Assistant Attorney General, 1981–1984. The subject of an investigation by Independent Counsel ALEXIA MORRISON, Theodore Olson was accused of obstruction of justice for allegedly impeding a congressional probe of the Environmental Protection Agency (EPA). He proceeded to challenge the authority of the independent counsel in court. On January 22, 1988, the D.C. Circuit Appeals Court ruled the independent counsel unconstitutional, but the Supreme Court announced its reversal of this decision on June 29. *MORRISON v. OLSON*, having established the legitimacy of the office, paved the way for the continuing investigation of Olson. On August 26, however, after a 28-month inquiry, Morrison announced that evidence against Olson was insufficient to warrant prosecution.

After graduating from Boalt Hall School of Law in 1965, Olson worked at the Los Angeles firm of Gibson, Dunn & Crutcher. During the 1970s, he was successful in defending the First Amendment rights of a series of clients. These included the 1975 representation of the California Newspaper Association and the *Los Angeles Times* against Burbank's prohibition of newspaper racks in 97 percent of their city; the 1976 defense of the *St. Louis Post-Dispatch* against a libel suit brought by the Church of Scientology; and representation of Metromedia in their challenge of San Diego's prohibition against billboard advertising. In February 1981, Attorney General WILLIAM FRENCH SMITH hired Olson as assistant attorney general in charge of the Office of Legal Counsel (OLC).

Although Olson was a supporter of President REAGAN's conservative agenda, it appears that he succeeded in maintaining the necessary objectivity required of OLC head. This is evidenced by two opinions he rendered: in 1982, Olson advised the attorney general that Congress could not deprive the Supreme Court of its jurisdiction in matters regarding busing and abortion; and in 1983, he advised the Central Intelligence Agency (CIA) that any employment of personnel in covert operations must be reported to Congress as mandated by the War Powers Act.

Despite the presence of the Superfund hazardous waste cleanup law, the Reagan administration's EPA had failed to refer a single toxic pollution case to the Justice Department by the end of 1982. EPA administrator Anne Gorsuch was accused of dereliction by environmental advocates. In response to requests for EPA documents by House subcommittees, OLC advised turning over most materials but retaining those that related to the executive branch's ability to enforce the law. When negotiations for the release of the remaining documents failed, Gorsuch, accompanied by Olson, invoked executive privilege. As a result, the House cited her for contempt and referred the matter to the U.S. attorney for prosecution. After the Justice Department filed suit against the House, the matter was settled in February 1983, when OLC reviewed the documents once more. They found three references suggesting that release of cleanup funds might be linked to timing of Senate elections. These documents were referred to the Justice Department's Criminal Division. The Reagan administration's claim of executive privilege, incapable of protecting wrongdoing, was dropped.

On March 10, 1983, Olson appeared before the House Judiciary Committee to answer questions regarding OLC's role in obstructing Congress's investigation of EPA. During his testimony before Chairman Peter Rodino (D-New Jersey), Olson denied that any EPA official had informed him the agency was in favor of submitting the requested documents to Congress, despite OLC's advice to the contrary. In addition, Olson claimed that all relevant OLC documents requested by the Judiciary Committee, for the purposes of the current hearing, had been turned over by the Justice Department. Three years later, the veracity of these two statements by Olson was contested by lawyers in the Public Integrity section of the Justice Department's Criminal Division. By this time, Olson had left the Justice Department in order to return to private practice.

On December 12, 1985, the Judiciary Committee sent a report to Attorney General EDWIN MEESE calling for an independent counsel investigation of several Justice Department officials, including Olson, Carol Dinkins, and Edward Schmults. Meese decided to dismiss allegations against Dinkins and Schmults. In April, the U.S. Court of Appeals Special Division named JAMES McKAY to conduct an investigation of Olson. One month later, McKay stepped aside due to conflict of interest, and Alexia Morrison replaced him.

While Olson's attorneys attempted to convince Morrison that the charges against him were unworthy of formal investigation, Morrison was working to have Dinkins and Schmults formally added to the scope of her inquiry. Both failed. Morrison proceeded to issue subpoenas against Olson, Dinkins, and Schmults. Olson's attorneys were unable to secure assurance from Morrison that compliance with the subpoena would not mean that they were waiving their right to mount a constitutional challenge to the independent counsel statute. Consequently, they advised Olson to ignore it. In August 1987, Olson, Dinkins, and Schmults were found in contempt. The citation was stayed while the three appealed, and Olson made his constitutional case against the independent counsel statute.

In January 1988, the Appeals Court declared the independent counsel statute unconstitutional by a 2–1 vote. Morrison appealed. On March 9, 1988, with the statute of limitations running out, Olson agreed to waive his rights in return for Morrison's promise to rule on his case within 60 days of the Supreme Court's decision. In June, the Supreme Court reversed the Appeals Court's decision on a 7–1 vote. In August, as promised, Morrison delivered her report on Olson, declaring that although his testimony before Congress had been less than forthcoming, it had been true in a literal sense. No further action was warranted.

The length of the investigation to which Olson was subjected prompted many to criticize the behavior of the independent counsel as excessive. Morrison answered that Olson's constitutional challenge to the independent counsel's authority helped contribute to the investigation's duration. Olson remains a pivotal figure in the history of the office. Though the effort expended in his investigation appeared out of proportion to the offenses alleged, the Supreme Court associated with the inquiry ended constitutional challenges to the mechanism.

References:

Frankel, Alison. "Ted Olson's Five Years in Purgatory." *American Lawyer* (December 1988): 68. Ten-thousand word article addresses questions regarding whether Olson was a scapegoat for the Justice Department, and whether Morrison used him as a hostage in attempting to obtain the right to prosecute Dinkins and Schmults.

Marcus, Ruth. "Ex-Official's Testimony Not Designed to Conceal; Decision against Prosecuting Olson Explained." *Washington Post*, 21 March 1989, sec. A, p. 4.

Ostrow, Ronald J. "Independent Counsel Explains Why She Didn't Prosecute Figure in '83 EPA Probe." *Los Angeles Times*, 21 March 1989, sec. A, p. 17.

Russakoff, Dale. "Theodore Olson Is Free at Last." *Washington Post*, 23 March 1989, sec. A, p. 25.

P

Pearson, Daniel S. (1930–   ) Independent Counsel, Ron Brown investigation, 1995–1996. On July 6, 1995, former federal prosecutor Daniel Pearson was named independent counsel to investigate whether Commerce Secretary Ron BROWN had violated any laws in conducting and/or reporting his private financial affairs. Pearson's inquiry began in earnest that September, after his office was fully staffed. He proceeded to conduct a discreet investigation that neither interfered with Brown's official cabinet duties nor rallied public opinion against him. His probe was abruptly halted on April 3 when Brown was killed in a plane crash.

A graduate of Yale University Law School, Pearson served as assistant U.S. attorney for South Florida (1961–1963). He established a reputation for integrity and fairness as a state appeals court judge during the next decade. Pearson also served as an instructor on the University of Miami Law School faculty, teaching classes in trial advocacy. He was working at the law firm of Holland & Knight, specializing in appellate work, when he was named independent counsel.

Pearson was charged with determining whether Brown had violated the law in accepting payments from former business partner Nolanda Hill, filing inaccurate financial disclosure reports, and making false statements on a loan application related to his purchase of a townhouse. Brown's troubles stemmed from $400,000 he received from Hill in a buyout of his interest in their company, First International, Inc. This included payment of $190,000 in debts Brown had accumulated. At the time of the buyout, Hill's company, Corridor Broadcasting, was in the process of defaulting on a $24 million debt to the government.

By February, congressional Republicans were concerned that Pearson's inquiry was foundering and were considering reopening their own investigation into the matter. Departing from his silence, Pearson briefed them on his progress to date. It was revealed that he had expanded his original mandate to include examination of possible violations of tax regulations and campaign spending laws by First International and Corridor. Both the IRS and FBI were actively involved in the process. Pearson's staff was also investigating Brown's link to Dynamic Energy Resources, a small natural gas company in Oklahoma. Brown's son, Michael, had been hired by the company, and two daughters of Dynamic Energy's owners went to work at the Commerce Department. The Republicans were satisfied by what they had learned.

At the end of March, a Washington grand jury convened by Pearson issued subpoenas to Dynamic Energy officials in order to ascertain the facts concerning Michael Brown's hiring. Dynamic was also being investigated by the Oklahoma Corporation Commission, which regulates utilities. Ron Brown's death days later effectively ended much of Pearson's probe. Pearson turned over information regarding Brown's son and business associates to the Justice Department. Pearson's investigation, which had not resulted in any indictments, cost a rather modest $262,500.

References:

Jackson, Robert L. "Ex-Prosecutor to Probe Ronald Brown's Finances." *Los Angeles Times*, 7 July 1995, sec. A, p. 17.
Knight, Jerry. "IRS Probes Firm Once Owned by Brown, Partner, Independent Counsel Investigating Commerce Secretary Requests Study of Company's Taxes." *Washington Post*, 16 February 1996, sec. A, p. 6.
———. "Ronald Brown Probe Widens." *Washington Post*, 30 March 1996, sec. C, p. 1.
"Questions Remain in Federal Probe." *Arizona Republic*, 4 April 1996, sec. A, p. 10.

Percy, Charles H. (1919–   ) U.S. Senator (R-Illinois), 1967–1984. The first U.S. senator to call for appointment of a special prosecutor after WATERGATE, Charles Percy effectively articulated the need to restore the public's faith in the integrity of government. Working with Senator HOWARD BAKER (R-Tennessee), he introduced S. 2734 (1973), one of the first pieces of legislation calling for establishment of a special prosecutor office. During the period between Watergate and the passage of the ETHICS IN GOVERNMENT ACT (1978), Percy was among a group of moderate Republicans who consistently pressed the executive branch to institute a mechanism aimed at convincing Americans that their government would not countenance similar misconduct in the future.

Born in Pensacola, Florida, Percy was educated at the University of Chicago and served in the Navy during World War II. He began working at Bell & Howell as a student, won election to their board of directors at age 23, and was named their president six years later. Although he never held elective office, Percy was seriously considered as a running mate for RICHARD NIXON in 1960. His victory over longtime Illinois Senator Paul Douglas in 1966 immediately established him as a serious presidential prospect. Percy's support for Nelson Rockefeller's candidacy in 1968 may well have cost him the vice presidency that year. His presidential ambitions in the 1970s suffered when Nixon was forced to resign in 1974 due to Watergate. After completing Nixon's term, GERALD FORD decided to run on his own in 1976. Rather than challenge his party's incumbent, Percy dutifully supported him. The Republican Party's increasing conservatism during the 1980s signaled the decline of Percy's popularity and influence. He was defeated by Democrat Paul Simon in 1984 while attempting to secure a fourth term.

During Nixon's presidency, Percy's opposition to the president's policies and decisions was commonplace. After opposing Nixon's conduct during the Vietnam War, level of spending on defense, and choice of Supreme Court nominees, Percy earned the enmity of the administration. Nevertheless, he won re-election by over a million votes in 1972 and had established his independence from the corruption that was revealed when the Watergate scandal erupted. During 1973, Percy joined Senator Howard Baker in an effort to legislate the establishment of a special prosecutor's office separate from the executive branch. Their bill, S.2734, was an early, unsuccessful effort in this direction.

In 1975, Percy and Baker offered an amendment to Senator ABRAHAM RIBICOFF's Watergate Reorganization and Reform Act (S.495). Because they did not believe that a permanent office of special prosecutor was well-advised, they proposed that the Justice Department establish a division of government crimes for the purpose of monitoring future executive-branch misconduct. The senate would exercise advise and consent authority over the appointment of the assistant attorney general in charge of this division. Although this arrangement would avoid constitutional objections to an independent office, it was subject to criticism for failing to eliminate the conflict of interest inherent when the executive branch investigates itself.

By 1976, following congressional hearings, Percy expressed serious reservations regarding any permanent office of special prosecutor. The testimony of many witnesses had convinced him that a temporary mechanism was preferable. Serving on the Senate Committee in Governmental Affairs in 1977, Percy supported Senator Ribicoff's new bill, S.555, which called for a temporary special prosecutor. His expectation that President CARTER would welcome Congress's approval of the bill was realized the following year with enactment of the ETHICS IN GOVERNMENT ACT.

Percy's determination to help craft a substantial response to the abuses of Watergate was of significant assistance in the passage of what would later be known as the independent counsel statute. Along with Baker, Jacob Javits (R-New York), and John Glenn (D-Ohio), he was part of a bipartisan coalition that facilitated its success.

References:

Bertozzi, Mark. "The Federal Special Prosecutor: Too Special?" *Federal Bar News and Journal* 29 (1982): 222–230. Discusses Baker-Percy bill S.2734 along with other 1973 legislative proposals addressing Watergate abuses.
———. "Oversight of the Executive Branch: A Policy Analysis of Federal Special Pros-

ecutor Legislation." Ph.D. dissertation, State University of New York at Albany, 1980. Includes S.2734 among bills aimed at removing special prosecutor from executive branch.

Harriger, Katy J. *Independent Justice: The Federal Special Prosecutor in American Politics.* Lawrence: University Press of Kansas, 1992. Chapter 3, "A Watergate Legacy," discusses Percy's role in helping establish an office of special prosecutor.

Neal, Steve. "Percy Endured and Endeared, But Was Nagged by Career as Might-Have-Been." *Chicago Tribune,* 13 January 1985, sec. C, p. 1. Reviews and assesses Percy's political life.

Pierce, Samuel R. (1922–) Secretary of Housing and Urban Development (HUD), 1981–1988. The only cabinet member to serve throughout President RONALD REAGAN's two terms, Samuel Pierce was the subject of Independent Counsel ARLIN ADAMS's investigation that lasted five years (1990–1995) and cost $18 million. Ultimately, Adams decided not to pursue an indictment against Pierce, but the former Secretary was criticized for lack of managerial rigor that permitted large-scale corruption to flourish. In the end, Pierce acknowledged as much.

A native of Glen Cove, Long Island, Pierce was educated at Cornell University (BA, 1947; JD, 1949). He served as assistant district attorney in New York (1949–1953), and assistant U.S. attorney for the Southern District of New York (1953–1955) before moving to Washington where he worked as an assistant in the Department of Labor (1955–1956) and associate counsel to the House of Representatives' Judicial Subcommittee on Antitrust (1956–1957). Pierce served as a judge on the New York Court of General Sessions (1959–1961) and was a member of the faculty at the New York University School of Law (1958–1970). Returning to Washington, he headed the U.S. Treasury's legal division for three years (1970–1973).

An associate of former New York Senator Kenneth Keating and Governor Nelson Rockefeller, Pierce's political affiliations were moderately Republican in nature. Consequently, his appointment to Ronald Reagan's conservative cabinet appeared somewhat out of character. And Pierce made it clear that he considered abortion a private matter—another irritant as far as conservatives were concerned. During his tenure at HUD, housing advocates waited in vain for the secretary to articulate a program that would replace traditional federal aid for those in need of adequate shelter. As the only African American in the Cabinet, Pierce was also frequently called upon to comment on the administration's absence of a civil rights program. His bland responses angered liberals. Clearly, Pierce's performance satisfied neither end of the political spectrum.

It was Pierce's relaxed managerial style, however, that would cause him the most difficulty. On November 2, 1989, 19 Democratic members of the House Judiciary Committee requested that Attorney General RICHARD THORNBURGH seek an independent counsel investigation of Pierce. Their committee's inquiry into HUD had convinced them that federal funds had been administered in a manner calculated to favor Republican businessmen, in violation of federal statutes. They charged Pierce with complicity in a conspiracy to defraud the government and with offering perjured testimony regarding the matter. Thornburgh, an opponent of the independent counsel arrangement, responded that the Justice Department was conducting an ongoing investigation of the situation. He intended to consider the request, but viewed it as politically inspired.

On February 1, 1990, Thornburgh formally requested appointment of an independent counsel to investigate Pierce and his management of HUD. The request specified the Moderate Rehabilitation Program, administered during the period 1984–1988, as the subject of inquiry. Perjury allegations against Pierce were not included in the request, because the attorney general believed that evidence to support that contention was lacking. The Special Division of the Court of Appeals named former federal judge Arlin Adams to head the probe.

On November 1, 1990, the House Government Operation Committee issued its final report on the HUD allegations. It found that Pierce, though not actually violating the law, did facilitate the awarding of grants to administration friends. His testimony before Congress was characterized as "misleading." Adams indicated that he would give the report serious consideration. Over the next five years, Adams mounted an investigation that led to 16 convictions, including those of Pierce's top aides Lance Wilson and Deborah Gore Dean. Adams decided against seeking an indictment of Pierce, however, citing the former secretary's age (72), a lack of criminal intent, and the fact that he had not profited from the misconduct. Pierce issued a statement on December 15, 1995, acknowledging that he had held meetings with friends who were lobbying for HUD contracts and that such contacts might well have led his staff to believe that these persons could receive assistance. Pierce also admitted failing to properly control the activities of his employees, which resulted in misappropriation of government funds. In his testimony before Congress, Pierce stated, he had been misleading and unresponsive.

In 1988, Pierce expressed confidence that he would receive the credit he deserved, once analysts examined his record in an impartial manner. He believed that HUD, under his direction, had achieved more with fewer resources. After all, the number of employees had been reduced by 20 percent, but the number of aid recipients had risen 34 percent. Representative Bill Green (R-New York) characterized Pierce as a one of the "stars of the administration." After surviving the independent counsel investigation of Arlin Adams, Pierce's record appeared to have been characterized by incompetence just short of criminality.

*

References:

Boot, Max. "Investigation of HUD in Full Swing." *Christian Science Monitor*, 12 January 1993, p. 6.
Cooper, Kenneth. "Pierce Misled Hill, Panel Concludes." *Washington Post*, 2 November 1990, sec. A, p. 23.

"Former Secretary Pierce Spared Trial in HUD Corruption Case." *New York Times*, 12 January 1995, sec. A, p. 16.

Pear, Robert. "Washington Talk: Cabinet; Secret of Survivor Is Topic of Hot Debate." *New York Times*, 26 January 1988, sec. A, p. 22. Reviews Pierce's career before investigation.

Saul, Stephanie. "Thornburgh Seeks Special HUD Probe." *Newsday*, 2 February 1990, p. 2.

Shaw, Gaylord. "Bid for Special Prosecutor in Pierce Case." *Newsday*, 3 November 1989, p. 15.

"Stonewall Sam." *Newsday*, 21 January 1995, sec. A, p. 20. Opinion piece expressing dismay at what paper considers to have been Pierce's successful efforts at impeding Adams's investigation.

Poindexter, John M. (1936–   ). The "IRAN-CONTRA Affair," as it came to be known, was the attempt by REAGAN Administration officials to effectuate a sale of weapons in exchange for the release of American hostages in Iran. The profit realized would be diverted to personal bank accounts and the Nicaraguan Contra rebels to support their fight against the existing regime.

Independent Counsel LAWRENCE E. WALSH was appointed in December 1986 to investigate and prosecute criminal acts perpetrated in relation to the Iran-Contra Affair. As a result of this independent counsel investigation, 14 people were charged with criminal offenses and 11 were convicted. Of the 14 cases, 2 persons were pardoned before trial and 1 case was dismissed as a result of the inability of independent counsel investigators to obtain classified information from the BUSH administration. Of the 11 people convicted, 2 convictions were overturned on appeal. Those convictions were of Lieutenant Colonel OLIVER NORTH and Navy Vice Admiral John M. Poindexter.

John Poindexter became a member of the National Security Council staff in June 1981. Before joining the Staff, he had a distinguished naval career during which he held high-ranking Pentagon posts and the prestigious post of commander of a U.S. battleship.

During October 1983 Poindexter became deputy to National Security Adviser ROBERT McFARLANE, and served as McFarlane's deputy for two years. While at this post, one of his subordinates was Oliver North. On December 4, 1985, Poindexter was appointed National Security Adviser. For the next year, he oversaw the Iran-Contra operations. As Poindexter's subordinate, North was directly involved in those operations.

In November 1986 the secret Iran-Contra operations were uncovered and made public by the REAGAN administration. Officials disclosed that some of the proceeds from the sale of U.S. arms to Iran had been diverted to the Nicaraguan Contras. As a consequence of this exposure, Attorney General EDWIN MEESE III asked for the appointment of an independent counsel to investigate any criminal activity arising from the covert operations, and, if necessary, the prosecution of those crimes. Specifically, the independent counsel was to investigate and prosecute any provision of assistance to the military activities of the Nicaraguan Contra rebels during an October 1984 to 1986 prohibition on such aid, and the sale of U.S. arms to Iran in contravention of stated U.S. policy and possible violation of arms-export controls.

There were opposing views as to whether Poindexter and the others should have been either investigated or prosecuted. Because the investigation surrounded foreign policy actions of the administration, some believed that prosecuting such actions was punishment for political opinion. The policies against dealing with terrorists and not providing aid to the Contras were political issues. However, a counterargument is that political opinion became law when Congress passed legislation forbidding the United States from aiding the Contras.

Those who supported Poindexter felt that his actions in aiding the Contras and in selling arms to Iran in exchange for the hostages were truly patriotic acts. According to administration and Reagan supporters, the goal of saving hostages and pursuing a consistent foreign policy in Central America justified the means Poindexter utilized.

Those who believed that Poindexter should have been investigated and prosecuted felt so out of a belief that constitutionally, foreign policy decisions, regardless of how inconsistent or unwise, are the role of Congress and not independent administration officials. Therefore, U.S. foreign policy toward Nicaragua, although inconsistent in its willingness to fund the Contras, was constitutionally the responsibility of Congress. People of this view argue that Congress is charged with the duty and power to control the purse of the United States; therefore, if Congress wishes to cut off funding to the Contras, such action is within their power. From this perspective, regardless of the ends, the administration does not have the freedom to pursue and fund policies without the consent of Congress.

Selling arms to Iran was considered by some to be inconsistent with U.S. foreign policy forbidding dealing with terrorists. The Iranian hostage-takers were considered terrorists. Further, those Americans involved in the Iran-Contra affair were potentially violating specific laws called the BOLAND AMENDMENTS. The Boland Amendments were enacted in response to the Reagan administration's foreign policy actions. That is, in December 1981, President Reagan authorized the CIA to undertake a covert program to support the Contra's opposition to the Nicaraguan government. Congress funded the program. Some legislators in Congress supported the CIA's effort as a check on the spread of communism; others feared that the Contras' activities would supply a convenient pretext for the current Nicaraguan regime to impose martial law and suppress all civil liberties. The conflict became a question of whether the CIA, in the guise of inhibiting arms traffic and inducing the Nicaraguan leader to negotiate with other Central American countries, was, in reality, trying to undermine and overthrow the Nicaraguan government.

To prevent such a broadening of influence, Representative Edward P. Boland of Massachusetts introduced a series of legislative limits on the use of government appropriations. The first of the Boland Amendments restricted U.S. activity to the interdiction of arms transfers to rebel guerrillas in El Salvador. As the CIA's efforts expanded, investigating congressmen concluded that the agency had exceeded the authority intended by Congress. Concerned that Congress would cut the funding or terminate the program altogether, the CIA—aided by the Department of Defense—began to stockpile arms for the Contras.

In 1984, congressional opponents of paramilitary activity obtained a cap of $24 million on CIA spending for the Contras. That amount was quickly exhausted. The Reagan administration continued to pursue increased funding for the Contras. Congress responded by enacting the most severe of the Boland Amendments, barring the CIA, the Defense Department, and "any entity engaged in intelligence activities" from assisting the Contras. The generalized prohibition included the National Security Council, which was responsible for coordinating intelligence activities. Misuse of government personnel and funds in contravention of the Boland Amendments could support a charge of conspiracy to defraud the government, even though the Boland Amendments carried no criminal penalties.

On December 19, 1986, the Special Division of the U.S. Court of Appeals for the District of Columbia Circuit appointed Lawrence E. Walsh as independent counsel. The Court charged Walsh with investigating five issues: (1) the sale of arms to Iran; (2) the transfer of either arms or funds to any government; (3) the financing or funding of any such transfer; (4) the diversion of proceeds to any foreign country; and (5) the provision of support for military insurgents in armed conflict with the government of Nicaragua since 1984. This investigation led to prosecution of some of the highest-ranking administration officials for the violation of U.S. law and executive orders.

As a result of the independent counsel investigation and prosecution, on March 16, 1988, Navy Vice Admiral John M. Poindexter was convicted on seven felony charges related to his role in the "Iran-Contra Affair," including making false statements, destruction and removal of records, and obstruction of Congress. The convictions were reversed on appeal.

Numerous obstacles faced Walsh in his investigation and prosecution, such as the complexity and number of documents involved and the political pressures of prosecuting high-ranking officials. One significant obstacle created an important legal challenge to Walsh, ultimately allowing the defeat of Poindexter's conviction. That obstacle was the Congressional grant of IMMUNITY given to Poindexter to compel his testimony before the Select Committees investigating the Iran-Contra affair. Congress, in its need to react quickly to what seemed a national scandal, wanted to uncover the sequence of events taking place between the administration, Iran, Israel, and Nicaraguan Contras. Arguably, Congress wanted quick answers with apparent little concern for future prosecution of criminal acts. This apparent need for expediency can be seen as a direct conflict with the independent counsel's mission. Granting immunity to Poindexter would allow him to testify before Congress without fear that his testimony would be used against him in any later prosecution. On May 2, 1987, Congress granted immunity to Poindexter. This immunity came before Walsh and his investigative team had time to complete their investigations of possible criminal activity by Poindexter.

The timing of the grant of immunity created a special challenge to Walsh and his prosecution team. Poindexter would be protected by the *Kastigar* defense. Named after *Kastigar v. United States*, 406 U.S. 411 (1972), this defense demands that the prosecution, when prosecuting an immunized defendant, demonstrate that the immunized testimony of the defendant has not been used in the prosecution. This defense was what eventually led to the overturning of Poindexter's conviction.

In light of the *Kastigar* defense, to preserve any possibility of conviction, the independent counsel investigators had to develop a scheme to insulate themselves from being "tainted" by the public hearings before Congress. The efforts to insulate the investigators included "canning" all evidence gathered prior to such hearings. In addition, Walsh and his staff could not read the papers, listen to the news, or be exposed to any source of information reporting the Poindexter testimony before Congress.

Insulating the prosecution team was an undefined challenge because no objective guide guarantees the survival of any potential conviction. The independent counsel team had to design a method of gathering evidence and preventing themselves from becoming exposed to immunized testimony. Then they could only hope that a court would find their methods sound.

Oliver North was prosecuted first. During his trial, the court applied a very narrow standard of "use." Under this standard, if a witness had listened to the immunized testimony, even if his or her trial testimony contradicted or expanded on what was said to Congress, the possibility still remained that the trial testimony had been influenced by the immunized testimony. The trial court in Poindexter's case had rejected this sweeping view as "absolutist," prior to the final decision in North. However, the Appellate Court in Poindexter's case found that Walsh and his prosecution team did not meet its standard in demonstrating that the evidence at trial had not been influenced by the immunized testimony. In addition, the Appellate Court interpreted the meaning of "obstruction of justice" to necessitate a showing of more than a "mere" false statement made to Congress. According to the Court, lying to Congress does not equal "obstruction" unless the individual has corruptly influenced someone else to do so. The views of the Appellate Court reversed the conviction.

The panel reviewing the conviction of Poindexter was contextually interesting. Poindexter was the highest official charged with illegal involvement in the Iran-Contra affair. He effectively provided a defense for President Reagan by adamantly denying informing President Reagan of the actions of the National Security Council. Poindexter's famous words were "The buck stopped here," alluding to the fact of his complete command and control over the operations. Walsh's team was unable to find sufficient evidence to charge and prosecute Reagan because the only physical proof of his involvement had been destroyed by North, and Poindexter voluntarily took all responsibility. As a result, Poindexter was viewed as a true patriot and a hero by Reagan supporters.

The three judges on the panel were Judge Douglas Ginsburg, Judge DAVID BRYAN SENTELLE, and Judge Abner J. Mikva. Ginsburg had served in the Reagan administration as the assistant attorney general in charge of the Justice Department's antitrust division, and then served in the Office of Management and Budget. Ginsburg was also nominated by President Bush for the Supreme Court. Sentelle was a Republican from North Carolina who was elevated to the Circuit by President Reagan. He was a supporter of Jesse Helms who opposed independent counsel investigations as unconstitutional. Mikva, a former congressman, was appointed to the Circuit by President Jimmy CARTER. Mikva was a staunch protector of the disadvantaged, including criminal defendants, but he also undoubtedly understood the great need for honesty on the part of government officials.

This three-judge panel held that Walsh had failed to show that Poindexter's immunized testimony had not been used against him at his trial. Mikva dissented. To appeal this decision, Walsh filed a writ of certiorari to the U.S. Supreme Court; however, the Court refused without comment to review the case.

References:

Abrams, Elliot. *Undue Process: A Story of How Political Differences Are Turned into Crimes*. New York: Free Press, 1993.
Cohen, William S., and George J. Mitchell. *Men of Zeal*. New York: Viking, 1988.
Draper, Theodore. *A Very Thin Line: The Iran-Contra Affairs*. New York: Hill and Wang, 1991.
McFarlane, Robert C., and Zofia Smardz. *Special Trust*. New York: Cadell & Davies, 1994.
Secord, Richard, with Jay Wurts. *Honored and Betrayed*. New York: John Wiley & Sons, Inc., 1992.
Walsh, Lawrence E. *Firewall: The Iran-Contra Conspiracy and Cover-up*. New York: W. W. Norton & Company, Inc., 1997.
———. *Iran-Contra: The Final Report*. New York: Times Books, 1994.

—ANDREA SHEMBERG

Poling, Daniel A. (1884–1968) Provisional Special Prosecutor, tax scandal, 1951. A spiritual leader of international repute, Daniel Poling was named by President HARRY TRUMAN as special prosecutor to investigate the tax scandals plaguing his administration. Poling was to share responsibility for the inquiry with THOMAS F. MURPHY, U.S. District Court judge and former prosecutor of Alger Hiss. After accepting the post, Poling was unable to agree upon a working relationship with Murphy. Murphy also encountered opposition to his service from his fellow judges and proceeded to withdraw. Poling's resignation followed. Truman charged Attorney General J. HOWARD McGRATH with finding a replacement. McGrath named former New York City reformer NEWBOLD MORRIS.

Born in Portland, Oregon, Poling was raised in the Evangelical Church. Both his parents were evangelists. After graduating from Dallas College, Oregon, an institution founded by his father, Poling moved to Ohio, where he began his long association with the Christian Endeavor Association, an organization he led from 1927 until his death. During this period, he also served as editor in chief of *Christian Endeavor World*, published in Columbus, Ohio. In addition, Poling was an international temperance leader, running as the Prohibition Party candidate for Ohio governor in 1912 and serving several times as president of the National Temperance Council of America. His temperance activities took him to England, France, and Germany during World War I, where he spoke under the sponsorship of the Prohibition Educational Commission. Poling logged over two million air miles, visiting 50 countries as part of his charitable activities. At the invitation of General Douglas MacArthur, he made several tours of the Far East. As publisher of the *Christian Herald*, Poling advocated religious fundamentalism, universal military training, and separation of church and state, while arguing against communism and pacifism. In 1951, he founded the Chapel of Four Chaplains in Philadelphia, an interfaith house of worship honoring the sacrifice of four military ministers (including one of his sons) who died during the sinking of the army transport *Dorchester* on February 3, 1943. That same year, Poling was an unsuccessful Republican candidate seeking the office of Philadelphia mayor.

Poling's reputation as spiritual leader largely transcended politics. His traditional, orthodox, religious values, however, led him to identify with the Republicans. As a result, his selection as special prosecutor in December 1951 served to balance the moderate Democratic leanings of Thomas Murphy. Both men were national figures of impeccable integrity. Their credentials as Cold War anticommunists were beyond reproach—Murphy had prosecuted suspected communist Alger Hiss, and Poling was named chairman of the All-American Conference to Combat Communism in 1950. Decisions regarding further action to be taken against any corrupt tax officials remaining in the Truman administration were not likely to be challenged if they were made by Murphy and Poling. Unfortunately, their investigation was never begun. The two were unable to agree on an organizational framework for their inquiry. Certainly, Murphy's experience as prosecutor greatly exceeded any related activities with which Poling had been associated, but his prospective service as tax scandal investigator was considered inappropriate by his fellow appeals court judges. Consequently, Murphy withdrew and Poling's resignation quickly followed. The investigation of their successor, Newbold Morris, was also aborted almost before it had begun.

It is impossible to predict the course that a tax scandal investigation led by Poling would have taken. It is entirely possible, however, that any such investigation may well have encountered the same difficulties Morris met. Morris's methods were deemed overly aggressive, and he was dismissed. Poling was a crusader of broad vision and bold action. Had he been able to work with Murphy, a tenacious investigator, it is not unlikely that Truman would have found their work unacceptably invasive. Such an eventuality would have strengthened the hand of those who championed establishment of a truly independent prosecutor.

References:

Dunar, Andrew J. "All Honorable Men: The Truman Scandals and the Politics of Morality." Ph.D. dissertation, University of Southern California, 1981. Mentions Poling's acceptance of the special prosecutor post and indicates that a third member was slated to join the Murphy-Poling team, reportedly "a prominent Chicago attorney."

National Cyclopedia of American Biography, Ann Arbor: University Microfilms, 1967, volume 54, under "Poling, Daniel A." p. 120.

Pomerene, Atlee (1863–1937) Special Prosecutor, Teapot Dome investigation, 1924–1929. Appointed by President CALVIN COOLIDGE to investigate the transfer of naval oil reserves to private developers, Atlee Pomerene, along with OWEN J. ROBERTS, conducted a thorough inquiry that resulted in the convictions of former Secretary of the Interior ALBERT FALL and oil magnate HARRY SINCLAIR.

A lifelong resident of Ohio, Pomerene was educated at Princeton University (B.A., 1884; M.A., 1887) and Cincinnati Law School (1886). He served as city solicitor in Canton, Ohio (1887–1891) and prosecuting attorney of Stark County (1897–1900) before becoming active in Democratic Party politics. Pomerene served as chairman of the Democratic State Convention and was elected lieutenant governor of Ohio in 1910. The following year, he was elected to the U.S. Senate, winning a second term in 1917.

When the TEAPOT DOME Scandal erupted in 1924, President Coolidge was pressured to take extraordinary measures to uncover the apparent corruption that had resulted in the private exploitation of national oil reserves. Teapot Dome was similar to several other public embarrassments experienced by the administration of President WARREN HARDING. After Harding's death in office, the cleanup was left to Coolidge. At first, Coolidge named former Attorney General THOMAS W. GREGORY and attorney SILAS STRAWN as special prosecutors. Both, however, were forced to step aside when their connections to the oil industry were revealed during Congressional hearings regarding the scandal.

Pomerene had completed his second term in the Senate in 1923 and was practicing law in Cleveland when Coolidge named him special prosecutor. Both Pomerene and Roberts, an attorney from Philadelphia, were widely respected in the legal profession. Nevertheless, opposition to their appointment surfaced immediately. Montana's Democratic Senators THOMAS J. WALSH and Burton K. Wheeler led a faction that contended that Coolidge's latest choices were no more likely to aggressively prosecute executive-branch misconduct than Gregory or Strawn. Wheeler's principal concern was the restoration of the nation's oil

reserves to public control. Walsh decried Pomerene's lack of experience regarding public land law. Senator Irvine Lenroot (R-Wisconsin) supported Pomerene's appointment, arguing that knowledge of contract law—not public
lands—formed the essence of the investigation at hand. Although Pomerene's
appointment was not unanimously supported, he was confirmed on February 16,
1924 by a 59–13 vote (24 not voting). Roberts was confirmed two days later.

On March 11, Pomerene and Roberts obtained court injunctions against Harry
Sinclair and EDWARD DOHENY, preventing them from continuing to extract
oil from reserves previously held by the government. On March 13, they filed
suit in Cheyenne against Sinclair's Mammoth Oil Company, citing fraud and
conspiracy by Sinclair and Fall as reasons for setting aside the Teapot Dome
oil lease contract. Four days later, they repeated the process in Los Angeles
with Doheny's Pan-American Oil Company as their target. On March 31, Sinclair was indicted by a Washington, D.C., grand jury for contempt of Congress,
a charge stemming from Sinclair's refusal to answer questions regarding the oil
leases because he maintained that the committee lacked jurisdiction in the matter. In April, a grand jury was convened in Washington, D.C., to hear evidence
on the oil lease cases.

In civil cases filed by Pomerene and Roberts, the U.S. District Court in Los
Angeles, on May 28, 1925, voided the contract between Doheny and the government due to evidence of bribery. On June 19, however, at Cheyenne, the
Wyoming District Court upheld the legality of Sinclair's lease at Teapot Dome.
The Wyoming decision was reversed on appeal, and in two separate decisions
in 1927, the Supreme Court upheld the government's claim to oil reserves that
had been operated by Doheny and Sinclair.

On December 16, 1926, both Doheny and Fall were acquitted of conspiracy
by a Washington, D.C., jury. Sinclair was found guilty of contempt of the Senate
on March 17, 1927, and during an aborted conspiracy trial involving Sinclair
and Fall, he was again cited for contempt. For this conviction, he entered prison
on May 6, 1929. On October 25, 1929, Fall was convicted of bribery, entering
prison on July 20, 1931.

Pomerene, along with Roberts, compiled an impressive record as special prosecutor. Public outrage over mishandling of the nation's oil resources empowered
the special prosecutors to act forcefully against corruption. The fact that they
served at the pleasure of the president did not inhibit them, for the president
was also pressured to act in a similar manner.

References:

Busch, Francis X. *Enemies of the State*. Indianapolis: Bobbs-Merrill, 1954. Chapter 2
        covers Pomerene and the Teapot Dome affair.
Ise, John. *The United States Oil Policy*. New Haven: Yale University Press, 1926. Chap-
        ter 25, "The Naval Reserves and the Teapot Dome Investigation," discusses Pom-
        erene's appointment.
Noggle, Burl. *Teapot Dome: Oil and Politics in the 1920's*. Baton Rouge: Louisiana
        State University Press, 1962. Chapter 6, "The Onrush of Scandal," covers Pom-
        erene's appointment. Chapters 7, "Teapot Dome and the Presidency," and 9, "In-

terlude," discuss the criminal and civil trials in which Pomerene acted as prosecutor.

Stratton, David Hodges. "Albert B. Fall and the Teapot Dome Affair." Ph.D. dissertation, University of Colorado, 1955. Chapter 11, "Oil Scandal in Court," details prosecution of Pomerene's case.

White, William Allen. *A Puritan in Babylon: The Story of Calvin Coolidge*. New York: Capricorn Books, 1965. Chapter 24, "And Sits in the Seat of the Mighty," covers Pomerene's appointment.

R

Rauh, Carl S. (1940–   ) Independent Counsel, W. Lawrence Wallace investigation, 1987. Longtime legal associate of famed trial attorney ROBERT S. BENNETT, Carl Rauh served as independent counsel during the early stages of an investigation into the manner in which former Assistant Attorney General W. LAWRENCE WALLACE reported his taxes. He was forced to resign on March 30, 1987, because his service violated Justice Department regulations regarding conflict of interest. The investigation was resumed five months later by Atlanta tax attorney JAMES HARPER, who cleared Wallace of any wrongdoing.

Carl Rauh was educated at Columbia University (B.A., 1962), the University of Pennsylvania (LL.B., 1965), and Georgetown University (LL.M., 1968). He served as assistant U.S. attorney for Washington, D.C. (1966–1969), and as an attorney in the Deputy Attorney General's Office in the Justice Department (1969–1971). During this period, Rauh met Robert Bennett, who would become his friend and associate during the ensuing years. Throughout the 1970s, Rauh rose in the ranks of the Justice Department, serving as U.S. attorney for the District of Columbia in 1979. In 1980, Rauh left the Justice Department to join Bennett at the Washington law firm of Dunnells, Duvall, Bennett & Porter as a partner. In 1990, Rauh and Bennett moved on to the firm of Skadden, Arps, Slate, Meagher & Flom.

Rauh's brief tenure as independent counsel was shrouded in secrecy. The Wallace case was sealed by the Special Division of the Court of Appeals, and the Justice Department refused to confirm the existence of the investigation. After Rauh's departure, the Special Division had difficulty locating a tax attorney to continue the investigation. Most qualified candidates had cases pending before the Department of Justice, thereby creating a conflict of interest. James Harper was finally appointed in August, and he concluded his inquiry four months later.

During the 1990s, Rauh assisted his partner Bennett in helping defend President Bill CLINTON against the sexual harassment lawsuit filed by PAULA JONES. Other high-profile clients included former Representative Dan Rostenkowski (D-Illinois), whom Rauh and Bennett defended in 1993 against allegations involving misuse of the House Post Office.

References:

Marcus, Ruth. "Harassment Trial Delayed While Clinton Is in Office." *Washington Post*, 29 December 1994. Includes Rauh's remarks on behalf of President Clinton, reacting to postponement of Jones trial.
————. "Justice Official Won't Be Charged in Tax Case." *Washington Post*, 19 December 1987, sec. A, p. 3.

Reagan, Ronald (1911–) U.S. President, 1981–1988. The independent counsel statute was not yet three years old when Ronald Reagan assumed the presidency. It had been invoked twice (the HAMILTON JORDAN and TIMOTHY KRAFT investigations) for relatively trivial reasons (allegations of drug use). During the Reagan years, seven separate independent counsel investigations were initiated (those of RAYMOND DONOVAN, EDWIN MEESE, MICHAEL DEAVER, THEODORE OLSON, the IRAN-CONTRA affair, LYN NOFZIGER, and W. LAWRENCE WALLACE), and the statute was reauthorized twice—in 1983 and 1987. Reagan came to Washington planning to shrink big government. Many Reagan administration officials, intent on dismantling substantial portions of the federal bureaucracy, regarded the ETHICS IN GOVERNMENT ACT (1978) as a major impediment. They perceived its financial disclosure and blind trust restrictions as adding to the regulatory burden already in place, and the independent counsel statute was considered a convenient weapon wielded by enemies of the Reagan Revolution. It was blamed for creating many of the ethics problems encountered by Reagan's associates.

Reagan regarded the special prosecutor/independent counsel office as an unconstitutional encroachment on executive authority. Nevertheless, he employed the independent counsel to his advantage on at least one occasion, and approved the statute's reauthorization twice. He also considered the independent counsel as a necessary device for convincing the public of the government's integrity. When Edwin Meese encountered significant congressional opposition to his appointment as attorney general, Reagan called for a special prosecutor to investigate the ethics charges that had been raised. The subsequent appointment of JACOB STEIN succeeded in quelling the gathering storm. Relative silence ensued as the special prosecutor conducted his inquiry. Meese was subsequently cleared of any wrongdoing, and his appointment approved. Some observers regarded Reagan's use of the special prosecutor as exceptionally skillful in this matter.

The 1983 reauthorization of the independent counsel statute was signed by Reagan on January 3 with few misgivings, because it incorporated amendments that granted the executive branch greater control over the process. The attorney general could use greater discretion before triggering an investigation by considering the credibility of the accuser and whether there were grounds to believe that further investigation was warranted. In addition, the special prosecutor could now be removed for "good cause," a marginally easier standard to meet than the original specification of "extraordinary impropriety." Crafted in reaction to the Jordan and Kraft investigations, these amendments to the statute were welcomed by an administration that would have liked to see the Office of Special Prosecutor disappear.

In 1986 the Reagan administration called for an independent counsel investigation of the IRAN-CONTRA affair, apparently hoping that such an inquiry would quiet the developing furor and clear the accused, much as the Meese investigation had done. Reagan did not anticipate LAWRENCE WALSH's six-year, $40 million inquiry that seriously hindered the president during his second term. Although Reagan suffered little politically, it took GEORGE BUSH's 1992 pardon of CASPAR WEINBERGER to halt Walsh's probe at the Cabinet level. Walsh himself deposed Reagan on July 24, 1992 and found the former president incapable of recalling persons and events related to the Iran-Contra matter.

On December 15, 1987, Reagan signed the second reauthorization of the independent counsel statute with serious reservations. His own Justice Department and several of his closest advisers recommended a veto. Amendments to the statute this time removed discretion from the hands of the attorney general. Congress was displeased with the fact that only 8 of the 38 criminal allegations received by the Reagan Justice Department since 1983 had resulted in an independent counsel appointment. During 1983 and 1984, three separate lawsuits had been filed attempting to force the attorney general to conduct preliminary investigations of alleged executive-branch misconduct. Now amendments to the statute sought to remedy the same unresponsiveness addressed in court by *NATHAN v. ATTORNEY GENERAL, DELLUMS v. SMITH*, and *BANZHAF v. SMITH*. The 1987 reauthorization required the attorney general to conduct more preliminary investigations and to expedite the referral process. Congress was given greater access and oversight roles, and the independent counsel's jurisdiction was expanded. Reagan repeated his belief that the statute unconstitutionally infringed upon the law enforcement prerogatives of the executive, but signed the reauthorization nonetheless.

Reagan's signature hurt Olson's case against the independent counsel in 1988. Had Reagan maintained a strong, unequivocal stance in opposition to the statute, there would have been an ideological consistency for the Supreme Court to consider. Instead, Reagan's ambivalence concerning the issue served to undercut his stated opposition to the arrangement. This assisted the Supreme Court in granting constitutional legitimacy to the independent counsel mechanism in *MORRISON v. OLSON* (1988). Reagan has also been criticized by those who found his support of the separation of powers doctrine rather selective. Although his administration stood by the principle in *INS v. CHADHA* (1983), *BOWSHER v. SYNAR* (1986), and *Morrison v. Olson* when the legislature took authority away from the executive, it did not apply the same reasoning in *MISTRETTA v. UNITED STATES* (1989) when the legislature transferred authority to the executive.

References:

Eastland, Terry. *Ethics, Politics, and the Independent Counsel: Executive Power, Executive Vice 1789–1989.* Washington, D.C.: National Legal Center for the Public Interest, 1989. Chapters 6, "The First Amendments to the Law: 1983," and 7, "The Second Amendments to the Law: 1987," discuss Reagan's approval of the independent counsel statute's reauthorizations.

Harriger, Katy J. *Independent Justice: The Federal Special Prosecutor in American Politics.* Lawrence: University Press of Kansas, 1992. Chapter 8, "Symbols and Politics," discusses Reagan's ambivalence toward the statute.

Roberts, Robert N., and Marion T. Doss, Jr. *From Watergate to Whitewater: The Public Integrity War.* Westport: Praeger, 1997. Chapter 10, "The Great Ethics Crusade," describes how the independent counsel statute interfered with the Reagan agenda.

Schoenbrod, David. "How the Reagan Administration Trivialized Separation of Powers (and Shot itself in the Foot)." *George Washington Law Review* 57 (1989): 459–473. Maintains that the Reagan administration acted inconsistently and opportunistically in its advancement of the separation of powers principle.

Walsh, Lawrence. *Firewall: The Iran-Contra Conspiracy and Cover-up.* New York: Norton, 1997. Chapter 22, "Nuclear War," describes Walsh's interview with an impaired, but still personally appealing, Reagan in 1992.

Reno, Janet (1938–   ) Attorney General, 1993–   . The longest-serving attorney general of the twentieth century, Janet Reno triggered seven different independent counsel investigations and came under criticism for failing to initiate at least one more. After launching the WHITEWATER investigation in 1994 with the appointment of Independent Counsel ROBERT FISKE, Reno proceeded to facilitate probes of Cabinet members MIKE ESPY (1994), HENRY CISNEROS (1995), RONALD BROWN (1995), BRUCE BABBITT (1998), and ALEXIS HERMAN (1998). She also approved an independent counsel inquiry of White House aide ELI SEGAL in 1996. In 1997, Reno refused to request an independent counsel to investigate 1996 Democratic fund-raising tactics, although it appeared evident that there were numerous violations of federal regulations. As the independent counsel statute prepared to lapse on June 30, 1999, Reno testified in favor of its demise, citing politicization of the process as reason enough for its nonrenewal.

Born in Miami, Florida, Reno was educated at Cornell (B.A., 1960) and Harvard (LL.B., 1963) universities. After admission to the Florida bar in 1963, she worked as an associate with the law firm of Brigham & Brigham (1963–1967). Following the establishment of her own firm (Lewis & Reno, 1967–1971), Reno became involved in state government—first, as counsel for Florida's Senate Criminal Justice Committee, which was revising the state's criminal code. She then worked as assistant state attorney in the 11th Judicial Circuit in Miami (1973–1976). Reno became state attorney in 1978, a position she maintained until her appointment as attorney general in 1993.

One year after becoming attorney general, Reno appointed Robert Fiske to investigate the developing Whitewater scandal. The independent counsel statute had lapsed in 1992 following the lengthy IRAN-CONTRA investigation. In the absence of governing legislation, Reno acted on her own initiative in making the appointment. As the Whitewater saga continued to unfold, Congress decided to revive the independent counsel statute. Fiske's preliminary report in July 1994 failed to implicate either President Bill CLINTON or his wife in wrongdoing.

Although Reno favored confirming Fiske as independent counsel under the newly renewed statute, Republicans favored replacing him with someone who was likely to be more aggressive in his approach. The Special Division of the Appeals Court apparently concurred in this regard, appointing KENNETH STARR as the new investigator in August. Starr undertook a lengthy investigation which took many detours (FILEGATE, TRAVELGATE, MONICA LEWINSKY). Starr's requests to expand his initial charge, including broadening of the Whitewater probe to include the activities of former Justice Department official WEBSTER HUBBELL and former Arkansas Governor JIM GUY TUCKER, were generally received favorably by Reno.

In September 1994, Reno requested an independent counsel investigation of Department of Agriculture Secretary Mike Espy in response to allegations that he had received gratuitites from businesses he was charged with regulating. DONALD SMALTZ conducted a four-year probe that resulted in judgments against Tyson Foods as well as Espy's indictment. In December 1998, however, Espy was acquitted on all counts. In 1995, Reno initiated investigations that resulted in the appointments of Independent Counsels DAVID M. BARRETT and DANIEL S. PEARSON, who investigated Housing and Urban Development Secretary Henry Cisneros and Commerce Secretary Ron Brown, respectively. Barrett's probe resulted in Cisneros's indictment on charges he gave false testimony regarding payments he made to a former mistress. Pearson's inquiry of Ron Brown's finances was halted following Brown's death in an airplane crash over Croatia in April 1996.

In 1996, Reno requested an independent counsel investigation to determine whether White House aide Eli Segal had violated conflict-of-interest regulations by engaging in fund-raising for a private group while functioning as head of the Americorps national service program. CURTIS EMERY VON KANN's inquiry ended the next year without an indictment.

In 1997, Reno's decision not to seek appointment of an independent counsel to investigate Democratic Party fund-raising violations, despite a well-publicized recommendation to the contrary by FBI Director Louis J. Freeh, signaled a change in what had been regarded as her early enthusiasm for the statute. She now seemed satisfied with permitting the voters to determine the fate of politicians charged with employing illegal campaign tactics. Reno also expressed greater confidence in the ability of Justice Department officials to conduct non-partisan investigations concerning politically sensitive issues. Republican charges that Reno's decision was politically influenced had to be balanced against a record of independent counsel requests that had angered Clinton administration officials in the past.

In 1998, Reno demonstrated that she had not abandoned employment of the independent counsel statute. Her requests resulted in the appointment of Independent Counsels CAROL ELDER BRUCE and RALPH I. LANCASTER who initiated investigations of Interior Secretary Bruce Babbitt and Labor Secretary Alexis Herman, respectively. Babbitt was charged with corruption regarding the issuance of a casino license to a Native American tribe. The subject of the Herman investigation concerned allegations that the Secretary engaged in influence peddling while soliciting illegal campaign contributions.

With the independent counsel statute set to expire on June 30, 1999, the Senate Governmental Affairs Committee opened hearings on its fate. Reno testified before the committee on March 17, expressing the opinion that the statute was unworkable and incapable of being satisfactorily amended. Basing her observations on a greater foundation of experience than any other attorney general could claim, she characterized the statute as fatally compromised by procedural questions that could not be solved under the Constitution. The attorney general was forced to request an independent counsel whenever further investigation of a matter was warranted. This represented too low a threshold, stated Reno, because further investigation was almost always warranted. The crucial question, Reno contended, was whether an investigation should proceed in instances where it is does not appear that a prosecutable case will result. Because the statute does not clearly address this point, the attorney general often attempts to inject his/her own judgment at this point, inevitably subjecting the Justice Department to criticism. In what many viewed as a thinly veiled reference to Kenneth Starr, Reno also stated her opposition to the tactics of many independent counsels who felt pressured to secure indictments in order to legitimize their expenditure of time and effort. She repeated the criticisms voiced by many previous opponents (usually targets) of the statute, in claiming that investigations strayed too far from their initial charges and concentrated too many resources in probing the affairs of single individuals. Revisions that had been proposed by the AMERICAN BAR ASSOCIATION and COMMON CAUSE, suggesting that either the Justice Department's Criminal Division or Public Integrity Section be reorganized as semiautonomous departments in order to carry on as independent investigative agencies, were characterized by Reno as interesting but probably not possible. She believed that the suggestions would cause additional organizational problems.

On March 18, 1999, the three appeals court judges who appointed Kenneth Starr ruled that they did not have the authority to prevent Reno from launching an investigation of alleged misconduct by the independent counsel. Issues to be examined included a pattern of improper leaks regarding Clinton's testimony before the grand jury, the conduct of Starr's staff toward Monica Lewinsky before she had secured legal representation, and failure of Starr to disclose contacts he had with PAULA JONES's legal team prior to his appointment as independent counsel.

References:

Eisler, Kim Isaac. "And Then There Was Janet." *Washingtonian* (April 1997): 43. Contends that because of Reno's incorruptible image, she is virtually unfireable.

Jackson, Robert L., and Eric Lichtblau. "Judges' Ruling Allows Reno to Pursue Starr Inquiry." *Los Angeles Times*, 19 March 1999, sec. A, p. 18.

Johnston, David. "Independent Counsel Law Is Too Flawed to Renew, Reno Tells Senate Panel." *New York Times*, 18 March 1999, sec. A, p. 22.

Labaton, Stephen. "Reno's Off-and-on Mood for Counsel Is Off Again." *New York Times*, 5 October 1997, sec. A, p. 28. Discusses Reno's decision not to request an independent counsel to investigate Democratic Party campaign fundraising.

Morgan, Dan. "Senate Coalition May Save Independent Counsel Law." *Washington Post*, 18 March 1999, sec. A, p. 2. Contains Reno's response to suggested revisions of the statute.

Reno, Janet. "Campaign Finance Investigation: Testimony before the Judiciary Committee." *Vital Speeches*, 1 November 1997, p. 34. Transcript of Reno's address before the House Judiciary Committee, October 15, 1997.

Ribicoff, Abraham A. (1910–1998) Senator (D-Connecticut), 1963–1981. Senator Abraham Ribicoff (D-Connecticut) was the primary sponsor of two prominent pieces of post-WATERGATE legislation, both calling for the creation of special offices to be charged with investigation and prosecution of executive-branch misconduct. The Watergate Reorganization and Reform Act (S.495, 1975) envisioned a permanent office of public attorney, whereas the Public Officials Integrity Act (S.555; 1977) called for a temporary special prosecutor. The 1975 initiative was passed by the Senate but not the House of Representatives. The 1977 effort eventually succeeded, forming the basis of the ETHICS IN GOVERNMENT ACT (1978), which created the Office of Special Prosecutor.

Born in New Britain, Connecticut, Ribicoff was the son of immigrant Polish Jews. He worked his way through New York University (1928–1929), the University of Chicago (1929–1930), and its law school (LL.B., 1933). Ribicoff practiced law in Hartford before winning a seat in Connecticut's House of Representatives in 1938. During the 1940s, he served as a judge in Hartford's Police Court and as Chairman of the Connecticut Assembly of Municipal Court Judges. In 1948, Ribicoff defeated Republican incumbent William J. Miller in election for U.S. Representative in Connecticut's first district. His 25,000-vote margin of victory was viewed as crucial to Democratic candidate Chester Bowles's gubernatorial victory. In 1952, Ribicoff suffered his only electoral defeat, losing to Prescott Bush in a bid for the U.S. Senate. In 1954 Ribicoff was elected governor, unseating incumbent John Davis Lodge. An early champion of John F. Kennedy, Ribicoff joined the president-elect's Cabinet in 1961 as secretary of health, education and welfare. In 1963, he was elected senator, serving three terms before stepping down in 1981. His denunciation of Richard Daley's treatment of antiwar protestors at the 1968 Democratic convention in Chicago provoked an angry, obscene response from the mayor that remains one of the more vivid images of the era.

Ribicoff's 1975 bill (S.495) called for creation of a permanent public attorney's office that would investigate allegations of executive-branch misconduct; receive referrals from the attorney general when the Justice Department perceived there to be a conflict of interest; receive referrals from the Federal Election Commission; and hear allegations of wrongdoing related to federal campaign and election laws. During hearings that began in July, Senators Lowell Weicker (R-Connecticut) and WALTER MONDALE (D-Minnesota) testified on the bill's behalf, but reservations concerning the constitutionality of a permanent attorney's office were expressed by Senators CHARLES PERCY (R-Illinois), HOWARD BAKER (R-Tennessee), Jacob Javits (R-New York), and John Glenn (D-Ohio). The bill failed to make its way through the House of Representatives, and President GERALD FORD's drastic amendment of the bill, placing the special prosecutor within the Justice Department, prevented its passage the following year.

In 1977, Ribicoff's bill (S.555), incorporating suggestions made by the AMERICAN BAR ASSOCIATION (ABA), called for a temporary special prosecutor. President Jimmy CARTER, supporting the concept, added provisions requiring financial disclosure by public officials. The new bill, reflecting Carter's changes (S.1446) was introduced by Ribicoff. After defeating an extended effort aimed at including Congress within the special prosecutor's jurisdiction, the House's version of the special prosecutor bill (H.R. 9705) was reconciled with the Senate's. The result became the Ethics in Government Act, signed into law by President Carter in 1978.

Ribicoff's persistent efforts on behalf of a special prosecutor law helped ensure the eventual success of the initiative. He keenly felt the need to restore public confidence in the political process following Watergate. In 1981, Ribicoff resigned from the Senate and left Washington to practice law in New York. In his last years, he lamented the fact that politics had become increasingly meanspirited. Ribicoff's much-publicized 1968 confrontation with Mayor Daley was unplanned and uncharacteristic. He did not welcome the development of a political process that relied upon personal attack. Ribicoff died at a rest home in the Bronx on February 23, 1998.

References:

Current Biography, under "Ribicoff, Abraham A." New York: H. W. Wilson, 1955, p. 503–505.

Harriger, Katy J. *Independent Justice: The Federal Special Prosecutor in American Politics*. Lawrence: University Press of Kansas, 1992. Chapter 3, "A Watergate Legacy," discusses Ribicoff's legislative efforts on behalf of the special prosecutor concept.

Morse, Charles F. J. "Abraham Ribicoff Dies at 87." *Hartford Courant*, 23 February
    1998, sec. A, p. 1. Comprehensive account of career.

Richardson, Elliot (1920–1999) Attorney General, 1973. In May 1973, as President RICHARD NIXON's attorney general, Elliot Richardson selected the Watergate Special Prosecution Force's first special prosecutor, ARCHIBALD COX. Five months later, Richardson resigned rather than obey Nixon's directive to fire Cox for conducting an investigation deemed too intrusive by the president.

Richardson was raised in Brookline, Massachusetts, and educated at Harvard University (B.A., 1941; LL.B., 1947). In the 1950s, he worked as an aide to Senator Leverett Saltonstall (R-Massachusetts) and Governor Christain Herter. After a stint in Washington as a U.S. attorney during the administration of President Dwight Eisenhower, he returned home in the 1960s, serving as his state's lieutenant governor (1965–1967) and attorney general (1967–1969). In 1969, Richardson accepted an offer from President Nixon to join his administration as undersecretary of state. The following year, he was appointed to the cabinet as secretary of health, education, and welfare. In 1973, Richardson was moved to secretary of defense, but after Watergate resulted in the resignation of many Nixon associates, the president named him attorney general, charged with completing the investigation in a satisfactory manner. Both houses of Congress were calling for appointment of a special prosecutor to handle the Watergate inquiry, and the President indicated that he was willing to permit Richardson to name such an individual to supervise the inquiry.

On May 7, 1973, Richardson announced that he would appoint a special prosecutor and submit his choice to the Senate Judiciary Committee for informal approval. Initially, Richardson encountered difficulty in finding an experienced trial attorney who would agree to assume responsibility for an investigation to be conducted under the watchful eye of the attorney general. New York Federal District Judge Harold Tyler, former Deputy Attorney General Warren Christopher of Los Angeles, retired Appeals Court Judge David Peck, and Colorado Supreme Court Justice William H. Erickson all declined his offer. After the Judiciary Committee proved successful in pressuring Richardson to draft a charter that granted the appointee substantial authority to conduct the investigation independently, the task of locating a person to serve became substantially easier. Unveiled on May 17, the charter promised that the attorney general would not interfere with the special prosecutor. Only "extraordinary improprieties" would constitute grounds for removal. This agreement also ensured Richardson's confirmation by the Senate.

On May 21, Archibald Cox, Richardson's former labor law professor, accepted appointment as special prosecutor. On May 25, both Richardson and Cox assumed their duties. As Cox conducted his investigation, Richardson was frequently called upon by the White House to communicate its displeasure at comments and actions that reflected badly on the President. Richardson, in turn, was politely rebuffed by Cox who frequently reminded him of the charter that defined their working relationship. Richardson attempted to assert an administration prerogative of screening allegations before turning them over to Cox. Cox rejected this proposal. In August, Richardson sought to restrict Cox's jurisdiction over allegations regarding illegal wiretaps and surveillance, citing national security as justification. Again, Cox balked. In September, Cox did acquiesce to Richardson's argument that activities occurring before January 1971 or after May 1973 should not be subject to the special prosecutor's scrutiny. In this fashion, Richardson and Cox worked out the boundaries within which the new special prosecutor mechanism would operate.

This relationship became further strained in July when White House aide Alexander Butterfield informed the Senate Judiciary Committee that Nixon routinely taped presidential conversations, and Cox determined to obtain them. Because the White House refused his requests, Cox resorted to the courts. When Judge JOHN J. SIRICA ruled in Cox's favor on October 12, Nixon attempted to reach a compromise by submitting summaries of the tapes. Richardson objected to the president's first proposal that called for Cox to receive summaries prepared by Nixon. In response, White House Chief of Staff Alexander Haig suggested that the summaries be verified by venerable senator and longtime Nixon supporter, John Stennis (D-Mississippi). Richardson presented this offer to Cox on October 15. The White House intended that Richardson communicate to Cox that no further tape requests would be honored. Richardson, hoping to reach a settlement on one aspect of the issue at a time, remained silent on this point. Cox rejected the compromise presented by Richardson. Instead, he suggested that Judge Sirica name persons to verify the accuracy of any tape summaries. The White House found this counterproposal unacceptable. Richardson was ordered to dismiss Cox. Rather than accede to this directive, Richardson submitted a letter of resignation. Deputy Attorney General WILLIAM RUCKLESHAUS followed suit. It was left to Solicitor General ROBERT BORK to carry out the order.

Public outrage at Cox's firing led to the the appointment of Special Prosecutor LEON JAWORSKI, whose investigation resulted in the resignation of Nixon. Richardson's decision to resign rather than participate in the obstruction of the Watergate investigation was vindicated. By refusing to violate the charter that granted Cox the autonomy necessary to conduct a thorough investigation, Richardson helped create the atmosphere that led to JAWORSKI's success. If the Justice Department was to retain responsibility for investigations of executive-branch misconduct, it was necessary to recognize when presidential interference threatened to jeopardize its operation, and refuse to sanction such transgression.

Richardson re-entered the Cabinet as President GERALD FORD's secretary of commerce in 1975. He worked in the Washington law firm of Milbank, Tweed, Hadley & McCloy as senior partner before returning to Massachusetts in 1984, where he was badly defeated in his attempt to capture the Republican Party senatorial nomination. Called upon to comment on occasional investigations of the executive branch, Richardson praised the TOWER COMMISSION report that criticized the Reagan administration's participation in the IRAN-CONTRA scandal, and suggested censure as an appropriate remedy for President CLINTON's LEWINSKY-related activities. In 1996, Pantheon published Richardson's book, *Reflections of a Radical Moderate.*

References:

Ben-Veniste, Richard, and George Frampton, Jr. *Stonewall: The Real Story of the Watergate Prosecution.* New York: Simon and Schuster, 1977. Chapters 1, "The First Special Prosecutor," and 6, "Saturday Night Massacre or Saturday Night Suicide?," discuss Richardson-Cox interaction. A detailed account of the attorney general's attempt to avoid Cox's dismissal is provided.

Doyle, James. *Not above the Law: The Battles of Watergate Prosecutors Cox and Jaworski.* New York: Morrow, 1977. Chapters 1, "Archibald Cox," 2, "Cox's Army," and 8, "Massacre," cover Richardson's role as Cox's nominal supervisor.

Eastland, Terry. *Ethics, Politics, and the Independent Counsel.* Washington, D.C.: National Legal Center for the Public Interest, 1989. Chapters 3, "Watergate: The Origins of the Law," and 4, "The Search for the Law: 1973–1976," describe Richardson's presentation of the special prosecutor's charter and the independence guranteed by it.

Harriger, Katy J. *Independent Justice: The Special Federal Prosecutor in American Politics.* Lawrence: University Press of Kansas, 1992. Chapter 3, "A Watergate Legacy," discusses Richardson's relationship with the first Watergate Special Prosecutor.

Roberts, Owen J. (1875–1955) Special Prosecutor, Teapot Dome investigation, 1924–1929. Selected by President CALVIN COOLIDGE, along with ATLEE POMERENE, to investigate the transfer of naval oil reserves to private developers, Owen J. Roberts proceeded to assist in conducting a thorough inquiry that resulted in the imprisonment of former Secretary of the Interior ALBERT B. FALL and the reacquisition of the oil deposits by the government.

Born in Philadelphia, Roberts was educated at the University of Pennsylvania (B.A., 1895; LL.B., 1898). During the next twenty years, he served on the university's law school faculty, rising to the rank of full professor. Roberts served as assistant district attorney of Philadelphia County (1901–1904), while also practicing law privately and representing the Pennsylvania Railroad and other large corporations. During World War I, Roberts prosecuted espionage cases for the Eastern District of Pennsylvania.

THOMAS W. GREGORY and SILAS STRAWN were President Coolidge's first choices to investigate the TEAPOT DOME affair. They were forced to resign, however, when it was revealed that they had ties to the oil industry. Roberts was chosen as a Republican who, along with Pomerene, former Democratic senator from Ohio, would ensure a nonpartisan investigation. Senator George W. Pepper (R-Pennsylvania), a fellow Philadelphian and University of Pennsylvania alumnus, had suggested Roberts to Coolidge. At the time of his appointment, Roberts was serving as director of the American Telephone and

Telegraph Company and several other large corporations. He also had openly opposed a proposed government investigation of the Standard Oil Company. Several senators argued that Roberts was unlikely to aggressively pursue action against the oil developers who were charged with corruptly obtaining control of government oil. Conservationist Gifford Pinchot, a friend of Roberts, advised him to decline, because he believed that the matter was outside of Roberts's area of expertise. The senate did confirm his appointment, however, on February 18, 1924, two days after Pomerene was approved. It was believed that the vote was intentionally postponed to a time when it was known that administration critic Senator THOMAS J. WALSH (D-Montana) would be absent.

Roberts was known for his deliberate, thorough, and conscientious approach to investigations. He and Pomerene succeeded in placing control of the large Teapot Dome and Elk Hills oil reserves back in the hands of government by filing injunctions and supporting their validity through the appeals process. After a four-year probe, HARRY SINCLAIR, director of the Mammoth Oil Company, was convicted of contempt, and Fall was found guilty of bribery. More comprehensive conspiracy charges against Sinclair, Fall, and Pan-American oil magnate EDWARD DOHENY were unsuccessfully prosecuted.

Roberts's work on the Teapot Dome affair had brought him to the attention of the nation. In 1930, President Herbert Hoover named Roberts to the Supreme Court. His confirmation was unopposed. Roberts served for 15 years, generally as a voice for conservatism and opponent of President Franklin Roosevelt's New Deal. In 1940, there was considerable sentiment for a Roberts presidential candidacy, especially among Republicans who opposed Thomas Dewey. The unexpected success of Wendell Willkie, however, proved to be an insurmountable problem for Roberts supporters. Roberts himself never expressed presidential aspirations.

References:

Busch, Francis X. *Enemies of the State*. Indianapolis: Bobbs-Merrill, 1954. Chapter 2 discusses Roberts and the Teapot Dome affair.

Current Biography, under "Roberts, Owen, J." New York: H. W. Wilson, 1941, p. 714–716.

Noggle, Burl. *Teapot Dome: Oil and Politics in the 1920's*. Baton Rouge: Louisiana State University Press, 1962. Chapters 6, "The Onrush of Scandal, 7, "Teapot Dome and the Presidency," and 9, "Interlude" discuss Roberts's appointment and his participation in the investigation.

Roosevelt, Theodore (1858–1919) U.S. President, 1901–1908. As an activist president committed to reform, Theodore Roosevelt twice presided over the naming of special prosecutors to lead investigations of executive-branch misconduct. In 1902, Roosevelt's Attorney General Philander Knox appointed FRANCIS J. HENEY to direct the investigation and prosecution of General Land Office personnel involved in fraud. The following year, Roosevelt appointed CHARLES J. BONAPARTE as Justice Department special assistant to aid in the investigation of corruption in the Post Office. Both inquiries resulted in substantial reform of the agencies in question, and conformed with the progressive nature of Roosevelt's approach to government.

A committed conservationist, Roosevelt, as president, was determined to protect public land from theft and exploitation. Working with chief forester and national conservation leader Gifford Pinchot, Secretary of the Interior Ethan A. Hitchcock, and Assistant Commissioner of the General Land Office William A. Richards, Roosevelt fought to combat fraudulent land transactions in the Pacific Northwest that had regularly placed thousands of acres of valuable timberland in the hands of corporations. The General Land Office, an administrative unit of the Department of the Interior, was run by Binger Hermann, former U.S. Representative from Oregon (1884–1897). Evidence suggests that Hermann was intimately involved in many of the fraudulent land deals processed by his office, although he was never convicted. Hermann repeatedly refused to take action when charges of malfeasance were brought to his office's attention. When action was taken by Richards in Hermann's absence, Hermann acted to obstruct the subsequent investigation. Hitchcock received permission from Roosevelt to demand Hermann's resignation. Before leaving office in February 1903, Hermann succeeded in destroying files of documents and correspondence that might conceivably have been used as evidence of his criminal involvement in the land frauds.

Exposure of a series of further fraudulent land sales in western Oregon prompted the U.S. attorney for Oregon, John Hall, to issue indictments against Commissioner of the Eugene Land Office, Marie Ware, local attorney Dan Tarpley, lumber assessor Steven A. D. Puter, and timber land speculator Horace G. McKinley. Hall asked Attorney General Knox to appoint popular Oregon Republican D. J. Malarkey special prosecutor for the investigation. Instead, Knox named San Francisco attorney Francis Heney, a Democrat. After assuming his duties in November 1903, Heney began an investigation that would last seven years. Its scope would expand to include John Hall and many Oregon Republicans. The Republican Party of Oregon prevailed upon Roosevelt to remove Heney, claiming that the California Democrat was intent on ruining the Republicans for partisan reasons. Roosevelt, whose progressive fervor transcended party loyalty, allowed Heney to continue. Even though he harbored doubts concerning the wisdom of Heney's aggressive methods, Roosevelt continued to support his decisions. By 1910, Heney's conviction record justified Roosevelt's faith in him.

In June 1903, Roosevelt named Charles J. Bonaparte, grand nephew of the Emperor Napoleon, to assist in the investigation of corruption within the Post Office. In 1902, Postmaster General Henry Clay Payne had initiated an investigation into reported violations of civil service regulations, fraud, and political favoritism in the department. When Payne was on leave due to health problems, Roosevelt charged one of Payne's assistants, Joseph L. Bristow, with pursuing the inquiry. John N. Tyner, assistant attorney general assigned to the Post Office, resigned in May 1903 after being charged with destruction of documents related to the case. Roosevelt became dissatisfied with the progress of the inquiry after Payne too quickly dismissed a postal employee's allegation that President McKinley's postmaster, Charles Emory Smith, had used the office to serve for political ends. Roosevelt's appointment of Bonaparte resulted in an expedited, well-focused probe. The resulting personnel changes appeared to address the problem in a satisfactory manner. Bonaparte was appointed attorney general by Roosevelt in December 1906, and in that capacity provided assistance to Heney in his continuing land fraud prosecutions.

Roosevelt allowed his special prosecutors the independence necessary to conduct an effective investigation. Dependent though they were upon the pleasure of the president, Heney and Bonaparte received the support they required in order to take decisive action against individuals involved in corrupt practices.

References:

Gould, Lewis L. *The Presidency of Theodore Roosevelt.* Lawrence: University Press of Kansas, 1991. Chapter 5, "The Square Deal," discusses both the Heney and Bonaparte investigations.

Messing, John. "Public Lands, Politics, and Progressives: The Oregon Land Fraud Trials, 1903–1910." *Pacific Historical Review* 35 (1966): 35–66.

Ruckleshaus, William D. (1932–   ) Deputy Attorney General, 1973. As deputy attorney general during the WATERGATE investigation, William Ruckleshaus followed the example set by Attorney General ELLIOT RICHARDSON in refusing to dismiss Watergate Special Prosecutor ARCHIBALD COX when directed to do so by President RICHARD NIXON. As a result, he was discharged. Solicitor General ROBERT BORK proceeded to relieve Cox of his duties.

Ruckleshaus was born into a family with a rich political history. Both his father and grandfather were active in county politics, and his uncle served in the state legislature. Educated at Princeton (B.A., 1957) and Harvard (LL.B., 1960) universities, Ruckleshaus entered private practice (Ruckleshaus, Bobbitt & O'Connor, 1960–1968) after graduation. At the same time, he served in state government as Indiana's deputy attorney general (1960–1965); chief counsel at the Office of Attorney General (1963–1965); minority attorney of the Indiana Senate (1965–1967); and member of the Indiana House of Representatives (1967–1969). Ruckleshaus was elected Indiana House majority leader in 1966 as a freshman legislator, the first time that a newcomer had ever been selected for that post. After an unsuccessful attempt at Democratic Senator Birch Bayh's seat in 1968, Attorney General John Mitchell appointed Ruckleshaus assistant in charge of the Justice Department's civil division in 1969. In 1970, President Nixon named Ruckleshaus first director of the new Environmental Protection Agency (EPA). After establishing that the EPA would confront municipalities and corporations that failed to act against air and water pollution, Ruckleshaus left in 1973 to become acting director of the FBI, and then deputy attorney general.

After being named Watergate special prosecutor by Attorney General Elliot Richardson, Archibald Cox asked Acting FBI Director Ruckleshaus for a complete report of FBI documents relating to the Watergate investigation. Cox had doubts concerning the FBI's involvement in the Watergate cover-up, because testimony had indicated that former Director L. Patrick Gray had destroyed potential evidence and passed agency reports along to presidential counsel John Dean. Ruckleshaus's report satisfied Cox that the integrity of the agency had not been compromised. Cox arranged with Ruckleshaus to have the Watergate Special Prosecuting Force work directly with FBI field agents, thereby avoiding headquarters bureaucracy. The relationship Ruckleshaus established with Cox nearly resulted in his being named deputy special prosecutor. Cox had difficulty hiring a distinguished Republican who would provide political balance to a staff that included many former Kennedy Democrats. Before Cox was able to offer him the job, however, Ruckleshaus had moved over to the Justice Department as Richardson's deputy.

When Nixon decided to have Cox dismissed rather than turn over his telephone tapes as the special prosecutor insisted, Ruckleshaus refused to carry out the executive order. Richardson had presented Cox with a proposed compromise that would permit the special prosecutor to receive summaries of the tapes. Cox refused. When ordered to fire Cox, Richardson delivered his own resignation to the president at a meeting in the Oval Office on October 20, 1973. White House Chief of Staff Alexander Haig instructed Ruckleshaus by telephone to discharge Cox. Ruckleshaus indicated that he would prefer to resign. Before he could formally submit his letter, he was fired. Questioned about his stance, Ruckleshaus indicated that he had made a commitment to Cox, just as Richardson had, pledging not to interfere in the conduct of the Watergate investigation. Even in the absence of such a commitment, Ruckleshaus stated that he would not have facilitated Cox's dismissal. Apparently, he believed such action to be against the public interest and in violation of his own standard of conduct.

After leaving the Justice Department, Ruckleshaus returned to private law practice with the Washington, D.C., firm of Ruckleshaus, Beveridge, Fairbanks & Diamond (1974–1976). He acted as senior vice president of the Weyerhaeuser Company in Tacoma (1975–1985) before returning to D.C. to reassume leadership of the EPA following the agency's problems under Anne Burford's direction. The Superfund scandal concerning proposed cleanup of toxic waste sites had indirectly led to the investigation of Assistant Attorney General THEODORE OLSON by Independent Counsel ALEXIA MORRISON. The subsequent Supreme Court case *MORRISON v. OLSON* (1988) established the constitutionality of the independent counsel statute. Ruckleshaus re-established the EPA's credibility during his two-year tenure (1983–1985). In 1985 Ruckleshaus resigned and returned to private law practice in Seattle with Perkins

Coie (1985–1988) before joining Browning-Ferris Industries as chairman of the board (1988–1995). In 1996, he founded the Madrona Investment Group.

Ruckleshaus's refusal to fire Cox had left Bork as Nixon's only remaining viable option. There is conjecture that had Bork followed the lead of Richardson and Ruckleshaus, the president would have been unable to dismiss Cox at all. Ruckleshaus acted in a manner consistent with the integrity necessary for permitting any special prosecutor to operate effectively within the Justice Department. If Richardson and Ruckleshaus had been permitted to set the standard for behavior in such situations, there may have been no need to create an independent counsel office outside the Department of Justice.

References:

Ben-Veniste, Richard, and George Frampton, Jr. *Stonewall: The Real Story of the Watergate Prosecution.* New York: Simon and Schuster, 1977. Chapter 2 "The Script and the Players," describes Cox's contacts with Ruckleshaus when the latter was Acting FBI Director. Chapter 6, "Saturday Night Massacre or Saturday Night Suicide," discusses Ruckleshaus's refusal to dismiss Cox.

Doyle, James. *Not above the Law: The Battles of Watergate Prosecutors Cox and Jaworski.* New York: Morrow, 1977. Chapter 8, "Massacre," discusses Ruckleshaus's last days as deputy attorney general.

Horning, Jay. "First EPA Chief Keeping Involved." *St. Petersburg Times,* 15 March 1992, sec. A, p. 15. Overview of Ruckleshaus's career.

Ruff, Charles F. C. (1939–   ) Watergate Special Prosecutor, 1975–1977. The fourth and final WATERGATE special prosecutor, Charles Ruff supervised the activities of the Watergate Special Prosecution Force (WSPF) during the last 20 months of its existence. While acting as the unit's caretaker in its last, anticlimactic days, he also opened a new investigation examining allegations that President GERALD FORD had misused campaign funds when he was a congressman. Ruff was also charged with the responsibility of deciding whether to retry former Attorney General John Mitchell's assistant, Robert Mardian, after his original Watergate-related conviction was reversed on appeal. Twenty years later, Ruff was retained by President Bill CLINTON to assist in his defense against charges brought by Independent Counsel KENNETH STARR. In this capacity, he effectively presented the president's case before the Senate, convened as a court of impeachment, on January 19, 1999.

A native of Cleveland, Ohio, Ruff was educated at Swarthmore College (B.A., 1960) and Columbia University (LL.B., 1963). During his career, Ruff has alternated between positions in academia and the Justice Department. He has taught law at the University of Liberia (1963–1965), the University of Pennsylvania (1966–1967), Antioch Law School (1972–1973), and Georgetown University (1973–1979). Ruff also worked as a research associate at Columbia University's African Law Center. While working in Liberia, he contracted an illness that has confined him to a wheelchair ever since. At the Department of

Justice, Ruff served as trial attorney in the Criminal Division (1967–1970); chief of the Management and Labor Section, Criminal Division (1970–1972); associate deputy attorney general (1978–1979); acting deputy attorney general (1979); and U.S. attorney for the District of Columbia (1979–1982). His work as both assistant Watergate special prosecutor (1973–1975) and the office's head (1975–1977) was conducted part-time, while he maintained his position at Georgetown University. Ruff also worked as chief inspector of the Drug Enforcement Administration (1975) and deputy inspector general with the Department of Health, Education, and Welfare (1977–1978). After 1982, Ruff entered the law firm of Covington & Burling in Washington, D.C.

When HENRY RUTH, the third Watergate special prosecutor, filed his final brief concerning Watergate defendants' appeal on cover-up charges in October 1975, it was anticipated that the WSPF might be disbanded. Ruth had already prepared a final report recounting all that the office had accomplished since its inception. Attorney General EDWARD LEVI, however, did not eliminate the force. It has been suggested that Levi might not have wanted to act in a manner that could prove politically unpopular during an election year. In any case, the office remained in business with Ruff, promoted from assistant Watergate special prosecutor, as its head. The office was moved to smaller quarters, and Ruff worked part-time only. Ruff's previous work with the WSPF entailed investigation of alleged NIXON campaign finance irregularities. His lengthy investigation into a $100,000 cash gift from Howard Hughes to Nixon's friend Charles (Bebe) Rebozo proved fruitless and frustrating.

When the Ford allegations were referred to his office, Ruff believed that they could have been adequately handled by the Justice Department. His investigation into the charge that, as a congressman, the president had illegally converted maritime union campaign contributions to his personal use resulted in no indictment. Ruff felt pressured to conclude the matter before election day in 1976. When the Court of Appeals reversed the conviction of Watergate defendant Robert Mardian, ruling that the former Justice Department official was entitled to have his case severed from that of his codefendants after his attorney was forced to withdraw due to illness. Rather than retry Mardian, Ruff announced on January 18, 1977, that the charges would be dropped. Ruff believed that it was time to close the door on Watergate. The nation's preoccupation with the scandal had gone on too long. There was nothing more left to investigate, Ruff asserted, and future executive-branch misconduct could best be handled by the Justice Department, unless the president himself or the attorney general were the subjects of a criminal investigation. Ruff filed a 74-page report as an addendum to Ruth's 277-page document (which had been conveniently renamed "Report" from "Final Report" once it was learned that the WSPF would continue past 1975). No dramatic revelations were to be found. When asked whether his work might be second-guessed at some time in the future, Ruff responded with a comment some believed foreshadowed his defense of President Clinton: He had learned that convenient failure of memory was the best defense against hostile investigators bent on making a perjury case.

In 1993, Ruff succeeded in extricating Senator Charles Robb (D-Virginia) from charges that he had obstructed justice and conspired to violate wiretap laws. Working largely behind the scenes, Ruff convinced the Justice Department to allow his client to testify a second time before the grand jury, enabling Robb to effectively refute allegations that might well have resulted in indictment. In private practice, Ruff successfully defended Senator John Glenn twice during the early 1990s. He convinced the Senate Ethics Committee that Glenn had been guilty of nothing more than poor judgment in accepting campaign contributions from Charles Keating, whose savings and loan company was found guilty of multiple violations of federal regulations. Ruff also persuaded the Federal Election Commission to allow Glenn to exceed the federal limit of $50,000 on personal funds used to repay election campaign debts.

On January 7, 1997, President Clinton named Ruff White House counsel. On January 19, 1999, Ruff appeared before the Senate to defend the President on charges that he had committed perjury and obstructed justice by urging others to do the same when faced with questions regarding his relationship with former White House intern MONICA LEWINSKY. Ruff refuted both charges during his presentation, while casting doubt on the facts as presented by the Independent Counsel Office. Offering alternative interpretations of the facts as presented by KENNETH STARR was considered risky strategy by some, because it might convince legislators that witnesses needed to be called, thereby extending the proceedings beyond the time frame originally envisioned. As it turned out, the Senate did not elect to call many witnesses. Even if the charges against the President were true, Ruff stated, the allegations would not amount to impeachable offenses. In responding to House Manager Henry Hyde's previous assertion that America's war heroes would be dishonored by Clinton's continuation in office, Ruff recalled his own father's military service at the invasion of Normandy and maintained that his father would feel that all those who faithfully discharge their constitutional duty honor America. Ruff's performance was credited with significantly helping to defeat the effort at removing the President.

References:

Ben-Veniste, Richard, and George Frampton, Jr. *Stonewall: The Real Story of the Watergate Prosecution.* New York: Simon and Schuster, 1977.

Howe, Robert F. "Two High-Powered Lawyers Facing Off in Robb Probe." *Washington Post*, 9 January 1993, sec. B, p. 1.

Mitchell, Alison. "Clinton Chooses His Fifth White House Counsel." *New York Times*, 8 January 1997, sec. B, p. 7.

Pertman, Adam. "Defense Tactic Called Effective But Risky." *Boston Globe*, 20 January 1999, sec. A, p. 21. Analyzes Ruff's presentation at President Clinton's impeachment trial.

Woodward, Bob. "The Last Prosecutor." *Washington Post*, 19 June 1977, sec. A, p. 1.

Ruff expresses weariness at investigation that has gone on too long; speaks against establishment of a permanent office of special prosecutor.

York, Byron. "The White House Plays Ruff." *American Spectator* (June 1997): 28–33. Expresses opinion that Ruff's appointment will make it more difficult for Republicans investigating Clinton. Author considers Ruff the most capable of Clinton's White House counsels to date.

Ruth, Henry S., Jr. (1931–   ) Watergate Special Prosecutor, 1974–1975. Deputy special prosecutor under ARCHIBALD COX and LEON JAWORSKI, Henry Ruth became the third Watergate Special Prosecutor on October 26, 1974 when Jaworski resigned. After the dismissal of Cox, Ruth helped orient Jaworski to the job, then served throughout the new special prosecutor's term in office. During this period, Ruth made many of the prosecutorial decisions, sanctioned by Jaworski, that resulted in the conviction of WATERGATE defendants, and the resignation of President NIXON. During his year as Watergate special prosecutor, Ruth suspended action on the weaker Watergate cases and, as required by charter, prepared a report detailing the activities of the Watergate Special Prosecuting Force (WSPF) from its inception.

Educated at Yale (B.A.) and the University of Pennsylvania (LL.B.), Ruth was recruited as deputy special prosecutor by James Vorenberg, Archibald Cox's executive assistant. Vorenberg had worked with Ruth on President Lyndon Johnson's Crime Commission. Ruth was director of New York City's Criminal Justice Coordinating Council when approached by Vorenberg. He was responsible for directing law enforcement planning, and dispersing law enforcement grant funds. Although Ruth's manner—soft-spoken and cynical—contrasted sharply with the outspoken, optimistic Cox, both men saw the WSPF job as thankless but necessary.

Ruth served as a loyal lieutenant to Cox, regularly participating in staff meetings, planning strategy for acquiring the Nixon tapes, and fearing the possible consequences of White House intransigence. Contemplating the possibility of Cox's firing should compromise on the tapes issue prove impossible, Ruth realized that without Cox, no one could sign an indictment. The WSPF might end up powerless, easily converted to serve President Nixon's purposes.

After Cox's dismissal on October 20, 1973, Ruth urged the WSPF to remain on the job. Reasoning that dramatic gestures—such as resignation or attempting to obtain a contempt citation of the president or his disbarment—would undercut the important work underway. He saw it as a matter of professional responsibility. If conditions became intolerable, they could always resign.

Public indignation at Cox's firing resulted in Leon Jaworski's appointment as the new special prosecutor on November 1. At first fearing that Jaworski might have pledged to cooperate with Nixon, Ruth quickly decided that the best way to approach Jaworski was by assuming the best and attempting to educate him concerning the state of affairs at WSPF. Ruth believed, as Cox had, that a sitting president should not be indicted. Instead, he felt that WSPF should turn over evidence gathered to John Doar, counsel to the House Impeachment Committee. Jaworski agreed with Ruth on the indictment issue, but was reluctant to work with the impeachment committee, because he was unsure of the course they would follow. At the same time, Jaworski was eager to obtain indictments on lesser Watergate-related cases that Ruth felt were not quite ready. Ruth also believed that Jaworski was too secretive, conducting lengthy private discussions with White House Chief of Staff Alexander Haig and conducting few meetings with WSPF staff. As a result, Ruth often convened the staff on his own in order to facilitate better communication.

As evidence against the President continued to mount, many on the WSPF staff moved in favor of indictment. Jaworski remained opposed, and Ruth acted as mediator. Jaworski's determination to obtain the Nixon tapes matched Cox's, and the courts supported him. Facing defeat, Nixon resigned on August 8, 1974. President FORD's pardon of Nixon in September was followed by Jaworski's resignation in October. Ruth was named the new special prosecutor.

Ruth considered Jaworski's resignation ill-timed. He was especially upset about a statement Jaworski had made to the effect that most of the Watergate work was finished. Ruth knew that much remained to be done, and that most of it was of the unpopular variety, including decisions about what cases not to prosecute. Ruth shunned the limelight, and he believed that dropping cases would subject him to both unfair criticism and undesired publicity. Fortunately for Ruth, the public quickly lost interest after Jaworski's departure, and Ruth largely achieved the anonymity he desired. On February 21, 1975, Judge JOHN SIRICA sentenced Watergate defendants John Mitchell, H. R. Haldeman, and John Ehrlichman to two and a half to eight years in prison. Robert Mardian received a sentence of 10 months to three years. Ruth considered the sentences too lengthy.

During July 1975, Ruth testified against ABRAHAM RIBICOFF's bill, S.495, seeking establishment of an office of special prosecutor. Ruth felt that, barring extraordinary circumstances, the Justice Department could handle investigations of executive-branch misconduct. After preparing a 277-page report that he considered final, Ruth resigned as special prosecutor on October 10, 1975, turning the job over to CHARLES RUFF.

In 1979, Ruth became involved in the first Ethics Act (1978) investigation, serving on the defense team for President Jimmy CARTER's Chief of Staff HAMILTON JORDAN, who was the target of a probe headed by Special Prosecutor ARTHUR CHRISTY. In 1985, Ruth served on a commission named by Philadelphia mayor Wilson Goode charged with investigating the violent confrontation between city authorities and the radical black group MOVE, which had resulted in a fire and the deaths of virtually all members of the sect. Eight years later, Ruth served on a special panel convened by Treasury Secretary Lloyd Bentsen investigating the actions of the Bureau of Alcohol, Tobacco, and Firearms following their deadly raid on the Branch Davidian complex in Waco, Texas. Ruth came to believe that there needed to be an alternative method of dealing with extremist cults other than delegating crisis resolution to law enforcement agencies. During President CLINTON's confrontation with Independent Counsel KENNETH STARR's office, Ruth noted similarities between the President's attempts at asserting executive privilege and Watergate-era efforts made by Richard Nixon.

Ruth's steadfast service on the WSPF under Cox and Jaworski was of great assistance in assuring the effective prosecution of Watergate-related crimes. The resolution of the crisis he helped in achieving as their successor supported his contention that one need not create an independent special prosecutor office in order to guarantee justice in such cases.

References:

Ben-Veniste, Richard, and George Frampton, Jr. *Stonewall: The Real Story of the Watergate Prosecution*. New York: Simon and Schuster, 1977.

Doyle, James. *Not above the Law: The Battles of Prosecutors Cox and Jaworski*. New York: Morrow, 1977.

S

Scalia, Justice Antonin (1936–) Supreme Court Justice, 1986– . Justice Antonin Scalia does not hesitate to employ excessive and angry rhetoric to support the controversial positions he articulates in his concurring and dissenting opinions. His personal attacks on colleagues are well documented. Of all of his angry opinions, perhaps his most vituperative, and interestingly his most prophetic, was his solitary dissent in *MORRISON v. OLSON*, where he argued that the Office of the Independent Counsel violated the separation of powers.

When the constitutionality of the Independent Counsel Statute came before the Supreme Court, the Republican Party controlled the Presidency and the Democratic Party controlled the Congress. At the time, independent counsels were considered tools of the political left who were out to make life difficult for conservative executive branch officeholders. This changed dramatically, of course, when KENNETH STARR began his investigation into President CLINTON's sexual behavior. Interestingly, Justice Scalia's dissent in *Morrison* cut through this political partisanship and boldly predicted that disaster would befall the country if the constitutionality of the Office of the Independent Counsel were sustained. Perhaps because of the frequency with which Justice Scalia employs such rhetoric, his warnings went unheeded.

In his dissent in *Morrison*, Justice Scalia first took issue with the majority's discussion of the separation of powers issues raised by the Independent Counsel Statute. He argued that Article I's directive that "The Executive Power shall be vested in a President of the United States," meant that "all" of the executive power must be vested in the President. Therefore, placing federal prosecutorial discretion in the hands of an officer not under the control of the President, such as the independent counsel, violated Article I. Responding to the majority's argument that the President retained sufficient control over the independent counsel to satisfy separation of powers concerns because he/she could be fired for "good cause," Justice Scalia argued that politically it would be virtually impossible for a President to actually terminate an independent counsel. In any event, Scalia argued that it did not matter how much control the President actually retained under the "good cause" requirement because unless he retained all of it, which he clearly did not under the statute, the law violated Article I.

Justice Scalia made several other arguments concerning broad separation of powers principles. He argued that the independent counsel was a principal officer under Article II, Section 2 and, therefore, his/her appointment by a panel of judges, as opposed to the President with the advice and consent of the Senate, was unconstitutional. And, he also believed that the restriction on the removal of the independent counsel to cases of "good cause" violated Presidential prerogatives. The real importance of Justice Scalia's dissent, however, lies not in his legal arguments but in his account of the practical evils caused by the existence of the independent counsel. His description of the potential abuses of the office predicted headlines that wouldn't appear for approximately ten years.

Justice Scalia began the "policy" section of his dissent by noting that federal prosecutors have great power and discretion to decide who will be prosecuted under federal law. The remedy for abuses of this power, according to Scalia, is a political one. Federal prosecutors are selected and removed by the President, and if federal crimes are prosecuted selectively or without a "reasonable sense of proportion, the President pays the cost in political damage to his administration" (*Morrison*, 728–729).

The independent counsel, however, is not selected by the President but by a panel of Article III judges. This feature of the statute breaks up the unity of executive powers and diminishes political accountability. Furthermore, Scalia suggested that these judges might be "politically partisan . . . and select a prosecutor antagonistic to the administration, or even to the particular individual who has been selected for this special treatment. There is no remedy for that, not even a political one" (*Morrison*, 730). Scalia went so far as to suggest that "even if it were entirely evident that unfairness was in fact the result—the judges hostile to the administration, the independent counsel an old foe of the President, the staff refugees from the recently defeated administration—*there would be no one accountable to the public to whom the blame could be assigned*" (*Morrison* at 731).

Scalia said that he was not suggesting that this kind of unfairness was present in the *Morrison* case. But, he added, "the fairness of a process must be adjudged on the basis of what it permits to happen, not what it produced in a particular case" (*Morrison*, 731). Ten years later, a panel of Republican judges appointed a leading conservative political figure to investigate a Democratic President, making Scalia's warnings seem pertinent and astute.

Scalia also argued that one of the great advantages of a unitary executive is that it leads to uniform application of federal criminal law. The independent counsel, however, operates in a solitary fashion "cut off from the unifying influence of the Justice Department, and from the perspective that multiple responsibilities provide"(*Morrison* at 732). Scalia writes:

What would normally be regarded as a technical violation (there are no rules defining such things), may in his or her small world assume the proportions of an indictable offense. What would normally be regarded as an investigation that has reached the level of pursuing such picayune matters that it should be concluded, may [to the independent counsel] be an investigation that ought to go on for another year. How frightening it must be to have your own independent counsel and staff appointed, with nothing else to do but to investigate you until investigation is no longer worthwhile—with whether it is worthwhile or not depending upon what such responsibilities usually hinge on, competing responsibilities. And, to have that counsel and staff decide, with no basis for comparison, whether what you have done is bad enough, willful enough, and provable enough, to warrant indictment. How admirable the constitutional system that provides the means to avoid such a distortion. And, how unfortunate the judicial decision that has permitted it. (*Morrison*, 732)

By pointing out the potential for abuse inherent in the Office of the Independent Counsel, and how that Office's responsibilities are inconsistent with our political system's normal balancing of discretion and accountability, Justice Scalia made a lasting and significant contribution to the political debate over the existence of the independent counsel. As noted at the outset, Justice Scalia's excessive rhetoric often drowns out the substance of his message. In the case of *Morrison v. Olson*, however, and in light of the great political debates over the impeachment of President Clinton, a process put in motion by independent counsel Kenneth Starr, Justice Scalia's rhetoric fit his message.

References:

Fleissner, James. "The Future of the Independent Counsel Statute: Confronting the Dilemma of Allocating the Power of Prosecutorial Discretion." *Mercer Law Review* 49 (1998): 427.
Morrison v. Olson, 487 U.S. 654 (1988).
Smith, Christopher. "Justice Antonin Scalia and the Institutions of American Government." *Wake Forest Law Review* 25 (1990): 783–809.
Symposium, The Independent Counsel Statute. *Mercer Law Review* 49, no. 2 (1998): 427–564. Includes articles by John Q. Barrett, GRIFFIN BELL and Katy Harriger in addition to Fleissner.

—ERIC J. SEGALL

Secord, Richard V. (1932–   ), retired Air Force Major General. A graduate of West Point, Secord served as a combat pilot in Vietnam, flying 285 missions and then heading the CIA's air war in Laos. Between 1975 to 1978 he was the Air Force section chief of the U.S. Military Assistance Advisory Group in Iran where he met ALBERT HAKIM, later his business partner in the IRAN-CONTRA matter. In May 1980, he was promoted to major general and was the ranking Air Force officer in charge of rescue efforts for U.S. hostages held in Iran between 1980 and 1981. He then served as deputy assistant secretary of defense for International Security Affairs. In the wake of allegations of improper dealings with a former CIA agent who had been convicted of smuggling arms to Libya, Secord was forced to resign from the Air Force in 1983.

CIA Director WILLIAM CASEY tapped Secord to assist marine Lieutenant Colonel OLIVER NORTH in keeping the Nicaraguan Contras alive "body and soul" after Congress passed the 1984 BOLAND AMENDMENT prohibiting U.S. military aid and assistance to the anti-Sandinista forces. Casey suggested Secord for the job despite deep reservations expressed by other CIA members. Secord and Hakim played the crucial role of middlemen and set up the tax-exempt Enterprise Corporation through which funds, supplies, and intelligence reports were channeled to the Contras. In particular, they arranged a series of shell corporations and Swiss bank accounts to which North had access and into which North deposited the money he had illegally solicited from third-party countries, wealthy individuals, and eventually the diversion of funds from the sale of arms to Iran. All told, more than $47 million flowed through the Enterprise Swiss bank accounts controlled by Secord and Hakim.

During 1985 and 1986, Secord received cash payments from the Enterprise. Some of the money was used for business expenses such as buying supplies for the Contras and providing them with military training. Overall, more than $11 million in arms and equipment were delivered to the Contras. However, much of the money also went unaccounted for after a U.S. plane was shot down and the Contra operation was subsequently shut down. In later investigations into the Iran-Contra affair, Secord said he had used the money to pay for the missiles shipped to Iran. For the most part, though, the Enterprise did not deal in cash on the Iranian side of the affair. Because of that, independent counsel LAWRENCE WALSH argued that Secord had kept much of the profits from the arms sales and tried to conceal them, asking others to deny their existence as well.

Secord became directly involved in the arms sales to Iran in 1985–1986 and served as the middleman in the transfer of funds and delivery of arms. Again the Enterprise Corporation served as the clearing house through which funds were transferred. Secord's involvement in this operation began with the ill-fated shipment of missiles to Iran in November 1985. He took over the delivery from Israel, which was having problems going through a western European country. Secord successfully shipped the missiles, though completing the operation involved the use of a CIA proprietary plane and subsequently required a presidential finding authorizing the use of CIA property in a covert action. Following this sale, the administration decided to deal directly with Iran rather than continue going through Israel. Secord then played a part in the diversion of funds to the Contras from these later arms sales. He and North marked up the prices on the CIA missiles sold to Iran (which themselves had been bought from the Department of Defense) by 300 percent.

In December 1986, Secord was subpoenaed by Congressional intelligence committees. He refused to testify and invoked the Fifth Amendment. In 1987, he changed his mind and agreed to testify without a grant of immunity before the Select Committees on Iran-Contra as the first witness. At the hearings, Secord said that his motives in the affair had been honorable. He claimed that he had acted as a volunteer for the benefit of the United States and that he did not profit personally from the Iran-Contra affair. He also said that his activities had been authorized, but now the administration had deserted him and the others involved, letting them take the fall. In his own investigation and prosecution, though, independent counsel Lawrence Walsh showed that Secord had accumulated untaxed wealth of at least $2 million, which he kept in secret bank accounts overseas. Furthermore, Walsh attempted to show that Secord did not act as a private individual but rather as a government agent in part of a larger conspiracy to defraud the U.S. government with unauthorized covert operations. The profits diverted from overcharging the Iranians were made on U.S. government property and should not have found their way into North's or Secord's hands to be used at their discretion (for personal gain or to support the Contras). In his testimony to Congress and to Walsh, Secord was, for the most part, truthful about the Enterprise's operational matters and the funneling of monies, but less so regarding his personal gain from the affair.

In 1988, Secord was charged with six felony counts, including conspiracy to defraud the United States deceitfully by supporting the Contras in defiance of the Boland Amendments and also using the sale of weapons to Iran to raise funds to be spent by North and not the United States government. He was also charged with endangering the administration's hostage-release effort by overcharging Iran for the arms and then diverting the profits to the Contras and to himself. The conspiracy indictment was severed because of the immunized testimony given to Congress by the others indicted on the same charge—JOHN POINDEXTER, North, and Hakim—and later dismissed because of problems with declassifying documents for the trial. In the end, Secord faced three counts of giving illegal gratuities to North. He had arranged for the installation of a security system at North's home as well as setting up a $200,000 Swiss investment account for the marine's family with funds from the Enterprise Corporation. In 1989, Secord was indicted on nine additional counts of impeding and obstructing justice before the Senate and House Select committees to investigate the Iran-Contra affair for making false statements on the proceeds of the arms sales. As part of a plea bargain, he agreed to cooperate with the independent counsel's investigation and trials and pleaded guilty to a felony charge that he had falsely denied to Congress that either he or North had benefited from the Enterprise Corporation and that he had given illegal gratuities to a government official. He was sentenced in January 1990 to two years probation.

References:

Draper, Theodore. *A Very Thin Line: The Iran-Contra Affairs.* New York: Hill and Wang, 1991.
Final Report of the Independent Counsel for Iran/Contra Matters. Washington, D.C.: GPO, 1993.

Secord, Richard, with Jay Wurts. *Honored and Betrayed: Irangate, Covert Affairs, and the Secret War in Laos.* New York: John Wiley and Sons, Inc., 1992.

Walsh, Lawrence E. *Firewall: The Iran-Contra Conspiracy and Cover-up.* New York: W. W. Norton and Company, 1997.

—JACLYN STANKE

Segal, Eli J. (1942–) administrative assistant to the President, 1993–1996. The subject of an investigation by independent counsel CURTIS EMERY VON KANN, former White House official Eli Segal was charged with conflict of interest arising from the fact that he participated in private fund-raising efforts during the time when he was head of the AmeriCorps service program. Von Kann's report, filed on August 21, 1997, cleared Segal of any wrongdoing. The independent counsel concluded that Segal did not benefit personally from his association with the private group, Partnership for National Service. Segal believed that funds raised privately represented legitimate avenues of support for the endangered AmeriCorps program.

Segal was a successful Boston game company and direct-mail executive when he joined Bill CLINTON's 1992 presidential campaign as chief of staff. He served as chief financial officer on the Clinton transition team, and assumed leadership of the AmeriCorps National Service Program in February 1993. The innovative program guaranteed college aid for middle- and working-class youth who participated in a year of national service. AmeriCorps participants repaired homes, instructed children, helped provide care for the aged, and engaged in conservation efforts. Segal was continually involved in efforts to save AmeriCorps from annual budget-cutting measures proposed by congressional Republicans. Segal's attempts at privately financing the program appeared to be based on success he had achieved with the Boston-based CityYear organization, an AmeriCorps prototype. CityYear augmented federal funding with substantial corporate support. Segal succeeded in organizing significant corporate support for these programs by publicizing a General Accounting Office (GAO)-certified study that indicated for every federal dollar spent, AmeriCorps projects returned between $1.60 and $2.60 in measurable community benefits and leveraging of private dollars. Republicans countered with a GAO study that found each volunteer costing the government $18,000.

Segal's fund-raising efforts, which were organized through the private Partnership for National Service, precipitated an independent counsel investigation initiated in 1996. Von Kann's probe was sealed by the courts, its existence not revealed until the final report was made public in December 1997. Segal, who was exonerated, left the Clinton administration early in 1996 to join the Welfare to Work Partnership. He was also named to the Home Shopping Network's board of directors. In 1997, Segal joined the board of the Citizen's Financial Group of Providence, Rhode Island.

References:

"Investigation Clears Former Clinton Aide." *New York Times*, 20 December 1997, sec. A, p. 9.

"Segal Gets Job with Clinton." *Advertising Age*, 8 February 1993, p. 41.

Woodlief, Wayne. "Politics Inside Out: Segal Goes to Bat for AmeriCorps." *Boston Herald*, 26 September 1995, sec. A, p. 19.

Sentelle, David B. (1943–) U.S. Appeals Court Judge, 1987– . In 1994 Federal Judge David Sentelle conferred with North Carolina's conservative Republican Senators Jesse Helms and Lauch Faircloth shortly before participating in the decision to replace independent counsel ROBERT FISKE with KENNETH STARR. Sentelle's behavior prompted accusations of unethical conduct, which resulted in a formal complaint filed with the District of Columbia Judicial Council. Sentelle was cleared of any wrongdoing, but the incident raised serious questions regarding the extent to which judicial appointment of the independent counsel is influenced by politics.

Until he was named to the Court of Appeals, David Sentelle had spent his life entirely within the boundaries of North Carolina. Educated at the University of North Carolina (B.A., 1965; JD, 1968), he joined the law firm of Uzzell & Dumont in Asheville (1968–1970) before assuming the post of Assistant U.S. Attorney in Charlotte (1970–1974). In 1974, Sentelle became District Judge of that city, a position he held for three years before leaving to become a partner in the firm Tucker, Hicks, Sentelle, Moon & Hodge. His appointment to the U.S. District Court in 1985 allowed him to remain in Charlotte for another two years. In 1987 Sentelle was named to the U.S. Court of Appeals in Washington, D.C. Three years later, he participated in the decision that overturned OLIVER NORTH's IRAN-CONTRA convictions.

Sentelle had been active in Republican politics at the University of North Carolina, where he served as president of the Young Republicans and chairman of the conservative Young Americans for Freedom. He became acquainted with Senator Jesse Helms in the mid-1970s. Helms recognized Sentelle as a young man with principles similar to his own, and became his political patron. Sentelle served as Mecklenburg County Republican chairman in 1979, and ran unsuccessfully for a seat on the county commission in 1980.

In 1992 Sentelle became the presiding judge of the Special Division charged with appointment of independent counsels. The independent counsel statute lapsed in 1994. On January 20, Attorney General JANET RENO, acting on her own, appointed Robert Fiske independent counsel to investigate the WHITEWATER affair. Fiske, regarded as a moderate Republican, issued a preliminary report on July 30 that found the CLINTONs innocent of any wrongdoing. Two weeks before Fiske's report became public, Sentelle had joined Senators Faircloth and Helms for lunch in the Senate dining room. On August 5, Fiske was replaced by Starr, a Republican whose political principles were closer to those of Sentelle's patrons.

Conservatives had claimed that Fiske could not be relied upon to conduct an impartial inquiry because he was appointed by the Clinton Justice Department. The independent counsel statute, revived in June, called for a truly independent appointment. In addition, Fiske had other possible conflicts of interest: He had represented Prudential-Bache and Smith Barney Shearson, firms involved with the Arkansas Development Finance Authority, during the time that Clinton was governor; Fiske's firm had represented the International Paper Company, which had sold land to the Whitewater Development Corporation; in private practice, he had twice collaborated with BERNARD NUSSBAUM, a former White House Counsel who had resigned over Whitewater-related problems; and he had collaborated with Clinton attorney ROBERT BENNETT in defense of Bank of Credit and Commerce International (BCCI) officials Clark Clifford and Robert Altman.

Sentelle's critics claimed that Starr's conflicts were more obvious: member of the Reagan administration's Justice Department; BUSH administration Solicitor General; former head of the Quayle Commission on Civil Justice Reform; past representative of Independent Women's Forum, which prepared a legal brief opposing Clinton's claim of IMMUNITY against PAULA JONES's lawsuit; and association with the Lynde & Harry Bradley Foundation, which provided substantial funding to organizations that had helped create the Whitewater controversy—the Free Congress Association, *American Spectator* magazine, and the Landmark Legal Foundation. In addition, it was argued that, unlike Fiske, Starr intended to continue his private law practice while he served as independent counsel.

Criticism of Sentelle's behavior was prompt and widespread. Five former presidents of the AMERICAN BAR ASSOCIATION (ABA)—Chesterfield Smith (1973–1974), W. Reece Smith, Jr. (1980–1981), Robert McCrate (1987–1988), Robert D. Raven (1988–1989), and John J. Curtin, Jr.(1990–1991)—issued a statement characterizing Sentelle's actions as "unfortunate, to say the least." They formally requested that Special Division judges demonstrate greater respect for the principles of impartiality in the future. Two private citizens filed a complaint with the D.C. Court of Appeals requesting disciplinary action against Sentelle for his alleged violation of the Judicial Conduct Act of 1980 (Pub.L. No.96–458). In November, Judge Harry Edwards ruled that Sentelle was not guilty of any such violations. Edwards found that the rules governing a judge's behavior during a trial do not apply to appointment of an independent counsel. Even if the allegations against Sentelle were true, stated Edwards, no violation would have occurred. A judge is not prohibited from consulting with others before making an appointment.

Some of Sentelle's colleagues, including political opponents, did not believe that his actions were deserving of criticism. In Charlotte, most of Sentelle's associates felt that any decision he rendered would have to be based on the law, not politics. Some felt that, at most, Sentelle had demonstrated a lapse of judgment. Others praised Helms's political skill in cultivating Sentelle's loyalty and reaping political benefits from it years later.

The role Sentelle played in Starr's appointment, and the political events that may have influenced it, helped fuel the arguments of those who doubt the possibility of the independent counsel office ever achieving the impartiality necessary to guarantee the neutrality of its operations. Public confidence, the driving force behind the independent counsel statute's creation, suffers whenever the integrity of the judicial appointment process appears compromised.

References:

Applebome, Peter. "Judge in Whitewater Dispute Rewards Faith of His Patron." *New York Times*, 17 August 1994, sec. A, p. 1.

Krotoszynski, Ronald J., Jr. "On the Danger of Wearing Two Hats: *Mistretta* and *Morrison* Revisited." *William and Mary Law Review* 38 (1997): 417–485. Argues that *MORRISON v. OLSON* and *MISTRETTA v. U.S.* decisions help undermine judicial integrity by entangling judges in politics.

Reske, Henry J. "Lunch Not Unethical." *ABA Journal* (January 1995): 27.

Ryan, Peter M. "Counsels, Councils and Lunch: Preventing Abuse of the Power to Appoint Independent Counsels." *University of Pennsylvania Law Review* 144 (1996): 2537–2569. Argues that provisions of the Judicial Conduct Act (Judicial Councils Reform and Judicial Conduct and Disability Act of 1980, 94 Stat.2035) should apply to actions of judges on the Special Division. Details arguments on both sides of Sentelle controversy. Reminds us that SCALIA's dissent in *Morrison* warned that there would be no remedy for a biased independent counsel.

Seymour, Whitney North (1923–   ) Independent Counsel, Michael Deaver investigation, 1986–1988. The first independent counsel to bring a case to trial, Whitney North Seymour secured a conviction against former White House aide MICHAEL DEAVER for lying to Congress and a federal grand jury regarding his activities as a lobbyist immediately after leaving his post with the REAGAN administration.

Born in Huntington, West Virginia, Seymour was educated at Princeton (B.A., 1947) and Yale (LL.B., 1950) universities. He entered private practice in New York City with the firm Simpson Thacher & Bartlett, where his father was a partner. Seymour remained with the firm for 32 years (1950–1982), becoming a partner himself in 1961. As Assistant U.S. Attorney (1953–1956), special state counsel (1960–1961), and U.S. Attorney for the Southern District of New York (1970–1973), Seymour built a record of accomplishment by investigating racketeering, police corruption, and narcotics trafficking. He served one term in the New York State Senate (1966–1968), but was unsuccessful in his attempts to capture seats in the U.S. House of Representatives and the Senate. In 1983, Seymour returned to private practice on a smaller scale, forming the firm Brown & Seymour.

Named independent counsel on May 29, 1986, Seymour conducted his investigation out of the public view, refusing to speak to the press or even supply them with an office address or telephone number. Seymour explained his behavior as an attempt to avoid doing a disservice to Deaver. Journalists were not understanding. Seymour claimed that William Safire tried to blackmail him into providing information. Safire, according to Seymour, threatened to subject the independent counsel to criticism unless Seymour returned his calls. Seymour refused to do so, and Safire penned several articles critical of him.

Seymour became convinced that he would be unable to prosecute Deaver for violating antilobbying provisions of the ETHICS IN GOVERNMENT ACT (1978), because Deaver effectively prevented such action by lying. Accordingly, Seymour determined to secure an indictment against Deaver for perjury. Deaver attempted to prevent such an indictment by suing in U.S. District Court. In *DEAVER v. SEYMOUR* (1987), Judge Thomas Penfield Jackson denied Deaver's request on the grounds that adequate remedy existed after indictment, and Deaver had failed to demonstrate that he was likely to win on the merits of the case. On December 16, 1987, Deaver was convicted on three of five perjury counts. Seymour was aided inadvertently by Deaver's attorney, Herbert J. Miller, who decided not to present a defense. He justified his gamble by explaining that he did not believe he needed to. After agreeing to drop his appeal, Deaver was sentenced to a three-year suspended sentence and fined $100,000.

By most accounts, Seymour's 18-month inquiry was successful, resulting in the first conviction obtained by an independent counsel. Although the cost of the investigation, $1.5 million, was more than the total of the previous four inquiries combined, succeeding investigations would prove much more expensive. Some of Seymour's tactics, however, prompted charges of abusive behavior. Twice Seymour attempted to subpoena the Canadian ambassador to the United States, Allan Gotlieb, in an effort to obtain testimony regarding Deaver's lobbying activities related to the issue of acid rain. These attempts clearly violated the concept of diplomatic immunity. The State Department intervened on behalf of Gotlieb, and the subpoenas were invalidated by the district court. Seymour also prompted criticism by accepting large fees to lecture about government ethics after condemning the influence of money in politics on the occasion of Deaver's conviction.

Seymour designed his own seal, featuring an eagle's head turned in a direction opposite that of the Department of Justice's, because he wanted a visual reminder of the office's total independence. Some found that creation illustrative of what they regarded as Seymour's arrogance. Seymour's supporters saw him as a man dedicated to the public's welfare, someone who led his family in an annual reading and discussion of the Declaration of Independence every July 4. Objective consideration must conclude that, whatever his personal merits, Seymour's independent counsel investigation was probably effective in giving pause to lobbyists who sought to profit quickly from recent government service.

References:

Ayres, B. Drummond. "The Independent Style of Deaver's Prosecutor." *New York Times*, 8 June 1987, sec. A, p. 14.

Eastland, Terry. *Ethics, Politics, and the Independent Counsel: Executive Power, Executive Vice 1789–1989*. Washington, D.C.: National Legal Center for the Public Interest, 1989.

Harriger, Katy J. *Independent Justice: The Federal Special Prosecutor in American Politics*. Lawrence: University Press of Kansas, 1992.

McAllister, Bill. "Deaver Is Found Guilty of Lying about Lobbying." *Washington Post*, 17 December 1987, sec. A, p. 1.

Shultz, George P. (1920–   ) Secretary of State, 1982–1989. George Shultz was born in New York City on December 13, 1920. He began his career as an academic and taught economics at several colleges. Shultz served in the U.S. Marine Corps during World War II and then went on to earn a doctorate in economics from the Massachusetts Institute of Technology (MIT). However, in the 1950s Shultz was called upon to serve on a number of presidential advisory boards after he developed a reputation for his negotiating skills in labor disputes. President John F. Kennedy made use of his talents in the 1960s by appointing him to chair several task forces on manpower and labor relations, and President RICHARD NIXON nominated Shultz to serve in several senior posts in his administration. He served as secretary of labor (1969–1970), the first director of the Office of Management and Budget (1970–1973), and secretary of the treasury (1973–1974). When Secretary of State Alexander M. Haig, Jr., resigned in 1982, REAGAN asked Shultz to replace him.

Shultz soon distinguished himself as the leader of the moderate faction in Reagan's Cabinet, and he often quarreled with Secretary of Defense CASPAR WEINBERGER. Shultz's cautious diplomacy and quiet nature contrasted sharply with the aggressive, flamboyant nature of his predecessor. Nonetheless, Shultz proved adept at the bureaucratic infighting that marked the Reagan administration. As secretary of state, he worked to initiate arms control measures with the Soviet Union, and his efforts culminated in the Intermediate-Range Nuclear Force (INF) Treaty and the Strategic Arms Reduction Talks (START) negotiations. Nonetheless, Shultz was a committed Cold Warrior, supporting the Reagan Doctrine with its emphasis on containment and rollback of Soviet influence. He often found himself at odds with other members of the Cabinet and threatened to resign on several occasions. One of the most significant of these episodes concerned the IRAN-CONTRA scandal, where Shultz asserted that the State Department was deliberately left out of the decision-making process that initiated the operation to supply aid to the Contras.

From the beginning, Shultz opposed the arms-for-hostages deal that initiated the Iran-Contra scandal. In addition, he and the State Department were deliberately kept uninformed of the effort to supply weapons and aid to the Nicaraguan Contras as the National Security Council dominated the formulation of policy for Central America. Nonetheless, Shultz did support efforts to gain external funding of the Contras and was present at several high-level meetings where such endeavors were discussed. When the story of the arms deal broke in November of 1986, Shultz was on the verge of departing for Vienna to participate in a meeting of foreign ministers of the Conference of Security and Cooperation in Europe (CSCE). He was caught unaware of the true extent of the nature of the operation, and he and his top aides attempted to put together a coherent chronology of what Shultz knew and when he knew it. Upon his return to Washington, Shultz immediately began to counsel the President to be forthcoming about the episode so as to minimalize the potential political fallout. He also endeavored to regain control of foreign policy formulation toward Iran and Central America.

As the investigation of the matter unfolded, Independent Counsel LAWRENCE WALSH and his team were more concerned over what seemed to be inconsistencies in Shultz's testimony. During interviews, Shultz emphatically stated both his opposition to the arms sales to Iran and his denial of having participated in them. However, Walsh's investigation found that Shultz had a far greater knowledge of the operation than he led Congress and investigators to believe.

In 1985, when Admiral JOHN POINDEXTER first proposed the arms-for-hostages deal, Shultz vigorously opposed the idea on both policy and practical grounds. Once the decision was made to initiate the venture, Walsh found that the State Department had tried on two occasions to circumvent the operation by opening separate lines of communication and negotiation with Iran. After the news of the scandal broke in November of 1986, Shultz initially considered resigning. However, he regrouped and undertook a major effort to save the administration by counseling the President to end the sales and confront the public with an honest account of the sales. Shultz managed to regain control over the administration's Iranian policy and management of counterterrorism operations. He was able to convince Reagan to ban all future arms shipments to the Iranians in 1986. Nonetheless, he was isolated from most of the rest of the President's other senior officials in his opposition. The split in the administration became public when Shultz announced on a television news show that he personally opposed future arms deals, but that he could not speak for the rest of Reagan's senior aides.

Unlike most of the participants in the Iran-Contra investigation, Shultz was generally cooperative with Walsh. He ordered State Department officials to turn over relevant documents in a timely manner, and he seemed to emerge as one of the few heroes of the scandal. However, Walsh's investigation found from handwritten notes that Shultz and two of his senior aides, executive secretary Nicholas Platt and executive assistant M. Charles Hill, had misled investigators over the extent of the Shultz's knowledge of the arms shipments. Specifically, Walsh found that Shultz knew about weapons transfers from Israel to Iran in 1985. Walsh also found that Shultz was aware of direct arms shipments from the United States to Iran in 1986. Evidence emerged that reports from the State Department's antiterrorism units had made Shultz aware of OLIVER NORTH's activities and the arms sales.

When he deposed Shultz, the independent counsel found him a "combative and a skillful" witness. Shultz confirmed that he had not been entirely truthful

with Congress but claimed his errors were unintentional and the result of inaccurate chronologies that had been prepared for him by Hill. Shultz claimed
that some of Hill's notes on the actual events that transpired had been overlooked and that there were inconsistencies with the chronology that he presented
to Congress.

In spite of his erroneous testimony before Congress, the independent counsel
decided not to indict Shultz, because it could not be proven that his testimony
was willfully false. In addition, Walsh was hesitant to prosecute the figure that
he described as the "lone voice of reason" in the administration. The independent
counsel did find that Hill and Platt had deliberately withheld relevant notes and
documents from investigators. He believed that the two may have been in collusion to mislead investigators, but there was no strong evidence, and Walsh
decided not to indict either of the two.

After Shultz left office in 1989, he returned to private life and became the
Jack Steele Parker Professor of International Economics at the Graduate School
of Business at Stanford University and a fellow of the Hoover Institute. On
January 19, 1989, Shultz was awarded the Presidential Medal of Freedom, the
nation's highest civilian award. This was followed by the second Seoul Peace
Award in 1992, and the Koret Prize for contributions to Economic Reform and
Development in Israel. Shultz was also the recipient of numerous honorary degrees from various universities, including Notre Dame, Loyola, and Princeton.
In March of 1989, he was appointed director of the Boeing Company. Shultz
subsequently joined the board of directors of a number of companies, including
Charles Schwab & Company and Gulfstream aerospace. In 1993, Shultz published his memoir, *Turmoil and Triumph: My Years as Secretary of State*. That
same year he was appointed to the Governor's Council of Economic Advisors
in California. During the 1996 presidential campaign, Shultz served as an economic policy adviser to Senator ROBERT DOLE. Shultz continues to be an
active commentator on economic and foreign policy.

References:

Draper, Theodore. *A Very Thin Line: The Iran-Contra Affairs*. New York: Hill and Wang,
    1991.
Fagen, Richard R. *Forging Peace: The Challenge of Central America*. New York: Basil,
    1987.
Reagan, Ronald W. *An American Life: The Autobiography*. New York: Simon and Schus-
    ter, 1990.
Rodman, Peter W. *More Precious Than Peace: The Cold War and the Struggle for the
    Third World*. New York: Scribner's, 1994.
Shultz, George P. *Triumph and Turmoil: My Years as Secretary of State*. New York:
    Scribner's, 1993.
Walsh, Lawrence E. *Firewall: The Iran-Contra Conspiracy and Cover-up*. New York:
    W. W. Norton, 1997.
———. *Iran-Contra: The Final Report*. New York: Times Books, 1994.

Weinberger, Caspar W. *Fighting for Peace: Seven Critical Years in the Pentagon.* New
        York: Warner, 1990.

                                                                    —TOM LANSFORD

Silberman, Laurence H. (1935–   ) Judge, U.S. Court of Appeals (D.C. Circuit), 1985–   . On January 22, 1988, Judge Laurence Silberman delivered an
opinion that temporarily invalidated the independent counsel statute. His decision in *IN RE SEALED CASE* reversed the finding of the U.S. district court,
and was in turn reversed in *MORRISON v. OLSON.* Silberman, joined by Judge
Stephen F. Williams, ruled that the independent counsel statute represented an
unconstitutional intrusion upon the executive's law enforcement authority, and
conferred inappropriate powers upon the Judiciary. Judge RUTH BADER
GINSBURG dissented.

Born in York, Pennsylvania, Silberman was educated at Dartmouth College
(B.A.) and Harvard University (LL.B., 1961). He lectured on labor law at the
University of Hawaii (1962–1963) while practicing privately in Honolulu with
the firms Moore, Torkildson & Rice and Quinn & Moore (1961–1964). In 1964,
he became a partner in the firm Moore, Silberman & Schulze. Three years later,
Silberman relocated to Washington, D.C., where he worked as an attorney in
the general counsel's office at the National Labor Relations Board. In 1969, he
assumed the position of solicitor in the Labor Department. The next year, Silberman began a three-year term as Undersecretary of Labor. In 1973, he returned
to private practice with the firm Steptoe & Johnson in Washington. One year
later, he was appointed Deputy Attorney General, a position he left in 1975 to
become ambassador to Yugoslavia (1975–1977). Silberman worked as managing
partner with Morrison & Foerster in Washington (1978–1979) before accepting
the position of executive vice-president with the Crocker National Bank in San
Francisco (1979–1983). He served as vice chairman of the State Department's
Committee on Security and Economic Assistance (1983–1984) until his appointment to the Court of Appeals in 1985.

In *In re Sealed Case*, Silberman ruled that the independent counsel statute
violated Article II's appointments clause, Article III's limitations on judicial
authority, and the separation of powers doctrine. In addition, Silberman believed
that the statute interfered with the president's ability to faithfully execute the
law by restricting the executive's ability to remove the independent counsel from
office. This provision, he maintained, violated the principle established in *MY-
ERS v. U.S.* (1926) that the president must be able to remove at will officers
performing purely executive functions. Silberman rejected the notion that the
independent counsel was an inferior officer whose appointment might be constitutionally delegated to the Judiciary. He considered the independent counsel's
authority too broad for such a designation. Furthermore, the power to prosecute,
argued Silberman, must be regulated by an elected official in order to ensure
accountability and protect individual liberty. No such control existed for the
independent counsel. Silberman considered the independent counsel statute an

overreaction to WATERGATE abuses, and did not feel that executive misconduct created a conflict of interest that called for such a radical remedy. More
important, Silberman contended, was the damage done to the constitutional concept of a unitary executive by the creation of the independent counsel office.
Finally, Silberman believed that judicial supervision of the independent counsel's prosecutorial conduct effectively subverted that branch's constitutional
status as a neutral body designed to resolve disputes.

Silberman's decision threatened to invalidate Independent Counsel WHIT-
NEY NORTH SEYMOUR's investigation that had resulted in the conviction of
former White House aide MICHAEL DEAVER on perjury charges. Whereas
LAWRENCE WALSH and JAMES McKAY had accepted backup appointments from the Justice Department, Seymour had not. The Supreme Court's
quick consideration of the case, however, rendered the issue moot. Although
Morrison v. Olson would reverse Silberman's ruling, many of the complaints
he registered regarding the independent counsel arrangement would be resurrected when deliberations concerning the statute's renewal began in 1999.

Silberman's tenure on the Court of Appeals has continued well past *In re
Sealed Case*. On July 20, 1990, Silberman led the court in overturning OLIVER
NORTH's IRAN-CONTRA convictions, ruling that the grant of IMMUNITY
enjoyed by North had been violated. In 1992, it was reported that ideological
conflicts on the D.C. Court of Appeals between conservatives Silberman and
DAVID SENTELLE and liberal colleague Abner Mikva were threatening communication necessary to the effective operation of that judicial body. The partisanship, however, did not prevent the court from continuing to function. In
1994, Silberman delivered an opinion that supported the expulsion of a Navy
midshipman on the grounds that he was an admitted homosexual. The decision,
which reversed a lower-court ruling, was criticized in particular because it was
not alleged that the midshipman had participated in homosexual activity. In
1998, Silberman spoke for a three-judge panel that overturned a government
policy requiring radio and television stations to hire minorities. He continues to
represent judicial conservatism on the D.C. Court of Appeals.

References:

Harriger, Katy J. *Independent Justice: The Federal Special Prosecutor in American Politics*. Lawrence: University Press of Kansas, 1992. Chapter 5, "Is the Prosecutor
Constitutional?" discusses Silberman's ruling in *In re Sealed Case*. Harriger main-
tains that Silberman followed a "tortuous" path around established case law in
reaching his decision.
Holmes, Steven A. "F.C.C. Requirement on Minority Hiring Is Voided by Court." *New
York Times*, 15 April 1998, sec. A, p. 1.
Lewis, Neil A. "An Ideological Flap Ruffles a Court's Two Wings." *New York Times*,
13 March 1992, sec. B, p. 16.
Locy, Toni. "Appeals Court Backs Expulsion of Homosexual Midshipman." *Washington
Post*, 23 November 1994, sec. A, p. 2.

"Special Prosecutor Law Rejected by Appeals Court." *Los Angeles Times*, 24 January
   1988, sec. A, p. 1.

Silverman, Leon (1921–   ) Special Prosecutor, Raymond Donovan investigation, 1981–1982. The first of six special prosecutor/independent counsel investigations to occur during the REAGAN administration, Leon Silverman's probe
of Secretary of Labor RAYMOND DONOVAN involved allegations that Donovan's construction company maintained ties to organized crime. After a nine-
month inquiry, Silverman concluded that there was insufficient evidence to
warrant criminal charges.

A resident of New York, Silverman was educated at Brooklyn College (B.A.,
1942) and Yale University (LL.B., 1948). He also pursued postgraduate studies
at the London School of Economics (1948–1949). Silverman practiced law with
the New York firm of Riegelman, Strasser, Schwartz & Spiegelman (1949–
1953) before assuming the post of Assistant U.S. Attorney for the Southern
District of New York (1953–1955), working under J. Edward Lumbard, later
one of the judges who would appoint him special prosecutor. (Special Prosecutor
ARTHUR CHRISTY had also been selected by Lumbard after an earlier association with him.) He served as Assistant Deputy Attorney General in the Department of Justice (1958–1959), then began his long association with the New
York firm of Fried, Frank, Harris, Shriver & Jacobsen (1960–   ). In 1967,
Silverman was named counsel to the New York Governor's Committee to Review Laws and Procedures in the Area of Human Rights. During his service on
this committee, Silverman helped write many of the state's human rights laws.
He was also president of the New York Legal Aid Society (1970–1972) and
served on the Committee to Review Legislative and Judicial Salaries in 1972–
1973.

Silverman was appointed Special Prosecutor in the Donovan case on December 29, 1981. He accepted the appointment with a sense of urgency: Because
some of the allegations involving Donovan originated in 1977, the statute of
limitations was a concern. Attorney General WILLIAM FRENCH SMITH asked
for the appointment, requesting that the investigator's jurisdiction be limited to
the issues involving Donovan's alleged presence when an official of his construction company made a reported $2,000 payment to a union official, and
whether Donovan lied about the incident during his confirmation hearings. The
court presented Silverman with a broader mandate covering any other evidence
that might be developed during the investigation.

Silverman's probe grew out of allegations that Pellegrino (William) Masselli,
a confessed Mafia member and subcontractor for Donovan's Schiavone Construction Company, bribed Blasters Local 29 union official Louis Sanzo to keep
Tunnel Workers Local 147 from winning the right to work on Schiavone's
subway project. Because the Tunnel Workers received higher wages and better
benefits, their labor would have cost Schiavone more money. It was alleged that

Donovan was aware of the payoff. The allegations against Donovan were made by union official and ex-convict Mario Montuoro. Montuoro's charge remained unsubstantiated during Silverman's investigation.

Silverman convened a grand jury in May to hear evidence. In June, the body of one of Silverman's witnesses, career criminal Fred Furino, was found in the trunk of a car. It had been alleged that Furino had served as a "bagman," collecting payments from Donovan's construction company. During the course of Silverman's inquiry, many other allegations surfaced. Several of them were presented to the grand jury. They included charges that Donovan had made an illegal payoff to *The Trib*, a short-lived New York newspaper; possible violations of the Federal Elections Campaign Act (1971) by Donovan on behalf of Ronald Reagan during the 1980 presidential campaign; illegal entertainment of union officials by Donovan; and charges that Donovan illegally received inside information regarding work on a New Jersey Turnpike project. On June 28, 1982, Silverman reported that the grand jury had decided against indictment on all charges. The special prosecutor concluded that there was "insufficient credible evidence" to warrant further action. Silverman refused to share his private judgment concerning Donovan with the public, and specifically declined to apply the terms "exonerated" or "given a clean bill of health" to his subject. Silverman's investigation did corroborate one allegation made by Montuoro regarding the existence of "no-show" employees on the Schiavone payroll, but it could not be demonstrated that Donovan knew of the situation.

In early August, Silverman reopened his probe in order to investigate a new set of allegations against Donovan. One of the charges concerned the establishment of "no-show" jobs at Schiavone Construction. It was alleged that Donovan met with William Masselli near Miami in 1979 to establish these positions for members of the Genovese crime family. During this second phase of Silverman's probe, Nat Masselli, William's son was killed the night before his father was to have testified before a grand jury.

On September 13, Silverman again concluded that the available evidence did not warrant further action against Donovan. Although some charges against Donovan's company appeared credible, Silverman did not interpret his jurisdiction to include all transactions of the Schiavone Construction Company. If Donovan was not personally involved, Silverman did not believe that the special prosecutor should take action. Although he was closing his examination of the Donovan case, Silverman expressed amazement at the sheer number of allegations with which his office had been presented.

Silverman's investigation had disposed of a great number of charges in less than one year. The inquiry cost $333,000, a relatively modest amount when compared with the cost of inquiries that were to follow. Silverman also exhibited uncommon restraint in deciding not to pursue peripheral charges made against Donovan's construction company. Future prosecutors/counsels would refuse to define their jurisdiction as narrowly.

References:

Blumenthal, Ralph. "Inquiry on Donovan Again Yields 'Insufficient Evidence' to Prosecute." *New York Times*, 14 September 1982, sec. A, p. 1.

Lardner, George, Jr. "FBI Told Reagan Staff Donovan Had Mob Ties." *Washington Post*, 15 June 1982, sec. A, p. 1.

————. "No Basis Found for Prosecution of Donovan." *Washington Post*, 29 June 1982, sec. A, p. 1.

————. "Silverman Confirms New Donovan Probe." *Washington Post*, 3 August 1982, sec. A, p. 7.

Rowan, Roy. "The Payoff Charges against Reagan's Labor Secretary." *Fortune*, 31 May 1982, p. 80.

"Summary of Prosecutor's Report and a Transcript of Remarks by Donovan." *New York Times*, 29 June 1982, sec. A, p. 17.

Thornton, Mary, and George Lardner, Jr. "Court Names Prosecutor in Donovan Case." *Washington Post*, 30 December 1981, sec. A, p. 1.

Sinclair, Harry F. (1876–1956) petroleum producer. On 7 April 1922, Harry Sinclair's Mammoth Oil Company was granted a lease by Interior Secretary ALBERT FALL permitting extraction of oil from the TEAPOT DOME reserve in Wyoming. Subsequent investigation by Congress and Special Prosecutors ATLEE POMERENE and OWEN J. ROBERTS resulted in Sinclair's indictment for conspiracy. Although found not guilty on this count, Sinclair was convicted on contempt charges for refusing to answer questions regarding Teapot Dome and served a nine-month prison sentence in 1929.

Born in Wheeling, West Virginia, Sinclair was raised in Independence, Kansas and educated as a pharmacist at the University of Kansas. He was unsuccessful at this profession and in 1901 was forced to close the drug store his father had left him. Sinclair's collection of $5,000 in insurance money following a hunting accident permitted him to enter the oil business. At first, he dealt in "mud silles," large logs used as foundations for oil derricks. As profits accumulated, Sinclair began to trade in leases and wells. In 1905, his investment in Oklahoma's Kiowa Pool oil well earned $100,000 for him. With backing from partners he was able to purchase additional wells in Oklahoma and expand into refining and marketing of petroleum. In 1916, Sinclair separated from his partners, obtained support from Wall Street bankers, and created the Sinclair Oil and Refining Corporation, integrating all aspects of his oil operation. In 1917, President Woodrow Wilson appointed Sinclair to the oil subcommittee of the Committee on Raw Materials, part of the Council of National Defense. After World War I, Sinclair expanded his operation to include holdings in Costa Rica, Panama, Angola, and Portuguese West Africa.

When Albert Fall opened the naval oil reserves to private development, Sinclair joined oil man EDWARD L. DOHENY in obtaining leases. Teapot Dome, designated Naval Reserve No. 3 by the government, represented one of the richest deposits in the mid-continental region. Led by Progressive Wisconsin Senator Robert LaFollette, conservationists and congressional Democrats began their investigation into this transfer of massive government oil to private individuals. Testifying before the Senate's Public Lands Committee in December 1923, Sinclair denied presenting Fall with payment or gift of any kind in return for the oil lease at Teapot Dome. Sinclair explained that livestock he had sent to Fall in January was unrelated to the oil transaction. On 13 March 1924, President CALVIN COOLIDGE's Special Prosecutors Pomerene and Roberts filed suit in Cheyenne's Federal District Court against Sinclair charging fraud and conspiracy. They asked that the Teapot Dome contracts be invalidated. On 23 March, Sinclair appeared again before the Senate and, acting on the advice of counsel, refused to answer any questions on the grounds that the Committee lacked jurisdiction to interrogate him further regarding the oil lease. As a result, on 31 March, a grand jury indicted Sinclair for contempt.

On 17 March 1927, a Washington DC jury found Sinclair guilty of contempt of the Senate. Sinclair's attorney appealed the decision. On 17 October, Sinclair and Fall were tried for conspiracy. After two weeks, Pomerene moved for a mistrial on the grounds that Sinclair had hired Burns Agency detectives to stalk jury members. Although Sinclair maintained that the only reason he had hired the detectives was to ensure that the jurors were not approached by other interested parties, Judge Frederick J. Siddons declared a mistrial. In February 1928 Sinclair's behavior again resulted in a contempt citation. This citation was accompanied by a six-month jail sentence. Before the contempt citations could be decided on appeal, Sinclair again went on trial for conspiracy with Fall. In April 1928, following a two-week trial, Sinclair was acquitted of conspiracy in a surprise verdict. Sinclair had again refused to testify, and the Teapot Dome lease had already been invalidated and condemned by the Supreme Court as the result of illegal collusion.

On 8 April 1929, the Supreme Court upheld Sinclair's conviction for contempt before the Senate. On 4 June, Sinclair's contempt of court citation was affirmed, and on 6 May he entered prison. President Herbert Hoover refused to consider Sinclair's clemency plea.

Sinclair's prison sentence did not adversely affect his business interests. In 1930, he accumulated $28 million in a joint oil venture with John D. Rockefeller, Jr. During the Second World War, Sinclair served on the Petroleum Industry War Council. At the time of his death, Sinclair Oil ranked 14th on *Fortune* magazine's list of the top 500 industrial corporations.

References:

Busch, Francis X. *Enemies of the State*. Indianpolis: Bobbs-Merrill, 1954. Chapter 2 covers the Teapot Dome case and Sinclair's conviction.
Dictionary of American Biography, supplement 6, pp. 584–585.
Noggle, Burl. *Teapot Dome: Oil and Politics in the 1920's*. Baton Rouge: Louisiana State University Press, 1962.

Sirica, John J. (1904–1992) Judge, U.S. District Court for Washington, D.C., 1957–1986. As the judge primarily responsible for handling most of the court

cases related to the WATERGATE break-in, John Sirica has been largely credited with conducting legal proceedings in a manner that ensured that the truth
surrounding the affair would be revealed. His decision to uphold the Watergate
Special Prosecution Force (WSPF) subpoena of President RICHARD NIXON's
telephone tapes was instrumental in unraveling the White House attempt to avoid
responsibility for its misconduct. Sirica's effectiveness in uncovering the truth
regarding Watergate strongly influenced the framers of the independent counsel
statute to provide for judicial appointment of the special prosecutor, a feature
of the law that Sirica himself did not support.

Born in Waterbury, Connecticut, Sirica was the son of Italian immigrants.
After moving several times, the family settled in Washington, D.C., in 1918.
Initially intimidated after a one-month stint at George Washington University
Law School at the age of 17, Sirica later enrolled at Georgetown and received
his law degree in 1926. After trying his hand at boxing in Florida, Sirica returned
to practice law in Washington. He worked as Assistant U.S. Attorney (1930–
1934), while struggling to build his practice. Increasingly involved in Republican Party politics, Sirica campaigned for Wendell Willkie, Thomas E. Dewey,
and Dwight D. Eisenhower. He was one of the few Italian-Americans who
would regularly stump for Republican candidates. After working as counsel to
a House select committee investigating the Federal Communications Commission (FCC) in the mid-1940s, Sirica joined the Washington firm of Hogan &
Hartson. He was its chief trial attorney when named to the district court in 1957.
Acquiring seniority on that body in 1971, Sirica was able to assign himself to
the Watergate burglary case.

Some critics believed that Sirica should not have presided at the Watergate
trials, because he had made rulings that were responsible for having brought the
cases to court. Others felt that Sirica, nearing age 70, would lack the vigor to
withstand lengthy court proceedings. Sirica's stamina held, although a serious
heart attack he suffered in 1976, thirteen months after the end of trials, illustrated
the risk that had been taken. Sirica was an activist judge during the Watergate
trials, frequently characterized by the defense as another prosecutor. He participated in questioning of the defendants, and imposed severe sentences that were
provisional in nature, pending the defendant's decision to cooperate with investigators. This tactic has been credited with prompting Watergate burglar James
W. McCord to issue a letter to Sirica implicating his superiors in the affair.
Sirica's reading of this letter in open court on March 23, 1973, represented a
turning point in the investigation. Sirica was occasionally impatient and inatten-
tive during the trials, and his errors included uttering comments disparaging the
character of Watergate defendants. The Court of Appeals, however, a body that
had frequently reversed Sirica in the past, upheld his rulings. Sirica's errors,
they maintained, were harmless.

Sirica's relentless pursuit for the truth, and his refusal to defer to the President
on this issue, was necessary to the successful functioning of the WSPF. Without
his support for their subpoenas, and his continual refusal to accept the initial

explanations of McCord and G. Gordon Liddy, Watergate may never have been successfully prosecuted. Sirica achieved the status of folk hero as the Watergate story unfolded. He was selected *Time*'s man of the year in 1973. Although he was reluctant to believe that the President himself was personally involved in the matter, Sirica insisted on pressing for all the facts, wherever they may lead. Once it became clear that Nixon was implicated, Sirica felt betrayed. He did not believe that one could be both a statesman and a criminal. GERALD FORD should not have pardoned Nixon, stated Sirica. Had the President been successfully prosecuted in his court, Sirica declared, he would have been sent to jail. In his 1979 book *To Set the Record Straight* (New York: Norton) Sirica expressed the wish that "no political party will ever stoop so low as to embrace the likes of Richard Nixon again." Sirica believed that none of Nixon's achievements could hope to mitigate Watergate, and he feared the day when the American public would fail to concur.

Sirica believed the WSPF's accomplishments had demonstrated that the Constitution was well equipped to deal with instances of executive-branch misconduct. Although he had occasionally assumed a prosecutorial stance during the Watergate trials, Sirica contended that any statute calling for the judicial appointment of a special prosecutor would mean abandonment of the Judiciary's neutrality.

References:

Ben-Veniste, Richard, and George Frampton, Jr. *Stonewall: The Real Story of the Watergate Prosecution.* New York: Simon and Schuster, 1977.

Doyle, James. *Not above the Law: The Battles of Watergate Prosecutors Cox and Jaworski.* New York: Morrow, 1977.

Eastland, Terry. *Ethics, Politics, and the Independent Counsel.* Washington, D.C.: National Legal Center for the Public Interest, 1989. Chapter 4, "The Search for Law: 1973–1976," refers to Sirica's opposition to judicial appointment of the special prosecutor. He made this statement in concurring with Judge GERHARD GESELL's ruling in *NADER v. BORK.*

Harriger, Katy J. *Independent Justice: The Federal Special Prosecutor in American Politics.* Lawrence: University Press of Kansas, 1992.

Jackson, Robert L. "John J. Sirica, Watergate Case Judge, Dies at 88." *Los Angeles Times,* 15 August 1992, sec. A, p. 1.

Sirica, Jack. "My Dad Decided Nixon Was a Crook." *Newsday,* 28 April 1994, sec. A, p. 39. The author, John J. Sirica's son, was a *Newsday* staff writer.

"Sirica, 88, Dies." *New York Times,* 15 August 1992, sec. A, p. 1.

Smaltz, Donald (1937–) Independent Counsel, Mike Espy investigation, 1994– . The first independent counsel to begin operations following the 1994 revival of the independent counsel statute, Donald Smaltz proceeded to conduct a four-year investigation of MIKE ESPY, President Bill CLINTON's first Secretary of Agriculture. Though his probe resulted in the assessment of over $10.5 million in fines against corporations that had contributed illegal gifts to Espy, as well as conviction of several of Espy's aides, Espy himself was found not guilty on 30 counts of accepting illegal gratuities.

A native of Pennsylvania, Smaltz was educated at Pennsylvania State University (B.A., 1958) and the Dickinson School of Law in Carlisle where he received his law degree in 1961. For over two years, he served as trial attorney for the U.S. Army's Judge Advocate General's Corps at Fort Bragg, North Carolina, before accepting appointment as Assistant U.S. Attorney in Los Angeles. In 1967, Smaltz began private practice in Los Angeles, specializing in defense of white collar crime. In 1975, while representing Frank DeMarco, former president RICHARD NIXON's tax attorney, Smaltz won a dismissal of charges on the grounds that WATERGATE prosecutors had failed to present information that pointed toward his client's innocence. Other high-profile clients represented by Smaltz included the Teamsters and California Overseas Bank, the financial institution used by former Philippine dictator Ferdinand Marcos and his wife Imelda to extract much of their nation's wealth. A Republican, Smaltz worked with the Los Angeles firm of Morgan, Lewis & Bockius (1987–1992) and taught law at Southwestern University during the 1980s. In 1990 Smaltz chaired a Federal Bar Association conference in Los Angeles that heard testimony from Imelda Marcos and former independent counsel target Lyn NOFZIGER regarding the excesses of overzealous government prosecutors. Nevertheless, when Smaltz was named independent counsel for the Espy probe on September 9, 1994, he was quoted as welcoming the opportunity of "wearing the white hat again."

Smaltz was working at his own small law firm, Smaltz & Anderson, when appointed independent counsel. At first, he anticipated that the investigation would take no more than six months, even though he had been allowed a broad mandate to investigate any improper gifts Espy may have received. The inquiry would extend over four years and force Smaltz to dissolve his law firm in 1997. Because gifts allegedly provided by Tyson Foods prompted the investigation of Espy, Smaltz began his investigation by visiting the headquarters of the poultry operation in Fayetteville, Arkansas, in November 1994. Smaltz determined that Tyson had extended $12,000 in gifts to Espy over a period of 15 months. These included football tickets for a 1994 Dallas Cowboys game, plane fare to the Super Bowl, a birthday party, and a $1,200 scholarship for Espy's girlfriend Patricia Dempsey. This largesse was allegedly aimed at convincing Espy to delay implementation of U.S. Department of Agriculture (USDA) standards regarding fecal contamination of poultry. These measures, ultimately postponed by USDA, would have cost Tyson millions of dollars in compliance costs. In December 1997, Tyson agreed to pay $6 million in fines.

In 1996, Sun-Diamond Growers of California was convicted on eight counts of providing illegal gratuities to Espy. These consisted of meals, trips, and gifts valued at $14,000. Included was an attempt to contribute $5,000 toward helping pay off debts incurred by Espy's brother Henry during an unsuccessful congressional campaign in 1993. In addition, the international investing firm Smith-

Barney Inc., agreed to pay a $1 million fine for purchasing Espy's 1994 Super Bowl ticket. It was charged that the firm was trying to convince the Secretary to waive a $286 million prepayment penalty originating from a $3.1 billion loan extended to Smith-Barney client Oglethorpe Power Corporation of Georgia. Other businesses fined for allegedly bribing Espy included Crop Growers Corporation ($2 million) and AFLAC insurance ($80,000).

Smaltz's investigation also implicated several individuals besides Espy. Ronald Blackley, former congressional aide to Espy, was sentenced to 27 months in prison on March 18, 1998, for making false statements regarding receipt of $22,000 he received from USDA-regulated businesses. Espy's friend Richard Douglas was convicted for his role in extending bribes while working as a lobbyist for Sun-Diamond.

In August 1997, Smaltz secured a 39-count indictment against Espy for allegedly soliciting and accepting $35,000 in gifts from businesses regulated by his department. In November 1998, U.S. District Court Judge Ricardo Urbina dismissed several of the charges, including the $1,200 Tyson scholarship awarded to Patricia Dempsey. Espy stood trial on the remaining 30 counts, and was acquitted on December 2. It was perceived that Smaltz had failed to present convincing evidence that the gifts presented to Espy had resulted in favors returned by USDA. In the absence of a demonstrated *quid pro quo*, Espy was acquitted. Neither Dempsey nor Tyson Foods Chairman Don Tyson was called to testify at trial, reportedly because prosecutors feared that they would have supported Espy and attacked Smaltz. In retrospect, it was considered that this decision by the prosecution might have been a mistake.

Although Smaltz succeeded in penalizing unethical gift giving by USDA-regulated corporations, he failed to prove his case against the gift recipient. On April 27, 1999, the Supreme Court made it more difficult to penalize gift givers as well by ruling that unless the gratuity is linked to an official act on the part of the recipient, it would no longer constitute a crime. Smaltz had no immediate comment on the decision, but his probe appeared to be at an end.

The decision in the Espy case appeared to represent another in a series of recent setbacks for independent counsels. Smaltz's investigation has been compared to KENNETH STARR's WHITEWATER probe in several respects. Starr was named to his office shortly before Smaltz, and began his investigation shortly after Smaltz initiated his. Both have suffered criticism regarding prosecutorial excesses. During his investigation of Tyson Foods, Smaltz attempted to validate the accusations of disgruntled former Tyson employee Joe Henrickson who told prosecutors that he had delivered bribes to former Arkansas governor Bill Clinton. Critics charged that Smaltz was trying to compete with Starr by targeting the president. The Espy decision compares with Starr's unsuccessful prosecution of SUSAN McDOUGAL. Wrongdoing appeared evident, but juries perceived an overzealousness on the part of the prosecution that appeared to nullify whatever criminality might have occurred.

References:

Merelman, Diana. "Leading the Espy Probe." *American Lawyer* (November 1996): 32.
Ostrow, Ronald, and Henry Weinstein. "Independent Counsel Appointed to Investigate Espy." *Los Angeles Times*, 10 September 1994, sec. A, p. 14.
Russell, Keith. "Espy's Bitter Harvest." *Insight on the News*, 4 May 1998, p.7. Praises Smaltz's performance, detailing his successes; predicts victory in Espy trial.
"Secrets of an Independent Counsel" from the PBS television program *Frontline*. See www.pbs.org/wgbh/pages/frontline/shows/counsel, which features an interview with Smaltz in which he describes the course of his investigation.
Thomas, Pierre, and Howard Schneider. "Los Angeles Attorney Chosen to Head Investigation of Espy." *Washington Post*, 10 September 1994, sec. A, p. 3.

Smith, William French (1917–1990) Attorney General, 1981–1985. Firmly convinced that the ETHICS IN GOVERNMENT ACT violated the Constitution's separation of powers principle, William French Smith was nonetheless called upon to implement the statute's independent counsel provisions on numerous occasions during his tenure as attorney general. In two instances, he triggered special prosecutor/independent counsel investigations. In both cases, the targets of the inquiry—Secretary of Labor RAYMOND DONOVAN and Attorney General designee EDWIN MEESE—requested the probes in order to counter allegations of wrongdoing. On all other occasions, Smith exercised prosecutorial discretion consistent with his disdain for the statute by refusing to initiate such investigations.

A direct descendant of Uriah Oakes, fourth president of Harvard College, Smith was born in Wilton, New Hampshire. Educated at the University of California at Berkeley (B.A., 1939) and Harvard University (LL.B., 1942), he served as an officer in the Naval Reserve during World War II. Relocating to Los Angeles after the war, Smith joined the law firm of Gibson, Dunn & Crutcher, where he specialized in representation of corporate clients during collective bargaining negotiations. A member of RONALD REAGAN's "kitchen cabinet," Smith helped plan the political strategy that enabled Reagan to capture the California Statehouse and the presidency. He was rewarded by appointment to the University of California Board of Regents in 1968. In that capacity, he opposed the efforts of antiwar protestors to force the university to discontinue nuclear weapons research. Similarly, Smith resisted anti-apartheid group pressure to break university ties with countries that maintained business relations with South Africa. During the 1970s, Smith served as California Chamber of Commerce president (1974–1975), and helped direct the operations of numerous corporations including Pacific Telephone and Telegraph of San Francisco, Crocker National Bank, Pacific Mutual Life Insurance of Los Angeles, Pacific Lighting, and Pullman Inc. of Chicago.

As attorney general, Smith espoused the conservative principle of judicial restraint. This meant the end of any activist federal role in the area of civil rights. Smith considered affirmative action measures such as busing and racial quotas to be counterproductive. The principle of equal protection was distorted by these measures, according to Smith. It followed that Smith did not look favorably on the Ethics Act, since it created an Office of Special Prosecutor that infringed upon the prerogatives of the Justice Department. Smith soon realized, however, that the act might call upon the attorney general to request appointment of a special prosecutor in certain instances, but it could do little to force the issue.

On December 24, 1981, Smith announced that he would not appoint a special prosecutor to investigate National Security Adviser RICHARD V. ALLEN's acceptance of a gift from Japanese businessmen during the performance of official duties, and his failure to report it on financial disclosure forms. Following a preliminary investigation, Smith ruled that no further inquiry was warranted in the absence of any demonstrated criminal intent on the part of Allen. The gratuity was offered in social circumstances, stated Smith, and could reasonably be perceived by Allen as unconnected to any official function.

Three days later, Smith, responding to a request by Secretary of Labor Raymond Donovan, asked for a special prosecutor to investigate charges that Donovan had witnessed an official from his construction company tendering a bribe to a labor union officer. Donovan called for the appointment in order to demonstrate that the charge was without merit. After a lengthy, complicated investigation by LEON SILVERMAN, during which many other allegations surfaced, the special procecutor determined that no indictments were warranted.

In May 1982, Smith's personal finances came under scrutiny of the Justice Department when it was revealed that he had received a $50,000 severance fee from the Earle M. Jorgenson Company. It was alleged, by Senator Edward Kennedy (D-Massachusetts) among others, that the payment was made to supplement his government salary and possibly influence decisions Smith would make as attorney general. In July, the Justice Department ruled that the payment, which Smith returned in response to criticism, was intended as compensation for past services only. In a second instance, the Department declared that Smith had violated conflict-of-interest regulations by investing in a tax shelter. Because the attorney general oversees the Tax Division, which represents the Internal Revenue Service (IRS) in court, Smith's tax shelter placed him in a position of conflict with his official office. The violation, however, was mitigated by the fact that Smith took voluntary steps to rectify the situation by limiting his deductions. As a result, the investigation was ended with no action beyond the reprimand.

In 1983 and 1984, three attempts were made by individuals to force Smith to initiate independent counsel investigations. In *NATHAN v. ATTORNEY GENERAL* (1983), *DELLUMS v. SMITH* (1983), and *BANZHAF v. SMITH* (1984), the attorney general declined to pursue allegations of executive-branch misconduct either because the individuals lacked standing or the charges lacked specificity. In each case, the U.S. district court upheld the plaintiffs, but the court of appeals supported Smith. As Judge ROBERT BORK indicated, the attorney general is in control of the independent counsel's triggering mechanism, and revisions to the statute accompanying its 1982 reauthorization served to increase the amount of discretion the attorney general was allowed.

In 1984, Smith acquiesced to Edwin Meese's request for an independent counsel investigation of allegations of financial irregularities and favoritism that surfaced during Senate hearings following the president's designation of Meese as the next attorney general. Smith initiated the process, and the Special Division named JACOB STEIN independent counsel. Stein's investigation determined that Meese's behavior, though unethical, did not warrant criminal prosecution. Meese used the report to his advantage in securing his confirmation as Smith's replacement.

Smith's adherence to the principle of judicial restraint, and his reluctance to employ an independent counsel mechanism, which he considered unconstitutional, prompted the statute's further revision in 1987. These changes served to remove the very same discretion granted the attorney general five years earlier. This paved the way for a greater number of investigations, many of which have been characterized as abusive and excessive.

References:

Babcock, Charles, and Bob Woodward. "Attorney General Criticized; Justice Closes Investigations of Smith." *Washington Post*, 22 July 1982, sec. A, p. 1.

Boyer, Edward J. "William French Smith, 73 Dies; Reagan Adviser and Attorney General." *Los Angeles Times*, 30 October 1990, sec. B, p. 1. Obituary recounting Smith's career.

Harriger, Katy J. *Independent Justice: The Federal Special Prosecutor in American Politics*. Lawrence: University Press of Kansas, 1992. Chapter 4, "Implementation and Oversight," covers Smith's opposition to the independent counsel statute and his reluctance to employ it.

Pound, Edward T. "Allen Exonerated by Justice Department." *New York Times*, 24 December 1981, sec. A, p. 1.

Taylor, Stuart, Jr. "Attorney General's Power to Bar Special Counsel Upheld in Court." *New York Times*, 26 June 1984, sec. A, p. 1.

Wright, Michael, and Caroline Rand Herron. "Donovan Wanted a Prosecutor and He'll Get One." *New York Times*, 27 December 1981, sec. A, p. 4.

Starr, Kenneth W. (1946–   ) Independent Counsel, Whitewater investigation, 1994–   . Appointed to succeed ROBERT FISKE, following the revival of the independent counsel statute, Kenneth Starr launched a more aggressive and wide-ranging inquiry into President Bill CLINTON's affairs. What began as a probe of a failed Arkansas land deal a decade earlier expanded to include investigations of the 1993 suicide of White House counsel VINCENT FOSTER, the manner in which White House travel office staff had been dismissed (TRAVELGATE), alleged misuse of FBI files by White House personnel (FILEGATE), and consensual sexual activity between the president and former White House intern MONICA LEWINSKY. Starr's report of his findings, delivered to the

House of Representatives in September 1998, largely ignored all but the Lewinsky affair, which formed the basis of the president's impeachment on grounds
of perjury and obstruction of justice. Starr's prosecutorial tactics have come
under scrutiny as well, due in part to the manner in which information had been
continually leaked to the press during the investigation.

Born in Vernon, Texas, Starr was educated at George Washington (B.A.,
1968), Brown (M.A., 1969), and Duke (J.D., 1973) universities. Starr clerked
for Judge David Dwyer (5th Circuit Court of Appeals, Miami, Florida, 1973–
1974) and Supreme Court Chief Justice Warren Burger (1975–1977) before
serving as counselor to Attorney General WILLIAM FRENCH SMITH (1981–
1983). He also practiced privately with the firm of Gibson, Dunn & Crutcher
(Los Angeles, 1974–1975; Washington D.C., 1977–1981). In 1983, Starr was
appointed to the U.S. Court of Appeals (D.C. circuit) where he served for six
years. He left to accept the post of solicitor general at the Justice Department,
a position he held until 1993. Starr was a partner at the Washington, D.C. firm
of Kirkland & Ellis when called upon by the Special Division to assume the
duties of independent counsel for the WHITEWATER investigation.

To some, Starr's appointment appeared politically motivated. Because Fiske
had been appointed by Attorney General JANET RENO during the period in
which the independent counsel statute had lapsed, it was argued that Fiske's
work would not be perceived as truly independent. Starr's appointment occurred
shortly after Special Division Judge DAVID SENTELLE met with conservative
North Carolina Senators Lauch Faircloth (R-North Carolina) and Jesse Helms
(R-North Carolina), prompting critics to charge that the process had been tainted.
Although two private citizens filed suit alleging violations of the Judicial Conduct Act, and a group of past ABA presidents registered their protest, Starr's
appointment stood.

Starr's first year as independent counsel was a productive one. He succeeded
in obtaining indictments against Clinton associates WEBSTER HUBBELL
(fraud), JIM GUY TUCKER (bankruptcy-fraud), and JAMES and SUSAN
McDOUGAL (conspiracy). On December 6, 1994, Hubbell entered a plea of
guilty to defrauding the Rose Law Firm of over $400,000. The McDougal cases
might well have implicated the Clintons in Whitewater-related crimes. As
LAWRENCE WALSH had done during the IRAN-CONTRA investigation,
Starr was following standard prosecutorial procedure by pressuring persons perceived as mid-level conspirators, anticipating that they could be persuaded to
testify against those at the highest level.

After 1995, Starr's investigation slowed as his targets proved recalcitrant.
Hubbell remained silent despite serving a jail sentence and being reindicted.
Tucker waited almost three years before pleading guilty. Though Jim McDougal
agreed to provide testimony against Clinton in 1997, his credibilty had been
badly damaged by then. Susan McDougal elected to serve 18 months for contempt rather than answer any of Starr's questions. Her retrial in 1999 ended in
a hung jury.

In January 1996, HILLARY CLINTON's billing records relating to her legal work for Jim McDougal's Madison Guaranty bank were discovered. They had been subpoenaed by Starr's office in 1994. Starr required Hillary Clinton to testify before a Washington grand jury on January 26, and the White House residence was searched for further Whitewater documents. Neither approach proved fruitful. After Bill Clinton's re-election in November, it appeared that the investigation was nearing conclusion. On February 17, 1997, Starr announced that he was preparing to leave in order to accept a deanship at Pepperdine University. Four days later, apparently in reaction to Republican criticism of his decision, Starr decided to remain until the end of the investigation.

For the next year there was little news regarding Whitewater or any of the tangential inquiries that it had spawned. On January 21, 1998, however, it was revealed that the independent counsel office was investigating whether the president had suborned the perjury of former White House intern Monica Lewinsky and obstructed justice during the PAULA JONES sexual harassment lawsuit. Concerned that Clinton was attempting to buy the silence of witnesses, as Starr believed the president had done in the Whitewater affair, the independent counsel obtained tapes of Lewinsky discussing her sexual relationship with the president by wiring friendly witness LINDA TRIPP. Convinced by the new evidence that there was adequate reason for additional investigation, Attorney General Reno authorized Starr to expand his probe to include possible obstruction of justice in the Paula Jones case.

Starr proceeded to examine everyone who might have witnessed evidence of the president's relationship with Lewinsky. This resulted in grand jury appearances by Oval Office staff, former interns, attorney and Clinton friend Vernon Jordan, the president's personal secretary Betty Currie, Monica Lewinsky's mother Marcia Lewis, and Secret Service employees. He also investigated other allegations of sexual harassment such as the charge brought by former Clinton campaign worker Kathleen Willey. (Willey's story was at first supported, then denied by her friend Julie Hiatt Steele. In 1999, Starr unsuccessfully prosecuted Steele for recanting.) Starr offered Lewinsky transactional IMMUNITY in return for her testimony before the grand jury, and on August 18, 1998, obtained the president's appearance, a tape recording that was later televised. The president at first denied any sexual relationship with Lewinsky, then acknowledged "inappropriate" behavior, maintaining the absence of any contradiction by parsing words. Starr's report to Congress in September 1998 focused on the president's behavior in the Lewinsky affair, alleging perjury and obstruction of justice.

The House of Representatives succeeded in voting articles of impeachment in December 1998 based on the Starr report. However, an abbreviated trial in the Senate ended in February after failing to summon the necessary two-thirds vote on any of the counts. Most congressmen did not believe that the charges amounted to the high crimes and misdemeanors specified in the Constitution as proper grounds for removal of a president. In addition, Clinton's popularity remained high throughout the proceedings, and removal would likely have come at considerable political costs.

Although Starr was initially determined to avoid the pitfalls of Lawrence Walsh's inquiry, in many respects he repeated them, perhaps even exceeded them. The five years and $40 million consumed by Starr's probe rivals Walsh's totals. Starr's aggressiveness spurred criticism of an office that was unaccountable and unprincipled. His single-mindedness prompted accusations of a vendetta against the President. The charges were rendered more plausible by the fact that Starr had ties to old Clinton enemies such as Richard Mellon Scaife, and had offered to assist the Paula Jones legal team in prosecution of their suit before accepting the independent counsel appointment. Even though perjury and obstruction of justice are serious matters, even in a civil case, the sexual context within which the violations occurred caused many to question the appropriateness of the constitutional sanctions invoked. Consensual sex, even when it constitutes adultery, did not appear as subversive of the democratic process as arms-for-hostages deals and attempts at overthrowing governments that incur our displeasure. Yet, Starr's tactics, though much maligned, were not substantially different from those regularly employed by conscientious prosecutors faced with similar circumstances. Starr was forced to use them, however, in the highest of profile cases against a president who was able to maintain his popularity throughout the humiliating ordeal. Clinton's impeachment will likely stand as Starr's enduring accomplishment, although the indictment of the President after leaving office remains a possibility.

References:

Bleifuss, Joel. "School for Scandal." *In These Times*, 8 March 1998, p. 14. Presents Starr's investigation as a politically motivated attempt to criminalize the president's personal life.

Starr, Kenneth W. "Law and Lawyers: The Road to Reform." *Fordham Law Review* 63 (1995): 959–969. Blames current pervasive distrust in society on anti-power sentiment, individualism, and interest in scandal. Advocates revival of honor and integrity, virtues that should replace litigation as remedies for misconduct. Proposes abolishment of punitive damages.

Taylor, Stuart, Jr. "Kenneth Starr v. The Legal Profession." *National Journal*, 13 July 1998, p. 1347. Supports Starr's contention that unrestrained advocacy is responsible for many lawyers' current disregard for the truth. Contends that Starr's unpopularity within the legal profession stems from his criticism of the commonly adopted tactics of "concealment, deception and distortion."

Toobin, Jeffrey. "Starr Can't Help It." *New Yorker*, 18 May 1998, pp. 32–38. Evaluates Starr's performance in light of the weaknesses inherent in the independent counsel statute.

Stein, Jacob (1925–   ) Independent Counsel, Edwin Meese investigation, 1984. It has been said that Jacob Stein's investigation of EDWIN MEESE represents the only instance of an independent counsel investigation benefiting the subject of the investigation. Stein's five-month probe centered on Meese's financial transactions, his possible participation in campaign abuses, and the manner in which he secured military promotion. After Stein reported that there was no basis for prosecution, Meese and his supporters were able to use the findings to help secure his confirmation as attorney general.

A second-generation Washington attorney, Stein began practicing law in 1948 after receiving his law degree from George Washington University Law School. A partner with the firm Stein, Mitchell & Menzies, he is past president of both the voluntary District of Columbia Bar Association (1968–1969) and the District of Columbia Bar (1982–1983), an organ of the courts. Stein has been a faculty member at Harvard, Georgetown, and George Washington University law schools. Stein's legal experience consists primarily of criminal and civil representation of individuals rather than corporations. Considered apolitical, Stein has never voted. He has attributed this to having been raised in the District of Columbia when residents were not extended that privilege. Stein has always maintained an immaculate courtroom demeanor, scholarly in approach and elegant in appearance.

In 1974, Stein's successful defense of Kenneth Parkinson, attorney for the Committee to Re-elect the President (CRP), represented one of the rare successes for those accused of involvement in WATERGATE. He was able to portray his client as uninvolved with either any alleged misconduct or the other defendants in the case. He was also able to produce an impressive array of character witnesses who helped convince the jury that Parkinson was merely a conscientious attorney representing the CRP in a responsible manner.

When called upon by the Special Division to investigate Meese, Stein was involved in representing former Reagan press secretary James Brady in civil suits stemming from his injuries suffered during John Hinckley's attempt on Reagan's life in 1981. Meese called upon Attorney General WILLIAM FRENCH SMITH to initiate an independent counsel investigation, believing that such an inquiry would serve to demonstrate that the allegations against him were baseless. Stein was appointed on April 2, 1984. Specifically, he was charged with investigating whether Meese had filed false financial disclosure forms, engaged in illegal financial arrangements with persons later appointed to office, participated in illegal stock trading, secured preferential treatment for businesses in which he held an interest; obtained a promotion in the military reserve by illegal means, and/or participated in illegally obtaining President Jimmy CARTER's debate materials for use by the Reagan campaign in 1980. Stein managed to examine all these charges within five months, successfully shielding the probe from public scrutiny until the last few weeks when his decision not to prosecute was leaked to the press, allegedly by Meese's attorneys. Stein's report, filed on September 20, criticized Meese's careless approach to ethical concerns but decided against prosecution on any of the charges. The investigation had cost $312,000.

After the Meese investigation, Stein continued as an active participant in other independent counsel investigations. He defended Carol Dinkins, an associate of THEODORE OLSON, whose challenge to the independent counsel's authority resulted in *MORRISON v. OLSON* (1988), the case that established the constitutionality of the office. Stein was successful in helping prevent Independent Counsel ALEXIA MORRISON from adding a probe of his client to her investigation, as she desired. Stein was critical of the length of time Morrison needed to conduct her inquiry. He maintained that the 14-month process should have consumed no more than six.

In June 1998, Stein and Plato Cacheris assumed the defense of former presidential intern MONICA LEWINSKY. Unlike Lewinsky's former attorney, family friend William Ginsburg, Stein and Cacheris worked in relative secrecy. Avoiding confrontation with the office of Independent Counsel KENNETH STARR, they succeeded in negotiating an agreement granting transactional IMMUNITY to Lewinsky. This paved the way for her testimony before a grand jury and the Senate, the latter occurring during the failed impeachment trial of President CLINTON.

References:

Ben-Veniste, Richard, and George Frampton, Jr. *Stonewall: The Real Story of the Watergate Prosecution.* New York: Simon and Schuster, 1977. Chapter 15, "Truth . . . T-r-u-t-h . . . Truth," covers Stein's defense of Parkinson.

Eastland, Terry. *Ethics, Politics, and the Independent Counsel: Executive Power, Executive Vice 1789–1989.* Washington, D.C.: National Legal Center for the Public Interest, 1989. Chapter 7, "The Second Amendments to the Law, 1987," details Stein's charge in the Meese case.

Taylor, Stuart, Jr. "Man in the News; Unconventional Lawyer with a New Task." *New York Times*, 3 April 1984, sec. A, p. 20. A biographical profile depicts Stein as an "urbane intellectual" and skillful, respected trial lawyer with an admiration for Winston Churchill, Benjamin Franklin, and Oliver Wendell Holmes.

Strawn, Silas H. (1866–1946) Provisional Special Prosecutor, Teapot Dome Affair, 1924. On January 29, 1924, President CALVIN COOLIDGE named Chicago attorney Silas Strawn and former U.S. Attorney General THOMAS W. GREGORY special prosecutors to investigate the questionable transfer of naval oil reserves to private developers. Both men were revealed to have connections to the oil industry, which prevented their confirmation by the Senate. Strawn's difficulty stemmed from his having served as director for a bank that helped float stock for Mammoth Oil Company president HARRY F. SINCLAIR, a key figure in the TEAPOT DOME scandal.

Born in Ottawa, Illinois, Strawn learned the law while working in his cousin Lester's law firm (Bull & Strawn). He moved to Chicago in 1891, joining the firm of Winston & Meagher. Becoming a partner in 1894, Strawn helped build a large corporate practice for the firm. Its clientele grew to include the Union Stock Yards & Transit Company, Chicago & Alton Railroad, and the Mutual Life Insurance Company of New York. Strawn served as director of Electric

Household Utilities Company, the First National and First Trust & Savings Banks of Chicago, and Montgomery Ward & Co. He appeared to have the respect of both the legal and commercial communities. Politically a Republican, Strawn's appointment as Teapot Dome Special Prosecutor would serve as proper balance to Gregory's Democratic affiliations.

Gregory was forced to withdraw his name from consideration on February 4, 1924, after his association with oil magnate EDWARD L. DOHENY became known. Coolidge replaced him with Ohio politician ATLEE POMERENE. Nine days later, the president withdrew Strawn's name from consideration when Senator Irvine Lenroot (R-Wisconsin) reported that the Public Lands Committee would not approve the nomination. On February 15, Coolidge replaced Strawn with Philadelphia attorney (and future Supreme Court Justice) OWEN J. ROBERTS.

In 1925, Coolidge appointed Strawn a commissioner to represent the United States at the Chinese customs conference in Peking. The meeting was held in accordance with the terms of the Washington Conference for arms limitation (1921–1922). Strawn also served on the commission charged with investigating extraterritorial jurisdiction in China (1925–1926). Later associations included the American Society of International Law, the Carnegie Endowment for International Peace, and the International Chamber of Commerce.

References:

Ise, John. *The United States Oil Policy*. New Haven: Yale University Press, 1926. Chapter 25, "The Naval Oil Reserves and the Teapot Dome Investigation," explains Strawn's brief tenure as special prosecutor.
National Cyclopedia of American Biography, volume 34, p. 16.
Noggle, Burl. *Teapot Dome: Oil and Politics in the 1920's*. Baton Rouge: Louisiana State University Press, 1962. Chapter 6, "The Onrush of Scandal," discusses Strawn's selection and withdrawal as special prosecutor.

Sullivan, Brendan V., Jr. (1942–   ), attorney for Oliver North during Iran-Contra investigation. Sullivan played a central role in the IRAN-CONTRA affair. Born in Rhode Island, Sullivan was educated at Georgetown University, receiving his A.B. in 1964 and his J.D. in 1967. As a senior partner in the powerful Washington law firm of Williams and Connolly, Sullivan was hired by North after the Iran-Contra scandal broke in late 1986.

As a defense lawyer, Sullivan had a reputation of never cooperating with the prosecution. Working for NORTH, he lived up to his reputation. He practiced continuous delay, filing numerous defense motions and discovery demands that kept the prosecution team of Independent Counsel LAWRENCE WALSH busy. His law firm was also known for overpowering government counsels in staff and finances. Therefore, as Walsh investigated and then prosecuted North, he and his staff tried to match Sullivan's resources and subsequently incurred high expenses. The independent counsel's expenses themselves became an issue as the Iran-Contra investigation dragged on into the 1990s. Sullivan raised the issue himself, at times asking the Justice Department to look into Walsh's expenses. He even filed motions under the Freedom of Information Act to gain access to the information.

After taking North's case, Sullivan immediately filed a federal lawsuit in February 1987 in which he sought to nullify the law under which the independent counsel had been appointed. Sullivan argued that Walsh had been appointed by a panel of judges and only a presidential appointee had the power to prosecute cases against the United States. Sullivan claimed that the Independent Counsel Act was an unconstitutional violation of separation of powers. When Attorney General EDWIN MEESE gave Walsh a parallel presidential appointment, Sullivan filed another suit. Sullivan argued unsuccessfully that Meese could not appoint Walsh without the advice and consent of the Senate.

In the spring and summer of 1987, Sullivan sought the best terms possible for North's appearance before the Congressional Select Committees on Iran-Contra. Because Congress wanted to get the facts out to the American public as soon as possible, Sullivan was able to secure limited immunity for North. The "use IMMUNITY" agreement granted that anything North said before the committee could not be used against him in a trial. The independent counsel objected as the grant of immunity would impede his investigation and eventual prosecution of North. (At this point, Walsh had not yet formed an indictment against North because he hoped to get a full indictment with a conspiracy charge rather than a fragmentary one with only lesser offenses). Walsh therefore requested from Congress, and received, more time to gather outside evidence that he could use against North. The delay in North's appearance allowed Sullivan and his client to hear the congressional testimony of others before North's own, and thus learn what had already been made public and what had not. Sullivan also gained time to prepare for North's trial defense. For Walsh, North's immunity grant meant having to proceed in the dark in his investigation of the Iran-Contra affair. He and his staff could not listen to North's testimony to gain evidence or investigative leads. Rather, they had to remain "untainted" in order to allow for a fair trial of North later on.

Sullivan secured additional concessions from Congress in exchange for his client's appearance at the hearings. North would testify only once—either in public or private—but not both. Refusing to allow North to give the committee a private deposition with his testimony prior to his appearance before the committee, as other witnesses before him had, Sullivan forced Congress to put the witness on the stand without any idea of what he would say. Thus, Congress had no road map for inquiry. Sullivan also obtained a limit of 30 hours on North's testimony and a promise that Congress would not call North as a witness again. Sullivan did, however, agree to let North give limited private testimony as to whether President RONALD REAGAN knew of the diversion of funds from the Iranian arms sales to the Nicaraguan Contras. Sullivan also agreed to deliver all documents and notebooks to the committee, but North was allowed to black out "irrelevant" portions, which constituted about 30–40 percent of the material. Furthermore, the notebooks remained in Sullivan's possession while the independent counsel was trying to gain access to them.

In July 1987, Sullivan engineered North's six-day appearance before Congress. Wearing his uniform with six rows of medals, North looked like a patriotic hero, even though he had not worn the uniform to work in five years. Sullivan also stacked briefs and documents around North to make him look like a persecuted scapegoat besieged by a mound of paperwork. As letters and telegrams came pouring in from Americans in support of North, Sullivan piled them on the witness table. He then begged the committee to listen to the American public. Outside the courtroom, Sullivan read the telegrams and letters to the press.

At the Congressional hearings (and later in North's trial), Sullivan portrayed his client not as a loose cannon running a rogue operation within the government, but rather as a dedicated officer carrying out his assigned duty. North's actions, he argued, had been authorized and approved by his superiors, including ROBERT McFARLANE, JOHN POINDEXTER, and most importantly the President himself. If anything, Sullivan pointed out, North was the scapegoat being asked to take the fall now as the administration tried to distance itself from the marine.

Sullivan also engineered North's testimony to Congress. As the questioning began, Sullivan had North take the Fifth Amendment. Members of Congress reminded him that he had been granted immunity and his testimony could not be used against him. North then proceeded to answer questions, testifying that he had carried out a sacred duty to protect democracy. The duty was so sacred that the end justified the means, even if it had meant lying to Congress earlier about his actions. His appearance was so riveting that his public approval ratings soared.

Following North's appearance before Congress, Walsh continued to work on the charges to be included in the indictment against North. Walsh tried to negotiate a guilty plea from North because the prosecution's case would be stronger if he had the testimony of lower-level officials against the superiors who had authorized their actions. Sullivan rejected the bargain because he knew Walsh would face great difficulty in trying the case against his client. In March 1988, North was indicted on 16 felony counts, including conspiracy to defraud the United States Government by supporting the Contras in violation of the BOLAND AMENDMENTS, theft of government property with the diversion of funds spent at the direction of North and not the U.S. Government, and endangerment of the U.S. hostage release effort by overcharging the Iranians and diverting the funds to the Contras. He was also charged with lying to Congress, obstructing Congress, and accepting an illegal gratuity as a government official. He eventually stood trial on 12 of the charges. A defense motion to sever the conspiracy indictment against North, Poindexter, RICHARD SECORD, and ALBERT HAKIM was successful. With separate trials, the judge ordered Walsh to try a government official first, meaning either North or his superior Poindexter. Walsh chose to try North first.

Before the trial, Sullivan let his partner, Barry Simon, inundate the court with over 100 pretrial motions (the judge denied nearly all of them), delaying the trial for some time. As the trial began, Sullivan decided to GRAYMAIL the proceedings. In other words, he sought to terminate the prosecution of North by exposing national security secrets in his defense. (In particular, he hoped to get the conspiracy charge dropped). Because the trial was open to the public, any government documents used by either the defense or the prosecution had to be declassified first. Each side also had to explain to the court why they needed the documents as evidence. North complained that this procedure violated his constitutional right to a fair trial because he had to give away his position in advance. Sullivan supplemented his cause by asking to use numerous classified documents for North's defense even though many of them had little relevance to the case but contained many secrets of national security. Given the number of classified documents requested by Sullivan (the government refused to declassify many of them for use in the trial) and the fact that he planned to call the President to testify, the conspiracy charge was eventually dropped.

North's trial finally started in January 1989. During it, Sullivan once again painted North as a can-do officer who had simply carried out his orders. The witnesses, including McFarlane for the prosecution, glorified North. North himself was Sullivan's star witness. He admitted everything, but said he had simply followed orders that he believed the President had authorized. Therefore, his actions were not criminal in intent. In May 1989, a jury convicted North on 3 of the 12 criminal counts (altering and destroying documents, accepting an illegal gratuity, and aiding and abetting in the obstruction of Congress). He was fined $150,000, given a three-year suspended sentence, two years probation, and 1,200 hours of community service. Sullivan filed an appeal, and a three-judge panel reversed the judgments in July 1990 on the basis that the prosecution's witnesses had been tainted by North's 1987 congressional testimony. Walsh then appealed to the Supreme Court, but it declined to review the case. A remand hearing to retry the charges followed, but Walsh asked that the charges be dismissed. He realized it would be nearly impossible to prove that the witnesses had not been tainted. After four years as North's attorney, Sullivan was successful. The charges were dismissed.

References:

Bradlee, Ben, Jr. *Guts and Glory: The Rise and Fall of Oliver North.* New York: Donald I. Fine, Inc., 1988.
Martindale-Hubbell Lawyer Locator, lawyers.martindale.com
Walsh, Lawrence E. *Firewall: The Iran-Contra Conspiracy and Cover-up.* New York: W. W. Norton & Company, 1997.

—JACLYN STANKE

T

Tax Scandal. During 1951 and 1952, the Truman administration was embroiled in a scandal involving tax fixing by members of the Bureau of Internal Revenue and the Tax Division of the Department of Justice. When allegations of misconduct were made public, the House Ways and Means Committee and Judiciary Committee investigated the two agencies and uncovered widespread violations. Sixty-six internal revenue officers were forced to resign in 1951. In 1952, the former commissioner of Internal Revenue and one of his assistants were convicted of tax fraud. The Assistant Attorney General of the Tax Division was fired and convicted of conspiracy to fix a tax case.

In order to show his concern about the scandal, and to avoid congressional control of the investigation, Truman decided to set up an independent commission to investigate the tax-fixing allegations. He chose NEWBOLD MORRIS, a Republican lawyer who had been involved in corruption investigations in New York, to head the investigation. Morris worked with the Bureau of the Budget to design a questionnaire for government employees that would determine both their income and their expenses. The presumption of the questionnaire was that this information would show whether government employees were living beyond their means and might, therefore, be conspirators in the tax-fixing scheme. The Bureau believed that the information was to be gathered only from lawyers in the two agencies implicated in the scandal. Instead, in an early case of overreaching by the special investigator, Morris sought to extend the investigation to all federal government employees.

Attorney General JAMES HOWARD McGRATH resisted this effort by Morris, and many others in government complained about the far-reaching and intrusive nature of the questions. In a meeting with Truman, Morris acknowledged that it would be impossible to reach all federal employees but suggested that it would be possible to cover the top 10,000, thus setting an example for the rest. Truman expressed his concern about Morris's overreaching to McGrath, who turned around and fired Morris. Truman then fired McGrath. The ensuing controversy allowed the Republicans to characterize the Democrats as the party of corruption in the 1952 election.

The Tax Scandal demonstrates several important issues in the history of special prosecutor investigations. First, it illustrates the way in which congressional investigation and public attention can force a president to establish an independent investigative office. Second, the case offers an important contrast to Watergate in terms of the consequences of firing a special prosecutor. McGrath's firing of Morris did have political fallout and, in the short term, garnered much negative publicity. But Truman survived the initial outcry because he was not himself implicated in the scandal, and most government officials realized that Morris had overstepped his bounds. The Tax Scandal demonstrates that there is the potential for abuse of power by a special investigator and suggests that when that happens, presidential power of removal is an important check on that abuse.

References:

Donovan, Robert J. *Tumultuous Years: The Presidency of Harry S Truman, 1949–1953.* New York: W. W. Norton, 1982.

Gosnell, Harold F. *Truman's Crises: A Political Biography of Harry S Truman.* Westport, CT: Greenwood Press, 1980.

Morris, Newbold. *Let the Chips Fall: My Battles with Corruption.* New York: Appleton-Century Crofts, 1955.

U.S. Congress. House. Committee on the Judiciary. *Investigation of the Department of Justice. Hearings Before the Special Subcommittee to Investigate the Justice Department,* 82nd Cong., 2d sess., 1952.

U.S. Congress. House. Ways and Means Committee. *Final Report of the Subcommittee on Administration of Revenue Laws,* 82nd Cong., 2d sess., 1952.

—KATY J. HARRIGER

Teapot Dome Scandal. The presidential administration of WARREN HARDING (1921–1923) was characterized by allegations of misconduct among his Cabinet members and personal scandal involving a mistress. But it was after his death in August of 1923 that the biggest scandal of his tenure came to a head. The Teapot Dome Scandal grew out of conservationists' criticism of Harding's Secretary of the Interior ALBERT FALL. Fall was accused of failing to enforce conservation laws and protecting special interests to which he was beholden. By the spring of 1922 this criticism had provoked substantial press attention, and consequently, considerable concern in the U.S. Senate. In April, the Senate voted to begin an investigation into Fall's decision to lease U.S. naval oil reserves held at Teapot Dome. The hearings were delayed by Republicans who wanted to avoid attention to the scandal until after the 1922 congressional elections.

Albert Fall resigned from his Cabinet position in early 1923, but the rumors of scandal associated with the leases persisted. In addition, there were now allegations that the Department of Justice was involved in covering up the wrongdoing. Shortly after Harding's death, the rumors became full-blown charges of criminal conduct. In October of 1923, the Senate Committee on Public Lands and Survey finally began its hearings. With renewed public attention, President CALVIN COOLIDGE felt the pressure to respond in some way. He directed the Justice Department to send a representative to the hearings and to be prepared to act if law enforcement actions were necessary. Conservationists both inside and outside of Congress were not satisfied that the Coolidge Justice Department would aggressively pursue the allegations, and they began to advance the notion that a special counsel was needed to pursue any legal developments in the case.

In order to preempt congressional action, Coolidge decided to make a special counsel appointment himself. He announced his attention to "employ special counsel of high rank drawn from both political parties" to handle the litigation arising out of the case. In particular, counsel was needed to pursue the litigation necessary to cancel the fraudulent oil leases. The Senate endorsed this move with a resolution directing the President to make such an appointment. The choices were not without controversy. After submitting and then withdrawing his first two choices, Coolidge finally nominated former Democratic Senator ATLEE POMERENE of Ohio and OWEN ROBERTS, a Republican lawyer from Philadelphia. (Roberts would later become a justice on the United States Supreme Court.) The confirmation battle in the Senate was a bitter one, but eventually Pomerene and Roberts were confirmed and commissioned in February of 1924.

The two attorneys worked for the next four years on the legal matters surrounding the scandal. In addition to canceling the leases, Secretary Fall was successfully prosecuted for accepting a bribe for the oil leases. The men alleged to have offered the bribe were acquitted. During this time the Senate committee continued its hearings. A special committee was appointed to look into allegations that Attorney General HARRY DAUGHERTY had mishandled the case. As the investigation grew, Daugherty was forced to resign. Having lost his appeals, Albert Fall finally entered federal prison in July of 1931.

The Teapot Dome case is significant to our understanding of special prosecutors because it demonstrates that appointments of this type can be made without a statutory mandate to do so. Public exposure and congressional investigation put pressure on the president to make an appointment. The Senate's role in confirming the special counsels influenced the choice of individuals and helped create the appearance of independence from the president. It was a very real possibility that the Senate would reject Coolidge's nominees (in fact, his fear of this caused him to withdraw his first nominations). This forced Coolidge to look for men from different parties and with a reputation for independence and integrity. The historical record of this case suggests that despite the fact that Pomerene and Roberts were presidential appointees, they had sufficient independence to fulfill their mission effectively.

References:

Noggle, Burl. *Teapot Dome: Oil and Politics in the 1920's*. Baton Rouge: Louisiana State University Press, 1962.
U.S. Congress. Senate. Committee on Public Lands and Surveys. *Leases Upon Naval Oil Reserves*, 68th Cong., 1st sess., 1923.
Woodward, C. Vann, ed. *Responses of the Presidents to Charges of Misconduct*. New York: Delacorte Press, 1974.

—*KATY J. HARRIGER*

Thompson, Larry D. (1945–   ) Independent Counsel, HUD investigation, 1995–1998. An associate of Independent Counsel ARLIN ADAMS, Larry Thompson succeeded Adams in 1995 and produced the final report that brought the investigation of the Department of Housing and Urban Development (HUD) to a virtual conclusion in October 1998. The longest independent counsel investigation since the creation of the office in 1978, the HUD probe lasted 8.5 years before issuance of its final report. Technically, the probe was not yet fully concluded as of 1999, because Deborah Gore Dean, former HUD Executive Assistant to Secretary SAMUEL PIERCE, continues to appeal her conviction for influence peddling. The investigation cost $28.1 million.

Born in Hannibal, Missouri, Thompson was educated at Culver-Stockton College in Canton, Montana (B.A., 1967), Michigan State University (M.A., 1969), and the University of Michigan (J.D., 1974). He worked as industrial relations representative for the Ford Motor Company (1969–1971) and attorney for the Monsanto Company (1974–1977) before entering private practice with the Atlanta firm of King & Spalding (1977–1982). In 1982, Thompson, a Republican, was appointed U.S. Attorney for the Northern District of Georgia, a position he held for four years. During this period, he directed operations of the Southeastern Organized Crime Drug Enforcement Task Force. After returning to private practice in 1986, Thompson helped assist in the defense of Supreme Court Judge nominee Clarence Thomas against Anita Hill's sexual harassment charge during 1991 confirmation hearings.

When Thompson assumed direction of the HUD investigation in July 1995, it was assumed that the probe would be terminated shortly. Arlin Adams had obtained 16 convictions and collected $2 million in fines for influence peddling and misappropriation of federal funds. In addition, $10 million had been returned to government coffers. It was declared that the investigative phase of the probe was at an end. Thompson proceeded to conclude matters with former Secretary of the Interior James Watt who had been charged with illegally lobbying HUD on behalf of developers after leaving office in 1983. Thompson arranged a plea bargain agreement with Watt in 1996 calling for five years' probation, 500 hours of community service, and payment of a $5,000 fine. Still, the investigation could not be officially closed, because appeals of convictions were pending.

In October 1998, Thompson decided to issue a final report, even though Deborah Gore Dean's appeal was yet to be decided. Both Adams and Thompson signed the final, three-volume report that declared a symbolic end to their probe. The report found that HUD awards in the 1980s were made to personally benefit former HUD officials and their associates, not on the basis of merit. Samuel Pierce, HUD Secretary during this period, was cited for negligence but escaped without formal prosecution. In addition to Dean, those convicted during the investigation include former U.S. Treasurer Catalina Vasquez Villapando and former Assistant HUD secretaries Thomas Demery and Philip D. Winn.

The length of the HUD investigation has been cited by both friends and opponents of the independent counsel statute as excessive. Although the probe has resulted in numerous convictions, assessment of sizable fines, and the return of misappropriated funds to the treasury, it had taken what many consider to be an unconscionable amount of time to accomplish this. Even longtime supporter of the statute, Senator CARL LEVIN (D-Michigan), has characterized the length of the investigation as "scandalous." Certainly Adams did not foresee the inquiry consuming another three and a half years after he left in 1995. It is not clear, however, that Thompson can be faulted for this eventuality. Plea bargain negotiations and conviction appeals inevitably consume much time. Perhaps it would have been wiser to write the final report in 1996 following conclusion of Watt's case.

References:

Hamburger, Tom. "Latitude Given to Special Prosecutors Draws Fire." *Star Tribune* (Minneapolis, MN), 10 May 1998, sec. A, p. 17. Includes listing of all independent counsel investigations to date.

Johnston, David. "Independent Counsel Replaced in HUD Inquiry." *New York Times*, 2 July 1995, sec. A, p. 21.

Miller, Bill. "Report on HUD Details 1980's Pattern of Abuse." *Washington Post*, 27 October 1998, sec. A, p. 17.

Thornburgh, Richard L. (1932–   ) Attorney General, 1988–1991. Named by President RONALD REAGAN to succeed EDWIN MEESE as Attorney General, Richard Thornburgh was expected to restore respectability to a position that had been tarnished by his predecessor's penchant for ethical lapses. During his three-year tenure, Thornburgh triggered the independent counsel investigation of the Department of Housing and Urban Development (HUD) in 1990, initiated two other inquiries in 1989 and 1991 that remain sealed by court order, and represented the Justice Department during Independent Counsel LAWRENCE WALSH's ongoing IRAN-CONTRA investigation. Decisions made by Thornburgh in connection with the Walsh probe proved most influential in blocking prosecution of key figures in the affair.

A native of the Pittsburgh area, Thornburgh was educated at Yale where he received a degree in civil engineering in 1954, and the University of Pittsburgh Law School (law degree, 1957). He worked as attorney for the Aluminum Company of America (1957–1959) before leaving to practice privately in Pittsburgh. Thornburgh was named U.S. Attorney for Western Pennsylvania in 1969. In 1975, he was appointed Assistant U.S. Attorney, heading the criminal division during the administration of President GERALD FORD (1975–1977). Elected Governor of Pennsylvania in 1978, Thornburgh served two terms, the legal limit, resigning in 1986. He accepted an offer to head the Institute of Politics at Harvard's Kennedy School of Government, leaving on August 12, 1988, to assume the duties of attorney general.

In theory, Attorney General Thornburgh and Independent Counsel Walsh were allies, prosecuting possible executive branch misconduct related to the Iran-Contra affair. In reality, Thornburgh also represented the administration for which many Iran-Contra defendants claimed they were acting when they committed violations of the law. Complicating matters was the fact that several national security agencies held that many of the documents relating to the activities of the Iran-Contra defendants contained classified information, and could not be released. Only the attorney general had the authority to override such agency rulings. During preparations for the trial of OLIVER NORTH in January 1989, Judge GERHARD GESELL indicated that he considered many classified documents essential to North's defense. Because Thornburgh refused to permit disclosure of the information in question, Walsh was forced to agree to the dismissal of conspiracy charges against North. Thornburgh had to be pleased by this outcome. The previous November, he had filed a brief supporting North's motion to dismiss the conspiracy count on grounds that the prosecution was seeking to criminalize routine foreign policy debates between the executive and legislative branches of government.

In February, Thornburgh and Walsh attempted to come to an understanding that would allow the remaining charges against North and subsequent defendants to be tried. Walsh agreed to object should the defense attempt to introduce secret information into the trial. Thornburgh promised to refrain from interfering during trial unless he believed national security to be threatened. Both would be relying on the CLASSIFIED INFORMATION AND PROCEDURES ACT (CIPA) of 1980 to facilitate the use of sensitive documents during trial when necessary. The main point of contention remained Thornburgh's interpretation of the term "classified" with respect to intelligence information. Walsh maintained that much of what Thornburgh deemed sensitive was in fact already common knowledge, such as the governments that had assisted the United States in facilitating the arms-for-hostages deal, and the actual location of CIA posts in Central America. Termed "fictional secret" information by Walsh, Thornburgh firmly objected to its release. Whereas the North trial was concluded, the prosecution of CIA agent JOSEPH FERNANDEZ was fatally handicapped by Thornburgh's CIPA filings, and ultimately dismissed in November 1989. After dismissal, Thornburgh released the classified information, and Walsh was able to use it productively in subsequent questioning of Fernandez.

In 1990, Thornburgh requested appointment of a special prosecutor to investigate allegations of fraud and mismanagement against SAMUEL PIERCE, HUD Secretary. Once the Special Division had named ARLIN ADAMS independent counsel, Thornburgh asked for an expansion of the original probe in response to testimony obtained by congressional investigators indicating that Pierce's decisions were influenced by personal and political favoritism. The lengthy HUD investigation extended well beyond Thornburgh's tenure as attorney general. Arlin Adams left the investigation in 1995, and LARRY D. THOMPSON continued the inquiry.

Thornburgh has remained active in public affairs since leaving Washington. In 1995, he joined an international team of distinguished attorneys in an attempt to defend Chinese dissident Wei Jingsheng who was eventually exiled to the United States. In 1996 Thornburgh spoke out in support of Republican efforts to pass legislation limiting the ability of consumers to collect damages from businesses that produce defective products.

References:

Harriger, Katy J. *Independent Justice: The Federal Special Prosecutor in American Politics*. Lawrence: University Press of Kansas, 1992. Chapter 6, "Conflict of Interest," discusses Thornburgh's role in facilitating dismissal of conspiracy charges against Oliver North.

Picharallo, Joe. "Thornburgh Is Asked to Explain Blocking Iran-Contra Data." *Washington Post*, 2 December 1989, sec. A, p. 4.

Savage, David G. "Contrary Interests Provoke Thornburgh-Walsh Clash over North Trial." *Los Angeles Times*, 19 February 1989, sec. A, p. 28.

"Thornburgh Orders Wider Investigation of Pierce." *Orlando Sentinel Tribune*, 30 May 1990, sec. A, p. 6.

Walsh, Lawrence. *Firewall: The Iran-Contra Conspiracy and Cover-up*. New York: W. W. Norton, 1997.

Tower Commission Report (1987). Chaired by former Senator John G. Tower (R-Texas), the Tower Commission examined the IRAN-CONTRA affair, and reported its findings in a 304-page document issued on February 26, 1987. Based on interviews conducted with President RONALD REAGAN, his assistants and Cabinet members, the report found that Iran-Contra was attributable to the president's failure to properly supervise his National Security Council (NSC) staff. NSC staff and White House Chief of Staff Donald Regan were also criticized for failing to make judicious use of the responsibility granted them by the president. Instead of carefully and openly considering their options and possible consequences, they operated in a secretive, conspiratorial manner. The result was the creation of foreign policy initiatives by the NSC that ran counter to the stated policies of the administration itself regarding terrorism and relations with nations that support it. According to the report, the president had an incomplete understanding of the arms-for-hostages arrangement with Iran, and was totally ignorant of the diversion of arms sale profits to the Contras. Because the report supported the concept that the Iran-Contra affair was the product of conspiratorial behavior limited to the NSC, it helped promote the arguments of those who urged a quick end to Independent Counsel LAWRENCE WALSH's Iran-Contra investigation.

The Tower Report indicated that the Iran-Contra arrangements may have violated both the ARMS EXPORT CONTROL ACT (1976) and the NATIONAL SECURITY ACT (1947). The first made it illegal to export arms without a license. Unless the president approved the transactions, arms sales to Iran were illegal. The report, however, concludes that it was likely that the president did consent to the transactions. Even presidential approval of the arrangement would probably not be sufficient, according to the Tower Commission, to comply with the provisions of the National Security Act, which required a finding that such transactions were in the vital interests of the United States.

Aside from White House Chief of Staff Donald Regan, the person with whom the report found most serious fault was National Security Adviser JOHN POINDEXTER. According to the report, Poindexter actively worked to exclude other NSC members form Iran-Contra decisions, misled Secretary of State GEORGE SHULTZ on several occasions, and failed to appreciate the serious legal consequences of arms profit diversion to the Contras.

The Tower Commission study was hampered by an alarming absence of written records concerning NSC meetings, refusal of cooperation by the FBI and the independent counsel office, and invocation of the Fifth Amendment by both OLIVER NORTH and Poindexter. The commission was fortunate in discovering an unexpected source of information—internal NSC computer messages that partially compensated for the lack of written meeting records. The president's inability to recall details relating to Iran-Contra was also noted in the report. While many attributed this to political convenience, others wondered if it might be symptomatic of a pathological condition.

The Tower Commission Report provided the most complete account of the arms sale to Iran that existed in early 1987. It was also of assistance to the independent counsel office in expanding the information base from which investigation could proceed, and integrating evidence that was being discovered. Walsh believed, however, that the report ultimately harmed his efforts to trace the Iran-Contra conspiracy to its origins, and hold the top White House officials responsible for their misconduct. If the Tower Commission was to be believed, malfeasance was largely limited to the NSC. Walsh was to labor another five years in an attempt to disprove this conclusion.

References:

Battiata, Mary. "John Tower and His Arduous Mandate." *Washington Post*, 26 February 1986, sec. B, p. 1.

Gerstenzang, James. "Tower Report Blames Reagan, Aides." *Los Angeles Times*, 27 February 1987, sec. A, p. 1.

Pear, Robert. "The White House Crisis: Tower Inquiry Found There Is Much Reagan
    Can't Recall." *New York Times*, 28 February 1987, sec. A, p. 9.
"The Tower Commission Report; Excerpts: A Crisis of Confidence." *Los Angeles Times*,
    27 February 1987, sec. A, p. 18.
Walsh, Lawrence. *Firewall: The Iran-Contra Conspiracy and Cover-up*. New York: W.
    W. Norton, 1997. In Chapter 5, "The Bramble Bush," Walsh assesses the effect
    of the Tower Commission Report on the independent counsel investigation.
Watson, Russell, and John Barry. "A Stunning Indictment." *Newsweek*, 9 March 1987,
    p. 25. 4,700-word article discusses Tower Commission Report in light of question
    posed by Juvenal's "Satires": "*Quis custodiet ipsos custodes?*" or "Who will
    guard the guardians?"

Travelgate. In May 1993 the CLINTON White House announced the firing of
its travel office staff on grounds of mismanagement. Critics contended that the
dismissals occurred because the Clintons wished to favor an Arkansas firm with
the business. Matters were exacerbated when it was revealed that the White
House request for an FBI investigation of the travel office preceding the firings
was not made according to established procedure. Critics noted that RICHARD
NIXON had used the FBI to help conceal the true nature of the WATERGATE
scandal 20 years earlier. Interest in the "Travelgate" scandal was maintained
when former travel office director Billy Dale was acquitted of embezzlement
charges in 1995; charges were leveled the following year to the effect that
HILLARY CLINTON had pressured White House officials to fire the travel
office staff; and it was revealed that former White House counsel VINCENT
FOSTER was deeply troubled by his involvement in the travel office firings at
the time of his suicide in 1993. In March 1996 the attorney general requested
that WHITEWATER Independent Counsel KENNETH STARR expand his inquiry to include investigation of charges that White House personnel had lied
about Hillary Clinton's involvement in the travel office firings.

It has been maintained that serious mismanagement of the travel office had
been routinely ignored by the press because the office faithfully catered to their
needs over the years. Examination of the office uncovered the fact that contracts
were arranged with private contractors without bids. The contracts themselves
were frequently never even written. In addition, director Billy Dale had apparently appropriated over $50,000 for his personal use. Prior to his trial for em-
bezzlement, he offered a letter to prosecutors offering to return $69,000 and
serve a brief jail sentence. (After the Justice Department refused the settlement
offer, Dale was acquitted.) It was charged that Dale and his staff served as
personal valets for journalists, providing them with premium hotel bookings and
favorite liquors, and maintaining a discreet silence regarding their intimate secrets. Several journalists, including ABC's Sam Donaldson and Jack Nelson of
the *Los Angeles Times*, testified on behalf of Dale at his trial, aiding in his
successful defense. It appeared to some that the clumsy manner in which the

White House handled the firings served to obscure the genuine reasons for them. Similarly, the cries of cronyism that accompanied the White House's replacement of Dale with Little Rock-based Worldwide Travel overshadowed the fact that Worldwide handled $150 million in business each year and enjoyed a reputation as a leader in the field of travel management technology.

Some critics professed to see a wider conspiracy surrounding travelgate. Correspondence was discovered indicating that Hollywood executive and Clinton supporter Harry Thomason and his associate, aircraft consultant Darnell Martens, sought to obtain control of the travel office in order to achieve official status that could be used to launch a more grandiose project involving control of large segments of government aviation. Martens's consulting firm, TRM, maintained that it could save the government millions of dollars by running the government's aiplane fleet more efficiently. It appears that the president had reacted favorably to the Thomason/Martens proposal when it was broached in February 1993. Martens requested that the White House authorize an audit of existing government aircraft with the actual work to be done by Martens's firm. Given this more grandiose scenario, Vince Foster's suicide, and his note alluding to the travel office firings, appear more sinister in nature. The project was halted when a furor erupted following dismissal of the travel office staff. Conspiracy theorists pointed out that both Clintons were involved in this large scheme from the beginning.

In June 1996 the manner in which the Clinton administration had examined FBI files, beginning with Dale's, became an issue of controversy. FILEGATE joined travelgate as a public scandal. In October 1996 Representative William Clinger (R-Pennsylvania), chairman of the House Committee on Government Reform and Oversight, forwarded his committee's findings on both matters to the independent counsel. Clinger suggested that Starr might want to look at the congressional testimony of current or former White House officials Jane Sherburne, Craig Livingstone, Anthony Marceca, William Kennedy, BERNARD NUSSBAUM, and Thomas "Mack" McLarty in order to determine whether perjury and/or obstruction of justice had occurred. Democrats charged that Clinger's communication was politically timed to influence the presidential election.

Starr's investigation of Hillary Clinton's role in the Travelgate affair was hindered by a Supreme Court ruling in June 1998 that extended attorney-client privilege beyond the grave in criminal cases. The 6–3 decision meant that the independent counsel would not gain access to the notes of an attorney representing Vince Foster. The notes, taken nine days before Foster's suicide, were believed to contain information bearing on the case. It was argued before the Court that persons would be less likely to confide in their attorneys if they thought such confidence was likely to be betrayed after their deaths. The Supreme Court's decision reversed a 1997 lower court ruling.

Starr's report to the House of Representatives in September 1998 did not address the travelgate issue.

References:

Packer-Tursman, Judy. "Clinger Sends Travelgate Data to Prosecutor." *Pittsburgh Post-Gazette*, 16 October 1996, sec. A, p. 9.

Roberts, Robert N., and Marion T. Doss, Jr. *From Watergate to Whitewater: The Public Integrity War*. Westport, CT: Praeger, 1997. Chapter 12, "The Clinton Scandals," covers Travelgate.

Thomasson, Dan. "What Kind of Justice Favors the Dead over the Living?" *Houston Chronicle*, 30 June 1998, sec. A, p. 19. Criticizes Supreme Court ruling that blocked Starr's access to notes of Vince Foster's attorney.

" 'Travelgate': Mindless Howls of Cronyism." *Travel Weekly*, 28 June 1993, p. 84. Characterizes White House replacement of travel office staff with Worldwide Travel as wise business decision.

York, Byron. "The Hidden Tale of Travelgate." *Weekly Standard*, 22 January 1996, p. 18. Sees Travelgate as part of a broader conspiracy to create a "kitchen-cabinet Federal Aviation Administration."

Tripp, Linda R. (1949–   ) Pentagon assistant. After working as a White House aide for four years (1991–1995) during the presidencies of GEORGE BUSH and Bill CLINTON, Linda Tripp was transferred to the Pentagon. There she encountered MONICA LEWINSKY, befriended her, and became her confidante. Lewinsky's revelations concerning her sexual affair with the president were taped by Tripp and turned over to the office of Independent Counsel KENNETH STARR. Starr viewed the tapes as evidence that Clinton and Lewinsky had lied during their January 1998 depositions in PAULA JONES's sexual harassment lawsuit. Convinced that Lewinsky had been induced to lie by Clinton, Starr received permission to expand his investigation of Clinton to include the Lewinsky affair. Tripp's tapes became instrumental in Starr's refocused case against the president, which resulted in his impeachment.

Born Linda Rose Carotenuto in Whippany, New Jersey, Tripp attended secretarial school and was working for a catering firm in Montclair when she met Bruce M. Tripp, a biology major at Farleigh Dickinson University. He was an Army operations officer when they were married in 1971. During the next 20 years, Tripp followed her husband to a series of posts, including stints in the Netherlands and Germany, working in whatever government jobs she could land while raising two children. In 1991 she joined the White House secretarial pool after her husband was transferred to Washington. She enjoyed the professionalism of the Bush White House, but apparently disliked the more casual atmosphere of Clinton's. Transferred to the White House counsel's office, Tripp worked for VINCENT FOSTER and BERNARD NUSSBAUM. She found the secrecy surrounding counsel business frustrating. When Lloyd Cutler became White House counsel in 1994, he brought his own secretary. Tripp was left with little to do, and eventually was transferred to the Pentagon where she occupied a windowless cubicle in the basement.

When Lewinsky was transferred to the Pentagon in April 1996, Tripp developed a friendship with her. By the end of the year, Tripp had learned of Lewinsky's affair with Clinton. In March 1997, Tripp was questioned by a *Newsweek* reporter regarding White House aide Kathleen Willey's allegation of sexual misconduct by Clinton. When Tripp offered circumstantial evidence corroborating Willey's account of the incident, Clinton attorney ROBERT BENNETT characterized her as untruthful. It was Bennettt's remark, some maintain, that caused Tripp to document Lewinsky's confessions. Concerned that she might be called to testify in the Paula Jones case, Tripp was determined to possess evidence that would support her deposition statements. In December 1997, Tripp and Lewinsky were subpoened to testify in the Jones matter. On January 7, Lewinsky denied a sexual relationship with the president. Five days later, Tripp contacted the independent counsel's office with taped telephone conversations that contradicted Lewinsky's testimony. Starr, believing that Lewinsky's perjury had been suborned by Clinton, wired Tripp with a microphone the next day in order to obtain additional information. On January 14, Lewinsky presented Tripp with "talking points," proposed testimony that Tripp was being directed to offer at her deposition. Starr regarded this as another attempt by Clinton to suborn perjury.

Tripp's tapes represented important leverage employed by the independent counsel office in forcing the president to admit that his testimony before the Jones attorneys on January 17, 1998, was less than truthful. While this admission helped effectuate his impeachment by the House in December, it proved insufficient to support his removal from office. Tripp's tapes were less effective in supporting the subornation of perjury charge.

Tripp's taping of Lewinsky's conversations subjected her to villification by the press and public. In addition to the obvious betrayal of a friend's confidences implicit in such behavior, the fact that Tripp had attempted to obtain a contract for a book caused many to suspect her motives. Tripp hired an agent in an attempt to repair her public image.

References:

Priest, Dana, and Rene Sanchez. "Once-Trusted Civil Servant at Heart of Scandal." *Washington Post*, 23 January 1998, sec. A, p. 22.

Sciolino, Elaine, and Don Van Natta. "Testing of a President: The Confidant." *New York Times*, 15 March 1998, sec. A, p. 1.

Truman, Harry S (1884–1972) President of the United States, 1945–1952. In 1952, President Truman agreed to the appointment of NEWBOLD MORRIS as special prosecutor to assist Attorney General J. Howard McGrath in investigating misconduct within the Bureau of Internal Revenue (BIR) and the Tax Division of the Justice Department. When Morris's methods were deemed overly aggressive in nature, McGrath fired him. Truman, in turn, dismissed McGrath. The turn of events served to demonstrate the handicap under which an investigator of executive branch misconduct operates when not enjoying independent status. It also illustrated the advantage of presidential appointment: Abusive prosecutors can be summarily dismissed.

By the time that Truman agreed to appoint a special prosecutor, the tax scandals had been rather thoroughly investigated by Congress. Sixty-six internal revenue officers had been dismissed in 1951, including district tax collector James P. Finnegan, a Missouri friend of Truman's. Theron Caudle, Assistant Attorney General for the Tax Division, was removed by Truman and convicted of bribery in 1955. BIR Commissioner Joseph Nunan was also forced to resign. Still, Truman was urged to appoint an outside investigator to examine matters. Truman selected, and received acceptances from, Judge THOMAS F. MURPHY and Philadelphia clergyman Reverend DANIEL POLING. Disagreement over the team's leadership, combined with the opposition of Murphy's associates on the bench, led to Murphy's withdrawal. Poling's resignation followed. Truman then charged his attorney general with naming an assistant to handle the inquiry. Morris, an associate of former New York mayor Fiorello LaGuardia, was appointed. A questionnaire he determined to administer to thousands of federal officials was considered unnecessarily intrusive, and precipitated his dismissal.

Both Morris's dismissal and Truman's firing of McGrath resulted in considerable negative publicity, and helped the Republicans capture the White House in 1952. Truman was able to survive the tax scandal and surrounding events, probably because he himself was not implicated. It also appears that those who were responsible for tax-fixing and bribery were removed and duly prosecuted through normal channels without need for a special prosecutor.

References:

Abels, Jules. *The Truman Scandals*. Chicago: Henry Regnery, 1956. Chapter 1, "President Truman and Corruption," discusses the tax scandal, characterizing Truman as tolerant of corruption due to his association with Kansas City machine boss Tom Pendergast.

Dunar, Andrew J. "All Honorable Men: The Truman Scandals and the Politics of Morality." Ph.D. dissertation, University of Southern California, 1981.

Eastland, Terry. *Ethics, Politics, and the Independent Counsel: Executive Power, Executive Vice 1789–1989*. Washington, D.C.: National Legal Center for the Public Interest, 1989. Chapter 2, "The History before the Law, 1789–1973," covers the Truman tax scandal. Argues that conventional investigation of the matter helps make the case against the need for an independent counsel.

Ferrell, Robert H. *Harry S. Truman and the Modern American Presidency*. Boston: Little, Brown and Company, 1983.

Gosnell, Harold F. *Truman's Crises: A Political Biography of Harry S. Truman*. (Contributions in *Political Science*, No. 33). Westport: Greenwood, 1980.

Harriger, Katy J. *Independent Justice: The Federal Special Prosecutor in American Politics*. Lawrence: University Press of Kansas, 1992 Chapter 2, "Ad Hoc Appointment," discusses the Truman tax scandal. Stresses the value of presidential appointment when special prosecutor proves abusive: In addition to retaining power of removal, the president is forced to accept responsibility for an investigation that might be headed off track.

Tucker, Jr., Jim Guy (1943–) Arkansas Governor, 1992–1996. A participant in WHITEWATER-related transactions during the 1980s, Jim Guy Tucker was among those investigated by Independent Counsel KENNETH STARR who sought his testimony regarding the nature of the CLINTONs' involvement. In 1986, Tucker helped Jim McDOUGAL implement an illegal scheme to purchase land in rural Arkansas for residential development. Ten years later, Starr was successful in convicting Tucker along with the McDougals for bank fraud. Tucker proceeded to mount a legal challenge to Starr's authority as independent counsel that succeeded at the district court level, but was reversed on appeal in 1996. This decision in *United States v. Tucker* 78 F.3d 1313 (8th Cir. 1996) affirmed that an attorney general's referral to an independent counsel is not reviewable by the judiciary. In 1998, Tucker agreed to cooperate with Starr's investigation in return for avoiding a prison sentence.

Born in Oklahoma City, Tucker was educated at Harvard University (B.A., 1964) and the University of Arkansas (J.D., 1968). After practicing law privately with Rose, Barron, Nash, Williamson, Carroll & Clay in Little Rock (1968–70), he worked as prosecuting attorney for Arkansas 6th Judicial District (1971–1972). Between 1973 and 1975, Tucker served as the state's attorney general. In 1977, he was elected to the House of Representatives for one term. He returned to private practice as partner in the firm Tucker & Stafford in 1979. Tucker was elected lieutenant governor in 1991 and governor the following year.

Tucker's involvement in Whitewater stemmed from his collaboration in the 1985 Castle Grande real estate deal with the McDougals. Tucker helped them purchase 1,000 rural acres by participating in a scheme that would allow McDougal to circumvent state and federal banking regulations. The scheme, which involved DAVID HALE's Small Business Investment Corporation, Capital Management Services, consisted of a series of complicated loans that served to conceal the fact that McDougal was investing more of his own bank's funds in the Castle Grande project than the state would allow. In the process, Hale was misusing federal Small Business Administration funds that were intended to assist minorities and the poor. Tucker's role in the scheme included deliberate falsification of loan documents.

Starr targeted Tucker along with the McDougals for their real estate transactions, in order to encourage their cooperation in his investigation of the Clintons. Tucker was indicted for bank fraud with the McDougals in August 1995 and convicted on May 28, 1996. Whereas Jim McDougal began to cooperate with Starr at this point, his wife SUSAN remained silent. Tucker resigned the governorship on July 15 in order to pursue his appeal.

Although District Court Judge Henry Woods ruled that Starr had exceeded his authority in prosecuting Tucker, Appeals Court Judge Pasco M. Bowman II reversed that finding. Speaking for a unanimous three-judge panel, Bowman found that the independent counsel statute did not permit the judiciary to review decisions of the attorney general in this regard. Despite the fact that Tucker was not occupying a position specifically covered by the statute, and was not included in the independent counsel's original charge, his case was related to Whitewater, and the attorney general had properly exercised her discretion in permitting the independent counsel to expand his probe in Tucker's direction. The decision in *United States v. Tucker* served to support the expansion of the independent counsel's authority, and was criticized by those who interpreted the ruling as sanctioning abusive use of the office's power. It should not be permissible, critics contended, for the independent counsel office to employ use of limitless resources in the prosecution of individual citizens, especially when the crimes in question were essentially unrelated to the original subject of inquiry.

In February 1998, following an extended period of illness that necessitated a liver transplant, Tucker agreed to cooperate with Starr's office. In April, however, he attempted to have his conviction overturned, charging juror misconduct. On May 17, 1999, Tucker was ordered to pay $1 million in fines and was sentenced to four years probation. He indicated that he would appeal the decision.

There is no indication that Tucker has supplied Starr's office with information that would tend to implicate the Clintons in Whitewater-related misconduct. Starr's report to the House of Representatives in September 1998 was silent on the matter.

References:

Barnes, Steve. "Arkansas Governor Resigns after Furor." *New York Times*, 16 July 1996, sec. A, p. 10. Describes Tucker's attempt to belatedly rescind his resignation and take a leave of absence instead.

"Former Arkansas Governor Alleges Juror Bias in Fraud Convictions." *White Collar Crime Reporter* (April 1998): 12. Includes a chronology of the case. Tucker charged that one juror neglected to mention that her fiancé had been refused clemency by him.

Schmidt, Susan. "Ex-Governor to Cooperate with Starr; Tucker Plea Bargains in Whitewater Case." *Washington Post*, 21 February 1998, sec. A, p. 1.

Young, Rick. "The Castle Grande Deal" from the PBS television program *Frontline*, episode "Once Upon a Time in Arkansas." www.pbs.org/wgbh/pages/frontline. Summarizes Tucker's role in Whitewater/Castle Grande chronology.

U

United States v. Germaine 99 U.S. 508 (1878). By maintaining that inferior officers may be appointed by courts of law or heads of departments, *United States v. Germaine* belongs to the body of case law that serves to legitimize the manner in which independent counsels have been appointed. This case defined inferior offices as those that are not mentioned in Article II section 2 of the Constitution.

The defendant in this matter was a surgeon appointed by the Commissioner of Pensions to examine persons applying for pensions. Such arrangement was provided for in an act passed on March 3, 1873, and codified in Revised Statutes section 4777. For each examination performed, the surgeon was paid $2. The state of Maine charged that the surgeon was an officer of the United States, and therefore not entitled to collection of such fees. Citing an act of 1825, codified as 4 Stat. 118, the state indicted the surgeon for embezzlement. The Supreme Court received the case after the Circuit Court for the District of Maine certified that there was a division of opinion concerning the matter.

Justice Samuel F. Miller ruled that civil surgeons appointed by the Commissioner of Pensions are not officers of the United States, but rather agents or employees entitled to payment collected. Furthermore, the Commissioner of Pensions, stated Miller, is not the head of a department, as contended by the plaintiff. The term "head of department," as stated in Article II section 2, is synonymous with "principal officer," and applies to major subdivisions of the executive branch. (Addressing the Assistant Attorney General arguing the case for the government, Miller cites the newly created Department of Justice as an example of such a department.) Rather, Miller ruled, the Commissioner of Pensions was an inferior officer who may be appointed by a court of law or department head, as specified in the Constitution's Appointments Clause. Plaintiff's argument citing the case *United States v. Hartwell* 6 Wall. 385 (1867) was judged irrelevant, because the defendant in that case was an officer of the government, having been appointed by the acting head of the Treasury Department.

In his discussion, Miller clearly differentiated between principal and inferior officers of the United States, and the manner in which each is to be appointed, according to the Constitution. Crafters of the independent counsel statute relied upon such distinctions in providing for judicial appointment of what they conceived to be an inferior officer of the government.

References:

Eastland, Terry. *Ethics, Politics, and the Independent Counsel: Executive Power, Executive Vice 1789–1989*. Washington, D.C.: National Legal Center for the Public Interest, 1989. Chapter 8, "Is the Law Constitutional," mentions *Germaine* as defining the term "inferior officers," but argues that the definition is still subject to varying interpretation.

O'Keefe, Constance, and Peter Safirstein. "Fallen Angels, Separation of Powers, and the Saturday Night Massacre: An Examination of the Practical, Constitutional, and Political Tensions in the Special Prosecutor Provisions of the Ethics in Government Act." *Brooklyn Law Review* 49 (1982): 113–147. Cites *Germaine* as providing authoritative definition of "inferior officers." Argues for continued existence of independent counsel statute.

Simon, Donald J. "The Constitutionality of the Special Prosecutor Law." *University of Michigan Journal of Law Reform* 16 (1982): 45–74. Cites *Germaine* as authoritative in determining how inferior officers may be appointed. Defends constitutionality of independent counsel statute.

V

Von Kann, Curtis Emery (1942–) Independent Counsel, Eli Segal investigation, 1997. On August 21, 1997, Independent Counsel Curtis Emery von Kann issued a report that declared that former White House administrative assistant ELI SEGAL should not be prosecuted for simultaneously raising funds for a private group and heading the AmeriCorps program. The investigation had been sealed by court order; its existence was not discovered until the report was released on December 19, 1997. Von Kann asserted that technical violation of conflict-of-interest regulations existed, but because there was neither criminal intent nor personal gain involved, prosecution was not warranted. His investigation cost $381,712.

Von Kann served as an associate judge on the Washington, D.C. Superior Court (resigning in 1995) and practiced privately with the D.C. firm of Ross, Dixon & Masback (1996) before being named independent counsel. He has also worked with JAMS/Endispute, an arbitration organization. In 1994, Von Kann's statements in a *Legal Times* article, citing neglect of America's cities as cause for intractable urban crime, were reprinted in the *Congressional Record*.

In February 1999, Von Kann appeared before a Senate panel in order to advocate reform of the independent counsel statute as an alternative to its demise. Von Kann called for time limits to be placed on investigations and rotation of judges who serve on the Special Division that appoints independent counsels.

References:

"Independent Counsel Clears Ex-Clinton Aide in Funds Probe." *Chicago Tribune*, 20 December 1997, p. N6.

Morgan, Dan. "Restraint Urged on Changing Counsel Law." *Washington Post*, 25 February 1999, p. A4.

W

Wallace, W. Lawrence (1949–) Assistant Attorney General, 1985–1986. The subject of an independent counsel investigation sealed by court order, Wallace was exonerated by Independent Counsel JAMES HARPER in December 1987. Charged with failing to file personal income tax returns during a two-year period, subsequent investigation revealed that Wallace had filed the returns when informed they were due. In addition, the government had suffered no harm, because Wallace was entitled to a refund both years.

A native of Raleigh, North Carolina, Wallace was educated at Harvard Law School and worked for General Motors and North Carolina's Department of Natural Resources before being appointed to the Justice Department in 1979. When named assistant attorney general in 1985, Wallace became only the second African American to serve at that level. As assistant in charge of the department's management, Wallace supervised administrative services, budget, finances, and computer systems until resigning in November 1986. After leaving, Wallace joined the Washington office of Drinker, Biddle & Reath where he specialized in environmental law.

Investigation of Wallace was begun by Independent Counsel CARL RAUH who was forced to resign during the inquiry's early stages due to conflict of interest. After several months, Harper, an Atlanta tax attorney, assumed responsibility for the probe. It was originally alleged that Wallace had failed to file income tax returns for three years during the period 1979–1985, but it was discovered that a form had been received for one of the years in question. On December 17, 1987, Harper reported that the misdemeanor violations did not warrant further action.

The Wallace investigation was one of two such sealed inquiries that were being pursued during that time period. Details of the second probe, concluded in 1989 without indictment, were never revealed.

References:

Kurtz, Howard. "2 Independent Counsels Are Secretly Appointed; Justice Department Ex-Aide Reportedly Probed." *Washington Post*, 18 December 1986, sec. A, p. 10.

Marcus, Ruth. "Justice Official Won't Be Charged in Tax Case." *Washington Post*, 19 December 1987, sec. A, p. 3.

"Meese Names Black Assistant Attorney General." *Washington Post*, 10 August 1985, sec. A, p. 9.

Walsh, Lawrence (1912–   ) Independent Counsel, Iran-Contra investigation, 1986–1992. A lifelong Republican, Lawrence Walsh was the special prosecutor investigating a series of allegations against the REAGAN administration known as the IRAN-CONTRA affair. The attorney general appointed Walsh Special Prosecutor in late 1986, not long after rumors began circulating that the United States government had been selling arms to Iran, a government President Reagan earlier had condemned for supporting terrorists. When Walsh concluded his investigation six and one-half years later, he had spent $35.7 million and had indicted five members of the Reagan administration, three private citizens, and one corporation on felony or misdemeanor charges in connection with the scandal. Although Walsh later won convictions of several defendants in the scandal, many were later overturned on appeal. Several other defendants pled guilty following lengthy plea bargaining. In addition, one Reagan Cabinet member, Caspar Weinberger, Secretary of Defense, was pardoned by President GEORGE BUSH shortly before he left office. In all, Walsh had served as Special Prosecutor more than four times as long as the two principal WATERGATE scandal prosecutors, ARCHIBALD COX and LEON JAWORSKI, combined.

A native of New York, Walsh spent most of his professional career in that city. He earned undergraduate and law degrees from Columbia University. He began his legal career on the staff of the newly elected Manhattan District Attorney, Thomas E. Dewey. After Dewey was elected Governor of New York, he hired Walsh as assistant and later chief counsel. In 1954, President Dwight Eisenhower named Walsh a federal District Court judge in Manhattan. Later, Walsh was appointed chief deputy to Attorney General William Rogers, where they worked together in the Little Rock, Arkansas, school desegregation case. In the 1960s Walsh joined a major Wall Street law firm where he quickly rose to prominence and was widely considered to be among the top attorneys practicing corporate law. This undoubtedly contributed to his being elected to head the AMERICAN BAR ASSOCIATION. By the time of his appointment as Special Prosecutor, Walsh was in his mid-70s, semi-retired, and living in Oklahoma City.

By the time Walsh took office, the Iran-Contra scandal already had attracted three governmental investigations: inquiries from committees in each house of Congress plus the three-member "TOWER COMMISSION," which was created by and reported to President Reagan. Walsh went quickly to work assembling a staff of nearly 30 attorneys, plus a team of FBI and IRS investigators nearly as large. As a manager, Walsh generally gave subordinates maximum flexibility. He assigned a former law firm partner, ROBERT FISKE, JR,, primary responsibility for making many of the hiring decisions. In addition, Walsh organized his staff of attorneys into teams with jurisdiction based upon the nature of their investigation.

With the use of a federal grand jury, the Special Prosecutor's Office initially indicted four persons, including two members of President Reagan's National Security Council team, Vice Admiral JOHN POINDEXTER, national security advisor, and Lieutenant Colonel OLIVER NORTH, a Poindexter subordinate and deputy director for political-military affairs. Also indicted were RICHARD SECORD, a retired Air Force major general, and ALBERT HAKIM, an Iranian-born businessman. The four were charged with committing an array of crimes, ranging from perjury, theft of public funds, and conspiring to obstruct justice, to diverting public funds from munitions sales to Iran to arm the Contra rebels in Nicaragua.

Before taking the North case to trial, Walsh had to defeat a pair of legal challenges. First, the Reagan administration and defense attorneys failed to overturn the independent counsel law by arguing that Walsh had unconstitutionally attempted to deny executive powers granted the president. Later, defense attorneys failed in an effort to have the charges dismissed because they violated the defendants' fifth amendment rights against self-incrimination.

Meanwhile Walsh suffered a serious setback: Citing national security protection, the White House, supported by the Justice Department, declined to release important classified information pertinent to prosecuting the case. Thus, lacking essential evidence, Walsh was forced to withdraw the two more serious charges of diverting funds, and conspiring to obstruct justice.

Finally, with the pretrial challenges dispatched, in May of 1989, Walsh won a felony conviction against North, who was put on probation, fined $150,000, and sentenced to community service. However, a year later North won an appeal overturning each of his convictions. The verdict maintained that IMMUNITY protection granted North for his testimony before congressional committees contradicted his Fifth Amendment protection against self-incrimination.

Walsh confronted a similar scenario in his subsequent prosecution of Poindexter. Walsh won conviction, including a six-month prison sentence, on all five charges against the former National Security Advisor. On appeal, the conviction was dismissed because of the use of the defendant's congressional testimony against him during his subsequent trial.

Charges pending against subsequent Iran-Contra defendants were resolved with plea bargains that produced comparatively light misdemeanor sentences.

Next, Walsh prosecuted the most senior Reagan administration official involved in the Iran-Contra scandal, Secretary of Defense CASPAR WEINBERGER. In 1992 Walsh secured an indictment charging Weinberger with five felony counts involving perjury and obstructing justice. In addition, four days before the 1992 election, Walsh outraged his fellow Republicans by adding a charge to those pending against Weinberger. The allegation stemmed from a note Weinberger had written in 1986 that apparently contradicted President Bush's assertions that as Vice President he had never been involved in the arms-for-hostages program. However, in the end, President Bush defeated Walsh. On the evening of December 24, 1992 President Bush presented a Christmas present to Weinberger and five other Iran-Contra defendants in the form of a pardon. Walsh, outraged, responded by renewing allegations that President Bush participated in a cover-up.

Finally, saying that it would be too difficult to put a case together, Walsh declined to accuse Attorney General EDWIN MEESE III of perjury. Moreover, others said that had he lived, the late WILLIAM CASEY, a former director of the Central Intelligence Agency, would have been indicted on perjury and conspiracy charges in connection with the scandal. So, on August 6, 1993, Walsh submitted his final report on the Iran-Contra scandal, resigned his position, and returned home to Oklahoma City.

Unlike his famous predecessors in the Watergate scandal, Walsh was appointed and served under provisions of the ETHICS IN GOVERNMENT ACT of 1978, which Congress passed partially in response to President Richard Nixon's famous "Saturday Night Massacre" firing of Special Prosecutor Archibald Cox. Although President Reagan requested a special prosecutor be appointed to investigate Iran-Contra allegations, jurisdiction for doing so was in the hands of a panel of three federal appeals court judges. The objective of such a system clearly was to prevent another "Saturday Night Massacre." Hence, Walsh was granted a measure of independence.

However, Walsh did confront serious, and at times insurmountable, obstacles. First came a successful claim of national security that was used to shelter essential White House documents from the Special Prosecutor's office. Failure to win dismissal of this case forced Walsh to drop some of his most serious charges. Second, his efforts received unwelcomed interference from immunity granted key defendants while giving testimony during congressional hearings on the Iran-Contra scandal. Walsh, aware of this pending serious problem, sought unsuccessfully to have Congress delay its hearings until after he had finished his case. The action became the basis for attorneys for both North and Poindexter winning overturn of their convictions on appeal.

References:

Harriger, Katy J. *Independent Justice: The Federal Special Prosecutor in American Politics.* Lawrence: University Press of Kansas (1992). This is an analytic study of the Federal Special Prosecutor's Office throughout the twentieth century.

Walsh, Lawrence. *Firewall: The Iran-Contra Conspiracy and Cover-up.* New York: Norton, 1997.

—ROBERT E. DEWHIRST

Walsh, Thomas J. (1859–1933) U.S. Senator (D-Montana), 1913–1933. As a member of the Senate's Public Lands and Surveys Committee, Thomas Walsh assumed the role of chief congressional prosecutor investigating the TEAPOT DOME scandal in 1923. Ensuing revelations regarding the transfer of government oil to private developers prompted the appointment of special prosecutors ATLEE POMERENE and OWEN J. ROBERTS by President CALVIN COOLIDGE in 1924.

The son of Irish immigrants, Walsh was born in Two Rivers, Wisconsin. After teaching school for several years, he studied law at the University of Wisconsin (LL.B., 1884). He practiced with his brother in Redfield, South Dakota, for six years, before opening his own office in Helena, Montana, in 1890. Walsh built his practice by defending laborers, and earned a reputation as the state's most successful prosecutor of lawsuits against mining companies. After failing to win election to Congress in 1906, Walsh was chosen by the state legislature in 1912 to represent Montana in the Senate.

Walsh was not a conservationist. In fact, he had advocated the leasing of oil reserves in the past. Walsh also possessed a sympathetic understanding of the ranching and prospecting skills possessed by self-made frontiersmen like Secretary of Interior ALBERT FALL. Nevertheless, when progressive Senator Robert La Follette (R-Wisconsin) searched the Public Lands Committee for someone to lead the investigation of the Teapot Dome matter, Walsh's reputation for integrity made him an outstanding candidate. Already occupied with numerous committee assignments and facing a Republican majority on the Public Lands Committee, Walsh at first represented La Follette's cause in a rather perfunctory manner. Under his conscientious questioning, however, it was discovered that Fall had received $100,000 from Pan American Petroleum owner EDWARD DOHENY, one of the developers who benefited from the oil transfer. This revelation transformed the Teapot Dome affair from a minor concern to a major scandal. Witnesses, once reluctant to speak, now felt compelled to testify. Republican loyalists on the committee, such as Irvine Lenroot (R-Wisconsin) and Reed Smoot (R-Utah), could no longer attempt to portray the matter as insignificant. The criticism of the Republican press no longer appeared justified by circumstances. Walsh and La Follette were vindicated.

Coolidge's February 1924 appointment of special prosecutors to investigate the oil transfers was a direct result of Walsh's success. On June 6, 1924, Walsh forwarded the majority report of the Public Lands Committee to the Senate. In it, Fall was charged with corruption for his role in the oil transfers, but Walsh was scrupulous in drawing conclusions. His judicious approach angered as many Democrats who wanted to continue the crusade as Republicans who wished to bury the matter. The Walsh report was of use to Democrats who wished to use Teapot Dome as a campaign issue in the 1924 elections, but it did not prove decisive.

As the trials resulting from the investigations of special prosecutors Pomerene and Roberts drew to a close in 1928, Walsh emerged as a serious presidential contender. In addition to the national reputation he enjoyed thanks to his work on the Teapot Dome investigation, Walsh was viewed as a logical compromise candidate who could reconcile the forces supporting William McAdoo of California and New York's Al Smith. Walsh supported Prohibition like McAdoo and was Catholic like Smith. In addition, his appeal was not restricted to either the urban northeast or the rural south, and he was popular with the workers. In March 1927, McAdoo withdrew as a candidate and threw his support behind Walsh. Encouraged, Walsh began to campaign in earnest. He fared poorly in the primaries, however, and left the race in May.

Walsh remained a Democratic leader in the Senate. A staunch supporter of Franklin Roosevelt, he was rewarded with appointment as attorney general in 1932. His sudden death on March 2, 1933, preceded his assuming office.

References:

National Cyclopedia of American Biography, volume 24, pp.10–11.
Noggle, Burl. *Teapot Dome: Oil and Politics in the 1920's*. Baton Rouge: Louisiana State University Press, 1962.

Watergate. The political scandal that resulted from the break-in at Democratic Party headquarters on June 17, 1972, fueled the drive to create an independent counsel mechanism, and memory of the affair helped sustain the office's existence over the next two decades in the face of mounting criticism.

When revelations by Watergate burglar James McCord and presidential counsel John Dean implicated the White House in an attempt to conceal the true nature of the affair, President RICHARD NIXON was forced to agree to the appointment of a special prosecutor. ARCHIBALD COX assumed the post. Although technically an employee of the Justice Department, his charter allowed him considerable freedom to pursue his investigation. On July 16, 1973, it was revealed that Nixon had taped all White House telephone conversations. Cox's effort to obtain these tapes resulted in his dismissal in what became known as the "Saturday Night Massacre" of October 20, 1973. The subsequent furor led to the appointment of Special Prosecutor LEON JAWORSKI, whose continued investigation implicated the president and prompted his resignation on August 8, 1974. While the last two Watergate Special Prosecutors, HENRY RUTH and CHARLES RUFF, concluded prosecutions and prepared their final report, Congress labored to create a statutory independent counsel mechanism that would prevent future Watergates.

It has been argued that Watergate demonstrated that existing remedies were capable of providing justice in the face of widespread executive branch misconduct. The Watergate Special Prosecuting Force (WSPF), assisted by federal Judge JOHN SIRICA, the Senate's Select Committee on Watergate chaired by SAM ERVIN, the investigative press and public opinion combined to uncover the true nature of the scandal and apply appropriate penalties. Nevertheless, public confidence in the integrity of its public servants had been seriously damaged. It was deemed necessary to institute reform that would guard against repetition of such misconduct. Over two years had passed before justice was served. Nixon had been able to conceal the matter long enough to secure his re-election in 1972, and came very close to burying the truth permanently. His ability to fire Cox raised conflict-of-interest concerns that could not be answered within the existing governmental system. Even if the Justice Department was capable of conducting an impartial investigation of White House malfeasance, the appearance of conflict of interest would always present a problem, especially with Watergate a recent memory.

The impression made by Watergate on the public psyche was immense. It has been widely regarded as the most serious political scandal of the twentieth century. The name "Watergate" was affixed to the scandal because the break-in that precipitated it occurred at the Watergate Office Building in Washington, D.C. The term, however, quickly entered the language as a synonym for outrageous public behavior. Every ethical lapse by public officials became another "Watergate"—"gate" alone became a suffix attached to any noun descriptive of public scandal in order to evoke the memory of Watergate's severity—hence TRAVELGATE, FILEGATE, and Zippergate (some journalists' term for the LEWINSKY affair). It is not surprising, therefore, that many believed the existing governmental framework needed to be altered in order to allow for proper investigation of executive-branch misconduct.

Between 1973 and 1978, Congress labored continually in order to craft a mechanism that would facilitate investigation of the executive branch yet avoid violating the constitutional principle of separation of powers. In December 1973, the Hart-Bayh (S.2611), Taft-Hruska (S.2642), and Percy-Baker (S.2734) bills all made serious attempts to achieve this goal. Sam Ervin proposed a permanent prosecutor bill the following year. It would take several years, however, before fundamental questions regarding the new mechanism's nature and jurisdiction could be resolved. Would only the executive branch be the subject of inquiry, or should Congress also be covered? Should the creation exist as a permanent Office of Public Attorney, or would a temporary mechanism be preferable? In the end, the AMERICAN BAR ASSOCIATION and COMMON CAUSE helped fine-tune Senator ABRAHAM RIBICOFF's Public Officials Integrity Act of 1977 to create a statute calling for judicial appointment of an independent counsel, the process to be triggered by the attorney general. The continuing influence of Watergate is reflected in the fact that much criticism over the next several years focused on the role of the attorney general. It was alleged that the attorney general exercized too much influence over the process. Such conflict of interest, it was charged, should not be countenanced. It was unlikely, however, that the mechanism could ever have passed constitutional muster, as it did in *MORRISON v. OLSON* (1988), without an element of control exercised by the executive branch.

Reauthorization of the independent counsel statute in 1982 and 1987 continued to address the issue of the role played by the attorney general. The specter of Watergate caused many to reject the concept of an executive branch investigation of itself. As Watergate receded in memory, however, it became easier to find fault with the length, cost, and invasiveness of independent counsel investigations such as IRAN-CONTRA and WHITEWATER, especially when they appeared to be employed for political purposes. Once both Democrats and Republicans had suffered through years of excruciating examination by special prosecutors with unlimited resources, even Watergate began to appear an insufficient motivation for continuation of the office. Press and public appeared to concur.

Reauthorization hearings held in 1999 still produced those like Senator CARL LEVIN, and former independent counsels ARTHUR CHRISTY and CURTIS EMERY VON KANN who invoked Watergate's memory while arguing for the continuation of the independent counsel in some form; but they were in the minority. Perhaps if Independent Counsel LAWRENCE WALSH had not been thwarted by President GEORGE BUSH's Christmas Eve pardon in 1992, the Iran-Contra investigation might have implicated a White House as thoroughly as Watergate had, which might have resurrected popular support for the institution, and ensured its survival for another decade or two.

References:

Ben-Veniste, Richard, and George Frampton Jr. *Stonewall: The Real Story of the Watergate Prosecution.* New York: Simon and Schuster, 1977.

Bertozzi, Mark. "The Federal Special Prosecutor: Too Special?" *Federal Bar News & Journal* 29 (1982): 222–230.

Doyle, James. *Not above the Law: The Battles of Watergate Prosecutors Cox and Jaworski.* New York: Morrow, 1977.

Harriger, Katy J. *Independent Justice: The Federal Special Prosecutor in American Politics.* Lawrence: University Press of Kansas, 1992. Chapter 2, "Ad Hoc Appointment," discusses Watergate's influence on the creation of the independent counsel statute. Despite the "Saturday Night Massacre," Harriger argues that presidential appointment of special prosecutors resulted in healthy suspicion and vigilance by the Congress, courts, press, and public. This facilitated both support and proper oversight of the special prosecutor.

Weinberger, Caspar W. (1917–   ) former Secretary of Defense, 1981–1987. Weinberger took both his bachelor and law degrees from Harvard before going on to serve as an Army officer in the Pacific during World War II. Following the war, he joined a San Francisco law firm and became involved in California politics, taking up the post of Republican Party Chairman for the state in 1962. In the NIXON administration he held several high-ranking positions, including Chairman of the Federal Trade Commission and Secretary of Health, Education, and Welfare. However, it was his directorship of the Office of Management and Budget that earned him the nickname "Cap the Knife" because he drastically cut federal programs and spending. Returning to private practice, Weinberger served as general counsel for the Bechtel Corporation before being tapped by

REAGAN for the position of Secretary of Defense. In that post, he oversaw a massive military buildup in the early 1980s, was a strong proponent of the Strategic Defense Initiative ("Star Wars"), and attempted to end the nation's post-Vietnam reluctance to use military force in its foreign policy. He resigned as Secretary of Defense in December 1987 in the midst of the Iran-Contra affair.

In 1985, REAGAN administration officials discussed the possibility of trying to make connections with moderate factions in Iran to better relations with that nation once the Ayatollah Khomeini died. The sale of arms to Iran for its war with Iraq was considered one way to improve relations and make contacts. In the meantime, the arms sales might help with the release of American hostages being held by pro-Iranian factions in Lebanon. Weinberger objected to any arms-for-hostages deals with Iran. He advised the President that shipments of arms to Iran were illegal. Since 1979, the United States had barred weapon sales to Iran and in 1984 had placed Iran on the list of nations sponsoring terrorism, making sales to that country illegal under the ARMS EXPORT CONTROL ACT.

In spite of the opposition of Weinberger and Secretary of State GEORGE SHULTZ, the administration began shipping arms to Iran through Israel in August 1985. While Weinberger continued to oppose the change in policy, he eventually acquiesced and ordered the Department of Defense to provide the necessary arms. In November 1985, National Security Adviser ROBERT McFARLANE asked Weinberger for 500 Hawk missiles. Israel would sell its missiles to Iran and then the United States would replenish the Israeli stocks. Weinberger passed McFarlane's request on to Colin Powell, wanting to know about the legality and availability of the missiles. Weinberger reported back to McFarlane that to carry out the plan would require Congressional notification (and later he also told the president that transferring arms through Israel would not make it legal). McFarlane informed Weinberger that Reagan planned to go ahead without notifying Congress (in violation of the NATIONAL SECURITY ACT).

In late December 1985, Reagan administration officials made the decision to deal directly with Iran rather than go through Israel anymore. Thus, CIA shipments of covert arms to Iran were needed. Weinberger continued to object, but through Powell he directed the Department of Defense to make the missiles available to the CIA. The Department sold the missiles to the CIA, but Weinberger insisted that the Department was not to be involved directly in shipping arms to Iran. (The CIA then sold the arms to RICHARD SECORD's Enterprise Corporation, which in turn sold the arms to Iran.) On three occasions the Department sold missiles to the CIA (in May 1986, Hawk missile parts were sold; in February and October of that year TOW missiles were sold).

While giving testimony in 1987 (before the TOWER COMMISSION and Select Committees on Iran-Contra), Weinberger withheld information from members of Congress. In regard to the arms sales, he portrayed McFarlane and the NSC as running a rogue operation within the government. He said that neither he, nor high-level officials in the administration (including the president) had known about the sales. The investigation of Independent Counsel LAWRENCE WALSH later concluded that while opposing the arms sales, Weinberger's actions before Congress were an attempt to cover-up and protect a president who had violated U.S. laws regarding arms sales, violated his own policy, and failed to notify Congress as was required. In particular, Weinberger lied about his knowledge regarding the proposed or actual arms shipments to Iran during 1985–1986.

Weinberger also denied to Congress the existence of his own detailed diary notes. Walsh's investigative team only obtained the notes in 1991, after two lengthy searches through Weinberger's papers in the Library of Congress. By placing the notes with the unclassified portion of his personal papers (when in fact, they should have undergone a classification review and been classified), Weinberger made it difficult to locate them. Furthermore, Weinberger's permission was needed to look at the materials. Walsh interpreted these actions as a deliberate attempt to hide the notes.

When discovered, the notes indicated that Weinberger did not have only vague information about the proposed and actual shipment of arms to Iran as he had claimed. Rather he had detailed information, and had been kept informed constantly. He had received detailed intelligence reports disclosing that arms were the currency in American deals with Iran, and he knew by October 1985 that OLIVER NORTH was involved in the sale of arms to Iran. His notes further revealed that high-level administration officials had been aware of the sales and that they had held meetings in November 1986 to protect themselves and the president regarding the possible illegality of the arms sales. Weinberger's notes also revealed that he knew about the Saudi contributions to the Contras though the notes did not indicate that the Secretary of Defense was aware of North's Contra resupply operation or other activities on that end of the Iran-Contra affair.

Because Weinberger's notes went undiscovered for so long, he was not charged with any crime until 1992. At that point he was indicted on five counts of lying to Congress primarily with regard to his knowledge of the arms sales to Iran. The five felony counts included: obstruction of a congressional investigation by concealing and withholding relevant notes, making false statements to Congress regarding his knowledge of Saudi funding to the Contras, perjury before Congress regarding his knowledge of the planned shipment of Hawk missiles to Iran in November 1985, perjury before Congress regarding replenishing missiles that Israel had shipped to Iran, and making false statements to the Office of the Independent Counsel and the Federal Bureau of Investigation regarding his notetaking. Each count carried a maximum penalty of five years in prison and $250,000 in fines. He pled not guilty to all charges.

Following the original indictment, the presiding judge later dismissed the obstruction charge regarding the concealment of notes. Walsh was determined to prosecute Weinberger. First, Weinberger had gone out of his way to hide his notes and had repeatedly denied their existence. Secondly, Walsh wanted to show that the Iran-Contra affair was not simply a rogue operation carried out by North and the NSC. Rather, North's efforts had been authorized by those higher up. Thus, the Iran-Contra affair encompassed a government conspiracy by the executive branch to evade Congressional oversight and was followed by a concerted cover-up by top officials. The cover-up included Weinberger even though he had continually opposed the sale of arms to Iran. Walsh therefore sought, and received, a supplemental indictment with a false statements charge. This time the judge dismissed the charge because it had exceeded the statute of limitations.

In December 1992, President Bush pardoned Weinberger less than two weeks before he was to stand trial on the remaining charges. The pardon was unusual because Weinberger had not yet been convicted of anything. To many, the pardon confirmed the existence of a cover-up and especially President Bush's knowledge of it. (Weinberger's defense team planned to call Bush as a witness.) As Vice President, Bush had repeatedly insisted that he had been out of the loop on Iran-Contra, but his notes indicated otherwise. Bush's own diary was found only after Walsh had announced the conclusion of his investigation in 1993.

References:

Draper, Theodore. *A Very Thin Line: The Iran-Contra Affair.* New York: Hill & Wang, 1991.
Final Report of the Independent Counsel for Iran/Contra Matters. GPO: Washington, D.C., 1993.
Walsh, Lawrence E. *Firewall: The Iran-Contra Conspiracy and Cover-Up.* New York: W. W. Norton & Company, 1997.

—JACLYN STANKE

Whitewater. A 230-acre tract of land in rural Arkansas purchased in 1978 for residential development, "Whitewater" became the basis of an investigation that extended over five years, exceeded $35 million in cost and occupied two different independent counsels. The perceived excessiveness of the inquiry did much to turn public opinion against the independent counsel mechanism. Because of Whitewater, many Democrats came to view independent counsel investigations largely as political witch-hunts, a characterization already common among Republicans after IRAN-CONTRA.

In June 1978, the McDOUGALS and CLINTONs borrowed $203,000 to finance the purchase of land along the White River in Northern Arkansas. Susan McDougal named it "Whitewater." The Whitewater Development Corporation hoped to build and sell vacation homes on the land they had obtained. Unfortunately, land values fell during the 1980s, and the Whitewater venture failed. Jim McDougal proceeded to obtain the Bank of Kingston in 1980 and the Woodruff Savings & Loan in 1982. They were renamed the Madison Bank & Trust and Madison Guaranty Savings & Loan, respectively. What ensued was a series of intricately involved loans intended to conceal financial losses, avoid banking regulations, and finance additional real estate investments. It was hoped that a new project—the 1985 Castle Grande development, south of Little Rock—would produce profits, enabling Whitewater investors to recoup their losses and realize substantial profits. Instead, bank examiners uncovered aspects of a scheme that involved misuse of DAVID HALE's Small Business Administration (SBA) lending company, extension of unsecured loans, and establishment of "shell" corporations to conceal violations of banking regulations.

HILLARY CLINTON, a member of Little Rock's Rose Law Firm during the 1980s, performed legal work for Madison Guaranty. As a result, she was believed to be more knowledgeable than her husband regarding McDougal's financial transactions. By July 1986, the McDougals were forced to relinquish control of their bank. Jim McDougal was indicted for bank fraud in 1989, and tried and acquitted in 1990. During Bill Clinton's campaign for the presidency, questions were raised concerning the Whitewater investments. It wasn't until January 1993 that McDougal bought out Clinton's interest in Whitewater for $1,000. Six months later, removal of files from the office of White House attorney and former Rose Law firm associate VINCENT FOSTER following his suicide renewed interest in Whitewater.

Congress began investigation of the Clintons' Whitewater involvement in 1994. At the same time, Attorney General JANET RENO initiated an independent counsel investigation by appointing ROBERT FISKE to probe the matter. The Senate Banking Committee concentrated on the Clinton administration's contacts with the Resolution Trust Corporation, the agency responsible for examining what remained of McDougal's failed Madison Guaranty & Trust. The hearings that followed cost Deputy Treasury Secretary ROGER ALTMAN and Treasury General Counsel JEAN HANSON their jobs. Fiske, who had been appointed during a lapse in the independent counsel statute's existence, issued a preliminary report on June 30. He found no evidence of criminal misconduct. By this point, Whitewater had provided sufficient motivation for renewing the independent counsel statute. In August, KENNETH STARR was appointed by the Special Division, replacing Fiske who was deemed insufficiently independent, having been appointed by the attorney general. Critics of Starr's appointment charged that Special Division Judge DAVID SENTELLE had been unduly influenced by Clinton's political enemies during the appointment process.

Starr's examination of Whitewater began with a flurry of indictments against Clinton associates WEBSTER HUBBELL, JIM GUY TUCKER, and the McDougals. Although several convictions were obtained, these targets did not provide enough information to charge the Clintons. Susan McDougal in particular proved an especially recalcitrant witness, opting to serve a jail sentence rather than testify. Starr's probe gradually stretched well beyond the confines of the Arkansas real estate community. Approved expansions of his probe encompassed controversies involving dismissal of White House travel office employees (TRAVELGATE), and the questionable use of FBI files by the administration (FILEGATE). Charges that Clinton had used Arkansas law enforcement officers to procure women for him (Troopergate) during the time he was governor were also investigated. PAULA JONES's sexual harassment lawsuit led Starr to examine the allegations surrounding those deposed, specifically the testimony of former White House intern MONICA LEWINSKY.

What began as an investigation of an obscure real estate venture in Arkansas had become a lurid examination of the president's sexual behavior and his efforts to avoid its disclosure. Because those efforts included misleading/perjurious testimony before a grand jury and suspected attempts at influencing the testimony of others, Clinton's impeachment was effected. Specific Whitewater allegations faded as the Lewinsky-related drama unfolded.

Many Whitewater questions remain. Missing records, faulty memories and silent witnesses prevent a thorough understanding of the Clintons' involvement in the matter. Perhaps more important is the fact that the matter, decades old, never captured the interest of the public, and few would maintain that it justified the investment of resources devoted to its detailed examination. It is anticipated that the independent counsel will issue a report addressing Whitewater before he closes his office. His report to the House of Representatives in September 1998 was devoted almost exclusively to the Lewinsky affair. Two more trials of Webster Hubbell are still scheduled.

References:

"Once Upon a Time in Arkansas." *Frontline* episode. www.pbs.org/wgbh/pages/frontline
"Rough Whitewater Ride for Clinton." *Congressional Quarterly Almanac* (1994): 108–115.
"Whitewater Sparks New Hearings." *Congressional Quarterly Alamanc* (1995): 1–57 to 1–60.

Whittlesey, Faith Ryan (1939–   ) Ambassador to Switzerland, 1981–1983; 1985–1988. A friend of Attorney General EDWIN MEESE, Faith Whittlesey was accused of misusing funds donated to the American embassy in Switzerland, accepting a bribe, and obstruction of justice. Meese avoided triggering an independent counsel investigation into these matters by likely exercising more discretion than was permitted him under the independent counsel statute. His handling of the Whittlesey incident helped fuel the 1987 reforms that mandated the attorney general to expedite preliminary investigations into alleged misconduct, and refer more cases to the Special Division for assignment to an independent counsel.

Born in Jersey City, Whittlesey received her law degree from the University of Pennsylvania in 1963. She served as special assistant to the attorney general with the Pennsylvania departments of Justice (1964–1965) and Public Welfare (1967–1970) before appointment as Assistant U.S. Attorney for the Eastern District of Pennsylvania (1970–1972). In 1972, she was elected to Pennsylvania's House of Representatives where she served four years. Whittlesey was working with the Philadelphia firm of Wolf, Block, Schorr & Solis-Cohen when first appointed ambassador to Switzerland in 1981. She served on the White House staff from 1983 until 1985 before reassuming the ambassador's post for three more years. In 1988, Whittlesey joined the firm of Myerson & Kuhn in New York.

In 1985, Whittlesey established a fund to help finance her entertainment expenses in Switzerland. The fund's chairman, Fred Gottfurcht, solicited contributions, occasionally promising donors that they could expect to be guests of the ambassador in return for their donation. One donor's son was provided with a job by Whittlesey in return for his contribution. Gottfurcht himself also enjoyed official favors, such as dinners and concert tickets, in return for his assistance in establishing a fund that exceeded $82,000. When Whittlesey's deputy, Eric Kunsman, was discovered to be cooperating with a State Department investigation of her activities, Whittlesey threatened to dismiss him.

Meese's Justice Department avoided referring the allegations against Whittlesey to the Special Division by conducting what was termed a "threshold inquiry" into the matter. This inquiry was a screening process that enabled the attorney general to dismiss cases that did not appear to warrant a formal preliminary investigation. Avoiding a preliminary investigation meant that no report need be made to the court. Despite the fact that the allegations against Whittlesey-appeared to contain the "specific and credible evidence" necessary for triggering a preliminary inquiry, Meese decided against such action. He declared that Whittlesey's actions were without criminal intent. Meese claimed that the ambassador's hiring of a donor's son did not represent a *quid pro quo*, even though the donation occurred about the same time. Noting that there existed conflicting accounts of Whittlesey's communication with Kunsman, the attorney general ruled that a private citizen would not have been charged with obstruction of justice under such circumstances.

Because Meese was a personal friend of Whittlesey, many critics contended that he should have recused himself from deliberations in her case. Former WATERGATE Special Prosecutor ARCHIBALD COX, speaking as chairman of COMMON CAUSE, observed that Meese's decision appeared to be based on sympathy he felt for Whittlesey's plight. Such compassion, stated Cox, served to highlight the conflict of interest existing in this case, and encouraged the belief that personal association influenced the ultimate decision.

A congressional investigation conducted in 1987 discovered that a majority of allegations presented to the Justice Department in the preceding five years had been disposed of in the same manner as Whittlesey's. This prompted the 1987 revisions to the independent counsel statute that removed much of the discretion accorded the attorney general by the reforms of 1982.

References:

Eastland, Terry. *Ethics, Politics, and the Independent Counsel: Executive Power, Executive Vice 1789–1989*. Washington, D.C.: National Legal Center for the Public Interest, 1989. Chapter 7, "The Second Amendments to the Law," covers the

Whittlesey case. Argues against the necessity for Meese to have recused himself
in the matter.

Harriger, Katy J. *Independent Justice: The Federal Special Prosecutor in American Politics*. Lawrence: University Press of Kansas, 1992. Chapter 6, "Conflict of Interest," discusses the Whittlesey situation.

Ignatius, David. "Meese's Missing Sense of Propriety." *Washington Post*, 3 May 1987,
sec. B, p. 1. Contends that Meese's behavior in the Whittlesey affair would lead
one to believe that he was unaware of the ethical standards traditionally applied
to the position of attorney general.

Wiener v. United States 357 U.S. 349 (1958). By affirming that the president
does not possess absolute authority to remove from office all government employees performing executive functions, *Wiener v. U.S.* belongs to the body of
case law serving to support the limitations imposed on the executive branch by
the independent counsel statute.

The petitioner in this case was a member of the War Claims Commission, a
body charged with adjudicating claims filed by prisoners of war, internees, and
religious organizations who may have suffered injury or loss caused by the
opposition forces during World War II. The commissioner had been appointed
by President HARRY TRUMAN on June 2, 1950, and removed by President
Dwight D. Eisenhower three years later after refusing to resign as requested.
Eisenhower believed he possessed authority to select personnel of his own
choosing for the office in question. The petitioner sued in the Court of Claims
to collect salary lost as a result of his dismissal. The Court of Claims was divided
on the matter, and proceeded to dismiss the case.

Justice Felix Frankfurter, in delivering the opinion for the Supreme Court,
relied heavily on *HUMPHREY'S EXECUTOR v. UNITED STATES* 295 U.S.
602 (1935). That case, Frankfurter ruled, effectively limited the comprehensive
presidential power of removal asserted in *MYERS v. UNITED STATES* 272 U.S.
52 (1926). *Humphrey* defined the president's removal power as applying to only
those officials whose functions were purely executive in nature. This did not
include government employees performing quasi-judicial duties, especially when
the tenure of office is relatively brief. Frankfurter drew a clear distinction between officials who were part of the executive establishment, and therefore subject to presidential removal; and those whose duties required that they enjoy a
necessary independence from executive interference.

The Supreme Court, in this instance, drew a parallel between the functions
of the Federal Trade Commission (FTC), at the heart of the case in *Humphrey*,
and the War Claims Commission in *Wiener*. It was ruled that both bodies were
created by Congress with the intention that their members be able to exercise
judgment with substantial independence. Congress had specified that FTC members could be removed by the president for neglect, inefficiency, or specific
malfeasance only. Congress did not address the issue of removal at all in the
War Claims Act of 1948. The Court inferred in both cases, however, that due

to the nature of their functions, commissioners were not intended to be subject to arbitrary dismissal. The decision of the Court of Claims was reversed.

Wiener helped those who crafted the independent counsel statute to view with confidence their decision to protect the special prosecutor from easy removal by the president. They had reason to expect that a mechanism designed in this manner would likely pass constitutional scrutiny. *MORRISON v. OLSON* (1988) proved their confidence to be justified.

References:

Dudley, Earl C. "Morrison v. Olson: A Modest Assessment." *American University Law Review* 38 (1989): 255–274. Places *Wiener* alongside *Humphrey* in arguing that *Morrison* decision was plausible.

Eastland, Terry. *Ethics, Politics, and the Independent Counsel: Executive Power, Executive Vice 1789–1989*. Washington, D.C.: National Legal Center for the Public Interest, 1989. Chapter 4, "The Search for Law: 1973–1976," discusses *Wiener*. Points out that proponents of the independent counsel statute used *Wiener* to argue that the prosecutorial function was not exclusively held by the executive branch. Some carried the argument further, advocating the view that the special prosecutor's functions were not exclusively executive in nature.

Harriger, Katy J. *Independent Justice: The Federal Special Prosecutor in American Politics*. Lawrence: University Press of Kansas, 1992. Chapter 5, "Is the Prosecutor Constitutional?," covers the *Wiener* precedent.

O'Keefe, Constance, and Peter Safirstein. "Fallen Angels, Separation of Powers, and the Saturday Night Massacre: An Examination of the Practical, Constitutional, and Political Tensions in the Special Prosecutor Provisions of the Ethics in Government Act." *Brooklyn Law Review* 49 (1982): 113–147. Cites *Wiener* in arguing for maintaining the independent counsel office.

Tiefer, Charles. "The Constitutionality of Independent Officers as Checks on Abuses of Executive Power." *Boston University Law Review* 63 (1983): 59–103. Includes *Wiener* in recounting legal history supportive of independent counsel mechanism.

Y

Young v. United States 481 U.S. 787 (1987). By affirming the right of federal courts to appoint special prosecutors, *Young v. United States* served to support the constitutionality of this arrangement as specified in the independent counsel statute.

In 1982, French leather goods manufacturer Louis Vuitton obtained a court injunction against Sol Klayminc's handbag companies for trademark infringement. After gathering evidence of continuing violations, Vuitton's attorneys convinced the U.S. District Court to appoint them special prosecutors. The subsequent sting operation conducted by the special prosecutors resulted in conviction of Klayminc for contempt. On appeal, it was argued that attorneys possessing an interest in a case should not be appointed special prosecutors, because such an arrangement violated the principle of impartiality. The Court of Appeals rejected this argument, stating that, on occasion, interested attorneys are the only source of information in such cases. Furthermore, the supervision of such attorneys by the court should guarantee the impartiality of the prosecution.

On May 26, 1987, Supreme Court Justice William Brennan reversed the judgment of the Court of Appeals. His ruling found it improper for the district court to appoint attorneys as special prosecutors when these same lawyers stand to benefit from the court order in question. However, Brennan and the court majority specifically affirmed the right of the court to appoint private attorneys to prosecute violations of criminal contempt citations. Federal Rule of Criminal Procedure 42(b) should be interpreted to permit such appointments. Such power cannot be limited to the U.S. Attorney's Office, because the judiciary must possess independent means to execute its own authority.

Although the partiality of the specific special prosecutors in this case resulted in reversal of the lower court's decision, the mechanism permitting court appointment of special prosecutors was supported. Justices Marshall, Blackmun, Powell, Stevens, O'Connor, Rehnquist and SCALIA concurred in whole or part.

Justice White dissented, maintaining that there was no error in the appointment of interested parties as special prosecutors.

Curiously, Solicitor General Charles Fried, representing Attorney General ED-WIN MEESE's Justice Department, filed a brief in the *Young* case that relied on the validity of the independent counsel statute. In this instance, Fried argued that court appointment of special prosecutors did not violate separation of powers doctrine, a point of view that was at odds with comments made by Meese concerning the statute on other, nonjudicial occasions.

References:

Friewald, Aaron. "Fried Favorably Cites Counsel Law." *Legal Times*, 9 March 1987, p. 5.

Glitzenstein, Eric R., and Alan B. Morrison. "The Supreme Court's Decision in *Morrison v. Olson*: A Common Sense Application of the Constitution to a Practical Problem." *American University Law Review* 38 (1989): 359–382. Points out that *Young* permits court appointment of private attorneys to act as special prosecutors even when the executive branch declines or opposes such appointment, as long as no executive authority is usurped by such appointment. Article uses this argument to refute logic of decision in *IN RE SEALED CASE* 898 F.2d 476 (D.C Cir).

Youngstown Sheet & Tube Co. v. Sawyer, 343 U.S. 579 (1952) The United States Supreme Court decided a case of great magnitude on June 2, 1952. It was *Youngstown Sheet & Tube Co. v. Sawyer*, and the issue was whether the president of the United States could order a government takeover of the steel industry in order to prevent a nationwide steel strike. The court's decision would later serve to support *MORRISON v. OLSON* (1988) and the office of independent counsel.

The case originated five months earlier, when the United Steelworkers of America union asked for raises in its 1952 contract. The 253 steel companies said they could not comply until they raised their prices. However, the country was fighting a "police action" in Korea at that time, meaning that the President, HARRY S TRUMAN, was worried about mobilizing our resources and about the problems that would be caused by inflation. Accordingly, he asked his Wage Stabilization Board for its input in the matter. Before it gave its opinion, the union scheduled a strike four times but postponed it each time.

When the Board finally gave its recommendation, it called for a raise in wages in three stages plus a monetary increase in fringe benefits. The union accepted, but the companies did not. Therefore, the union re-scheduled the strike, and this one seemed to all parties to be one that would occur. Truman was faced with a dilemma. He could, of course, allow the companies to raise steel prices, but that seemed unlikely due to the demand for steel for national defense, not only for Korea but also for the country's atomic energy industry.

Another option was to invoke the 1947 Taft-Hartley Act provision, which allows the government to seek an eighty-day "cooling off" period during which time the parties seek a solution. This was not a mandatory solution, but was available when strikes threatened the country's health or safety. One must realize, however, the political facts of life; namely, Truman had vetoed the bill when it was passed by the Republican Congress, which he deemed the "do-nothing" Congress, and it had been passed over his veto. He considered it too pro-management and too anti-labor. As an illustration, it allowed management to complain to the National Labor Relations Board about unfair labor practices.

The remaining option was for Truman to seize the steel industry. That was an unprecedented move and would be sure to trigger an industry lawsuit. However, that is what Truman did. In a radio address to the nation, he explained that the increase in prices asked for by the industry was outrageous. He also said that Taft-Hartley would not prevent a shutdown of one to two weeks before its implementation. Therefore, his recourse was to order his Secretary of Commerce, Charles Sawyer, to become the custodian of the companies. One hour later, attorneys for two of the steel companies filed suit in the U.S. District Court in Washington, D.C., requesting a temporary restraining order from the takeover and indicating that they would also seek a permanent injunction against it. That next day the president of one of the country's steel companies gave a radio address rebuttal to Truman's speech.

The same day as the rebuttal speech, the case was argued before Judge Alexander Holtzoff. At that time, Truman sent Congress a message explaining his action. Although there was much debate, the only motion of any substance that passed was one in the Senate denying the president the power to use money that was being appropriated for the next fiscal year to carry out the seizure.

Meanwhile, Holtzoff denied the temporary restraining order, saying that if the seizure was illegal, the companies could sue for damages. Thus, the companies now asked the same court for a preliminary injunction, and this time Judge David Pine granted it, as he felt that money damages would be inadequate. The union then did call for a strike, and the government asked the Court of Appeals for the District of Columbia for a stay of the preliminary injunction until it could get the Supreme Court to look at the issue. The appellate court agreed to the stay by a 5–4 vote. The Supreme Court upheld the stay and agreed to hear the case, and the union agreed not to strike pending the outcome.

When the case was argued before the Court, a noted lawyer who had formerly been the U.S. Solicitor General, John W. Davis, spoke for the industry. Speaking in behalf of the government was Philip Perlman, who also had been the Solicitor General and was presently the Acting Attorney General. Also invited to speak was Arthur J. Goldberg, representing the union, who was later to become a member of the Supreme Court.

Some three weeks later, the Court rendered its decision, and stunned the president by voting 6–3 that he had exceeded his powers. Hugo Black wrote it, but each of the other five in the majority wrote concurring opinions explaining what caused them to vote as they did. Those five were Justices Frankfurter, Douglas, Jackson, Burton, and Clark. Black's opinion was that the Constitution did not expressly give the president the right to seize an industry, nor did it do it indirectly by the commander-in-chief power. Congress had not given him that power either. He said the president might have used Taft-Hartley, or even provisions of the 1948 Selective Service Act or the 1950 Defense Production Act, but he did not use any of them. In dissent, Chief Justice Fred Vinson spoke for himself and Justices Reed and Minton and argued that the president is allowed to act unless Congress says otherwise, and Congress had said nothing about seizing an industry in an emergency situation.

When the decision was announced, the union did strike, and stayed on strike for seven weeks. It ended on July 24 with the union getting an increase in wages and a monetary increase in fringe benefits, and the companies being allowed to raise their prices.

The importance of the steel seizure case is that even in times of national emergency, the Supreme Court will not grant power to the president that it does not find, either expressly or indirectly, in the Constitution nor in Congressional actions.

Along with cases such as *KENDALL v. U.S.* (1838) and *COMMODITY FUTURES TRADING COMMISSION v. SCHOR* (1986), this decision stressed that each branch's separate powers were also shared powers, not permitting the type of aggrandizement attempted by Truman. Justice Jackson, in particular, advocated this flexible cooperative approach in his concurring opinion. Such an analysis would later lend legitimacy to the independent counsel statute.

References:

Dudley, Earl C. "*Morrision v. Olson*: A Modest Assessment." *American University Law Review* 38 (1989): 255–274.

Sherry, Suzanna. "Separation of Powers: Asking a Different Question." *William and Mary Law Review* 30 (1989): 287–300.

Westin, Alan F. *The Anatomy of a Constitutional Law Case*. New York: Macmillan, 1958. The definitive book on the subject.

—ROBERT W. LANGRAN

Z

Zeldin, Michael (1951–   ) Independent Counsel, Clinton passport file search, 1992–1995. From 1992 to 95, Michael Zeldin served as deputy to Independent Counsel JOSEPH DiGENOVA during a probe of the manner in which Bill CLINTON's State Department passport file was employed by President GEORGE BUSH's campaign team. In 1995, DiGenova departed, and Zeldin concluded the inquiry. He proceeded to confirm DiGenova's finding that no criminal conduct was evident in the matter.

Zeldin received his law degree from George Washington University's National Law Center in 1976. He practiced privately with the Washington, D.C. law firm of Cole, Raywid & Braverman before joining the faculty at his *alma mater*. There, Zeldin served as supervising attorney of George Washington's poverty law clinic. After receiving a master of laws degree from Georgetown University in 1983, he moved into criminal defense work. The following year, he joined the Justice Department's Narcotics and Dangerous Drugs Section as a litigator. In 1989, he took over as director of the Department's Office of Asset Forfeiture. In that capacity, Zeldin supervised a staff of 15 lawyers who seized hundreds of millions of dollars in property from drug dealers, racketeers, and money launderers. Before leaving the Department three years later, he served as Criminal Division specialist on money laundering, and participated in the congressional investigation into the "October Surprise," which alleged that RONALD REAGAN's campaign team worked to delay the release of American hostages held in Iran in order to prevent President Jimmy CARTER taking credit for the achievement.

In 1992, Zeldin joined Joseph DiGenova's independent counsel investigation into charges that the Bush campaign used Bill Clinton's passport files in an unprincipled manner in order to portray the Democratic candidate's student antiwar activities as subversive. Zeldin concurred with DiGenova's finding that campaign officials used poor judgment, but were not guilty of criminal activity.

He brought the investigation to a formal conclusion after DiGenova departed in 1995.

In 1994, Zeldin assumed control of the Washington, D.C., office of Decision Strategies, which helps companies conduct internal investigations in order to guard against possible lawsuits. Three years later, he joined Price Waterhouse's global forensic investigations team charged with detecting and examining misconduct against the firm's clients. During the WHITEWATER investigation, Zeldin frequently appeared on television talk shows to comment upon the course that the inquiry was taking. He frequently supported the contention that KENNETH STARR was ill-advised to concentrate his efforts on the LEWINSKY affair.

References:

"Laundering His Career." *Legal Times*, 17 January 1994, p. 3. Recaps Zeldin's career.
Watson, Tom. "What a Job: If He Finds It, He Takes It." *Legal Times*, 20 March 1989, sec. S, p. 6.

Bibliography

Abels, Jules. *The Truman Scandals*. Chicago: Henry Regnery, 1956.

Abrams, Elliott. *Undue Process: A Story of How Political Differences Are Turned into Crimes*. New York: Free Press, 1993.

Alterman, Eric. "Scandal Sheet." *New Republic*, 20 April 1987: p. 17.

Amar, Akhil Reed, and Neal Kumar Katyal. "Executive Privileges and Immunities: The Nixon and Clinton Cases." *Harvard Law Review* 108 (1995): 701–726.

Applebome, Peter. "Judge in Whitewater Dispute Rewards Faith of His Patron." *New York Times*, 17 August 1994, p. A1.

Atlas, Terry. "Barr Forced to Weigh Probe of Iraqi Loans." *Chicago Tribune*, 16 October 1992, p. C3.

———. "Retired Judge Will Probe Iraq Loan Case." *Chicago Tribune*, 17 October 1992, p. C1.

Babcock, Charles R. "Lobbyist's Conviction Thrown Out in Espy Case." *Washington Post*, 4 March 1998, p. A7.

———. "No Special Prosecutor Needed in Miller Case." *Washington Post*, 12 March 1980, p. A2.

———. "Special Prosecutor Investigations Called 'Enormous Waste.'" *Washington Post*, 21 May 1981, p. A20.

Babcock, Charles R., and Tom Sherwood. "New Cocaine Allegation Cited in Jordan Inquiry." *Washington Post*, 14 September 1979, p. A3.

Babcock, Charles, and Bob Woodward. "Attorney General Criticized; Justice Closes Investigations of Smith." *Washington Post*, 22 July 1982, p. A1.

Baker, Senator Howard H., Jr. "The Proposed Judicially Appointed Independent Office of Public Attorney: Some Constitutional Objections and an Alternative." *Southwestern Law Journal* 29 (1975): 671–683.

Barfield, Deborah. "Hillary Scorns Scandal." *Newsday*, 12 February 1998, p. A7.

Barker, Jeff. "Babbitt Case About More Than Just Interior Chief." *Arizona Republic*, 24 March 1998, p. A2.

———. "Babbitt Investigator Draws GOP Fire." *Arizona Republic*, 20 March 1998, p. A1.

Barnes, Steve. "Arkansas Governor Resigns after Furor." *New York Times*, 16 July 1996, p. A10.

Barth, Alan. *Government by Investigation*. New York: Viking Press, 1955.

Battiata, Mary. "John Tower and His Arduous Mandate." *Washington Post*, 26 February 1986, p. B1.

Beale, Sara Sun, William C. Bryson, James E. Felman, and Michael J. Elston. *Grand Jury Law and Practice*. 2nd ed., St. Paul: West Group, 1997.

Beckwith, David. "The High Price of Friendship." *Time*, 28 December 1987, p. 23.

Behar, Richard. "On Fresh Ground." *Time*, 26 December 1994, p. 111.

Beinstein, Debra. "Making the Case against Nofziger." *The American Lawyer* (September 1987): 117.

Bell, Griffin B., Archibald Cox, Lloyd N. Cutler, and Lawrence E. Walsh. "A Roundtable Discussion on the Independent Counsel Statute." *Mercer Law Review* 49 (1998): 453–488.

Bendavid, Naftali. "Reno OK's Counsel to Probe Labor Secretary." *Chicago Tribune*, 12 May 1998, p. N3.

Bendavid, Naftali, and Jan Crawford Greenburg. "Bennett's Legal Plan under Fire." *Chicago Tribune*, 27 January 1998, p. N1.

Ben-Veniste, Richard, and George Frampton, Jr. *Stonewall: The Real Story of the Watergate Prosecution*. New York: Simon and Schuster, 1977.

Berry, John F. "Civiletti Affirms Miller Never Knew of Payments." *Washington Post*, 6 February 1980, p. C1.

Bertozzi, Mark. "The Federal Special Prosecutor: Too Special?" *Federal Bar News & Journal* 29 (1982): 222–230.

———. "Oversight of the Executive Branch: A Policy Analysis of the Federal Special Prosecutor Legislation." Ph.D. dissertation, State University of New York at Albany, 1980.

Biskupic, Joseph. "Looking at Human Problems with Judicial Restraint." *Washington Post*, 20 July 1993, p. A1.

Bleifuss, Joel. "School for Scandal." *In These Times*, 8 March 1998: p. 14.

Blumenthal, Ralph. "Inquiry on Donovan Again Yields 'Insufficient Evidence' to Prosecute." *New York Times*, 14 September 1982, p. A1.

Blumenthal, Sidney. "The Boland Achievement." *Washington Post*, 15 June 1987, p. C1.

Boot, Max. "Dakota Official Pleads Guilty in HUD Probe." *Christian Science Monitor*, 13 May 1993, p. 3.

———. "Investigation of HUD in Full Swing." *Christian Science Monitor*, 12 January 1993, p. 6.

———. "Uneven Results Mark HUD Corruption Cases." *Christian Science Monitor*, 17 February 1993: 3.

Borger, Gloria. "Scenes from a Marriage." *U.S. News & World Report*, 2 February 1998, p. 30.

Borger, Gloria, with Kenneth T. Walsh and Ted Gest. "White House Follies." *U.S. News & World Report*, 16 May 1988, p. 20.

Bork, Robert H. "Against the Independent Counsel." *Commentary* (February 1993): 21.

Bowermaster, David J., and Greg Ferguson. "The Clinton-Fiske Face-Off." *U.S. News & World Report*, 4 April 1994, p. 20.

Boyer, Edward J. "William French Smith, 73 Dies; Reagan Adviser and Attorney General." *Los Angeles Times*, 30 October 1990, p. B1.

Bradlee, Ben, Jr. *Guts and Glory: The Oliver North Story.* New York: Donald I. Fine, Inc., 1988.

Brazil, Eric. "Ex-Special Prosecutor Doubts Starr's Goals." *San Francisco Examiner,* 27 January 1998, p. A7.

Brill, Steven. "Anonymity and Dignity." *American Lawyer* (September 1994): 5.

Brinkley, Joel. "House Panel Calls C.I.A. Manual Illegal." *New York Times,* 6 December 1984, p. A3.

Brown, George D. "When Federalism and Separation of Powers Collide—Rethinking *Younger* Abstention." *George Washington Law Review* 59 (1990): 114–156.

Brown, Jonathan P. "*Banzhaf v. Smith*: Judicial Review under the Independent Counsel Provisions of the Ethics in Government Act." *Iowa Law Review* 70 (1985): 1339–1352.

Brown, Warren. "Carter Aide Steps Down Amid Probe." *Washington Post,* 15 September 1980, p. A1.

Busch, Francis X. *Enemies of the State.* Indianapolis: Bobbs-Merrill, 1954.

Cannon, Carl M. "Probe of Cisneros Will Not Let Go." *Baltimore Sun,* 30 November 1997, p. A1.

Cannon, James. *Time and Chance: Gerald Ford's Appointment with History.* New York: HarperCollins, 1994.

Carter, Betsy, Stephan Lesher, and Tony Fuller. "Saturday-Night Survivors." *Newsweek,* 20 October 1975, p. 14.

Cerio, Gregory. "Tainted Evidence." *Newsweek,* 4 January 1993, p. 7.

Chandler, Clay. "For Treasury's Top Lawyer, Cross-Examination Awaits." *Washington Post,* 1 August 1994, p. A19.

Church, George J. "Acid Raining on Deaver's Parade." *Time,* 5 May 1986, p. 20.

Clayton, Cornell W. *The Politics of Justice: The Attorney General and the Making of Legal Policy.* Armonk, N.Y.: M. E. Sharpe, Inc., 1992.

Clines, Francis X. "Hillary Clinton Tells Grand Jury She Cannot Account for Records." *New York Times,* 27 January 1996, p. A1.

Cohen, Richard. "What's His Secret?" *Washington Post,* 28 March 1997, p. A29.

Cohen, William S. "Reforming the Special Prosecutor Process." *American Bar Association Journal* 68 (1982): 278–281.

Cohen, William S., and George J. Mitchell. *Men of Zeal.* New York: Viking, 1988.

Cooper, Kenneth. "Pierce Misled Hill, Panel Concludes." *Washington Post,* 2 November 1990, p. A23.

Corn, David. "Instant Karma—Eventually." *The Nation* 255 (1992): 532.

Cox, Archibald. "Reflections on a Firestorm." *Saturday Review,* 9 March 1974, pp. 12–14, 56.

Cromer, Brian A. "Prosecutorial Indiscretion and the United States Congress: Expanding the Jurisdiction of the Independent Counsel." *Kentucky Law Review Journal* 77 (1989): 923–950.

Danelski, David J., and Joseph S. Tulchin, eds. *The Autobiographical Notes of Charles Evans Hughes.* Cambridge: Harvard University Press, 1973.

Daugherty, Harry M., and Thomas Dixon. *The Inside Story of the Harding Tragedy.* New York: Churchill, 1932.

DeMott, John S. "The Bill Comes Due for Deaver." *Time,* 30 March 1987, p. 23.

Devroy, Ann, and Helen Dewar. "Republicans Seek Travel Office Probe." *Washington Post,* 12 June 1993, p. A5.

Doan, Michael, and Patricia A. Avery. "Michael Deaver." *U.S. News & World Report*, 14 April 1986, p. 8.

Donovan, Robert J. *Tumultuous Years: The Presidency of Harry S Truman, 1949–1953*. New York: W. W. Norton, 1982.

Doyle, James. *Not above the Law: The Battles of Watergate Prosecutors Cox and Jaworski*. New York: Morrow, 1977.

Draper, Theodore. *A Very Thin Line: The Iran-Contra Affairs*. New York: Hill and Wang, 1991.

Drew, Christopher. "Iran-Contra Charge for CIA Aide." *Chicago Tribune*, 21 June 1988, p. C3.

Dudley, Earl C. *" Morrison v. Olson*: A Modest Assessment." *American University Law Review* 38 (1989): 255–274.

Dunar, Andrew J. "All Honorable Men: The Truman Scandals and the Politics of Morality." Ph.D. dissertation, University of Southern California, 1981.

Eastland, Terry. *Ethics, Politics, and the Independent Counsel: Executive Power, Executive Vice 1789–1989*. Washington, D.C.: National Legal Center for the Public Interest, 1989.

Eisler, Kim Isaac. "And Then There Was Janet." *Washingtonian* (April 1997): p. 43.

Elliott, E. Donald. "Why Our Separation of Powers Jurisprudence Is So Abysmal." *George Washington Law Review* 57 (1989): 506–532.

Elsasser, Glen. "Iran-Contra Figure Tells of Casey Ties." *Chicago Tribune*, 1 August 1992, p. C10.

———. "North Judge Reluctant to Call Bush, Reagan." *Chicago Tribune*, 28 January 1989, p. C4.

Engelberg, Stephen. "Washington Talk: Profile—North's Attorney." *New York Times*, 6 July 1987, p. A10.

Epstein, Lee, and Thomas G. Walker. *Constitutional Law for a Changing America: Institutional Powers and Constraints*. Washington, D.C.: CQ Press, 1995.

Ervin, Sam, Jr. *Preserving the Constitution: The Autobiography of Senator Sam Ervin*. Charlottesville: Michie, 1984.

———. *The Whole Truth: The Watergate Conspiracy*. New York: Random House, 1980.

Fagen, Richard R. *Forging Peace: The Challenge of Central America*. New York: Basil, 1987.

Farrell, John Aloysius. "Special Prosecutor to Sift Iraq Aid Sought." *Boston Globe*, 10 July 1992, p. 1.

Feldmann, Linda. "What's Behind the Latest White House Scandal?" *Christian Science Monitor*, 21 June 1996, p. 4.

Fenyvesi, Charles. "Washington Whispers." *U.S. News & World Report*, 26 September 1994, p. 40.

Ferrell, Robert H. *Harry S Truman and the Modern American Presidency*. Boston: Little, Brown and Company, 1983.

Fleissner, James. "The Future of the Independent Counsel Statute: Confronting the Dilemma of Allocating the Power of Prosecutorial Discretion." *Mercer Law Review* 49 (1998): 427–452.

Fletcher, Martin. "Clinton Aide Quits as Inquiry Begins into Files Scandal." *The Times*, 27 June 1996.

Ford, Gerald R. *A Time to Heal: The Autobiography of Gerald R. Ford*. New York: Harper and Row, 1979.

Frankel, Alison. "Ted Olson's Five Years in Purgatory." *American Lawyer* (December 1988): 68.

Freiwald, Aaron. "Fried Favorably Cites Counsel Law." *Legal Times*, 9 March 1987, p. 5.

———. "New Prosecutor Takes Over Wallace Probe." *Legal Times*, 7 December 1987, p. 4.

Fried, Charles, and Paul M. Bator. "Debate: After the Independent Counsel Decision: Is Separation of Powers Dead?" *American Criminal Law Journal* 26 (1989): 1667–1681.

Frieden, Terry. "McDougal Criminal Contempt Trial Rescheduled for February." *CNN Interactive*. ⟨http//cnn.com/ALL POLITICS/stories/1998/11/16/mcdougal/⟩

Friedman, Alan. "BNL Hell: An Iraqgate Primer." *New Republic*, 9 November 1992, p. 18.

Germond, Jack, and Jules Whitcover. "Hillary Clinton"s Chief Role May Be to Save Her Husband's Career." *Baltimore Sun*, 13 February 1998, p. A17.

Gerstenzang, James. "Tower Report Blames Reagan, Aides." *Los Angeles Times*, 27 February 1987, p. A1.

Gerwitz, Paul. "Realism in Separation of Powers Thinking." *William and Mary Law Review* 30 (1989): 343–354.

Gleick, Elizabeth, and Alan Freedman. "Secord on the Record." *People*, 12 October 1992, p. 133.

Glitzenstein, Eric R., and Alan B. Morrison. "The Supreme Court's Decision in *Morrison v. Olson*: A Common Sense Application of the Constitution to a Practical Problem." *American University Law Review* 38 (1989): 359–382.

Goodpaster, Gary. "Rules of the Game: Comments on Three Views of the Independent Prosecutor Case." *American University Law Review* 38 (1989): 383–393.

Gordon, Greg. "Minnesotan Is Cleared in Telling White House about Probe." *Minneapolis Star Tribune*, 1 July 1994, p. A7.

———. "Whitewater Briefing Defended by Lawyer." *Minneapolis Star Tribune*, 2 August 1994, p. A1.

Gormley, Ken. *Archibald Cox: Conscience of a Nation*. Reading, MA: Addison-Wesley, 1997.

Gosnell, Harold F. *Truman's Crises: A Political Biography of Harry S Truman*. (*Contributions in Political Science*, No.33). Westport: Greenwood, 1980.

Gould, Lewis L. *The Presidency of Theodore Roosevelt*. Lawrence: University Press of Kansas, 1991.

Greene, John Robert. *The Presidency of Gerald R. Ford*. Lawrence: University Press of Kansas, 1995.

Gressman, Eugene. "Introduction." *Hofstra Law Review* 16 (Fall 1987): 1–10.

Grove, Lloyd. "Say It Again Sam." *Washington Post*, 23 April 1996, p. D1.

———. "That Other Southern President." *Washington Post*, 14 January 1993, p. C1.

Gugliotta, Guy. "Iran-Contra Figure Shot Down Again." *Washington Post*, 18 June 1996, p. A11.

Gurdon, Hugo. "Top Lawyers Denounce White House Starr 'War.'?" *Daily Telegraph*, 7 March 1998, p.15.

Gwyn, William B. "The Indeterminacy of the Separation of Powers and the Federal Courts." *George Washington Law Review* 57 (1989): 474–505.

Halstuk, Martin. "Weinberger Prosecutor Lashes Out." *San Francisco Chronicle*, 26 December 1992, p. A2.

Hamburger, Tom. "Latitude Given to Special Prosecutors Draws Fire." *Star Tribune* (Minneapolis, MN), 10 May 1998, p. A17.

Harriger, Katy J. "The History of the Independent Counsel Provisions: How the Past Informs the Current Debate." *Mercer Law Review* 49 (1998): 489–517.

———. *Independent Justice: The Federal Special Prosecutor in American Politics*. Lawrence: University Press of Kansas, 1992.

Hayes, Andrew W. "The Boland Amendment and Foreign Affairs Deference." *Columbia Law Review* 88 (1988): 1534–1574.

Hayward, Ed. "Dole Favors Independent Probe into Dem Funds." *Boston Herald*, 16 April 1997, p. 15.

Hendrickson, Paul. "Counsel at the Warehouse Door." *Washington Post*, 9 April 1979, p. C1.

Henry, John C. "Judge Dismisses Hubbell Charges, Rebukes Starr." *Houston Chronicle*, 2 July 1998, p. A1.

Hickey, Jennifer G. "The Last Refuge of a President." *Washington Times*, 23 March 1998, p. 14.

Holmes, Steven A. "F.C.C. Requirement on Minority Hiring Is Voided by Court." *New York Times*, 15 April 1998, p. A1.

———. "Giving in to 'Graymail.' " *Time*, January 16, 1989: p. 24.

Horning, Jay. "Donovan's Government Experiences Haven't Soured His Labors." *St. Petersburg Times*, 10 October 1993, p. A7.

———. "First EPA Chief Keeping Involved." *St. Petersburg Times*, 15 March 1992, p. A15.

Howe, Robert F. "Two High-Powered Lawyers Facing Off in Robb Probe." *Washington Post*, 9 January 1993, p. B1.

Howlett, Debbie. "HUD Prober Not an 'Activist.' " *USA Today*, 11 April 1990, p. A2.

Hyde, William. *Encyclopedia of the History of St. Louis*, volume 2, p. 1016–1017. New York: Southern History Company, 1899.

Ignatius, David. "Meese's Missing Sense of Propriety." *Washington Post*, 3 May 1987, p. B1.

Ise, John. *The United States Oil Policy*. New Haven: Yale University Press, 1926.

Isikoff, Michael. "The Night Foster Died." *Newsweek*, 17 July 1995, p. 20.

———. "N.Y. Lawyer Fiske Is in Line to Head Whitewater Inquiry." *Washington Post*, 20 January 1994, p. A3.

———. "The Paula Problem." *Newsweek*, 26 January 1998, p. 24.

Isikoff, Michael, and Mark Hosenball. "Why Vince Foster Died." *Newsweek*, 11 July 1994, p. 17.

Isikoff, Michael, and Evan Thomas. "Clinton and the Intern." *Newsweek*, 2 February 1998, pp. 30–34.

Jackson, Robert L., "Dole Calls for Investigation of Iran-Contra Counsel." *Los Angeles Times*, 9 November 1992, p. A23.

———. "Ex-Prosecutor to Probe Ronald Brown's Finances." *Los Angeles Times*, 7 July 1995, p. A17.

———. "GOP Lawyer Picked to Probe Whitewater." *Los Angeles Times*, 21 January 1994, p. A30.

————. "John J. Sirica, Watergate Case Judge, Dies at 88." *Los Angeles Times*, 15 August 1992, p. A1.

————. "Nofziger Faces Inquiry on Lobbying." *Los Angeles Times*, 5 November 1986, p. A16.

————. "Prosecutors Urge Special Counsel for Alexis Herman." *Los Angeles Times*, 9 May 1998, p. A10.

Jackson, Robert L., and Eric Lichtblau. "Judges' Ruling Allows Reno to Pursue Starr Inquiry." *Los Angeles Times*, 19 March 1999, p. A18.

Jackson, Robert L., and Ronald J. Ostrow. "Allegations Covered by Ethics Act, Justice Dept. Rules." *Los Angeles Times*, 25 November 1986, p. A17.

————. "Ex-HUD Secretary Indicted, Accused of Lying to FBI." *Los Angeles Times*, 12 December 1997, p. A1.

————. "Special Counsel Named in Babbitt Probe." *Los Angeles Times*, 20 March 1998, p. A18.

Jacoby, Tamar. "William Casey: Silent Witness." *Newsweek*, 18 May 1987, p. 46.

Jaworski, Leon. *Papers*. Texas Collection at Baylor University, Waco, Texas.

————. *The Right and the Power: The Prosecution of Watergate*. New York: Reader's Digest Press, 1976.

Johnston, David. "Ex-Agent Is Bitter Over Iran Affair." *New York Times*, 26 November 1989, p. A31.

————. "Independent Counsel Law Is Too Flawed to Renew, Reno Tells Senate Panel." *New York Times*, 18 March 1999, p. A22.

————. "Independent Counsel Replaced in HUD Inquiry." *New York Times*, 2 July 1995, p. A21.

————. "Lawyer Linked to 80's HUD Scandal Is Named to Investigate Housing Chief." *New York Times*, 25 May 1995, p. B10.

————. "Lawyers in North Trial: Alike Only in Their Passion to Win." *New York Times*, 18 April 1989, p. B6.

Jones, Joyce. "The Best Commerce Secretary Ever." *Black Enterprise* (June 1996): p. 90.

Jones, Tamara. "Henry and Linda." *Washington Post*, 22 February 1998, magazine section, p. W10.

Jordan, Sandra D. "Classified Information and Conflicts in Independent Counsel Prosecutions: Balancing the Scales of Justice after Iran-Contra." *Columbia Law Review* 91 (1991): 1651–1698.

Kalt, Brian C. "Pardon Me?: The Constitutional Case against Presidential Self-Pardons." *Yale Law Journal* 106 (1996): 779–809.

Kelly, James. "Allen Exit, Shake-Up at the White House." *Time*, 11 January 1982, p. 23.

————. "Donovan Probe." *Time*, 11 January 1982, p. 23.

Kiernan, Laura A. "Former Carter Aide Challenges Constitutionality of Ethics Law." *Washington Post*, 20 November 1980, p. A4.

————. "Jordan Cocaine Tests '78 Ethics Law." *Washington Post*, 3 September 1979, p. B1.

Kilberg, William J. "Jones v. Clinton." *Employee Relations Law Journal*, 22 September 1994, p. 173.

Klaidman, Daniel, and Ann Woolner. "Craig Gillen Takes the Stage in Iran-Contra." *Legal Times*, 22 June 1992, p.1.

Kmiec, Douglas W. *The Attorney General's Lawyer: Inside the Meese Justice Department.* New York: Praeger, 1992.

Knight, Jerry. "IRS Probes Firm Once Owned by Brown, Partner, Independent Counsel Investigating Commerce Secretary Requests Study of Company's Taxes." *Washington Post*, 16 February 1996, p. A6.

————. "Ronald Brown Probe Widens." *Washington Post*, 30 March 1996, p. C1.

Koh, Harold Hongju. *The National Security Constitution: Sharing Power after the Iran-Contra Affair.* New Haven: Yale University Press, 1990.

————. "Why the President (Almost) Always Wins in Foreign Affairs: Lessons of the Iran-Contra Affair." *Yale Law Journal* 97 (1988): 1255–1342.

Kornbluh, Peter, and Malcolm Byrne, eds. *The Iran-Contra Scandal: The Declassified History.* New York: The New Press, 1993.

Kranish, Michael. "Still-Silent Susan Is Indicted." *Boston Globe*, 5 May 1998, p. A1.

Krotoszynski, Ronald J., Jr. "On the Danger of Wearing Two Hats: *Mistretta* and *Morrison* Revisited." *William and Mary Law Review* 38 (1997): 417–485.

Kurkjian, Stephen. "Brooke Reportedly Is Focus of HUD Probe." *Boston Globe*, 22 August 1992, p. 1.

Kurtz, Howard. "Evidence of Crime Distinguishes Watergate from Debate Case." *Washington Post*, 29 May 1984, p. A4.

————. "2 Independent Counsels Are Secretly Appointed; Justice Department Ex-Aide Reportedly Probed." *Washington Post*, 18 December 1986, p. A10.

Kurylo, Elizabeth. "Carter Says Gore Deserves Support." *Atlanta Journal and Constitution*, 21 October 1997, p. A11.

Kutler, Stanley I. *The Wars of Watergate: The Last Crisis of Richard Nixon.* New York: Alfred A. Knopf, 1990.

Labaton, Stephen. "Labor Secretary's Nemesis Now Finds Himself Impugned." *New York Times*, 16 January 1998, p. A18.

————. "Reno Is Said to Choose New Yorker as Counsel." *New York Times*, 20 January 1994, p. A12.

————. "Reno's Off-and-on Mood for Counsel Is Off Again." *New York Times*, 5 October 1997, p. A8.

————. "A Report on His Suicide Portrays a Deeply Troubled Vince Foster." *New York Times*, 11 October 1997, p. A1.

Lacayo, Richard. "Hale Storm Rising." *Time*, 13 April 1998, p. 54.

————. "Jones v. The President." *Time*, 16 May 1994, p. 44.

Lacovara, Philip A. "Graymail, Secrets and the North Trial." *Los Angeles Times*, 5 January 1989, p. B7.

Lardner, George, Jr. "Abrams Pleads Guilty in Iran-Contra Affair." *Washington Post*, 8 October 1991, p. A1.

————. "Abrams Sentenced to 2 Years' Probation." *Washington Post*, 16 November 1991, p. A20.

————. "Administration, Senators Air Ethics Law Changes." *Washington Post*, 29 April 1982, p. A5.

————. "Crux of Babbitt Probe: Recollections in Conflict." *Washington Post*, 29 March 1998, p. A8.

————. "FBI Told Reagan Staff Donovan Had Mob Ties." *Washington Post*, 15 June 1982, p. A1.

————. "Grand Jury Clears Jordan." *Washington Post*, 29 May 1980, p. A1.

————. "Insufficient Credible Evidence." *Washington Post*, 14 September 1982, p. A1.

————. "No Basis Found for Prosecution of Donovan." *Washington Post*, 29 June 1982, p. A1.

————. "Prosecutor Appointed in Jordan Case." *Washington Post*, 30 November 1979, p. A1.

————. "Prosecutor Labels Meese 'a Sleaze.' " *Washington Post*, 23 July 1988, p. A3.

————. "Senate Chairman Favors End to Independent Counsel Law." *Washington Post*, 11 December 1998, p. A29.

————. "Silverman Confirms New Donovan Probe." *Washington Post*, 3 August 1982, p. A7.

Lardner, George, Jr., and Walter Pincus. "Notebook Reveals North-Bush Meeting." *Washington Post*, 9 May 1990, p. A1.

Leach, Jim. "Those International Vigilantes Were Wrong." *Washington Post*, 29 September 1984, p. A17.

Leavitt, Paul, Tom Squiteri, and Bill Nichols. "Maine Lawyer Appointed to Investigate Herman." *USA Today*, 27 May 1998, p. A6.

Lee, Rex E. "Boland Does Not Apply to the President." *Los Angeles Times*, 22 June 1987, part 2, p. 5.

Levin, Carl. "A Record of Shame: Why Meese Must Resign." *Washington Post*, 22 May 1988, p. C1.

Levin, Carl, and Bill Cohen. "Save the Special Prosecutor Law." *Washington Post*, 27 September 1992, p. C7.

Levinson, L. Harold. "Balancing Acts: *Bowsher v. Synar*, Gramm-Rudman-Hollings, and Beyond." *Cornell Law Review* 72 (1987): 527–552.

Lewis, Ephraim. "Tiptoeing Around Goobergate." *Businessweek*, 9 April 1979, Industrial ed., p. 129.

Lewis, Neil A. "An Ideological Flap Ruffles a Court's Two Wings." *New York Times*, 13 March 1992, p. B16.

————. "Ex-CIA Official Testifies Boss Knew About Iran-Contra Affair." *New York Times*, 29 July 1992, p. A1.

————. "Ex-Spy Chief Is Convicted of Lying to Congress on Iran-Contra Affair." *New York Times*, 10 December 1992, p. A1.

————. "Former Spy Weeps at Iran-Contra Trial." *New York Times*, 30 July 1992, p. A10.

————. "Iran-Contra Trial of Ex-CIA Man Ends in a Deadlock." *New York Times*, 27 August 1992, p. A1.

————. "The Nation: How to Build a Better Independent Counsel." *New York Times*, 17 May 1998, p. D1.

Liberman, Lee S. " *Morrison v. Olson*: A Formalistic Perspective on Why the Court Was Wrong." *American University Law Review* 38 (1989): 313–358.

Locy, Tony. "Appeals Court Backs Expulsion of Homosexual Midshipman." *Washington Post*, 23 November 1994, p. A2.

————. "Ex-Agriculture Secretary Indicted." *Washington Post*, 28 August 1997, p. A1.

Locy, Toni, and Guy Gugliotta. "Court Appoints D.C. Lawyer as Special Counsel in Cisneros Case." *Washington Post*, 25 May 1995, p. A8.

————. "Independent Counsel, Witness in Cisneros Probe at Odds." *Washington Post*, 16 November 1996, p. A4.

Lowther, William. "Standing By Her Man—Fiercely." *Macleans*, 9 February 1998, p. 28.

Maas, Peter. "Oliver North's Strange Recruits." *New York Times*, 18 January 1987, p. F20.

Madison, Christopher. "Old Scandal Rides Again." *National Journal* 14 (1992): 2620.

Magnuson, Ed. "Death of an Expert Witness." *Time*, 18 May 1987, p. 37.

———. "Pawn among the Giants." *Time*, 17 April 1989, p. 22.

Maitland, Leslie. "Revision of Law on Special Prosecutors Is Backed." *New York Times*, 9 September 1982, p. B14.

Malone, Julia. "Whitewater: Good News So Far.' *Atlanta Journal and Constitution*, 1 July 1994, p. A10.

Mantius, Peter. "Can 'Mr. Fixit' Solve Bush's Lingering Legal Woes? Griffin Bell Tackles Former President's Iran-Contra Problems." *Atlanta Journal and Constitution*, 24 January 1993, p. A8.

Marcus, Ruth. "Common Cause Seeks Independent Counsel Probe of Parties' Spending." *Washington Post*, 10 October 1996, p. A23.

———. "Dole and Mitchell Spar over Starr." *Washington Post*, 15 August 1994, p. A9.

———. "Ex-Official's Testimony Not Designed to Conceal; Decision against Prosecuting Olson Explained." *Washington Post*, 21 March 1989, p. A4.

———. "Harassment Trial Delayed While Clinton Is in Office." *Washington Post*, 29 December 1994, p. A1.

———. "Judge Ruth Ginsburg Named to High Court." *Washington Post*, 15 June 1993, p. A1.

———. "Judges Weigh Independent Counsel Law." *Washington Post*, 17 September 1987, p. A19.

———. "Justice Official Won't Be Charged in Tax Case." *Washington Post*, 19 December 1987, p. A3.

Martin, Thomas S., and David E. Zerhusen. "Independent Counsel—Checks and Balances." *George Washington Law Review* 58 (1990): 536–548.

Mathews, Tom, Elaine Shannon, and Susan Agrest. "A Peanut Prosecutor." *Newsweek*, 2 April 1979, p. 31.

Mathews, Tom, with Holly Morris and Elaine Shannon. "Did Billy Cook His Books?" *Newsweek*, 26 March 1979, p. 50.

Mathews, Tom, with John Walcott, Elaine Shannon, Vern E. Smith, and Joseph B. Cumming, Jr. "Those Carter Loans." *Newsweek*, 12 February 1979, p. 33.

Matraia, Michael T. "Running for Cover behind Presidential Immunity: The Oval Office as Safe Haven from Civil Suits." *Suffolk University Law Journal* 29 (1995): 195–231.

Mauro, Tony. "ABA Begins Study of Court Nominee." *USA Today*, 15 July 1991, p. A3.

Mayer, Allan J., and Elaine Shannon. "The Peanut Probe: Case Closed." *Newsweek*, 19 October 1979, p. 35.

Mayer, Allan J., and Kim Willenson. "The Senators Scold Billy and Jimmy." *Newsweek* 13 October 1980, p. 47.

Mayer, Allan J., with Eleanor Clift, Elaine Shannon, Gloria Borger, Kim Willenson, Holly Morris, and Vern E. Smith. "A Storm over Billy Carter." *Newsweek*, 4 August 1980, p. 14.

McAllister, Bill. "Deaver Is Found Guilty of Lying about Lobbying." *Washington Post*, 17 December 1987, p. A1.

McDonald, Marci. "A Superspy Comes Clean." *Macleans*, 22 July 1991, p. 28.

McFarlane, Robert C., and Zofia Smardz. *Special Trust*. New York: Cadell & Davies, 1994.

McFeely, William S. *Grant: A Biography*. New York: W. W. Norton, 1981.

McGrory, Brian. "Dole, Baker Reject Talk of a Quick Deal on Clinton." *Boston Globe*, 28 September 1998, p. A1.

McGrory, Mary. "One More Battle of Principle." *Washington Post*, 20 December 1984, p. A2.

———. "SHHHH! Congress Doesn't Want to Wash Our Dirty Little War in Public." *Washington Post*, 16 December 1982, p. A3

McNeely-Johnson, K. A. "*United States v. Nixon*, Twenty Years After: The Good, the Bad and the Ugly—An Exploration of Executive Privilege." *Northern Illinois University Law Review* 14 (1993): 251–301.

Merelman, Diana. "Leading the Espy Probe." *American Lawyer*, (November 1996): 32.

Merida, Kevin. "Explaining Whitewater; Leach Vows 'Straightforward House Hearings.' " *Washington Post*, 7 August 1995, p. A1.

———. "Republicans' Dive into Whitewater Scores Some Points." *Washington Post*, 14 August 1995, p. A1.

Messing, John. "Public Lands, Politics, and Progressives: The Oregon Land Fraud Trials, 1903–1910." *Pacific Historical Review* 35 (1966): 35–66.

Miller, Bill. "Espy Pleads Not Guilty." *Washington Post*, 11 September 1997, p.A10.

———. "Espy's Former Chief of Staff Sentenced to 27 Months." *Washington Post*, 19 March 1998, p. A5.

———. "Report on HUD Details 1980's Pattern of Abuse." *Washington Post*, 27 October 1998, p.A17.

Mintz, Howard. "Brosnahan to Prosecute Weinberger." *The Recorder*, 16 October 1992, p. 1.

Mitchell, Alison. "Clinton Chooses His Fifth White House Counsel." *New York Times*, 8 January 1997, p. B7.

Mixter, Stephen Charles. "The Ethics in Government Act of 1978: Problems with the Attorney General's Discretion and Proposals for Reform." *Duke Law Journal* (1985): 497–522.

Mollenhoff, Clark R. *Game Plan for Disaster: An Ombudsman's Report on the Nixon Years*. New York: Norton, 1976.

———. *The Man Who Pardoned Nixon*. New York: St. Martin's Press, 1976.

Morain, Dan. "Ready for Combat." *Los Angeles Times*, 12 January 1989, p. A1.

———. "Restraint Urged on Changing Counsel Law." *Washington Post*, 25 February 1999, p. A4.

———. "Senate Coalition May Save Independent Counsel Law." *Washington Post*, 18 March 1999, p. A2

Morgan, Peter W. "The Undefined Crime of Lying to Congress: Ethics Reform and the Rule of Law." *Northwestern University Law Review* 86 (1992): 177–258.

Morganthau, Tom, and Elaine Shannon. "Ham Jordan's Prosecutor." *Newsweek*, 10 December 1979, p. 55.

Morganthau, Tom, John Walcott, and Elaine Shannon. "The Carter Warehouse Probe." *Newsweek*, 4 June 1979, p. 23.

Morris, Newbold. *Let the Chips Fall: My Battles against Corruption.* New York: Appleton-Century-Crofts, 1955.

Morrison v. Olson 487 U.S. 654 (1988).

Morse, Charles F. J. "Abraham Ribicoff Dies at 87." *Hartford Courant*, 23 February 1998, p. A1.

Nader v. Bork, Civil Action No. 1954–73, U.S. District Court for the District of Columbia.

Neal, Steve. "Percy Endured and Endeared, But Was Nagged by Career as Might-Have-Been." *Chicago Tribune*, 13 January 1985, p. C1.

Neikirk, William R., and Glen Elsasser. "Meese Disputes North on Casey's Role." *Chicago Tribune*, 30 July 1987, p. C1.

Nelson, Jack. "Clinton's Trust in Carter Rests on Long Relationship." *Los Angeles Times*, 26 September 1994, p. A1.

Noggle, Burl. *Teapot Dome: Oil and Politics in the 1920's.* Baton Rouge: Louisiana State University Press, 1962.

North, Oliver. *Under Fire: An American Story.* New York: HarperCollins Publishers, 1991.

Novak, Viveca. "Chasing Good-Time Charlie." *Time*, 8 September 1997, p. 58.

O'Keefe, Constance, and Peter Safirstein. "Fallen Angels, Separation of Powers, and the Saturday Night Massacre: An Examination of the Practical, Constitutional, and Political Tensions in the Special Prosecutor Provisions of the Ethics in Government Act." *Brooklyn Law Review* 49 (1982): 113–147.

Osgood, Russell K. "Government Functions and Constitutional Doctrine: The Historical Constitution." *Cornell Law Review* 72 (1987): 553–597.

Ostrow, Ronald J. "Ex-CIA Official Faces Iran-Contra Charges." *Los Angeles Times*, 27 November 1991, p. A18.

———. "Independent Counsel Explains Why She Didn't Prosecute Figure in '83 ERA Probe." *Los Angeles Times*, 21 March 1989, p. A17.

———. "Labor Secretary Comes Under Scrutiny." *Los Angeles Times*, 15 January 1998, p. A4.

———. "Panel Suggests Four Possible Law Violations." *Los Angeles Times*, 28 February 1987, p. 1.

———. "William Barr." *Los Angeles Times*, 21 June 1992, p. M3.

Ostrow, Ronald J., and Robert L. Jackson. "Investigator Grants Immunity to Cisneros Ex-Mistress." *Los Angeles Times*, 10 May 1996, p. A11.

Ostrow, Ronald, and Henry Weinstein. "Independent Counsel Appointed to Investigate Espy." *Los Angeles Times*, 10 September 1994, p. A14.

Packer-Tursman, Judy. "Clinger Sends Travelgate Data to Prosecutor." *Pittsburgh Post-Gazette*, 16 October 1996, p. A9.

Parry, Robert. "The Man Who Wasn't There." *The Nation* 256 (1993): 226.

Pear, Robert. "Civiletti Discloses He Spoke to Carter on Brother Case." *New York Times*, 26 July 1980, p. A1.

———. "F.B.I. Is Said to Be Checking New Allegations on Donovan." *New York Times*, 2 August 1982, p. A8.

———. "Washington Talk: Cabinet; Secret of Survivor Is Topic of Hot Debate." *New York Times*, 26 January 1988, p. A22.

———. "The White House Crisis: Tower Inquiry Found There Is Much Reagan Can't Recall." *New York Times*, 28 February 1987, p. A9.

Pianin, Eric. "Common Cause Calls for Probe of Rostenkowski." *Washington Post*, 22 December 1992, p. A19.

Picharallo, Joe. "Thornburgh Is Asked to Explain Blocking Iran-Contra Data." *Washington Post*, 2 December 1989, p. A4.

———. "Weinberger Highlights a Problem: Did '85 Sales to Iran Break Law?" *Washington Post*, 15 August 1987, p. A10.

Pincus, Walter. "Walsh Rejects Call to Fire New Prosecutor." *Washington Post*, 11 November 1992, p. A18.

Pooley, Eric. "Red Face Over China." *Time*, 1 June 1998, p. 46.

Pound, Edward T. "Agents of F.B.I. Told to Resume Inquiry on Allen." *New York Times*, 21 November 1981, p. A1.

———. "Allen Exonerated by Justice Department." *New York Times*, 24 December 1981, p. A1.

———. "Carter Associates Still Under Inquiry." *New York Times*, 1 February 1981, p. A23.

———. "Inquiry Set on Alleged Drug Use by Kraft, Carter Campaign Aide." *New York Times*, 14 September 1980, p. A1.

———. "Kraft Charge Laid to an Aide of Party's." *New York Times*, 17 September 1980, p. A1.

Press, Aric, and Diane Camper. "A Justice-in-Waiting." *Newsweek*, 31 August 1981, p. 37.

Priest, Dana, and Rene Sanchez. "Once-Trusted Civil Servant at Heart of Scandal." *Washington Post*, 23 January 1998, p. A22.

Radcliffe, Donnie. "The Notable Nofziger." *Washington Post*, 12 April 1981, p. L1.

Raines, Howard. "Nofziger Leaves Reagan: Take Three." *New York Times*, 23 January 1992, p. A9.

Rankin, Robert A. "The Case against Hillary." *Tampa Tribune*, 23 January 1996, p. 4.

Reagan, Ronald W. *An American Life: The Autobiography*. New York: Simon & Schuster, 1990.

Reeves, Richard. *A Ford, Not a Lincoln*. New York: Harcourt Brace Jovanovich, 1975.

Reno, Janet. "Campaign Finance Investigation: Testimony Before the Judiciary Committee." *Vital Speeches*, 1 November 1997, p. 34.

Reske, Henry J. "Lunch Not Unethical." *ABA Journal* (January 1995): 27.

Rich, Spencer. "Kraft Is Cleared of Allegations He Used Cocaine." *Washington Post*, 25 March 1981, p. A1.

———. "Senator Is Insistent on Perjury Probe of Treasury Chief." *Washington Post*, 15 February 1980, p. A16.

Roberts, Robert N., and Marion T. Doss, Jr. *From Whitewater to Watergate: The Public Integrity War*. Westport, CT: Praeger, 1997.

Rodman, Peter W. *More Precious Than Peace: The Cold War and the Struggle for the Third World*. New York: Scribner's, 1994.

Rosen, Jeffrey. "The New Look of Liberalism on the Court." *New York Times*, 5 October 1997, p. F60.

Rosenbaum, David E. "Ex-CIA Aide Called a Principal in Iran Affair." *New York Times*, 23 April 1987, p. A10.

Rosenfeld, Megan. "A 21-Gun Send-off, California's Ron Dellums Departs House with Bittersweet Memories and Fond Farewells." *Washington Post*, 7 February 1998, p. B1.

Rowan, Carl. "Lessons Americans Can Learn from the Life of Ron Brown." *Buffalo News*, 9 April 1996, p. B3.

Rowan, Roy. "The Payoff Charges against Reagan's Labor Secretary." *Fortune*, 31 May 1982, p. 80.

Rowley, James. "Mondale, Kassebaum Baker Urge Ban on 'Soft Money' Gifts." *Buffalo News*, 30 September 1997, p. 12D.

Russakoff, Dale. "Theodore Olson Is Free at Last." *Washington Post*, 23 March 1989, p. A25.

Russell, Keith. "Espy's Bitter Harvest." *Insight on the News*, 4 May 1998, p. 7.

Ryan, Peter M. "Counsels, Councils and Lunch: Preventing Abuse of the Power to Appoint Independent Counsels." *University of Pennsylvania Law Review* 144 (1996): 2537–2569.

Safire, William. "Unclosed Filegate." *New York Times*, 23 July 1998, p. A25.

Saikowski, Charlotte. "Iran-Contra Probe: Reagan's View of Law Called into Question." *Christian Science Monitor*, 21 May 1987, p. 1.

Salans, Marc R. "Independent Counsel: The First Ten Years." *George Washington Law Review* 56 (1988): 900–936.

Salant, Jonathan D. "Ex-Associate of Clinton Aide to Probe Babbitt." *Buffalo News*, 20 March 1998, p. A6.

Salgado, Richard P. "Government Secrets, Fair Trials and the Classified Information Procedures Act." *Yale Law Journal* 98 (1988): 427–446.

Sargentich, Thomas O. "The Contemporary Debate about Legislative—Executive Separation of Powers." *Cornell Law Review* 72 (1987): 430–487.

Saul, Stephanie. "Thornburgh Seeks Special HUD Probe." *Newsday*, 2 February 1990, p. 2.

Savage, David G. "Cisneros Former Mistress Admits Lying to Buy Home." *Los Angeles Times*, 16 January 1998, p. A13.

———. "Contrary Interests Provoke Thornburgh-Walsh Clash over North Trial." *Los Angeles Times*, 19 February 1989, p. A28.

Schapsmeier, Edward L., and Frederick H. Schapsmeier. *Gerald R. Ford's Date with Destiny*. New York: Peter Lang Publishing, 1989.

Schmickle, Sharon. "Minnesota Native at Storm's Center Built Reputation as Brilliant Lawyer." *Minneapolis Star Tribune*, 9 March 1994, p. A1.

Schmidt, Susan. "Executive Privilege Claim Covers First Lady's Talks with Blumenthal." *Washington Post*, 24 March 1998, p. A6.

———. "Ex-Governor to Cooperate with Starr; Tucker Plea Bargains in Whitewater Case." *Washington Post*, 21 February 1998, p. A1.

———. "Interference Seen in Whitewater Case." *Washington Post*, 22 March 1996, p. A19.

Schmidt, Susan, and Serge F. Kovaleski. "Hubbell Says Nussbaum Kept Probers from Files." *Washington Post*, 20 July 1995, p. A1.

Schneider, Howard. "Down the Whitewater Rapids." *Washington Post*, 13 January 1994, p. C1.

———. "Ex-Judge: SBA Loans Mocked Law." *Washington Post*, 15 February 1994, p. A1.

Schoenbaum, Eleanora W., ed. *Political Profiles: The Nixon/Ford Years*. New York: Facts on File, Inc., 1979.

Schoenbrod, David. "How the Reagan Administration Trivialized Separation of Powers (and Shot Itself in the Foot)." *George Washington Law Review* 57 (1989): 459–473.

Schorr, Daniel. "Even an Ethicist Can Get Splashed by Whitewater." *Christian Science Monitor*, 3 May 1996, p. 19.

Schram, Martin. "Jordan Affair: A Dilemma for Carter, Media, Justice Dept." *Washington Post*, 25 September 1979, p. A7.

Sciolino, Elaine, and Don Van Natta. "Testing of a President: The Confidant." *New York Times*, 15 March 1998, p. A1.

Secord, Richard, with Jay Wurts. *Honored and Betrayed: Irangate, Covert Affairs, and the Secret War in Laos*. New York: John Wiley and Sons, Inc., 1992.

Seematter, Mary E. "The St. Louis Whiskey Ring." *Gateway Heritage* (Spring 1988): 32–42.

Shane, Peter M. "Presidents, Pardons and Prosecutors: Legal Accountability and the Separation of Powers." *Yale Law and Policy Review* 11 (1993): 361–406.

Shapiro, Walter. "Bush Bites Back." *Time*, 18 January 1988, p. 16.

Shapiro, Walter, Thomas M. DeFrank, Gloria Borger, and Howard Fineman. "Has Mike Deaver Gone Too Far?" *Newsweek*, 14 April 1986, p. 23.

Shapiro, Walter, Margaret Garrard Walker, and Howard Fineman, "Cashing In on Reagan." *Newsweek*, 3 March 1986, p. 21.

Shaw, Gaylord. "Bid for Special Prosecutor in Pierce Case." *Newsday*, 3 November 1989, p. 15.

Shenon, Philip. "Independent Counsel Is Named in Inquiry over E.P.A. Documents." *New York Times*, 25 April 1986, p. A13.

———. "More Republican Lobbying of H.U.D. Is Disclosed." *New York Times*, 11 December 1989, p. A21.

Sherman, Mark, and Rebecca Carr. "Whitewater Investigation Prison Tapes Controversy." *Atlanta Constitution*, 6 May 1998, p. A10.

Sherry, Suzanna. "Separation of Powers: Asking a Different Question." *William and Mary Law Review* 30 (1989): 287–300.

Shultz, George P. *Triumph and Turmoil: My Years as Secretary of State*. New York: Scribner's, 1993.

Sidey, Hugh. "Did Washington Kill Vincent Foster?" *Time*, 23 August 1993, p. 76.

Simon, Donald J. "The Constitutionality of the Special Prosecutor Law." *University of Michigan Journal of Law Reform* 16 (1982): 45–74.

Simon, Roger. "Counsel Indicts Clinton Friend a 2nd Time." *Chicago Tribune*, 1 May 1998, p. A1.

Sirica, Jack. "My Dad Decided Nixon Was a Crook." *Newsday*, 28 April 1994, p. A39.

Smith, Christopher. "Justice Antonin Scalia and the Institutions of American Government." *Wake Forest Law Review* 25 (1990): 783–809.

Smith, Jeffrey R., and Howard Kurtz. "Meese Was in Wrong Job." *Washington Post*, 17 February 1989, p. A25.

Starr, Kenneth W. "Law and Lawyers: The Road to Reform." *Fordham Law Review* 63 (1995): 959–969.

———. "Starr Report to the House of Representatives." 9 September 1998.

Stein, Jonathan. "Czech It Out." *The Nation* 258 (1994): 149.

Stewart, James B. *Blood Sport: The President and His Adversaries*. New York: Simon & Schuster, 1996.

Strasser, Fred. "North Case Appears on Course for Trial." *National Law Journal*, 26 December 1988, p. 3.

Stratton, David H. *Tempest over Teapot Dome: The Story of Albert B. Fall* (Oklahoma Western Biographies, vol. 16), Norman: University of Oklahoma Press, 1998.

Stratton, David Hodges. "Albert B. Fall and the Teapot Dome Affair." Ph.D. dissertation, University of Colorado, 1955.

Strauss, Peter L. "Formal and Functional Approaches to Separation-of-Powers Questions—A Foolish Inconsistency?" *Cornell Law Review* 72 (1987): 488–526.

———. "Was There a Baby in the Bathwater? A Comment on the Supreme Court's Legislative Veto Decision." *Duke Law Journal* (1983): 789–819.

Susolik, Edward. "Separation of Powers and Liberty: The Appointments Clause, *Morrison v. Olson*, and the Rule of Law." *Southern California Law Review* 63 (1990): 1515–1567.

Swire, Peter, and Simon Lazarus. "Reactionary Activism: Conservatives and the Constitution." *The New Republic*, 22 February 1988, p. 17.

Symposium, The Independent Counsel Statute. *Mercer Law Review* 49, no. 2 (1998): 427–564.

Tachmes, Alexander I. "Independent Counsels under the Ethics in Government Act of 1978: A Violation of the Separation of Powers Doctrine or an Essential Check on Executive Power?" *University of Miami Law Review* 42 (1988): 735–765.

Tackett, Michael. "Reno Asks to Renew Special Prosecutors but Dole Says Law Wastes Money." *Chicago Tribune*, 15 May 1993, p. N3.

Taylor, Stuart, Jr. "Attorney General's Power to Bar Special Counsel Upheld in Court." *New York Times*, 26 June 1984, p. A1.

———. "4 Rebut Testimony of Rehnquist on Challenging of Voters in 60's." *New York Times*, 2 August 1986, p. 1.

———. "The Great House Bank Holdup Scandal Is Phony and the Inquiry Is Suspect." *San Diego Union-Tribune*, 31 May 1992, p. C3.

———. "Her Case against Clinton." *American Lawyer* (November 1996), 57.

———. "Judges Hear Case on 1980 Campaign Documents." *New York Times*, 21 June 1984, p. B9.

———. "Kenneth Starr v. The Legal Profession." *National Journal*, 13 July 1998, p. 1347.

———. "Man in the News; Unconventional Lawyer with a New Task." *New York Times*, 3 April 1984, p. A20.

———. "Reagan's Defenders Arguing He Can Defy Congress's Ban." *New York Times*, 17 May 1987, p. 14.

Taylor, Stuart, Jr., and Daniel Klaidman. "Bob Bennett Got to the Top by Doing a Great Job for His Clients. But He Failed Rostenkowski When He Said Yes to the President." *The American Lawyer* (July/August 1994): 65.

Taylor, Stuart, Jr., Daniel Klaidman, and William W. Horne. "What Kind of Lawyer Is Bob Bennett?" *The American Lawyer* (July/August 1994): 68.

terHorst, Jerald. *Gerald Ford and the Future of the Presidency.* New York: The Third Press, 1974.

Thomas, Evan, and Michael Isikoff. "Clinton v. Paula Jones." *Newsweek*, 13 January 1997, p. 26.

Thomas, Evan, and Daniel Klaidman. "A Star's Fall from Grace." *Newsweek*, 22 December 1997, p. 70.

Thomas, Pierre, and Howard Schneider. "Los Angeles Attorney Chosen to Head Investigation of Espy." *Washington Post*, 10 September 1994, p. A3.

Thomasson, Dan. "What Kind of Justice Favors the Dead over the Living?" *Houston Chronicle*, 30 June 1998, p. A19.

Thornton, Mary. "Independent Counsel Quits to Avoid Conflict." *Washington Post*, 30 May 1986, p. A17.

———. "New Position Spotlights Lance's Past." *Washington Post*, 17 July 1984, p. A7.

Thornton, Mary, and George Lardner, Jr. "Court Names Prosecutor in Donovan Case." *Washington Post*, 30 December 1981, p. A1.

Tiefer, Charles. "The Constitutionality of Independent Officers as Checks on Abuses of Executive Power." *Boston University Law Review* 63 (1983): 59–103.

Toobin, Jeffrey. "Starr Can't Help It." *New Yorker*, 18 May 1998, pp. 32–38.

Torry, Saundra. "At 87, Erwin N. Griswold Is the Dean of Supreme Court Observers." *Washington Post*, 15 July 1991, p. F5.

Totenberg, Nina. "For the U.S.: Griffin Bell, Esq.; A Closing Argument on the Departing Attorney General, Who Hopes to Leave a Legacy of Integrity, Patriotism and Nonpartisan Justice." *Washington Post*, 1 July 1979, magazine section, p. 10.

Ullmann, Owen. "Who Killed Roger Altman?" *Washingtonian*, October 1994, pp. 71–75.

U.S. Congress. House. Committee on the Judiciary. *Investigation of the Department of Justice. Hearings Before the Special Subcommittee to Investigate the Justice Department*, 82nd Cong., 2d sess., 1952.

U.S. Congress. House. Ways and Means Committee. *Final Report of the Subcommittee on Administration of Revenue Laws*, 82nd Cong., 2d sess., 1952.

U.S. Congress. Senate. Committee on Public Lands and Surveys. *Leases Upon Naval Oil Reserves*, 68th Cong., 1st sess., 1923.

Van Gelder, Lawrence. "Thomas Murphy, Police Head and Prosecutor of Hiss, 89." *New York Times*, 31 October 1995.

Van Natta, Don. "Testing of a President: The Prosecutor; Hardball Tactics Appear to Fall Short against a Defiant McDougal." *New York Times*, 6 May 1998, p. A20.

Van Natta, Don, Jr., and Jill Abramson. "Web of Influence." *New York Times*, 11 January 1998, p.1.

Verkeuil, Paul R. "Separation of Powers, The Rule of Law and the Idea of Independence." *William and Mary Law Review* 30 (1989): 300–341.

Victor, Kirk. "Lost Cause?" *National Journal*, 1 March 1997, p. 410.

———. "On the Firing Line." *National Journal* 29 (1997): 828.

Von Drehle, David. "Key Clinton Player Finally on the Program." *Washington Post*, 3 April 1993, p. A1.

Wallace, Don, Jr., and Allen Gerson. "The Dubious Boland Amendments." *Washington Post*, 5 June 1987, p. A27.

Walsh, Lawrence E. "Final Report of the Independent Counsel for Iran/Contra Matters." Washington, D.C., GPO, 1993.

———. *Firewall: The Iran-Contra Conspiracy and Cover-up*. New York: W. W. Norton, 1997.

———. *Iran-Contra: The Final Report*. New York: Times Books, 1994.

———. "Political Oversight, the Rule of Law, and Iran-Contra." *Cleveland State Law Review* 42 (1994): 587–597.

Walsh, Mark. "Brosnahan Speech Tops Bar Installation Dinner." *The Recorder*, 25 January 1993, p. 3.

Wassenaar, Sheri L. "Watt Draws Probation in HUD Probe." *Los Angeles Times*, 13 March 1996, p. 13A.

Watson, Russell, and John Barry. "A Stunning Indictment." *Newsweek*, 9 March 1987, p. 25.

Watson, Tom. "What a Job: If He Finds It, He Takes It." *Legal Times*, 20 March 1989, p. S6.

Weaver, Maurice. "Republican Clamour Grows for Whitewater Investigator." *Daily Telegraph*, 8 January 1994, p. 11.

Weinberger, Caspar W. *Fighting for Peace: Seven Critical Years in the Pentagon*. New York: Warner, 1990.

Weiser, Benjamin. "Company Man." *Washington Post*, 17 May 1992, p. W10.

———. "Ex-CIA Operative Chooses to Stand and Fight Charges." *Washington Post*, 8 September 1991, p. A27.

Westin, Alan F. *The Anatomy of a Constitutional Law Case*. New York: Macmillan, 1958.

White, Jack E. "An Empty Seat at the Table; Ronald Harmon Brown, 1941–1996." *Time* 15 April 1996, p. 72.

White, William Allen. *A Puritan in Babylon: The Story of Calvin Coolidge*. New York: Capricorn Books, 1965.

Wilkie, Curtis. "Remembering a Southern Rogue." *Newsweek*, 23 March 1998, 35.

Will, George. "The 'Spirit' of Boland, a Pseudo-Law." *Washington Post*, 24 May 1987, p. D7.

Williams, Robert H. "FBI Investigating Alleged Cocaine Use by Jordan." *Washington Post*, 25 August 1979, p. A1.

Wines, Michael. "Thornburgh Abandons Choice for Top Justice Post." *New York Times*, 7 July 1989, p. A1.

———. "Thornburgh Choice for Deputy Is Under Fire." *New York Times*, 30 April 1989, p. A25.

———. "Washington at Work: Quintessential Spy Undone by His Own Loyalty." *New York Times*, 30 July 1991, p. A12.

Wolf, Stephen A. "In the Pursuit of Power without Accountability: How the Independent Counsel Statute Is Designed and Used to Determine the Energy and Independence of the Presidency." *South Dakota Law Review* 35 (1990): 1–39.

Woodlief, Wayne. "Politics Inside Out; Segal Goes to Bat for AmeriCorps." *Boston Herald*, 26 September 1995, p. A19.

Woodward, Bob. *Veil: The Secret Wars of the CIA 1981–1987*. New York: Simon and Schuster, 1987.

Woodward, C. Vann, ed. *Responses of the Presidents to Charges of Misconduct*. New York: Delacorte Press, 1974.

Wright, Michael, and Caroline Rand Herron. "Donovan Wanted a Prosecutor and He'll Get One." *New York Times*, 27 December 1981, p. A.

Wright, Ronald F. "Congressional Use of Immunity Grants after Iran-Contra." *Minnesota Law Review* 80 (1995): 407–468.

York, Byron. "The Hidden Tale of Travelgate." *Weekly Standard*, 22 January 1996, p. 18.

———. "Vince Foster, in the Park, with the Gun." *Weekly Standard*, 27 October 1997, p. 25.

———. "The White House Plays Ruff." *American Spectator*, June 1997, p. 28–33.

———. "Why Ron Brown Won't Go Down." *The American Spectator*, April 1996, p. 32–34.

Young, Rick. "The Castle Grande Deal." From the PBS television program *Frontline*, episode "Once Upon a Time in Arkansas." ⟨http://www.pbs.org/wgbh/pages/frontline⟩

Zaradich, Linda. "Outside Counsel Urged in Ethics Case." *The Courier-Journal*, 4 May 1989, p. A6.

Zehren, Charles V. "FBI Counsel Rapped." *Newsday*, 29 March 1997, p. A13.

———. "Fonz in with a Splash." *Newsday*, 30 November 1994, p. A24.

———. "Her Triple Threat." *Newsday*, 7 January 1996, p. A5.

———. "I Was Right: Senators Hear Nussbaum's Side." *Newsday*, 10 August 1995, p. A3.

Zehren, Charlie. "McDougal Lived Life Large." *Newsday*, 11 March 1998, p. A33.

Index

Page numbers for main entries are in **bold**.

About the Contributors

SUSAN ROTH BREITZER is a Ph.D. candidate in U.S. History at the University of Iowa. She received her B.A. in American Studies from Grinnell College, her M.L.S. from the University of Pittsburgh, and her M.A. in history from Eastern Illinois University. Her scholarly interests include U.S. social, immigration, and political history.

THOMAS CLARKIN received his doctorate in American history from the University of Texas at Austin in 1998. He is an adjunct faculty member at San Antonio College. His book on federal Indian policy during the 1960s will be published in 2001 by the University of New Mexico Press.

CYNTHIA M. CLINE received her Juris Doctor from Duquesne University in Pittsburgh. She has been a legal practitioner for 20 years in Southwestern Pennsylvania and Northern West Virginia. Currently, she is pursuing her Ph.D. in Political Science at West Virginia University where she teaches a course in Introduction to Law and the Legal System.

ROBERT E. DEWHIRST is Professor of Political Science at Northwest Missouri State University. He has written articles about politics in Missouri and America that have appeared in several academic journals. He has also written and coedited several books on Congress, public policy, and elections. These include *Rites of Passage: Congress Makes Laws* (Prentice-Hall, 1997); *Passage, Implementation, and Feedback* (Kendall/Hunt, 1998); and *Government at Work: Issue Evolution Passage, Implementation, and Feedback* (Wadsworth, 2000), the latter two coedited with Sunil Ahuja. He currently is writing a biography of Mrs. Mamie Eisenhower and a reference book on Missouri politics.

GERALD S. GREENBERG is a Reference Librarian and Associate Professor at Ohio State University's Education, Human Ecology, Psychology & Social Work Library where he also oversees a larger freshman library instruction program and serves as collection manager for the subject areas of Physical Education and Sports. His recent publications include "Caleb Emerson, Nineteenth-Century Newspaper Publisher of Marietta, Ohio" in *Publishing History* and *Tabloid Journalism: An Annotated Bibliography of English-Language Sources* (Greenwood, 1996).

KATY J. HARRIGER is an Associate Professor of Politics at Wake Forest University, where she teaches American politics and constitutional law courses. She is the author of *Independent Justice: The Federal Special Prosecutor in American Politics* (University Press of Kansas, 1992) and the 2nd revised edition entitled *The Special Prosecutor in American Politics* (University Press of Kansas, 2000). She has testified before Congress about the independent counsel statute.

ROBERT W. LANGRAN is a Professor of Political Science at Villanova University. He began teaching there in 1959, and chaired the Department from 1968 to 1978. He won the Lindback Award for Distinguished Teaching in 1972, and the Faculty Service Award in 1997. He has published four editions of a book on the Supreme Court, numerous articles, and has a coauthored book forthcoming on government and the American economy. He is also a member of the Villanova athletic hall of fame, having coached their men's tennis team for 27 years and the women's tennis team for 25 years, retiring from coaching in 1993.

TOM LANSFORD is an Assistant Professor of Political Science at Kent State University, Tuscarawas Campus. He has previously published articles in journals such as *European Security, Defense Analysis, The Journal of Conflict Resolution*, and *Strategic Studies*. Along with Wayne Lesperance he has coauthored *Untying the Gordian Knot: Great Power Interests in the Persian Gulf* (Pearson, 1999) and *Teaching Old Dogs New Tricks: International Organizations in the 21st Century* (Pearson, 2000).

ERIC J. SEGALL is Professor of Law at Georgia State University College of Law where he teaches constitutional law and federal courts. His articles on constitutional law have appeared in, among other journals, the UCLA, University of Pittsburgh, and George Washington law reviews, and he is currently writing a book review of Laurence Tribe's third edition of *American Constitutional Law* for *Constitutional Commentary*. He is a former trial attorney for the United States Department of Justice and in that capacity represented the National Archives when it received document requests from the Independent Counsel during the Iran-Contra investigation.

ANDREA SHEMBERG is a 1997 graduate of The Ohio State University College of Law. She is an associate in the Labor and Employment Department of Squire, Sanders & Dempsey L.L.P., specializing in workers' compensation, discrimination, employment at will, and labor relations cases. Her litigation experience includes representation before federal and state courts, administrative agencies, and other alternative dispute resolution mechanisms.

PETER M. SHANE, Professor of Law and former Dean of the University of Pittsburgh School of Law, is a specialist in separation of powers law and the application of law to the presidency. A former Justice Department lawyer and assistant general counsel to the Office of Management and Budget, he is the coauthor of two major casebooks on separation of powers law and on administrative law, respectively, and has written over 25 law review articles on constitutional and administrative law issues.

JACLYN STANKE teaches American and European history at Campbell University in Buies Creek, North Carolina. She is currently completing her dissertation, "Danger and Opportunity: Eisenhower, Churchill, and the Soviet Union after Stalin, 1953–1955," at Emory University in Atlanta.

RONALD WRIGHT is a Professor of Law at Wake Forest University. He teaches and writes about issues in criminal justice administration, including the congressional use of immunity grants. Wright is also the coauthor of a law school casebook, *Criminal Procedures: Cases, Statutes and Executive Materials* (Aspen, 1998). Before joining the faculty at Wake Forest, he worked as a criminal prosecutor for the U.S. Department of Justice.